# Sewing

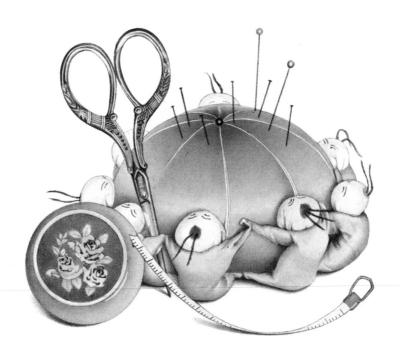

# Sewing

## ANN LADBURY

Mitchell Beazley Publishers Limited, London

*Sewing* was edited and designed by
Mitchell Beazley Publishers Limited, Mill House,
87–89 Shaftesbury Avenue, London W1V 7AD

*The Joy of Living Library*
© Mitchell Beazley Publishers Limited 1976
*The Joy of Living Library Sewing*
© Mitchell Beazley Publishers Limited 1978
All rights reserved
First edition published 1978
Reproduction of any kind in part or in whole in any
part of the world is reserved by Mitchell Beazley
Publishers Limited

ISBN 0 85533 103 8

*Sewing* was written by Ann Ladbury. The
following specialists contributed to the home
and decorative sewing sections: Jeanne
Argent, *Sewing for the Home*; Jane Stevens,
*Embroidery*; Eirian Short, *Quilting*; June
Thorpe, *Appliqué*; Marian Bryan, *Patchwork*;
Ann E. Gill, *Beading*.

| | |
|---|---|
| *Editor* | Daphne Wood |
| *Art Editor* | Val Hobson |
| *Assistant Editor* | Jinny Johnson |
| *Technical Editor* | Louise Callan |
| *Editorial* | Ruth Binney |
| | Viv Croot |
| *Assistant Art Editor* | Flick Ekins |
| *Art Assistant* | Allison Blythe |
| *Picture Researcher* | Susan Pinkus |
| *Editorial Assistants* | Margaret Little |
| | Anne Cannon |
| *Production* | Lis Blackburn |
| *Publisher* | James Mitchell |
| *Executive Editor* | Iain Parsons |

Typeset by Keyspools Ltd, Golborne, Lancashire    Reproduction by Fotomecanica Iberico, Madrid
Printed in Spain by Printer industria gráfica s.a. Sant Vicenç dels Horts    Barcelona    1978
Depósito Legal B-48.201-1977

# *Before You Begin to Sew . . .*

In *The Basics of Sewing* and *Perfect Dressmaking*
a range of four brown tones and textures has been
used to differentiate the right and wrong sides of
the main fabric and the right and wrong sides of
lining or facing. Starting with the darkest and
finishing with the lightest, the tones indicate:
    Lining or facing, right side; the facing may be in
    lining fabric or in self-fabric
    Main fabric, right side
    Lining or facing, wrong side
    Main fabric, wrong side
A similar range of green tones and textures has
been used in *Sewing for the Home* and *Decorative
Sewing* and grey for *Fitting, Beading* and *Repairs*.

Adhesive tape

Interfacing

Bias binding (except on pp. 49–52)

Pattern pieces appear white.

In the captions right side has been abbreviated to
RS, wrong side to WS.

The Imperial and metric measurements given
throughout the book are working equivalents
rather than exact conversions.

Arrows at the foot of a righthand page indicate
that a method continues on the following page.

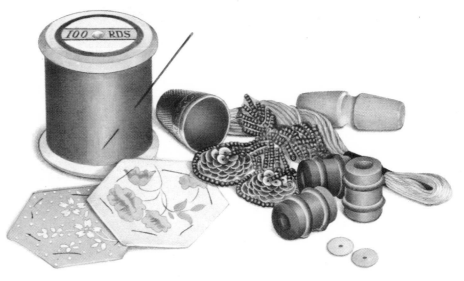

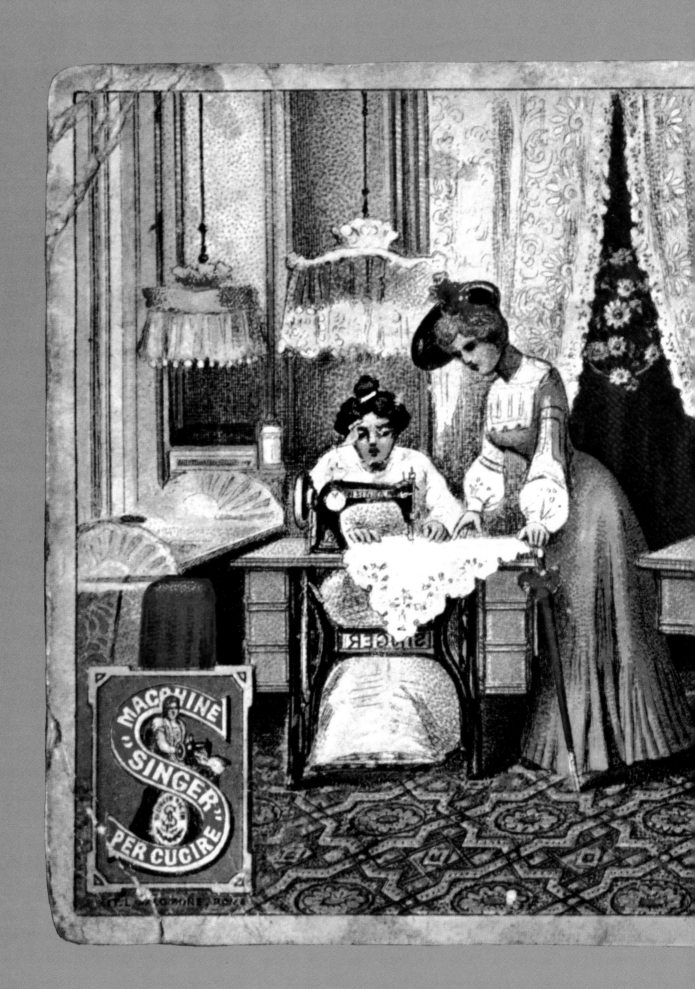

# THE BASICS OF SEWING

*"Needle, needle, dip and dart,*
*Thrusting up and down,*
*Where's the man could ease a heart*
*Like a satin gown?"*

**Dorothy Parker**

# Sewing Machines

Mob violence and lengthy and acrimonious litigation are but two of the problems that have beset the evolution of one of the most useful of all domestic and industrial appliances, the sewing machine.

Although the first patent was taken out by an English cabinetmaker, Thomas Saint, in 1790, the first person to make his model truly productive was a French tailor, Barthélemy Thimonnier. His heyday was, however, short. In 1830 he had 80 machines in a Paris workshop making French army uniforms; the next year the machines were destroyed by rival tailors fearful for their livelihoods.

Thimonnier's machine worked a chain stitch in imitation of a form of embroidery. The first to design a machine that broke away from the principles of hand sewing was the American Walter Hunt. Hunt's needle had an eye at the point, thus eliminating the need for the needle to go right through the fabric as in hand sewing. The stitch formed was known as lock stitch and was more secure than the earlier chain stitch. Hunt never patented his machine, however, and it was his compatriot, Elias Howe, who developed and in 1846 patented a very similar machine, which heralded the start of the sewing machine industry.

Litigation ensued when Howe discovered that other inventors, among them Isaac M. Singer, were beginning to produce imitation models. Like Howe's, Singer's machine had a shuttle that created a considerable noise. Relief for the noise-afflicted ears of seamstresses and tailors came with the invention, in 1852, of a machine that, instead of a shuttle, had a crude version of the bobbin used today. Two years later its American inventor, Allen B. Wilson, added the further refinement of a four-motion feed so that fabric was automatically moved on between stitches. Here at last was the prototype of the modern domestic machine.

Eventually, to avoid further litigation, four companies agreed, in 1856, to pool their patent interests, thereby setting up the first large-scale patent pool. The manufacturers were Howe, Singer, Wheeler & Wilson and Grover & Baker.

Although few machines were manufactured before 1850, in 1860 more than 111,000 were produced by 74 US companies, and the production figures had risen to 700,000 at the beginning of the 1870s. By 1900 patents had been issued worldwide for machines that could hem stitch (the inventor's name, Gegauf, became synonymous with the process in Germany), zigzag, stitch buttonholes and sew two parallel seams simultaneously.

The industry was responsible for more than just alleviating the burden of home sewing and, eventually, placing ready-made clothes within the economic reach of everybody. The farthest-reaching of its many by-products, the social and economic effects of which have been even greater than those of the sewing machine, was introduced by Isaac Singer's partner to boost sales—hire purchase.

*Rescued from obscurity in 1874, the design for the first sewing machine was patented by a London cabinetmaker, Thomas Saint, in 1790. Although Saint considered his invention suitable for "stitching, quilting, or sewing", it is unlikely that he constructed it, as its rescuer, Newton Wilson, a sewing machine manufacturer, had to modify the mechanism below the table to make the machine work. An awl made a hole in the fabric and a notched needle carried the thread through. A loop of thread was held underneath by a hook, or looper. When the next stitch passed through, the loop was released. The resulting stitch was a form of straight stitch on top and chain stitch beneath.*

*The first patented sewing machine to have a needle with the eye at the pointed end and to work lock stitch, a primitive version of the modern machine stitch, was the 1846 model by Elias Howe. Fabric was held vertically by pins on a sliding metal plate and moved on between stitches. A curved needle entered the fabric horizontally to leave a loop of thread, through which a shuttle passed more thread. The two threads then locked together in the fabric. The plate had to be returned continually to its original position and the fabric reset.*

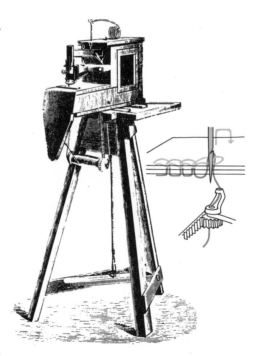

*Barthélemy Thimonnier's curiously elongated model of 1830 was driven by a treadle. It had a barbed needle that drew thread up through the cloth from a reel and rotating mechanism below the table. After passing through a kind of presser foot, the needle, with the loop of thread round it, went through the cloth to pick up more thread. As the needle rose it drew the lower thread through the upper loop to form a chain stitch. The needle rotated partially at each up and down movement, so preventing the barb from catching the upper loop of thread. The barb did, however, tend to catch in the fabric.*

*Packed in a box that could be converted into a stand and work table, Isaac Singer's first cumbersome model of 1851 incorporated other innovatory features. The lock stitch was formed by the vertical action of a straight needle and the horizontal, and noisy, movement of a shuttle beneath the fabric. The machine was driven by a novel form of treadle, which was connected to the balance wheel and worked by a heel-and-toe action. Because of its weight, it was more suitable for industrial than domestic use.*

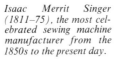

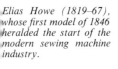

Elias Howe (1819–67), whose first model of 1846 heralded the start of the modern sewing machine industry.

Isaac Merrit Singer (1811–75), the most celebrated sewing machine manufacturer from the 1850s to the present day.

Promoted as the smallest sewing machine ever, this German pocket model of 1885 had to be clamped to the table for use.

Cruelly denied success in his lifetime, the French tailor Barthélemy Thimonnier (1793–1859) received posthumous recognition, here in the form of a cover story, for the invention of the first truly productive sewing machine.

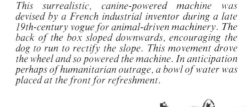

This surrealistic, canine-powered machine was devised by a French industrial inventor during a late 19th-century vogue for animal-driven machinery. The back of the box sloped downwards, encouraging the dog to run to rectify the slope. This movement drove the wheel and so powered the machine. In anticipation perhaps of humanitarian outrage, a bowl of water was placed at the front for refreshment.

The true ancestor of the modern lock stitch machine first appeared on the market in the 1860s, manufactured by its inventor Allen B. Wilson and his financial backer, Nathaniel Wheeler. Attractively decorated, no doubt to appeal to female buyers, the machine was driven by a treadle.

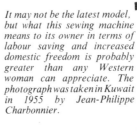

The 1860s Wheeler and Wilson model incorporated a feed mechanism that moved fabric on automatically between stitches and worked a strong, secure lock stitch. A rotating hook beneath the fabric caught the needle thread and passed it under a bobbin holding the under-thread. The two threads then interlocked. The top loop was released and drawn up to form the first stitch as the next loop of thread passed through.

An advertisement inspired the ingenious model by James Gibbs. Not realizing that the advertised machine had an under-thread, Gibbs devised a system of chain stitch with, under the fabric, a rotating hook to replace the noisy shuttle. He patented the model in 1857 and manufactured it with Charles Willcox.

It may not be the latest model, but what this sewing machine means to its owner in terms of labour saving and increased domestic freedom is probably greater than any Western woman can appreciate. The photograph was taken in Kuwait in 1955 by Jean-Philippe Charbonnier.

# Sewing Machines

Apply the same rules to buying a sewing machine and to deciding on the make and model as you would to buying a car. Have a good look round at the variety of makes on the market and study brochures of models that are in your price range. (Considerable discounts are often obtainable on a cash payment or if you trade in another machine in part-exchange.) Discuss the choice of machine with friends and try out their machines. Find out from dressmaking students which is the most popular and reliable make used in their schools and colleges.

Once you have narrowed down the choice, look at the machines you are interested in. Be wary if the dealer tries to persuade you to take a particular one as he may be receiving additional commission for disposing of an obsolescent model. Beware, too, of enormous price reductions as these may indicate that the model is about to be withdrawn. Be suspicious of a manufacturer who has many different machines on the market and is constantly offering them at give-away prices. The few manufacturers who make high-quality precision machines of well-finished durable metal have no need to keep offering new models.

Do not be impressed by the ease with which the demonstrator uses the machine; try it out yourself. Lift it up and make sure you can carry it. Even if you have a sewing room you will have to move the machine sometimes.

Take with you to the showroom a selection of fabrics of different thicknesses, including a thin silk and a synthetic jersey, and try them, folded double, in the machine. Do this yourself after being shown how to operate the machine and after carefully reading the instruction manual. Remove the demonstrator's fabric as it will have been specially chosen because the machine operates perfectly on it.

Although the demonstration model should be in perfect working order, always try out the threading procedure. Unthread the machine and rethread. Was it easy, and in sequence? Were they easy loop-over actions or did you have to keep licking the thread and peering through a hole? Do not worry unduly about bobbin ▶

Although sewing machines vary enormously in design and in the position of various knobs and dials, they have many similar basic features, which are labelled on the standard free-arm model below. Refer to the machine manual for detailed instructions on how to thread your machine correctly at top and bottom.

**Inserting needle** Push needle firmly up into needle hole as far as it will go, with groove of needle facing in same direction as final threading point above it. Tighten needle clamp. The thread fits into groove for length of needle and passes through eye from groove side.

**Feed teeth** For normal sewing the teeth feed fabric under foot. If they are too sharp for some fine fabrics cover them with tissue paper. They can be partially or completely lowered for special stitching. The grooved lines on plate beside teeth are a useful guide for keeping stitching straight. The long needle hole is for all stitching, the smaller round hole for feeding in cord, elastic, etc.

**Take-up lever** Make sure lever is at its highest point when threading machine so that needle is also at its highest point, with eye raised above foot, for threading.

**Lamp switch**

**Face plate** Remove for oiling and cleaning and to change light bulb.

**Needle clamp**

**Presser foot** To insert and remove fabric, raise foot by raising upper lever at back; for all stitching lower foot by lowering lever. To remove foot, raise clamping lever, the metal bar at top of foot, also used for cutting threads.

**Inserting bobbin in free-arm machine** Open hinged door on free arm. Pull out central bar on back of bobbin case to grip bobbin, insert case into socket in machine so bar extending from case fits into upper groove beneath machine bed. Shut door.

**Tension disc** Use for controlling tension of thread as it is wound on to bobbin.

**Top tension control wheel** Move to adjust tension control of top thread.

**Thread tension and thread guide**

**Final threading point**

**Needle**

**Hinged door to bobbin holder**

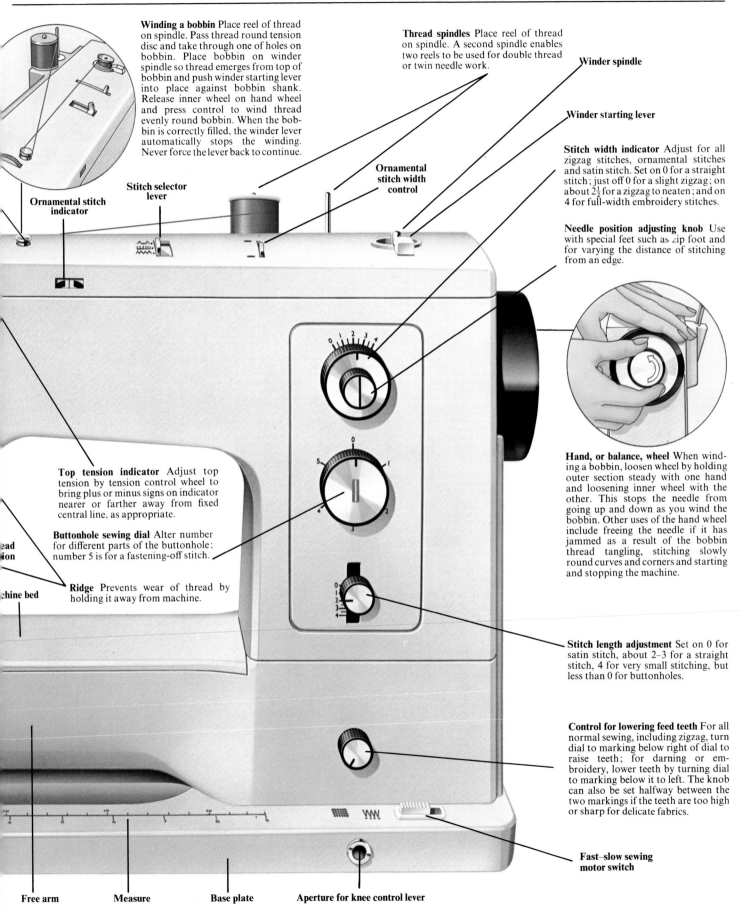

**Winding a bobbin** Place reel of thread on spindle. Pass thread round tension disc and take through one of holes on bobbin. Place bobbin on winder spindle so thread emerges from top of bobbin and push winder starting lever into place against bobbin shank. Release inner wheel on hand wheel and press control to wind thread evenly round bobbin. When the bobbin is correctly filled, the winder lever automatically stops the winding. Never force the lever back to continue.

**Ornamental stitch indicator**

**Stitch selector lever**

**Ornamental stitch width control**

**Thread spindles** Place reel of thread on spindle. A second spindle enables two reels to be used for double thread or twin needle work.

**Winder spindle**

**Winder starting lever**

**Stitch width indicator** Adjust for all zigzag stitches, ornamental stitches and satin stitch. Set on 0 for a straight stitch; just off 0 for a slight zigzag; on about $2\frac{1}{2}$ for a zigzag to neaten; and on 4 for full-width embroidery stitches.

**Needle position adjusting knob** Use with special feet such as zip foot and for varying the distance of stitching from an edge.

**Top tension indicator** Adjust top tension by tension control wheel to bring plus or minus signs on indicator nearer or farther away from fixed central line, as appropriate.

**Buttonhole sewing dial** Alter number for different parts of the buttonhole; number 5 is for a fastening-off stitch.

**Ridge** Prevents wear of thread by holding it away from machine.

**Hand, or balance, wheel** When winding a bobbin, loosen wheel by holding outer section steady with one hand and loosening inner wheel with the other. This stops the needle from going up and down as you wind the bobbin. Other uses of the hand wheel include freeing the needle if it has jammed as a result of the bobbin thread tangling, stitching slowly round curves and corners and starting and stopping the machine.

**Stitch length adjustment** Set on 0 for satin stitch, about 2–3 for a straight stitch, 4 for very small stitching, but less than 0 for buttonholes.

**Control for lowering feed teeth** For all normal sewing, including zigzag, turn dial to marking below right of dial to raise teeth; for darning or embroidery, lower teeth by turning dial to marking below it to left. The knob can also be set halfway between the two markings if the teeth are too high or sharp for delicate fabrics.

**Fast–slow sewing motor switch**

**Free arm**   **Measure**   **Base plate**   **Aperture for knee control lever**

threading as this is always the most difficult part of the process and comes with practice.

Check that the light is over the needle. On old machines, on which it was an optional extra, it was nowhere near it. Look at the construction of the machine for easily breakable plastic in the inner works. Look at the plugs on the flex connecting the machine to the foot; they should be moulded to prevent them coming loose.

During the test, find out if the machine is versatile but still simple to use. Whatever the machine, the basic operations are the same, such as winding the bobbin and threading up. Do not select a model if there is anything irritating or awkward about any of these operations. Check that the machine is easy to clean and oil.

Check the following points when trying out the stitching. Do the two unbasted layers of fabric travel evenly under the foot or are you left with a surplus on the top? (This indicates teeth that are too high or an uneven feed.) Does the machine stop quickly when you lift your foot, or, if you prefer a knee control, your knee, or does it run on? An electronic control stops at once, a good electric one stops within three stitches.

After you have taken all these points into account, consider what else you want the machine to do. As so many fabrics fray and have to be neatened, it is helpful to have a swing-needle machine that does a zigzag stitch. The needle is swung from side to side in a variety of widths by means of a stitch regulator. There are two kinds of swing-needle machine: the semi-automatic and the fully automatic. The semi-automatic works a limited range of stitches, including buttonhole, and on most machines the top has to be opened up and a disc inserted for each change of stitch. The fully automatic performs a wider range of stitches; the extra ones, however, are mainly for embroidery. The stitches are selected simply by turning a knob or dial. Check which machine feet are included in the purchase price.

Consider, too, whether you require a free-arm model or a flatbed. The flatbed, the original type, has a solid base and is useful for big articles such as curtains and sheets. On the free-arm, the plate, or bed, and the bobbin case are fitted into an arm that stands free of the base, so that fabric can easily be moved across and round underneath when sewing. This model is useful for such purposes as setting in sleeves and cuffs and for children's clothes. The ideal solution is to buy a free-arm model that has a table plate to add on, and a cabinet with a special lifting and lowering mechanism so that by moving a lever you convert the machine from free-arm to flatbed and vice versa.

Ask the dealer about servicing, repairs and speed of repair. If in doubt, check these points with the wholesaler.

Read the guarantee carefully. If you are not going to use the machine much, a year will go by very quickly.

## Buying second-hand

Test a second-hand machine thoroughly, preferably in two separate sessions, and do not buy it until you have checked that the make is not obsolete, that the machine works and that you can get it repaired. Be very suspicious if it is a new model; it may be for sale because it is defective.

Since they were invented, sewing machines have been heirlooms, handed down, still functioning perfectly, for generations. Buy a good-quality machine, pay as much as you can afford, and you might well have something to hand on in your family. But, if you buy a cheap machine, regard it purely as an interim measure, a stepping stone to a Rolls Royce—but do not complain if it does not perform like a Rolls Royce.

## Looking after your machine

Use the machine as much as possible and each time you use it check that the flex casing is not badly worn and exposing wires. Store the machine in a warm place and keep it dust free. If you leave it out between sewing sessions, make a loose protective cover for it. Brush out all fluff repeatedly—several times when making a garment. New models can be stiff and are easier to use when run in.

## Cleaning

Clean and oil your machine regularly, preferably at the end of each garment. If it is being put away for any length of time, clean and oil it beforehand.

To clean the machine, remove the needle and throw it away. Open all doors, remove all plates, take out the bobbin case and remove the bobbin. Clear out any pins from the bottom of the machine. Brush out all fluff and bits of thread, especially on and under the teeth, with the machine brush. Blow hard to remove the last traces. Wipe all parts with a clean rag.

## Oiling

Many machines have the oil points marked; put only one drop of sewing machine oil in each. Run the machine and watch the oil being absorbed. If any other moving parts look dry, apply one drop of oil to each and run the machine again. If oil points are not marked, apply oil to all obvious moving parts and to holes. Put one drop of oil in the bobbin socket. Wipe away excess oil with a clean rag. Close all doors and polish the machine. Place a piece of fabric under the foot to catch excess oil and lower the foot.

When you next use the machine, wipe the needle socket to remove any oil, remove the fabric and then insert a new needle. Before threading up, run the machine on a piece of fabric until you are sure no more oil is coming from the needle socket.

## Position

The machine should be about 10 cm/4 in away from the front edge of the supporting surface, and your eyes should be between 15 and 24 cm/6 and 9 in diagonally above and directly in front of the needle. Try a chair or, preferably, an adjustable stool for comfort—when sewing you should be able to lean forward with both hands on the machine bed. If the chair or stool is the wrong height it will cause backache. If the chair is too low, put blocks under the legs rather than adding a cushion. If you have a foot control, make sure your foot rests easily on it. Have the maximum table space to the left to take the weight of the fabric. When making large items, place a chair near the machine with its back to the table and push the fabric on to it as you sew.

### Thread

Buy enough thread—an all-purpose synthetic or a mercerized cotton, unless otherwise directed under the individual stitches—to complete the garment. If seams are to be neatened, you will generally need two reels; a long dress or other garment with long edges to be neatened will usually require three reels.

### Needles

For normal sewing, needles range in size from small, 70 (11), to medium, 90 (14), and large, 110 (18). Choose the one most suitable for the fabric. In general, the finer the fabric the smaller the needle so that it does not make ugly

| *Large* |
| *Medium* |
| *Small* |

holes. A medium size is suitable for most medium-thickness fabrics, but sometimes a very close weave or knit is better stitched with a finer needle. Change to a new needle frequently, particularly when working on synthetic fabrics.

### Attachments

All machines have attachments for special kinds of stitching. Some make sewing easier on certain fabrics, some save time and some are essential, sometimes in conjunction with a particular needle, for forming various stitches.

The machine manual will explain how to attach and use the feet. Those illustrated here are the most useful ones; some may have to be purchased as extras, but they are worth the investment for a more professional result. Keep the additional feet near the machine so that you will be more inclined to use them.

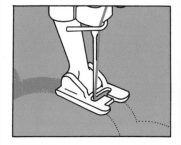

**Embroidery foot** Use for satin stitch and machine embroidery. Short toes allow greater visibility and accuracy; underside is raised to take the thickness of the stitch.

A special needle is available in a range of sizes for leather and suede.

*Leather/suede*

This has a spear-shaped point, which cuts the fabric. Never use it on any other types of material.

A ball-point needle, also available in a range of sizes, prevents missed stitches on synthetic jersey, the ball-

*Ball-point*

point pushing into the fabric easily to ensure that every stitch is properly formed.

*Twin*

Certain stitches require particular needles, such as, for double stitching, the twin needle.

*Double-eyed*

The double-eyed needle obviates the need to change needles for a lot of alternate basting and stitching. The needle is simply rethreaded, with basting thread through the upper eye, or with ordinary thread through the lower one.

**Bobbins**
There is little variation in size and shape. Some bobbins have holes all round which make it easy to see how much thread is left. At the start of winding the bobbin, the end of thread can be passed through either of the two smaller holes, whichever is uppermost, but this is not essential. Others have a groove at the top and bottom to fit on to certain types of bobbin winder. Metal bobbins are more durable than plastic ones.

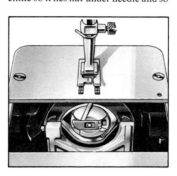

**Inserting threaded bobbin in case** Place in socket of bobbin case and pull thread round under spring until it emerges from hole in socket.

**Inserting bobbin in flatbed machine** Draw back needle plate. Pull out central bar on back of bobbin case to grip bobbin, and insert case in machine so it lies flat under needle and so

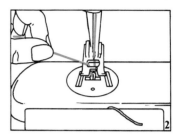

bar extending from side of case fits into upper groove beneath machine bed. Close needle plate.

**Raising bobbin thread** Insert threaded bobbin case. On a flatbed machine

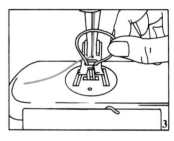

leave needle plate door open; on a free-arm shut hinged door of bobbin holder. Hold top thread loosely and turn hand wheel towards you until needle is right down in bobbin area (**1**).

Continue to turn hand wheel to bring needle up to its highest point. As it comes up, it will have a loop of bobbin thread round it (**2**).

Let go of top thread and pull loop with fingers or pin to bring free end of bobbin thread up through the hole in the plate (**3**).

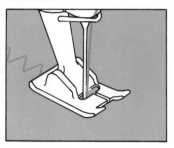

**Straight stitch foot** The general all-purpose foot for all straight and zig-zag stitching.

**Hemming foot** Most suitable for fine fabrics. Has a long toe and a central curl that turns under the raw edge to form a narrow hem, which is fed under the needle.

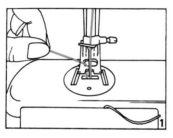

**Binding foot** Fabric is fed through the central groove inside the raised cone and encased in binding wrapped round and shaped by outer grooves. Bought pre-shaped binding is fed through slit at top of cone.

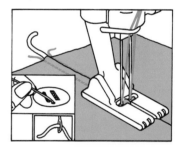

**Pin tuck foot** Makes narrow tucks that fit into the grooves on the front of the foot. Use with twin needle. Tucks can be filled with cord, which is fed up through the hole in the needle plate.

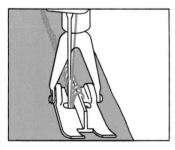

**Tailor's tacking foot** Raised centre lifts thread, making loops on surface of fabric; the loops are then cut to leave tufts of thread. A quick method of marking a large area.

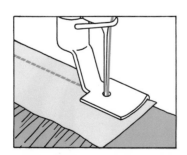

**Gathering foot** Gathers a length of fabric in fixed amounts as you stitch. Some gathering feet will also gather one piece of fabric while stitching it to another flat, ungathered piece.

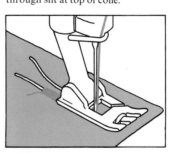

**Buttonhole foot** Large foot for machined buttonholes; position middle toe on marked line and watch line and stitching progress through wide needle hole.

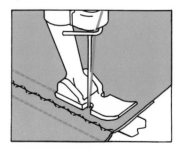

**Zip foot** Slender foot with semicircular holes on either side for stitching close to zip teeth; adjust needle to enter appropriate hole. Also used for applying piping.

# Hand-sewing Equipment

Small scissors

Tape measure

Silk buttonhole twist and silk sewing thread

Mercerized thread 40 and 60

Tailor's chalk

Multicoloured thread plait

Polyester thread

Sharps, left, and betweens, right

Bodkins

Battery-operated scissors

Elastic thread

Beeswax

Thimble and open-ended thimble

Basting thread

Pincushion and emery bag

Plastic-headed pins

Large cutting-out scissors

Button thread

Rouleau turner

Unpicker

Pattern tracing wheel

Needle threader

Polyester thread

Polyester thread

Nylon invisible thread

Metre rule

Left-handed scissors

Medium scissors

Lightweight all-purpose scissors

Adjustable marker

Good sewing equipment is not merely desirable but essential for professional results. Although the range of gadgets and aids for hand sewing is continually increasing, the basic items required are few.

### Scissors

Good-quality scissors that not only cut well but are comfortable to hold are an essential part of sewing equipment. Drop-forged steel scissors are a good buy as they have sharp blades and can be reconditioned. Although you can rely solely on a pair of lightweight all-purpose scissors, it is best to have several pairs of different sizes. For snipping threads and seam turnings use a small pair with large finger holes; for trimming seams and fabric edges a medium-sized pair with 17 cm/6½ in blades; and for cutting out fabric accurately, a large pair with 28 cm/11 in blades. All except the small pair should be side-bent—shaped so that the handles fit the hand comfortably and the blade rests flat on the table to give an accurate cutting line. Special scissors with handles and blades reversed right to left are available for left-handed sewers. Battery-operated scissors, although less accurate, are useful for those who have problems manipulating ordinary scissors; they also make cutting out less tiring. Never use dressmaking scissors for any other purpose or they will become blunt.

### Needles

Betweens are short needles, ideal for hand sewing as it is easier to make small, correctly formed stitches with a short needle. Keep a variety of sizes and select needles according to the weight of the fabric. Sharps, long needles, are used for fly-running or for gathering when a lot of stitches are collected on the needle. These are also available in different sizes. Very long needles known as "straws" are used for working through many layers. Needles soon become blunt so replace them often.

### Thread

Sewing thread is available in different fibres and thicknesses. For general hand and machine sewing there is a choice of mercerized cotton, synthetic thread and silk. A slightly shiny cotton thread, mercerized cotton is available in two thicknesses—60 for lightweight fabrics and 40 for heavy. It is suitable for use on natural fibre fabrics but is not strong enough for synthetics. A multicoloured plait of mercerized cotton is a handy way of keeping small quantities of a variety of colours for minor hand-sewing tasks. Polyester synthetic thread is suitable for all types of fabric. Pure silk thread may be used for sewing on silk and good-quality wool.

All threads are available in a range of colours but if you cannot find a colour that exactly matches the fabric, choose a shade darker because it will show less than a light thread. On a multicoloured fabric, do not necessarily match the thread to the background colour.

Choose one to match the predominant effect—sometimes this may not even be one of the colours in the fabric.

Other threads have special uses. Basting thread is a loosely twisted cotton, easy to break and remove, which is used for temporary stitching. Elastic thread is for gathering and shirring, and nylon invisible thread is useful for stitching hems. Button thread is a thick, slightly shiny linen thread for attaching buttons to heavy items such as coats. Silk buttonhole twist, a thick pure silk thread, is suitable for working buttonholes on thick fabrics and for decorative stitching.

### Thimble

A thimble is worn on the middle finger of the hand holding the needle and makes hand sewing more comfortable and efficient. In addition to the thimble with a top there is an open-ended thimble, which is pleasant to use as air can reach the finger.

### Beeswax

It is essential to strengthen double thread for sewing on buttons by coating it with beeswax, and it is generally helpful to wax double thread to prevent the two strands from parting. A light covering of wax on synthetic thread stops it twisting in use.

### Bodkin

Once made in bone or ivory, bodkins are now available only in plastic. Use them instead of scissors for removing basting stitches as scissors may harm the fabric. Bodkins can also be used for threading elastic or cord through a casing. The elastic is tied round the grooves at one end of the bodkin and then inserted.

### Tailor's chalk

Stitching lines, darts and alterations can all be marked with tailor's chalk. Always use white chalk as colours may not brush out easily—even on white fabric it is visible as a dull mark. Keep the chalk sharp by shaving the edge carefully with the medium scissors.

### Measures

A fibreglass tape measure, marked with metric and Imperial measurements, is the best buy. Linen and other fabric tape measures eventually stretch a little. An adjustable marker, a short metal rule with a movable arrow, is useful when the same measurement has to be used repeatedly as, for example, when making tucks or buttonholes. The arrow is set at the beginning of the work at the required measurement and left in position until the work is complete. Use a metre rule or yardstick for long straight measurements and checking grain lines and hems. It should be made of smooth wood so it does not catch on fabrics.

### Pins

Buy good steel pins in a container. Always keep the dark absorbent paper with the pins

as it prevents rust. Cheap pins are difficult to insert and can damage or mark fabric because they are too thick and do not have good points. Long pins with coloured plastic heads are too long for normal use, but are suitable for fitting or for open or hairy fabrics where they are easily visible. Pincushions are a safe and handy means of storing pins when pinning. Some have an emery bag, which contains an abrasive for cleaning pins and needles.

### Notions

Many other items of equipment are useful if not essential. To minimize fraying and to hold edges and turnings down, two kinds of iron-on adhesive strip are available—a fine web strip and one with a peel-off paper backing. They are both sandwiched between two layers of fabric. The paper-backed one has the advantage that the backing can be left on until you press the top layer of fabric on to the strip.

A needle threader is helpful if you have difficulty threading needles or have bad eyesight; instructions for use are supplied on the packet. Seams may be quickly ripped open with an unpicker. The sharp point is inserted under the first stitch and the unpicker moved along the seam so the curve cuts the stitches; see also p. 37. The point is also useful for picking out odd threads. A tracing wheel can be used with dressmaker's carbon to transfer pattern markings to fabric. This is less efficient than tailor's tacks as it marks only one side.

A rouleau turner, a long metal needle with a blunt end, is handy for turning through rouleau. For threading elastic, cord, ribbon, etc., through a casing, an elastic threader can be used instead of a bodkin. A flat metal needle, it has an oblong eye, through which one end of the cord is threaded and knotted to anchor it. Elastic must be sewn to the eye.

All these additional notions and many others are helpful and often time-saving, but it is essential to provide yourself first with the best basic equipment, which will be of long-lasting assistance to your sewing.

*Porcelain thimbles, very popular as courting gifts, were made, often by apprentice potters, in all the great English potteries from the 18th century onwards.*

# Hand-sewing Equipment

The history of hand sewing is one of refinement rather than of development. Methods and equipment are universal and have changed very little.

The basic tool, the needle, is a perfect piece of functional design developed more than 14,000 years ago. Needles and pins began life as crude awls made of thorn, bone or flint, used to punch lacing holes in animal skins. Gradually, the needle emerged as a specific tool, at first notched like a crochet hook so that hair or sinew could be attached and ultimately refined by the drilling of an eye. By the Bronze Age, needles and pins were commonplace.

Suitable thread came a little after the advent of the needle: cotton appeared in India and Egypt in 3000 BC, silk in China in 2640 BC and wool and linen in Europe in the 7th century BC. The processes established at these early dates for producing yarn from raw material have not been superseded, merely mechanized.

Topless bronze and brass thimbles, bronze and iron pins, one-piece, curved, cloth-cutting shears and a flourishing cotton industry were ancient Rome's contribution to sewing. In contrast, medieval Europe almost sank into regression, producing only iron wire pins and needles and leather thimbles. Help was on its way, however: slowly the Arabs were bringing silk to Europe, and by the 12th century sericulture was established in Italy. By the 14th century a thriving thimble industry had been established in Nüremberg, where craftsmen specialized in making ornate brass thimbles.

In the 15th and 16th centuries, the English pin industry, slowly changing over to brass, ran foul of officialdom, Richard III banning imports in 1483 and Henry VIII restricting the sale of pins to two days a year. Steel needles, which probably originated in China, were brought to Europe by the Moors. Thimbles were being produced in every conceivable material from shagreen to porcelain, and in Renaissance France the first tape measures appeared, ribbons embroidered with lines a fixed distance apart. Centimetre markings were not introduced until 1799. Double-bladed steel scissors, originating from the East, were produced in 16th-century Venice, and their distinctive shape encouraged much ingenious decoration, culminating in an extremely rude 18th-century French design known as *jambes de princesse* (princess's legs).

Naturally, the Industrial Revolution made its mark. With the invention in 1824 of the solid-headed pin machine, pins were made for the first time from a single strand of wire. Another first was the production of thread sold ready-wound on wooden bobbins instead of in skeins for the buyer to wind at home. Mercerization made cotton thread stronger and smoother by treating it with caustic soda. The needle industry was automated, but scissor-making remains a craft. Our own century's contribution is manmade yarns, but it is beyond the technocrats to redesign the basic sewing tools.

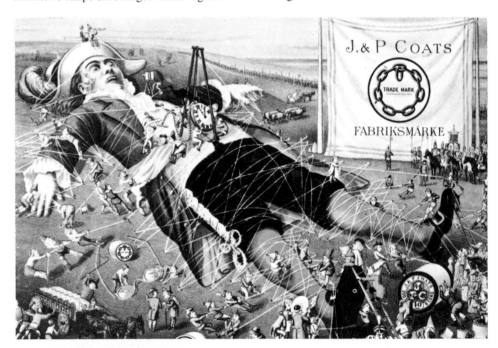

*Enterprising Lilliputians immobilize the luckless Gulliver and demonstrate the remarkable strength and versatility of the various kinds of factory-wound thread first produced in the mid-19th century.*

*After the invention of the eye-drilling machine in 1826, needle-making in England graduated from the status of a cottage industry, albeit sophisticated, to full mass production. Needles of all sizes and degrees of sharpness were made and artfully packaged, usually in strong paper envelopes.*

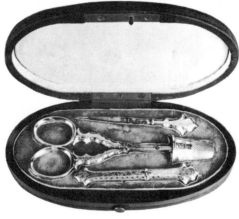

*A late Victorian silver sewing set, nestling compactly in a velvet-lined case. The set comprises a needle case, thimble, scissors and a stiletto, a decorously fiendish device used to stab sewing holes, either on closely woven material or for metal threadwork.*

*A maple leaf pincushion, right, bristling with pearls and patriotism, made in 1900 in Canada.*

# Fibres and Fabrics

At one time it was fairly easy to identify the fibre used to make a fabric. Not only were the natural fibres such as cotton and wool recognizable, but so were nylon and polyester. Consequently, it was possible to make a reasonable guess at how the fabric would behave in wear and how it would have to be treated during making up. The fabrics, too, were fairly standard, but due to great technological advances in mixtures of fibres it is now rarely possible to distinguish the fibre content instantly.

Fortunately, rolls of fabric now have to have their fibre content labelled. The fibres are listed in order of predominance; those present in quantities of 5 per cent or less do not need to be named unless they significantly affect the behaviour of the main fibre. It is, therefore, important to be familiar with all the main fibres, both natural and manmade, and with their properties in order to know what to expect from the fabric. All fibre names have been standardized and rayon, now known as viscose, has been broken down into its different types for identification. If the trade name is used on the label, the generic name is also shown.

Fibres are produced either in staple form, as short tufts, or in filament form, as long continuous strands. The spun fibre is known as yarn. All synthetics are produced as filaments, but most can also be processed to form staple yarn. Silk is produced in filament form only, whereas wool and cotton come only in staple form.

Natural and manmade fibres may be blended with other fibres before spinning, or spun first and then combined with other fibres, before being made into cloth.

## Natural fibres

The first to make clothing out of natural fibres, either from animal hairs or from parts of plants or vegetables, was prehistoric man. The fibres were spun to form yarn. The oldest evidence of fibre use is probably the specimens of flax and wool fabrics found in primitive lake dwellings in Switzerland, which date back to the 6th and 7th centuries BC. Mummies wrapped in linen bandages and wall paintings depicting the process of preparing the fibre indicate that linen was well known to the Egyptians more than 5000 years ago. The first cotton cloth is believed to have been woven in India in 3000 BC, and the production of silk was an industry in China in 2640 BC.

These four principal natural fibres—cotton, linen, silk and wool—continued to monopolize the textile market until the late 19th and early 20th centuries, when the first manmade fibre—rayon—and later the first synthetic fibre—nylon—were introduced. Even today, despite the rapid increase in the range of manmade fibres, natural fibres maintain their lead in the world's fibre production.

Among the other natural fibres are ramie, which resembles linen and is taken from the stalk of a species of nettle, and the luxurious hair fibres, rabbit, angora, mohair, cashmere and vicuna.

Ramie, a lustrous pure white fibre, is sturdy and coarse and can be blended in small amounts with wool, cotton, nylon and viscose to increase their durability. As it withstands wear and heat, treat the resulting fabric according to its main fibre.

Of the hair fibres, rabbit has been used in Europe as a fibre for clothing for more than a century and is warm, soft and lightweight. As the hairs are short they are unsuitable for spinning on their own and so are usually mixed with wool. Many woven and knitted fabrics have a small percentage of rabbit hair included, for extra beauty and warmth. Angora rabbit hair is occasionally used alone for knitwear and expensive dress fabrics.

Mohair, a very fine, thin, smooth fibre, is derived from the hair of the Angora goat. The most valued mohair comes from Turkey. Mohair is commonly combined with wool to make top-grade, lightweight, fine suitings for men. It is also used for scarves, sweaters and stoles as well as dress materials, linings, velvets and imitation furs.

Cashmere was originally produced in Kashmir from the hair of the indigenous goat, but now comes also from Mongolia, Tibet, Iran and Iraq. Smooth and soft, cashmere is used mainly for sweaters and some woven fabrics. The finest and costliest of all hair fibres is vicuna, from the animal of the same name, a member of the llama family found in the Andes.

Follow the care instructions on the fabric label closely for all luxury hair fibres. In general, if the fibres are washable, treat them the same way as wool. The characteristics and uses of the four main natural fibres—cotton, silk, linen and wool—and laundering, dry cleaning and pressing instructions are on p. 218.

## Manmade fibres

When future historians and archaeologists name and categorize the present era, the Stone Age, Iron Age and Bronze Age may well be joined by the Age of Manmade Fibres. Although the history of these fibres begins in the last century, it is during the 20th century, particularly in the 1930s and 1940s, that the most rapid changes have taken place.

Manmade fibres owe much to the producer of a natural fibre, the silkworm. Although silk was first produced commercially in China in 2640 BC, it was not until 1664 that an English chemist and mathematician, Robert Hooke, suggested that the silkworm's work could be emulated by man.

The first to put this idea into practice was Count Hilaire de Chardonnet. In 1885 he was granted the first manmade fibre patent and in 1891 his first artificial silk factory went into production in France. The fibre was based on cellulose. In this De Chardonnet was indebted to the discovery of his compatriot A. Payen, who, in 1839, had extracted cellulose from wood, so providing the basis for all the early manmade fibres.

A new impetus to the industry came with the manufacture of viscose. (The name comes from the Latin *viscosus*, treacly.) A cellulose-based fibre, it was invented in 1892 by the three British scientists Cross, Bevan and Beadle, and proved to be a more economic means of producing artificial silk than any previous methods—as such it was responsible, among its many other uses, ▶

---

## MAKING FIBRES

*The basic method of making almost all manmade fibres is a direct imitation of nature. A viscous liquid chemical substance is forced through fine holes in a nozzle, or spinneret, to form filaments, below right. The filaments are then solidified in various ways. Similarly, the silkworm extrudes liquid silk through a gland in its head known as a spinneret. The liquid solidifies to form a cocoon, below left.*

*There are two different forms of manmade fibres—continuous filament yarn and staple fibre. A continuous filament yarn can be made up* *of a single filament or several hundred fine filaments, and in this form it is then woven or knitted into a fabric. Staple fibre consists of thousands of filaments from several spinnerets which form a tow, a thick rope-like structure. This is then cut into exact lengths and re-spun before being made up into a fabric. Different fibres can be blended to form staple fibres, so giving a wide variety of textiles. Staple fibre can be processed more quickly and easily than continuous filament, and the yarns are usually cheaper than the corresponding continuous filament ones.*

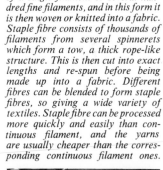

# Fibres and Fabrics

for the birth of the modern stocking.

Acetate, the nearest to silk of all manmade fibres, finally went into production at the end of World War I. Like viscose, acetate revolutionized women's clothing and was widely used for underwear and for nightwear.

The ultimate breakthrough in the production of manmade fibres came in 1931 with the so-called "Pe-Ce" fibres, the first completely synthetic textile fibres manufactured from the chemical polyvinyl chloride by the German company IG-Farben. The manmade fibres industry no longer had to rely on natural substances or regenerated extracts from them, such as cellulose, for making fabrics, but could instead turn to the increasingly wide range of petroleum or coal-tar chemicals for the production of fully synthetic fibres.

### The pin-up era

The greatest textile revolution was the development of nylon in 1938. Not only did it inaugurate, in 1939, the era of the nylon stocking and the pin-up, but, because nylon was thermoplastic, for the first time fabrics and garments could be set by heat so they kept their size and shape in wear and wash. Within months of each other, Du Pont de Nemours in the United States and IG-Farben in Germany patented the fibres which, although made quite differently, were almost identical in their characteristics.

It was Du Pont who called theirs nylon. Originally made from coal-tar products, nylon is now mainly made from petroleum chemicals.

The 1940s saw the discovery of acrylic and polyester, both synthetic fibres. Polyester was developed by two British researchers, Whinfield and Dickson, in 1941 and manufactured by Imperial Chemical Industries (ICI)—the biggest of the European chemical concerns—and Du Pont. Acrylic was patented first by a German fibre chemist, Herbert Rein, in 1942 and two months later by Du Pont.

Since the 1940s other cellulosic and synthetic fibres including triacetate and modacrylics have been invented. In 1962 the production of synthetic manmade fibres exceeded the million tons mark. By 1975 the figure had risen to above seven million tons. For many years the cellulose-based fibres dominated the manmade market, but in 1968 synthetics overtook them.

At their best manmade fibres produce textiles that are tough, washable, crease-resisting, hardwearing and less likely than their natural counterparts to shrink, fade or felt. They have also had considerable effect on how textiles are made up. More suitable, because of their smoothness, than natural fibres for other methods of fabric production besides weaving, manmade fibres are continually increasing the range of fabrics available.

For many, the word laundering still conjures up thoughts of "Black Monday", despite the numerous labour-saving appliances and cleansing agents available today which have so drastically reduced the amount of effort expended to obtain a clean wash.

The oldest and most primitive method of laundering, still in use in some parts of the world, is to pound the cloth with stones or trample it in water until the dirt is removed by friction. In the Middle Ages grease stains were removed by rubbing the cloth with a mixture of fuller's earth and lye, or by soaking it in warm wine for a couple of days. Washerwomen also used wooden bats to beat dirt from clothes.

In the 16th century it was customary for household washing to be done in large amounts every two or three months. The famous 17th-century diarist Samuel Pepys hinted at the domestic upheaval washday brought when he wrote: "Home, and being washday, dined upon cold meat."

Homemade soap, melted to a jelly, was commonly used for household laundry in the 1600s. Tallow, olive oil and ashes dissolved in water were the basic ingredients. Once a cheap way of producing the alkali needed for soapmaking was discovered in 1793, and the heavy soap tax in Great Britain was repealed in 1853, commercial supplies became abundant and consumption

rose steadily. The turn of the century brought more specialized soaps for different purposes, but it was not until a petroleum derivative became available in 1950 that the first soapless detergent appeared. At the end of the 1960s a wash product was produced that was neither a soap nor a soapless detergent but combined their best qualities.

During the 19th century other aids to lessen the drudgery of washday became widely used, such as the wooden dolly, a long pole for agitating the clothes in a tub, the washboard and the wringer. The principles behind these early aids are reflected in the toss, tumble and spin action of washing machines today.

The later 19th century also witnessed the advent of the free-standing boiler for heating water by gas or electricity, as well as one of the earliest home washing machines, which was operated by turning a crank. Patented in 1858 by Hamilton E. Smith of Pennsylvania, it unfortunately tangled or tore most of the clothes. Not until 1907 was there a home washer run by a motor, but by 1912 nearly all home laundry manufacturers in the United States and many in Europe were making machines driven by electric power. Today most home washing machines are automatic, thus freeing their owners from the backbreaking toil and drudgery of "Black Monday".

*Camouflage-coloured acetate was applied to the linen wings of World War I aircraft to make them wind- and water-proof. As its fumes also destroyed the liver, British workers were given an antidotal pint of milk or pound of cheese a day.*

*At the beginning of the century, heavily soiled clothes were generally cleaned with a heavy-duty soap like Foamo, which was melted in boiling water to make a washing solution. Satisfactory soap powder was not manufactured until 1925.*

One of the first soap flakes, Lux was introduced in 1900 for fine fabrics and woollens, as recommended in the above advertisement of 1910 by Will Owen.

The drudgery and rigour of washday without mechanized aids is epitomized in this 19th-century beckside scene in the Scottish highlands.

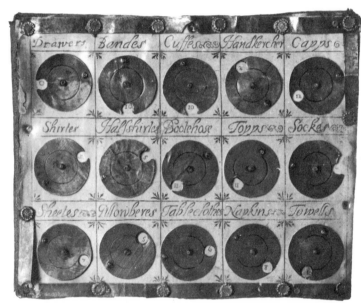

Until the 18th century, all but the poorest sent their laundry out or had it done by servants. The number of items being laundered was recorded by wooden dials on washing tally boards.

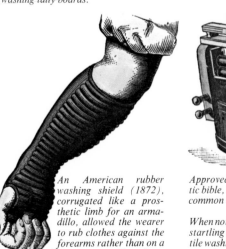

An American rubber washing shield (1872), corrugated like a prosthetic limb for an armadillo, allowed the wearer to rub clothes against the forearms rather than on a damaging washboard.

Approved by Mrs Beeton in her domestic bible, the hand-driven wringer was a common aid in the 19th century.

When not demonstrating its many other startling talents, this ingeniously versatile washing machine from 1928 packed up to become an ironing table.

# Fibres and Fabrics

Yarns of different colours, strengths and thicknesses can be combined to produce a wide range of woven fabrics. The thickness of a yarn is defined by its denier, the weight per standard length of fibre (9,000 metres/ 9,846 yards); the lower the denier the finer the yarn and the lighter the resulting cloth. In some fibres single spun yarns are weak, so they are often twisted together in sets of two, three or four to strengthen them and sometimes also to produce a combination of colours within a yarn. The resulting yarns are referred to as two ply, three ply and four ply.

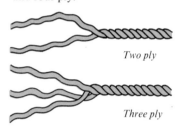

*Two ply*

*Three ply*

When fabric is woven, the vertical threads, or warp yarns, which run the length of the finished fabric, are held on the loom and the horizontal, or weft, yarns inserted through them. The warp yarns are sometimes known as selvedge threads because they run parallel with the strengthened edge, or selvedge, of the fabric.

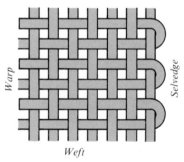

*Warp*  *Selvedge*

*Weft*

The most common pattern of weaving the weft through the warp is alternately over and under the warp threads. This produces a plain-weave fabric. If both weft

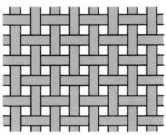

*Plain weave*

and warp yarns of the plain weave are of identical weight, the finished fabric is known as even-weave. When yarns of different strengths are used, the warp threads are the stronger, so it is wise to cut out with the warp running in the direction of most strain. Other patterns in the weave are produced by varying the order in which weft threads pass over and under the warp. Hopsack and twill are examples of two-over-

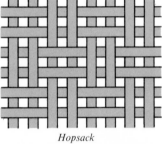

*Hopsack*

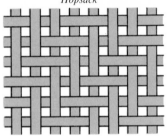

*Twill*

two-under weaves. Patterns, as in brocade, can be woven into a fabric by passing the weft over many warp threads. This process is known as Jacquard weaving after the special apparatus and loom and their French inventor Joseph Marie Jacquard.

*Brocade*

*Jacquard weave, RS and WS*

## Knitted fabrics

Knit or jersey fabrics are produced from a continuous length of yarn, and most yarns can be used to make them. There are two basic knit structures—weft and warp. Weft knit is modelled on hand

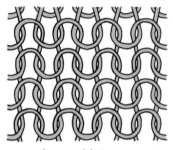

*Loose weft knit*

*Single-warp knit*

knitting with one yarn knitted in the horizontal, weft, direction. For a warp knit several yarns are knitted at once in the lengthways, warp, direction. Warp knits generally have less stretch than weft because each yarn interlocks with the one beside it.

Knits can be close and firm, loose and ribbed like hand knitting, or lacy. A surface pattern may be created by introducing another yarn, but the back of the fabric will show that it is knitted. Knits can also be identified by their cut edges, which do not fray. All knits stretch across the width, sometimes by an enormous amount. There may be no selvedge, but if there is, it may be rough and uneven or curled.

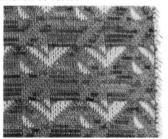

*Weft knit with selvedge*

## Bonded fabrics

Bonds, or laminates, are woven or knitted fabrics specially produced for sticking to a backing, which is often thin acrylic or nylon knit. A very thin sheet of polyurethane foam may be placed between the fabric and the backing. This adds warmth to the fabric and reduces creasing. The two or three layers are permanently stuck together with an adhesive.

*Bonded*

## Stretch fabrics

Elastomer yarns have long been woven into fabrics used for making garments such as swimsuits, but today stretch versions of woven fabrics, including gabardine, denim, lace, twill and many others, can be produced. The stretch usually runs lengthways, with the warp, but can be incorporated into both warp and weft.

## FABRIC FINISHES

Demand for easy-care, resilient and hard-wearing fabrics has led to rapid development in fabric finishing. The handle and performance of a fabric is greatly improved by finishing, but unless the treated fabric is particularly smooth, rough, dull or shiny the finish may be invisible to the purchaser. Because finishes may be destroyed by incorrect treatment and often are not labelled, it is best to enquire before buying.

## Colour fast

Most fabrics, such as cotton and silk, that are liable to fade in sunlight are treated to resist fading unless, as in denim, fading is deliberately required.

## Shrink resistant

Absorbent fibres such as cotton often shrink when penetrated by water. Many fabrics (voile and loosely woven cotton are two of the most notable exceptions) can be pre-shrunk, but the process is sometimes known as "shrinkage control" because it is virtually impossible for manufacturers to guarantee no further shrinkage.

## Crease resistant

Fabrics made from fibres such as cotton, silk, linen and viscose tend to crease badly and thus benefit from the application of a crease resistant finish. Because all fabrics crease, if only for a moment, when placed under pressure, manufacturers often call this a "crease recovery" finish. Crease resistance is achieved by various processes and fibres react differently, so guarantees vary accordingly. For example, some fabrics are guaranteed to shed creases within a quoted period out of wear, whereas for others the period is not quoted.

## Non-iron

Many manufacturers name their non-iron finishing process "minimum iron" or "drip dry" because the results after washing may not satisfy everyone and most fabrics do not dry entirely flat, especially where the fabric is double. Repeated washing eventually destroys a non-iron finish.

## Water repellant

Various chemical methods are used to treat fibres to reduce water absorption. The finish, applied to gabardine, poplin and nylon, is not completely waterproof and is often described as "shower-proof". Spray-on finish to reduce water absorption can be bought to treat fabric at home.

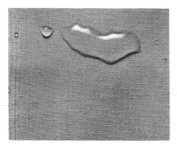

*Water repellant*

## Stain and alcohol repellant

A few fabrics such as dress velvet are treated to resist staining and repel alcohol. Always check fabric care instructions.

## Flame resistant

Fabrics cannot be made fireproof, but those that flare up readily, such as cotton and viscose, can be treated to make them slow to catch fire. When choosing fabric for children's nightwear, clothes for the elderly, or when buying dress net check

*Textiles were the major industry of the Middle Ages. This woodcut from a 12th-century manuscript at Trinity College, Cambridge, shows the progress of wool from the sheep through spinning, left, to cloth woven on a primitive loom.*

whether it is flame resistant. The finish is usually destroyed by boiling or bleaching the fabric.

*Flame resistant*

## Mothproof

Fabrics such as wool and silk that form the food of clothes-moth larvae can be treated to prevent them from being eaten in this way. A spray can be used for home treatment of fabric.

## Anti-bacterial

Fabrics liable to rot when attacked by mildew or the bacteria that break down human sweat can be treated by a process undetectable on the fabric. The treatment is usually applied only to more expensive materials.

## Brushed

Cotton, viscose, acrylics and nylon can be finished so that they have a soft, slightly furry surface. Brushed fabrics are warmer than unbrushed ones because additional air pockets are formed on their surface, but the brushing

process weakens the fibres and increases their flammability.

## Glazed

A polished effect, which reduces soiling, is produced on the fabric surface. Furnishing fabrics made from absorbent fibres and some dress fabrics, particularly cottons, may be glazed.

*Glazed*

## Mercerized

Caustic soda is applied to cotton and other natural fibres to create a slight shine and increase fibre strength. This important finish is applied to cotton sewing yarn as well as to cotton fabric.

## Embossed

Most fabrics can be embossed with a raised design by passing them between engraved rollers. The finish is not always permanent, so follow washing instructions carefully.

*Embossed*

## Moiré

A moiré, or water mark, effect is created by spraying silk, viscose, and sometimes cotton fabrics with water and then heating them. Do not damp press these fabrics or the effect is destroyed. A more permanent water mark is produced by making small engravings on the right side of the fabric. The life of the finish depends on both the fibre and the way it is treated, so follow care instructions meticulously.

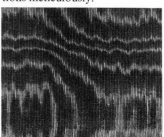

*Moiré*

# Fibres and Fabrics

Successful sewing depends very much on a careful choice of fabric. It is wise not to buy entirely on impulse, nor to have a totally preconceived idea, although the type of garment to be made narrows the choice. A tailored garment, for example, needs crisp fabric. To make a good choice, follow these guidelines:
● Stand in front of a mirror and hold the fabric over you to see if the colour is suitable. Check by comparing it with a colour you know to be unflattering.
● Hold the fabric against you flat, pleated, gathered or draped, depending on the garment style, to check that it reacts correctly.
● To see how the fabric looks against your legs, hold it so one end reaches your hemline. If choosing fabric for trousers or a long dress, lower its edge to the floor. Examine the effect of the fabric over the whole area of the planned garment, particularly if the fabric is checked, striped or has a very large or small pattern.
● Crush a corner of the fabric to see if it creases badly or springs up. Note that springy fabric is hard-wearing, but can be difficult to sew.
● Examine the raw edge to see if the fabric frays. If the fabric has no other disadvantages, fraying can be coped with by cutting out with turnings 5 mm/¼ in wider than usual, or more if necessary.
● Hold the fabric up to the light to examine the weave or knit. Use close weaves and knits for garments that will have heavy wear.
● Pull jersey fabric lengthways and widthways to check its give. Make sure that the fabric springs back after stretching.
● Look at the design or weave to see if the fabric has nap or is "one way" (see Nap).
● Check the straightness of the grain (see Grain).
● For checked or striped fabric fold over one corner to make sure the lines match (**1**). If they do not match, the fabric cannot be used on the cross because the pattern is uneven.
● Unroll the fabric and look for any flaws (see Flaws).
● Check the washability of the fabric and the finishes, such as crease and flame resistance.
● Select the fabric you like best, that will be most suitable for the garment and will mix well with existing clothes and accessories.

## Flaws

Flaws in fabric include knots or uneven patches in the weave, knit or print, dirty marks and, particularly in synthetics, dirt along the folded edge of the fabric. On good-quality fabric flaws are marked at the selvedge with coloured thread. Fabric with a flaw on the wrong side may be acceptable. If a flaw is on the right side, work out whether you have sufficient length to accommodate the pattern pieces before the flaw appears or estimate whether main pattern pieces can be placed on either side of the flaw to avoid it. By asking for extra fabric you should be able to avoid one flaw, but do not buy a length with several imperfections.

## Remnants

If bought wisely, remnants can be bargains, but remember that if the length was saleable for its purpose, as with trouser fabric, it would not be offered as a remnant. Small remnants are always usable. Cotton, for example, can be used for patchwork, repairs and contrasting yokes and cuffs, and fabrics of all kinds are ideal for toys. Larger remnants can be made into headsquares, aprons and children's clothes, while whole lengths make blouses. When buying a remnant, check that it is sufficient for the garment you have in mind.

## Grain

The grain is the straight thread of a woven fabric. The warp threads are usually known as the lengthways grain, the weft threads as the cross grain. Knitted fabrics do not in fact have a grain, although the term is used to refer to the lines of knitting.

If fabric is "off grain", the selvedges will not meet when the fabric is folded in half along the cross grain—the simplest check

*Couched in purple prose, this advertisement was intended to captivate the female interest and thereby promote the sale of the Aberfoyle range of fabrics. The advertisement appeared in 1928 in* McCall's, *the American fashion bible.*

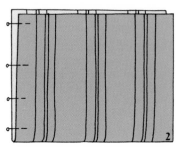

(**2**). Forcing the selvedges to meet causes wrinkling (**3**) and the fabric will not lie flat with both the straight grain of the fabric

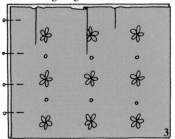

and the straight grain lines of the pattern pieces matching. (The straight grain is generally the warp, but small pieces of fabric are often cut on the weft.)

Woven fabric in a natural fibre can be straightened by pulling it from the two opposite "short" corners (**4**), although synthetics

may not respond to this treatment. If the fabric has a finish that prevents this method of straightening, dampen the whole length, pull it to correct the grain, fold it lengthways in half and baste it together round all edges before drying and pressing it. The

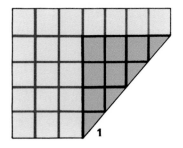

*Japanese silks such as those being selected by the women, left, are traditionally block printed or stencilled, a technique dating back in the Japanese textile industry to the 8th century AD.*

motif—to make it match. When cutting out, add an extra 1 cm/$\frac{3}{8}$ in turning allowance for a small pattern, more for a larger one, so the seams can be moved at fitting to improve matching. If in any doubt about matching, choose plain fabric for part of the garment, or turn some pieces such as yokes on to the cross to avoid matching.

Wherever possible, matching should be perfect at garment

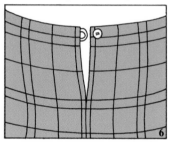

seams (**6**). It is not always possible to do this completely if, for example, the two matching edges are cut at different angles or one

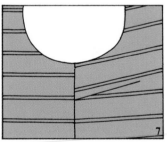

edge of a seam has a dart (**7**). A stripe or check may be perfectly matched round the body, includ-

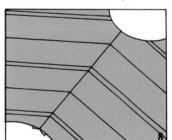

ing shoulder seams (**8**), but it may be impossible to chevron vertical lines at the side seams. Always try to match patterns perfectly at the centre front and centre back and, on a skirt, at the side seams. If a shoulder dart prevents matching, leave it out and adjust the fit.

basting can then be removed. Knitted fabrics can be straightened in a similar way. It is impossible, however, to straighten synthetic jersey because it is made from a thermoplastic fibre, which is permanently set by heat.

Fabric such as brocade that has the pattern woven into it can also be straightened, unless it is synthetic, but fabric that has been printed off grain cannot be corrected and the pattern pieces must be cut according to the print, ignoring the straight grain. If a piece of off-grain fabric must be used, choose a pattern with many small pieces and cut each out on single fabric one at a time.

## Nap

A true nap is a pile or finish on the fabric surface that lies in one direction only. If two pieces of fabric are joined with the nap facing in different directions, the piece with the nap lying the wrong way will appear lighter than the other one (**5**). If in doubt about the direction, brush your hand across the fabric in both

directions to see which way the pile lies smoothly. Examples of fabrics with a true nap are faced cloth, velours and velvet. A large number of other fabrics are "one way" for different reasons. Many fabrics have prints, checks or uneven stripes that lie in one direction. Satins, gabardines, knits and fabrics containing metal loops should be treated as one way because of the direction

of the weave or the effect of light on them.

If you are in any doubt about a fabric, always buy extra to allow for nap. Check the pattern envelope for the amount to buy. Cut all pattern pieces with the nap lying in the same direction.

## Matching patterned fabrics

Successful matching of prints, checks and stripes can depend on careful choice of fabrics and garment patterns. Before selecting a checked or striped fabric, make sure that the pattern envelope does not advise against it. If matching is necessary, avoid a pattern with many joins or panels and remember that gathers, pleats and folds are easier to manage. Buy enough extra fabric so that there is room to move each main pattern piece one whole pattern repeat on the fabric—it may be a stripe or block of checks or a big floral

# A-Z of Fabrics

Both natural and manmade fibres can be made up into such a wide variety of cloths that it is impossible to give detailed sewing instructions for each fibre. Refer to the individual fabrics in the following list of popular, widely used materials. If in doubt about how to handle a particular fabric, stitch and launder it in the same way as a fabric of a similar weight and thickness. For example, silk tweed should be treated as any other form of tweed of the same weight. Machine needle size, hand needle size, the type of thread and stitch length are given at the end of the entry for each fabric. For further information on fibre characteristics and care see pp. 218 and 219.

**ALPACA** The soft, fine hair of the South American alpaca makes a thin fabric that is both lustrous and crisp and also warm and durable. Used mainly for men's wear. Alpaca also denotes fabric made from other fibres and blends, such as viscose and acetate, with a similar finish. 70–90 (11–14); 7–9; silk or synthetic; medium.

**ANGORA** Formerly described any long, white rabbit hair included in fabric; now refers only to the hair of the Angora rabbit. Expensive and generally mixed with other fibres. 70–90 (11–14); 7–9; silk; medium.

**ASTRAKHAN** Very expensive curly fur simulating the fleece of the young astrakhan lamb. Astrakhan fur fabric, usually made from acrylic fibres, is a good imitation. Do not press. Used for hats and as coat trim. 100–110 (16–18); 6; synthetic; large.

**BARATHEA** Very closely woven, smooth, fine fabric usually of wool. Used for coats, skirts and suits. Marks easily in pressing. 90 (14); 6; synthetic or mercerized; medium to large.

**BATISTE** Soft, fine fabric, usually in plain colours. Can be of cotton or polyester yarn. Easy to sew. Washable. Used for dresses, lingerie, handkerchiefs, blouses and children's wear. 70–90 (11–14); 7; synthetic or mercerized; small.

**BEDFORD CORD** Long-wearing corded fabric, first made in New Bedford, Massachusetts. Made from wool, cotton or polyester. Can be attractively top stitched. Used for coats, jackets, riding habits and trousers. 100 (16); 6; synthetic; medium to large.

**BONDED FABRICS** Layers of fabric of any fibre, but usually acrylic, joined to a jersey backing, generally of nylon. The layers are held by adhesive, but sometimes a thin layer of polyurethane foam is also added. Non-fraying, easy to handle but springy. Top stitch seams. Used for loose coats and jackets. 90 (14); 6–7; synthetic; large.

**BOUCLE** Woven or knitted fabric in various weights, characterized by surface loops. May be wool, mohair or acrylic, or a mixture of several fibres. Used for ladies' coats, jackets and dresses. 90 (14); 6–7; synthetic; medium to large.

**BROCADE** Fancy-patterned fabric produced by mixing dull and shiny yarns in matching or contrasting colours and sometimes including metallic yarns. Additional threads are often introduced which run along WS and come to the surface only occasionally. Can be made from any yarn but now usually acetate. Frays, particularly if there are additional threads on WS. Dry press. Avoid too close a fit. Used for wedding and evening dresses; thicker types for furnishings. 70–90 (11–14); 8–10; synthetic; medium.

**BUCKRAM** Plain-weave, specially stiffened, coarse cotton fabric. Used for hats, belts and upholstery, including curtain pelmets. Not usually washable as the stiffening agents wash out. 90–100 (14–16); 5–6; synthetic; large.

**CALICO** A firm, plain-weave cotton fabric, originally made in Calicut, India. Generally cream coloured but also available in a variety of colours and patterns. Strong and hard-wearing. Used for dresses, shirts, blouses and children's clothes. 90 (14); 6–7; synthetic or mercerized; medium.

**CAMEL CLOTH** Any woollen or blend the colour of camel hair. Usually coat weight with a slightly brushed surface. "Camel hair" denotes very expensive cloth containing real camel's hair; sheep's wool is often added to reduce the price. 100 (16); 6–9; synthetic, mercerized or silk; large.

**CANVAS** Various types and weights of plain-weave cotton and linen yarns made for use as interfacing in tailored clothes. Also, in open weave, used for embroidery. Choose needle size and thread according to weight of canvas.

**CASHMERE** Expensive, fine, soft, lightweight fibre from hair of Kashmir goat. Often mixed with wool, it is made into knitwear and top-quality coatings. 70–90 (11–14); 6–9; silk or mercerized; medium to large.

**CHALLIS** A fine, lightweight fabric previously made from wool but now from any fibre or blend. Often printed with a floral or paisley pattern. Used for blouses, dresses and children's wear. 70 (11); 7–8; synthetic or mercerized; medium.

**CHAMBRAY** Cotton fabric made by using white weft yarns and coloured warp, forming a variety of stripes and patterns. Hard-wearing and easy to wash. Used for dresses, shirts, trousers and children's clothes. 70–90 (11–14); 6–8; synthetic or mercerized; medium.

**CHEESECLOTH** Originally used for wrapping cheese. A rough-surfaced fabric, usually Grade 4 pure cotton, with an unfinished look, but soft and comfortable in wear. In natural ecru or coloured. Washes well; need not be ironed. Used for blouses, skirts, shirts and dresses. 70 (11); 7–8; mercerized or synthetic; medium.

**CHENILLE** Thick, tufted, expensive fabric made from cotton, sometimes mixed with manmade fibres such as viscose; also made occasionally from silk or wool. Dry cleaning advisable. Do not press. Once confined to furnishings but now produced for coats, dressing gowns and jackets. 100 (16); 5–6; synthetic; large.

**CHIFFON** Sheer, soft fabric, sometimes made from silk, more often from nylon or polyester. Difficult to handle, especially the synthetic chiffons, which fray readily. Dry press. Used for scarves, blouses, dresses and evening wear. 70 (11); 8–10; synthetic or silk; small.

**CHINTZ** Closely woven cotton fabric with glazed or permanent finish. Usually printed with flowers or birds. Wears well. Used for furnishings. 90 (14); 5–6; mercerized or synthetic; large.

**CIRE** Fine, silky fabric with a shiny wet look. Made from silk or, more usually, nylon or polyester and sometimes acetate. Used for bathing suits, blouses, dresses and rainwear. 70 (11); 7; synthetic; small to medium.

**CORDUROY** *Cord du roi*—cloth of the king—is a ribbed fabric usually of cotton but it can contain some polyester or be entirely synthetic on a knitted backing. The pile, running the length of the fabric, is made by weaving additional threads into a plain- or twill-weave fabric and looping them over the surface. The loops are cut after weaving is complete. As the pile shades, cut out with it running upwards on the body. Press lightly on WS only. Used for jackets, trousers, suits, skirts, dresses and furnishings. 90 (14); 6; synthetic or mercerized; medium to large.

**CREPE** Fabric with crinkled appearance produced by chemically twisting the yarn before weaving. Made in wool, acetate, cotton, silk, polyester and acrylic yarns. Liable to shrink. Drapes well; used for dresses and blouses. 70–90 (11–14); 6–7; synthetic or mercerized; medium.

**DAMASK** Jacquard-weave fabric, mixing shiny and dull yarns. Pattern textures or colours on WS are exact reverse of those on RS. Made from cotton or linen for table wear and soft furnishings; from acetate, viscose and other synthetics for dresses. 90 (14); 6–7; mercerized or synthetic; medium.

**DENIM** Name derives from French town of Nîmes ("de Nîmes"). Hard-wearing twill-weave cloth of white yarns mixed with blue or another colour. Usually cotton but sometimes mixed with polyester. Washes well. Cotton varieties fade. Top stitches well. Used for work clothes and informal wear, particularly jeans. 90 (14); 6; synthetic or mercerized; medium to large.

**DOESKIN** Close-weave plain or twill cloth, usually fine wool, with a soft nap on RS producing a silky sheen. Press on WS only with steam iron or dry iron using a damp muslin cloth as the fabric iron-marks easily. Used for coats, skirts and dresses. 90 (14); 6–8; silk, mercerized or synthetic; medium to large.

**DONEGAL** Rough tweed of wool or mixtures including cotton, polyester, viscose, acrylic, characterized by a white knobbled effect. Used for coats, jackets, trousers and skirts. 90–100 (14–16); 5–7; synthetic or mercerized; medium to large.

**DRILL** Very strong, twill-weave cotton. Launders well. Used in white and khaki for uniforms and can also be striped. 110 (18); 6–7; synthetic or mercerized; large.

**DUCK** Very strong, closely woven heavy cloth, usually of cotton. Plain-weave canvas effect. Used for furnishings, protective clothing and trousers. 100 (16); 6; synthetic; large.

**DUPION** Comparatively inexpensive silk fabric, made from a thick, uneven yarn reeled from double cocoons. The effect can be imitated in acetate and synthetic yarns. Creases easily. Press dry if silk. Used for dresses and coats. 70 (11); 8–9; silk or synthetic; medium.

**DUVETYN** (also Duvetyne) Fabric with a smooth, brushed RS resembling suede finish. Often wool but can also be cotton or synthetic fibre. Cut pattern pieces with nap in one direction. Used for lightweight jackets, coats and dresses. 90 (14); 6–8; synthetic or mercerized; medium.

**FACED CLOTH** Any fabric that has a raised or brushed surface on RS, or face side. Unlike pile fabrics such as velours, these are not one-way fabrics. Usually wool but may also contain synthetic fibres such as acrylic or polyester. Medium- and heavyweight fabrics used for dresses, suits, coats and blazers. 90 (14); 7–8; synthetic or mercerized; medium to large.

**FAILLE** Cross-ribbed fabric with close weave. Sometimes silk but generally acetate or polyester. Used for dresses and coats. 70 (11); 7; synthetic; medium.

**FELT** Non-woven fabric with no grain made by pressing short lengths of wool fibre, cotton or synthetics and bonding them with heat and moisture. Weak, not washable, and fairly expensive. Available in a variety of colours. Used primarily for soft toys, decoration, boleros and hats, but not for durable clothes. 90 (14); 6; synthetic; large.

**FELT CLOTH** Woven fabric made of wool or blends with surface brushed or felted to obscure weave. Treat as ordinary plain-weave fabric. Used for coats and jackets. Sew as for felt.

**FLANNEL** Soft, warm, all-wool fabric with a slightly napped surface on RS. Often made into sports' clothes, blazers and skirts. 90 (14); 6–7; silk, mercerized or synthetic; medium to large.

**FLANNELETTE** Soft plain-weave cotton fabric with brushed surface. Warm and washable. Used for baby clothes, nappies and sheets. Also suitable for nightwear if flame-proofed. 70 (11); 7–8; mercerized or synthetic; medium.

**FUR FABRIC** Smooth or curly fur pile on woven or jersey backing. Pile usually acrylic but can be nylon or another synthetic. Backing generally synthetic. Cut all pieces with nap in same direction. Do not press. Used for jackets, coats and trimming. 100–110 (16–18); 5 or 6; synthetic; large.

**GABARDINE** Closely woven twill-weave cloth in wool, cotton or polyester. The diagonal twill weave discourages water absorption, making gabardine ideal for raincoats. 100–110 (16–18); 6–7; synthetic; large.

**GEORGETTE** Fine sheer fabric with crêpe appearance, made from twisted yarns of silk, nylon or polyester. The synthetic fabrics tend to slip and fray. Dry press. Uses include blouses and evening dresses. 70 (11); 8–10; synthetic or silk; small.

**GINGHAM** Hard-wearing cotton fabric in which white and dyed yarns form checks and, less commonly, narrow stripes. Used for casual clothes, children's wear, tablecloths, bedspreads and curtains. 70 (11); 7–8; mercerized or synthetic; medium.

**GROSGRAIN** One-way horizontal-ribbed fabric, often narrow. Made from acetate, polyester or even silk. Used for ribbons and evening wear. 70 (11); 7–8; synthetic; medium.

**HABUTAI** Very light, soft, silk fabric in plain or twill weave, at one time produced exclusively in Japan. Creases easily; needs mounting to add body. Used for dresses and also for linings.

70 (11); 8; silk or synthetic; medium.

**HARRIS TWEED** Durable plain or herringbone woollen cloth made from coarse wool showing slightly white hairs. Officially the term refers to cloth from the Outer Hebrides only but it is often used to describe a Harris-type tweed. Used for coats and jackets. 100 (16); 6; silk or mercerized; large.

**HOLLAND** Fine linen cloth usually natural in colour. Used in furnishings and upholstery under the main fabric and also in tailoring for reinforcing pockets. 90–100 (14–16); 5–6; synthetic or mercerized; large.

**JERSEY** First made on the island of that name. Any knitted fabric may be so called, although the word is usually reserved for plain or stocking-stitch knits. Jersey fabric was always made of wool, but it can now be of any fibre and can be plain, printed or jacquard. 70 (11), ball-point if necessary; 7–8; synthetic; medium, slight zigzag.

**KNIT** Normally used to describe knitted fabrics with a lot of give; they may be thick, ribbed, lacy or open. Knits are made in all fibres and blends, but some lose their shape and should be avoided for trousers. 90 (14); 6–7; synthetic; large, slight zigzag.

**LACE** Fine openwork fabric made in various ways from a range of fibres such as cotton, nylon, polyester and blends. Some lace includes acetate. Wash carefully or dry clean. Hand wash old lace in a pillowcase. Piece lace is used for dresses and bridal gowns, lace edging for decoration. 70–90 (11–14); 6–10; synthetic or mercerized; medium.

**LAME** Fabric made from any of various fibres into which metallic threads, often gold or silver, have been woven. Used for evening wear. 70 (11); 7; synthetic; medium.

**LAWN** Name derives from Loan, France, the place where it was initially made. Fine plain-weave fabric of cotton, polyester or linen. Crisp finish. Used for blouses, dresses, nightwear, for mounting other fabrics and for lining yokes and small areas. 70 (11); 7–10; mercerized or synthetic; small.

**LUREX** Metallic thread covered with polyester film to prevent tarnishing. Mixed with polyester, acrylic, wool, acetate or other yarns in woven or knitted fabrics, for evening wear and blouses. Also available as a sewing thread. Cut fabrics containing lurex thread with nap in one direction. 70 (11) —insert a new needle for each garment; 7–8; synthetic; medium.

**MADRAS** Cheap cotton fabric, often unfinished, so may shrink. Hand-woven in Far East in bright-coloured stripes or checks. Used for dresses and shirts. 70 (11); 6–7; mercerized or synthetic; medium.

**MATELASSE** Fabric with a raised pattern producing a quilted effect. An extra weft thread is added, making it look almost like double fabric. Dress fabrics are often acetate or nylon, furnishing fabrics usually viscose or cotton. 90 (14); 6–7; synthetic; large.

**MOIRE** Ribbed or corded fabrics subjected to heat and heavy pressure after weaving to give a rippled appearance. Made from synthetics, acetates and triacetates and, occasionally, silk and cotton. Used for evening wear. 70 (11); 7–8; synthetic; medium.

**MOLESKIN** Closely woven twill cotton fabric, with a slightly velvety finish on RS. Used for jackets, shirts and trousers. 90 (14); 6; mercerized or synthetic; large.

**MOUSSELINE** Shiny, soft, satin-weave fabric of silk, acetate or polyester. Used for evening blouses. 70 (11); 8; synthetic; medium.

**MUNGO** Cheap woollen cloth made from short, waste-wool fibres. Often blended with cotton or other wool. Used for duffle coats, casual trousers and unlined wear. Does not wear well. 90 (14); 6; synthetic; medium.

**MUSLIN** Cheap, open-weave cotton fabric with a tendency to crease and shrink. Often used for lining lightweight materials. Plain white household muslin is excellent as a pressing cloth; bleached and dyed muslin are used for dresses and blouses. 70 (11); 7–8; mercerized or synthetic; small.

**NEEDLECORD** Lightweight cotton or synthetic fabric with short, fine-ribbed pile. Often printed. Washable. Used for blouses, shirts, skirts, dresses and children's clothes. 70 (11); 6–7; synthetic or mercerized; medium.

**NINON** Sheer, plain-weave fabric made from cotton or synthetics such as polyester or nylon. Used for sheer curtains. 70 (11); 9–10; synthetic; medium.

**OMBRE** From French word meaning "shaded". Refers to many knitted or woven fabrics with a design in which the colour graduates from light to dark. 70 (11), ball-point if necessary; 7–8; synthetic; medium to large.

**ORGANDIE** Fine, plain-weave, transparent, permanently stiffened cotton. Creases readily. Used for accessories, blouses, dresses, curtains, bedspreads and in book binding. 70 (11); 7; mercerized or synthetic; small.

**ORGANZA** Slightly lustrous, transparent, plain-weave fabric in silk or synthetic yarn. Used for evening wear, bridal veils and linings. 70 (11); 9–10; synthetic or silk; small.

**PANNE** Pile fabric, usually velvet, with pile pressed flat in one direction to give a lustrous surface. Made from any fibre. Jersey-backed panne velvet is very easy to sew. Cut with pile running upwards. Press lightly on WS. Used for dresses and trousers. 70 (11); 7–9; synthetic; medium.

**PERCALE** Plain close-weave fabric, generally cotton but may also contain some polyester. Sometimes has a slight sheen. Used for nightwear, children's clothes and blouses. 70 (11); 7–8; mercerized or synthetic; medium.

**PETERSHAM** Usually refers to the narrow-width ribbed belting material for skirts and trousers. Can be viscose, polyester or cotton. Sew by hand with small needle and use same thread as for garment.

**PLISSE** Cotton fabric with part of the design, usually stripes, puckered. Washable but do not iron. Used for childrens' clothes and also for blouses and underwear. 70 (11); 7; mercerized or synthetic; medium.

**POLYESTER/COTTON** A small percentage of polyester fibre added to cotton produces a soft hard-wearing fabric with less tendency to crease than pure cotton. Easy to sew. Used for all types of garment. 70–90 (11–14); 6–9; mercerized or synthetic; medium, large.

**POPLIN** Closely woven fabric made of cotton fibre that is mercerized before weaving. Thick weft thread gives fabric its distinctive appearance—a smooth tight weave with a slight shine. Difficult to sew—stitching is very obvious—and press. Seams liable to wrinkle. Pins may leave holes. Used for shirts and dresses. 70 (11); 7–9; synthetic; medium.

**PVC** Abbreviation for polyvinyl chloride, knitted or woven fabric, often cotton, which is coated to add a dull or shiny waterproof finish. May be quiet and soft if vinyl in coating is porous, or noisy if vinyl is non-porous. Do not press. Sponge to clean. Avoid bringing the fabric into contact with sharp edges as it splits easily. Used for children's clothes, aprons, rainwear and furnishings. Apply a spot of oil to machine needle before stitching. 90 (14) and roller foot; 6–7; synthetic; large.

**REVERSIBLE CLOTH** Double-sided fabric made by joining together two, sometimes weak, layers with adhesive or thread. Usually wool but can be acrylic. Used for coats, capes, duffle coats and jackets. No lining needed. 100–110 (16–18); 6–7; synthetic or mercerized; large.

**SAILCLOTH** Thick, strong fabric usually made from cotton but can include some polyester. Creases, so normally treated for crease resistance. Can be attractively top stitched. Used for crisp outfits, dresses, suits, trousers and jackets. 90 (14); 6–7; synthetic; medium to large.

**SATEEN** Satin-weave cotton fabric, shiny on RS. Used for curtain linings, draperies and bedspreads. Not hard-wearing under strain. 90 (14); 6; mercerized or synthetic; medium.

**SATIN** Slippery fabric, shiny on one side. Fabrics for evening wear, lingerie and blouses made from silk, acetate or polyester. Cotton and crêpe-backed satin look similar and are used for dresses and blouses. All satin with attractive finish on WS can be made up with dull side out. Dry press on WS only. 70–90 (11–14); 7–9; synthetic or mercerized; small to medium.

**SEERSUCKER** One of first non-iron dress fabrics. Usually made of cotton with rows of warp threads pulled tightly to create wrinkled effect. Generally produced in coloured stripes. Washes well. Ironing flattens but does not eliminate wrinkles. Used for summer suits, dresses, table and sports' wear. 70 (11); 6–7; mercerized or synthetic; medium.

**SHANTUNG** Originally a natural-coloured Chinese silk used for blouses, suits and dresses. The term now denotes a plain-weave cloth with an uneven surface; made of any fibre, from yarns of irregular thickness. 70–90 (11–14); 6–7; synthetic; medium.

**STRETCH TOWELLING** Cotton or polyester loop-pile fabric with soft velours-type finish on RS. Used for beachwear, robes and children's clothes. 90 (14); 6; synthetic; medium, slight zigzag.

**SUEDE CLOTH** Any fibre, knitted, woven or non-woven, and often brushed on RS, which resembles real suede. Cut woven or bonded suede cloth with nap in one direction. Sew jersey suede cloth as for heavy synthetic jersey. 90 (14); 6; synthetic; medium, slight zigzag.

**SURAH** Fine twill-weave fabric made from polyester, acetate, triacetate or occasionally silk. Often printed. Used for blouses, dresses and men's ties. 70 (11); 8–9; synthetic; medium.

**TAFFETA** Plain-weave, smooth, crisp fabric made from acetate, polyester or triacetate and occasionally silk. Creases easily. Dry press. Used for evening wear and trimmings. 70 (11); 9; synthetic or mercerized; medium to large.

**TICKING** Firm cotton fabric, usually twill weave, often striped. Washes well. Very hard-wearing. Used for mattress and pillow covers when down-proofed, but also for dresses, shirts and trousers. 100 (16); 6; cotton or synthetic; large.

**TOWELLING** Sometimes called Terry weave or Terry cloth. Additional cotton threads are inserted to form loops on one or both sides. Can be plain or printed. Varieties with loops on both sides are thick and bulky to handle. The loops fall off when cut, so the edges must be neatened. Soft and highly absorbent. Used for beachwear, towels, curtains and robes. 90 (14); 5–6; mercerized or synthetic; large.

**TWEED** Any thick, rough, heavy-weight woollen fabric with white hairs in surface. Can be in plain herringbone or twill weave. Used for coats, jackets and suits. 100 (16); 5–6; synthetic or mercerized; large.

**UNCUT VELVET** Made from any fibre. Some of the pile is left uncut, so forming loops. Often used for furnishings. Cut with nap in one direction. Press and sew as for velvet.

**VELOURS FRAPPE** Velvet with a raised pattern. The smooth parts between the pile areas can be flattened or cut away. Uses as for velvet and also suits and coats. Treat as velvet.

**VELVET** Rich-looking pile fabric made from cotton, silk, polyester, nylon or other synthetics. Additional warp threads used to form the pile, which is even but shades. Cut out with pile running upwards. Various types of velvet dress and furnishing fabrics are available, including printed, figured and velours. Press lightly on WS only, with another piece of velvet RS up on pressing board. When stitching insert tissue between layers of velvet to prevent wrinkled seams. 70 (11); 8–9; synthetic or mercerized; medium to large.

**VELVETEEN** Has rich appearance of velvet but made of cotton. The pile is added by inserting additional weft threads. These are looped in the weaving and cut afterwards. Usually frays readily as pile is not well anchored. Cut out with pile running upwards. Press lightly on WS only, with a piece of velveteen RS up on the pressing surface. Used for dresses, trousers and suits. 90 (14); 7–8; synthetic or mercerized; medium to large.

**VOILE** From French word meaning "veil". Sheer, plain-weave fabric, made from cotton or polyester; cotton voile is softer and more comfortable. Used for full sleeves, gathers, frills and curtains. 70 (11); 9–10; synthetic or mercerized; small to medium.

**WINCEYETTE** Lightweight, brushed cotton or viscose fabric. Washes and wears well. Used for sheets and nightwear but must be treated for flame resistance. 90 (14); 7; mercerized or synthetic; medium.

# Pressing

One of the most important processes in sewing, pressing contributes more than anything else to a professional result. It is essential at each stage in the construction of a garment to build in shape and set the seams; it can also, if properly done, greatly improve the look of slightly unsatisfactory sewing. Besides an iron and ironing board there are other pieces of useful pressing equipment.

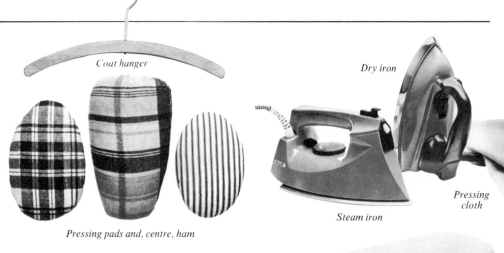

Coat hanger

Dry iron

Pressing cloth

Steam iron

Pressing pads and, centre, ham

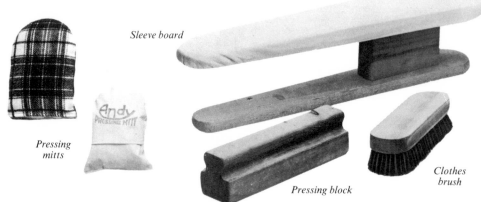

Sleeve board

Pressing mitts

Pressing block

Clothes brush

## Pressing surface
The ideal surface is a firm, custom-built bench padded with one or two layers of blanket and a layer of sheeting or other cotton material. Alternatively, use an area of an unpolished table or part of the kitchen work surface padded with a blanket and sheeting. Have a piece of asbestos on which to stand the iron. The ironing board can be used for pressing, although it may wobble under the pressure.

## Irons
Ideally, have two irons—a steam iron for light- and medium-weight fabrics and for the final pressing of finished articles, and a dry iron to use with a damp pressing cloth for other materials. Choose the heaviest type of dry iron. Steam irons can be used dry with a cloth, but they tend to be too light in weight.

When pressing, stand steam irons on their specially constructed heel to prevent water leaking on to the ironing surface. Lay dry irons flat on the ironing board well or an asbestos mat. Always unplug irons after use and empty steam irons. Clean the sole plates by wiping with a little washing-up liquid on a damp cloth or use an iron-cleaning stick.

## Pressing cloths
A fine, open-weave cotton such as muslin makes a good general pressing cloth. Thicker cotton cloths hold more water and are useful for the heavier fabrics of some tailored clothes. Alternatively, fold the muslin cloth so that it holds more moisture.

## Water
Ideally, there should be a wash basin in the work room. If there is no tap nearby have a bowl of water to hand.

## Sleeve board
An essential piece of pressing equipment, the sleeve board is padded on one or both sides and has a selection of different-sized ends for different areas of a garment. Wooden sleeve boards are stable and easy to use; the metal ones supplied with some ironing boards are rather springy. When pressing, stand the sleeve board, preferably, on a table covered with a blanket and sheeting, or on the ironing board.

## Pressing block
This is a smooth block of wood for banging steam into heavy fabrics immediately after the iron has been applied and for making strong creases such as trouser creases. Pressing blocks

are sometimes shaped into a ridge along the top to make a handle. If you cannot obtain a block, use a book or the back of a large clothes brush when necessary.

## Clothes brush
Keep a brush handy for bringing up the nap on fluffy fabrics when they are still warm from pressing. Use it also to remove tailor's chalk marks from the fabric, preferably before pressing so that they do not "set".

## Coat hangers
Have a few shaped wooden hangers, some with bars, for hanging each piece of pressing while the fabric cools.

## Pads, hams and rolls
Buy a small, oval, lightweight pressing pad that can be held in the hand while pressing such areas as shoulders and sleeve heads, which are difficult to press flat. A pressing mitt can also be used in these areas. A bigger, harder ham or pad is useful for larger areas and a padded seam roll for pressing sleeve seams. Alternatively, make all three with cotton covers and a filling of cut-up tights. As a temporary substitute for all three types of pressing pad use a folded towel.

## Ingredients of pressing
Pressing, as the word suggests, is the application of pressure—and also heat and usually moisture—to the fabric for as long as is

necessary to achieve the desired shaping. Experience teaches you how to achieve the right result on every fabric, but there are a few basic principles, which, if followed, will produce good results. Before pressing, take into consideration the fibre content, weave, thickness and texture of the material, all of which determine the correct degree of heat, moisture and pressure needed.

Most irons are thermostatically controlled to keep them at the chosen temperature setting. The settings are cool, warm and hot, but the indicator can also be set between the three main settings. Some irons have fibre names instead of temperatures on the indicator, others have both.

Before pressing the garment, allow the iron to heat up fully and test the temperature by pressing a crease into a spare piece of fabric. Adjust the temperature if necessary. If you are pressing with a damp cloth, select a higher temperature as the cloth prevents the heat fully penetrating the fabric.

One method of providing moisture for pressing is by using a steam iron. Water drips on to a hot plate inside the iron and the resulting steam escapes through holes in the sole plate. The amount of steam available from most irons is sufficient only for light-weight fabrics. Some irons also have spraying equipment, but be careful when using this on the right side of the fabric, or on unfamiliar materials, as water can leave a mark. One disadvantage of steam irons is that the sole plate may leave an imprint on some thick, soft fabrics.

An alternative method of providing moisture is to use a damp muslin pressing cloth, which enables you to control the amount of steam going into the fabric. The damp cloth can be used with a dry iron or a steam iron set to dry. Wring out the cloth thoroughly for pressing lightweight fabrics, but leave water in it for fabrics requiring more steam. The cloth cools the base of the iron so the damper the cloth the hotter the iron must be to ensure that the water is converted to steam immediately.

Do not cover the whole of the work with the pressing cloth—use only a small area of the cloth at a time to cover the section to be pressed. Lift the cloth off the fabric as soon as you raise the iron to stop water soaking into the garment. Keep the cloth damp, wringing it out with care, so that the amount of water in it remains constant during one pressing operation. When pressing small, difficult areas, cover only the toe of the iron with the cloth.

Pressure is applied by the weight of the iron and by leaning on it. The iron is never actually allowed to rest on the fabric, but its weight is controlled according to the fabric being handled. Only light pressure is needed on soft fabrics and on fabrics with a pile or surface that you do not want to flatten. Much more weight and pressure are needed on heavy, closely woven and springy fabrics. Lean on the iron to apply extra pressure when pressing features such as pleats or trouser creases. Apply pressure in short, sharp, almost banging movements, not sliding ones. Press for a couple of seconds only, less on some fabrics.

### The pressing sequence
After testing the temperature on a piece of fabric, arrange and smooth out a section of the part to be pressed on the pressing surface. Wring out the pressing cloth. Arrange a part of it on the work and immediately apply the iron. Lift the iron and cloth and examine the fabric. It is unlikely to be completely pressed so arrange another damp part of the cloth on the fabric and press again. Continue until satisfied that the fabric is permanently shaped into its new position. Quickly re-press any wrinkles while the fabric is warm and easy to handle. The muslin is sufficiently transparent to enable you to see whether the iron is being applied correctly. If using a steam iron, follow the same procedure without the cloth. With both dry and steam irons use only as much of the iron as is necessary—the whole plate can leave an iron imprint on the fabric.

After pressing a section leave it to cool for a moment before moving on to the next section or the fabric may crease; some fabrics may also stretch. If the work has been pressed on the wrong side, check the right side, as most fabrics need pressing on both sides.

Pressing is a slow, time-consuming job, but more than justifies the time spent by the professional finish it gives to your sewing.

The search for ways of keeping clothes neat and well pressed is an age-old preoccupation, dating back to the ancient Egyptians and Chinese, the Greeks and the Romans. It is also a fascinating testimony to man's powers of ingenuity.

Most of the methods of pressing in the ancient world relied on pressure rather than heat being applied to damp material, a principle that lasted until the 1780s. The earliest surviving examples of ironing equipment date not from the ancient world, however, but from the Viking era. Buried in the graves of Viking women were mushroom-shaped black glass irons known as *gnidestein*, rubbing stones or slykstones, a name they inherited from even earlier, similarly shaped versions in stone and wood.

A different technique, but still reliant on pressure, was the mangling, or smoothing, board, which appeared in Denmark in the 16th century. Long and flat, the board had a handle at one end. Damp material was wrapped round a roller, placed on a smooth surface and rolled under the board until free of wrinkles. In 17th- and 18th-century Holland large rolling pins, which worked on the same principle, were used.

Cumbersome though more sophisticated, the rock mangle was widely used in the United States in the late 1700s. It was up to five feet wide and ten feet long, with a wooden box on top of the frame that held up to a ton of stones. The weighted box rolled back and forth over material wrapped round rollers.

The Chinese were among the earliest to use heat rather than just pressure to smooth their clothes. The first of these irons, intricately decorated and resembling an open bed pan, survive from the Ming dynasty (1368–1644). The Chinese refined other pressing processes. Instead of the old method of holding water in the mouth and blowing it on the cloth when needed, they used a water can. ▶

Ladies preparing silk *(detail) is the earliest known picture of ironing, a 12th-century copy by Emperor Hui-Tsung of an 8th-century painting. Intricately decorated, Chinese irons, as this one, were cast in iron and the detailed work was finished by hand. The handles varied from teakwood to bone, jade or ivory.*

# Pressing

By the beginning of the 17th century the tailor's goose was widely used in Europe, its name deriving from the handle, which protruded forwards in a curve like a goose's neck. These irons varied in weight from eight to as much as 60 pounds, but were usually from 16 to 22 pounds. They were never used very hot; the weight did most of the work.

It is uncertain when the first flat, smoothing, or sad, irons were made, but they were the precursor of the modern iron. The origin of "sad" is also lost, but it may come from the Old English word *saed*, solid. There were two types of flat iron—the original iron made from one solid piece of metal with the handle moulded in, and the later type with detachable handles, which had a disconcerting tendency of falling off, or of taking so long to attach that the iron cooled. The first iron with a detachable handle that was trustworthy and easy to use was patented in 1870 by Mary Florence Potts of Iowa, USA. The oval shape, pointed at both ends, was popular well into this century as the iron could be worked in opposite directions without being lifted up and reversed.

By the 1700s, the flat, box and charcoal irons were in use. The early irons were made of crude ore. Later they were made mostly of cast steel or cast iron, notably in England, and of brass, particularly in Scandinavia. However, the use of brass slumped dramatically in Denmark by the 1880s as it was widely held responsible for the grimy, yellow look of clothes after washing and ironing.

The flat iron was heated in front of the fire. Box irons were hollow with a swing or lift-up gate at the back to cover the opening where a "slug", or "bolt", of hot iron was inserted. Charcoal irons were similar, but were filled with charcoal chips which were then lighted.

Chief among ironing instruments with specialized uses was the goffering, or talley, iron, a small iron that could reach into pleating, ruffles, tucks and gathers, although it was primarily a fluting and crimping iron. It was first used in Italy, probably in the early 1600s, and spread rapidly through Europe, an essential fashion aid.

During the first half of the 19th century self-heating irons appeared, warmed by natural gas, carbide-acetylene, alcohol, kerosene, gasoline, steam and, finally, electricity. Many could be heated by more than one kind of fuel. Some travelling irons even provided a pan in which water could be heated for shaving or a morning cup of tea.

One of the earliest electric irons was patented by two Americans, R. N. Dyer and H. W. Seely, in 1883. Each time the iron was set down the wires had to be re-connected to complete the circuit and re-heat it. Designs continued to improve, but the real revolution in ironing did not come until the 1950s with the introduction of the steam iron. Even now, however, flat, charcoal and self-heating irons are manufactured for use in areas where gas and electricity are still unknown.

*Three 18th-century irons. The English box iron with the slug of metal partially inserted, left, is made to the first box iron patent taken out by the British inventor Isaac Wilkinson in 1738. The charcoal iron, centre, is mid-European. The dragon figure was used repeatedly for decoration. The box iron, right, is hand made of bronze and is probably Danish.*

*A polisher, an iron with a curved base, was used to iron starched garments until they shone. The model, left, with its trivet is 18th-century English. The utilitarian flat iron, centre, typical of its kind, came in a range of sizes; this model was first manufactured in 1896. Right, a more elegant 18th-century French flat iron decorated with an embossed hand.*

*Made early this century this 18-pound tailor's goose is identical to those used 300 years ago and known for a time in England as "weasels". Hence the old rhyme: "Up and down the City Road, In and out the Eagle, That's the way the money goes—Pop goes the weasel." Pop is to hock or pawn; the Eagle was a public house.*

*A later development of the goffering iron, the fluter made ruffling and pleating far less irksome. The most popular hand model, with a rocker action, was the American one, above left, first made in 1866. The English fluter with rollers, above right, dates from the late 1800s. The fluting scissors, or tongs, in the foreground were used when travelling.*

*One of the most successful flat irons was the Mrs Potts iron, patented in 1870 and named after its inventor. Sold in sets of three, the bases were of differing weight and size and the handle was detachable. The oval shape of the bases, with a point at either end, was ideally suited to the gathered and tucked clothes of the period.*

*Two self-heating irons. The electric steam iron, left, was made in Germany in the early 1900s. The water was put in at the front and the steam escaped through five tiny holes in the base plate. The "Brilliant" kerosene iron, right, also German and made at the end of the 1800s, became a popular spirit iron. Air holes at the sides aided combustion.*

**Seams** Place seam WS up on sleeve board. Open it out with fingers and closely follow fingers down seam with toe of iron (**1**). Press same section again

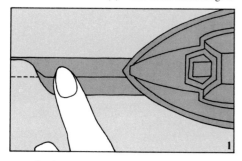

more firmly until seam stays open. Continue to end of seam. Turn work RS up and press again lightly, protecting the fabric with a cloth if necessary and correcting any wrinkles (**2**).

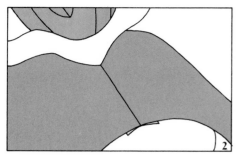

**Darts** Place fabric WS up with point of dart at the end of a sleeve board or pressing pad. On fine- and medium-thickness fabric, fold dart towards the centre of the garment or upwards, depending on its position, and press lightly down to its point (**3**).

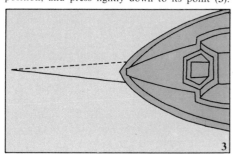

Return iron to wide base of dart and press more heavily to flatten. Turn fabric RS up and press again lightly, keeping the point of the dart at the end of the board to avoid flattening the shaping. On thick fabrics cut darts open before pressing.

On small darts with a piece of tape or lining stitched into them, press the dart one way and the tape the other (**4**), following the method above.

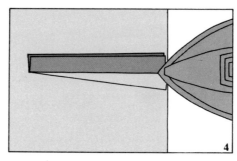

**Bindings** With binding stitched to RS, place fabric on pressing surface RS up; if stitched to WS place fabric WS up. Run toe of iron along join, lifting strip to make a good line (**5**). Do not run iron right over strip or turnings will make a ridge.

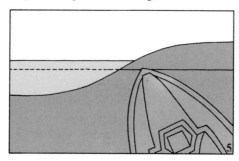

**Buttonholes** Place work RS down on a folded towel. Press back of buttonholes with toe of iron; work toe into each opening to flatten and straighten it (**6**).

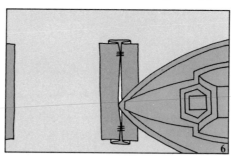

**Zips** Open zip and lay flat on sleeve board, RS up. Wrap damp pressing cloth round toe of iron and run toe along stitching (**7**), not over zip teeth.

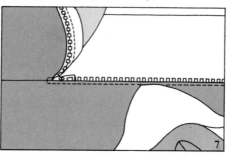

*Mrs Tiggywinkle, the indefatigable laundress in Beatrix Potter's tale, checks the temperature of her flat irons.*

**Sleeve heads** With garment and sleeve RS out and sleeve hanging loose, arrange a pressing pad or folded towel in armhole of garment. Hold pad in one hand to avoid creasing. Place a small section of damp cloth over the sleeve head seam and press round seam with toe of iron (**8**).

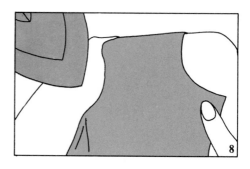

**Sleeves** Roll up a towel long enough to fill the entire length of the sleeve and push it into the sleeve, RS out. For extra firmness roll a magazine inside the towel. Place damp cloth over sleeve and press lightly (**9**), revolving sleeve and towel together after each section is pressed.

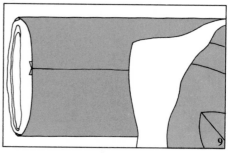

**Pleats** Lay finished pleat, basted into position, WS up on sleeve board and press well with a damp cloth, pressing inverted and box pleats open (**10**) and knife

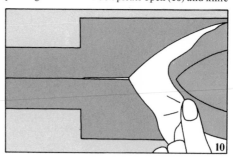

pleats to one side, as in (**11**). Remove iron and cloth and bang in the steam with a block (**11**). Allow to cool slightly before pressing next pleat. When all pleats have been pressed on WS, turn work to RS and press again lightly, removing any unevenness in the pleat line.

# Pressing

To press the hem of finished pleats, turn up hem and, one by one, place pleats, basted into position, RS up on sleeve board. Lift top section of pleat and re-press fold of pleat underneath (12). Rearrange pleat

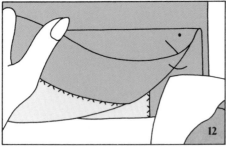

with top section in place and RS up. To avoid an imprint on fabric under pleat fold, place a folded towel under garment and press pleat on RS (13).

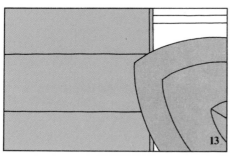

**Collars** When making a collar, arrange neck join of under-collar to neckline WS up on the end of a sleeve board or pressing pad and press as an open seam using toe of iron (14). Move neck join round as each

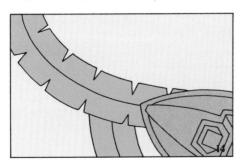

section is pressed. Finish by turning work over to RS and pressing again lightly as for an open seam.

On a finished collar with a fold or roll, baste roll diagonally and arrange collar RS out on a dummy or stand, or on a pressing ham, or round a rolled-up towel, all of which act as a neck. Press along the roll, using the other hand to shape the collar by easing it round the neck as you press (15).

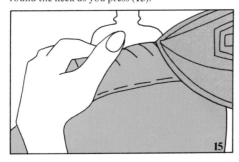

**Hems** Arrange basted hem WS up on sleeve board, with weight of garment resting on surface beneath to prevent stretching. Use side of iron and press basted

fold in sections (16). Do not press over top, raw edge of hem. Allow to cool before pressing next section.

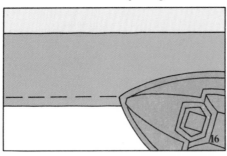

For a finished hem, place garment WS up on sleeve board and arrange a piece of fabric of equal thickness to hem, or a piece folded to equal its thickness, against bottom edge of hem. Press lightly over edge using a damp cloth (17) to avoid a ridge.

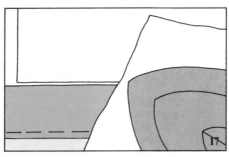

**Double fabric** On a garment that is almost completed, the iron is likely to press the outline of double areas such as facing joins, tucks, cuffs or collars through on to the garment. Avoid this by slipping part of a dry pressing cloth between the garment and the section to be pressed (18).

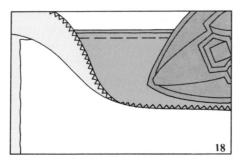

**Finished edges** On edges such as cuffs, facings and certain kinds of collar such as a straight stand, the join is often rolled slightly to the inside of the garment. To stop the join making a ridge on RS, press on the inside with toe of iron only (19).

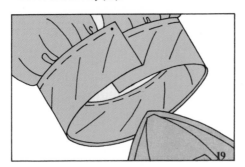

On a collar that turns over such as the shirt collar, the join is generally rolled slightly to the underside; press from this side using toe of iron (20).

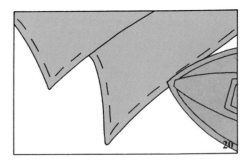

**Trousers** Baste seams, darts and any waist pleats and press creases in each leg before fitting or stitching legs. Hold one trouser leg up, RS out, by the hem; arrange leg seams with inside seam 1 to 2 cm/$\frac{3}{8}$ to $\frac{3}{4}$ in towards front. This places the front crease centrally over the knee and gives a better hang than when the seams are together. Arrange trousers RS up on pressing surface, with inside leg uppermost and front fold running from hem up to a point at waist about 7.5 to 10 cm/3 to 4 in from centre front seam. Do not force it to meet a dart point on women's trousers or the crease may not be straight. On some styles of men's trousers the crease runs into the front pleat. Use a damp cloth for all trouser pressing. Place cloth over front crease and press up crease a little way from hem (21). Remove iron and bang steam in with a

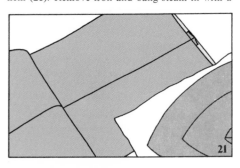

block (22). Press across leg from this point to

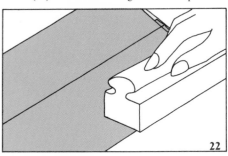

establish back crease (23). Continue pressing up to crutch area. Complete front crease up to waist. Press back crease so it meets centre back seam at waist. Allow the first trouser leg to cool and then repeat the procedure for the other leg.

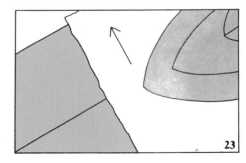

# Hand Sewing

To achieve the best results in hand sewing, try not to hurry your work and allow enough time at each session to complete a particular feature, such as a hem or set of buttonholes. It is also important not only to have the right equipment but to know how to use it properly. The instructions given below should be reversed by the left-handed sewer.

### Threading a needle
Pull the thread from the reel, bite off or cut and smooth the end with your teeth. Holding the needle close to the eye with the left hand, rest both hands lightly against each other to steady them while pushing the thread through the needle. Transfer the needle to the right hand and pull the thread through the eye with the left thumb and forefinger. The thread pulled through should be about one-quarter of the total length. With some synthetic thread that unravels it is often necessary to cut the end again cleanly if it does not thread the first time.

### Making a knot
After threading the needle, keep hold of the thread between the left thumb and forefinger and wind it once round the forefinger, about halfway along the pad (1)—not less or it will be impossible to form the knot. With the thumb pad roll the thread to the end of the forefinger to make a loop (2). Turn that into a knot by running both thumb and second finger nail down the thread to the end (3). The dampness of the thread end helps to form the knot. Do not make big knots and keep practising if you find that "tails"—spare lengths of thread beyond the knot—persist in forming.

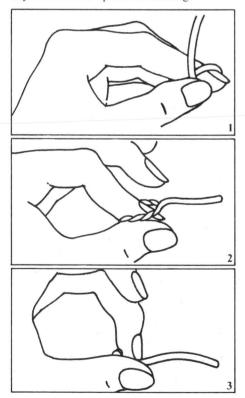

### Holding the needle
Hold the needle fairly near the point with the right thumb and forefinger. The other fingers should be bent, almost clenched, under the hand. The thimble, on the third finger, should have its side resting on the eye of the needle (4).

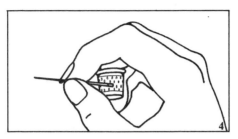

Insert the needle through the fabric, pushing the blunt end with the thimble. With the thimble still against the needle, move thumb and forefinger to grasp the needle point and pull the needle through the fabric. Stitches should generally be made in a smooth, continuous movement, not in a series of jabs and pushes. The fingers should control the needle all the time and hardly ever let go while working a row of stitches.

### Starting off
Most permanent stitches and also basting are best started with a knot, as it is strong. Hide the knot on the wrong side under a fold or an edge of the fabric for permanent stitching. Knots in thick thread are later cut off, as, for example, in sewing on buttons. Sometimes, knots are hidden well away from the stitching, as in buttonholes.

If the fabric is transparent or the work delicate, start with two small backstitches on top of each other (5). The easiest way to do this is to use a knot, make the stitches and then cut off the knot. Work them under a fold or an edge of the fabric.

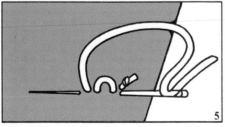

### Finishing off
Fasten off with at least two backstitches worked on top of each other, hiding them under a fold or an edge. Cut off the thread close to the surface of the fabric. See individual stitches for exceptions to this rule.

### Working temporary stitches
The main temporary stitches are tailor's tacks and basting. They are quicker and easier to work and the results more accurate if the fabric is flat on the table. It is also better and generally quicker to work temporary stitches standing up, so that your eyes are directly

above the stitches and your body weight is forward. Not only is this more comfortable than working with outstretched arms, but, as such stitches are generally worked over a large area, it is easier to gain an overall picture and to watch for wrinkles.

Use a long piece of basting thread, stretching from shoulder to wrist when threaded, and a large between needle—4 to 7, depending on the thickness of the fabric. Arrange the work on the table and stitch, using the other hand to ease and push the fabric on to the needle. The table surface is used almost to bounce the needle point off again and up into the fabric, and so wood, which is soft, is the best surface on which to sew.

### Working permanent stitches
Sit on a comfortable chair, near a window or directional lamp, as good light is essential. It can even be an armchair if you sit sideways and on the edge (the padded arm is handy for needles and pins).

Bend well over the work and relax. Even if sitting at a table, always hold the work, as it is important to retain the shape already inserted. Tailors sit cross-legged, or with one leg crossed over the other while sitting on the edge of a table or work board, so that they can build shape into a garment over their knees.

Unless otherwise indicated under the individual stitch, use a small between needle—8 to 12, depending on the thickness of the fabric—and a short piece of thread, no longer than from elbow to wrist when threaded, so that when you stitch, only the forearm should move, from hand to elbow. Working with a short thread makes the tension easier to control and also leads to neat identical stitches.

Have small scissors, thread and wax handy, and a bodkin for pulling out basting. Use the wax for smoothing out synthetic thread if necessary. Always press the stitching when finished, after removing basting stitches.

### Tension
Correct tension in hand sewing is just as important as in machining. To produce perfectly uniform stitches, the tension must be correct for the fabric, neither too tight nor too slack, and the tension of all the stitches must be even. This is one of the reasons for trying to complete a particular feature in one sitting, so that the same tension is maintained throughout the work.

Pull the thread through to finish each stitch with the same amount of tug. This takes concentration and practice because the thread becomes shorter and shorter and so the pull has to be adjusted fractionally for each stitch. Some hand stitches are pulled taut to embed the thread in the fabric. If several stitches are being made at one point, some are left taut on the surface, either for effect or to prevent wrinkling of the fabric, and others are deliberately left fairly slack to make sure a line does not show on the right side of the fabric.

# A-Z of Hand Stitches

## BACKSTITCHES
### Backstitch
Strong stitch used for fastening off almost all hand stitches, for repairing seams and for small areas where machining might be awkward. The stitches should form a continuous row.

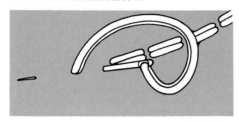

Use waxed double thread for strength. Work from right to left keeping stitches as small as possible, no more than 4 mm/$\frac{1}{8}$ in on top of work. Stitches on WS are twice the length of those on top and look rather untidy. Start with a knot. If knot is on RS, bring needle up to RS 4 mm/$\frac{1}{8}$ in farther on. Insert needle back by knot and bring out 4 mm/$\frac{1}{8}$ in in front of this first stitch. Take needle below by end of first stitch bringing it up another 4 mm/$\frac{1}{8}$ in in front of where it last emerged. If starting with knot on WS, bring needle straight through to RS and insert 4 mm/$\frac{1}{8}$ in behind knot. Bring out 4 mm/$\frac{1}{8}$ in in front of this first stitch and take further stitches as described above.

### Half backstitch
Neater, more attractive and stronger than an ordinary backstitch, although still untidy on WS so use only where this does not matter. The stitches do not form a continuous row; the space between them equals the length of the stitches—2 mm/$\frac{1}{16}$ in. Suitable for setting in sleeves by hand and for other places where a full backstitch would produce too large a stitch, causing the fabric to part.

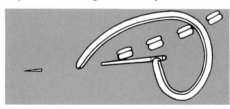

Work as for backstitch, using double waxed thread, but take needle back and through to WS only 2 mm/$\frac{1}{16}$ in behind emerging thread. Bring up to RS 4 mm/$\frac{1}{8}$ in in front of stitch as in backstitch. Pull thread tight with each stitch if working on a seam to ensure that the seam does not open up in any part and show threads.

### Prick stitch
A type of backstitch which, although untidy on WS, can be almost invisible on RS if worked with single thread. Use where hand stitching will enhance the finished appearance or where the pressure of machining would cause a ridge on layers of fabric, e.g. holding a binding over a hem, holding a jetting or binding over a pocket, stitching through a seam join from RS, as at the back of a collar. On fine fabrics such as chiffon and georgette insert zips with prick stitch rather than by machine.

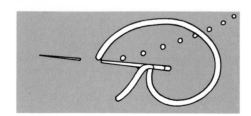

Use single thread and work from right to left. Begin with a knot or backstitch and bring needle through to RS. Make stitch by inserting needle again slightly behind point where it emerged, but almost in same hole. Take needle underneath for shortest distance fabric allows, 2 to 5 mm/$\frac{1}{16}$ to $\frac{1}{4}$ in depending on thickness of fabric, and bring up to RS. Do not pull thread too tight.

### Bar tack
Strengthening bar used across ends of sleeve opening and base of zip opening to prevent fabric tearing. Use ordinary sewing thread.

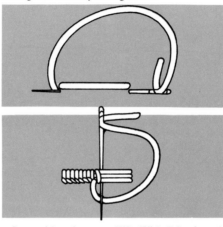

Start with a knot on WS. With RS of work towards you, bring needle through to RS and take three or four satin stitches on top of each other through fabric at point of strain. If there are several layers of fabric to be held, make stitches with stabbing motion. The length of the stitches will be the length of the bar tack. Cover these threads with closely spaced loop stitch, taking needle under strands. Pass needle to WS and fasten off firmly with a backstitch.

## BASTING STITCHES
### Diagonal basting
A big stitch used to cover large areas quickly. Keeps fabric flat, whereas ordinary straight basting would cause ridges. Particularly suitable for inserting interfacings, holding linings and holding roll line of collars. Unless working to a moulded curve, keep material flat on table and stand up to sew.

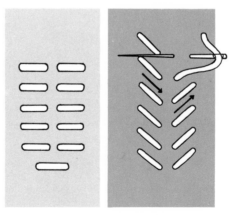

Work on RS, starting with a knot. Take a small horizontal stitch from right to left through fabric. Working towards you, take another stitch the same size as, and parallel to, the first, so that a diagonal stretch of thread on RS links end of first stitch with beginning of second. The parallel horizontal stitches show only on WS. Do not pull thread tight or ridges will form. The length of the parallel stitches and the distance between them varies according to the amount of control required. Take short stitches close together for greater control, longer ones more widely spaced if less control is needed. Several rows can be worked, about 3 cm/1$\frac{1}{4}$ in apart. Finish each with one loose backstitch for ease of removal.

### Even basting
Used to hold two or more layers of fabric together or for marking lines.

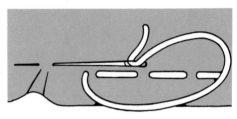

Start with a knot on RS and work from right to left. Stand up when stitching long straight lines and work on a flat surface. Push needle through fabric in one continuous in-and-out movement, making stitches about 2 cm/$\frac{3}{4}$ in long, shorter 'round curves or difficult areas. Pick up on needle as little fabric as possible between stitches—about 3 mm/$\frac{1}{8}$ in. If too much fabric is picked up, the layers of fabric part and seams open when the garment is being fitted, or the fabric moves when it is machined. Finish with one backstitch, or two if preparing for fitting. To remove, pull starting knot gently.

### Flash basting
Limited almost entirely to attaching seam allowances of loose linings to seam allowances of garments, e.g. at shoulders and side seams.

Work as a single row as for diagonal basting, strengthening the bottom of each diagonal with a backstitch instead of the ordinary horizontal stitch. Finish as for diagonal basting.

### Slip basting
Worked from RS to hold together pieces of fabric on which the design has to be matched or where a folded edge has to be caught down accurately before being pressed or stitched permanently.

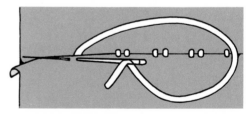

Fold top layer of fabric under at fitting line and pin at intervals to hold. Start with a knot on RS. Working right to left, slip needle into fold and bring out about 5 mm/$\frac{1}{4}$ in farther on. In single layer of fabric, directly opposite point at which needle emerges from fold, take a horizontal stitch of about 3 mm/$\frac{1}{8}$ in. Directly opposite the end of this stitch, insert needle in fold and take another 5 mm/$\frac{1}{4}$ in stitch, and so on. Finish with one backstitch. If the two joined pieces form a seam, the top layer is flapped over to reveal a row of ordinary straight basting stitches.

## Uneven basting

Used for the same purpose as even basting and also on fine or slippery fabrics for a better grip.

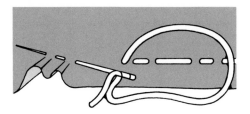

Work as for even basting, with same needle movement, but take a small stitch, e.g. 5 mm/¼ in, alternately with a long one, keeping space between stitches equal. Finish and remove as for backstitch.

**Blanket stitch** see **Loop stitch**

## Buttonhole stitch

Used for hand-worked buttonholes, and also for neatening a short length of raw edge to prevent fraying. Difficult to work neatly because a knot is formed with each stitch and an even tension must be kept on all knots. For hand-worked buttonhole method see p. 62. Follow the method below for neatening a raw edge.

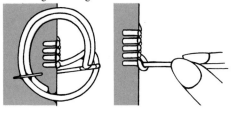

Begin with a knot on WS and work towards you with cut edge to right (to left, if left-handed). Take thread over edge and insert needle from WS beside knot. Bring needle point through to left of edge on RS. To form a knot rather than a loop, wind double section of thread by eye of needle round needle point towards you. Although the fingers should leave the needle at this stage, keep thimble in place at eye of needle to steady it while knot is formed. Let go of thread and finish pulling needle through fabric. To settle knot on edge of fabric, grasp thread near knot and tug it gently into position. Work next stitch beside it, nearer to you. The depth of stitch depends on how much the fabric frays; the more it frays the deeper the stitch (a fabric adhesive strip on WS helps to lessen fraying). The closeness of the stitches depends upon the thickness of the thread but keep spacing even and make sure that the knots touch.

## Catch stitch

Used almost entirely to hold up hems in medium and heavy fabrics, and sometimes over a raw edge in short lengths. Although weak, it is invisible on RS. It serves the same purpose as herringbone, but is smaller and neater.

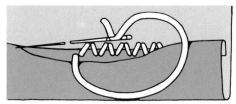

To avoid a ridge on hems, work stitch just under hem edge, 3 to 5 mm/⅛ to ¼ in down, depending on thickness of fabric. If it is worked lower, the weight of the edge eventually pulls and makes a line; you may also catch your heel in it. Work from right to left. Lift up hem edge and fasten thread inside with a knot or backstitch. Take a very small stitch in hem

fabric and 3 to 5 mm/⅛ to ¼ in to left, depending on thickness of fabric, a small stitch in garment. If possible, pick up one thread or less in garment, a little more in hem edge, keeping thread loose. If working over an edge, make stitches same size.

## Chain stitch

Although mainly an embroidery stitch, it has its uses in dressmaking and can be worked, with single or double thread or buttonhole twist, to make a chain to form a belt loop or French tack.

Start with a knot on WS and bring thread through to RS. Make a small loop and insert needle at point

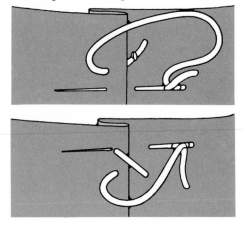

where it emerged, holding loop out to a length of 2 mm/1/16 in. Bring needle out just inside end of this first loop and continue to form chains until desired length is reached, holding line of chains away from fabric. Fasten off by taking needle through last loop and working several backstitches on WS.

## Cross stitch

Like chain stitch, it is mainly an embroidery stitch, but is useful in dressmaking for finishing off a raw edge and, in groups of a few stitches, for strengthening weak areas such as pocket ends. The needle must be stabbed through the work with each movement. This makes the other side untidy so use only inside a garment, e.g. for linings and turnings. Work on RS for decoration only.

Working from left to right, start with a backstitch and bring needle through to RS. To form first

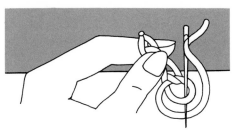

diagonal of cross, take needle below the point at which it emerged and insert same distance to right, bringing it up again at left exactly below start of diagonal. The distance the needle is taken down and across is 3 to 5 mm/⅛ to ¼ in, depending on thickness of fabric. To form second diagonal, insert needle at top righthand corner of cross and bring out at start of first diagonal. If room, work another two or three stitches beside initial stitch, but if space is limited and more strength needed, work second cross stitch over first.

To finish off a raw edge with cross stitch, work first diagonal of each stitch, from top left to bottom right, in a row towards you. When row is finished, work back in opposite direction, forming diagonals from bottom left to top right to complete each cross.

**Diagonal basting** see **BASTING**

## Draw stitch

Mostly confined to tailoring, but also used in dressmaking to join two folded edges invisibly from RS, e.g. collar and lapel. The join is often shaped or has more fullness in one edge than the other, so it is important to draw up thread on each stitch.

Begin with a knot well tucked away. Working from right to left, take a tiny stitch of 1 mm/1/16 in

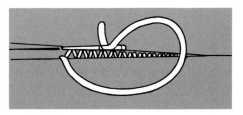

through one fold and insert needle in opposite fold slightly behind this first stitch. Pull thread through and draw folds together. Move forward 1 mm/1/16 in and repeat stitches. Do not pull thread too tight or fabric will wrinkle. Keep an even tension on all stitches. If join is curved, take a slightly longer stitch in concave curve to keep edges even. Slide needle to WS and fasten off well away from join.

**Even basting** see **BASTING**

## Feather stitch

When used in dressmaking, this embroidery stitch can be both decorative and functional; particularly suitable for faggoted seams and sewing on braid.

Use ordinary sewing thread or embroidery thread and work on RS towards you. Start with a knot or, on fine fabrics, a backstitch. Bring needle

through to RS of fabric and take a small stitch towards you, holding thread down against fabric to form loop and bringing needle out just above loop to form stitch. The amount of fabric picked up should be between 2 and 5 mm/1/16 and ¼ in depending on thickness of fabric. Begin second stitch slightly below loop to left, the distance below depending on thickness of fabric and size of stitch, and work third stitch slightly below second loop to right, and so on.

## Felling

A tailoring stitch used in dressmaking for attaching loose linings to the neck, front edges and seams of coats and jackets.

Baste lining in position with raw edge folded under. Hold work with fold of lining away from you. Start with a knot hidden under fold and, working from right to left, take a tiny deep stitch into fabric of garment, bringing needle out in edge of lining, no

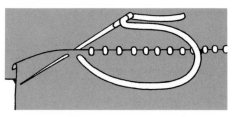

more than 2 mm/1/16 in away. Insert needle again in garment fabric slightly behind where thread emerged for an almost invisible stitch. Pull thread ▶

just far enough for the stitch to disappear; if it is pulled too tight the lining will wrinkle. Fasten off with two backstitches under the fold but in the garment. Although the stitch must be so small that it is virtually invisible, it is extremely strong. For a more professional result and a stronger finish, it can also be used as an alternative to hemming stitch to hold down a fold of fabric.

**Flash basting** see **BASTING**

**Fly-running** see **RUNNING STITCHES**

**Half backstitch** see **BACKSTITCHES**

### HEMMING STITCHES
#### Hemming stitch
Moderately strong and worked on WS to hold down a fold of fabric. It shows on RS and is, therefore, unsuitable for skirt and dress hems. It should also be avoided on jacket and trouser hems.

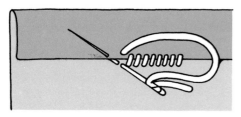

Work towards you. Begin with a knot, on WS of edge if possible, but if working on sheer fabric start with a small backstitch on WS. Take a slanting stitch 1 mm/$\frac{1}{16}$ in long, picking up part of single fabric and fold in one movement. Take another slanting stitch 1 mm/$\frac{1}{16}$ in farther forward. The length of the stitches and the distance between them can be a little more on thicker fabrics.

#### Hemming into machining
Stronger and more versatile than hemming. Use anywhere where a row of machining has been worked, e.g. on WS of waistbands or on cuffs.

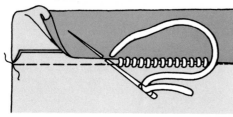

Work towards you. Instead of picking up fabric, pick up thread of machine stitch and then run needle into fold at a slight slant. Pull thread fairly tight. Work a hemming stitch into every machine stitch for maximum strength and neatness.

#### Shell stitch
A decorative stitch, equally visible on both sides, and used on fine fabrics only to hold a narrow hem or for making tucks.

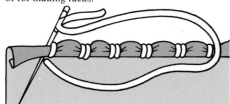

Work from right to left over a folded edge, usually 5 mm/$\frac{1}{4}$ in deep. Begin with a small backstitch—on WS if working a hem, on one of the two RS if working a tuck. Take needle over and behind folded edge, insert below it and bring through at same level

towards you. Pull thread sufficiently to wrinkle fold attractively. Hold thread with thumb of other hand, take another stitch over fold in same place as first and pull thread tight to hold stitch firmly. If working tucks, make three tiny running stitches between shells. If holding down an edge, run needle through fold for 5 mm/$\frac{1}{4}$ in or, if fabric is springy, work three hemming stitches along fold. Take needle over fold twice to make second shell, and so on. Press carefully to avoid squashing shells, pushing toe of iron into each shell.

#### Slip hemming
Used for holding down a folded edge, e.g. skirt hem, on light fabrics. Stitched with care, it can be almost invisible on both sides.

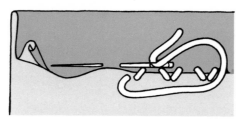

Work from right to left, beginning with a knot or a backstitch in fold. In one continuous movement take up one thread of single fabric on needle and, slightly in front of this, pass point into fold. Slip needle through fold for 2 to 5 mm/$\frac{1}{16}$ to $\frac{1}{4}$ in and bring out. Below the point at which the thread emerges and 1 mm/$\frac{1}{16}$ in farther on, take up another thread of fabric and insert needle in fold. Keep thread fairly loose as the hem shows if it is taut.

#### Slip stitch
Used for joining two folded edges. It can be invisible if carefully worked, so is useful for anything that has to be sewn from RS, such as a split in a seam, the gap in a belt, the ends of a tie, cuffs and collars.

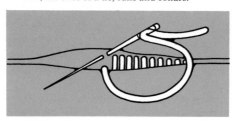

Start with a knot hidden inside one of folds. Working from right to left, take a tiny stitch along this fold and then take another in opposite fold about 1 mm/$\frac{1}{16}$ in farther on. Pull thread tight enough to join folds but not to wrinkle them. Fasten off slightly away from join.

#### Herringbone stitch
Similar to cross stitch, but not an even cross and quicker to sew. Worked over a raw edge to hold it down, e.g. on facings, and, worked in embroidery thread, to attach ric-rac or zigzag braid. Used frequently on medium and heavy fabrics, less on lightweight materials as the edge tends to curl up under the stitch. Can be used to neaten the hem of a thicker fabric, but inclined to be visible as a ridge after some wear.

To work over a raw edge, sew from left to right

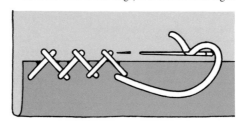

and begin with a knot or backstitch slightly below edge. In garment fabric above edge, diagonally to right of starting point, take a small stitch, 2 to 4 mm/$\frac{1}{16}$ to $\frac{1}{8}$ in long, depending on thickness of fabric, from right to left. Diagonally to right below first stitch and below raw edge, take another small horizontal stitch in same direction. Take a third stitch to right above second stitch on same level as first, and so on. Do not pull thread tight. Rows of horizontal stitches should be between 4 and 8 mm/$\frac{1}{8}$ and $\frac{3}{8}$ in apart.

Herringbone can be worked in various ways to attach braid, depending on the width and style of the braid. It is worked across thin braid, down the middle of a wider strip and, with ric-rac braid, the horizontal stitches are taken in opposite curves.

#### Loop stitch
Also called blanket stitch. Sometimes confused with buttonhole stitch but less lumpy and a loop is made rather than a knot. The stitches can be close together or spaced out, depending on where they are used. Close loop stitch, with no space between stitches, is used over bar tacks, at the back of buttons and for eyelet holes (where there would be no room for the knots of buttonhole stitches); open loop stitch is used as an alternative to herringbone for neatening raw edges or holding them down.

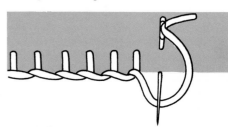

Work from left to right with edge towards you and start with a backstitch on WS. Bring needle and thread round to RS and insert needle above edge on RS, holding thread below edge. Bring needle out below edge over held thread. Pull thread and settle so that it lies along edge. The distance from the edge at which the needle is inserted varies according to the fabric—on non-fraying fabrics from 3 to 5 mm/$\frac{1}{8}$ to $\frac{1}{4}$ in, depending on thickness of fabric, on fraying from 4 to 8 mm/$\frac{1}{8}$ to $\frac{3}{8}$ in. Hold thread below edge and take another stitch a little to right for open loop stitch, immediately to right for close.

#### Overcasting
Used for neatening raw edges. If the material frays badly, work a row of machining first and trim away very close to it before overcasting over it.

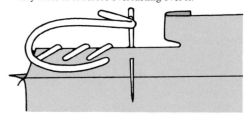

Work from left to right and start with a knot on WS if possible. Take needle over raw edge and insert in back of edge at right angles to fabric, bringing it through to front at same level. Pull thread through quickly to form sloping stitch, but not too tightly as edges will curl. If worked slowly, the stitches become upright and unattractive. Use thumb of other hand to hold edge flat while working. The depth of stitch and the distance between stitches depend on the thickness of the fabric, but make the depth as shallow as possible without pulling the fabric away.

#### Oversewing
Used for joining two folded edges where greater strength is needed than slip stitching can provide.

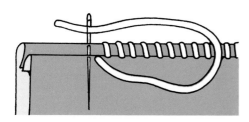

With the two folded edges together, work from right to left, starting with a hidden knot in back fold. Pass needle at right angles to body through top of both folds, picking up one fabric thread from each. Pull sewing thread through fairly tightly. Repeat to produce a row of tiny, neat, slanting stitches on RS. The distance between the stitches varies from 1 to 3 mm/$\frac{1}{16}$ to $\frac{1}{8}$ in, depending on thickness of fabric.

**Prick stitch** see **BACKSTITCHES**

## RUNNING STITCHES
### Fly-running
Quicker to work than running stitch and used where several long rows of running stitches are to be inserted, as, for example, in preparation for smocking.

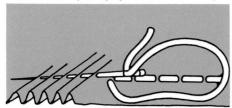

Use a sharps needle and work from right to left in a straight line. Start with a small backstitch. Hold needle near point and, instead of taking single stitches, wiggle point in and out of fabric at speed.

### Running stitch
Weak stitch used for inserting gathering threads, for preparing for smocking or for working French seams by hand on lingerie or baby wear—for seams practise the stitch first to ensure a good finish.

Start with a small backstitch and, working from right to left in a straight line, pass needle in and out of material at regular intervals. The stitches should be as small as possible and approximately the same size as the spaces between them (it is impossible to make them exactly the same). If working running stitch for gathering or in preparation for smocking, do not fasten off but leave an end of thread for pulling up gathers when all rows are in place. On a French seam, insert an occasional half or full backstitch for extra strength.

### Saddle stitch
Decorative top stitching worked from RS only.

With chalk or basting, mark out a line to follow, as stitch is invariably parallel with a finished edge and any deviation from its line is immediately noticeable. Using thick top-stitching thread and a needle large enough to take the thread, e.g. 4, begin with a well-hidden backstitch, especially if thread is a contrasting colour to fabric. Working from right to left, take a stitch 6 to 13 mm/$\frac{1}{4}$ to $\frac{1}{2}$ in. Take needle back almost to where it was first inserted and take it below, bringing it out 6 to 13 mm/$\frac{1}{4}$ to $\frac{1}{2}$ in in front of the first stitch. Take needle back almost to end of first stitch on RS and pass through to WS, and so on. The stitches should be longer than the gaps between them.

When working on a completed edge, or if stitching is to show on both sides, e.g. where a revers turns over, do not take needle through all thicknesses, but just stitch the surface. Turn work over and repeat on other side if stitching is to show.

### Satin stitch
Primarily an embroidery stitch, but useful for strengthening where a bar tack would be too lumpy, e.g. at ends of pockets and of hand-worked buttonholes.

Work in ordinary sewing thread, or, for buttonholes, buttonhole thread. Begin with a knot on WS and on RS make parallel small stitches on top of each other or very close together. With thick fabrics, stab needle back and forth from RS to WS. Pull thread tight.

**Shell stitch** see **HEMMING STITCHES**

**Slip basting** see **BASTING**

**Slip hemming** see **HEMMING STITCHES**

**Slip stitch** see **HEMMING STITCHES**

### Stab stitch
Strong stitch worked in a short length through several layers of fabric, e.g. at the base of a zip. The effect should be like prick stitch—an almost invisible dent rather than a stitch—but stronger.

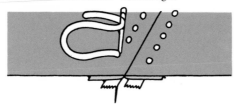

On WS a row of small stitches will show, so work stitch from whichever side is the more important to the appearance of the garment. Work as for prick stitch, but instead of running the needle through the fabric, stab it backwards and forwards through all layers.

### Tailor tacking
Also called tailor's tacks. The best and most accurate way of making marks through two layers of fabric. Used for marking turnings, balance marks, pleat lines, etc., after cutting out but before removing the pattern; also for marking two sides of a garment accurately, e.g. after making a fitting adjustment, or for marking position of pockets after the garment has been fitted.

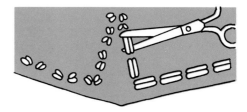

Follow the rules for temporary stitches on p. 31, using double basting thread. Work from right to left. Do not use a knot, but take a small stitch in double fabric about 2 to 4 mm/$\frac{1}{16}$ to $\frac{1}{8}$ in long depending on thickness of fabric. Move forward about 2.5 cm/1 in, less if working a curve, and take another small stitch. On a long straight line, the stitches on the surface can be longer, but never pick up more on needle than 4 mm/$\frac{1}{8}$ in. Do not fasten off end of thread but leave on surface and carefully snip in half all stitches on surface. Open the two layers of fabric until thread is revealed and snip across each pair of threads, leaving equal tufts on either side. This produces an accurate marking on two layers of fabric. Good tailor's tack tufts are so short they can be hard to remove (use teeth or tweezers). To save thread on long runs, pull thread through at end of each stitch until it leaves a small tuft and snip before making next stitch.

If tailor's tacks worked this way fall out prematurely, it is for one of the following reasons: you are not using proper basting thread, which is hairy and grips the fabric; you are not using double thread, which jams the tuft in the material; you are using too big a needle, making a hole in the fabric that allows the threads to escape; you are leaving long ends of thread that trail, get caught in your fingers and so come out.

**Uneven basting** see **BASTING**

### Whipping
Use to finish a rolled hem on fabrics such as silk, chiffon and georgette.

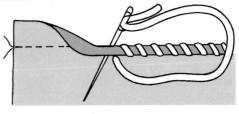

Work from right to left with a fine needle, 9 or 10 between. Anchor thread in raw edge with backstitch and roll raw edge under towards you between left thumb and forefinger. Pass needle over rolled edge to RS, insert at back of edge at an angle and bring through to garment fabric below roll. Re-roll next short section and hold with other hand while taking second stitch, and so on. The distance between the stitches varies according to the type of fabric—fairly close together on fine fabrics and more widely spaced on thicker ones. On fabrics such as polyester chiffon, polyester georgette, nylon chiffon and polyester lawn, work a row of machining first about 4 mm/$\frac{1}{8}$ in from raw edge and trim edge close to machining. Roll edge over towards you and whip stitch as above.

# Machine Stitches

Learn to control a new machine by practising first on paper and then on spare fabric. Do not thread the machine up but put a sheet of lined or squared paper under the foot, lower the foot and stitch on the lines. Practise lines, curves and corners, practise reversing and stopping and starting at marked points and try going very slowly.

When you are thoroughly familiar with the feel and speed of the machine, thread it up and do the same things on a double piece of check fabric. Then fold a piece of fabric and practise edge stitching. Finally, start on a garment, but confine yourself to straight and zigzag stitching for a while before embarking on more ambitious features such as buttonholes and automatic patterns. Work slowly at first, stitch by stitch, for good, professional-looking results.

### Rules for good machining
● Make sure that the fabric is flat and smooth before machining. Press it if it has been folded away.
● Insert the correct new needle for the fabric.
● Check that all dials are on 0 or set for straight stitch.
● Set the stitch length to approximately what you think will be correct—between 2 and $3\frac{1}{2}$ for most fabrics—and try out the stitching on a folded piece of spare fabric. Press and then examine both sides of the fabric to see if the length needs adjusting.
● Pull stretch jersey fabric to make sure that the amount of zigzag is correct for the fabric.
● Use the same colour and type of thread top and bottom, unless decorating.
● After machining, press the line of stitching on the upper side to smooth it out and to help embed the thread in the fabric.
● Trim off any fraying edges of fabric after pressing.

### How to start
Turn hand wheel towards you until thread take-up lever and needle are at their highest point. Check that needle and bobbin threads are long enough—about $6\,cm/2\frac{1}{4}$ in—and that they pass under foot and out towards back (1).

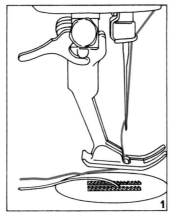

Place a test piece of double fabric right under foot, not part-way, with bulk of fabric to left and seam allowance in your line of vision to right of foot. Place forefinger on threads behind foot to stop them being sucked into needle hole. Turn

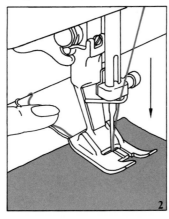

hand wheel towards you until needle is down in fabric. Lower foot (2). Turn hand wheel towards you to start and take over with foot or knee control of machine.

### Testing the stitch
Try out straight and zigzag stitches on a folded piece of fabric and adjust size until satisfactory. Also check any other stitches you intend using; some may not look right on the fabric and you may thus have to consider an alternative one. If the stitch proves to be unsatisfactory, rather than immediately twiddling knobs, quickly unthread machine, check that needle is in correctly, reinsert bobbin, rethread top, bring bottom thread out on to plate and test again. If the stitch is still unsatisfactory, consult the list of machine faults on p. 217.

### Tension
The thread on the top of the machine, coming from the spindle, passes through five or six points of control before going through the needle. The underneath thread, wound evenly on to the bobbin, is controlled only by a spring. The two threads loop together to form each stitch, the carefully controlled top thread catching as much or as little of the underneath one as is needed to form the stitch. It is, therefore, usually only the top thread that needs to be adjusted if the stitch is not properly formed.

Many modern machines have a self-adjusting tension mechanism and sew perfectly on all fabrics; in fact, any machine, even an old one, should stitch correctly if it has been cared for and the springs have not been strained. Never make any large adjustment to a tension control; a very small one should be enough to correct the feed of the thread. If it is not, have a new disc or spring fitted.

To check tension, work a row of straight stitching through double fabric. Examine both sides of fabric and run a finger along stitching. It should feel smooth. If it feels lumpy on either side, the tension needs some adjustment.

### Top tension too loose
Top thread forms loops on surface of fabric because too much thread is being allowed through controls (3). The underneath stitching feels lumpy where loose top thread has passed right through fabric (4) and the two threads interlock (5). Correct by tightening top tension control wheel; on most machines this is done by

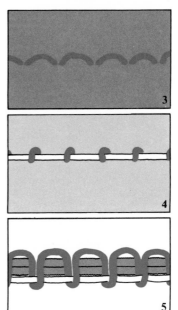

bringing plus sign on tension indicator nearer to central line.

### Top tension too tight
Top thread pulls on bottom one, drawing it up through fabric to RS (6).

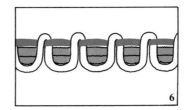

The stitching on top feels lumpy where underneath thread has come through. Correct by loosening top tension control, taking plus sign slightly farther from central line.

### Correct tension
The two threads loop together evenly, almost between the two layers of fabric. The stitching on both sides feels smooth and looks alike (7).

If adjusting top tension does not correct stitch, slightly loosen or tighten tiny screw on side of bobbin case or socket. This remedy should only rarely be necessary, possibly on very thick fabrics or when using shirring elastic or a top-stitching thread, and should not be regarded as a regular remedy for a poor stitch. When adjusting for a particular thread or stitch remember to readjust after use.

### Direction of stitching
Always have a guide on, or beside, which to stitch, such as tailor's tacks, basting, a chalk line or an edge. Do not machine on a row of basting but beside it, on raw edge side, so that it can be removed easily afterwards (8). Work from the wide to the narrow end of a seam.

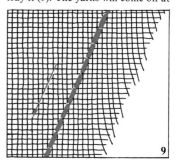

On edges that are not exactly on lengthways or cross grain the finished result is improved if you stitch, both by machine and by hand, in direction of grain. Take a piece of plain-weave cloth, cut it at an angle and slightly fray it (9). The yarns will come off at a sharp outward angle in one direction, but will lie flat against the fabric in the other. Whenever possible, stitch to keep angled fibres lying as close to raw edge as possible, especially when zigzagging (**10**).

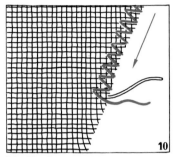

## Feeding in

Except for certain special effects, such as fluting an edge or working embroidery with a hoop, your hands should only guide the fabric; you should not need to push at the front or pull at the back.

## Keeping straight

Run edge of fabric level with one side of machine foot, or watch needle closely for accuracy on fabric motifs such as stripes (**11**). Some machines have marked measured lines on

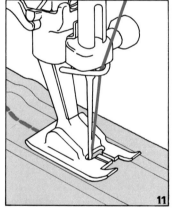

needle plate for guiding edge.

## Turning corners

Stop machine and insert needle into corner by turning hand wheel. Lift foot, turn fabric (**12**), lower foot and continue stitching.

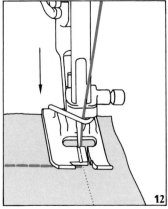

## Turning corners to be trimmed

Stop one stitch away from corner with needle down. Raise foot, swivel fabric and lower foot. Using hand wheel, work one stitch across corner. With needle still in fabric, raise foot again, swivel fabric so that you can

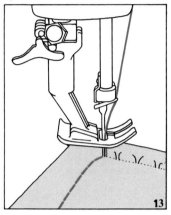

stitch along fitting line (**13**), lower foot and continue stitching.

## Working curves

On a gentle curve, stitch very slowly, holding fabric in both hands and easing it round gradually. For tight curves, stop at beginning of curve, and, with needle still in fabric, lift foot and turn fabric slightly into curve. Lower foot and work two stitches, using hand wheel for greater control. Repeat this sequence until end of curve, making sure that the stitching remains at the same distance from the edge of the fabric all the way round.

## How to stop

Near end of row of stitching, slow down, put your hand on hand wheel to act as a brake and lift your foot or remove your knee from control. If necessary, work last stitch by using hand wheel. Never machine off end of fabric. To ensure a neat line of stitching right to the edge, place a piece of folded fabric against edge and stitch on to it (**14**). Cut stitching between the two pieces of fabric.

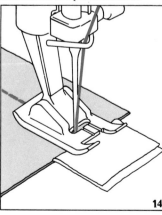

Turn wheel until needle and take-up lever are at highest point. Raise foot. Draw fabric out to back with threads still between toes of foot. Pull fabric backwards until 12 cm/4½ in of both

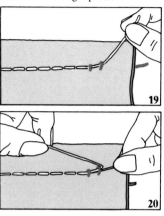

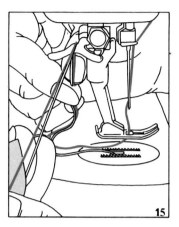

threads appear and cut threads midway on machine cutter (**15**), so leaving 6 cm/2¼ in on the machine and 6 cm/2¼ in on fabric.

## Fastening off ends

Reversing is the quickest way of finishing, but it adds a little stiffness and should be avoided on luxury or examination articles. Start machining a little way in from edge—1 cm/⅜ in is enough—and reverse to edge before going forwards (**16**). On reaching end

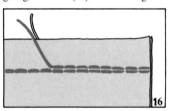

of line of stitching, reverse as at beginning of stitching to fasten off.

Alternatively, fasten off both RS and WS ends of thread in turn by backstitching a little way along machine stitching on WS (**17**) or by

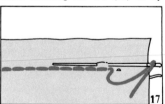

running the threads, again in turn, in and out of stitches on WS (**18**). A knot is awkward to tie and not very

durable in washing. To fasten off ends of thread when stitching on RS of fabric, pull ends of WS thread gently until a loop of RS thread forms (**19**). Pull loop up with pin or fingers to bring thread through from RS (**20**). Fasten off both ends by above methods. Cut off thread close to fabric. This keeps the work neat,

prevents the ends from being caught in the machine and avoids marks when the stitching is pressed.

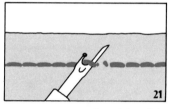

## Unpicking

Never open a seam and cut machine stitches between two fabric pieces because the tugging tends to stretch the fabric and little ends of thread are left to be removed.

To unpick machine stitching quickly on all fabrics except very fine ones, slip end of pin or unpicker under a stitch on upper side of work and lift and cut thread with small scis-

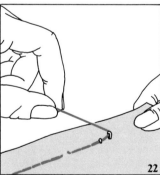

sors or on curve of unpicker (**21**). Continue to undo stitches by lifting, but not cutting, until you have enough thread to grip firmly between thumb and forefinger (wet fingers for a firmer grip). Tug very hard on thread against line of stitching—towards part not yet unpicked. The thread will snap six or seven stitches farther on (**22**). Turn fabric over, lift

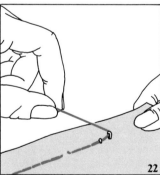

end of thread on WS and pull hard to snap it. Turn to RS again, lift thread and snap, and so on. This will not harm the fabric and is soon mastered with practice. On very fine fabrics such as chiffon unpick stitch by stitch, lifting and cutting each one in turn.

Place unpicked area on sleeve board and press with steam iron or with dry iron and damp cloth to smooth out fabric and close up holes.

# Machine Stitches

## STRAIGHT STITCHES

### Straight stitching

The most widely used stitch for joining two pieces of fabric. Suitable for all except stretch fabrics.

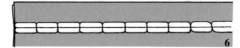

Following tailor's tacks, chalk marks or basting, machine slowly to keep straight and to avoid top layer of fabric moving (1). If working parallel with an edge, use edge of foot as guide.

### Edge stitching

Straight stitching or zigzag (see zigzag) worked on the edge of a fold, as for seam neatening. Place

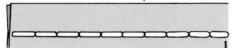

fabric under foot, with raw edge facing downwards to avoid wrinkling. Stitch slowly as near folded edge as possible, watching needle not foot (2). Press. Trim away surplus raw edge of fabric on WS.

### Stretch stitch

Most modern machines have a stretch stitch that should be used on fabrics with a great deal of give, such as jersey, velours and stretch towelling. The

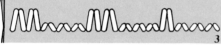

stitch is usually made up of about three small fairly straight stitches followed by a few tight zigzags (3). Do not use on crisp fabrics where a neatly pressed open seam is required.

### Basting

Most modern machines can be set to baste, generally using a special foot and needle. Although a fast method of basting, this must be carefully controlled to keep it straight. Useful for preparing several garments with long seams for fitting. Do not use on

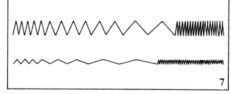

fine fabrics. Take care the top layer does not move while stitching. Use basting thread. To anchor the thread the first three or four stitches are automatically smaller than the subsequent ones (4).

### Top stitching

Decorative stitching, which is normally straight but can be a zigzag or embroidery stitch. It helps to keep edges flat on bulky fabrics such as quilting and breaks up the surface of plain fabrics, particularly cottons and denim. With all kinds of top stitching use a big stitch for the best effect. Always work from RS and leave long ends of thread that can be neatly sewn in on WS. There are several methods of top stitching:

With ordinary, matching sewing thread top and bottom. On many fabrics the stitch does not show on RS but an attractive ridge results on both sides.

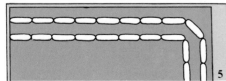

With two reels of ordinary sewing thread on top of machine, to match or contrast with fabric, threaded and put through needle together. Thread bobbin with ordinary thread to match fabric. This produces a slightly heavier, more obvious stitch (5).

With a twin needle and two reels of ordinary sewing thread on top and bobbin threaded in usual way with thread to match fabric. The two top reels can match the fabric or be a contrast. This produces two parallel lines of stitching (6).

With a large needle, no. 110 (or 18), and heavy top-stitching thread on top and ordinary sewing thread on bobbin. This produces a very bold single line of stitching on RS only. If the effect of the heavy thread is required on both sides, wind bobbin with top-stitching thread. Both threads should be the same colour and either match the fabric or contrast with it. Test stitch; you may have to loosen top tension slightly to prevent bobbin thread coming through to RS or loosen tension on bobbin case slightly to obtain a good stitch. If so, remember to re-adjust tension screw. Stitch very slowly. Bold or top-stitching thread may strain the bobbin case if used a lot. To prevent this, buy a spare case, adjust it and keep it only for top stitching.

## ZIGZAG STITCHES

### Zigzag

Used for neatening edges and for decoration. If using the stitch for decoration, experiment with the length and width to achieve the desired effect, which

can range from close-up stitches, barely discernible as zigzags, to more widely spaced, more obvious zigzags (7).

For zigzagging along an edge, the length and width of the stitch must be carefully set for each fabric to ensure that the zigzag prevents fraying. Try out various sizes of stitch until you find a satisfac-

tory one. The stitch should be as small and narrow as possible for the fabric (8), as with a wide zigzag the fabric frays between stitches. If the fabric frays badly or tends to curl up when stitched, set to widest stitch but run raw edge of fabric under needle. Half the zigzag is, therefore, lost and curling eliminated.

On fine fabrics turn under raw edge, baste it down, press and work a very small zigzag over fold (9). Trim away surplus fabric on WS.

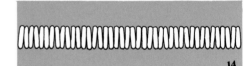

If any version of a zigzag stitch makes edge of fabric flute or stretch, lay an extra length of thread on fabric and zigzag over it (10). Use this thread to pull fabric flat after completing stitching.

### Slight zigzag

Useful for seams on fabrics that have give, such as jersey, as the stitch also has give and thus prevents seams splitting in wear. It can be used as an alternative to stretch stitch and gives a neater seam finish. Always use synthetic thread. Set zigzag

control to slightly off 0. Test stitch and pull to make sure there is enough give. The zigzag should be so slight that it is barely distinguishable from a straight stitch (11). If it is too wide, it prevents the seam from being pressed open correctly.

### Blind hem stitch

Used for holding up the hem on firm, fairly heavy fabrics and as a seam-neatening stitch on non-fraying jersey fabrics, where it helps to prevent the edge from curling up. It should not be used on hems of lighter weight fabrics as it shows. The stitch is made up of several straight stitches followed by a zigzag to the left of the needle and away from the edge (12). On a hem work the stitch so that the zigzag

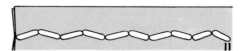

catches down the top edge of the hem on to WS of garment; use hemming foot and make sure fabric is folded and fed into machine accurately.

### Overlock stitch

Many modern machines have an overlock stitch for neatening edges that is similar to a commercial overlocking stitch. It consists of a zigzag to one side followed by two straight stitches and prevents fraying better than a normal zigzag. Work zigzag part right over raw edge and not within it (13).

### Satin stitch

Used mainly for machine-made buttonholes and machine appliqué; also for embroidery and for bar tacks through several layers if hand bar tacks would look wrong or inexpert. Use ordinary sewing thread

or, for embroidery or appliqué, machine embroidery thread and the satin stitch foot, which allows you to see the fabric more easily than the ordinary foot and helps to make the stitching more accurate. Watch hole in centre of foot while stitching. The stitches, tightly worked zigzags, should be very short and appear as closely packed parallel lines (14).

### Machine shell edge

Successful only on fine fabrics, it can be worked using the hemming foot and a small zigzag.

Alternatively, on non-fraying fabric, turn under raw edge and feed under needle with stitch on no. 4

zigzag. Allow needle to go off edge of fold on righthand side, which will draw fabric into shells. If fabric frays, turn and baste a narrow hem before machining. The machine can also be set to a blind hem stitch, which is worked so that, when the needle jumps to the side, it goes right over the edge (15). Use a long stitch and no. 4 stitch width.

### Machine embroidery stitches See p. 190.

# Seams

There are two basic types of seam—the functional, which holds the pieces of a garment together, and the decorative. Most functional seams have some shaping. The edges of the fabric pieces can be either angled or curved so that when joined they form a shaped area. This shaping provides style, or allows for the slopes and bulges of the body, or both. Sometimes, however, a functional seam is perfectly straight, as, for example, when joining narrow widths of fabric together to form one piece of a garment. Generally, the fewer functional seams on a garment the looser it is and the more seams there are the more shaping it has.

The fabric, the type of garment, possible strain of constant wear and washing and the effect wanted on the right side should all be taken into consideration when deciding on the type of functional seam to use.

Seams in lace and fine transparent fabrics such as chiffon, georgette and ninon, need special handling, particularly if the fabric is made from synthetic fibres. Seams in patterned fabrics must also be stitched with great care to ensure that pattern motifs match.

## Handling seams

The same preparatory stages apply to all seams, but certain things, including the seam allowance, vary according to the type of seam. For accuracy, mark all fitting lines before beginning to sew. Where possible—this depends on the type of seam—place the pieces of fabric flat on the table. Whether they are right or wrong sides together is again governed by the kind of seam.

With raw edges towards you, lift and flap (rather than drag or pull) the fabric until the fitting lines are level. Pin only if there is ease to control or if it is imperative to match the pattern of the fabric on both sides of the seam. Insert pins across the seam, not along it.

Baste the seam on the fitting line, keeping the fabric flat, but helping it on to the needle with each stitch. Machine close to raw edge side of basting rather than on top of it. This enables you to remove the basting easily and ensures a correct fit.

Unless, for example, you are working with material cut on the cross, always baste and stitch with the grain: from the wide part to the narrow, skirt hem to waist, neck to shoulder point, underarm to wrist, and so on. Press seam with the grain to prevent stretching. Press curved areas over a pad or the end of a sleeve board.

Listed below are the main types of functional seam for all weights and kinds of material.

## Open seam—straight stitched

Often called plain seam. The most widely used functional seam because it is flat and neat, produces the most tailored look of all seams, and is one of the most inconspicuous. Can be used anywhere except where there is gathering and on any material except transparent or fine fraying ones. As there is only one row of stitching, a split shows up immediately, so the seam may not be suitable for children's clothes or other garments intended for hard wear, such as jeans.

## Open seam—zigzag

Seams on jersey and other fabrics with give, such as crêpe, are best stitched with a slight zigzag for additional stretch. Pressed open, this looks like an open seam, but will not split in wear.

## French seam

A narrow seam that looks identical to an open seam on the right side but forms a ridge on the wrong side, so restrict to fine fabrics. Useful if fabric frays as edges are enclosed and excellent for blouses, nightwear and children's clothes. Can be worked by hand on fine garments. It is started on the right side, which makes fitting awkward.

## Narrow finish seam

Use only on lightweight or transparent fabrics as both turnings lie to one side.

## Taped seam

A method of reinforcing or stabilizing seams in areas such as the shoulder or the crutch of trousers. Particularly useful if fabric tends to stretch.

## Machine fell seam

Strong and flat and suitable for all medium-weight fabrics, including denim, drill, sailcloth, twill weaves and poplin, but not for very fine or bulky fabrics. Use on shirts, jeans, dungarees, pyjamas, wrap-over or beach robes and shorts.

Two rows of stitching show on one side of the fabric. If you have difficulty in working neat edge stitching (the second row), work the seam so that this is visible on the wrong side only. If the seam is worked so that the edge stitching appears on the right side, you will have to undo the seam basting and rebaste when fitting the garment. This seam can be worked in a thread that contrasts with the colour of the material.

## Curved seam

Often provides shaping for the bust and, therefore, the two edges of fabric to be joined differ in shape, one of the edges generally being more curved than the other.

## Angled seam

The angle formed by the seam is part of the design, but there is usually some additional shaping, which may prevent the two edges from fitting together easily.

## Self-neatened seam

Useful for fraying fabrics as raw edges are enclosed, but forms a bulky ridge so confine to thin materials. Very useful on curves such as armholes and where one edge is gathered, as on yokes and waistlines.

## Double-faced seam

Use for joining reversible fabric, if you want to be able to reverse the garment, and where a facing rolls back to show a join. Suitable only if the two layers of fabric are joined by threads, not adhesive.

## Welt seam

A strong seam that can be used on most fabrics, except very fine fraying ones. As a row of stitching shows on RS, the welt seam is an effective way to add interest to plain fabrics and to add style to casual coats, safari suits, shirt-waister dresses and trousers.

## Mantua-maker's seam

Used on fine fabrics. There is only one row of stitching so confine to loose-fitting items as otherwise the seam may pull open in wear.

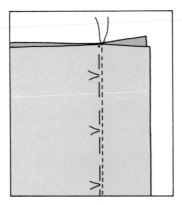

**Open** With fabric RS together, baste along fitting line and machine with straight stitch or, on stretch fabrics, zigzag. Remove basting and tacks. If zigzagging, use synthetic thread and set stitch width dial to slightly off 0. The stitch is slightly wobbly, not a defined zigzag.

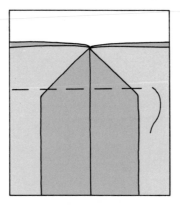

**2.** Where open seams meet, cut away turnings at an angle before stitching to reduce bulk.

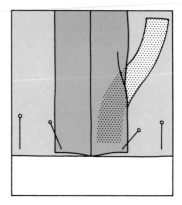

**3.** Open seams in fine jersey wrinkle for the last 20 cm/8 in to the hem because there is no weight to pull them down. Correct by stretching out this section and pinning it down to a sleeve board. Slip narrow strips of fabric adhesive tape under seam turnings and press. Leave to cool before removing pins.

# Seams

**NEATENING OPEN SEAMS**

To prevent fraying and to help keep turnings flat, always neaten the raw edges of open seams. Neatened turnings should be 1 to 1.5 cm/$\frac{3}{8}$ to $\frac{5}{8}$ in wide to support the seam. Choose a neatening method that will be effective on the fabric without adding bulk. Neaten raw edges for the whole length of the seam, even if you intend to insert a zip later on.

To neaten by hand on any type of fabric, overcast, trimming away surplus fabric as you sew (**1**).

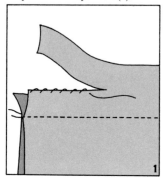

To neaten medium or heavy fabrics by machine, place fabric with raw edge under machine and zigzag over raw edge (**2**).

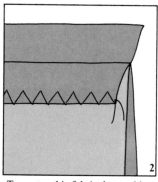

To neaten thin fabrics by machine, turn edge under 5 mm/$\frac{1}{4}$ in and zigzag or straight stitch close to fold. Press and trim away surplus on WS almost down to stitching (**3**).

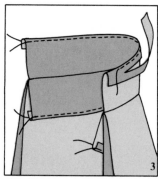

On fraying medium to heavy fabrics, trim 5 mm/$\frac{1}{4}$ in off seam turnings and machine each turning separately a little way in from the trimmed edge—not too close to the edge as this encourages fraying.

Overcast, taking stitch down almost to top of machining (**4**).

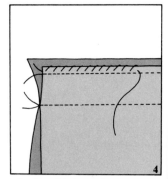

On firm fabrics such as polyester that fray only a little, loop stitch raw edges of seam (**5**).

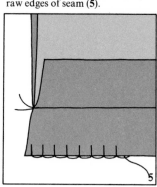

Badly fraying lightweight fabrics, e.g. brocade, can be bound with bias binding or net (**6**).

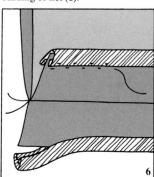

Prevent raw edge of fine jersey from rolling up by working blind hem stitch or any wide decorative machine stitch along it (**7**).

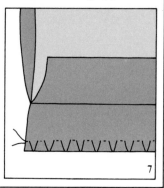

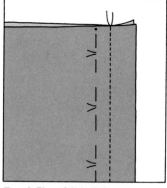

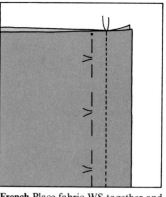

**French** Place fabric WS together and baste along fitting line. Work first row of stitching about 5 mm/$\frac{1}{4}$ in from fitting line (a little more on firm fabrics such as cotton). Remove basting and press stitching flat. Press turnings open on to RS, turn work over and press seam again from WS.

**2.** On RS press turnings together lightly. Trim both turnings down to within 3 mm/$\frac{1}{8}$ in of stitching.

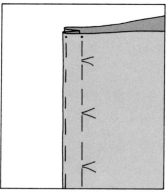

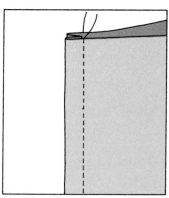

**3.** Open out fabric, fold so that RS are together, roll seam so that join appears right on edge and baste fabric together near edge. Hold seam to light to find edge of turnings on inside and baste slightly beyond edge. Press.

**4.** Machine beside second lot of basting. Remove basting and tacks and press stitching. Open out fabric and press seam towards back of garment. Press again on RS. Where two French seams cross, press each one in a different direction to eliminate excess bulk.

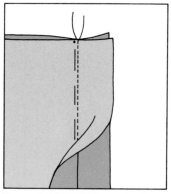

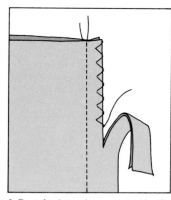

**Narrow finish** With RS together, baste along fitting line and machine. Remove basting and press seam open.

**2.** Press both turnings to one side. To finish by machine, trim raw edges down to 5 mm/$\frac{1}{4}$ in from machine stitching and zigzag over both together. Press on RS.

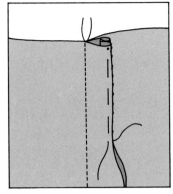

**3.** To finish by hand, fold turnings in to meet each other, baste, press and slip stitch together. Press on RS.

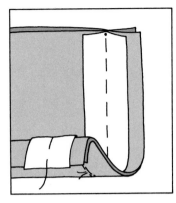

**Taped** Place fabric RS together and baste on fitting line. Baste a length of seam binding or tape (pre-shrunk) with centre over fitting line. Ease it round a curve. The tape can be applied to either piece of fabric and can be cut the same length as the seam before starting, or cut to size when the seam is finished.

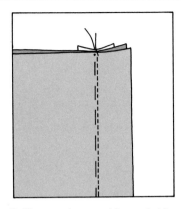

**2.** Turn work over with taped side down and machine beside basting. Remove basting and tacks. Press stitching, press seam open and neaten turnings as for open seam.

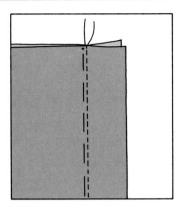

**Machine fell** Place fabric RS together if second row of stitching is to show on WS, WS together if to show on RS. Baste on fitting line and machine. Remove basting and tacks and press stitching. Press turnings open on WS and RS to remove wrinkles and produce a clean line.

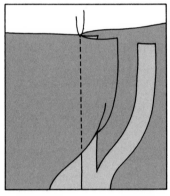

**2.** Press both turnings to one side—towards either the back or the front, but be consistent throughout the garment. Lift top turning and trim underneath one to 5mm/¼in. Press both turnings again to one side to flatten them.

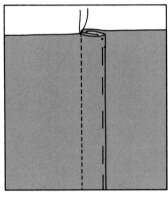

**3.** Turn under raw edge of upper turning and tuck it down as far as it will go under narrow trimmed edge. If seam appears clumsy, trim a little off wide turning before turning it under. Baste turning down to garment, keeping its folded edge an even distance from original machining. Press on RS.

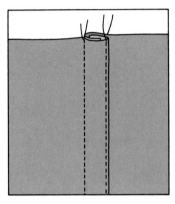

**4.** Machine on fold, with exactly the same size stitch as the initial row of machining. Press on RS.

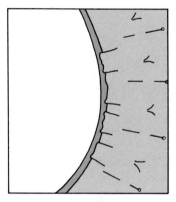

**Curved** With the more curved piece on top, match balance marks and pin fabric RS together, exactly on fitting line, taking care to pick up only a little fabric. Ease shaped piece into position and hold seam over your hand to pin so that it remains in a curve. There is no need to insert pins along a straight part of the seam.

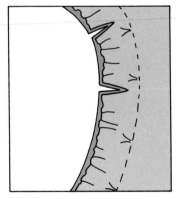

**2.** Baste on fitting line with small stitches along curve. If the fabric is stiff or unyielding, as you baste snip turnings at intervals almost down to basting. Remove pins.

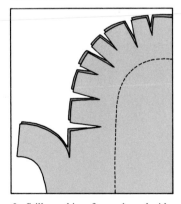

**3.** Still working from shaped side, machine slowly beside basting, following curve. Remove basting and tacks and press stitching. Trim turnings and snip them at more frequent intervals. Press seam either open or to one side and neaten turnings separately or together.

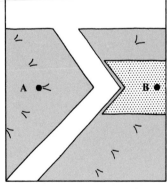

**Angled** Mark exact point of inner corner on both pieces of fabric at **A** and **B** and press a small piece of lightweight iron-on interfacing over **B** on WS. Cut interfacing down to fit shape of angle.

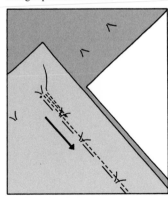

**2.** With RS together and corner marks matching, baste on fitting line parallel with two aligned edges from corner right to end of seam. Lower machine needle into corner, lower foot, stitch forward a little, reverse to corner and sew forward beside basting to end of seam. Remove basting and tacks. ▶

# Seams

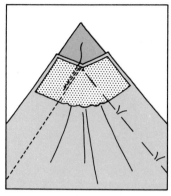

**3.** Press and neaten as a normal open seam. Turn work over and snip reinforced corner to within a thread of start of machine stitching. Swing fabric round with RS still together until the two unstitched edges align. With this side of work towards you, baste parallel with two aligned edges from corner to end of seam.

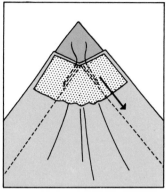

**4.** Lower machine needle into corner exactly where previous stitching ends. Stitch as before, reversing to fasten ends. Remove basting and tailor's tacks, press seam open and neaten. If you are unsure of reversing accurately at the corner, leave long enough ends of thread to sew in by hand.

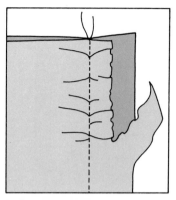

**Self-neatened** With RS together, baste along fitting line and machine. Remove basting and tailor's tacks and press turnings to one side. Trim down upper turning—always the gathered edge if there is one—to 5 mm/¼ in.

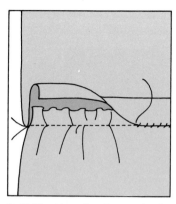

**2.** Fold wider edge down twice by rolling and bring it over to meet machining. Baste and press. Hem into machine stitches to finish or, for speed but a harder ridge, machine near bottom fold on WS. Remove basting and press seam.

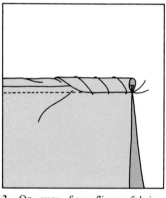

**3.** On very fine, flimsy fabrics, particularly at waists and armholes, make seam narrower so that it shows less. Trim down wider turning to 6 mm/¼ in, fold down as in (**2**) and whip stitch over edge, bringing needle through just above machining.

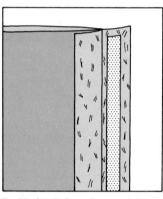

**Double-faced** Open layers of fabric and snip threads in from edge to a depth of about 4cm/1½in along seam edges to be joined. Counteract stretching by slipping narrow strips of paper-backed adhesive beside opened raw edges on WS of two outer layers, press with a damp cloth and peel off paper backing.

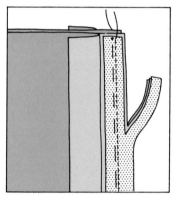

**2.** Place edges of two reinforced pieces RS together and baste, taking usual seam allowance. Machine beside basting, trim raw edges, remove basting and press seam open.

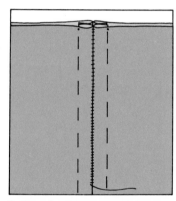

**3.** Turn in the two remaining raw edges so that they meet over centre of seam, baste and press. Slip stitch edges together. Remove basting and press both sides of fabric.

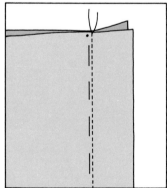

**Welt** With fabric RS together, baste on fitting line and machine. Remove basting and tailor's tacks, press seam open and press turnings to one side—towards the back or front of the garment, depending on where you want the additional stitching to show, but be consistent in the direction throughout the garment.

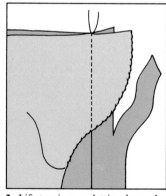

**2.** Lift turnings and trim down the underneath one to a little less than 1 cm/⅜ in. Neaten raw edge of wider turning unless fabric is non-fraying or garment is to be lined.

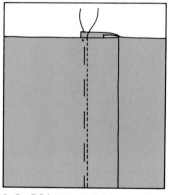

**3.** On RS baste parallel to seam line, stitching through wider turning and encasing the narrower one. Press lightly. Add a row of machine stitching or prick stitch parallel with seam, making sure that you stitch through the wider turning underneath. Remove basting and press seam on RS.

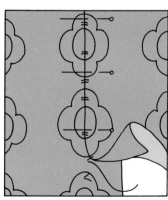

**Seams in patterned fabrics** Make sure pattern matches exactly at seams by working first from RS. Fold under one edge of fabric on fitting line and place it on RS of second piece, matching fitting lines and pattern of fabric. Place a few pins across seam at main points of pattern. Slip baste fabric together.

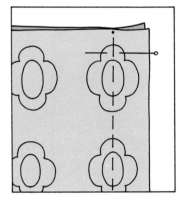

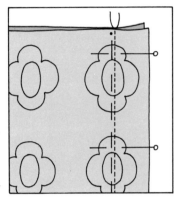

**2.** Remove pins. With fabric RS together, replace pins across seam at start of each motif or of alternate ones if the motifs are small. Check the underneath to make sure pattern is level. The pins should be inserted so that the heads project well beyond the raw edge or they may get caught under the machine foot.

**3.** Machine seam, stitching over pins, but slow down as you approach them so that the needle slides in easily to one side of them. (Fast stitching may jar needle against a pin and break it.) Alternatively, stop at each pin and work machine by hand wheel. Remove pins and basting and press. Neaten as for an open seam to finish.

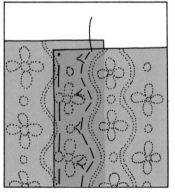

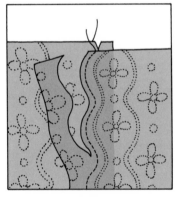

**Seams in lace** Cut out the pieces of lace with slightly wider turnings than usual and mark fitting lines. Matching fitting lines, with both pieces RS up, lap one piece over the other and baste together. Near fitting line on top piece use basting to mark out a stitching line round each motif of the lace pattern.

**2.** Using a perfectly matching thread, work over basted line with satin stitch or a close machine zigzag. Remove basting and tailor's tacks. Close to stitching snip away surplus lace on both top and bottom pieces. Press RS down on a folded towel.

*Popular in the late 17th and in the 18th century, the mantua was made by early dressmakers, or mantua-makers, who had little experience of fitting garments (hitherto, men's and women's clothes had been made by tailors). Its loose fit was ideal for the ample figure, such as that of the English aristocrat Lady Vyner in this detail from a painting of 1673 by John Michael Wright.*

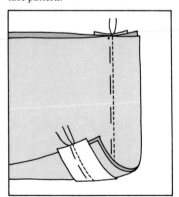

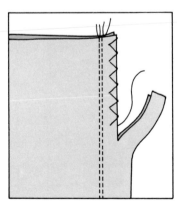

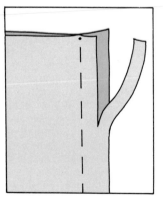

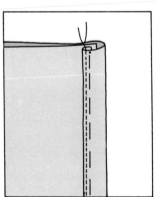

**Seams on transparent fabrics** To stop wrinkling when machining and to ensure the machine stitches properly and the teeth do not mark the fabric, place strips of tissue or thin typing paper under the fabric as you baste the seam. Machine with paper underneath, stitching through it, and tear it away when removing basting.

**2.** Use narrow finish, French or mantua-maker's seams on these fabrics. On the narrow finish, work a second row of machining to stabilize edges, trim edges down to within 3 mm/⅛in of this machining and zigzag or overcast together.

**Mantua-maker's** With RS together, baste fabric on fitting line. Trim down one layer to within 3 mm/⅛in of the basting.

**2.** Bring wider turning over trimmed layer, fold down twice and baste down on fitting line. On very fine fabric make a neater seam by trimming down wider turning a little before folding over. Machine along edge of fold. Remove basting and on WS press seam to one side.

# Seams

Decorative seams add style to an outfit and provide a focal point. It is important, however, not to over-do the decoration. Consider the type and design of the fabric, the outfit itself and the finished effect before working a decorative seam. Many look best on plain fabrics.

As decorative seams can be difficult, do not attempt any of the following until you have mastered the decorative stitches involved and have tried out the techniques on spare fabric.

## Piped seam

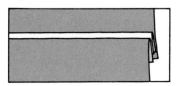

Matching or contrasting piping can be inserted into a seam to provide a focal point on clothes and soft furnishings. As it tends to make the seam more rigid, it is unsuitable for most softly draped styles. It can be soft, or unfilled, or filled with a length of cord that has been pre-shrunk.

## Lapped seam

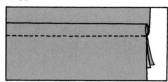

One side of the seam laps over the other. Suitable for any fabric.

## Top-stitched seam

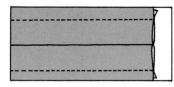

Any open seam can be decorated with additional stitching, worked in matching or contrasting bold or double thread, or using a twin needle to produce double stitching. The stitching can be on one side of the seam or both; try it out on correct number of thicknesses first. If you wish to stitch farther from the seam than the standard width of the trimmed turning—1 to 1.5 cm/$\frac{3}{8}$ to $\frac{5}{8}$ in—remember to add extra fabric at seams when cutting out the garment pieces.

## Faggoted seam

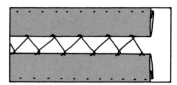

The seam is joined with faggoting, or feather stitch, to leave a gap between the seam edges. This can be a weak area, so avoid on clothing that will be subjected to a lot of wear. If the pattern does not include the seam, work it on fabric larger than you will need and cut the fabric around the pattern piece later.

## Insertion seam

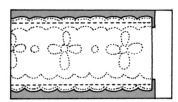

Lace is the usual insertion on fine fabrics for blouses, lingerie, etc., but any suitable open-weave braid or trimming can be used, and on almost any garment. The insertion can be added after the pattern pieces have been cut out; no extra allowance is needed.

## Slot or channel seam

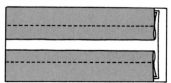

Use on any fabric, but most effective on plain, firm materials. Backing, cut from a contrasting coloured or patterned fabric, shows between the seam edges. It should be similar in weight to the garment fabric; if it is lighter, mount it on iron-on interfacing. The width of the backing depends on the weight and bulk of the fabric and on how visible the backing is to be. Generally, the maximum that should show is 5 mm/$\frac{1}{4}$ in, but on some styles the gap can be larger between the two fabric edges.

If the pattern does not include the seam, cut through a large enough piece of fabric, work the seam and cut out the fabric around the pattern piece later.

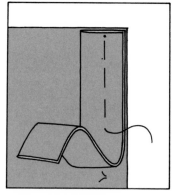

**Piped—soft** Cut and join enough crossways strips of fabric, 3 cm/1$\frac{1}{4}$ in wide, to make the required length. Fold joined strips in half, WS together, and press. Baste strip to RS of one of seam edges along fitting line, allowing fold of piping to extend beyond fitting line—the amount depends on the fabric.

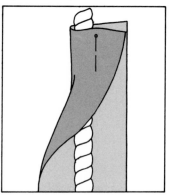

**Piped—corded** Cut a small piece of fabric on the true cross or on the bias, wrap it round the piping cord, pin and trim, leaving two 3.5 cm/1$\frac{1}{4}$ in turnings. Unpin and measure width of strip. Prepare strip this width and required length.

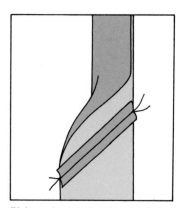

**Piping a circular edge** If the fabric has been joined so that it is no longer flat, make piping about 12 cm/4$\frac{1}{2}$ in longer than seam and join before applying it. Join soft piping or fabric of filled on straight grain as for crossways strips. Insert cord and stitch, leaving area unstitched where cord ends are to be joined.

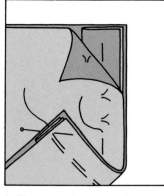

**2.** Place second garment piece over strip RS down. Baste, piercing top and bottom layers of fabric with pins and turning fabric back to check fitting lines coincide. Machine beside basting. Remove basting and tailor's tacks and press seam so that on RS piping is either upright or to one side. Trim off excess piping.

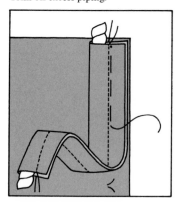

**2.** Wrap strip RS out round cord and machine with zip foot as close as possible to cord. Do not baste first as the stitches pull open. Baste piping down to seam line, machine and finish as for soft piping.

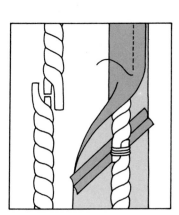

**2.** To join the cords of filled piping, trim ends of cord so they overlap slightly, unravel them a little and cut half the strands so their ends touch and the ends of the others overlap. Wrap overlapping strands round shorter ones and work a stitch over and over across join. Wrap fabric strip over cord.

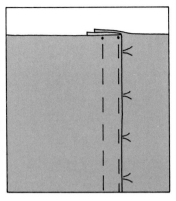

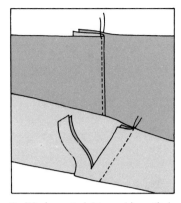

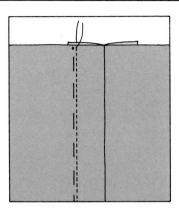

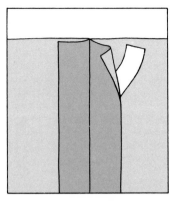

**Lapped** Decide which way seam is to lap, e.g. towards front if it is a shoulder or yoke seam. Turn under top layer of fabric on fitting line, baste fold and press. Place this WS down on to RS of underneath piece, matching balance marks and fitting lines and baste two pieces of fabric together slightly away from fold.

**2.** Work a straight machine stitch along fold or use a hand or machine embroidery stitch. Remove basting and tacks and press. On WS trim and neaten the two raw edges together.

**Top-stitched** Press and neaten open seam. At desired distance from seam, baste through garment and turning. Machine beside basting on RS, using machine foot as a guide, or work a hand or machine embroidery stitch. If stitching both sides of seam, sew in same direction. Remove basting. Press RS down on a folded towel.

**2.** For a more raised effect, cut bias strips of lining or other thin material such as cotton lawn and slip these under the turning on WS before basting. Baste and stitch as before. (The strips can be folded double; do not neaten their edges but, after completing stitching, trim away raw edge under turning.)

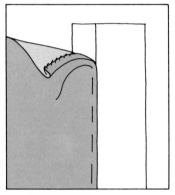

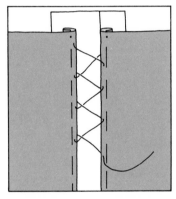

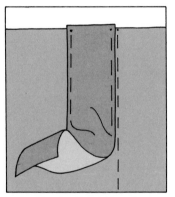

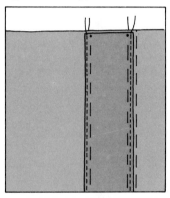

**Faggoted** Baste a line on RS of fabric to mark position of faggoting. Cut on line and turn in about 3 mm/⅛ in on each edge and stitch. Press. If seam is on bias, make sure you do not stretch it while hemming. On fine typing paper or tissue, pencil a straight line, place one hemmed edge WS down on line and baste to paper.

**2.** Place other hemmed edge about 3 mm/⅛ in away and baste. On wool or thicker fabrics the hems can be a little wider and the gap on the paper 1 cm/⅜ in. Join edges with feather stitch, worked in a thread of a suitable thickness, keeping gap between edges even and slipping needle along fold. Remove paper and basting.

**Insertion** The insertion can be as wide or as narrow as desired. Mark position of one edge of insertion with basting or tailor's tacks on RS of main fabric. Place one edge of insertion along this row of basting and baste to garment. Hold insertion flat and baste second edge to RS of garment.

**2.** Attach insertion to RS by machine with a straight, zigzag or embroidery stitch, or by hand with hemming or an embroidery stitch. If the insertion is not the same colour as the fabric, match the thread to the insertion for less conspicuous stitching. Remove basting. Press stitching and insertion with RS down on a folded towel.

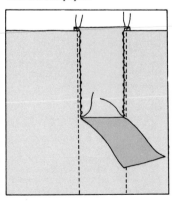

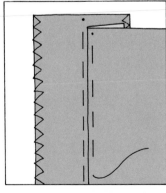

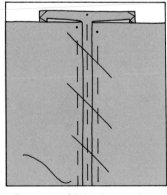

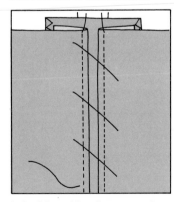

**3.** On WS cut fabric carefully between rows of stitching, about 4 mm/⅛ in away from each row. Trim edges and neaten—hand overcasting is easier than machine zigzag. If insertion is very transparent and you do not want the fabric edges to show through, roll them back into a narrow hem beside insertion and hem.

**Slot** Turn in raw seam edges on fitting line, baste and press. Remove basting and neaten edges. Cut backing strips on bias, at least 3 cm/1¼ in wide. Baste along centre of strip, neaten edges and press. Baste one folded edge of fabric, RS up, to strip 2 mm/¹⁄₁₆ in from centre and with top edge slightly below edge of backing.

**2.** Baste other fabric edge to strip the same distance away from the centre. Work a row of diagonal basting across folds and backing strip. Fit garment carefully, adjusting seam if necessary.

**3.** On RS machine along seam edges, 3 mm/⅛ in away from each fold, using machine foot as a guide. Remove basting from centre of backing and also diagonal basting holding backing in place. Press seam RS down on a folded towel.

# Hems

By the time you turn up a hem you should be sufficiently familiar with the fabric, through handling and pressing it, to be able to decide on the type of hem finish. However, if the decision seems difficult, consider whether a plain invisible hemline is best or whether the fabric lends itself to a machined or decorative finish. Consider, too, the weight of the material and remember that narrow hems work well on fine fabrics such as voile, cotton, polyester cotton, but that a deeper hem is needed for heavier materials.

Wherever it is essential that the hem is absolutely level—at the bottom edge of dresses, skirts and trousers—leave it until all other processes have been completed, as these may affect the hang of the garment. At the fitting stage, however, it is sometimes easier to assess the finished effect if the hem is turned up to its approximate length and basted.

Hems on nightwear, blouses and other tops can be turned up and finished fairly early in the construction. It is also simpler to hem certain kinds of sleeves before inserting them in the garment—those with cuffed and elasticated finishes and short sleeves. If, however, the sleeves are loose at the wrist and full length, they must be set in before being hemmed, as the extra fullness makes them appear longer.

## Measuring the hem
Pins, tailor's chalk, a full-length vertical mirror, a hand mirror—to see the sides and back—and a hem marker are needed for measuring and marking the hemline. There are various kinds of hem markers: some merely gauge the hem level, which is then marked with pins; others also mark it by puffing chalk on to the fabric or by firing pins. Alternatively, screw a long ruler or a straight length of wood on to a block of wood.

## Deciding on the length
Put the garment on and fasten it. Wear a belt or anything, such as a jacket, that may affect length. When deciding on the length of a skirt or dress, remember to make it $1 \text{cm}/\frac{3}{8}$ in shorter than the coat with which it will be worn. Wear shoes that correspond in style and height of heel to those you will wear with the outfit. With a special occasion outfit buy the shoes to go with it before completing the hem.

When turning up the hem on a sleeve before setting it into a garment, measure underarm seam of a sleeve on an existing garment as a guide to correct sleeve length.

Turn up and pin front of hem to approximately the required length. Look in mirror and adjust until correct. Consider overall height and any proportional problems: for example, avoid hemlines low across the calf if your legs are short from knee to ankle. Put one pin on turned-up fold of fabric to mark length at front and remove all other pins.

## Marking the length
If possible enlist help in marking the length. Adjust hem marker to level of pin (1). If using a length of wood or ruler, make a pencil mark on it at level of pin. Stand still while your helper moves round inserting pins horizontally at this level at intervals of about $6 \text{cm}/2\frac{1}{4}$ in. If the marker has a container of powdered chalk, pins need not be used. The marker must be close to the skirt so that the fabric is not pulled out at an angle.

If the skirt is full and hanging in folds, mark outer folds and re-arrange skirt so that remainder can be marked. Before marking a level hem on a skirt that is flared, circular or cut on the cross at any point, hang

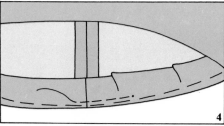

the garment on a hanger or dressmaker's dummy for a few days to allow the bias areas to drop. Avoid a dragged or lop-sided finish on a slightly shaped wide skirt hem by turning up and pinning first across centre front area, then centre back, then sides.

Trousers cannot be measured from the floor, but should be turned up and pinned to rest on shoes at front and slope down about $1 \text{cm}/\frac{3}{8}$ in at back (2).

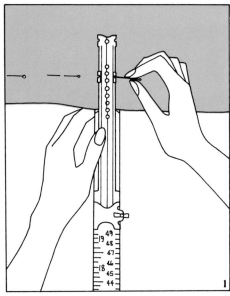

They should be fractionally shorter at inside leg than outside. Pin up both trouser legs, inserting pins vertically and checking that the two hems are equal in length by placing leg seams together and adjusting hems if necessary. If you still have difficulty in deciding on correct length, use inside leg seam of an existing pair as a guide.

Take off garment and spread hemline out on table RS up. Using tailor's chalk, make chalk dashes between pins (3). Do not attempt a continuous line

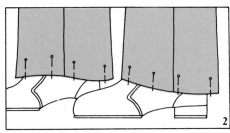

as it will invariably be uneven. Remove pins, one by one, and insert more chalk marks where pins were. If a chalk puffer was used, mark line again with chalk dashes as powdered chalk rubs off easily. If tailor's chalk is not visible on fabric, baste round hem at level of pins, picking up fabric between them and removing them afterwards. Correct any pins or chalk marks that are obviously out of line. The hem should appear as a curve—the more flared the hem, the more curved the line.

With fabric RS out, fold back upper layer of

garment to leave under layer clear to work on. Turn up the section of hem in front of you so chalk or basting is exactly on fold. Holding a short section with one hand, baste with stitches no longer than $1.5 \text{cm}/\frac{3}{4}$ in just inside fold (4). The exact position of

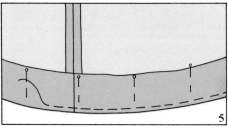

this row of basting varies with the fabric: with thin fabrics it should be about $2 \text{mm}/\frac{1}{16}$ in from the fold; with thick or springy ones about $4 \text{mm}/\frac{1}{8}$ in.

Hold up surplus fabric on inside by inserting pins at intervals, ignoring any fullness (5). Try on

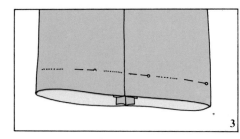

garment and check that hem is level and required length. Remove garment and all pins. If your posture is upright and your hips are level, measure length of side seams and any pairs of seams in front or back sections. Adjust hem if necessary. The length of all seams to the hem should be equal unless you are lop-sided and, therefore, need seams of varying lengths. Do not compare the length of the centre front seam with that of the centre back seam as these are rarely equal.

On check fabric make sure curve of hem runs evenly on checks on either side of centre front and centre back, even if you have lop-sided hips.

## Marking length unaided
If you have no one to help, pin the hem up and check that it is level in a mirror. Check that corresponding seams are equal in length (except centre front and centre back), allowing for any hip peculiarities. Mark hemline in a curve with chalk or pins, paying great attention to grain to see that angles of threads in weave are the same on either side of centre front and centre back. Turn up and baste as above but try on and check carefully from front, back and sides before proceeding. Alternatively, if you have a dressmaker's dummy that has exactly the same posture as you, put the garment on it to mark the hemline, following the above method.

## Pressing the bottom fold
Use sharp, heavy movements, never leaving the iron in position for more than an instant. It is preferable to bang the iron down in several sharp bursts rather than to apply prolonged pressure. Work slowly in short stretches and press only the bottom fold, not along edge of surplus fabric or a mark will be visible on RS. The final result should be a crisp line along hem fold.

## Depth of hem
The depth of the hem depends partly on the style and general finish of the outfit, but mainly on the fabric and the shape of the hem. Use narrow hems—2 mm to $1.5 \text{cm}/\frac{1}{16}$ to $\frac{5}{8}$ in—on long skirts and dresses, sleeves, frills, blouses, nightwear and shirts and on circular or flared edges. Straight or nearly straight hems can be wide—4 to $7 \text{cm}/1\frac{1}{2}$ to $2\frac{3}{4}$ in—in all fabrics. Short skirts and coats need a deep hem to

provide weight and, therefore, a better hang. Trouser hems should be between 2.5 and 4 cm/1 and 1½ in. The hem on all these garments can be single or double, depending on the fabric and style.

Mark depth of hem by using a ruler or adjustable marker and tailor's chalk and measure evenly from pressed edge, marking all round hem. If chalk does not show, insert pins horizontally through hem only (**6**). If you want to use strips of adhesive to hold hem

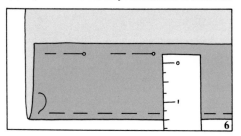

down, make hem the depth of the adhesive, allowing an extra 3 mm/⅛ in for basting at fold and the same for neatening. If the hem edge is to be turned under to form a double hem, allow slightly more fabric than the depth of the hem.

If the fabric is transparent and a neater finish is required, make hem deep enough to allow raw edge to be turned down as far as bottom fold.

### Seams within hem depth
After marking depth of hem, unpick basting at seams, open out fabric and cut down seam turnings of open seams within hem depth to 3 to 5 mm/⅛ to ¼

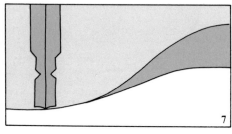

in to reduce bulk. On curves, snip these trimmed turnings exactly at pressed fold of hem (**7**).

### Neatening the raw edge
There are various methods of finishing raw edges, but the neatest and least visible methods—and the most widely used—are overcasting, machining and overcasting, and zigzagging.

To overcast, trim hem down to chalk line or pins and sew along edge (**8**). Work in small sections to minimize fraying. Pull thread fairly tight to bring edge up slightly and so counteract stretching.

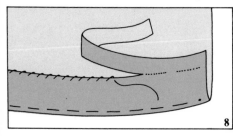

If the fabric frays badly or is a loose weave, work a row of straight machine stitching along chalk line marking raw edge. Trim close to machining, a little at a time, and overcast, taking needle just below machining and pulling thread fairly tight (**9**).

To zigzag, stitch along edge. This will probably cause stretching, so do not use on stretch fabrics.

A hem edge can be neatened with herringbone stitch or binding, but do not cover a wide hem edge

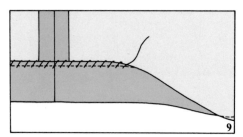

with straight seam binding, tape (Prussian binding), or even with herringbone, because the hemline will eventually show on RS.

### Holding the hem down
Hems can be held down in a variety of ways, depending on the type and weight of fabric and on whether the stitching is to show on RS.

On medium and thick fabrics catch stitch (**10**) is used for an invisible deep hem on coats, dresses, trousers and skirts. Baste neatened edge, just below

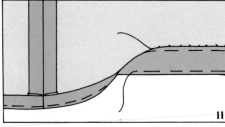

neatening, to WS of garment. Pull back edge towards you and start thread under it. Keeping edge away from garment, work catch stitch between hem and garment, stitching slightly below neatened edge. Do not pull thread tight or hemline will show on RS. Finish off in hem edge, remove basting and press up to, but not over, edge.

On fine or thin fabrics the raw edge can be turned under and held down by slip hemming (**11**). Turn

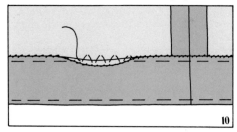

edge under about 1 cm/⅜ in and baste. Open out hem, press turned-under edge and baste it down to WS. With edge towards you, slip hem along it. Do not pull thread tight. Remove basting on WS and press up to, but not over, turned-under edge.

If the hem is likely to be let down later, edge stitch top of hem allowance by machine after basting and before slip hemming.

Hold the hem down by machining (**12**) only if you want a decorative effect or if the stitching is to show, e.g. on narrow hems and jersey. Turn raw edge under and baste. Open out hem, press turned-under edge and baste it down to WS. Place under the

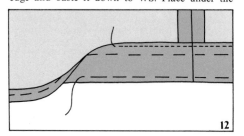

machine with WS of garment uppermost. Lower needle into turned-under edge, lower foot and complete hem with edge stitching. Remove basting and press. The appearance of a machine-finished hem is often improved by working another row of stitching on lower fold. Press stitching with toe of iron to remove wrinkles.

All widths of hem can be held down with an adhesive strip (**13**), but try this method out on a small piece of fabric as it is not always successful on

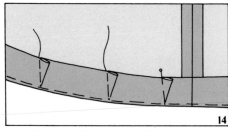

fine materials. It is ideal for trousers, giving a lasting crisp finish. Turn up, baste and press lower fold as usual and trim and neaten raw edge. Place hem on sleeve board and slip adhesive strip under hem edge so that it is covered. Insert only about 20 cm/8 in at a time. As the strip tends to break, it may not be possible to use one continuous piece. Butt edges of strips or overlap. Take hold of fabric, not adhesive, and pull gently outwards to counteract any slight drawing up. Press hem well until adhesive is melted, using a medium hot iron over a damp cloth and placing it three or four times on each spot. Remove basting and press again lightly.

### Dealing with fullness
If a wide hem is made on a shaped edge, fluting occurs. The method of dealing with this varies according to the weight and thickness of the fabric. Counteract slight fullness by overcasting and drawing up the edge as you sew. Excess fullness in lightweight or thin fabrics can be made into very small darts (**14**). Before trimming and neatening

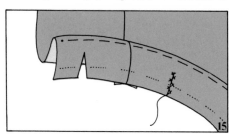

edge, pin darts, all in same direction, exactly where flutes occur, which is often near seams, and baste in place. Do not force them in for the sake of symmetry. Remove basting before final press.

To counteract fullness in thick or heavy fabrics, lay hem on table and, where fluting occurs, cut fabric down through hem edge to within 3 mm/⅛ in of basting at fold (**15**). Snip out a "V" of fabric at

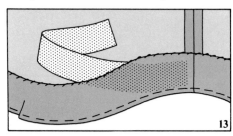

this point so that hem lies flat with raw edges close together. Take care not to cut too much. Re-join raw edges with a wide zigzag or herringbone. Trim hem edge on chalk marks, neaten and finish.

# *Hems*

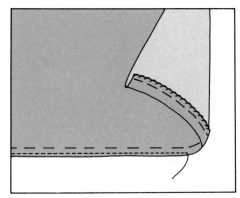

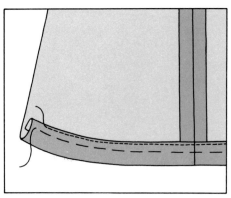

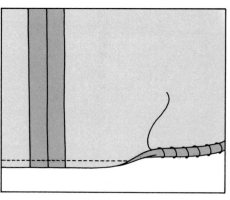

**Narrow** Use where weight is not needed, e.g. blouses and sleeves. The trimmed hem depth should be 2 mm to 1.5 cm/$\frac{1}{16}$ to $\frac{5}{8}$ in. On medium or thick fabrics neaten raw edge, baste to garment and hold down by catch stitching on WS or by machining along fold on RS, using machine foot as a guide. Remove basting and press. On fine fabrics turn raw edge under 1 cm/$\frac{3}{8}$ in, baste and press. Slip hem or machine, on WS, along bottom of turned-under edge.

**Curved** If the hemline is very curved, make the hem narrow to minimize fullness. On medium fabrics allow 5 mm/$\frac{1}{4}$ in beyond marked hemline, cut off surplus, neaten edge and catch stitch to garment. On fine fabrics cut away surplus 1 cm/$\frac{3}{8}$ in beyond mark, fold hem twice, baste and press. To finish slip hem or machine on WS, using a straight stitch close to top of hem or a zigzag over it. Remove basting and press.

**Circular** As little of a circular hem is on the straight grain it easily stretches and flutes, and should be as narrow as possible. Mark hemline and machine with a straight stitch 5 mm/$\frac{1}{4}$ in below line. Trim surplus, a little at a time, very close to stitching. Lick thumb and forefinger and roll a section of raw edge towards you. Hold down immediately with whipping or slip hemming and proceed to next section.

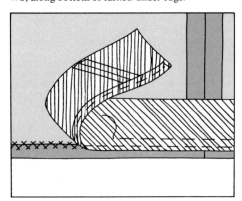

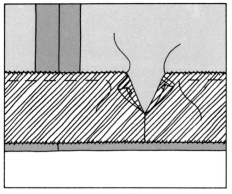

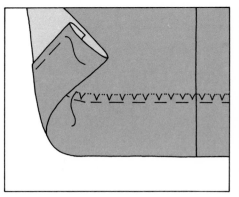

**Faced** Useful if there is not enough material to turn up a suitable hem. Trim raw edge to within 1 cm/$\frac{3}{8}$ in, or whatever is available, of marked hemline. Turn up hem, baste and press. Catch stitch or, on medium or thick fabrics, herringbone raw edge down. Remove basting and press up to edge. Cut and join crossways strips of lightweight fabric 5 cm/2 in wide. Fold in one edge of strip 5 mm/$\frac{1}{4}$ in, baste and press. Place fold 2 mm/$\frac{1}{16}$ in over hem edge and baste down.

**2.** Attach centre of strip to garment with diagonal basting. Turn in other raw edge 5 mm/$\frac{1}{4}$ in and baste to garment. Press edges of strip lightly. Slip hem upper edge to garment, turn fabric round and hem lower edge down. Turn in ends and slip stitch together. Remove all basting.

**Decorative finish—blind hem stitch** Hems on light-weight fabrics for loose linings, lingerie and nightwear can be finished decoratively by machine. Turn under raw edge of hem, baste and press. Set machine to blind hem stitch, or to an embroidery stitch, place work under machine with RS of garment uppermost and stitch close to turned-under edge with matching or contrasting thread. Remove basting and press.

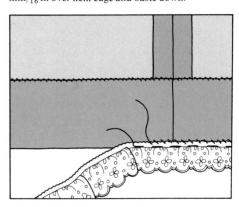

**Decorative finish—lace** Press turned-up hem. Attach narrow lace (stretch lace eliminates wrinkling), broderie anglaise or other trimming to WS of hem either by basting and oversewing top edge to fold of hem (so making the garment a little longer) or position trimming on RS of hem so that bottom edge aligns with fold of hem. Attach top edge to RS of hem with hemming, feather, herringbone, zigzag or machine embroidery stitch.

## JERSEY HEMS

The width of hem on jersey fabrics depends on the shape of the hemline, the weight of the fabric and the type of garment.

To make a wide hem, neaten raw edge of hem by zigzagging or overcasting over a length of

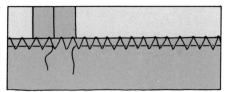

synthetic thread laid on RS of garment near raw edge. Leave ends of thread loose and long enough to grasp. Baste hem to WS of garment, pulling up loose ends of thread to draw edge up and so correct any stretching. Catch stitch edge to garment, cut off loose ends, or pull the whole length of thread out, remove rest of basting and press.

To make a narrow hem, zigzag along chalk line marking depth of hem on RS and trim away surplus close to stitching. Baste hem edge to WS of

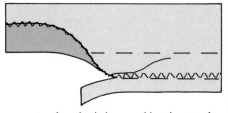

garment and catch stitch or machine close to edge on RS. Remove basting and press.

To achieve an attractively fluted edge on fine jersey, trim away surplus fabric to leave 5 mm/$\frac{1}{4}$ in beyond hemline mark. Place garment RS up under machine and turn under the 5 mm/$\frac{1}{4}$ in. (The machine bed holds it in place.) Set machine to a medium-width stitch—2$\frac{1}{2}$—and medium length. Zigzag over fold, but pull fabric to stretch it as it goes under foot to give a close satin stitch. On WS trim surplus fabric close to stitching. Do not press.

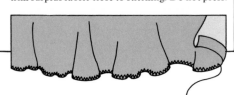

# Bindings

Binding is a method of neatening an edge by enclosing it in a strip of fabric. It is easier to work neatly with strips of fabric cut on the bias, as fabric cut like this stretches, making it possible to bind shaped edges such as curves.

Binding can be single or double except on bulky fabrics, where single binding should be used. It can be in the same fabric as the edge to which it is to be joined but a different colour, or it can be a contrasting print or texture. A lighter weight fabric can be used to bind a heavier one, but the reverse is more difficult and may entail doing all the sewing by hand to avoid puckering. Often binding can be cut from left-over scraps. If a lot of strips are needed, buy additional fabric to avoid cutting from small pieces and having a lot of joins.

Single binding can also be bought in several widths, pressed and folded ready to apply, but its use is limited as it comes only in cotton, mercerized cotton and nylon.

### True cross and bias

As a general term, bias binding denotes all binding cut diagonally to the grain of the fabric. More specifically, it refers to binding cut at an angle of less than 45° to the selvedge, as opposed to true cross, which is cut at an angle of 45°. True cross, or crossways, strips have maximum stretch, the amount varying according to the fabric. If a patterned fabric such as stripe or check or a plain fabric with a distinctive weave is used for binding, the strips must be cut in this way or the pattern will not look right. True cross strips must also be used on very concave edges such as scallops.

Some stretch fabrics, notably jersey, should be cut on the bias rather than the true cross as otherwise they have too much stretch and become unmanageable. The resulting edge finish can also be bubbly.

The amount of material available also determines the way in which the binding is cut; if you have plenty, cut non-stretch fabrics on the true cross; if not, cut on the bias.

Both crossways and bias strips have numerous other uses besides neatening edges. They can be worked into rouleau to form ties and skirt or coat tabs; they can be used to lengthen garments; and they can also be applied decoratively, either as strips or as piping.

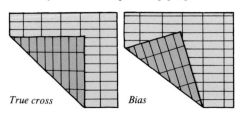

True cross      Bias

### FOLDING THE FABRIC

If possible use a piece of fabric that will produce long strips, so minimizing joins. For true cross strips, fold with WS together so a warp thread lies exactly over a weft thread and the fold is at 45° to the selvedge. If true cross binding is not essential, or if you are short of fabric and need a long strip of binding, refold so that warp and weft are not quite together, and so produce bias strips.

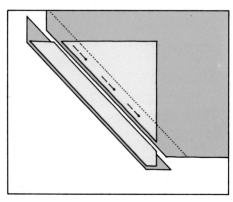

**Cutting the strips** To cut both crossways and bias strips, insert a few pins to hold folded fabric in place, leaving the fold free. Flatten the fold against the table and, using medium-sized scissors, cut carefully along the crease or, to ensure that you keep straight, run the toe of the iron lightly along the fold, unpin, open out and cut, but place the cut edges together again afterwards.

**2.** Using an adjustable marker, mark and cut a straight line parallel with edges to give a pair of strips. The top ones may get shorter but the underneath ones become longer as you go on cutting if the fabric piece is not square. Continue cutting strips of even width, inserting a couple of pins near the cut edges before measuring the next strip if the fabric is slippery or springy.

### CALCULATING THE WIDTH

The finished width of the binding depends on the thickness of the fabric. It is easy to apply a narrow binding made with thin fabric, but a narrow binding looks bulky in thick fabric. Aim for a finish of between 3 and 6 mm/$\frac{1}{8}$ and $\frac{1}{4}$ in. To calculate the width, cut a short piece of fabric, pin it to an edge and fold it over to see if the width is correct. Adjust and then measure width needed.

For single binding cut strips twice the finished width, plus a narrow turning on both sides of about 5 mm/$\frac{1}{4}$ in (less is difficult to handle). The strips can be trimmed later if they are too wide, although it is difficult to keep the edges straight.

Double binding strips should be four times the finished width, plus two turnings of 5 mm/$\frac{1}{4}$ in. The width cannot be reduced without unpicking.

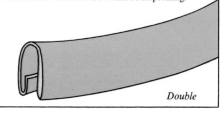

Single             Double

### JOINING CROSS AND BIAS STRIPS

Join strips of equal width end to end to form a strip about 7.5 to 10 cm/3 to 4 in longer than needed. The ends of the strips and the joins must be on the straight grain of the fabric as otherwise the joins bubble. When cutting bias from odd-shaped scraps that are not on the straight grain, lay all the strips end to end WS up and trim each one on the straight grain (**1**), pulling out a thread as a guide if necessary. Cut off ends with selvedges.

Press a small turning to WS at end of each strip. Lay strips out again end to end and WS up (**2**). Lift each pair of adjacent pressed turnings and place creases together, so the long edges are still running level. If these edges start making "steps", adjust until the steps disappear. (As you do this little triangles of fabric will jut out at each side.)

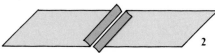

Joining the strips accurately is difficult and the easiest and most satisfactory method is to backstitch or half backstitch them together by hand, while they lie flat on the table (**3**). Joins can

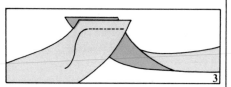

be machined, but even if previously pinned and basted they often end up slightly off the grain or with the long edges out of line. Also, fastening off by machine can produce hard, almost knotted, lumps in the joins. Press all joins and cut off extending triangles (**4**).

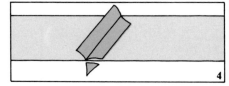

**Pressing the strips**

If the strips are in a very stretchy fabric, remove any excess stretch that might cause bubbling. (This is not necessary for bought binding.) Pin end of strip WS up on to ironing surface or sleeve board. Pull gently from other end; press pinned end, preferably using a steam iron. Move pin along and continue pressing whole length, shaping strip into a curve if it is for a scalloped or curved edge.

# Bindings

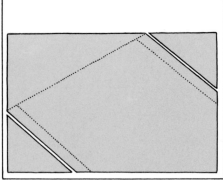

**Cutting continuous binding** If a long strip of single or double bias is needed and a large piece of material is available, at least 35 by 15 cm/13 by 6 in, trim fabric to a rectangle. At no less than 10 cm/4 in from the corner, cut off two diagonally opposite corners so the two cut edges are on the true cross. Mark 1.25 cm/½ in seam turnings with chalk along both edges and then chalk a line between ends of crossways edges.

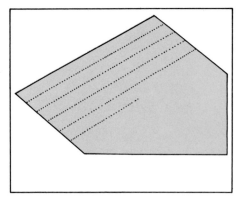

**2.** Cut fabric on chalk bias line. Experiment with a spare piece of fabric to establish the width of binding needed and on WS of main fabric mark chalk line this distance from long bias edge and parallel with it. Mark further parallel chalk lines the same width apart across the entire fabric piece.

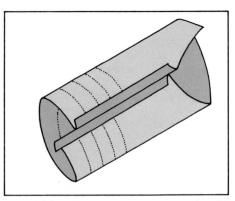

**3.** Fold fabric with two short crossways edges RS together, but with one edge extending on the long bias side, so that the other edge lines up with the first chalk line. Baste and stitch along marked seam line to form a tube. Remove binding. Press seam open and trim turnings down. Start cutting the continuous strip at the extension and cut round and round, following the marked lines exactly and thus keeping the strip an even width.

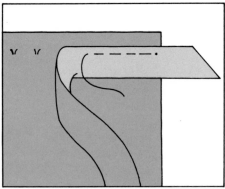

**Attaching single binding** Place one edge of binding RS down against RS of edge to be bound, taking 5 mm/¼ in turning on the strip but normal turning on the garment. Leave about 2 cm/¾ in of strip extending at the start for joining or finishing. Anchor difficult sections by pinning across the strip, but do not pin the entire length as the binding stretches to fit round the pins. Baste about 2 cm/¾ in of the fabric at a time, taking small stitches.

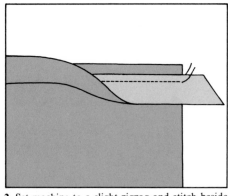

**2.** Set machine to a slight zigzag and stitch beside basting, strip uppermost, making sure turnings are even all along. Remove basting and press stitching. On RS push toe of iron up under strip towards stitching and edges and run it along join, lifting strip slightly. Trim raw edges to fractionally less than finished binding width, to give an attractive plump edge. On a very curved edge, snip turnings in towards the machining every 5 mm/¼ in.

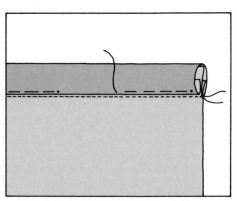

**3.** With WS of garment towards you, fold over raw edge of binding 5 mm/¼ in and bring fold on to machining. Baste into position in sections of about 6 cm/2¼ in, starting in the centre, followed by the ends, then the sections between. If you baste along from one end, the binding may not lie flat. Run toe of iron lightly along fold by machining.

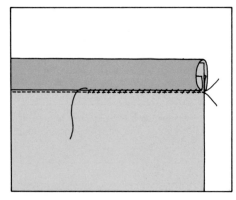

**4.** Hem into machining, picking up every stitch. Remove basting. Press WS lightly with edge on a folded towel to avoid compressing the binding. Alternatively, apply binding to WS of garment and fold over to RS so folded edge covers machining. Finish with hand or machine embroidery along fold. If the fabric of the edge to be bound is bulky, bind it with dress net cut on the straight grain. Trim edge so that fabric fills net.

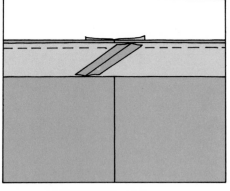

**Joins—single binding** On a continuous edge put the final join of the binding strip in an inconspicuous place, e.g. at underarm, back of neck or at side seam on hem. Baste strip to garment, leaving 2.5 cm/1 in surplus and unstitched at the start and about 1.25 cm/½ in unstitched at end. Fold back the two ends on to WS on straight grain so folds meet and press. Backstitch together along fold, press open and trim off ends. Machine binding to garment.

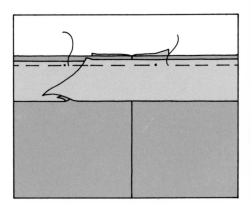

**2.** An easier method of joining the ends is to fold back the 1.25 cm/½ in on one end of the strip and lay the other end, unfolded, on top, overlapping at least 1 cm/⅜ in. Baste ends to garment along fitting line. With binding uppermost, machine beside basting. Remove basting.

## QUICK METHOD BINDING

An ideal method of single binding if you do not want to spend time on careful application and finishing. It is difficult to join the ends of the strip neatly, so apply the binding before joining the main seam on the area on which you are working so that the joins can be made in the seam. Cut a strip of binding wide enough for equal turnings to be folded in along each side so that edges of turnings almost touch.

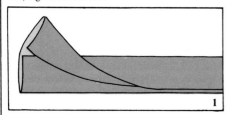

Fold strip again slightly off centre (1) and press. The narrower section is the finished binding width. Alternatively, for a more accurate and even finish, use bought bias binding, which is already pressed, as long as it is suitable for your chosen fabric. If you intend to attach the binding with a binding foot, make sure that the width of whichever type of binding you use fits the foot.

Trim raw edge of garment to a little less than the finished width of the binding. Place the binding over the trimmed edge so that the edge is sandwiched between the two turned-in edges of the binding. On RS baste through all layers and edge stitch (2), using a wide stitch such as zigzag or blind hem to ensure that the underneath fold is caught in place on WS. Remove basting and press binding carefully on WS and RS.

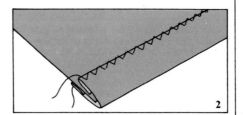

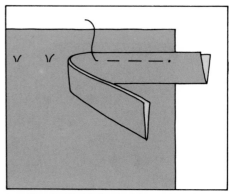

**Attaching double binding** Quicker and easier than applying single binding, but the strip must be very carefully cut. It can be bulky so confine to thin fabrics. Fold strip in half WS together. Press lightly. Baste raw edges of double strip to RS of garment edge, taking the normal turning on garment and 5 mm/$\frac{1}{4}$ in on edge of strip and leaving 2.5 cm/1 in surplus and unstitched at the start and about 1.25 cm/$\frac{1}{2}$ in unstitched at the end.

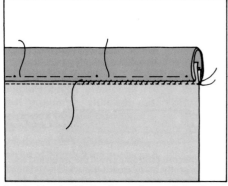

**2.** Machine beside basting, using a slight zigzag. Remove basting and press stitching and join as for single binding (2). Trim all turnings, but not too narrow. Turn work over and, with WS facing you, roll fold of binding over to meet machining. Baste, starting at the centre, then two sections at either end, followed by the areas between. Press lightly. Hold down by hemming into machining. Remove basting.

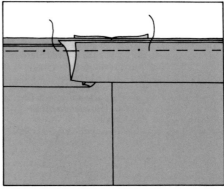

**Joins—double binding** Can be made on the straight grain as for single binding. This is, however, difficult to do neatly after the strip has been basted in position as the strip has to be completely opened out before joining. It is generally easier to use the overlapping method described in single binding.

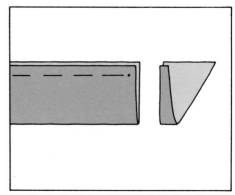

**Double edge finish** A quick, wide finish for a sleeve or hem. Useful for lengthening as it extends beyond the edge. It can be in a contrasting fabric, with the finished width varying from 1 cm/$\frac{3}{8}$ in to about 4 cm/1$\frac{1}{2}$ in. If possible apply when there is still one seam to complete; otherwise unpick a seam on the edge to be bound 6 cm/2$\frac{1}{4}$ in. Cut, join and press strips as for single binding. Fold in half WS together. Baste, press lightly and trim ends straight.

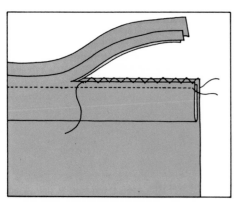

**2.** Baste raw edges of binding to RS of garment edge, taking 5 mm/$\frac{1}{4}$ in turnings on strip and usual turning allowance on garment. Machine with a slight zigzag. Remove basting. Trim turnings so they are all 3 mm/$\frac{1}{8}$ in. Neaten raw edges of binding and garment together with zigzag or overcasting.

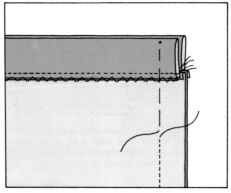

**3.** Press stitching. Fold binding over to hang below garment edge, turn work over and on WS press turnings up into garment. On RS press strip downwards. Join or rejoin seam, basting and machining from the binding up to keep lower edges level. Remove basting.

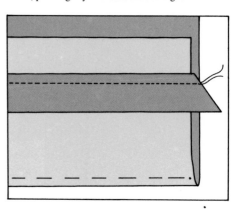

**Coat hem edge** Finish the raw hem edge of a loose-lined heavy coat with binding cut from lining fabric. Turn up hem, baste, press and mark depth. Prepare and join single bias binding 2 cm/$\frac{3}{4}$ in wide. Take 5 mm/$\frac{1}{4}$ in turning on binding and place RS down on WS of hem along marked hem edge and baste. Machine on binding, stitching slowly to prevent wrinkling. Remove basting. ▶

# Zips

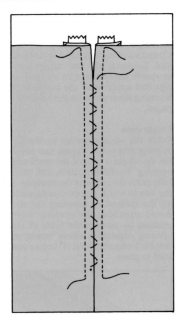

**Even hems** Equal amounts of fabric are left between the stitching and the zip on either side and the fabric edges meet down the centre of the zip teeth. There are two easy methods of doing this, but neither is suitable for bulky fabrics. Both methods can be used at side openings, wrists, centre front, underarm, short neck openings and centre back. If possible, select a zip with coloured teeth to match the fabric.

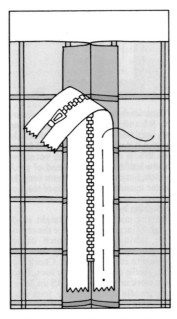

**2.** For first method, if the seam is curved, make small snips every 5 cm/2 in on neatened edges where zip is to be inserted. Turn in both edges along marked fitting lines. Baste and press without stretching seam turnings.

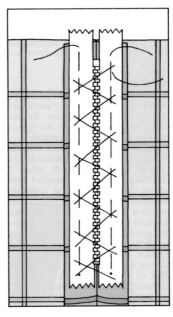

**3.** With both zip and fabric RS up, place one of pressed folds along centre of closed teeth. Hold zip in correct position with one hand, so slider is just below seam line at top of opening, and use other hand to baste approximately in centre of zip tape, about 5 mm/¼ in from fold. Start at appropriate end and take care not to stretch the fabric—ease it on to the zip. Baste second side from same end with folds of opening meeting.

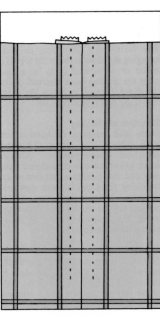

**4.** To prevent fabric being pulled off teeth when stitching, hold folded edges together with big oversewing stitches or catch stitch, both worked in basting thread through edges only. Stitch zip from RS by hand or by machine. Remove all basting. Work a bar tack at base of zip and remove oversewing or catch stitching. Press on RS along stitching and on WS with zip RS down on a folded towel.

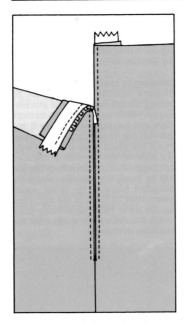

**Alternative even hems** This method is easier for curved seams and more accurate on fabrics with a pattern to be matched as the edges of the opening are held together more firmly while the zip is inserted. Place fabric edges RS together and baste on fitting line, matching pattern if necessary. Machine with a large stitch close to basting from base of opening to top. Remove basting. Press seam open, making small snips along curves.

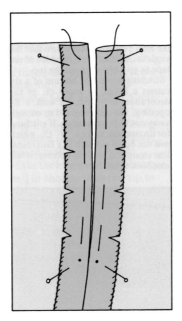

**2.** With garment WS up, place closed zip RS down on to seam. Centre teeth over seam and baste both sides of tape to seam turnings, stitching approximately in centre of tape, 5 mm/¼ in from teeth, or a little more if a heavy zip is being inserted.

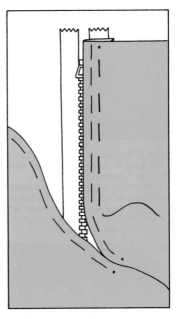

**3.** To keep zip in position if inserting by machine, anchor it further by working a row of close herringbone stitch on WS right across zip; use basting thread.

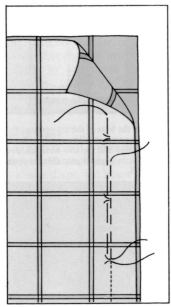

**4.** Sew zip in by hand or machine from RS. Remove all basting. Press the stitching from RS and press again RS down on a folded towel.

## QUICK METHOD BINDING

An ideal method of single binding if you do not want to spend time on careful application and finishing. It is difficult to join the ends of the strip neatly, so apply the binding before joining the main seam on the area on which you are working so that the joins can be made in the seam. Cut a strip of binding wide enough for equal turnings to be folded in along each side so that edges of turnings almost touch.

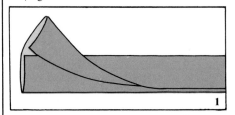

Fold strip again slightly off centre (**1**) and press. The narrower section is the finished binding width. Alternatively, for a more accurate and even finish, use bought bias binding, which is already pressed,

as long as it is suitable for your chosen fabric. If you intend to attach the binding with a binding foot, make sure that the width of whichever type of binding you use fits the foot.

Trim raw edge of garment to a little less than the finished width of the binding. Place the binding over the trimmed edge so that the edge is sandwiched between the two turned-in edges of the binding. On RS baste through all layers and edge stitch (**2**), using a wide stitch such as zigzag or blind hem to ensure that the underneath fold is caught in place on WS. Remove basting and press binding carefully on WS and RS.

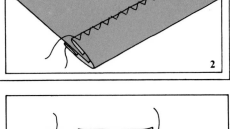

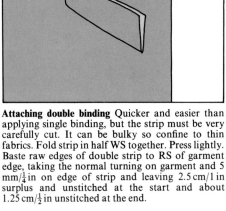

**Attaching double binding** Quicker and easier than applying single binding, but the strip must be very carefully cut. It can be bulky so confine to thin fabrics. Fold strip in half WS together. Press lightly. Baste raw edges of double strip to RS of garment edge, taking the normal turning on garment and 5 mm/$\frac{1}{4}$ in on edge of strip and leaving 2.5 cm/1 in surplus and unstitched at the start and about 1.25 cm/$\frac{1}{2}$ in unstitched at the end.

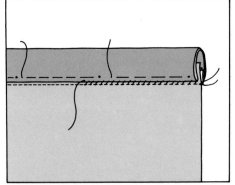

**2.** Machine beside basting, using a slight zigzag. Remove basting and press stitching and join as for single binding (**2**). Trim all turnings, but not too narrow. Turn work over and, with WS facing you, roll fold of binding over to meet machining. Baste, starting at the centre, then two sections at either end, followed by the areas between. Press lightly. Hold down by hemming into machining. Remove basting.

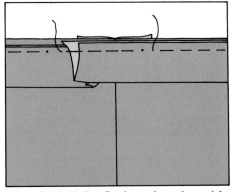

**Joins—double binding** Can be made on the straight grain as for single binding. This is, however, difficult to do neatly after the strip has been basted in position as the strip has to be completely opened out before joining. It is generally easier to use the overlapping method described in single binding.

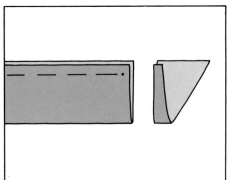

**Double edge finish** A quick, wide finish for a sleeve or hem. Useful for lengthening as it extends beyond the edge. It can be in a contrasting fabric, with the finished width varying from 1 cm/$\frac{3}{8}$ in to about 4 cm/1$\frac{1}{2}$ in. If possible apply when there is still one seam to complete; otherwise unpick a seam on the edge to be bound 6 cm/2$\frac{1}{4}$ in. Cut, join and press strips as for single binding. Fold in half WS together. Baste, press lightly and trim ends straight.

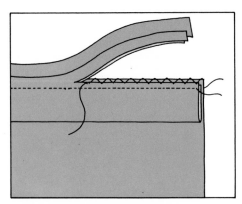

**2.** Baste raw edges of binding to RS of garment edge, taking 5 mm/$\frac{1}{4}$ in turnings on strip and usual turning allowance on garment. Machine with a slight zigzag. Remove basting. Trim turnings so they are all 3 mm/$\frac{1}{8}$ in. Neaten raw edges of binding and garment together with zigzag or overcasting.

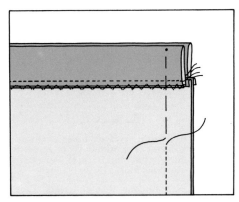

**3.** Press stitching. Fold binding over to hang below garment edge, turn work over and on WS press turnings up into garment. On RS press strip downwards. Join or rejoin seam, basting and machining from the binding up to keep lower edges level. Remove basting.

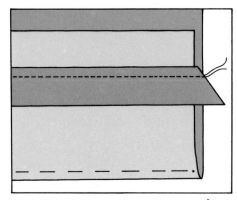

**Coat hem edge** Finish the raw hem edge of a loose-lined heavy coat with binding cut from lining fabric. Turn up hem, baste, press and mark depth. Prepare and join single bias binding 2 cm/$\frac{3}{4}$ in wide. Take 5 mm/$\frac{1}{4}$ in turning on binding and place RS down on WS of hem along marked hem edge and baste. Machine on binding, stitching slowly to prevent wrinkling. Remove basting.

▶

# Bindings

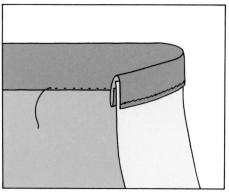

**2.** Press stitching and push toe of iron up under binding towards stitching and edges and run along join to push strip upwards. Trim raw edge of coat hem to 5 mm/¼ in. Roll bias over and behind edge to fit it closely; hold with thumb and forefinger and work prick stitch exactly in join of cloth and binding. Do not pin or baste as this lifts the fabric and makes it snake. Press lightly. Follow this method for binding open seams.

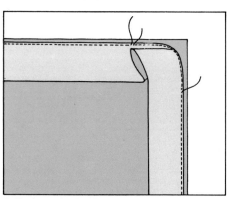

**2.** Tuck surplus binding in at the corner and press flat. Complete stitching at corner—this is easier by hand than by machine.

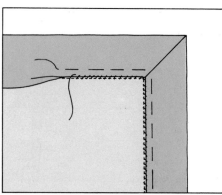

**3.** Turn binding over to WS and baste up to corner along both sides. Tuck surplus fabric under at corner and press flat. Hem binding into machining. At corners on WS and RS, slip stitch folds of surplus binding together. Remove basting.

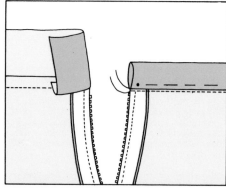

**Binding at a zip opening** Baste binding to garment edge, RS together, catching in top of zip tape and leaving at least 2 cm/¾ in extending at each end. Machine, remove basting, trim garment turnings to finished width of binding, but cut zip tape almost to stitching. Fold binding to WS, turning in ends to align with zip edge, and press. Trim off surplus at ends at an angle. Baste and hem binding in place. Slip stitch open ends by zip. Remove basting.

## ROULEAU

Rouleau is a tube made from fabric cut on the true cross or, if the fabric pattern does not matter, on the bias. Cut jersey on lengthways grain, or the stitching will break as the tube is turned through. Practise the following method with a small strip.

Press strip to stretch it and to remove excess ease. Fold strip in half, RS together; do not baste. Machine with a slight zigzag close to middle of strip, leaving long thread ends (**1**) at start and finish. Trim down raw edges fractionally.

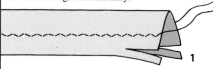

Slip an elastic threader or rouleau turner (long metal needle) into end of tube and, using ends of machine thread, sew eye of threader or turner to turnings at end of tube (**2**).

Ease fabric over eye. Section by section wrinkle tube on to turner and gently pull, turning tube through to RS (**3**). (It may be necessary to experiment with the position of the machining until the rouleau turns through easily.) Cut a strip four times the finished width of practice rouleau and proceed as above.

When the rouleau is turned through, cut threads anchoring turner and trim tube ends neatly, pushing at least 1 cm/⅜ in into tube (**4**). Do not stitch or press. Tie a knot in ends for decoration.

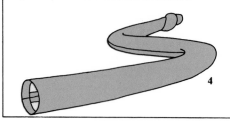

**Angled corners** These are difficult to keep neat. To attach single or double binding to a garment edge with an angled corner, baste a strip of binding to garment, stitching up to within 2 cm/¾ in of corner on either side. Machine to end of basting on each side. Remove basting.

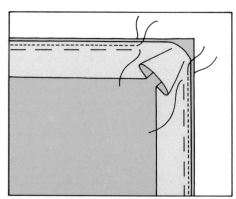

Rouleau is firmer and often looks better if filled with white string or pre-shrunk thin piping cord. Cut and join crossways strips. Cut cord twice length of strip, find its centre and start wrapping strip, WS out, round cord slightly past centre. Stitch across strip through cord to anchor end, and, using the zip foot, beside cord (**5**).

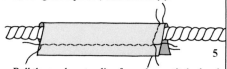

Pull the cord protruding from the unstitched end of strip gently away from strip while wrinkling fabric along cord towards stitched end (**6**). Working a section at a time, pull strip through to RS. Cut off surplus cord and finish as before.

**Tie finish**
To bind a neckline or wrist and add ties, cut a single or double bias or crossways strip the length of the edge to be bound, plus the extra needed for the ties. Attach binding. Where ends extend, turn in edges to meet each other; baste and slip stitch together (**7**). Finish as for ordinary rouleau.

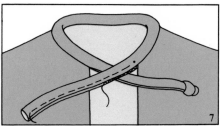

**Skirt and coat tabs**
Use bias strips of lining fabric as crossways strips stretch and split under the garment weight. For skirt tabs fold in half 15 cm/6 in of rouleau and stitch to garment when finishing the waistband.

For a coat tab turn in 5 mm/¼ in at each end of 8 cm/3⅛ in of rouleau. Pin across centre to inside back neck. Baste down the whole length. On RS of tab stitch ends in a square, hemming the three sides and working prick stitches across top of square.

# Zips

Fastening high-buttoned shoes while remaining comfortably seated proved a problem for portly Whitcomb L. Judson of Chicago. His solution was the invention, in 1891, of the first slide fastener—a metal chain of hooks and eyes, which were mechanically fitted into each other by a sliding cam, or metal tab. On the outside of the chain was a simple series of eyes through which shoe lacings could be inserted. The shoes were put on ready laced and the zipper closed by pulling a long string attached to the cam.

The invention caught the eye of a Colonel Lewis Walker of Pennsylvania, who saw in it the beginnings of an alternative to the time-consuming fastenings of the period—buttons, buckles, brooches, lacings and hooks and eyes. In 1894 Walker and Judson set up the Universal Fastener Company. The original design proved impractical for mass-production and, after experimenting with several others, the company began promoting the most promising, although this, too, had to be hand made.

In 1905 Walker and Judson introduced the C-Curity fastener, a series of interlocking hooks on a cloth tape not unlike the modern zip tapes. Advertised as an easy, reliable way to fasten skirts, this was the first slide fastener to be marketed and was sold door to door. Despite its name, however, it had a disconcerting habit of coming open inopportunely.

By 1908, machinery had at last been designed for manufacturing fasteners on a commercial scale, and the first one to be marketed profitably was called the Plako. Although it proved more secure than C-Curity, it was still not wholly reliable.

Not content with designing the Plako, the engineer Gideon Sundback developed in 1912 a new kind of fastening, Hookless No. 1. Instead of hooks, metal clamps were attached to one side of a cloth tape and as the slider was pulled it wedged a cord on the opposite tape between the clamps. The drawback of this zip was that it wore out too quickly to be commercially viable.

The following year the tireless Sundback invented Hookless No. 2, the prototype of the zip used today and the first to incorporate interlocking metal teeth. Public acceptance was slow as many people had had unfortunate experiences with C-Curity or Plako. The new zip was used by clothing manufacturers as a novelty rather than a practical alternative to accepted fasteners. Among its first uses were custom-made money belts, sold to sailors on the waterfront of New York, and the Locktite tobacco pouch. In 1918 the US Navy recognized the zip's practicality, substituting it for buttons in its flying suits to make them more windproof.

The term zipper came into existence as a trademark for Hookless fasteners on galoshes in the early 1920s and gradually became accepted as the name for all slide fasteners. The zip continued to be refined and improved, the most recent development taking place at the end of the 1950s, when nylon filament was introduced as an alternative to metal teeth. Today there are zips for every use, in every weight, and as invisible or blatant as needed.

*Crude and ungainly, the first zip fastener, invented in 1891, was originally designed as a device for doing up shoes. The shoe laces were inserted into the eyes on the outer edge of the metal chain. On the inner edge of the chain were hooks and eyes, which were fitted together by the sliding metal tab.*

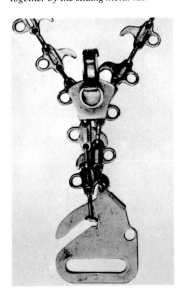

*Rear-Admiral Robert E. Peary, the first man to reach the North Pole in 1909, wears a flying suit from World War I. Zips were ideal for such outfits, cocooning the wearer in a draught-proof garment free from projecting fastenings that could become entangled in machinery—with fatal results.*

# Zips

It is often advisable to leave buying a zip until you are ready to insert it in the garment. You will find it easier to decide on the kind of zip and on its length and position after handling the fabric and fitting the garment. A small or short person may, for example, be able to insert a shorter zip more in proportion to the total length of the garment than that specified by the pattern; a larger figure may need a longer zip. You may decide to insert the zip in a different position from that on the pattern or even dispense with it altogether.

Never insert a zip at the centre back of trousers or a skirt if it can be placed elsewhere. The back of the figure is hollow, so a zip always appears to bulge outwards. And, on trousers, a zip prevents the back seam from giving as you move.

## Choosing the type of zip

There are three main types of zip—nylon, concealed and metal (the metal teeth can be coloured). Choose the nearest available colour to the fabric or one a shade darker. With multicoloured materials match the zip to your thread colour. If a closely toning colour is not available, or if your fabric is ombré, border patterned, striped or checked, insert the zip either by an uneven hems method or, preferably, use a concealed zip, which, correctly inserted, will be invisible.

## When to insert

A long zip is easiest to insert while the fabric is flat, before it is joined into a tube shape, but insert it at this stage only if you are sure that this area of the garment will not require any fitting alterations. Short zips are easier to insert and often, as in trousers and at wrists, they are left until the main parts of the garment are joined.

## Choosing the method of insertion

The method depends on the position of the zip in the garment, the effect desired and the fabric. Take into consideration the type of edge at the top of a zip opening and whether the zip is a good colour match. If you are a beginner, bear these factors in mind, but, even more importantly, choose one of the easier methods.

## Rules for all zips

● Make sure the zip opening is long enough for you to put the garment on easily without strain.
● If the zip has been folded, press the tape flat.
● Always have at least 1.5 cm/ $\frac{5}{8}$ in turning allowance on both sides of the zip opening. If fitting has reduced this, stitch on fabric or tape to make up the width.
● Make the length of the opening 3 mm/$\frac{1}{8}$ in shorter than the zip to prevent the end stop showing.
● With the zip basted in position, try the garment on to check the fit. Adjust fitting line if necessary.
● Keep all zips, except concealed, closed while inserting.
● If the zip is stiff, run a special wax pencil, beeswax or lead pencil along the teeth.

## Types of zip

Metal zips have nickel alloy teeth attached to a strong, coloured, twill tape. The teeth can be small and coloured to match the tape (**1**) or uncoloured (**2**). The coloured zip is lightweight and of medium strength; use wherever the teeth may show. The zip with uncoloured teeth is stronger and heavier weight; use in all garments, but insert so teeth do not show.

The nylon spiral zip (**3**) consists of two continuous coiled filaments of nylon, which are attached to a coloured tape. The tape is usually lightweight, and sometimes in matching nylon. When the zip is closed, the coils interlock. They part easily under strain, so do not use this zip on tight-fitting clothes. Soft and smooth-edged, it can be used on all fine fabrics and jersey.

When inserted, the concealed zip (**4**) looks like a seam on the right side, the slider rolling the nylon teeth on to the back of the zip. The tape can be nylon or cotton. Use on fabrics such as velvet and satin to avoid visible stitching, but not on tight-fitting garments.

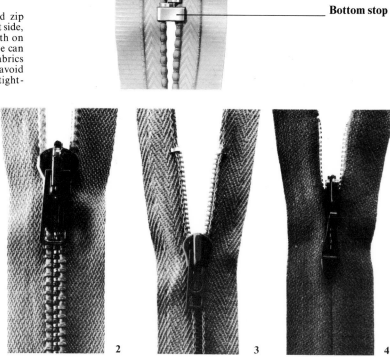

Top stop

Tape

Slider

Tab

Teeth

Stitching line

Bottom stop

1  2  3  4

## PREPARING AND STITCHING

From preparing a zip opening before starting to insert a zip to basting in a zip and stitching it by hand or machine and finishing off, the same basic processes are common to all types of zips and apply to all the methods of inserting them given on the following pages.

### Preparation

Stitch the seam right up to the zip opening and press. Neaten raw edges for the whole length of the seam and opening. Turn under, baste and carefully press the edges of the opening—the way in which you do this depends on the method of inserting the zip. Avoid stretching the opening when pressing by pinning the folds of the opening edges to a sleeve board, so that both edges are level (1) before you start to press.

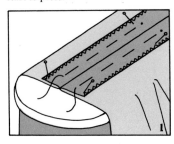

### Position of slider

With all zips and with all methods of inserting them the slider must be set slightly below the seam line at the top of the zip opening. If a facing is to be attached at the top, the slider should be 2 mm/$\frac{1}{16}$ in below the line on fine fabrics, 5 mm/$\frac{1}{4}$ in on bulky materials. The facing can then roll to WS, bringing the slider right to the top. If a collar or waistband is to be added after the zip has been inserted, place the slider 2 mm/$\frac{1}{16}$ in below the seam line when positioning the zip.

### Direction of stitching

Baste and machine or hand stitch both sides of the zip in the same direction where possible. Always work towards a raw edge if you have one and away from a finished edge. Stitching from the bottom upwards prevents a bulge at the bottom. If it is not possible to work in this direction, avoid the bulge by hand stitching rather than machining.

### Basting

Hold the zip in position at the slider end and baste it down to the edges of the opening. Do not use pins; they cause the zip to snake and become uneven, which makes it impossible to insert the needle correctly and quickly enough to ensure that the zip is fitted into the opening properly.

If you need to anchor the zip while you check the position of the slider or the length of the opening, place one pin from RS across and under teeth close to where you intend to start basting. With RS up, hold 2 cm/$\frac{3}{4}$ in at a time in position with one hand and, with a small needle, take two basting stitches (2). Remove pin and continue basting. Always baste right to both

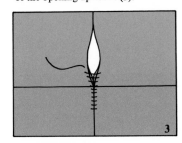

ends of the tape to help anchor the zip and keep it straight. The tape ends may be trimmed later.

If inserting a zip where two seams meet, e.g. at a waistline join, oversew the join together firmly from RS before basting in zip from the bottom of the opening upwards (3).

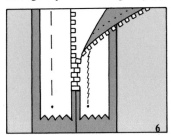

### Permanent stitching

All zips can be inserted by hand or machine, depending on how confident you are (it is easier by hand); on the position of the zip; on whether you want to make a feature of the zip with decorative machining; and on the strength required. Machining is stronger than hand sewing, but no quicker—by the time you have prepared the machine and adjusted the foot you can be halfway down one side by hand.

### Where to stitch

Do not stitch too close to the teeth; it makes the zip look bulky and shortens its life. The optimum distance away varies according to the type of zip and the method of insertion.

Stitching must be parallel with the fabric edge or zip teeth, particularly if it will show down both sides. A stitching line can be marked with sharp chalk, but learn to judge the distance from the fabric edge. With practice this is the more accurate method as sometimes you can follow the grain of the fabric. With visible zips work the final row of stitching from RS.

Some zips have a stitching line woven in the tape, but, as this is on WS of garment, use it only if in difficulty as a guide for basting.

If inserting a zip with a big slider (4), stitch at the usual distance from the

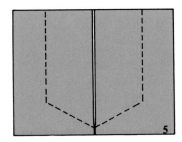

teeth nearly to the top and then, to prevent a bulge, stitch outwards at an angle, still keeping the line straight, for the final 1 cm/$\frac{3}{8}$ in. Make sure that the angle is the same on both sides of the tape to give a Y-shape at the top.

Stitching across the bottom of a zip causes a bulge, so avoid except for decoration or unless, as with a fly opening, the stitching is far enough away not to cause a bulge. If stitching for decoration, make a "V" (5), which will not bulge as much as a horizontal line straight across the bottom; it will also look much better.

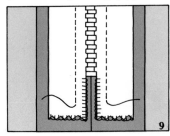

### Stitching by hand

This is much easier than machining, as you have more control and it is easier to keep the stitching straight. Always stitch a bulky fabric by hand. Using a small needle, begin with a knot and backstitch on WS, stitching through tape and turning only (6).

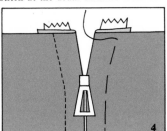

Turn work over and bring needle up to RS and work prick stitch, making the stitches as short as possible. Do not pull thread tight. Fasten off firmly on WS. If the stitching will not show, use a half backstitch instead of prick stitch, but make sure that you keep the same tension on both sides of the zip.

### Stitching by machine

Set the machine to a straight stitch slightly larger than that for the rest of the sewing; a small stitch causes puckering. Attach the zip foot and adjust to correct position. Check that the needle does not hit the foot. Place the work under the foot, RS up, lower the needle and then the foot, and machine very slowly (7). If stitching at

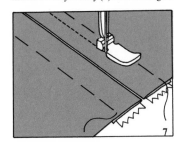

an open end, e.g. at a neckline, do not finish off by reversing but stitch to the end of the tape. At the bottom of the zip leave long ends of thread to sew in by hand on WS.

### Stitching by hand and machine

If hand stitching alone will not be strong enough, add a row of machining on WS along edge of tape through tape and turning only. This will not prevent the hand stitching breaking, but it will avoid a gap if it gives way. To achieve the decorative effect of machine stitching when inserting the zip by hand, first machine along the prepared edges of the fabric where you intend to stitch in the zip. Then set the zip in by hand, working prick stitch but taking the needle over the machine stitches (8).

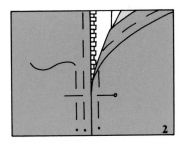

### Finishing off

On WS trim tape ends if desired and neatly loop stitch excess tape at the base of the zip to the seam turnings to prevent the tape rolling up (9).

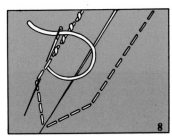

Neaten the base of the zip opening by working a very small bar tack by hand (10). If this will be too obvious, for example on a plain pale fabric, work it on WS.

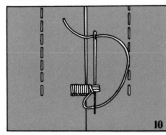

For additional strength on trousers, jeans and other articles of clothing or home furnishings, such as cushions, that will be subjected to hard wear, work a second row of machining on WS through tape and turning only, 2 to 3 mm/$\frac{1}{16}$ to $\frac{1}{8}$ in from edge of tape.

# Zips

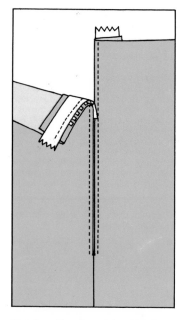

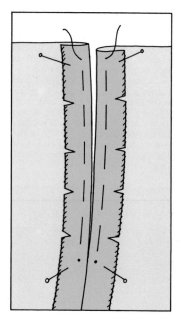

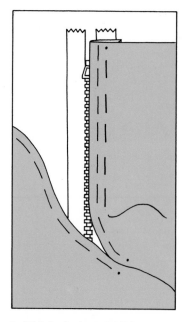

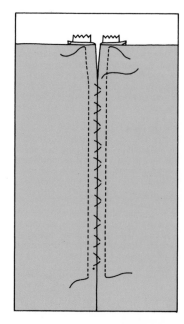

**Even hems** Equal amounts of fabric are left between the stitching and the zip on either side and the fabric edges meet down the centre of the zip teeth. There are two easy methods of doing this, but neither is suitable for bulky fabrics. Both methods can be used at side openings, wrists, centre front, underarm, short neck openings and centre back. If possible, select a zip with coloured teeth to match the fabric.

**2.** For first method, if the seam is curved, make small snips every 5 cm/2 in on neatened edges where zip is to be inserted. Turn in both edges along marked fitting lines. Baste and press without stretching seam turnings.

**3.** With both zip and fabric RS up, place one of pressed folds along centre of closed teeth. Hold zip in correct position with one hand, so slider is just below seam line at top of opening, and use other hand to baste approximately in centre of zip tape, about 5 mm/$\frac{1}{4}$ in from fold. Start at appropriate end and take care not to stretch the fabric—ease it on to the zip. Baste second side from same end with folds of opening meeting.

**4.** To prevent fabric being pulled off teeth when stitching, hold folded edges together with big oversewing stitches or catch stitch, both worked in basting thread through edges only. Stitch zip from RS by hand or machine. Remove all basting. Work a bar tack at base of zip and remove oversewing or catch stitching. Press on RS along stitching and on WS with zip RS down on a folded towel.

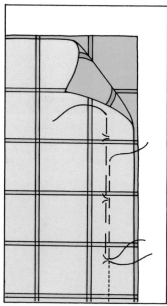

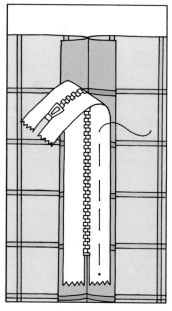

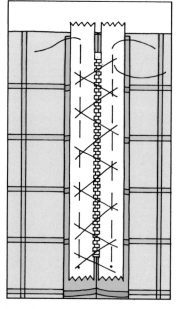

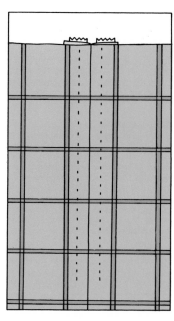

**Alternative even hems** This method is easier for curved seams and more accurate on fabrics with a pattern to be matched as the edges of the opening are held together more firmly while the zip is inserted. Place fabric edges RS together and baste on fitting line, matching pattern if necessary. Machine with a large stitch close to basting from base of opening to top. Remove basting. Press seam open, making small snips along curves.

**2.** With garment WS up, place closed zip RS down on to seam. Centre teeth over seam and baste both sides of tape to seam turnings, stitching approximately in centre of tape, 5 mm/$\frac{1}{4}$ in from teeth, or a little more if a heavy zip is being inserted.

**3.** To keep zip in position if inserting by machine, anchor it further by working a row of close herringbone stitch on WS right across zip; use basting thread.

**4.** Sew zip in by hand or machine from RS. Remove all basting. Press the stitching from RS and press again RS down on a folded towel.

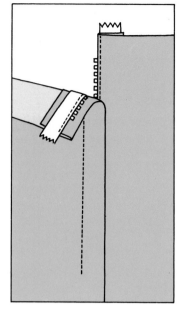

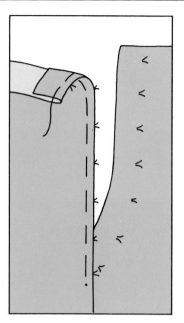

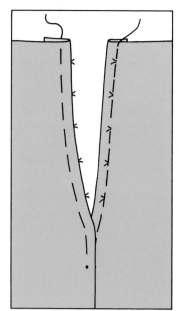

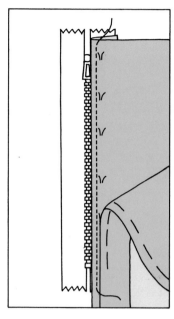

**Uneven hems** There are two uneven hems methods of inserting a zip. In both, one edge of the opening is wider than the other and the zip teeth are completely covered by a fold of fabric, so they are ideal methods if the zip is not a good colour match. Select uneven hems methods for skirts, front or side trouser openings and long back openings.

**2.** Cut out fabric, leaving slightly more than 1.5 cm/$\frac{5}{8}$ in seam allowance on both edges of zip opening. Decide which side of the opening will be the wider edge. At the front, the wide edge is to the right; at the left side to the front; at the back it is on the right side of the body (or left if left-handed), to make it easier to fasten the neck. Fold under wider turning on fitting line and baste. Press without stretching.

**3.** On second, or under, side turn under neatened edge 3 mm/$\frac{1}{8}$ in from fitting line to make a narrower turning. This ensures that the zip is well under the top edge and prevents it from being seen. The narrower turning should extend as far as the bottom of the zip tape. Baste on fitting line and press along it without stretching. If the seam is curved, make a few small snips in edge of both turnings to help them lie flat.

**4.** Starting at the top, with both zip and garment RS up, place fold of underside against teeth of closed zip and baste to zip tape. Stitch by hand or machine close to fold of fabric right to end of tape. Remove basting but not tailor's tacks. Press up to zip teeth.

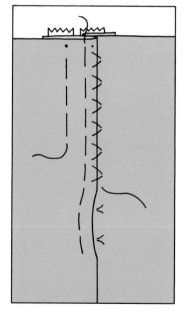

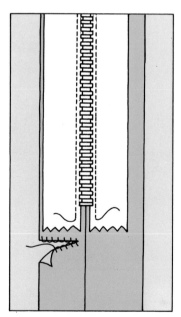

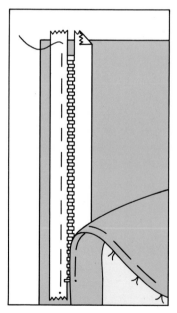

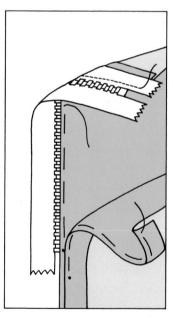

**5.** Bring wider fold over teeth until it meets original seam line of underside. This ensures that the garment fits correctly and that the zip is covered. Starting at the top, catch stitch fold down to underside with basting thread. Baste fold to free side of tape beside teeth and stitch close to basting by hand or machine. Remove basting but not catch stitching. Press stitching on RS and remove catch stitching and tailor's tacks.

**6.** At base of zip, snip narrower turning in towards the zip so that it lies flat. Loop stitch snipped raw edges of turning to neaten. Press well on WS.

**Alternative uneven hems** Use this method for extra strength; it has the same top fold as in the first method, but as no stitching shows on the fold underneath, the zip can be attached to the under fold by machine. Prepare and press wider fold as in previous method. Place closed zip RS down on RS of second, or under, side, centring teeth on fitting line, and baste along one side of tape beside zip teeth.

**2.** Machine or backstitch 2 mm/$\frac{1}{16}$ in from zip teeth. Remove basting and press stitching. Roll both zip and seam edge over so that zip is RS up. Baste along narrower turning side of zip through all layers—garment, turning and zip tape. Press up to teeth. Complete wide fold as in previous method, snipping and neatening narrower turning on WS so it lies flat.

57

# Zips

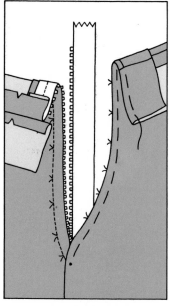

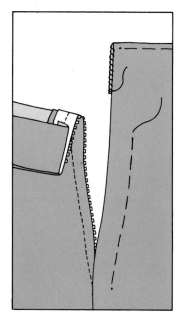

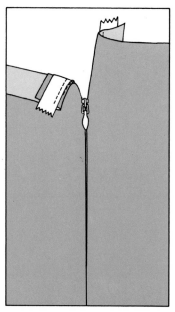

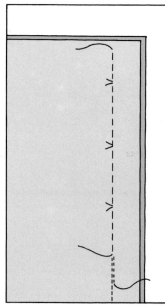

**Uneven hems—faced edge** If the edge above the zip is to be faced, baste and stitch narrow turning to zip tape as far as seam line, leaving top of tape free to be trimmed. Remove basting and press. Attach facing to neck in the usual way. Snip seam turnings and trim, with tape, so that one turning is smaller than the other. Fold under wider edge of both zip opening and facing on marked fitting line. Baste and press.

**2.** Roll facing to WS, baste along neck edge and press. Slip stitch edges by zip together. Lay wider turning over zip, baste and complete. Hold neck edge together neatly at top with a very small hook and thread bar.

**Concealed zip** The easiest and quickest of all zips to insert and so the best choice for beginners. Invisible from RS. Use when a good colour match is not available or when any other type of zip and method of insertion would break up the pattern on the fabric. It is ideal, too, for fabrics that are difficult to sew. A special foot that straddles the teeth may be available for your machine; otherwise use the ordinary zip foot.

**2.** Close up zip section of seam with a large machine stitch (this section should be 1 cm/$\frac{3}{8}$ in shorter than the zip as the bottom part is difficult to reach). Carefully press open entire seam length as it will be impossible to press the zip section again.

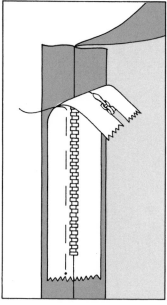

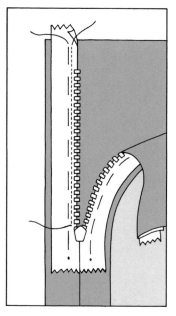

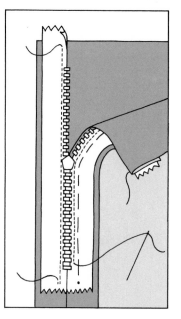

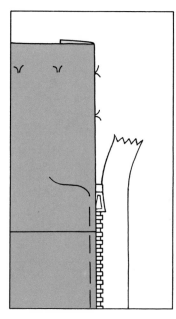

**3.** Place closed zip on WS of seam, centring teeth over join. Baste both sides through tape and turning only, not right through to garment. To do this, slip your fingers underneath the turning as you baste.

**4.** Undo original line of large machine stitches and open zip right to its base. Roll teeth over so they are flat. Open out fabric and machine or backstitch down each side of zip beside teeth, stitching through tape and turning only and working from WS of garment. Sew down as far as the slider, leaving ends of thread long enough to thread into a needle and to sew in by hand if stitching is done by machine.

**5.** Move the slider up a little and backstitch from previous stitching down to end of tape. Remove basting. Run slider up and down gently a couple of times to roll teeth into position again. If zip needs pressing, place it on a folded towel WS down and press lightly on RS.

**Finishing with a roll collar** Machine roll collar to neckline, but do not finish. Turn in edges of zip opening and collar and press. Insert zip by an even hems method, placing top of zip so that it extends into the collar by less than a quarter the depth—2 to 3 cm/$\frac{3}{4}$ to 1$\frac{1}{4}$ in. This conceals the slider and holds the collar upright. Complete collar in the usual way.

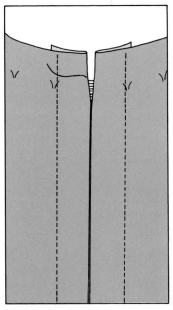

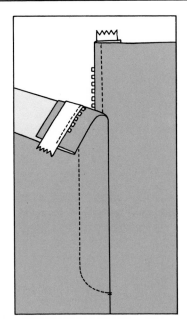

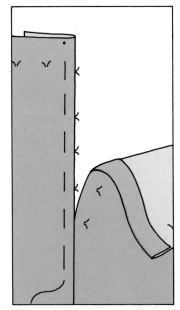

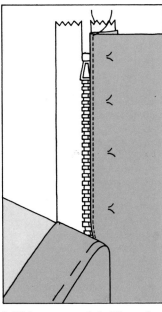

**Side seam zip** A short, back neck zip and an underarm zip are easier to reach than a long back zip and avoid a long row of stitching. Before setting in sleeves, insert back neck zip by appropriate method and underarm zip by an even hems method keeping tape 5 mm/¼ in below seam line of armhole. Continue the stitching right up to the armhole edge. Slip stitch folded edges together above zip to underarm edge.

**Fly insertion** Use at centre front of women's and children's trousers, tunics, jackets or wherever a concealed but flat zip insertion is needed, or where a wide edge is part of the design. Extra turnings of a total of 3 cm/1¼ in are needed for trousers, but allow a little more for a jacket. Add this on when cutting out or join an extra piece of fabric to wider edge. On trousers curve extra allowance at its base to reduce bulk.

**2.** On the side that is to form the wide covering flap, fold under turning on seam line, baste near fold and press. On second, or under, side turn under neatened edge 5 mm/¼ in from seam line to make a narrower turning. Baste into position and press. Snip narrower turning at the base to ensure that the zip lies flat.

**3.** With garment and zip RS up, place narrower fold against zip teeth and baste to tape. Stitch to end of tape by hand or machine. Remove basting and press stitching. With zip still closed, bring wider fold over until it meets seam line on fabric on underside of opening. This ensures that the garment fits correctly and that the zip is completely covered.

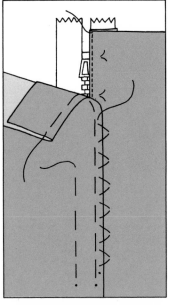

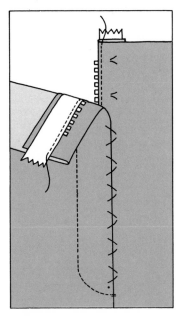

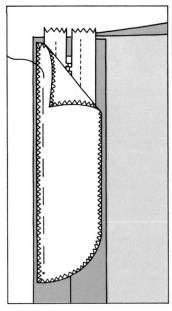

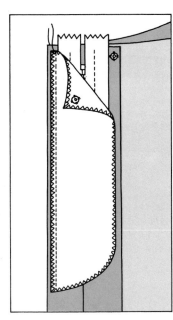

**4.** Hold down wider fold on fitting line of narrower one with large catch stitch worked in basting thread. Baste fold to zip close to teeth. To ensure that the distance between the stitching and the edge is even, use an adjustable marker to mark out, close to basting, an accurate stitching line with sharp chalk, or work another more accurate row of small basting stitches in coloured thread that will show up well on fabric.

**5.** Machine or hand stitch along marked line. At the base of the zip the stitching is usually curved round to meet the seam; make sure the point at which the stitching and seam meet comes below the end of the zip. Remove basting and press stitching. Work a bar tack at base of zip. Remove catch stitch.

**Guards** Add a guard to the back of a zip to protect sensitive skin or fine underwear. Cut a piece of lightweight fabric to the length of the opening, curved at one side of the base to keep it flat, and neaten it all round. Petersham ribbon is less bulky at the back of a dress than fabric as it needs neatening only at the ends, with hemming. Place guard on WS with one edge level with edge of one of seam turnings and baste together.

**2.** Machine near edge through guard and turning. Remove basting. If adding a guard to the back zip of a dress, finish by sewing a very small press stud to the unattached top corner and opposite garment edge. This helps to keep the zip closed during wear.

# Fasteners

Fasteners fall into three main groups: decorative fasteners such as frogs and rouleau loops; hooks, press studs and Velcro, which are concealed; and visible functional fasteners such as buttons and buttonholes. However, many fasteners are decorative as well as functional. For example, the positioning of buttonholes and buttons can produce a decorative effect and so can fancy buttons. Special press studs are available which can be covered with a button mould, or use a solid press stud with a decorative metal cap.

Before choosing the fasteners, consider the requirements and features of the garment. If there is likely to be strain at the fastening point, choose strong fasteners such as hooks or buttons. Press studs are not strong by themselves, but can be used with other fastenings or a single one can be placed at, for example, the neckline of a garment that has buttons as the main fastening. Use frogs on loose garments only as they are not strong and tend to come undone easily.

## Positioning

Consider the position of every fastening. Lumpy fastenings at the back of a garment can be uncomfortable, while hooks at the back tend to be rather unmanageable. Think about who will be wearing the garment and use a fastening the wearer can manage, and in an accessible position. For example, back fastenings are unsuitable for young children who dress themselves and the elderly.

In general, on everyday garments choose fasteners that are easy to use. Complicated ones such as rouleau loops should be confined to special garments that are not often worn. Many fastened openings must have an overlap, so bear this in mind when deciding on the type of fastener as some, such as hooks and eyes, cannot be used in this way.

Buttons and buttonholes are suitable for any fabric provided that the right type of buttonhole is made. Other fastenings should be chosen carefully to suit the fabric and garment. Do not spoil the appearance of the garment by choosing unsuitable decorative fastenings, and avoid mixing different kinds of decorative fasteners on one garment.

## BUTTONHOLES

There are four methods of making buttonholes. Whatever the method, always calculate the exact size of buttonhole needed, rather than abiding by the pattern markings. A buttonhole that is too small for the button stretches and flutes and one that is too large allows the button to come undone too easily. Work buttonholes before attaching buttons.

To calculate the size, measure the diameter of the button and allow for its thickness and for ease—the amount of ease required varies with the thickness of the fabric and the type of buttonhole. After calculating the size, make a trial buttonhole. To ensure a uniform set of buttonholes, use an adjustable marker set to the measurement.

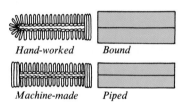

*Hand-worked*  *Bound*

*Machine-made*  *Piped*

### Piped buttonholes

The easiest method and suitable for all other than fine fabrics. Allow 2 mm/$\frac{1}{16}$ in ease on medium fabrics and 4 mm/$\frac{1}{8}$ in on thicker fabrics. Work first eight stages early on in the garment.

### Machine-made buttonholes

Suitable for all fabrics, these are easy to make once you have mastered the machine controls. They can fray a little so do not use on special garments or expensive fabrics. Work them when the rest of the garment is complete. Allow 3 mm/$\frac{1}{8}$ in ease on fine fabrics, 5 mm/$\frac{1}{4}$ in on thicker ones.

### Bound buttonholes

Difficult to work neatly and best restricted to lightweight fabrics. Allow 2 mm/$\frac{1}{16}$ in ease. Work early on, but finish off the backs when the garment is complete.

### Hand-worked buttonholes

These should be attempted only by those who are very experienced and enjoy hand sewing. With the correct thread, they are suitable for all fabrics. Allow 2 mm/$\frac{1}{16}$ in ease on fine fabrics, 4 mm/$\frac{1}{8}$ in on heavier ones. Work them when the garment is complete.

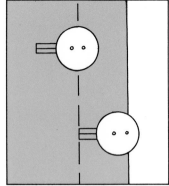

**Horizontal buttonholes** Place buttonholes horizontally at points of strain such as cuffs, waistbands, straps, belts and close-fitting dresses. The amount of fabric extending beyond button placement line limits the size of the button and buttonhole. The button must never be so large that it hangs over garment edge.

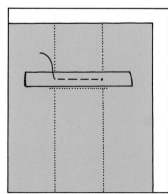

**Vertical buttonholes** Use on loose-fitting clothes or for decorative purposes, such as on pocket flaps, as the button tends to come undone easily if strained. Suitable also where the style limits buttonhole width, as on a narrow fly opening.

**Marking positions** If the centre front or buttonhole placement line is not marked, place one side of button against garment edge and mark position of other to establish outer end of a horizontal buttonhole, or placement line for a vertical one. Chalk a parallel line the buttonhole diameter away to mark inner end of horizontal.

**2.** Lay the buttons out on the garment to decide how many are needed to look attractive and provide an effective fastening. Do not place them too near the top or bottom where it might be difficult to make buttonholes. Calculate the buttonhole length and, using an adjustable marker, mark the positions with chalk lines.

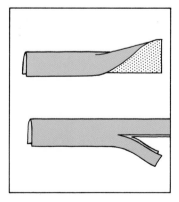

**Piped** Mark position of buttonholes. Cut a long strip of fabric 2.5 cm/1 in wide on straight grain, unless a special effect such as checks on the bias is required. Press paper-backed adhesive to WS of strip to minimize fraying. Fold strip WS together and press well. Trim width to 4 mm/$\frac{1}{8}$ in for fine fabrics, 6 mm/$\frac{1}{4}$ in for thick.

**2.** Cut a strip of piping the required length and place with cut edges against the buttonhole mark on RS of garment, leaving at least 1 cm/$\frac{3}{8}$ in extending on each side of buttonhole. Baste along centre of piping, stitching through garment and interfacing only, not through facing.

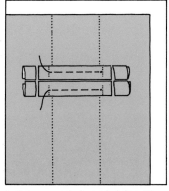

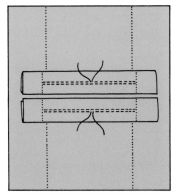

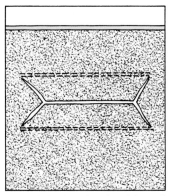

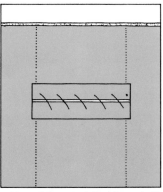

**3.** Cut a second piece of piping. Place on other side of buttonhole mark with cut edges close to first strip. Baste in position as in (**2**). Trim piping to 1 cm/⅜ in from buttonhole ends. Attach piping to the rest of the buttonholes in this way. Re-mark the exact length of the buttonholes by chalking firmly across the piping.

**4.** Starting in middle of one piece of piping, machine with a small stitch to chalk mark. Turn and, counting the stitches, machine to the other chalk mark. Turn and stitch back to centre. Stitch second piece, counting stitches to ensure lines of equal length on both pieces. Remove basting and cut off ends of thread.

**5.** On WS of work, snip with small scissors between the parallel rows of stitching. Cut diagonally out to ends of machine stitching through garment and interfacing only. To make sure you do not cut the piping, insert a finger between the piping strips.

**6.** From RS push piping through slit to WS and also the triangles of garment fabric at ends of buttonhole. Work piping flat with fingertips. Diagonally baste folded edges of piping together. Place work on folded towel and press WS with toe of iron.

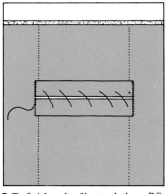

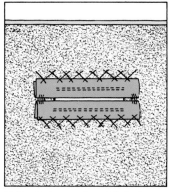

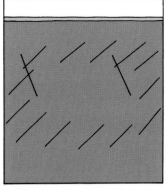

**7.** To finish ends of buttonhole on RS, work stab stitch across each end, taking needle down through fold at ends of buttonhole and up through piping. Press stitching lightly on RS using a cloth.

**8.** On thick or springy fabrics it may be necessary to hold raw edges of piping down on WS by herringboning them to interfacing. On all fabrics oversew ends of piping beyond the buttonhole opening to hold them together securely.

**9.** When garment is complete there will be a facing covering the back of the buttonholes. If fabric frays badly, press a strip of paper-backed adhesive to WS of facing. Diagonally baste all round each buttonhole on RS of garment and through facing. At each end of buttonhole stab a pin through to facing layer underneath.

**10.** On WS of garment snip facing between pins. Remove pins and snip into holes left by them. Turn raw edge under with point of needle and hem round making an oval shape. If the fabric is bulky, cut a larger shape to correspond to buttonhole shape and hem. Press buttonhole again on RS and WS and remove basting.

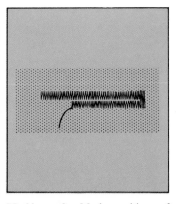

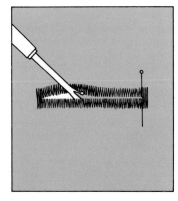

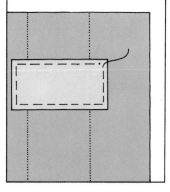

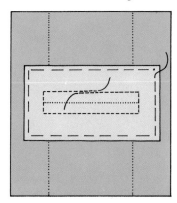

**Machine-made** Mark position of buttonholes. Attach buttonhole foot and set machine as shown in handbook. Press a strip of paper-backed adhesive between garment and facing to minimize fraying. Work buttonholes as shown in handbook, beginning at inside end. Work round twice on some fabrics for best results.

**2.** With small sharp scissors snip between rows of stitching and cut diagonally out to ends, as for piped buttonhole (**5**). Alternatively, slit the buttonhole with an unpicker, but place a pin at end of buttonhole to prevent unpicker cutting too far if it happens to slip.

**Bound** Mark position of buttonholes. Cut rectangles of fabric on the straight grain which are 3 cm/1¼ in wide and at least 3 cm/1¼ in longer than the buttonhole. Place rectangle RS down on RS of garment over position mark. Baste.

**2.** Re-mark buttonhole length on rectangle. Starting in centre, work a rectangle of stitching around position mark exactly the length of the buttonhole and three or four machine stitches wide. To finish off, work the final stitches over the first ones and cut off thread ends on WS and RS. Remove basting and press. ▶

61

# Fasteners

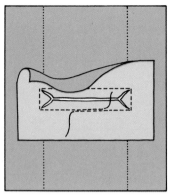

**3.** Snip centre of buttonhole with small scissors. Cut out to corners of rectangle, snipping right up to the machining. Press sides of rectangle towards centre by running toe of iron round seam on RS between garment and rectangle.

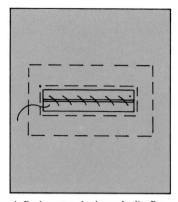

**4.** Push rectangle through slit. Press join from RS. Roll fabric until two folds of equal width fill the buttonhole opening. Hold the narrow seam edges on each side away from buttonhole and baste rectangle to garment. Press. Baste folds diagonally together at buttonhole centre.

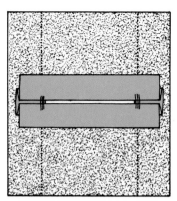

**5.** On WS of garment the rectangle should form inverted pleats at each end of buttonhole. Work bar tacks just beyond ends to hold pleats. Attach sides of rectangle to garment with very small pieces of fabric adhesive. Press buttonhole. Complete garment. Finish back of buttonholes as for piped method (**9**) and (**10**).

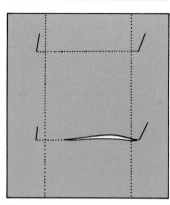

**Hand-worked** Mark position of buttonholes. On fraying fabrics it may help to press a strip of adhesive to underside of work, but this makes the edge stiffer to sew. Insert a pin at each end of mark and cut between pins. Start with an inconspicuously placed buttonhole—your technique will improve as you work.

**2.** Work on RS with a small needle and single thread with a knotted end—thick on heavy fabrics, otherwise normal sewing thread. Start between garment and facing, hiding knot slightly away from buttonhole. For a vertical buttonhole start at either end, for a horizontal one start at inside.

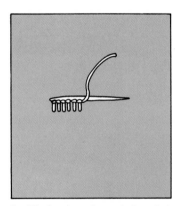

**3.** Work close buttonhole stitch through garment and facing towards you down first side. Pull thread to settle each knot on raw edges; the knots should touch.

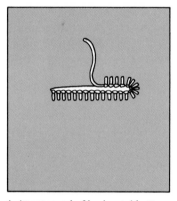

**4.** At outer end of horizontal buttonhole, nearest garment edge, work five stitches in a semicircle, bringing the needle into position for working second side. The five stitches must be shorter than the side stitches and the knots should lie on top of the fabric. This end accommodates the shank of the button.

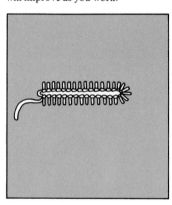

**5.** Work down second side in same way as first until inner end. Pass needle through knot of first stitch worked on first side and draw sides together.

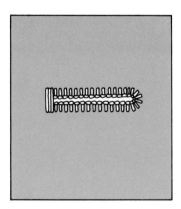

**6.** Work a bar of short satin stitches across end of buttonhole to depth of both rows of stitching. Pull the thread fairly tight. Pass needle to WS and loop stitch over bar to finish. (Do not stitch over bar on RS or you will have a clumsy end just where the buttonhole is always visible.) Cut off the thread end.

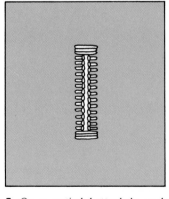

**7.** On a vertical buttonhole work another satin stitch bar at the other end of the buttonhole. On RS oversew both horizontal and vertical buttonholes with basting thread to draw sides together. Press lightly on RS and WS. Remove basting thread. Work all buttonholes at one sitting to achieve an even result.

## BUTTONS AND LOOPS

Thread or rouleau loops may be substituted for buttonholes if appropriate for the garment style. Both suit an edge-to-edge opening and rouleau can also be used for an overlap.

For a single small fastening, use a thread loop with a button. This can be made on a folded edge, but a seamed edge is desirable for rouleau, so that the loops can be sewn into the seam. Rouleau is preferable, and stronger, if more than one fastening is needed. Rouleau loops look best in groups or in a continuous line.

Rouleau can also be formed into decorative ball buttons, which are fastened with rouleau loops or frogs—intricate loops made with rouleau or cord.

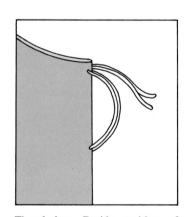

**Thread loop** Decide position of loop and button. Using double thread, work a backstitch on WS and bring needle up in loop position on garment edge. Allowing for button diameter, insert needle into edge a little below, leaving enough thread extending to pass over button. Work three more equal stitches in the same place.

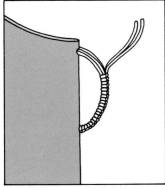

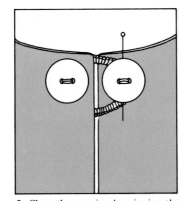

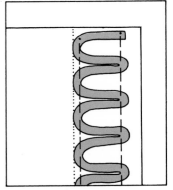

**2.** Work loop stitch closely over the extending stitches. Fasten off with a backstitch on WS of fabric.

**3.** Close the opening by pinning the loop in fastened position. Stitch button (see p. 64) to garment at farthest end of loop. If the button and loop are at the centre front, improve the appearance by sewing a second button beside the loop to balance the first one.

**Rouleau loops** For separate loops make a paper diagram as a position guide. Cut paper to length of opening. Mark seam line and loop positions. Cut pieces of rouleau to correct length for buttons. Baste loops to paper with ends extending past seam line towards garment edge and curves of loops level.

**2.** For a continuous row of loops, cut paper and mark seam line as before. Mark extent of loops according to button size. Baste rouleau to paper in snake-like curves, keeping loops close together. Allow outer edges to project over seam line and snip to ease strain. For a single loop, cut rouleau to the required length.

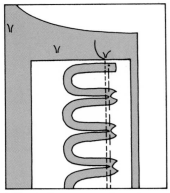

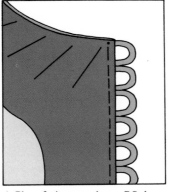

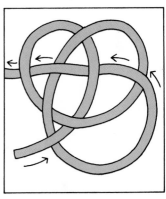

**3.** For both separate and continuous loops, place paper on RS of garment with seam line on garment seam line and loops extending back into garment. Baste. Machine through loops, paper and garment on seam line. Remove paper and basting. For a single loop, position on garment and attach as above.

**4.** Place facing over loops RS down and baste on seam line. Stitch through facing, loop ends and garment; work from garment side and follow first machine stitching. Remove basting. Turn facing to WS and baste diagonally in position. The loops now extend from the garment edge. Press facing.

**Ball buttons** To form a button, take a piece of rouleau and, with one end at the lower left, make a loop and hold it. Make another loop to the right of the first. Pass the long end of second loop over and back under the starting point from left to right.

**2.** Weave the long end over and under across the four strands of the two loops. Pull the long end gently to ease the rouleau loops into a ball.

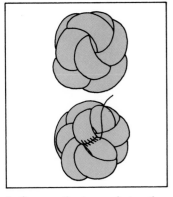

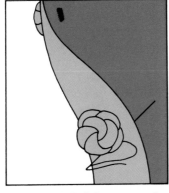

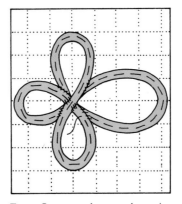

**3.** Oversew the two ends together. This join now becomes the underside of the button. Use the buttons with rouleau loops or frogs.

**4.** To attach ball buttons on fine fabrics, position button on RS of fabric. Working from WS, backstitch over and over through fabric and base of button. Loop stitch over the bar of stitches on WS. On thicker fabrics, sew button on from RS, working stab stitch through base of button to WS of fabric until firm.

**Frogs** On squared paper draw size and shape, making one horizontal loop the correct size for the button. Following the design, baste rouleau or cord to paper. Secure frog by oversewing ends and hemming loops to each other at centre.

**2.** Remove frog from paper. Tucking ends out of sight at the back, position frog on RS of garment with button loop extending from edge. Slip stitch in place up to edge of garment. Alternatively, to anchor frog more securely, backstitch it to garment from WS, working through fabric into back of rouleau.

# Fasteners

## BUTTONS

Choose buttons to suit the garment. For functional fastenings on casual or work clothes, use plain buttons that blend with the fabric. Decorative buttons will be noticeable, so make sure they harmonize with the garment. They will also draw attention to buttonholes. If in doubt, or if your chosen type of button is not available, use buttons covered in the garment fabric.

Spacing is important: use plenty of small buttons close together, but spread large ones out. Small buttons are best for fine fabrics and large ones for heavy fabrics. Before buying buttons, however, check the size recommended on the pattern as the fastening overlap is calculated for that size.

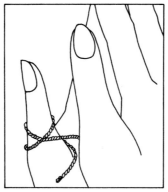

**Sewing on buttons** Thread a slightly larger needle than for most hand sewing. Pull thread through until double and knot ends. Run beeswax along thread, once for fine and four times for thick thread. Twist a section by rubbing it between the palms of your hands. Wind twisted part round thumb and twist next section.

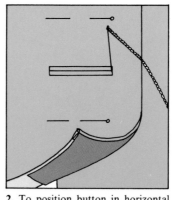

**2.** To position button in horizontal buttonhole, pin buttonhole overlap on to button side in the position it will be during wear. Insert needle into buttonhole at end nearest garment edge, where button shank will rest, and into fabric below. Remove pins and turn back overlap, to leave the button side free to work on.

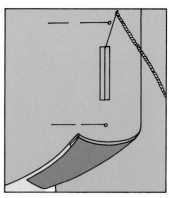

**3.** The button sits at the top of a vertical buttonhole. To position, pin overlap in place as in (**2**). Insert needle at top of buttonhole opening and pass through to fabric beneath. Remove pins and turn back overlap.

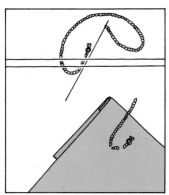

**4.** With RS uppermost, pass needle through to WS of work, leaving knot on RS. Bring needle up $2 \text{mm}/\frac{1}{16}$ in to left of knot—if working vertical buttonhole, turn the work sideways. Insert needle again by knot and bring up to the left to make another stitch. Cut off knot. The next stages vary according to the type of button.

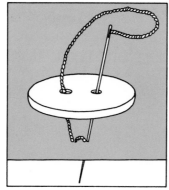

**Purely decorative buttons** may be stitched flat against the fabric. If the button has two holes, align them with buttonhole. Slip button on to needle and slide it down to rest on RS of fabric. Insert needle into other hole and through fabric. Bring up through first hole and stitch with a stabbing action until button is firmly attached.

**2.** If using a four-hole button, begin stitching as above. Work across a pair of holes in line with buttonhole. Make about four stitches—more make the centre lumpy. Bring the needle up through one of other pair of holes and work four stitches. Alternatively, work stitches in star formation diagonally across button.

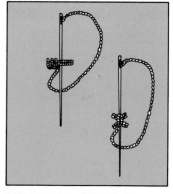

**3.** Turn work to WS and, for a two-hole button, work loop stitch over the bar of stitches. Fasten off with two stitches through fabric under bar. Cut off thread. For a four-hole button, draw the threads together on WS and work a few loop stitches over them. Pass needle through fabric and cut off the thread end.

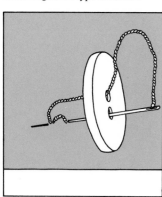

**Functional buttons** must be lifted off the fabric by a shank of 2 to $5 \text{mm}/\frac{1}{16}$ to $\frac{1}{4}$ in, depending on thickness of fabric. Start as for decorative buttons. Slip button on to needle and hold slightly above fabric. Pass needle through to WS and up through second hole of button, making a stitch over starting stitch.

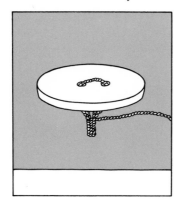

**2.** Continue working two- or four-hole button as for decorative buttons until shank is strong enough for fabric and button. Finish shank so needle is between button and fabric. Wind thread round shank from base to button. Pull to tighten and wind back to base of shank. Pull sharply again. Pass needle to WS and work bar tack.

**Dome buttons** have a metal loop at the back that acts as a shank. Start as in (**4**) and attach by taking a stitch through fabric, then passing needle through loop and so on. Make plenty of stitches until firm. Finish with a bar tack on WS.

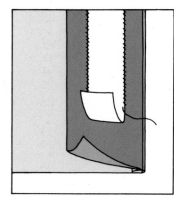

**Reinforcing** Always sew on buttons through two layers of fabric with interfacing or other reinforcement between them. If there is no interfacing in the garment, hem a length of tape or straight seam binding to WS of opening before sewing on buttons. To reinforce one button, fold tape into a small square and hem to WS.

"Once you have missed the first buttonhole, you'll never manage to button up", observed Goethe with depressing if unsublime accuracy. People have been fumbling with their buttons since long before Roman times, but surprisingly no one thought of the buttonhole until the 13th century.

Buttons were manufactured as early as 1166, and by 1250 they had become so popular in England that Henry III was obliged to pass a law limiting the number and kind permissible. But the golden age of the industry began in the reign of Elizabeth I—herself such a button devotee that she had several important royal heirlooms melted down to make new buttons—and lasted well into the button-hungry 19th century.

Bone is the oldest known material, but over the years buttons have been made from such diverse substances as wood, horn, ivory, animal hoofs, cut steel, pewter, cast brass, hand-painted porcelain, glass and lacquered papier mâché. The 19th century saw the apotheosis of the pearl button, made from the mother-of-pearl once discarded as valueless by pearl fishers.

Most buttons today are mass-produced from a variety of plastics. This makes them practical and adaptable to almost any weight and style of garment, but also rather unimaginative. It is worth collecting old buttons both for their intrinsic value and to add sparkle to home dressmaking.

Pearl cutters from Indonesia, Africa, India and Australia supplied the tons of mother-of-pearl demanded by the insatiable 19th-century market for pearl buttons and buckles.

The traditional, intricately patterned pearly suits worn by the kings and queens of London's costermonger fraternities were devised by ratcatcher Henry Croft in 1870. A suit—studded with 40,000 buttons—can weigh 20 kilos.

1. Ivory button, early 19th century; 2. Pictorial button with gilt surround, late 19th-century German; 3. Raised gilt design on gilt on silver plate, mid-19th century; 4. Silver and enamel button, probably late 19th-century Japanese; 5. Carved mother-of-pearl button, c. 1880; 6. Plastic art deco button; 7. Edwardian fabric button, c. 1900, hand-painted with ribbon flower; 8. Marble waistcoat button, probably late 19th-century Italian; 9. Painted enamel button, late 19th century; 10. Modern stag-horn button; 11. Crystal button with ammonite centre set in gold, c. 1920.

Frogging, ornamental loops of braid, was a standard feature of 19th-century military dress, as on the British officer's uniform above.

Plate-size buttons bedeck a curious character from a Dalby print of 1777.

# Fasteners

## HOOKS, EYES, BARS AND PRESS STUDS

Usually available in black and silver metal, these fasteners come in a range of sizes to suit different types of fabric and garment. The largest sizes are used mainly in soft furnishings. Press studs are also available in a few colours but the size range for these is limited. Although they are not very strong, and are unsuitable for clothes that will undergo heavy wear, transparent plastic press studs are useful on some garments as they are almost totally invisible when attached.

Attach fasteners to double fabric or to one layer of fabric and one of interfacing. Work with single synthetic thread that matches the fabric or with black thread to co-ordinate with black hooks and press studs.

Hooks and bars are strong and give a firm fastening for openings such as waistbands. In some openings, where the bar would be too noticeable, the hook can be used with a hand-worked thread bar. Hooks and eyes provide a slightly movable fastening but they are easier to use.

On overlapping openings, use hooks and bars—an eye would be visible. The hook is placed slightly back from the edge of the garment on the wrong side of the upper part of the overlap. The bar is positioned on the right side of the other edge, or underside, so that it is just under the edge of the upper layer when fastened.

Hooks and eyes are best where they will be invisible as, for example, on the inside of the garment or where there is a flap to cover them. Edges which are to meet, as at the back of a collar, can be brought loosely together with a hook and eye.

Press studs are generally suited to overlapping openings. On an opening where the two edges meet, press studs can be attached if the second half, the well section, is sewn to the edge through one hole only and thus extends from the edge. Tape with press studs already attached is available. It is stitched into position by machine and can save time if a large number of press studs is needed. It is often useful for fastening openings on clothes for babies and children.

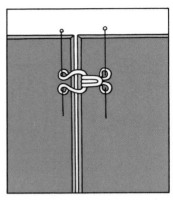

**Hooks and eyes** Fasten hook into eye and place them in position on WS of garment. The hook is set back from one edge and the loop of the eye should project from the other edge. Making sure that garment edges are in the correct position, insert a pin through loops of hook and one through loops of eye. Unfasten hook.

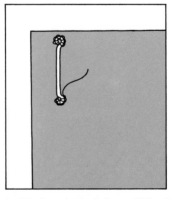

**2.** Work a backstitch beside end of hook. Pass thread under head of hook and take a stitch through the fabric, passing needle under hook. Work at least six stitches across the hook in this way to hold it down. Be careful not to go through to RS of garment.

**3.** Pass needle through fabric, again taking care not to go through to RS, and bring through beside one loop of the hook. Remove pin. Work close buttonhole stitch towards you round the first loop. Continue around the second loop. Fasten off with a backstitch beside hook.

**4.** Fasten hook into eye and check position of eye on garment. Adjust until correct. Unfasten hook. Start with a backstitch and bring needle up beside one loop of the eye. Work close buttonhole stitch round each loop, removing pin after starting stitching. Fasten off with a backstitch.

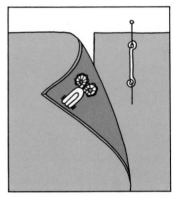

**Bars** If garment edges overlap, use bars for fastening hooks rather than eyes. Attach hook, as before, slightly back from edge on WS of upper part of overlap. Pin opening together. Pin bar in position through loops on RS of underside of opening. Fasten hook and bar to check opening closes properly. Unfasten hook.

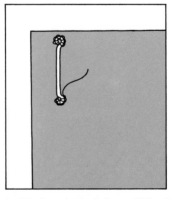

**2.** Work a backstitch on WS of garment beneath bar. Bring up thread beside bar. Remove pin and work close buttonhole stitch round first loop of bar. Take needle underneath fabric, bring up at second loop and stitch as first. Fasten off with a backstitch.

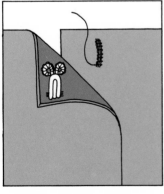

**3.** Make a thread bar if the metal bar is liable to be conspicuous. Close and pin opening after attaching hook. Insert needle in bar position and work a bar of four stitches the length of the hook head. Work close loop stitch over threads. Fasten off thread on WS with a backstitch.

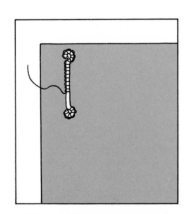

**4.** If a metal bar is required to give strength but is too obvious on the fabric, work loop stitch across central part of bar when it is attached. Use thread that matches the fabric, thus camouflaging the bar.

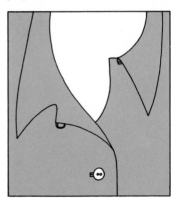

**5.** For a neck fastening that can be adapted to form a revers, use a hook and thread bar. Do not make the top buttonhole. Sew a tiny hook under the collar and make a thread loop on top corner of other side of opening. Attach a top button to upper layer of opening to give an even appearance when neck is fastened.

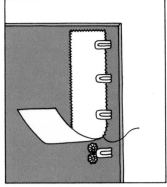

**6.** If using a row of hooks that may appear unsightly, cover ends of hooks with a piece of coloured seam tape to match fabric. Hem all round tape.

**7.** On a faced edge hooks can be inserted into a seam. Turn in garment edge and baste. Sew hooks, with head extending, to WS of edge. Turn in edge of facing and attach by hemming to WS of garment over hooks.

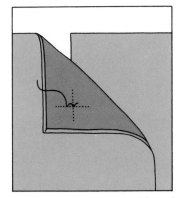

**Press studs** Decide on position of knob section on WS of top layer of opening overlap and mark position with chalk. Knot end of thread and take a stitch at the press stud position. Be careful not to take needle through to RS.

**2.** Place press stud over knot and anchor with one oversewing stitch worked through each hole.

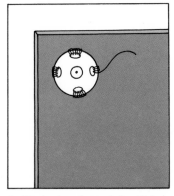

**3.** Work close buttonhole stitch in each hole of press stud, settling knots on fabric at edge of stud. Take three to five stitches in each hole, depending on size of press stud. Pin up garment opening.

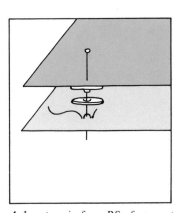

**4.** Insert a pin from RS of garment through hole in centre of press stud. Slip the under, or well, section on to pin and insert tip of pin into under layer of opening, to position the well. Start with a backstitch and work an oversewing stitch through each hole of well. Proceed as in (**3**).

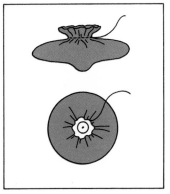

**5.** Press studs can be covered with lining fabric to match the garment. Cut two circles of woven lining to size. Work a row of gathering round edges. Place circles over both halves of stud, draw up gathering at back and fasten off. Trim surplus. Attach as for ordinary press studs.

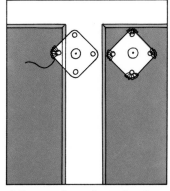

**6.** Press studs can be used to fasten edges that meet rather than overlap. Attach first half of press stud in usual way. Sew well, or second half, to other edge attaching it by only one hole. Leave remainder of stud extending from garment edge. Use a transparent plastic press stud for an invisible opening.

## VELCRO

A versatile fastener, Velcro can replace or augment many other fastenings. It is a nylon tape with two parts, one covered with tiny rigid hooks and the other with soft looped threads. When they are pressed together, the two parts adhere to each other.

Velcro is available in a wide range of colours and in several widths. Keep it fastened when not in use and when washing so the hook section does not catch on other things. When attaching Velcro, position the hook part so that it is not in contact with the skin during wear; otherwise it is likely to scratch the skin and be uncomfortable.

Velcro can fasten waistbands, cuffs and belts. It is also ideal for attaching bibs, frills and detachable collars. Or, cut in circles, it may be sewn at the back of buttons to replace buttonholes.

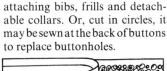

*Hook*  *Loop*

**For an edge-to-edge opening** cut strip to required length and separate the two parts. On WS place one part level with one edge and hem or work a small zigzag all the way round. Sew second part to WS of other edge so it extends beyond the edge. Trim Velcro so that none of hook part is exposed when fastened.

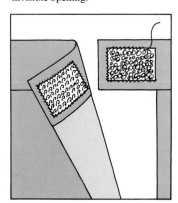

**For an overlap opening** cut strip to required length. Separate the two parts and trim 3 mm/⅛ in off hook section to stop it extending and catching. Position one part on WS of top layer, one on RS of under layer. Hem each part of the Velcro into position or work a small zigzag stitch all the way round.

# *PERFECT DRESSMAKING*

# Patterns

Paper patterns for dressmaking are available in a variety of makes. As each pattern company designs from its own set of basic pattern shapes, or blocks, you may well find that certain makes are better suited to your figure than others.

Ease for movement in the garment is allowed for when the pattern is produced but the amount allowed varies with different makes of pattern. Some garments require more ease than others; a blouse, for example, has more ease allowed than a fitted dress, and a coat more than a jacket. Some patterns have the instruction "use knit fabrics only", which indicates that very little ease has been added as the fabric itself should stretch to allow room for movement and shaping. More ease is allowed on large-size patterns.

Some patterns contain two or more sizes—this is an advantage as sizes can be mixed to accommodate individual figure needs.

Seam allowances of 1.5 cm/$\frac{5}{8}$ in are usually included but some patterns are the exact garment size and seam turnings must be added.

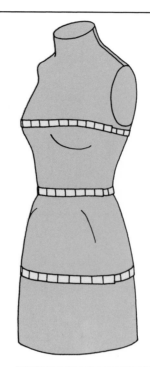

## Taking measurements

Before buying a pattern, take a few important body measurements to use as a guide when choosing the size of pattern. A chart of the measurements for each size is usually found at the back of pattern catalogues and on the pattern envelope.

Measure the bust or, on men and children, the chest firmly round the fullest part of the figure, taking the tape measure under the arms, and measure the waist firmly round the natural waistline. Take the hip measurement round the widest part of the hips on the pelvic bone.

A back neck-to-waist measurement is often indicated on the chart but as this is easy to adjust it need not be considered when buying the pattern unless you are very short-waisted and there is a special pattern.

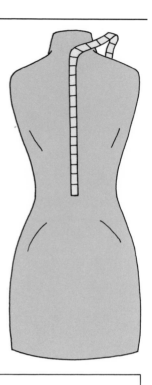

*"Pollock's garment fitting frame", designed to take intimate measurements with maximum propriety, ensured a wrinkle-free cut after only one session.*

## FIGURE TYPES

When choosing a pattern select the size which most closely resembles the measurements of the wearer of the garment although it is unlikely to be a perfect fit. As a general rule, choose patterns for tops and full-length clothes by the bust or chest size, and for skirts and trousers by the hip size.

There may be exceptions to this, however. A short, small-boned person with a large bust will have fewer alterations to make if a small pattern to suit the rest of the figure is used and the bust shaping enlarged. A tall person with a large bony frame may use a large pattern, reducing it at small features such as bust or hips. Buy the size that fits in the most places.

If dealing with a particular figure problem other than length, choose a pattern with a seam, dart or gathers at that point so that it can be adjusted easily. Select styles that flatter and draw attention to good points and disguise problem areas. Place emphasis such as any style features, decoration or colour contrast where it is most flattering. Examples of points to avoid with particular figure problems are: large hips—avoid low-waisted styles; large thighs—avoid straight skirts and keep to A lines, pleats and gathers; large bust—avoid gathers and excess fabric; thick waist—avoid waist joins and belts, and place the emphasis higher or lower; tall and thin—avoid vertical seams and princess lines. Beginners have more success with loose styles which do not need detailed fitting.

*Extremes of size have always been fair game for caricature, whether it be the simpering disparity displayed by the Misses Price—Half, Full, Low and High—above, or the elephantine joie de vivre of a seaside postcard lady, right.*

# CHECKING THE PATTERN

Before cutting out, check all the measurements on the pattern even if the basic measurements of bust or chest, waist and hip suggest it will fit. As the pattern is chosen by its width measurements these should be virtually correct. It is difficult to measure widths on the pattern because no indication is given of the amount of ease allowed. If, however, the pattern is not wide enough at any point, add extra fabric when cutting out.

The important feature to check on the pattern before cutting out in fabric is the length of each pattern piece, as this makes a great difference to the fit of the garment. Compare the length of each body area with the length of the pattern and adjust accordingly to ensure that the balance of each piece is correct. Solve any remaining problems when fitting the garment.

Keep a list of measurements for future use except when sewing clothes for children—they need measuring every time.

**Back neck to waist**
Establish waist level by tying a tape round waist or wearing a narrow belt. Measure from top spinal bone to natural waist. Add 5 mm/$\frac{1}{4}$ in for ease of movement.

**Back neck to underarm**
Measure from top spinal bone down centre of back to underarm level.

**Underarm to waist**
An exact measurement can be taken from an existing garment. Alternatively, measure at centre back from underarm level to waist.

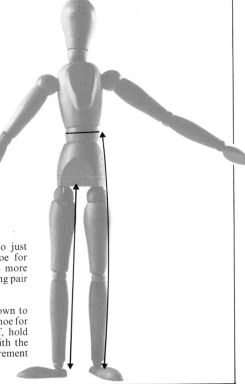

**Waist to hip level**
Measure at side from waist down to level of pelvic bone. This ensures skirt balance is correct as pattern hip level is often too low. Make a note of how far down this measurement is taken.

**Waist to hem**
Measure at centre front from waist to hemline. This gives a rough guide and the exact length is established when fitting the garment. To measure yourself, hold the tape so the end is level with your hem and read off the measurement at the waist.

**Front neck to waist**
Measure from hollow of neck straight down to waist level.

**Neck to chest**
Measure from hollow of neck to chest level—about halfway down armhole level but just before bust rises. Make a note of how far down the bust rises.

**Shoulder to bust point**
Measure from centre of shoulder down to point of bust. The bust dart position is established from this measurement.

**Sleeve seam**
Measure from underarm to wrist and add on 2.5 cm/1 in for ease. Alternatively, take the measurement from an existing garment.

**Underarm to elbow**
Measure with arm bent or take from existing garment. This measurement is needed when establishing elbow shaping position.

**Inside leg**
Measure from crutch point to just below top of appropriate shoe for trousers. This measurement is more accurate if taken from an existing pair of well-fitting trousers.

**Outside leg**
Measure at side from waist down to just below top of appropriate shoe for trousers. To measure yourself, hold the tape so the end is level with the ankle and read off the measurement at the waist.

# Patterns

Originally clothes patterns were communal. First used in the 1850s, they were simple designs made in rough paper which tailors and seamstresses paid a rental to cut from. Commercially produced paper patterns became available during the next decade. In 1863 a Massachusetts tailor, Ebenezer Butterick, sold his first set of graded patterns for men's shirts and children's clothes. Made from cardboard, these early patterns were difficult to pack and transport and were replaced first by lightweight paper and a little later by tissue paper. The tissue patterns were wrapped in a separate piece of paper with a sketch of the garment on the front.

By 1866 women's fashions were included in the range. Business boomed, aided by the invention of the sewing machine and its increased use in the home, and in 1867 Butterick formed E. Butterick and Company.

The first "counter" pattern book with fine woodcut illustrations appeared in fabric stores about 1875, and in 1919 paper patterns were first marketed in an envelope, accompanied by a separate instructions sheet. The formidable full-length title of this new package was "The Deltor—The New and Improved Illustrated Instructions Presenting in Pictures the *Cutting and Putting Together* with Complete Directions for *Finishing*".

Butterick did not hold its monopoly for ever. Other companies sprang up, and in 1927 the Simplicity Pattern Company was founded, later to become one of Butterick's main competitors. As the patterns improved and developed, so styles became more complicated than the very early, basic patterns. From 1948 patterns of original designs with increasingly detailed instructions were available. These became known as Vogue Paris Originals.

In 1950 the first printed pattern appeared, allowing pieces to be named and construction details such as seam allowances and darts to be shown on the pattern surface. These instructions became multilingual, and some are now replaced by symbols such as scissors for the cutting line and a machine stitch foot marking the sewing line. Today patterns cater for all tastes, all occasions and every dressmaker's capabilities.

*Garibaldi, top, gave the world a unified Italy, the currant biscuit and the heroic, red Garibaldi jacket, one of the first pattern designs, above. (Courtesy of Butterick Pattern Archives Library.)*

*Ebenezer Butterick lost no time in publicizing his paper pattern industry and in 1868 brought out a monthly magazine called* The Metropolitan, *later* The Delineator. *This was a curious alliance of dressmaking and literature, which lasted until April 1937. Theodore Dreiser edited it in the early 1900s and John Galsworthy and A. A. Milne contributed, as did the humorist H. L. Mencken and thriller-writer Edgar Wallace. However, patterns were its mainstay, and as this page from the October 1915 issue shows, their presentation has not changed much. The necessary yardage and possible variations in length or detail were indicated separately and each pattern then cost 6 pennies, the same price as a copy of the magazine.*

---

## UNDERSTANDING PATTERN MARKINGS

Pattern markings enable the manufacturer to convey information about the construction of a garment to the dressmaker. Many markings are accompanied by verbal instructions, often in several languages, and some, such as those for a zip or hemline, vary from manufacturer to manufacturer. Most markings should be transferred to the fabric before the pattern is removed and used as a guide when making up the garment.

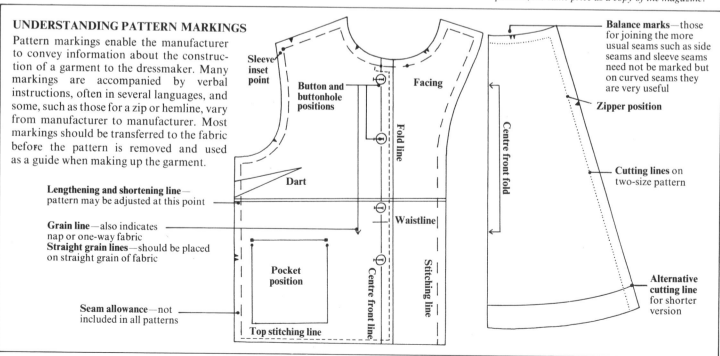

Sleeve inset point

Button and buttonhole positions

Facing

Fold line

Balance marks—those for joining the more usual seams such as side seams and sleeve seams need not be marked but on curved seams they are very useful

Zipper position

Centre front fold

Dart

Lengthening and shortening line—pattern may be adjusted at this point

Grain line—also indicates nap or one-way fabric
Straight grain lines—should be placed on straight grain of fabric

Waistline

Centre front line

Stitching line

Cutting lines on two-size pattern

Pocket position

Seam allowance—not included in all patterns

Top stitching line

Alternative cutting line for shorter version

## ALTERING PATTERN PIECES

Assemble the necessary equipment: a ruler, tape measure, pencil or felt pen, transparent adhesive tape, pins and extra paper. Using old scissors cut out the pattern pieces from the sheet of tissue on which they are printed; cut exactly on the printed outline or, on a multi-size pattern, on the line for your size.

Press pattern pieces flat with a cool iron. Draw a line in pencil or felt pen to mark the chest level on the front bodice, measuring from the front neck to the depth previously noted (see p. 71). Draw in the hip level on the skirt in the same way. Draw a line across the back bodice at underarm level.

Spread out each piece in turn and check against all the figure measurements taken. If the pattern has seam allowances included, measure within them; otherwise measure from the edge. Measure and mark at each point. If the pattern differs from the figure by more than 1 cm/⅜ in at any measuring point, it must be altered. Less than 1 cm/⅜ in can be adjusted when fitting or may even be taken up in ease.

Make the alteration at the measuring point. If an adjustment of, say, more than 2.5 cm/1 in is needed, make two smaller parallel alterations, about 2.5 cm/1 in apart, as too big an adjustment at one point may disturb the balance of the pattern too much. Some patterns have a printed line as a position guide for lengthening or shortening the pattern piece. Use this only if it is close to your marked adjustment point. The length of a skirt or trousers or the length of a bodice below the armhole can generally be adjusted on this line.

Make sure the paper is still flat after the alteration has been made.

### Checking edges

Adjusting the pattern may throw out edges slightly, so check the following points:
- Straighten or gently curve any seam edges that are uneven.
- If darts are affected by alterations, fold and pin them and cut the seam edge across the folded paper. Unpin the dart to give the correctly shaped edge.
- Make sure the straight grain line is still straight. If not, draw a new grain line parallel with main edge or, on a sleeve for example, exactly down the centre of the piece.
- If the depth of the armhole is shortened, take a small pleat across the sleeve head at the same point so that the sleeve fits.
- Check the length of all seam edges to make sure they match corresponding edges. For example, measure side seam edges of front and back bodices if an alteration has been made to one of them.

### Mounting patterns

If you intend to use a particular pattern fairly often, make it more durable by pressing the pieces on to lightweight iron-on interfacing. An adjusted pattern can be a useful reference for altering other patterns.

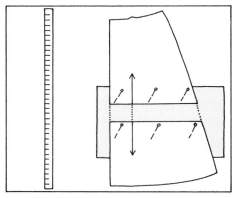

**To lengthen** a pattern place the pattern on a piece of paper. Cut the pattern on the adjustment line drawn when measuring or on the line printed on the pattern. Separate the pieces until the distance between them is equal to the length to be inserted. Pin pattern to paper beneath. Check that the overall measurement is correct and replace the pins with transparent adhesive tape. Trim away the surplus paper to even pattern edges.

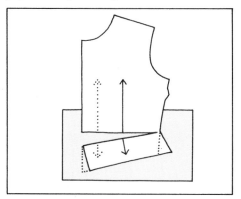

**Uneven alterations** are needed if, for example, the back neck-to-waist measurement is long but the side seam and front match pattern. To lengthen, cut pattern from edge to be lengthened across to, but not through, other edge. Swing lower half of pattern down to insert extra length. Pin to paper and check measurement. Replace pins with adhesive tape. Trim side seam, straighten lengthened edge and re-draw straight grain line parallel with edge.

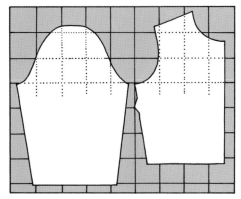

**Placing checks on pattern** Decide how checks are best placed on the body, taking into account any figure problems. Dealing with problem pattern piece first, draw guidelines on pattern piece tracing checks of fabric. Mark other pattern pieces, matching checks to first. If there is no problem area start by marking front pattern. When all pattern pieces are marked, place on fabric and cut out, matching checks and guidelines.

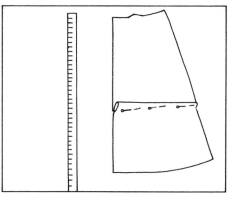

**To shorten** a pattern fold the pattern piece on the adjustment line drawn when measuring or on the line printed on the pattern. Make a pleat equal in total to the length to be removed, remembering that the fold is double. Pin the pleat and check that the pattern is the correct length. Replace the pins with transparent adhesive tape. Trim pattern edges if necessary to make them even.

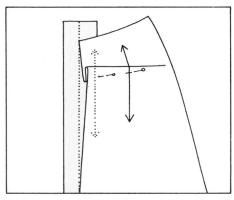

**2.** To shorten unevenly, make a tapering fold across the pattern at the point where it is to be shortened and pin. Smooth out from the fold to the opposite edge so nothing is taken up at that edge. Check the measurement and replace pins with transparent adhesive tape. To straighten the shortened edge, add an extra strip of paper or correct when cutting out pattern in fabric. Re-draw straight grain line parallel with edge of pattern piece.

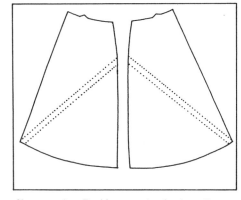

**Chevron stripes** Decide on angle of stripes. Draw a stripe on front pattern piece at that angle. Place back pattern beside front and draw a stripe at same angle, but in other direction, to match first one. When cutting out fabric, arrange pattern on fabric so that drawn stripe aligns with fabric stripe. Use the same method if cutting a pattern piece such as a skirt or sleeve on the cross instead of on the straight grain.

# Patterns

After sewing a few garments and dealing with length alterations, you will probably become more familiar with the problems of fitting. If you have to make the same fitting alterations on each garment the patterns are not absolutely correct for the figure. Once you are sure where these differences lie, and of the degree of adjustment necessary, make the alterations on each pattern before cutting out so that fitting the garment will be a much simpler operation.

The following adjustments may affect the shape within the pattern piece but the basic method and equipment are the same as for lengthening and shortening. Remember to correct any edges affected by the alterations.

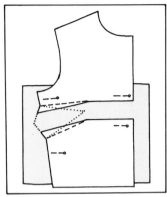

**Prominent bust** To enlarge the shaping area and accommodate a large bust, pin pattern on a piece of paper and cut along centre of dart to point. Cut across to centre front edge. Separate pieces by the amount to be added and re-draw edge of dart. Stitch dart from original base to new point by usual method.

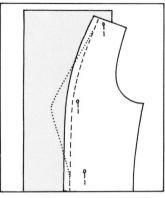

**2.** On a princess style dress, where shaping is in the seam of the front panels, adjust both side panels. Pin pattern to paper and extend bust point. Re-draw seam line from new bust point, tapering it to join original seam lines above and below the bust.

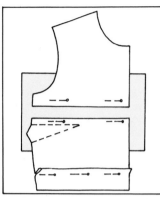

**Low bust** Move whole bust dart down. Place pattern on a piece of paper and cut across it between side seam and centre front above bust dart level. Separate the pieces, inserting amount needed to bring dart down to correct level and pin to paper. Fold and pin pattern below dart to take up any extra length.

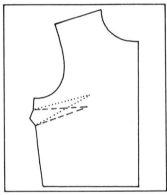

**High bust** Mark the new bust point on the pattern. Re-draw dart to this higher point from the original base. To raise or lower bust line on a princess style, lengthen or shorten pattern pieces above and below bust point to bring shaping to correct level for figure.

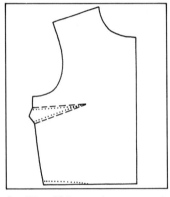

**Small bust** If dart produces too much fullness for a small bust, reduce width at base of dart and re-draw stitching lines. This makes the front side seam longer than the back, so match patterns at underarm and trim surplus at waist. Alternatively, take a fold in across pattern from side edge if pattern has no waist seam.

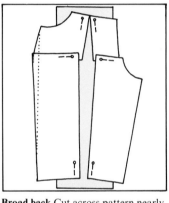

**Broad back** Cut across pattern nearly to edges, above or below armhole, depending on where width is needed. Cut down centre from shoulder to waist. Pin to paper and open out at horizontal cut to insert extra width. Keeping shoulder edges together, overlap horizontal cut edges and pin. Straighten centre back.

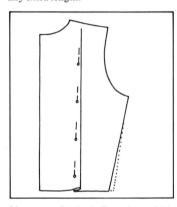

**Narrow or flat back** To reduce width of pattern, take a fold down centre of back pattern piece from shoulder to waist. If the shoulder is the correct width, take the fold upwards from the waist, tapering it away at shoulder edge. If the waist width is reduced too much, add a little at side seam to compensate when cutting out.

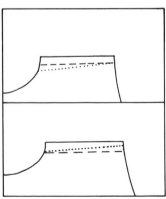

**Square shoulders** If square shoulders cause surplus fabric to appear at neck edge, draw a new lower shoulder seam line from neck, tapering it to original level at outer edge. To allow extra height at the shoulder, raise the seam line at outer edge, tapering it to original level at neck edge. Alter back and front.

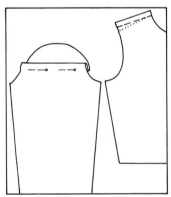

**Sloping or hollow front shoulders** To accommodate sloping shoulders, draw a new shoulder line from original neck point, lowering it towards armhole edge. Do this on front or back, or both, as required. Adjust front only for hollow front shoulder. If size of armhole is reduced, take small pleat across sleeve head to fit.

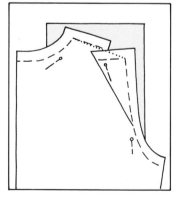

**Narrow shoulders** Cut pattern at an angle from the middle of the shoulder to halfway down armhole but not through armhole edge. Overlap pieces at shoulder and pin on to a piece of paper. Re-draw the shoulder seam line across overlap from original neck point to original shoulder point. Trim paper. Alter back and front.

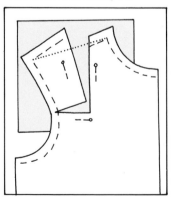

**Broad shoulders** Cut pattern down from mid-shoulder to a point level with middle of armhole. Cut across to armhole but not through edge. Swing cut piece back to add extra width on shoulder. Pin to paper and re-draw shoulder seam from original points. Alter back and front. Adjust shoulder line when fitting.

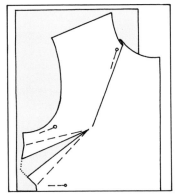

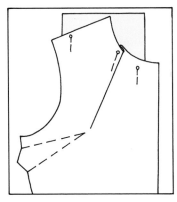

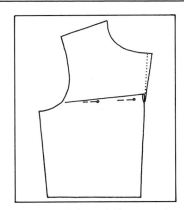

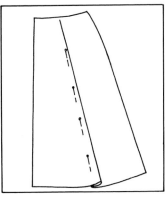

**Gaping neckline** This can be caused by a prominent bust or a hollow chest. If it is the former, cut pattern through centre of bust dart and place on paper. Fold and pin surplus at neckline, open dart wider and re-draw neckline. Re-draw outer edge of dart. Stitch along original lines.

**2.** If a hollow chest is the cause of a gaping neckline, pin pattern to paper and take a tapering fold from neckline only towards point of bust dart. Re-draw neckline.

**Flat chest** Take a fold across the pattern from the centre front edge above armhole level, tapering it away at armhole edge. To straighten the centre front line, it is usually helpful to take a little off the neckline.

**Thin thighs and legs** To adjust a skirt, take a fold up the centre of the pattern piece, tapering it away towards waist. Add fabric at side seam when cutting out if hip width has been reduced too much. Alter back and front.

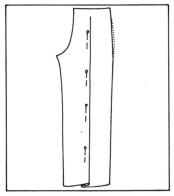

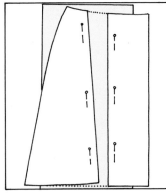

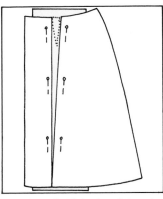

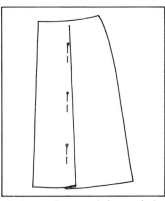

**2.** To adjust trousers for thin thighs and legs, take a fold up the centre of each leg, tapering it away towards waist. Add fabric at side seam when cutting out if hip width has been reduced too much. It is not always necessary to alter back and front.

**Prominent stomach or thick waist** If omitting darts is insufficient to accommodate figure, cut down centre of pattern from waist to hem. Pin to paper, separating pieces to allow extra width at waist and stomach area. Re-draw hemline and waistline.

**Large buttocks** If the size of the waist allows, increase width of waist dart or add a dart to provide extra buttock shaping. If there is no surplus at the waist, cut down centre of pattern from waist to hem. Open out pieces at waist only and pin to paper, inserting sufficient width at waist level to make a new dart. Draw in new dart.

**Flat bottom** One remedy is to omit the waist dart and take in the resulting surplus at waist in side seams. If this is insufficient, take a fold in centre of back at the hemline and taper it away at the waistline.

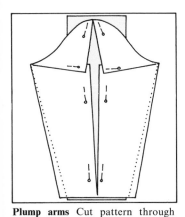

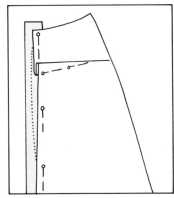

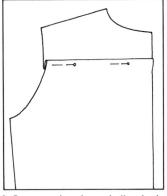

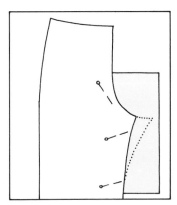

**Plump arms** Cut pattern through centre from sleeve head to wrist and cut across it just below underarm; do not cut through edges. Spread pattern on paper and open at horizontal cut to extra width needed, overlapping horizontal cut edges to keep pattern flat. If arm is thin below muscle area, adjust sleeve seam lines.

**Hollow back** To alter either a skirt or trousers, take a small fold across pattern from centre back edge about 5 cm/2 in below waist. Taper fold away at side seam. Re-draw centre back edge, curving it slightly at alteration point. Try to choose a pattern with a centre back seam so the garment can be shaped to the body.

**2.** On a one-piece dress a hollow back produces excess material at waist. Take out a pleat across centre back, level with the middle of the armhole. Adjust the slight reduction in armhole size when constructing the dress and inserting the sleeve.

**Thick thighs** If thighs are thick at inside leg, extend crutch point of a trouser pattern. Pin pattern to paper. Extend inside leg seam line from about 12 cm/5 in below the crutch upwards. Extend centre back seam line, in a curve, by a maximum of 5 cm/2 in to meet inside leg seam. Adjust at fitting if necessary.

# Patterns

Once the pattern is adjusted satisfactorily, check the fabric carefully before cutting out the garment. Examine the whole length and mark any flaws, marks or faded patches to be avoided with chalk.

Press out creases, such as the centre fold crease, with a damp cloth. It is particularly important to do this on synthetic jersey although sometimes the crease cannot be removed and has to be avoided when cutting out. Synthetics tend to attract dirt particles on the fold, which, if folded on the right side, will show up as a dirty mark when pressed. Wash the fabric, or have it dry cleaned if necessary, to remove this mark.

Jersey fabrics often have an untidy selvedge which should be cut off. On all fabrics straighten one end of the length. If the grain is not perfectly straight, the fabric should be stretched from opposite corners.

If the fabric contains natural fibres, test it for shrinkage. Using a ruler and a chalk pencil, measure and mark out a square of about 16 cm/$6\frac{1}{4}$ in at the centre of the fabric. Press the square with a damp cloth and allow the fabric to cool. Measure the square again and note any difference in its dimensions. Any slight shrinkage on that small square is multiplied if it occurs on the whole length so before use the fabric must be shrunk. Washable fabrics may be squeezed in warm water, or put in a washing machine without soap, then dried and pressed. Alternatively, press the single thickness of fabric all over with a damp cloth. Take care to press evenly and keep the cloth damp. Another method is to fold the fabric lengthways, place it on a damp sheet, roll it up and leave overnight. The next day press the fabric until it is completely dry.

Fold fabric right side out so that marks, flaws and pattern designs are visible. Pin straightened ends together and pin selvedges together at wide intervals. If short of space on the cutting-out surface, roll up the surplus length of fabric to prevent it from hanging off the table and stretching.

## Placing the pattern

Place each pattern piece in position on the fabric, checking that the grain line is straight by measuring an even distance from the fold or selvedge at each end of the grain line. Anchor the grain line to fabric with two pins. Position all the main pattern pieces to check that everything fits. Position smaller pieces but do not pin finally or cut until after fitting. Observe all instructions such as "place to fold" or "cut twice". Leave room between the pieces for seam allowances if the pattern does not include them, and for any extra width or length to be added for fit. When using patterns with no seam allowances, draw in the cutting line with tailor's chalk as a reminder.

On particularly bulky fabric, pinning the pattern to the fabric can tear the pattern and cause the fabric to lie unevenly. Anchor the pattern pieces on the fabric with a few heavy objects such as scissors or a pin box and chalk round the pattern. Remove the pattern and cut out, using the chalk line as a guide.

---

## FOLDING THE FABRIC

Each pattern piece is usually only half the garment area and is cut out on double fabric, sometimes on the fold. The material, therefore, must be folded in such a way as to accommodate all the pattern pieces on the correct grain.

Wide fabric, 140 to 175 cm/54 to 70 in, can usually be folded down the centre for cutting out the pattern. If one pattern piece is very wide and

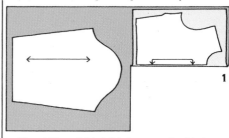

will not fit on folded fabric, open the fabric out and cut the piece on single fabric (1). Fold all narrower fabrics down the centre, provided pattern pieces are not too large.

Alternatively, if some large pattern pieces have to be cut, measure and cut off the length needed and fold and cut the fabric across the width. Turn the top piece of fabric round so that any nap or

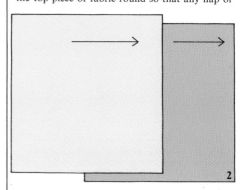

pattern is facing in the same direction on both pieces of fabric (2).

Where there is a pattern instruction "place to fold", the fold must be made on the straight grain

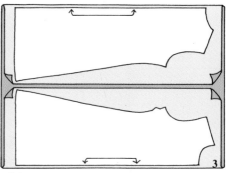

of the weave or on a straight line of knitting on a jersey fabric. If most, or all, of the main pattern pieces have to be placed against the fold, fold the fabric sides to middle with selvedges meeting at centre (3). Make sure the grain is straight on both the folded edges.

If short of fabric, fold in one side of fabric to a width just sufficient to take pattern pieces which

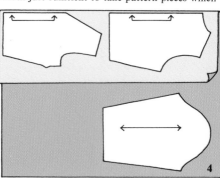

have to be cut on the fold. This leaves a wide strip along the other side where smaller pieces, such as the sleeve, can be cut on single fabric (4). Turn the pattern piece over to cut the second piece where necessary.

Facings, pockets and other small pattern pieces can be cut from any fabric that is left over after the main pieces have been cut out, but make sure that you leave enough room for them when cutting out the main pieces.

---

*Wasp stripes transformed into bold chevrons by clever cutting and careful matching at the skirt and bodice seams and front bodice opening.*

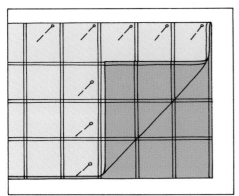

**Checked fabric** Fold fabric along a stripe suitable to fall at the centre of any pattern piece. Pin along the fold. Beginning in the centre of the length of fabric, insert pins across the width, ensuring that the checks match exactly on both the layers lengthways and crossways. Continue inserting pins across width and matching checks at intervals of 8 to 10 cm/3 to 4 in. Do not remove these pins or cut on them when cutting out fabric.

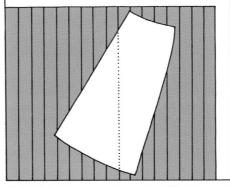

**Striped fabric** Prepare as for checked fabric to match the stripes. For chevron stripes, mark the pattern as on p. 73. Lay the fabric out as a single thickness and place the pattern pieces so that the chevron lines marked on the pattern line up with the stripes on the fabric. Turn each pattern over to cut it the second time if necessary.

**Geometric or floral fabric** Large bold designs must be carefully positioned on a garment. They are often placed centrally or on either side of a central seam. To help balance the design when cutting out, cut an additional paper pattern for a sleeve or cut a whole pattern piece for a back skirt or bodice front instead of placing a pattern piece on folded fabric. Each piece can then be cut out in single fabric and the design attractively placed.

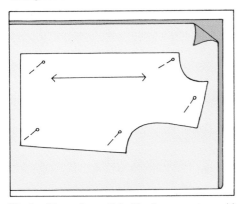

**Pinning** Place pins well inside the paper to avoid disturbing pattern edge, and pin at each corner of the pattern and between corners on a long edge. Insert pins diagonally, as the fabric gives and lies flatter than if pins lie with straight grain. Use only a few pins—too many make the fabric uneven and inaccurate when cut out.

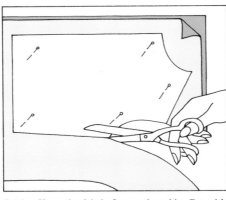

**Cutting** Keep the fabric flat on the table. Cut with the bulk of the pattern to the right of the scissors; reverse if left-handed. Use the whole blade and close the scissors right to the tips; do not make short chopping movements. Make sure the open blade fits snugly into the cut each time to avoid a chopped edge. Move round to reach all parts rather than moving fabric.

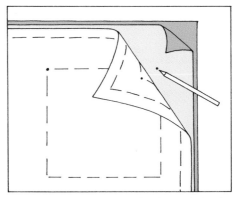

**Marking** Mark all seam allowances, folds, pleat positions, gathering and other features on the fabric before removing the pattern. Tailor's tacks are the best method of marking seam lines as they mark both sides and do not harm the fabric. If the pattern has a seam allowance, fold it back on the seam line and snip at curves to help it lie flat. Work tailor's tacks on fabric close to edge of paper to mark seams. Tailor's chalk can also be used.

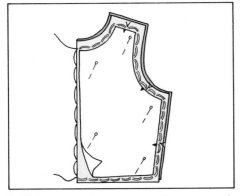

**2.** If the pattern has no seam allowance, work tailor's tacks round edge. Work single tacks at right angles to the seam to mark balance marks. Mark a fold with a row of basting along the fold before removing the pattern.

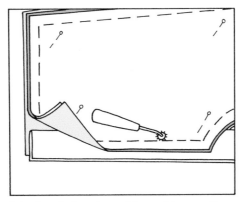

**A tracing wheel** can be used for marking seam lines. Place pattern piece on a surface that will not be harmed by tracing wheel. Cut dressmaker's carbon paper into strips about 5 cm/2 in wide. Fold strips carbon side out. Slide folded carbon between two layers of fabric so carbon is against WS of fabric. Pressing hard, run wheel along seam lines on pattern; check that marks are transferred to WS of fabric before removing pattern.

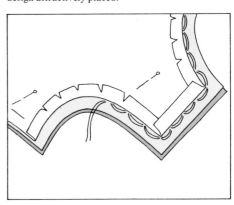

**Marking with a chalk pencil** Chalk is suitable for making occasional marks, such as a pocket position, but not for marking seam allowances all round a pattern piece. To mark with chalk, cut fabric out RS together, fold pattern back and make marks on WS of both layers of fabric. Pencils are available with a device that slides on to the fabric and marks both layers at once.

# *Interfacing*

Most garments have areas that need added reinforcement in the form of interfacing. This extra layer provides strength in areas that are frequently handled, such as openings with buttons and buttonholes or pockets. It helps edges such as necklines keep their shape and gives collars, cuffs and pocket flaps a crisp appearance. Applied to the wrong side of the fabric, interfacing is often later covered by a facing—hence its name.

Decide whether to use interfacing where the pattern suggests as it may be undesirable for the type of fabric and the effect desired. Then, if you decide to use it, choose the correct weight for the fabric. With the exception of belts and waistbands, interfacing should provide only slight stiffening. It should not change the nature of the fabric or drastically affect the appearance of the part of the garment to which it is applied.

It is only comparatively recently that interfacing has been available to home dress-makers in suitable weights for dress fabrics. There is now a wide range of types and weights of both woven and non-woven interfacings. Woven interfacings include canvas of various weights, lawn, cambric, net and organdie. In the newer, non-woven range there is a wide selection of weights from fine transparent to firm, including stretch interfacings, heavy-weights for pelmets and strong pliable types for waistbands. There are also fusible interfacings, with heat-sensitive adhesive on one side, which are ironed on to the fabric.

Keep a small stock of interfacings as it is not always possible to decide which weight is most suitable for the garment until you have started to handle the fabric.

A jacket showing interfacing (the textured areas) applied to the parts that need to be given shape, body and support. In a more tailored garment it is advisable to interface the entire front and back pieces in order to hold the shape across the chest and upper back areas.

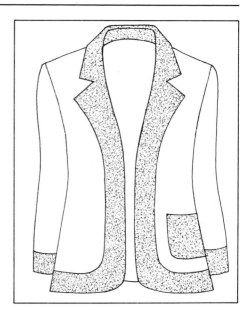

| FABRICS | INTERFACING |
|---|---|
| **Fine:** Chiffon, georgette, voile, organdie, muslin, ninon. | Transparent iron-on (test first), light woven such as organdie or net, or self-fabric. |
| **Lightweight:** Lawn, polyester/cotton, cheesecloth, seersucker, plissé, percale. | Transparent iron-on or lightweight sew-in non-woven. |
| **Medium-weight:** Poplin, denim, madras, calico, cotton, needlecord, gingham, lace, fine wool, fine synthetic mixtures, ticking, woven polyester, woven acrylic. | Soft iron-on, soft sew-in non-woven, or woven iron-on. |
| **Medium-weight with give:** Wool jersey, polyester jersey, acrylic jersey, bonded jersey, tweed, knits, soft wool. | Stretch iron-on or medium-weight sew-in non-woven. |
| **Medium-weight with "surface":** Brocade, matelassé, taffeta, satin, grosgrain velvet, moire, mousseline, habutai, bouclé, dupion, lurex, lamé. | Medium-weight sew-in non-woven. |
| **Soft but thick:** Angora, camel cloth, suede cloth, chenille lace, embroidered fabric, velours, doeskin. | Soft sew-in woven or non-woven. |
| **Firm-woven:** Coating, suiting, barathea, Bedford cord, gabardine, tweeds, woollens. | Heavy sew-in, heavy iron-on non-woven interfacing or tailor's canvas. |

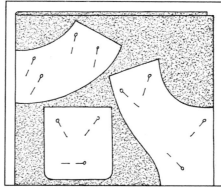

**Cutting** Use the pattern pieces for the parts of the garment to be interfaced. Place pattern on double layer of interfacing—on fold if necessary. On non-woven interfacing, place the pattern pieces in the most economical way as there is no grain to be followed. Pin and cut. Keep any pieces that are left over for future use.

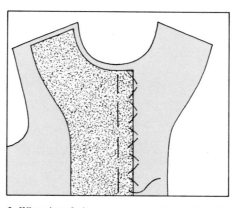

**3.** When interfacing a garment section where the facing is cut all in one with the garment and folded back, cut the interfacing to extend 1 cm/⅜ in beyond fold line. Place interfacing on WS of garment with fold lines matching. Baste it down diagonally and catch stitch edge beyond fold line. Fold interfacing extension back with facing so a double layer of interfacing lies on fold line.

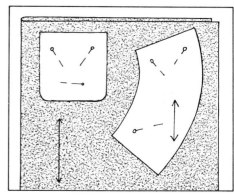

**2.** If using a woven or a stretch interfacing, place the pattern pieces with grain line on straight grain of interfacing. Cut collar interfacing in two pieces on the true cross and from a single layer to enable the collar to be shaped. On stretch interfacing place pieces so that give in interfacing matches stretch of garment fabric—usually widthways. Cut collar interfacing with stretch running end to end to allow collar to shape correctly round neck as above.

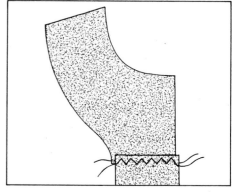

**Joining** Joins in interfacing should normally fall at garment seams. If it is necessary to join pieces because there is not enough interfacing to cut a pattern piece, cut sections of interfacing a little longer than required and overlap at join. Work zigzag stitch along join.

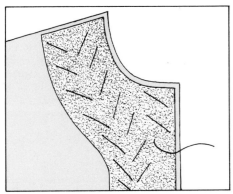

**Attaching lightweight sew-in interfacing** Cut out pieces of interfacing. Place fabric WS up on table and place interfacing on top. Work rows of diagonal basting up and down each piece, through fabric and interfacing, almost to edges. Always start basting in the centre of each piece to prevent the interfacing moving in either direction.

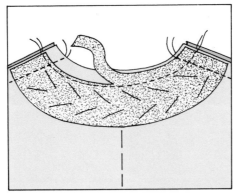

**2.** Make up the garment, stitching through interfacing and garment fabric. After stitching, trim interfacing away close to seam line to avoid bulk.

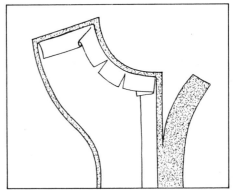

**Attaching medium and firm sew-in interfacing** Cut pieces of interfacing exactly to size of garment area, excluding seam turnings. To do this, either trim off or fold back seam turnings on pattern before cutting out interfacing, or cut interfacing to pattern and then trim off 1.5 cm/⅝ in, plus an extra 2 mm/1/16 in. Position interfacing on WS of garment and work rows of diagonal basting up and down almost to edges, as for lightweight interfacing.

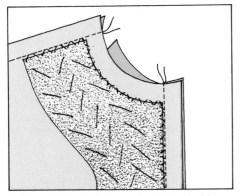

**2.** Trim away interfacing so that it lies inside any corners. Work catch stitch round the edges of the interfacing that lie against garment turnings. Baste and machine garment sections. The stitching should fall just beyond the edge of the interfacing to prevent bulky seams.

## IRON-ON, OR FUSIBLE, INTERFACING

Quick to insert, iron-on interfacing is now available in a wide range of weights to suit all fabrics from chiffon to tweed. There are also stretch iron-on interfacings for use with jersey and other soft, stretchy fabrics. Most are non-woven and, provided the correct weight is used for the fabric, they are all excellent and produce a crisp finish. Experiment first on a piece of the garment fabric as iron-on interfacing becomes slightly stiffer when attached.

If, on the test piece, a line is visible at the edge of the interfacing, use a lighter weight or, if already using the lightest, attach interfacing to the facing. This is less satisfactory because it is the garment, not the facing, that needs support. Alternatively, try attaching the finest weight of interfacing to both garment and facing. This solution is particularly successful on collars made in flimsy or sheer fabrics where trimmed turnings may otherwise show through the fabric.

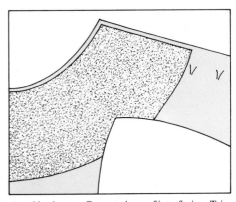

**Attaching iron-on** Cut out pieces of interfacing. Trim 3 mm/⅛ in off outer edges of interfacing to prevent it extending beyond garment edge and sticking to pressing surface. Place garment piece WS up and interfacing with adhesive side down on fabric. Using a medium iron, press interfacing firmly for three seconds; do not use moisture. Continue to press in sections until interfacing adheres to the fabric.

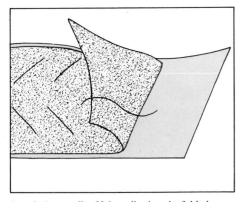

**Interfacing a collar** If the collar is to be folded, use a lighter weight of interfacing than for a flat area. Attach interfacing to WS of under-collar.

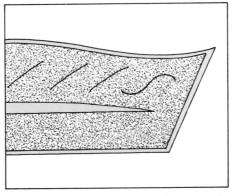

**2.** Firm non-woven interfacing may be bulky at the fold of a collar. To achieve a good roll line, press collar along fold and then cut away an oval slit in the interfacing on the fold line. At its widest point the slit should be about 3 mm/⅛ in wide, and it should extend to within 1 cm/⅜ in of the edges.

**TIPS**
- When interfacing an area for which no specific pattern piece is provided, mark the extent of the interfacing on the pattern of the garment section and cut from that. Try to avoid darts and other shaped areas.
- If the interfaced area is to be folded, as for example on collars or cuffs, use a slightly lighter weight interfacing than for flat areas such as pockets or single cuffs.
- If the interfaced areas prove difficult to handle, the interfacing is probably too heavy for the fabric. Unfortunately, the only remedy is to remove it and insert a lighter one.
- Before deciding on interfacing check that it can be washed or dry cleaned as required and check whether it will shrink.
- For future reference, note which type and weight of interfacing you have found suitable for use with different fabrics.

# Shaping

Pattern pieces are shaped so that, when they are joined, the garment fits the curves of the figure. Additional shaping is often needed within the pattern pieces to arrange or to take up fullness as a style feature or in order to accommodate parts of the body. Fullness is controlled by various methods, the amount of fullness allowed depending on the figure, the style of garment and the fabric.

Suitable for any fabric, darts, or tapering folds of fabric, are often used to arrange fullness. With correct adjustment, they give a smooth and comfortable fit.

Tucks, or parallel folds of fabric, can, if short, provide fullness. They can also be stitched over an entire area, as on a skirt or on the bodice of a dress, to give a purely decorative effect.

Fullness can also be controlled or created by gathers. The excess fabric is wrinkled or gathered up along the edge before the seam is made and the gathered part of the garment hangs loosely over the body. Several rows of gathering can be worked to produce different effects such as shirring, gauging or waffling, which may be decorative rather than functional. Use synthetic thread for all processes where threads are to be pulled or where there will be strain, as in shirring.

Frills and ruffles can also provide fullness, but usually only as an attractive style feature.

*A variety of ruffs modelled by some of the members of the Somerset House Conference of 1662. Surely the most uncomfortable of all fashions, these neck ornaments were made from layers of tightly gathered, stiffened linen frills.*

*Tailored chic was the hallmark of women's clothes in the late 1930s. An unusual feature of this 1937 autumn costume, below, is the reversal of the waist darts so that they both shape the jacket and provide decorative interest.*

*Shirring, the regular, repeated gathering of material with narrow elastic, can be used to shape an entire garment, like this elegant, clinging evening gown or, as is more usual, to define waists, wrists and yokes.*

*Softly flounced lacy frills, décolletages and shaped bodices characterized the indulgent ultra-feminine dresses of the 18th century. The fashion was set by Marie Antoinette, the subject of this painting by Mme Vigée-Lebrun.*

## DARTS

The size of the pocket of fullness at the point of a dart depends on the width of the fold of fabric at the base. Small, or narrow, darts are used where only a little shape is needed, as at shoulders or elbows, while wider darts create fullness at the bust or bottom.

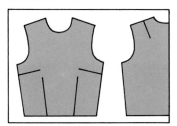

*Above left, bust and front waist darts; above right, shoulder darts.*

On garments without a waist seam the fullness can be controlled by a double-ended dart that is wide at the middle but runs to points at each end. If fullness has to be taken out as a curve, fit and cut dart before stitching.

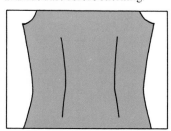

*Double-ended darts*

All darts should be as inconspicuous as possible. Very small ones, which may make a visible ridge if pressed to one side, may be balanced by sewing a piece of fabric into the dart.

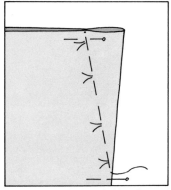

**Standard** Mark the stitching lines of the dart with tailor's tacks and fold fabric RS together with marked lines meeting. Insert two pins to hold the dart—one just beyond the point. Baste on stitching line from base to slightly beyond the point and remove pin at base.

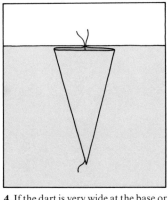

**4.** If the dart is very wide at the base or if it makes a noticeable ridge on the garment, press it so that the fabric lies evenly on each side of the stitching.

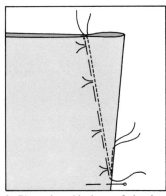

**2.** Place the wide base of the dart under the machine with the point directly in front of the foot. Stitch slowly beside basting from base to point, ending exactly on the fold. Reverse along fold to fasten ends or leave ends to sew in later. Remove basting and tailor's tacks and take out second pin.

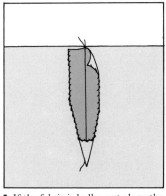

**5.** If the fabric is bulky, cut along the fold of the dart, almost to the point, after stitching. Trim and neaten the raw edges by hand. It is hardly worth using the machine for sewing such a short distance.

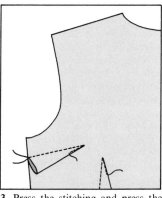

**3.** Press the stitching and press the dart to one side with the bulk pressed either downwards or towards the centre of the garment, depending on the pattern piece.

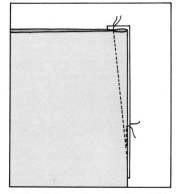

**6.** Small darts that may be visible from RS when pressed can be made even. Fold and baste the dart in the usual way. Place a piece of straight seam tape or a piece of selvedge from some lining fabric under the dart and stitch dart and tape together. To balance the dart, press the dart to one side and the tape to the other.

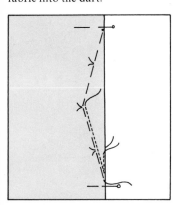

**Double-ended** Mark the dart as for standard dart. Fold fabric RS together matching the tacks. Insert a pin at each end of the dart beyond points and one at the centre. Baste, remove centre pin and press dart if fabric is springy. Starting at the centre, machine to one point reversing along fold. Turn the work round.

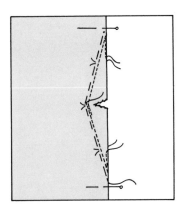

**2.** Overlapping the first stitching, stitch from the centre to the other point, reversing along fold. Remove tailor's tacks, pins and basting. Press dart, WS up, as two separate darts. Snip the fold at the centre of the dart and neaten the cut edges with loop stitch or overcasting. Press finished dart firmly.

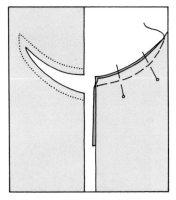

**Curved** As two curved edges have to be joined, this dart cannot be folded in the usual way. Mark seam lines of dart and cut away the centre, leaving 1.5 cm/⅝ in seam turnings. Place cut edges RS together and pin the dart, matching seam lines and lifting the fabric as you pin. Baste the seam. Remove pins.

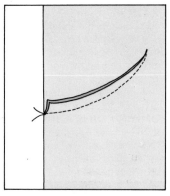

**2.** Place under machine and stitch slowly from base to point. Remove basting. Press stitching flat and then press both edges upwards. Trim edges to 5 mm/¼ in and neaten. Press dart again.

# Shaping

## TUCKS

The style of garment and the type and amount of fabric available govern the width of tucks. The spacing between each tuck depends on the effect desired in the finished garment.

Short, or released, tucks are a useful method of providing fullness on children's clothes and maternity wear. The amount of fullness required determines the size and number. Pin tucks are very narrow tucks, ideal for dainty garments in fine fabrics such as lingerie or baby clothes. Narrow tucks can also be made on the machine using the pin tuck foot and twin needle. These are purely decorative and do not provide fullness.

If a complete section, such as a yoke or cuffs, is to be tucked and tucks are not allowed for in the pattern, make the tucks on a large piece of fabric and then cut out the appropriate pattern piece.

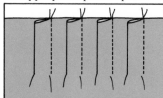

*Released tucks*

 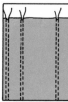

*Pin tucks*          *Machine tucks*

## GATHERS

Areas such as the shoulder, cuff, yoke or waist can have gathers set into them to introduce fullness. Gathers also allow for growth. The amount of gathering and of extra fabric needed depends on the fabric. Experiment first.

Gathering threads can be inserted by hand or by machine, or fabric can be gathered automatically, in fixed amounts, with the gathering foot or ruffler.

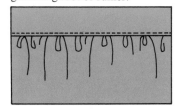

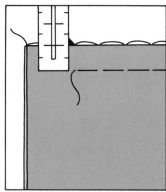

**Wide** To mark the centre of the first tuck, work a row of small basting stitches exactly on the straight grain of the fabric. Fold fabric WS together with basting on fold. Using an adjustable marker, measure required width of tuck. Mark stitching line and baste along it through both layers of fabric.

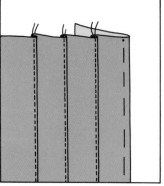

**Pin** Mark centre of first tuck as for wide tucks. Fold fabric WS together and baste about 3 mm/⅛ in from fold. Press lightly. Stitch right on the fold with a straight or zigzag machine stitch, running stitch, or a hand or machine embroidery stitch. Remove basting and press. Work the following tucks in the same way.

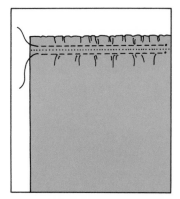

**Gathering** To insert gathering threads by hand, take pieces of thread longer than the edge to be gathered. Knot one end. Work two parallel rows of running or fly-running, one slightly below seam line and one above. Leave thread ends of each row free. Do not make the rows too long; work in sections on a long edge.

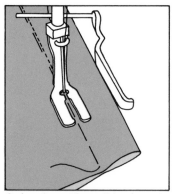

**2.** Attach machine quilting foot with adjustable bar. Adjust the end of the bar to the width of the fold and, using it as a guide, stitch the tuck. Alternatively, use the ordinary foot and hold the adjustable marker just in front of the foot to act as a stitching guide.

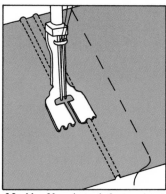

**Machine** Use pin tuck foot and twin needle with two reels of thread. Work a row of basting on straight grain of fabric as a guide for straight stitching. Stitch tuck on RS with edge of foot on basting. Move fabric so that stitched tuck fits under one of grooves on foot and machine second and subsequent tucks. Remove basting.

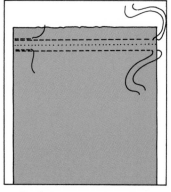

**2.** To insert gathering threads by machine, adjust machine to largest straight stitch. Reverse to anchor the thread and on RS machine two parallel rows on either side of seam line. Use a different coloured thread in the bobbin to distinguish it from that in the needle. Leave long ends of thread for pulling up the gathers.

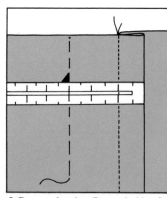

**3.** Remove basting. Press stitching flat and press tuck to one side. Note the tuck width and use the marker to mark a line indicating the centre of the next tuck, placing it at the desired distance from the previous one. Fold fabric and baste and stitch second and subsequent tucks as for first tuck.

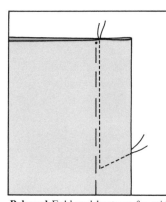

**Released** Fold and baste as for wide tucks with RS together. Stitch from raw edge to release point (end of tuck). Lift machine foot, turn fabric slightly and lower foot. Stitch across to fold at an angle. Repeat for subsequent tucks. Remove basting. Press tucks to one side or evenly on each side of stitching.

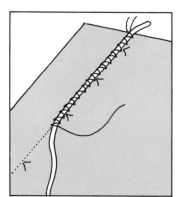

**3.** Alternatively, set the machine to a medium to wide zigzag. Feed a thick thread, such as buttonhole or fine crochet cotton, under the foot and, using ordinary matching thread, stitch over this thread, with fabric WS up. Some machines have a feed hole in the needle plate through which to pass the thicker gathering thread.

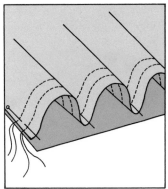

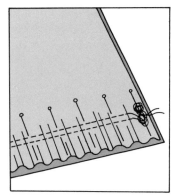

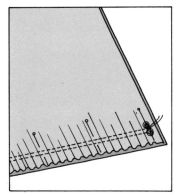

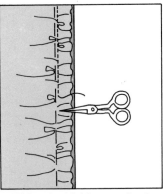

**4.** Mark centre of gathered edge and of flat piece to be joined to it. If gathered section is long, divide both edges into four or more sections. Mark centre and ends of each section with pins or chalk. With flat piece RS up and raw edge towards you, place gathered piece on top RS down. Match centres, ends and other marks and pin.

**5.** Grasp the ends of the gathering threads; if they have been inserted by machine, hold the bobbin threads. Do not pull them but gently ease the fabric along them. When gathers lie flat on top of ungathered edge, insert a pin across loose threads at end of gathers and wind threads round pin.

**6.** To even out the gathers, take hold of the fabric on either side of the gathering and tug sharply. Hold the two layers together by inserting a pin in the centre of the gathering and one at opposite end from pin anchoring threads. Insert more pins until each section is evenly divided. Even out gathers. Baste and remove pins.

**7.** With gathered side upwards, place fabric under machine. Stitch slowly, exactly on seam line and adjusting the gathers as they pass under the foot. Use points of small scissors to flatten or rearrange gathers and prevent them being folded in bunches. Remove basting and gathering threads.

## SHIRRING AND GAUGING

Two forms of functional and decorative gathering, shirring and gauging are used on areas such as bodices or cuffs. Shirring is worked in parallel rows with shirring elastic, which gathers the fabric as it is sewn. The gathering stretches in wear. Gauging gives the same outward effect, but as it is worked with normal thread it does not stretch. It is rather weak so the back must be covered.

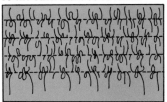

## WAFFLE

An attractive decoration for plain fabrics, waffle is suitable for yokes, sleeves and cushions. Use synthetic thread for strength. The gathering is slight; use the gathering foot or insert rows of gathering threads by hand or machine. Almost any fabric is suitable for waffling, but experiment first. It is best to work the waffling on a large piece of fabric and cut out the pattern piece afterwards.

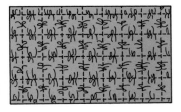

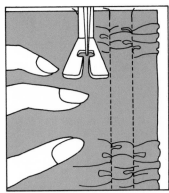

**Shirring** Mark area to be gathered. Using the bobbin winding mechanism on the machine, wind shirring elastic on to bobbin. Use synthetic thread on top. Set machine to a large straight stitch and sew on RS. (The first row may not gather at all.) Work subsequent rows using the side of the machine foot as a spacing guide.

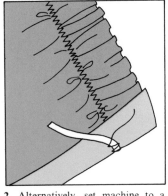

**2.** Alternatively, set machine to a medium zigzag stitch with synthetic thread top and bottom. Thread end of shirring elastic up through hole in needle plate. Place the reel of elastic on the floor so the elastic stretches slightly as it is machined down. The ends of elastic can be pulled up to tighten the shirring.

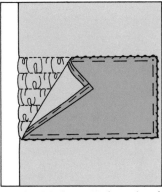

**Gauging** Mark area to be gathered. Using normal thread, work parallel rows of gathering. Pull up bobbin threads evenly and sew them in on WS. Cut a piece of lining fabric or soft cotton to the size of the gathered area and baste it to WS. Turn in raw edges and baste. Slip hem all round and remove basting.

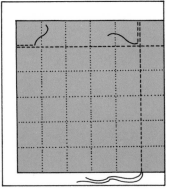

**Waffle** Mark area of fabric to be gathered on RS with horizontal and vertical rows of chalk dots. Insert gathers by hand or by machine, with large straight stitch, on RS along vertical rows and then horizontal. Reverse at the start of each row to anchor the threads and leave long threads at ends.

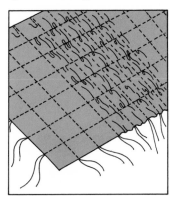

**2.** When all the rows are gathered, take hold of one set of threads (the bobbin ones if gathers were inserted by machine) and ease the fabric along them. Pull the threads up the desired amount and then pull the other set to balance.

### TIPS
● Work parallel rows of tucks, gathers, shirring, gauging and waffling in the same direction on the fabric.
● To judge how much material you will need for a gathering process, measure a small piece of fabric and try out the process. Re-measure fabric to see how much fabric has been taken up.
● When joining seams, stitch with the gathered piece uppermost so that you can keep a check on the gathering.
● Hold a newly shirred area in the steam of boiling water for a few seconds to shrink the elastic and give it more grip.

# Shaping

## ELASTIC

Lengths of elastic can be used to control fullness and can be substituted for cuffs on long sleeves. The elastic is inserted along an edge that is sewn to form a casing. Buy the elastic before stitching the edge to ensure that the casing is the correct size. Check the elastic is a suitable colour and that it is pre-shrunk and can be boiled if necessary. Fine fabric is adequately held by narrow elastic, but heavier fabric needs a wider type. If the elastic is to be threaded through bought binding, buy elastic of correct width to fit the binding.

If you decide to use an elastic finish instead of cuffs after cutting out and you are short of material, make a casing of lining fabric or bought bias binding.

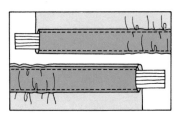

*Integrated casing, top, and separate casing, above.*

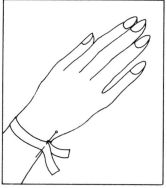

**Elastic sleeve finish** Measure elastic round wrist. Pull up a little, but not too much as allowance must be made for the thickness of the fabric. Pin elastic round wrist and leave it on for half an hour to check it is comfortable before cutting. Adding 1 cm/⅜ in for joining the ends together, cut the elastic to length.

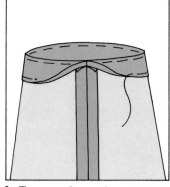

**2.** Turn up sleeve edge to length required and baste on fold. Press. Trim raw edge if necessary and turn under to form a casing the depth of the elastic width plus 4 mm/⅛ in for ease and the extra bulk and another 2 mm/1/16 in to allow for stitching. Baste, leaving an opening at seam line to insert elastic. Press.

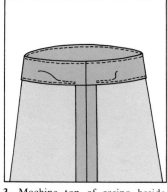

**3.** Machine top of casing beside basting with a straight stitch or small zigzag. Should an additional row of machining be required at the sleeve edge, allow an extra 2 mm/1/16 in on the casing depth. Press stitching and casing and remove basting.

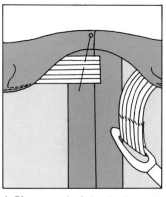

**4.** Pin one end of the elastic to the garment at the opening of the casing. Stitch the eye of an elastic threader to the other end of the elastic and thread the elastic through the casing to emerge at the opening. Alternatively, insert elastic with a bodkin; tie elastic in the grooves at one end of the bodkin before inserting in casing.

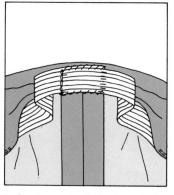

**5.** Overlap ends of elastic and pin. Check elastic is not twisted within the casing. Oversew overlapping sides of elastic. Remove pin and loop stitch raw ends of overlap. Pull elastic inside and prick stitch up opening of casing.

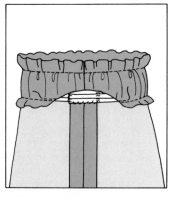

**Frilled edge** Turn up casing as for elastic sleeve finish, allowing extra fabric below the casing for the frill. Machine along top and bottom of casing. Insert elastic and finish as in previous method.

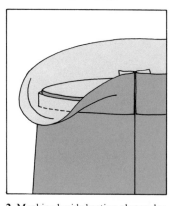

**Separate casing** is cut from binding or a crossways strip of lining or self-fabric. Calculate depth as in elastic sleeve finish method. Place binding or lining strip RS down on RS of sleeve edge with ends extending just beyond either side of sleeve seam. Baste to sleeve edge and fold back ends to meet at seam. Press folds and baste down.

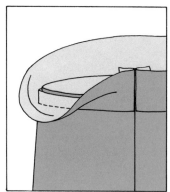

**2.** Machine beside basting along edge and ends. Remove basting. With RS of work uppermost, press seam of binding and sleeve downwards so that binding extends below sleeve edge.

**3.** With WS of sleeve towards you, roll binding over to WS so the join lies just over the sleeve edge on WS. Baste along edge on WS and press. For a frilled edge, roll the binding and join farther over to give desired depth of frill before basting.

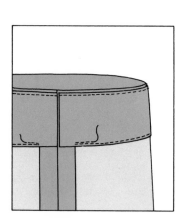

**4.** Turn under raw edge of binding and baste, leaving an opening to insert elastic. Press. Machine beside basting with a straight or small zigzag stitch. If desired, work a second row of stitching at sleeve edge, or at casing bottom if frilled edge. Remove all basting. Insert elastic and finish as for elastic sleeve finish.

## FRILLS

Frills can be made in most fabrics, other than bulky ones, and can be in matching or contrasting material. The amount of fullness depends on the fabric. Half as much again as the garment edge gives a slight gathering effect; twice as much provides a very gathered frill. The depth of the frill depends on its position. For example, a neck frill should not extend past the shoulders.

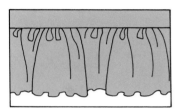

## RUFFLES

A decorative finish on necklines and cuffs, a ruffle is a piece of fabric cut in such a way that the outer edge is longer than the inner. This causes the ruffle to flute decoratively when attached. Make ruffles in fine fabrics so that they are not too bulky.

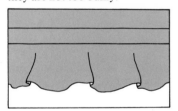

**Frills** Make frills from a straight piece of fabric. For skirt or sleeve frills, join ends to form a circle. Hem outer edge. Insert two rows of gathers along other edge. Pin frill to garment edge, RS together. Pull up gathers to fit. Baste and machine frill down. Remove basting and gathers. Neaten edges. Press frill away from garment.

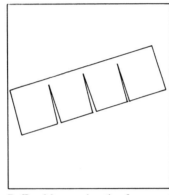

**Ruffles** Measure length of garment edge. Cut a piece of paper to that length by the approximate width of the ruffle. Fold the paper into equal squares. Open paper out and cut along each fold from one edge of the paper almost to the other.

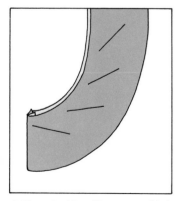

**4.** For a double ruffle, cut two fabric pieces and baste, RS together, along the outer edge. Machine beside basting and trim edges to 3 mm/⅛ in. Turn through until WS are together and join is right on edge. Press outer edge of ruffle and diagonally baste inner raw edges together.

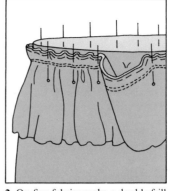

**2.** On fine fabrics make a double frill for extra body. Cut and join pieces as in previous method, but make the frill twice the finished depth. Fold frill WS together and press. Baste raw edges together. Insert two rows of gathering threads through both layers and attach to garment edge in the same way as a single frill.

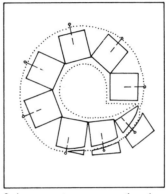

**2.** Arrange cut paper on another piece of paper, spreading out the cut sections. Draw round the outlines of the first piece of paper and cut along the drawn line; if the ruffle is to end in a point, trim off a corner. Use this cut shape as a pattern to cut out a piece of fabric for the ruffle.

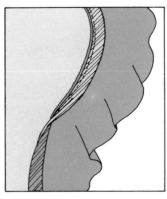

**5.** If the ruffle is to lie back on the garment, place hemmed ruffle RS up on RS of garment. Lay bias strip RS down on raw edge of ruffle. Baste and stitch through all layers. Remove basting. Fold strip over trimmed seam edges so they are encased. On WS hem neatened strip edge into machining. Press bias strip and fill.

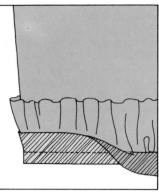

**3.** If the frill is to lie back on the garment, place hemmed frill RS up on RS of garment. Lay bias strip RS down on raw edge of frill. Baste and stitch through all layers. Remove basting. Fold strip over trimmed seam edges so that they are encased. On WS hem neatened strip edge into machining.

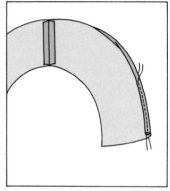

**3.** Join pieces if necessary to give the correct length for the garment edge. For skirt or sleeve ruffle, join ends to form a circle. Turn up a narrow rolled hem on the outer edge of the ruffle and hold it down by machining or by working whip stitch along it.

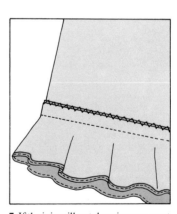

**6.** If the ruffle is to extend from the garment, attach it with a facing or a bias strip. Baste ruffle to garment, RS together. Baste bias strip or facing RS down on top of ruffle and machine through all layers. Remove basting. Take bias strip or facing to WS; hem bias into machining and hold down facing in usual way.

**7.** If the join will not show in wear, as at the end of a tight sleeve or the bottom of a skirt, attach the ruffle direct to the garment, RS together. Trim raw edges and neaten together. Press neatened edges into garment.

# Facings

A facing is a method of neatening an edge such as a neckline or armhole by applying a piece of fabric to one side of the edge and turning it completely to the other side. It is often called a shaped facing because one edge is cut to the same shape as the garment edge. The facing is usually finished on the wrong side of the garment and is invisible. If turned to the right side, it becomes decorative, but good results are difficult to achieve.

For best results with invisible facings, cut them from the garment material if the fabric is light- or medium-weight, but from lining material, nylon jersey or thin cotton if the garment material is bulky. Make decorative facings in any fabric of contrasting colour, pattern or texture, or in self-fabric.

Facings are sometimes in one piece, but more often are in several pieces that are joined, for neatness, in places corresponding to the garment seams. If short of material, join pieces to form a large facing piece, but in decorative facings make sure the joins fall at garment seams.

Before applying facing, stitch, neaten and press as many garment seams as possible and mark the seam turnings on the garment edges clearly and accurately. Seam turnings on facings need be marked only if the facing is decorative. Interface any areas that need support or will undergo strain before facing. To ensure that the facings lie flat, and to prevent stretching, always attach facing pieces to the garment before joining them. Basic processes, such as interfacing and joining, which apply to all facing methods, are dealt with fully in the basic shaped facing method.

## LAYERING AND SNIPPING FACINGS

Eliminate bulk in seams and help facings to lie flat by layering the edges and then snipping them. Trim interfacing, if used, very close to stitching; trim raw edge of facing to 3 mm/⅛ in. Trim garment edge to 5 mm/¼ in. Cut off corners diagonally close to stitching. If edge is concave

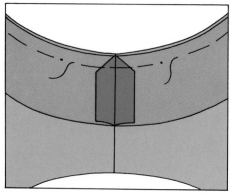

and fabric bulky, snip out small V-shapes every 5 mm/¼ in. On convex edges snip almost down to machining every 5 mm/¼ in.

*Concave, left, and convex, right, seen from WS*

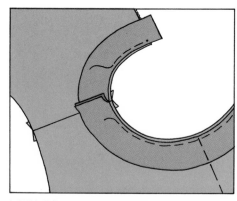

**Basic shaped facing** Used to finish curved edges such as necklines and armholes. If interfacing is needed, interface before facing. Cut out interfacing using facing pattern pieces. Trim 5 mm/¼ in from outer edge of each piece of interfacing to ensure that it will not extend beyond the finished edge of the facings. Diagonally baste interfacing to WS of garment.

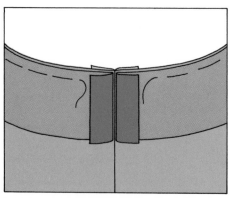

**3.** Make sure the facing is lying flat. Lightly press back all the unstitched facing ends so that the folds of each adjacent pair meet exactly over the garment seam line beneath them. These turnings may not be equal in depth if an alteration has been made or the facing has stretched.

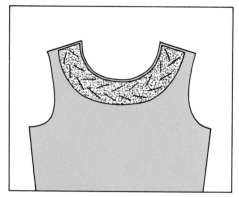

**5.** Press joins open and finish basting the facing to the garment by stitching across them.

**2.** With RS together, place facing pieces in position on garment, matching shaped edges. Insert a few pins to hold. Baste along seam line finishing 2 cm/¾ in away from any joins that have to be made in the facing. On a neckline with a zip at the centre back, baste to the end. (The turning of 1.5 cm/⅝ in on the facing extends beyond the zip.) Remove pins.

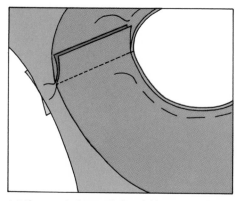

**4.** Lift pressed edges and place folds together. Insert one pin centrally across folds if fabric is slippery or springy. Baste along fold lines and remove pin. Keeping join away from garment, machine or backstitch along fold line. Remove basting. Trim turnings to 5 mm/¼ in and trim off corners at seam edge diagonally.

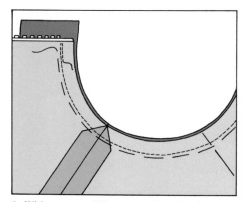

**6.** With garment WS up, machine slowly along marked seam line rather than on basting, which may not be accurate. On a neckline with a zip, start just inside zip, reverse for a few stitches, then sew forward. Stop frequently to turn work and guarantee a smooth curve. Lift work to make sure seams lie flat and face in the right direction and that facing joins are open and flat. Finish by reversing for a few stitches.

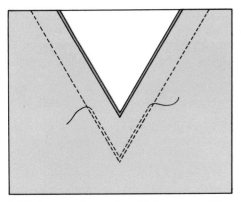

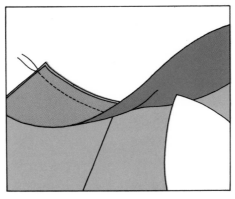

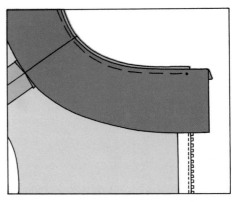

**7.** Work a second row of machining on top of first row round a sharp curve or at the point of a V-neck to prevent the fraying that will otherwise occur when this area is later snipped. Remove basting.

**8.** Place garment on sleeve board RS down. Press stitching flat, taking care not to distort the shaping of the edge. With RS up, slide iron under facing and run toe round join, lifting facing up vertically. Finish off, using the method outlined in the layering and snipping panel. For a V-neck, snip from point at outer edge almost down to point of machining.

**9.** With WS of garment uppermost, turn facing to WS; hold fabric across join and roll facing between thumb and forefinger to bring join right out to edge. Baste, rolling facing $2\,mm/\frac{1}{16}$ in farther on to WS at each needle insertion so join does not show on RS. Baste about $2\,mm/\frac{1}{16}$ in from edge on fine fabrics, $4\,mm/\frac{1}{8}$ in on heavier ones. If basting is too close to edge it will not anchor facing, if too distant the join will roll back to RS.

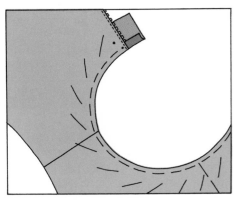

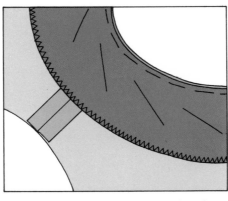

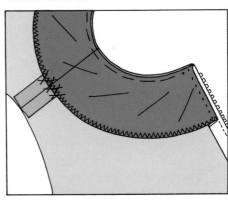

**10.** Press edge well on WS and RS. With RS of garment uppermost, hold faced edge over one hand to keep it in shape. Work a row of diagonal basting below edge to hold facing flat and in position.

**11.** On WS trim any fraying sections from lower edge of facing and neaten as for an open seam. A zig-zag machine stitch tends to straighten a curved edge, so press with a damp cloth or steam iron after stitching to flatten any flutes. When pressing, keep facing edge away from garment to avoid making an imprint on garment.

**12.** On WS attach facing to garment wherever facing edge crosses a seam. Use hemming stitches if facing edge has been turned under to neaten. Work herringbone stitch if facing edge is flat. For jersey fabric, which is likely to move during wear, lift facing edge and work a bar tack about $2\,mm/\frac{1}{16}$ in long between seam turning and facing. Turn under facing end by the zip and prick stitch folded edge to zip tape beside zip teeth. Remove basting.

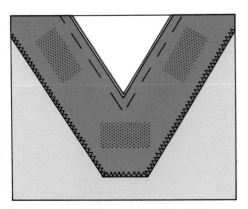

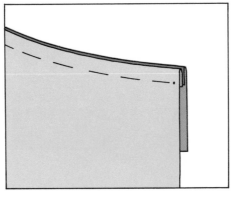

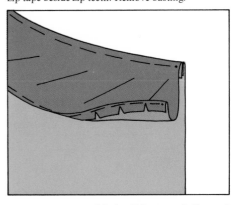

**13.** To anchor facing more securely—this is particularly important at armholes and V-necks—insert pieces of fabric adhesive strip between facing and garment. Cut pieces 2 to 2.5 cm/$\frac{3}{4}$ to 1 in long. Place garment WS up on sleeve board. Slip pieces of adhesive one at a time under facing every 2.5 to 4 cm/1 to 1$\frac{1}{2}$ in, or wherever the edge is very shaped or the fabric is springing up. Press well, using a damp cloth, to melt adhesive.

**Decorative facing** Follow (**1**) to (**8**) of basic method, but place facing RS down on WS of garment. Hold garment with WS up and turn facing over to RS. Roll edge between finger and thumb to reveal join and then roll it towards you until $2\,mm/\frac{1}{16}$ in of facing shows on WS of garment so that join is invisible on RS. Baste on WS with small stitches placed close to edge and press on WS and RS as for (**9**) and (**10**) of basic shaped facing method.

**2.** With garment and facing RS up, work diagonal basting beside top edge of facing. Mark hem turning on lower edge with tailor's chalk or a row of basting, measuring from top edge or following a pattern motif on the fabric. Turn in facing on marked line and baste it down beside fold. Trim raw edge to about 5 mm/$\frac{1}{4}$ in and snip any curves. Holding facing away from garment to avoid making an imprint, press turning along basting line. ▶

# Facings

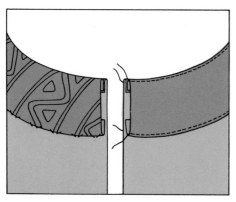

**3.** Baste facing flat to RS of garment. Finish by slip hemming, which may be preferable on patterned fabrics, or by machining with a straight or zigzag stitch along top and bottom edges. Alternatively, finish with a machine embroidery stitch along neck and facing edges. Remove all basting and press.

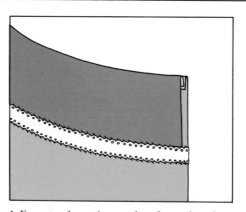

**4.** For extra decoration, mark or baste along hem turning as in (2) and trim fabric exactly on this line. Baste facing flat to garment and cover raw edge with braid. Baste braid in place, turn in ends and hem them down. Attach braid along both edges by hemming or machine stitching. For a shaped facing, choose a braid that will ease round the curves. Remove all basting and press.

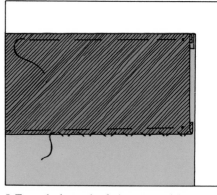

**5.** To apply decorative facing to a straight or nearly straight edge such as a hemline, cut strips of fabric on the bias or true cross and join to give required length. Baste to WS of garment with ends of strip joining over left side seam of skirt. Follow (3) to (8) of basic method. Roll facing over to RS as for standard decorative facing, baste and press. Hold down lower edge by any method suitable for the type and design of the fabric. Remove basting.

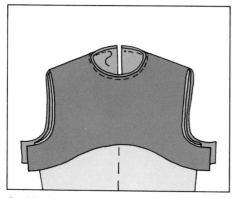

**Combination facing** If neck and armhole facings cut in the usual way will overlap at the shoulder, one large facing can be cut to combine the two if there is plenty of fabric. Pin facing pattern pieces together to correct shape before cutting out facing; the lower edge of the facing must curve upwards from the armhole to avoid restricting the shaping in the bust or back. Follow (1) to (9) of basic method, but do not join underarm seams of facing.

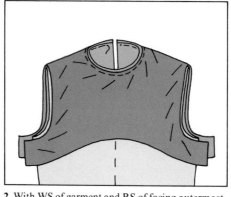

**2.** With WS of garment and RS of facing outermost, hold faced edge over one hand to keep it in shape. Work a row of diagonal basting round neck below edge to hold facing flat and in position against garment. Holding raw edges together, baste diagonally round armholes, but do not take basting too close to the edges.

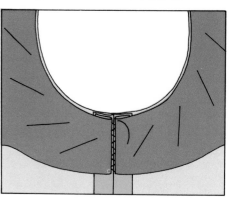

**3.** At underarm seam, turn in two facing edges to meet over seam. Slip stitch together.

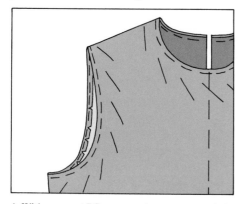

**4.** With garment RS out, turn in garment armhole edges along marked seam line. Baste along fold. Snip any curves using the method outlined in the layering and snipping panel. Press fold. If fabric is thick or springy, finish raw edges with herringbone stitch on WS.

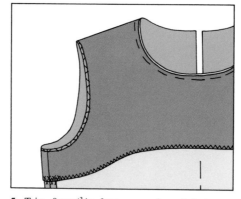

**5.** Trim 8 mm/$\frac{3}{8}$ in from raw edge of facing at armhole edge. Turn in trimmed edge to WS of facing so the fold is 2 mm/$\frac{1}{16}$ in from garment edge. This ensures that it is invisible during wear. Baste to garment and press. Finish by working hemming or felling stitch round armhole on WS. Neaten lower edge of facing. Where facing crosses underarm seam hold down with herringbone stitch. Remove all basting and press again.

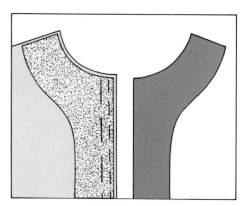

**Neckline with front opening: facing separate** Use this method if front edge is shaped or of contrasting fabric, or if loops or ties are used. If attaching interfacing, make sure centre front and seam lines are marked. Work first stages of piped or bound buttonholes; baste loops or ties in place. Follow (2) to (7) of basic method. When machining, start at bottom of centre front; continue round neck and down opposite centre front edge. Remove basting.

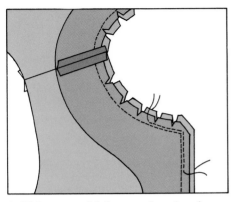

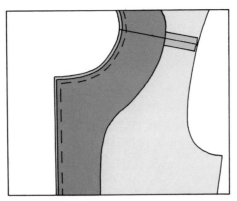

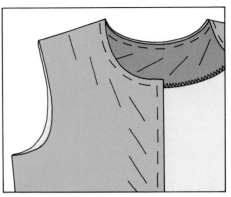

**2.** With garment RS down on sleeve board, press stitching flat. With RS up, slide iron under facing as far as possible and, lifting facing, run toe round join. Layer edges and snip neck edge, following method in layering and snipping panel. Do not snip front edge, unless it is curved (as for revers), because this will weaken it and may lead to an uneven appearance. Trim top corners at neck edge diagonally.

**3.** With WS of garment uppermost, roll facing to WS as for (**9**) of basic method so that join is 2 mm/$\frac{1}{16}$ in to WS. Baste close to edge. Work corner out by rolling it with the fingers or pushing it out with a collar point turner. Press edge well on WS and RS.

**4.** On RS of garment work a row of diagonal basting all round near edge. On WS neaten lower edge of facing and attach facing to shoulder seams with herringbone or hemming stitch, or a bar tack, as for (**11**) and (**12**) of basic method. Remove basting, unless buttonholes are to be worked or completed.

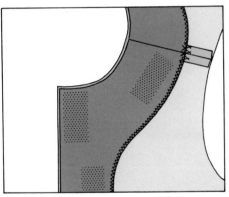

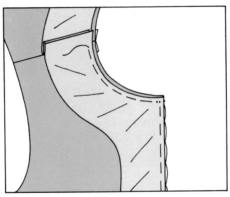

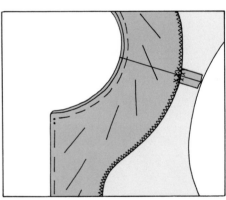

**5.** To prevent fraying, push a small piece of fabric adhesive into each corner of neckline front with a bodkin and press firmly. As for final stage of basic method, insert small pieces of adhesive strip between facing and garment at back of neck and in several places down front edges. Press well. If buttonholes are to be worked or completed, do not insert the adhesive until this has been done.

**Neckline with front opening: facing attached** To avoid bulky front-edge joins, cut front facings as garment extensions. Interface garment if desired. Mark centre front and seam lines. Work first stages of piped or bound buttonholes. Fold front facing to RS. Baste along fold and round neck and diagonally up front to within 2 cm/$\frac{3}{4}$ in of shoulder joins. Attach self-fabric back facing as for basic method (**2**).

**2.** Join back neck facing at shoulders to front facing, following (**3**) to (**9**) of basic method. With garment RS up, machine all round neck, reversing a few stitches at both centre front edges. Finish facing as for last three stages of front neck opening with separate facing.

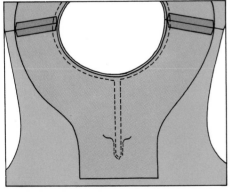

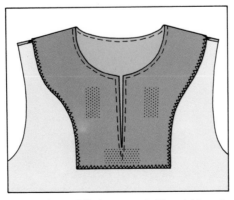

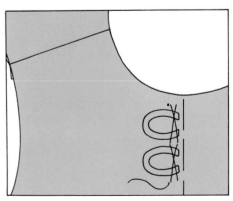

**Neckline with slit opening** Front facing extends 4 cm/1$\frac{1}{2}$ in below slit. Follow (**1**) and (**2**) of basic method, basting back neck and front facings in position. On WS of garment, mark position and depth of slit at centre front. Follow (**3**) to (**6**) of basic method, leaving 3 mm/$\frac{1}{8}$ in between lines of stitching down sides of slit and stitching to a point at its base. Work a second row of stitching round point. Remove basting. Press as for basic method (**8**).

**2.** Cut slit carefully between stitching right up to machining at point. Layer all edges and snip neck edges, following method in layering and snipping panel. Turn facing to WS and proceed as for basic method (**9**) to (**11**), attaching lower edge of facing at shoulder seams. Remove diagonal basting and insert short pieces of fabric adhesive on each side of opening and at corners as for final stage of front neck opening with separate facing. Remove basting and press well.

**3.** If ties or rouleau loops are to be used to fasten slit, position them on RS at centre front edge so that they face away from the slit. Baste them down before applying facing. Place facing over ties or loops and complete opening as above. As the facing is rolled to WS the loops or ties will extend beyond the edge. For loops, attach buttons on other side of slit.

# Waists

The position of the join between bodice and skirt varies with style and fashion from a high empire line to a low line on the hips. Whatever the style, the method of making a waist join is the same.

Fitting is particularly important in linking the bodice and skirt because the join must be in exactly the right place and neither too tight nor too loose. Patterns sometimes give instructions for joining the front of the bodice to the skirt front, the back of the bodice to the skirt back and then stitching the side seams from underarm to hem. This is a very unsatisfactory method, as the waist cannot be fitted properly.

Before making a waist join, make up the dress skirt except for the hem. Stitch the darts and seams in the bodice, but not the shoulder seams—the work is much easier to handle if these are left open. Leave openings of the correct length in both the skirt and the bodice for inserting the zip or any other fastening.

*The waist approximating to its natural position in an elegant late 1930s gown. Drawstrings create the sculptural effect. Photo by Hoyningen Huene.*

*At the beginning of the century, the waist fell to an all-time, just below the knee, low. The lovely, lively (but fictitious) Bessie McCoy stalked the pages of contemporary magazines, modelling the current fashions, and here she achieves the seemingly impossible task of walking in this 1905 model.*

*Waist elimination was the craze of the 1830s and ladies crammed themselves into stays, often by force, to achieve the desired spindliness. This rib-crushing fashion, deservedly much lampooned, as above, was probably the sole cause of that most genteel of 19th-century ailments, the vapours.*

*To achieve the empire line, the waist crept shyly upwards to nestle under the bosom. The style, which seems to evoke a professional innocence, was named for the Napoleonic ladies of the First Empire, but dates from earlier. This detail is from Carpaccio's Le Cortigiane, a 16th-century work.*

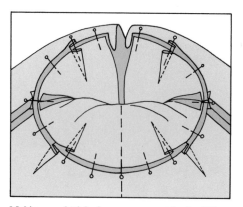

**Making a waist join** Arrange garment bodice RS up on a table with waist edge towards you. Place RS of skirt on top of bodice. Pin together at centre front and/or centre back, inserting pins vertically on WS of bodice. Match side seams and edges of opening and pin. Match any darts on skirt with those on bodice and pin; if such matching is impossible as a result of fitting adjustments, place darts evenly. Match all other fitting lines and pin.

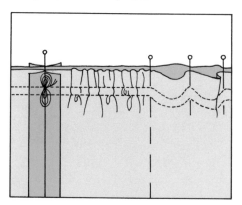

**2.** If a section or the entire length of the skirt, or both skirt and bodice, is to be gathered, insert two rows of gathering before pinning. Arrange bodice and skirt RS together as before and pin side seams, edges of opening and centre front and/or centre back, inserting pins vertically. Pull up gathering threads to fit and wind ends round pin. Insert extra pins round waist on gathered and ungathered joins, but use more, close together, if gathered.

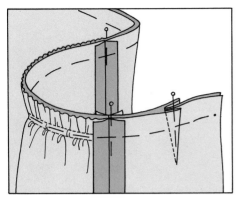

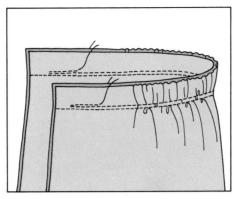

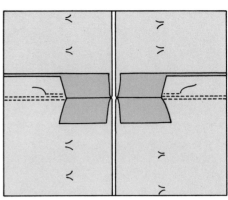

**3.** Baste all round waist with small stitches, working from the gathered side if appropriate, but from either side if both bodice and skirt are gathered. When basting across darts, make sure that they lie open or flat and face towards the centre. Remove all pins except those at seams and darts.

**4.** Machine waist join with gathers uppermost, stitching slowly over pins and making sure all darts remain in position. Remove pins. For additional strength, work a second row of stitching $2\,\mathrm{mm}/\frac{1}{16}\,\mathrm{in}$ above the first, starting and finishing $2\,\mathrm{cm}/\frac{3}{4}\,\mathrm{in}$ from opening. Reverse for a few stitches at each end. Remove basting and gathers. To prevent jersey fabric from stretching, stitch seam binding into the join on bodice side, as for taped seam.

**5.** Trim raw edges to $1\,\mathrm{cm}/\frac{3}{8}\,\mathrm{in}$. Snip into skirt turning close to machining, $2\,\mathrm{cm}/\frac{3}{4}\,\mathrm{in}$ from opening, and press seam open. This reduces bulk and makes the opening easier to finish.

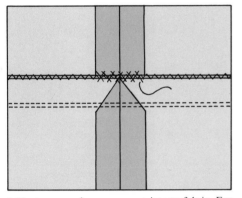

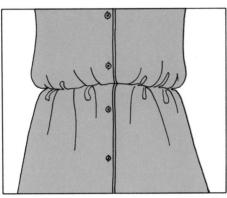

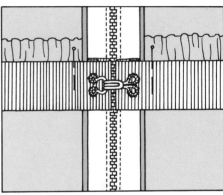

**6.** Neaten raw edges as appropriate to fabric. For fine fabrics, and garments that will be washed frequently, bind the edges, use a zigzag stitch, or work another row of machining and overcast. On WS press waist turnings up towards bodice. Press again on RS. At side seams hold waist join turnings in position with herringbone stitch.

**Stays** The appearance of a dress with a full skirt, or one made from fabric that is heavy or gives, is greatly improved by a stay inserted in the waist. A blouson dress needs a stay to lift the bodice so that the waist is in the correct position. If the dress is to be worn with a belt, a stay prevents the waist join from dropping and helps to ensure that the join remains invisible during wear.

**2.** Do not insert stay until dress is finished or zip has been put in. Cut curved or straight petersham (or, for fine fabrics, grosgrain ribbon), not wider than $2.5\,\mathrm{cm}/1\,\mathrm{in}$, to waist size, plus $3\,\mathrm{cm}/1\frac{1}{4}\,\mathrm{in}$. Turn in ends and attach hook and eye (see Fastenings panel). Press waist join up into bodice. With dress WS out and zip closed, pin fastened petersham to waist join on either side of zip, with top edge of petersham on waist join.

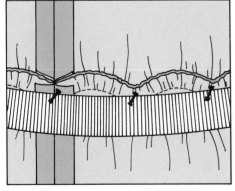

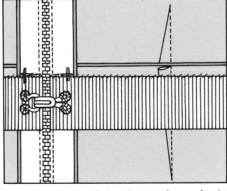

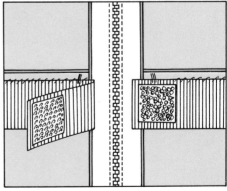

**3.** If the petersham is curved, place the concave edge on the waistline so the convex edge hangs below the waistline. In loose-fitting or gathered blouson dresses the waist join is longer than the petersham. Insert more pins at intervals round waist join so garment waist is evenly positioned along petersham. Attach petersham with bar tacks at intervals round the waist—at side seams, centre front or centre back and once between these points. Remove pins.

**4.** If the dress is close fitting, the petersham and waist join should be exactly the same length. After pinning at regular intervals, hold petersham firmly in place by hemming its top edge to turnings on waist join. On each side of zip finish hemming at edge of tape and work a strong bar tack to anchor petersham to tape, $2\,\mathrm{cm}/\frac{3}{4}\,\mathrm{in}$ from zip teeth. Remove pins.

**5.** For easy fastening at the centre back use two $2.5\,\mathrm{cm}/1\,\mathrm{in}$ pieces of Velcro rather than a hook and eye. Cut the petersham long enough to allow for the Velcro overlap (see Fastenings panel). Attach one piece of Velcro to underside, or underlap, of petersham, the other to overlap. Hold overlap down with a bar tack $5\,\mathrm{cm}/2\,\mathrm{in}$ from edge of zip tape. When fastening the dress, do up the stay before the zip.

# Waists

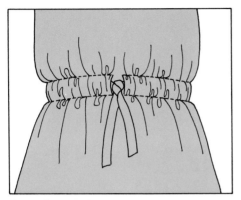

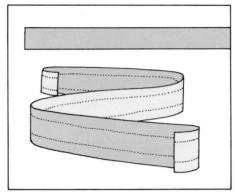

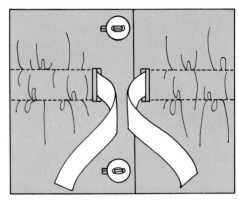

**Drawstring waistline** A casing—a length of fabric through which a tie or elastic is threaded—applied to RS or WS of a garment can be used instead of a waist join. The tie can be contrasting or self-fabric rouleau, a flat tie belt, cord, twisted or plaited wool, crochet, macramé or elastic with fabric tie ends. On a lined garment, make the casing by working two rows of stitching through the fabric and lining at the required distance apart.

**2.** For the casing width, measure width of tie insertion, allowing for its thickness, and then add 5 mm/$\frac{1}{4}$ in for ease and 3 cm/$1\frac{1}{2}$ in for turnings. For casing length, add 5 cm/2 in for turnings to garment waistline measurement. Cut a strip or strips of fabric, preferably on the cross but on the straight grain if there is insufficient material, and join to make up correct length. For a casing on WS of garment bought bias binding may be used.

**3.** If drawstring is to emerge on RS of garment, work two large vertical buttonholes on the garment before attaching casing. Make them slightly narrower than width of casing and place 2.5 cm/1 in apart or, if the garment opening is fastened with buttons, far enough for opening to lie flat. The buttonholes may be worked by machine, but on medium-weight or good-quality material piped buttonholes give the best finish.

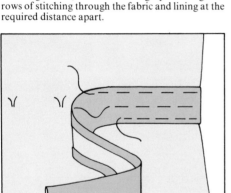

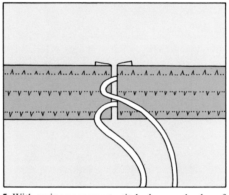

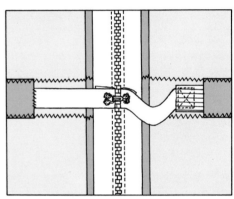

**4.** For a casing on WS of garment, mark garment waistline on WS with a row of basting or tailor's tacks. Centre casing, RS up, over marking and baste along centre. Turn in raw edge 1.5 cm/$\frac{5}{8}$ in on one side of casing and baste down. Using an adjustable marker, turn in 1.5 cm/$\frac{5}{8}$ in allowance on other side and baste. Turn in ends to meet, or turn them in at edges of zip tape or just behind worked buttonholes.

**5.** With casing uppermost, stitch along each edge of casing. A straight stitch may look crooked on RS of garment so use a small zigzag or blind hem stitch for a neater look, especially on plain fabrics. For an attractive effect, stitch again through the centre of the finished casing to allow space for two fine cord or rouleau ties. Remove basting and insert ties.

**6.** Attach casing for elastic before inserting zip or finishing opening. Position casing, turn in edges and baste as in (**4**). Turn in ends 5 cm/2 in from opening and baste. Machine along both edges to opening. Remove basting. Insert zip or finish opening. Cut elastic to fit waist and attach 5 cm/2 in of cotton tape to ends with machining. Thread elastic into casing and hem tape to casing to anchor ends. Turn in tape ends, hem and attach hook and eye.

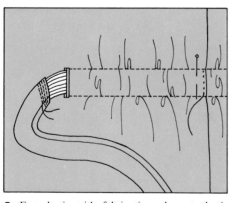

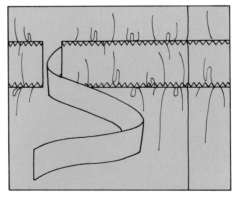

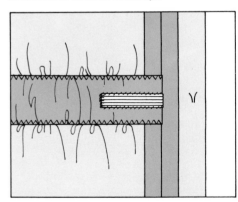

**7.** For elastic with fabric tie ends, cut elastic slightly shorter than waist and make a length of rouleau. Turn rouleau RS out, slot ends of elastic inside and machine across ends of rouleau several times to hold elastic. Slot elastic into casing, put on garment, arrange gathers and pin at side seams. Remove garment and prick stitch from RS through garment and elastic at side seams. Remove pins. Arrange gathers for all drawstring waists in this way.

**8.** For a casing applied to RS of garment, a strip cut on the cross often improves the design, as with checked fabric. Any joins in the casing should correspond with garment seams. Fold under turnings on casing sides and baste casing to waist join, with RS up. Turn in ends so they are 1 cm/$\frac{3}{8}$ in apart. Machine along both edges of casing using matching or contrasting thread and straight, zigzag or embroidery stitch. Remove basting. Insert tie.

**9.** If casing is applied to only part of a garment, such as round the back of the waist, cut casing and baste in position as in (**4**) and turn in ends. Machine casing sides and remove basting. If elastic is to be threaded through casing, allow enough to turn back over casing and hem sides and loop stitch raw ends of elastic firmly in position.

The method of completing the waist edge of a skirt or a pair of trousers depends largely on practical considerations such as figure shape, the strength required and the bulk of the fabric.

Many people find a waistband restricting, and a soft, more comfortable waist can be created by turning in the edge of the garment and adding tape, ribbon or, more usually, petersham. Petersham comes as a ribbon in different widths or as fabric. The fabric variety may be soft or boned, straight or curved. Curved petersham that fits slightly below the waist is often more comfortable than straight as it does not ride up during wear. Whichever petersham you choose should be washable and no wider than 4 cm/$1\frac{1}{2}$ in or it will curl up.

Stitch the petersham in place after the waist edge has been turned in, not before, or the petersham will quickly work itself out again. Because the edge of petersham is stiff to sew, use a very small needle and synthetic thread and hem into each bead at the petersham edge. Petersham is also used for stiffening straight and curved waistbands.

For the best results do not use the waistband piece provided by the pattern. Instead, establish the waistband length by measuring your waist and allowing for turnings and any overlap. Calculate the width according to personal taste, the style of the garment and the amount of fabric available. Do not cut out the waistband until you are ready to make it.

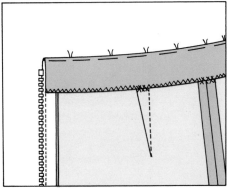

**Petersham waist finish** Insert zip into garment. Turn top edge of garment to WS along marked waistline above zip. Baste along fold. Press, taking care to avoid stretching. Neaten raw edge with overcasting or zigzag. Where edge crosses a dart or a seam hold it in place with herringbone stitch. At the zip hem ends down and across zip tape and turnings.

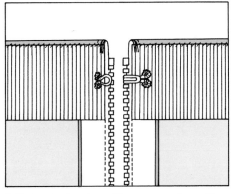

**3.** Baste petersham in position, remove pins and hem top edge to garment. Anchor ends of top edge of petersham on each side of zip with a bar tack into zip tape. Remove basting. Press.

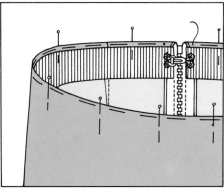

**2.** Cut petersham ribbon or petersham (curved or straight, soft or boned) to the waist length plus 3 cm/$1\frac{1}{4}$ in. Turn in 1.5 cm/$\frac{5}{8}$ in at ends and attach a hook and eye so petersham fits waist when fastened (see Fastenings panel). Fasten zip. With garment RS out, slip fastened petersham inside waist with hook and eye under zip. With top edge of petersham 2 mm/$\frac{1}{16}$ in below waist edge, pin on each side of zip. Pin all round from RS to ease any fullness.

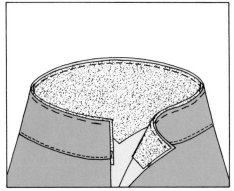

**Faced waistband** On casual clothes and those with yokes a soft waistline finish can be created with a facing. Baste interfacing to WS of waist area, over the yoke if there is one. Make up garment. Insert zip.

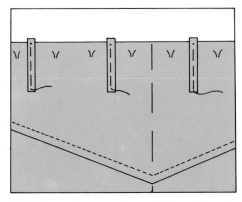

**2.** If belt carriers are a feature of the style, make them up and baste in position on RS of garment up to raw edge of waist, basting along full length of each carrier to prevent ends from being caught in subsequent stitching. Alternatively, hold them in position with transparent adhesive tape. The minimum number of carriers should be one at each side seam, two at the back and two at the front.

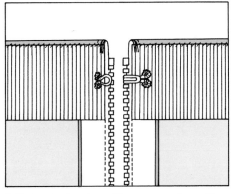

**3.** Place waist facing, which may be as large as the yoke, RS down on RS of garment. Baste and make joins as for other facings. Machine along seam line with garment uppermost. Remove basting. Layer as for facings, trimming turnings to no less than 3 mm/$\frac{1}{8}$ in on fine fabrics or 5 mm/$\frac{1}{4}$ in on thicker ones. Do not snip. On soft or jersey fabrics prevent stretching by inserting seam binding on WS of garment into waist join, as for taped seam.

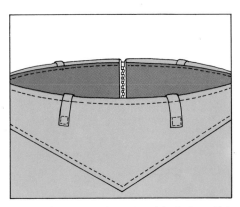

**4.** Roll facing to WS so that join is 2 mm/$\frac{1}{16}$ in towards inside of waist edge. Baste close to join. Press. The belt carriers now extend from join. Bring them over to RS, turn ends under and baste down. Stitch carriers in a square, hemming round three sides and working prick or stab stitch, depending on the fabric, across top of square. Remove basting. For a decorative effect, machine round carriers or work a row of top stitching round waist.

# Waists

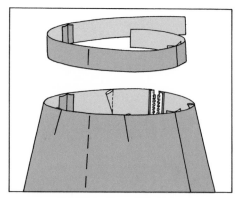

**Straight waistband** Cut a length of stiffening—petersham or petersham ribbon, or firm or pelmet interfacing—to size of waist, plus at least 7.5 cm/3 in to allow for an overlapping or underlapping extension. Cut fabric waistband twice the width of the stiffening, plus turnings and 3 cm/1¼ in longer than it, if possible on lengthways grain of fabric. If joins are necessary to make up the length, make sure they fall at garment seams.

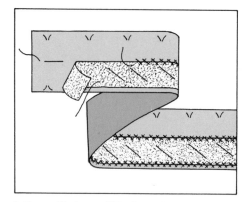

**2.** Place stiffening on WS of waistband so that it is 1.5 cm/⅝ in from each end and with one edge along waistband centre. Baste diagonally along centre of stiffening and either machine just inside both edges of stiffening or work herringbone stitch over them. Remove basting.

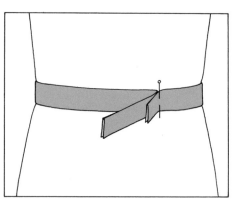

**3.** Fold waistband in half, RS out. Place round waist and pin ends together so that band fits comfortably. Insert pin so that it is 1.5 cm/⅝ in from one end of the band, leaving the other end longer, as an extension.

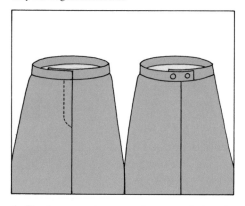

**4.** The longer end can overlap or underlap the shorter, depending on the style of the garment and the position of the fastening. Underlapping is preferable for side and back openings, because it is neater and less conspicuous, while an overlap looks more attractive for a front opening and creates a slimming effect if fastened with two buttons.

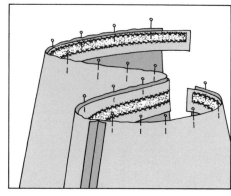

**5.** With garment RS out, unfold waistband and place it RS down on RS of waist, matching raw edges and with interfacing at top. Arrange extension and pin band to garment at start of extension. Pin other end so end of stiffening aligns with zip edge. Pin at intervals round waist. If there is much extra fabric in waist turn garment WS out and, working from WS, pin band at frequent intervals to RS, easing fullness. Baste. Remove pins.

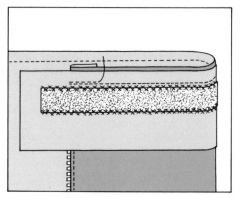

**6.** With waistband uppermost, machine just above edge of stiffening, finishing at edges of zip and reversing for a few stitches at each end. Remove basting. Trim turnings to about 3 to 5 mm/⅛ to ¼ in—too much trimming makes finishing difficult and may lead to stretching. Open out band away from garment and press waist join from RS so that turnings are pushed up into band.

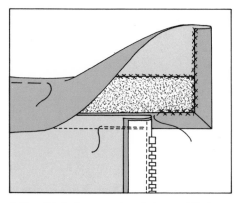

**7.** Turn fabric down over interfacing or stiffening to WS of waistband, baste along fold, starting and finishing a little in from each end. Press. Turn in ends of band over interfacing, baste and press. On extension end hold down turnings with herringbone stitch and remove basting.

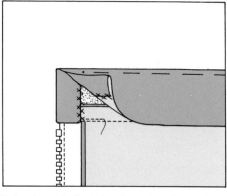

**8.** At other end of waistband turn in end to lie flush with zip edge. Hold down turning to interfacing with herringbone stitch and remove basting.

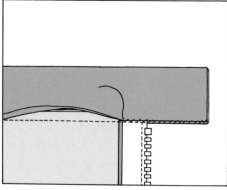

**9.** Turn under raw edge of waistband and baste it down so that fold falls on line of machine stitching on WS of garment. Hem along band into machining. Remove basting. Slip stitch ends of band and lower edge of extension up to edge of zip. Finish extension with hooks and eyes, buttons and buttonholes backed up with press studs, Velcro, or any other fastenings appropriate to the style of the garment (see Fastenings panel).

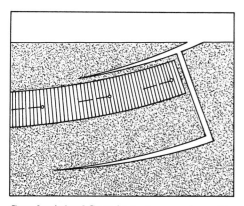

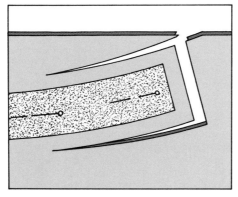

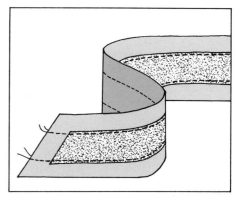

**Curved waistband** Curved petersham may be used to stiffen this band. If it is not the correct width for the band, use it as a guide to the waist curve and stiffen band with heavy or pelmet interfacing. Measure a length of petersham to fit waist, allowing for an extension as for straight waistband. Pin to interfacing. Cut round sides and edges of petersham not more than 5 mm/¼ in above concave edge and to desired width below convex edge.

**2.** Lay out a piece of lining material and a piece of fabric RS together, or two pieces of material, one of which will act as lining. The fabric can serve as lining with medium- and lightweight fabrics, but bulky fabric waistbands are best lined with lightweight cotton or nylon jersey or with lining material. Pin stiffening to the two fabric pieces and cut round, allowing 1.5 cm/⅝ in for turnings all round. Remove stiffening from fabric.

**3.** Place stiffening centrally on WS of fabric and baste down centre. Machine just inside both edges of stiffening, continuing stitching to ends of fabric, or work herringbone stitch over edges. Remove basting and press.

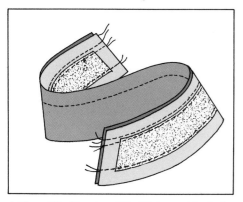

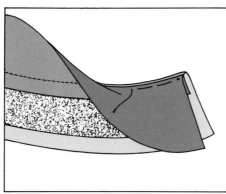

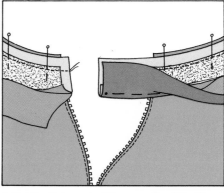

**4.** Place RS of band on RS of lining and baste the two raw edges together along the top, concave, edge just above edge of stiffening. Machine 3 mm/⅛ in from concave stiffening edge. This ensures that the lining does not show on the finished garment. Remove basting. Trim turnings as for faced waistband (3). Press.

**5.** Roll lining over to WS of band so that join is slightly to WS and baste near edge. Press. Put waistband round waist and decide which end will be extension; the extension can overlap or underlap. Adjust length as for straight waistband (3) and mark extension with tailor's chalk.

**6.** Holding lining out of the way, place RS of band on RS of garment. Because the waistband is curved it will sit a little below the waist, so it must be fitted carefully and usually needs to be set below top edge of garment. Match chalk line on extension end of band to zip edge and pin vertically. Match end of stiffening on short end of band to the other zip edge and pin. Insert pins all round waist at intervals and baste band into position. Remove pins.

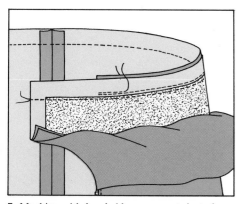

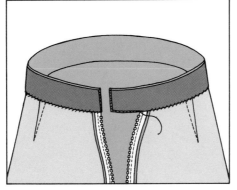

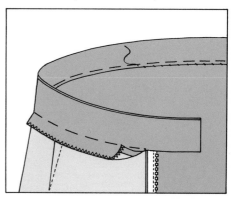

**7.** Machine with band side uppermost, just above edge of stiffening, stopping at zip edge and reversing for a few stitches at each end. Remove basting. Trim turnings to between 3 and 5 mm/⅛ and ¼ in. Open out band away from garment and press so that turnings face up into band.

**8.** Turn in ends of band and extension as for straight waistband (7). Turn up lower edge of lining along machining on WS and baste. Turn under lining edge on extension and short end of waistband and baste down. Press. Slip stitch ends of band and lining and lower edge of extension up to zip. Hold lining down by hemming into machining round waist. Remove all basting and press. Attach fastener to ends of extension (see Fastenings panel).

**9.** If using self-fabric lining on bulky fabric, attach waistband as in steps (1) to (7). Treat band and extension ends as in (8), but instead of turning in lower, raw, edge and hemming into machining, baste raw edge flat on to machining. Neaten edge as appropriate to fabric and hold in place by working prick stitch through from RS at join of band and garment. Remove basting.

# *Waists*

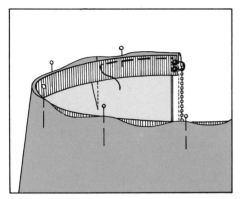

**Elastic petersham** may be attached to a waist edge for comfort. Stretch petersham slightly and measure to fit waist, plus 3 cm/$1\frac{1}{4}$ in for turnings. Turn in each end and attach hook and eye (see Fastenings panel). Prepare waist edge of garment. With RS of garment outermost, place fastened petersham inside waist. Pin vertically at intervals and then pin in between, stretching petersham to fit waist. Unfasten petersham, baste and hem to waist turning.

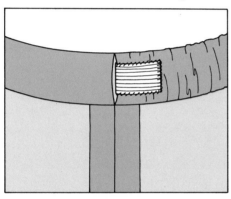

**Insert elastic** rather than stiffening in garments for adults and children with variable waistlines. Cut waistband, allowing for joins to fall at side seams. Stitch joins, leaving section on inside of band open. Attach as appropriate to straight or curved waistband. Thread wide elastic through one of join openings round back of band and bring other end out at second side seam. Turn ends over band towards back, oversew sides and loop stitch ends.

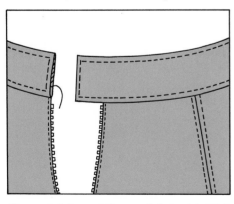

**On casual clothes** and those made from plain fabric such as denim, the waistband may be applied to WS of garment and then rolled over and finished by machining on RS so that the stitching matches any other top stitching on the garment. The stitching can also be worked in a contrasting colour thread.

## WAIST FASTENINGS

The style of the garment and the type of waist finish both determine the kind of fastener to be used. When selecting a suitable fastener, also take into account the ease with which it can be manipulated and whether it should be small and neat, and totally or partially concealed, or whether it should be a conspicuous feature.

**Petersham or petersham ribbon** Turn in ends 1.5 cm/$\frac{5}{8}$ in and turn in raw edges and hem round

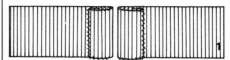

(**1**). Fasten ends with a large or medium hook and eye on RS (**2**), so hook faces towards body in wear.

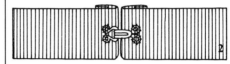

When fastened, petersham should fit waist loosely. Alternatively, oversew a large hook and bar down to ends through each hole (**3**).

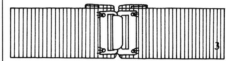

A large flat metal clip can also be attached to the petersham. Slip 1.5 cm/$\frac{5}{8}$ in of petersham through slots on clip, turn in raw edges and hem round (**4**). Attach a hook and bar with a slot in the same way. The hook should face outwards so that it is towards the body during wear.

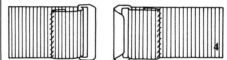

For Velcro, cut petersham 3 cm/$1\frac{1}{4}$ in longer than required, overlap ends and turn in and neaten end of underlap. Attach a 2.5 cm/1 in length of Velcro to WS of overlap and RS of underlap (**5**).

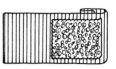 

**Overlap or underlap** Attach a hook and eye supported with a press stud (**6**). Press studs are not strong enough to hold a waistband on their own. Place the well section of the press stud on RS of underlap and the other part directly above it on WS of end of overlap. Stitch eye to end of underlap on WS and hook to overlap. The hook should face outwards so that it is towards the body during wear.

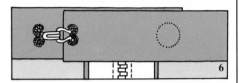

Alternatively, attach Velcro (**7**), but cut overlap or underlap side of band slightly longer than usual to create an effective hold. Cut Velcro to exact length of overlap or underlap minus 1 cm/$\frac{3}{8}$ in.

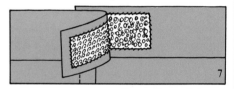

One or more buttons and buttonholes can also be used, but back them up with a press stud (**8**) to prevent buttonholes losing their shape in wear. Attach one part of press stud to end of underneath section, the other directly above to WS of overlap. Make buttonhole at end of overlap and attach button to underlap.

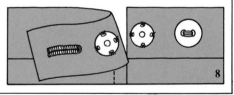

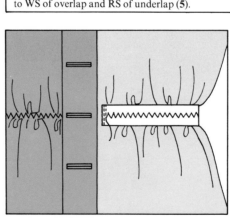

**If a dress is styled** to a straight pattern but is to be drawn in by a belt, help keep the fullness even by attaching a length of elastic round inside of dress, exactly on waistline. The elastic should fit the waist perfectly when slightly stretched. Arrange ends so they meet or lie on either side of an opening. Anchor with a few machine stitches and then zigzag down centre, stretching elastic a little during machining. The stitching is covered by the belt.

## TIPS

A well-fitting waist is not hard to achieve if these important points are borne in mind:
- Always measure the band to fit your waist and make the garment fit the band. If a length of material is basted on to the waist of a garment without being measured, the waist will invariably be too big as the top edge of the garment is likely to stretch.
- Cut a length of petersham exactly to waistband length and keep it as a guide for future bands.
- Always baste on a band when fitting a garment, especially trousers, as it helps the hang. A length of petersham can be used.
- Do not trim waist turnings too much as they act as support during wear. A guide is 5 mm/$\frac{1}{4}$ in on bulky fabrics, 3 mm/$\frac{1}{8}$ in on medium- or lightweight ones.
- Never snip waist turnings or the waist will stretch during wear.

# Sleeve Openings and Cuffs

There are several methods for making an opening at the end of a long sleeve. You do not have to use the one in your pattern.

If the fabric frays, choose an opening such as the faced slit in which the cut edges are reinforced and the raw edges hidden. For bulky fabric select any flat opening, and for springy material avoid openings such as the bound type that involve layering several pieces of narrow fabric. Instead choose the faced slit or flat dart opening.

Before making an opening consider its finished look. This will depend on the style of the cuff and the length of the opening, but any opening must be long enough to prevent strain at the top.

If the sleeve is not altered to its correct length before the opening is made, any subsequent shortening will shorten the opening. Establish the sleeve length by measuring the seam of an existing garment or by pinning the head of the sleeve pattern to the garment you are wearing.

Always cut and make the openings on both sleeves at the same time to ensure that they are correctly positioned. With the exception of the simple concealed opening, which falls at the underarm seam, the openings fall at the back of the sleeve, usually at the lowest part of the curve on the sleeve edge or in line with the little finger. Ideally, make the opening before joining the sleeve seam.

*The ultimate in sleeve openings, worn by a falconer (detail, Carpaccio's* Arrivo degli ambasciatori, *c. 1498).*

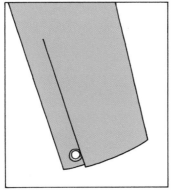

**Flat dart opening** This uncuffed sleeve is darted from the wrist. The lower part of the dart is left unstitched and split open to give a neat, flat opening suited to all fabrics. The bottom of the sleeve may have a narrow hem or be bound or faced, then fastened with loops and buttons, press studs or Velcro strips.

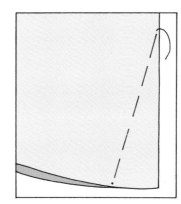

**2.** On WS of sleeve in usual opening position measure 15 cm/6 in up from bottom edge and mark a line for length of dart. Fold sleeve RS together along marked line and measure along sleeve edge about 4 cm/1½ in from fold for width at base of dart. Baste, tapering stitches to meet end of opening mark on fold.

**3.** Stitch top 5 cm/2 in of dart, reversing for a few stitches at end, and press dart towards front of sleeve. Cutting on fold, split lower section of dart as far as the end of the dart stitching. Remove dart basting.

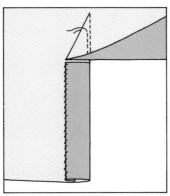

**4.** With dart still facing front of sleeve, lift back top edge and snip lower front edge horizontally in to end of stitching. Trim raw front edge vertically to 3 cm/1¼ in from marked line. Turn under raw edge and slip hem to sleeve to hold in position.

**5.** Similarly, snip back edge in to stitching and trim to 1.5 cm/⅝ in, neaten and fold back. Overcast remaining raw edges of dart. Press.

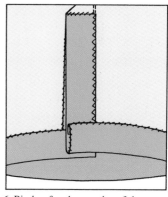

**6.** Bind or face lower edge of sleeve or turn up hem and complete. Because this lower edge is curved the hem should not be too deep. Attach fastenings after completing hem and if necessary hold down back edge of opening with a narrow piece of fabric adhesive, to prevent it from showing during wear.

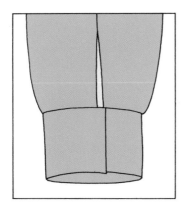

**Simple concealed opening** Easy for beginners. As it is flat it is suitable for any fabric and is the best choice of opening for adding an embroidered, beaded, quilted or other fancy cuff. As the opening falls at underarm seam on inside arm the cuff cannot have buttons. Fasten it instead with press studs or Velcro.

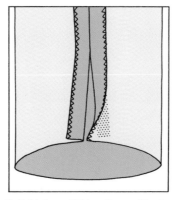

**2.** Fold sleeve RS together and baste and stitch underarm seam to within 7 cm/2¾ in of wrist, reversing for a few stitches at top of opening. Neaten raw edges right to wrist. Remove basting. Press seam open to wrist. The narrow turnings on the opening can be held down with fabric adhesive strips. Attach cuff.

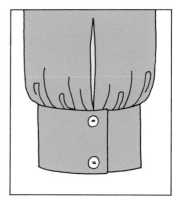

**Faced slit opening** A flat, neat, edge-to-edge opening. Quick to make and ideal for children's and casual clothes or on springy, fraying or bulky fabrics. For the latter, use lining or fine material for the facing. On adults' garments the opening should be about 7 cm/2¾ in long.

▶

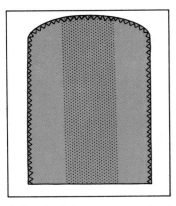

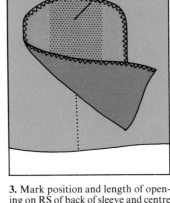

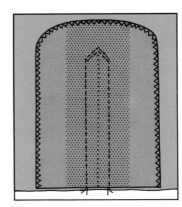

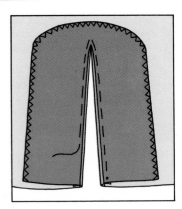

**2.** For the facing cut a rectangle of fabric or lining on straight grain 9 by 5 cm/$3\frac{1}{2}$ by 2 in. Cut one end in a curve and neaten both long sides and curved end. To prevent fraying and to hold facing in position press a strip of paper-backed adhesive 2 cm/$\frac{3}{4}$ in wide down centre of WS of facing. Peel off paper.

**3.** Mark position and length of opening on RS of back of sleeve and centre facing, RS down, over it. Push a pin through from sleeve side at top of marked opening and draw a dotted chalk line from this point to bottom of sleeve on WS of facing. Hold down facing with diagonal basting round neatened edges.

**4.** With facing side up, stitch 2 mm/$\frac{1}{16}$ in away from one side of the chalk line almost to its top. Turn fabric and stitch diagonally to end of chalk line. Turn again and stitch away from line at same angle for same distance. Turn fabric and stitch back to lower edge, 2 mm/$\frac{1}{16}$ in from line. Machine round point again. Remove basting.

**5.** Cut carefully between the two lines of stitching right to point. Roll facing to WS of sleeve, so that join is slightly to WS. Baste round opening to hold join in position and press—pressing makes the adhesive hold the facing back more firmly. Do not remove basting until cuff has been attached.

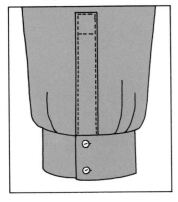

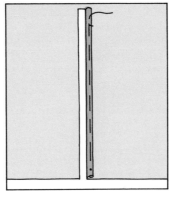

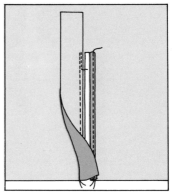

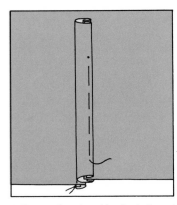

**Shirt sleeve opening** Suited to casual clothes, shirts and jackets. There are several ways of making this opening, all with similar results on RS of garment, but the method described here is an easy one. The opening should be up to 15 cm/6 in long on a man's shirt to avoid strain and to allow the sleeve to be rolled up.

**2.** With sleeve RS out, measure and mark opening at back of sleeve. Cut along mark. Make a narrow turning on back edge of opening, snip across at top of slit for 3 mm/$\frac{1}{8}$ in and roll hem that width to WS of sleeve. Baste hem, press and machine it, reversing for a few stitches at the top of the slit. Remove basting.

**3.** Cut fabric strip on straight grain 6 cm/$2\frac{1}{4}$ in longer than the opening and 4 cm/$1\frac{1}{2}$ in wide. Put one side RS down on WS of front edge of opening with raw edges level. Baste. Stitch, 2 mm/$\frac{1}{8}$ in from edges, from wrist to top of slit, reversing a little at top. Open out strip and press, RS up, to extend across slit. Remove basting.

**4.** Turn under other side of strip 3 mm/$\frac{1}{8}$ in to WS. Press. Bring strip through to RS of sleeve. Baste down turned-under edge of strip so that it covers machine stitches. The strip now extends beyond slit on RS of sleeve. Press strip.

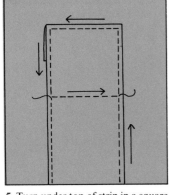

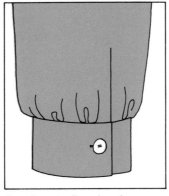

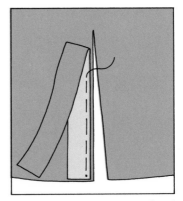

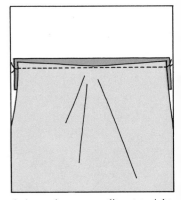

**5.** Turn under top of strip in a square or point a square is easier. With sleeve RS up, baste and stitch up the turned-under edge, across top of opening and down the other side to slightly below start of slit—stitch across strip for strength at this level. Outer slit edge may also be machined. Remove basting. Press. Attach cuff.

**Bound opening** Sometimes known as a continuous strip opening because it is made by attaching one piece of fabric. Its advantage is that it does not gape as the edges overlap. Use only on light- and medium-weight materials as it is often too bulky for heavy fabrics. It can replace the conventional shirt sleeve opening.

**2.** On RS at back of sleeve mark and cut slit for an opening about 7 cm/$2\frac{3}{4}$ in long. For all but fine fabrics, cut fabric strip on straight grain twice length of slit and 2.5 cm/1 in wide. Place one end, RS down, at bottom of sleeve, RS up, and with edge of slit and one side of strip level. Baste along strip 5 mm/$\frac{1}{4}$ in from edge.

**3.** As you baste, open slit out straight; the turning on the slit edge becomes smaller until it is only a few threads at centre (top of slit). Make sure turning on strip stays 5 mm/$\frac{1}{4}$ in all the way along. Machine on WS of sleeve, catching in the threads of material at centre. Remove basting.

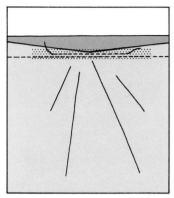

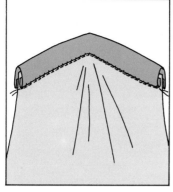

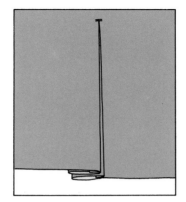

**4.** Reinforce top of slit by machining again on top of first row for 2 cm/¾ in across centre. For further reinforcement cut a small narrow strip of paper-backed adhesive and press it down on WS of sleeve at centre of slit so it extends from machining out to raw edges. Remove paper backing on adhesive strip.

**5.** Fold over raw edge on other side of binding strip. Place fold on line of machining on WS of sleeve. Baste. Hem into machining or, on casual clothes, machine the binding down. Remove basting. For fine fabrics cut a bias or crossways strip 1.5 cm/⅝ in wide; press to stretch and apply as for double binding.

**6.** To finish opening for both wide and narrow binding strips, turn sleeve RS up and bring opening edges together. Press so binding on edge to front of sleeve is folded back on to WS of sleeve and so binding on back edge extends forwards across the opening. Work a bar tack on RS of sleeve at top of opening.

**7.** On WS of sleeve at top of strip adjust fold to lie flat and backstitch through fold of strip from top of inside edge downwards, at an angle, to outer edges. This keeps the binding in position during wear. Attach cuff.

## CUFFS

A cuff may draw a sleeve in at the wrist or be a decorative addition. It usually fastens from the front on to the back of the sleeve. Choose fastenings according to style, fabric and convenience. For example, rouleau loops and buttons, like flat hooks and bars, are difficult to manipulate, whereas Velcro and press studs are easier. Hooks and eyes are not firm enough and cannot be hidden by the overlap. Buttons and buttonholes are most suitable for thin and medium fabrics. On all but very deep cuffs, work only one central buttonhole. Attach cuffs, except the easy wrap, after working the sleeve opening and joining the sleeve underarm seam.

### INTERFACING CUFFS

All cuffs except the bias, turn-back cuff need some reinforcement. Select interfacing according to fabric; it may need to be slightly stiffer than that on rest of garment. Mark centre line of a one-piece cuff before applying interfacing. (See also Interfacing.)

**Lightweight fabric** Iron or baste on interfacing to cover whole of WS of

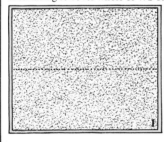

cuff (**1**) or to extend from one side to just over centre line. The edges are caught in the machining when the cuff is attached.

**Medium-weight fabric** Attach interfacing to WS of the cuff half that will be machined to sleeve first (the top, outside piece). Iron on, or baste on and catch stitch inner edge on marked centre line of cuff (**2**).

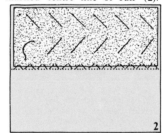

Alternatively, trim back interfacing beyond turning lines at outer edges and catch stitch all round.

**Heavyweight fabric** Cut interfacing to cover WS of cuff half that will be machined to sleeve first (top, outside piece). Trim so it will not catch in turnings and lies 2 mm/1/16 in from centre (**3**). Cut off corners. Iron or baste and catch stitch to WS of cuff.

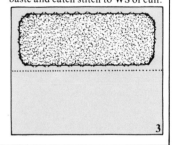

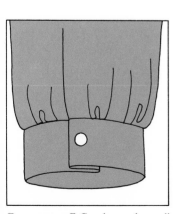

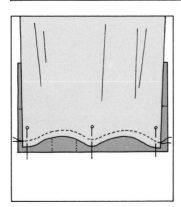

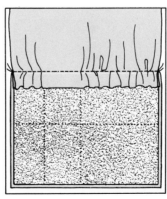

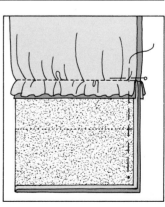

**Easy wrap cuff** Can be used on all light- and medium-weight fabrics, but may be too bulky on heavier ones. Excellent for all fraying materials because no opening is necessary in sleeve. Cuff wraps over from front to back of sleeve, in line with little finger. Interface whole cuff with lightweight interfacing (see panel).

**2.** Mark turnings and length and position of wrap-over on cuff. In lower edge of sleeve insert tucks or a row of gathering in seam allowance near seam line. Pin RS of one long cuff edge to lower edge of RS of sleeve, matching raw edges. Pull up gathering thread or adjust tuck width until sleeve fits cuff.

**3.** Arrange fullness so there is a flat section at cuff wrap-over. Baste sleeve to cuff. Remove pins and machine with tucks or gathers uppermost, taking usual seam turnings. Remove basting and gathers. Trim turnings to 5 mm/¼ in. Open out cuff to extend beyond sleeve end and press turnings towards cuff.

**4.** Fold sleeve RS together. With raw edges level down sleeve and cuff, pin cuff at wrist to hold both sides of join level. Baste along cuff and underarm sleeve seam. Starting from bottom edge of cuff machine beside basting up to underarm, making sure that the turnings remain flat all the way up. Remove pin and basting.

# Sleeve Openings and Cuffs

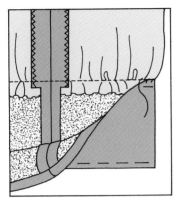

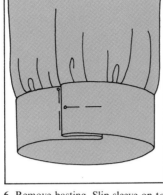

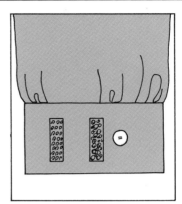

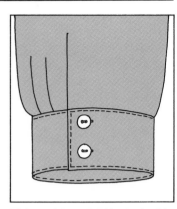

**5.** Press seam open and neaten raw edges to suit fabric, to just beyond cuff join. Trim away a little of seam turnings within cuff. Fold cuff on marked line along centre and baste close to fold. Turn under raw edge and baste to WS of sleeve so fold covers machining at join of cuff and sleeve. Press. Hem into machining.

**6.** Remove basting. Slip sleeve on to arm and pin sleeve head to shoulder of the garment you are wearing (it is not necessary to try on the garment you are making). Fold over wrap in cuff, in line with little finger, towards back of sleeve. Pin. Mark end of wrap on under section of cuff with pins or chalk. Unpin cuff and take off sleeve.

**7.** Open cuff out again and attach fastening—either press studs or Velcro—so that cuff fits when fastened. Remove any marker pins. For a decorative effect attach a button or buttons on outside of cuff overlap near folded edge.

**Plain straight cuff** This classic shirt cuff can be made in almost any fabric and top stitched when complete. If there is insufficient material, make the cuff from two pieces of fabric joined lengthways. This cuff can also be made very wide and then folded back and fastened with cuff links.

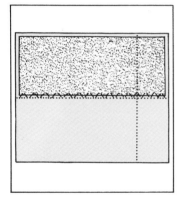

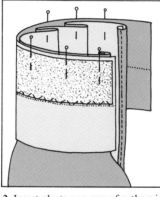

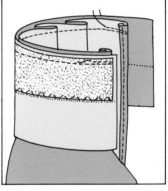

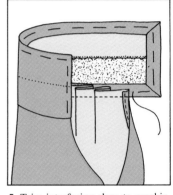

**2.** Interface WS of cuff to suit fabric (see p. 99). Mark turnings and fold lines. Except if attaching cuff to a shirt sleeve opening, mark length of underlap either from pattern or by trying on cuff round wrist—the underlap extension will be on the back of the sleeve.

**3.** Insert pleats or a row of gathers in lower edge of sleeve. Pin RS of cuff to RS of lower sleeve edge, matching raw edges and with back edge of sleeve opening on mark for start of underlap extension. Allow cuff to extend $1.5\,cm/\frac{5}{8}$ in beyond opening at front of sleeve. Draw up gathers or adjust pleats to fit cuff.

**4.** For a shirt sleeve opening, pin both cuff ends level with ends of opening. For all types of sleeve opening, baste and machine on WS of sleeve, which is easier to reach, making sure that pleats or gathers stay in place and taking usual seam turning. Start and finish at edges of opening by reversing a little. Remove basting and gathers.

**5.** Trim interfacing close to machining, raw edge of cuff to $5\,mm/\frac{1}{4}$ in and sleeve edge to slightly less. With cuff extending away from sleeve, press turnings into cuff. Fold in outer edge and ends of cuff along marked seam lines. Baste near edge. Trim raw edges to $5\,mm/\frac{1}{4}$ in to reduce bulk.

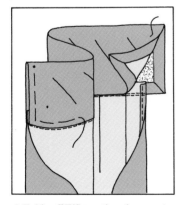

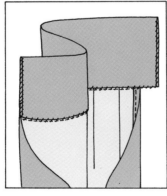

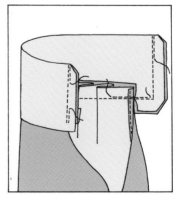

**6.** Fold cuff WS together along centre fold line so ends are level and basted outer edge of cuff lies on machining joining cuff to sleeve on WS. Baste ends and along edge over machining; baste diagonally along length of cuff.

**7.** Press. Slip stitch ends and lower edges of extension. Hold down cuff edge to WS of sleeve by hemming into machining. Remove all basting and then press again.

**8.** If fabric is fine or has a lot of give it may be better to fold cuff in half RS together after attaching interfaced side to sleeve and then to stitch across ends and extension. Trim turnings to $5\,mm/\frac{1}{4}$ in. Trim corners diagonally. Turn cuff RS out. Turn under free lower edge, baste and hem into machining. Remove basting.

*In the 17th century, smaller versions of the stiffly corrugated neck ruff found their way to the wrists.*

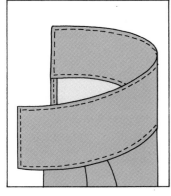

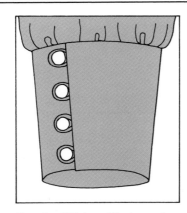

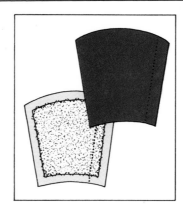

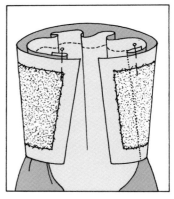

**9.** If cuff made by either method is to be top stitched, work this stitching round all four sides of completed cuff. Check for fit by trying cuff on as in (**2**). Attach fastenings as desired, but remember to choose ones that are easily manipulated.

**Shaped cuff** If the cuff is deeper than about 6.5 cm/2½ in it must be shaped to fit the curve of the arm above the wrist. A shaped cuff is cut in two parts and has a seam along its lower edge. It looks very attractive decorated with top stitching and fastened with rouleau loops and buttons.

**2.** Cut two pieces (one may be in lining) for each cuff. Pin top piece of each pair round wrist, allowing for 5 mm to 2 cm/¼ to ¾ in extension. Mark where front end of cuff falls on back to give length of underlap, allowing usual turnings on both ends. Interface top piece of each pair (see p. 99). Mark turnings.

**3.** Insert a row of gathers in bottom of sleeve. Place interfaced cuff piece RS down on RS of sleeve with convex edge on bottom of sleeve. On both sides of sleeve opening insert a pin from cuff side so cuff seam allowance extends beyond front edge of opening and underlap extension mark aligns with back edge.

*The scalloped cuff framing this maidenly wrist is bound with plaited rouleau. Embossed transfers such as this were collected in Victorian albums.*

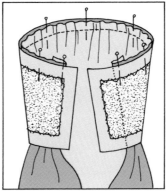

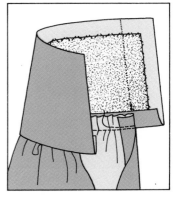

**4.** Pull up gathers to fit cuff. Pin round cuff from gathered side. Baste sleeve to cuff. Remove pins.

**5.** Machine, from gathered side, to edges of opening, reversing for a few stitches at each end. Remove basting and gathers. Trim turnings to 5 mm/¼ in, open out cuff to extend beyond sleeve end and press turnings into cuff.

*Impractically romantic wear for a bracing day by the seaside. As a concession to holiday activity, the forearms on this outfit of 1860 were left free, but shaded from the sun by a cascade of lace frothing from elbow-level cuffs.*

**6.** If rouleau loops are being used as fasteners, make up and baste into position on front edge of RS of cuff so loops face away from raw edges. Machine across loop ends beside seam line. Remove basting.

**7.** Place RS of second cuff (or lining) piece on RS of attached piece. Baste round wrist edge and along front edge. With outer, interfaced piece uppermost, machine round wrist curve, turn corner and machine along front edge. Stop exactly where interfaced cuff joins sleeve. Reverse a little at each end. Remove basting. ▶

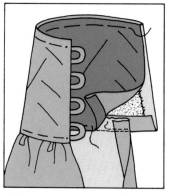

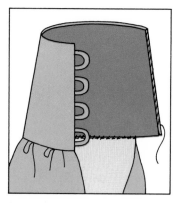

**8.** Trim turnings to 5 mm/¼ in and trim interfacing very close to stitching. Trim corners diagonally. Turn cuff RS out. Roll edges until wrist join on cuff is slightly to WS. Baste wrist edge close to join. Press. Baste diagonally along centre of cuff and across ends.

**9.** Turn in raw edge along bottom of cuff on to machine stitching on WS joining interfaced cuff section to sleeve. Baste. Hem into machining.

**10.** At extension end remove basting. Turn in cuff edges to meet at end and along extension. Slip stitch together. Add any decoration such as top stitching. Remove all basting. Press.

**11.** For an easier method of attaching second cuff piece to first on fine, flimsy fabrics, stitch, starting at front edge, round wrist curve and down back edge. Trim interfacing close to stitching, trim turnings and turn whole cuff RS out before finishing as in (**8**) to (**10**), slip stitching lower edge of extension only.

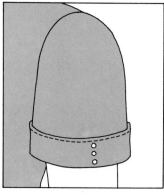

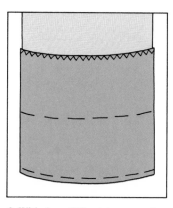

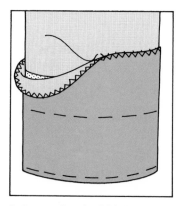

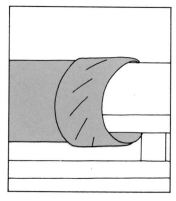

**Turn-back cuff** This cuff is a rolled back extension of the sleeve and is decorative rather than functional. It is not interfaced but stiffened with fabric adhesive web, which also holds the cuff in position and prevents it from rolling down during wear.

**2.** With sleeve WS out, turn up a deep hem on sleeve on fold line marked at desired depth. Baste close to fold. Neaten raw edge to suit fabric but do not press. Measuring from basted fold, mark fold line at the depth of turn-back of cuff.

**3.** Insert a length of fabric adhesive web round sleeve under neatened edge and along the turn-back fold line. Press round fold line to attach adhesive and catch stitch neatened hem edge to WS of sleeve.

**4.** Turn sleeve RS out and roll cuff back over RS of sleeve to turn-back fold line. Diagonally baste cuff to sleeve all round. Arrange on sleeve board RS up and press lightly. Remove all basting. Press on WS to melt adhesive. Work top stitching if desired round top of cuff turn-back, stitching through turn-back only.

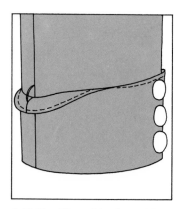

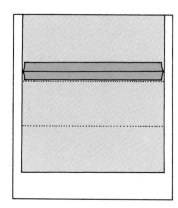

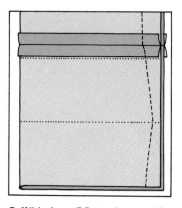

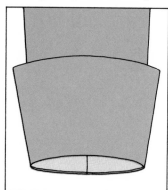

**5.** Hold cuff in position by working a bar tack at the sleeve seam, hidden between seam and cuff. Work another bar tack between seam and cuff on opposite side of sleeve or attach decorative buttons there through all layers of fabric.

**6.** For a decorative cuff in fabric of contrasting colour, pattern or texture, attach a piece of fabric twice desired cuff depth, plus seam allowances, to end of sleeve before joining sleeve seam. Press join open. Mark hem as in (**2**) and turn-back fold line 2 mm/1/16 in below join.

**7.** With sleeve RS together, machine down sleeve seam, taking usual turnings, and then chalk a stitching line 2 to 3 mm/1/16 to 1/8 in closer to raw edges as far as hem fold line midway down cuff. Stitch this section and complete seam, taking usual turnings. This ensures that the cuff is slightly bigger than the sleeve. Complete as before.

**Shaped turn-back cuff** This purely decorative cuff is considerably wider at the top than at the wrist. If the fabric is bulky, the inside of the cuff should be made from lining material. If there is a slit or a shaped part on the lower sleeve edge on the outside of the arm, the cuff pieces are also shaped.

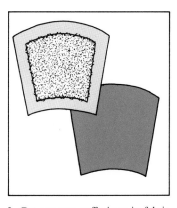

**2.** Cut out two cuff pieces in fabric and interface (see p. 99). Cut out two cuff pieces in lining material. The cuff join should fall at the underarm sleeve seam, but if the cuff has a break in it, as a decorative feature, make sure the break falls exactly at the seam when attaching the cuff.

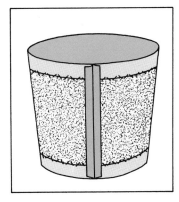

**3.** Fold interfaced cuff piece with RS together and join side seam. Trim turnings to 5 mm/¼ in, but do not neaten. Press seam together. Join seam in lining and trim in the same way. Turn cuff RS out.

**4.** Place RS of cuff to RS of lining, matching side seams, and baste together diagonally along seams. Baste cuff layers together diagonally all round. Baste wide, outer, edges of cuff together.

**5.** Machine outer edges beside basting. Remove all basting. Trim outer edges to 5 mm/¼ in and trim interfacing close to machining. Turn cuff RS out. Roll edge until join is slightly to inside of cuff. Baste round outer edge close to join. Press well. Baste diagonally round centre of cuff to hold cuff pieces together.

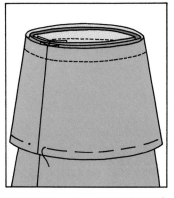

**6.** If cuff has a break in it, bar tack ends together on fitting line. Then, with sleeve RS out, slip cuff, RS out, over sleeve end and match raw edges at wrist and side seam joins. Baste round cuff at wrist edge on marked seam line through all layers and machine. Remove wrist edge basting.

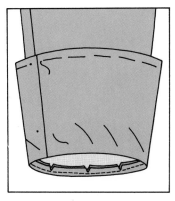

**7.** Move cuff down sleeve towards wrist so fold at wrist is slightly inside sleeve. Push raw edges at join up inside sleeve so they are hidden during wear. Snip turnings close to machining so they lie flat inside sleeve. Baste diagonally near lower cuff edge. Press cuff lightly, revolving it on a sleeve board or rolled towel.

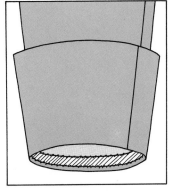

**8.** Turn sleeve WS out. Neaten raw edges of medium-weight or heavy fabric with herringbone stitch; neaten those of fine fabric by covering with a bias strip and hemming along both edges. Turn sleeve to RS and remove basting. If sleeve is lined, as for a coat, bring lining over unneatened raw edges and fell stitch in place.

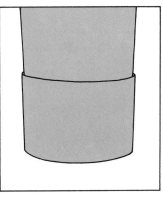

**Simple bias cuff** This cuff is made from bias material, often in a contrasting colour or pattern, joined to the end of the sleeve. The material can either be rolled back to form a cuff, or used as an extension to the sleeve end—a useful way of adding length.

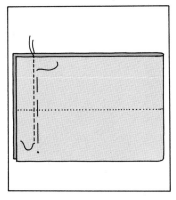

**2.** Cut crossways strip twice desired depth of cuff (at least 5 cm/2 in), plus 4 cm/1½ in for turnings and an allowance for roll on a turn-back cuff. Press strip to stretch it. Mark turn-back line. Place strip round bottom of sleeve. Pin ends together to fit sleeve and, with RS together, baste and machine ends. Remove basting.

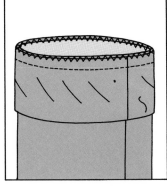

**3.** Press seam open. Fold strip in half lengthways, WS together, and work diagonal basting all round. Slip cuff over RS of sleeve so cuff join falls at underarm seam and outer edges match. Baste and machine along seam line at bottom of sleeve. Remove basting. Trim raw edges to 5 mm/¼ in and neaten together.

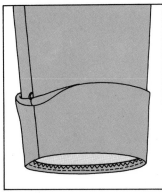

**4.** For turn-back cuff, pull cuff down until the join disappears inside the sleeve. Hold cuff in position and baste diagonally all round. Press. In lined sleeve cover the neatened edges with lining. Remove basting. Work bar tack at side seam between cuff and sleeve at least 1 cm/⅜ in from cuff edge.

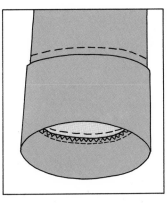

**5.** For an extended cuff, pull binding strip down and press turnings up into sleeve. For a decorative effect, work a row of top stitching on RS of sleeve, just above top edge of cuff; take stitches through all layers of fabric.

103

# Sleeves

*Short sleeves turned the formal dinner frock of 1932 into a casual, more versatile garment, wearable at other, less socially demanding times of day.*

*The simple, roomy, untailored sleeves of the traditional T-shaped Japanese kimono, worn here by a theatrical dancer from Kyoto, are comfortable to wear and easy to sew.*

*The severely shaped riding habits fashionable in 1896 featured exaggerated leg o' mutton sleeves. Long tight cuffs kept excess material out of harm's way.*

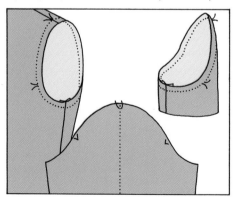

**Plain set-in sleeve** Mark armhole seam line on bodice and seam line at top of sleeve. It may also help beginners to mark the head point on the sleeve, which is exactly in the centre of the fabric cross grain, and the balance points halfway down the armhole on sleeve and bodice. Remember that balance and head marks are only guide lines and may be moved in fitting. Join and neaten sleeve seam. Turn bodice and sleeve RS out.

The style and line of sleeves, like other parts of a garment, are subject to the influences of fashion, but there are essentially only three types of sleeve—set-in, kimono and raglan.

The plain set-in sleeve is joined to the garment armhole with a seam that follows the underarm curve of the body exactly and then extends over the shoulder bone. The part of the seam on the shoulder may be high to give a cut-in look, be raised on a pad for a military style, or the sleeve head may be gathered into the armhole to create a high-standing sleeve; the section from shoulder to underarm always follows the same line on the body.

The kimono is the easiest sleeve to make. Simply an extension of the bodice, it is particularly suited to leisure clothes, but has the disadvantage of being bulky under the arm. This is because there is no shaped join at the shoulder and thus the sleeve must be loose fitting to allow for movement.

Commonly used on garments needing a fairly loose fit, the raglan sleeve is reasonably easy to construct. The seams joining sleeve to bodice run from neckline to underarm.

There are many possible variations on the three basic sleeves. For example, the sleeve may be set into a square armhole; the bodice yoke may be cut in one piece and the lower part of the sleeve gathered in; or a plain, short, set-in sleeve may have a gathered or circular lower section. The dropped shoulder line creates a shape similar to the kimono, but a separate sleeve section is joined to the bodice with a straight seam running across the arm (from the underarm) a little way below the shoulder bone. This style uses less fabric than the all-in-one kimono. Use appropriate seams, such as a lapped seam or an open seam, to make all these types of sleeves.

Except for men's shirt sleeves, sleeves are generally attached to the garment after their seams have been joined and neatened and their cuffs or sleeve ends finished.

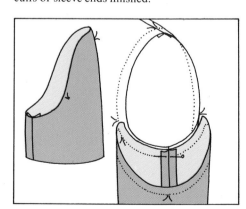

**2.** Check sleeves to establish the right and the left. On both sleeve and bodice the back of the armhole extends while the front is scooped. This shaping gives extra width across the back, where it is needed for ease of movement. Place RS of sleeve seam on RS of bodice seam, with raw edges at underarm matching, and pin across seams. Remember that seam positions may have been altered by fitting adjustments to sleeve or bodice.

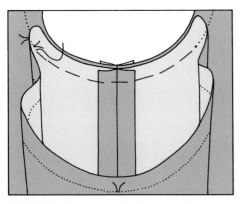

**3.** Hold RS of sleeve and bodice towards you. On underarm section only, and with raw edges together, match fitting lines and pin on each side of first pin for about 10 cm/4 in (approximately the length of deeply curved section of sleeve). Do not worry if balance marks on sleeve and bodice do not coincide, because of fitting or because they were inaccurately marked on the fabric. Baste underarm section. Fasten off basting, Remove all pins.

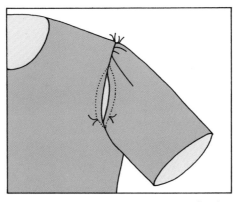

**4.** Put one hand inside shoulder at neck edge, bringing it out through the bodice armhole to grasp the sleeve head. Bring sleeve head up to end of shoulder seam and hold the two together.

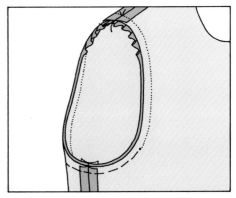

**5.** Pull bodice over sleeve so that bodice is WS out with sleeve hanging inside it and RS of sleeve and bodice are still together. In this position the sleeve head, which is larger than the armhole to allow for the shape of the shoulder, is wrinkled within the armhole because of the excess fullness.

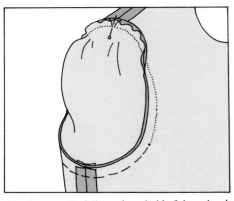

**6.** To disperse the fullness, keep hold of sleeve head and shoulder seam, and turn bodice and sleeve edges back over hand so that sleeve is on top, WS up. Pin sleeve head to bodice across marked seam line. There are now only two short stretches of sleeve head to attach to armhole and the fullness has been largely eased away by holding the sleeve and bodice correctly. Use this method for all types of fabric.

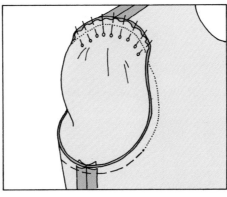

**7.** Keeping sleeve on top of bodice, insert pins at intervals across seam line, picking up fabric on fitting line only. Continue round armhole to meet basting. Add more pins in between until they are close together. The fullness in the sleeve head flutes at the sleeve edge but contracts to slight bumps of fabric where the pins are inserted. Adjust pins until most ease lies over shoulder and there is very little fullness down the back of the armhole.

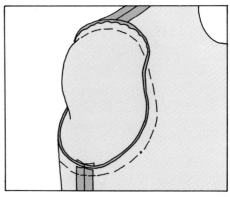

**8.** With sleeve still in same position, baste with small stitches across centre of pins, removing each pin as it is reached. Do not allow ease to form pleats. If this is a problem, take smaller stitches to divide up fullness. Try on garment, fit sleeve and adjust sleeve head basting if necessary.

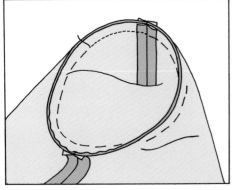

**9.** Sew in sleeve, preferably by hand, starting from underarm seam and using a small half backstitch. Remove basting. Sewing the sleeve in by hand enables you to hold the sleeve correctly, so that you can continue to control and take up the fullness in the sleeve head.

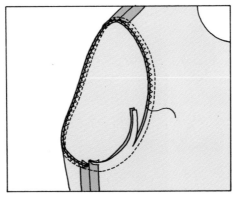

**10.** To machine sleeve in, stitch very slowly from sleeve side, starting at underarm seam. Use points of small scissors to prevent any pleats from forming, as for gathers. Remove basting. After stitching by hand or machine, trim turnings to no less than 13 mm/½ in and neaten both edges together. Press seam into sleeve head for support. At underarm press stitching on WS and leave seam upright.

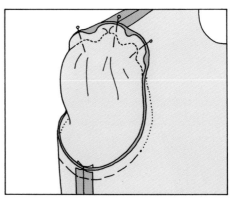

**Gathered head** Mark balance points as for set-in sleeve and insert one gathering thread in sleeve head between them. Proceed as for set-in sleeve (**1**) to (**5**). Pin again between top of sleeve head and end of underarm basting. Pull up gathering thread until sleeve lies loosely on top of armhole. Do not pull tight. Arrange gathers. Pin frequently. Finish as for plain set-in sleeve (**8**) to (**10**), always machining from sleeve side to control the gathers.

# Sleeves

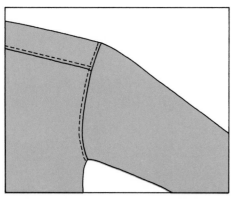

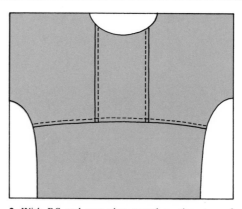

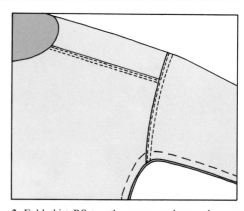

**Shirt sleeve** A man's tailored shirt sleeve usually has a loose, low armhole and a shoulder line that is almost dropped; the seam joining the sleeve to the bodice is only slightly shaped, especially if machine fell seams are used, which are difficult to make on a shaped armhole. Mark shoulder point on yoke with a tailor's tack.

**2.** With RS and raw edges together, place top of sleeve piece along open armhole edge on shirt, making sure that marked sleeve head aligns with shoulder point on yoke. Pin at sleeve head and at each end of seam. Baste, easing any fullness at top of sleeve evenly. Remove pins. Stitch together, using a machine fell, narrow finish or top-stitched seam. Remove basting and press.

**3.** Fold shirt RS together so raw edges and seam lines meet on sleeve underarm seam and on bodice side seam. Match ends of armhole seam at underarm and pin. Baste bodice side seam from hem edge to underarm. Remove pin at underarm and baste down sleeve underarm seam to wrist edge. Join bodice and sleeve seams with a continuous machine fell seam from hem edge of bodice to sleeve wrist edge. Remove basting. Press on WS and RS. Attach cuff.

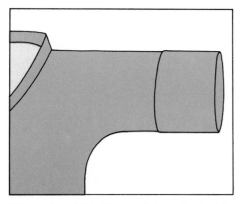

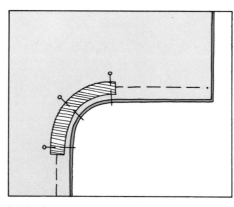

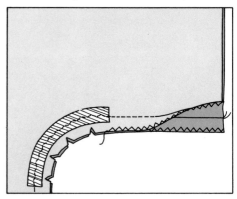

**Kimono sleeve** With this type of sleeve the shoulder seam is usually fairly straight or may even be eliminated by cutting out the pattern with the seam laid on a fold in the fabric so that the sleeve is all in one piece with the bodice. The more horizontal the shoulder seam or shoulder line the more room there is for movement (but this increases garment bulk).

**2.** With front and back garment pieces RS together, baste and machine shoulder seams, if any. Baste underarm seams. Cut a length of bought bias binding (pressed out flat and folded in half for neatness) or stretch lace to match length of most curved section of seam. Pin and baste binding or lace round curved section, centring it over seam line. The binding reinforces this section, allowing it to stretch but preventing splitting.

**3.** Machine seam using a stitch suitable for the fabric, but along reinforced section change to a slight zigzag to retain necessary give in seam. Remove basting. Along the curve, snip turnings, but not reinforcement, halfway to machining. Press seam open. The curved section may spring up again, but do not try to press it too flat. Neaten raw edges of seam; it is often quicker to overcast the snipped section by hand.

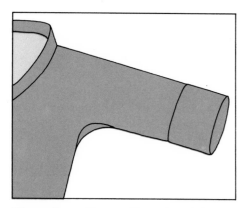

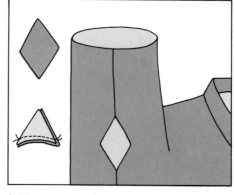

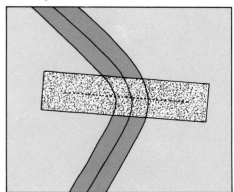

**Kimono sleeve with gusset** For a closer fitting, less bulky kimono sleeve, it is necessary to slope the shoulder more and sometimes, therefore, to narrow the sleeve at the wrist as well. The part of the seam round the underarm is then raised, which reduces the depth between shoulder and underarm, thus placing breaking strain on the seam when the arm is raised. To prevent this, a gusset, an extra piece of fabric, is inserted into the seam under the arm.

**2.** The gusset may be a diamond-shaped piece of fabric or two triangles joined to make a diamond. The latter fits into the armhole better because the edges of the two triangles that are joined are cut and sewn in a concave curve. The gusset may also be combined as part of a side panel in the garment.

**3.** A gusset can also be added to the preceding kimono sleeve if the underarm seam has already been stitched but found to be too tight. With garment WS out, chalk a line across seam at highest point under arm to extend 5 cm/2 in on each side of seam. On WS of garment apply a rectangle of light iron-on interfacing 6 cm/2¼ in wide to cover chalk line and extend 2 cm/¾ in over it at each end.

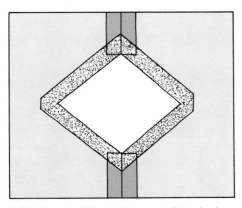

**4.** Cut along chalk line and open out slit to give four reinforced edges and a diamond-shaped hole. If no gusset pattern piece is provided, measure the four sides of the diamond and cut a piece of fabric to fit, allowing for usual seam turnings on each edge. If cutting two triangles to make gusset, add seam allowances for curved join in centre. Whichever gusset style you use, make sure that one side of it is on the straight grain.

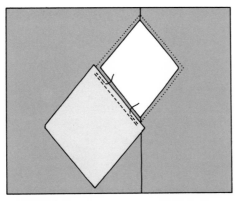

**5.** If gusset piece is provided, mark position of gusset opening and baste and machine underarm seam to start of each end of it. Reinforce raw edges of opening on WS with iron-on interfacing $3\,\text{cm}/1\frac{1}{4}\,\text{in}$ wide and open out into a diamond-shaped hole. To insert all types of gusset, place gusset RS down on RS of garment with edges of one gusset side and one opening side level. Baste and stitch along edge, reversing at each end. Remove basting.

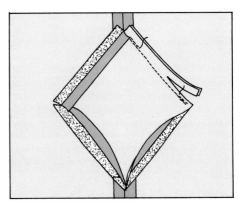

**6.** Trim turnings of stitched seam to $1\,\text{cm}/\frac{3}{8}\,\text{in}$. Press seam open. Snip garment turning at each end of machining right in to last machine stitch. Proceed as for an angled seam. Swing gusset round to work second side. Trim turnings and snip into corners as before. Turn work over to WS to complete third and fourth sides of gusset.

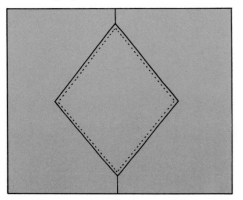

**7.** To further reinforce gusset seams and area, work a row of prick stitch from RS of gusset $3\,\text{mm}/\frac{1}{8}\,\text{in}$ inside join, stitching through all layers of fabric and round all four sides of gusset.

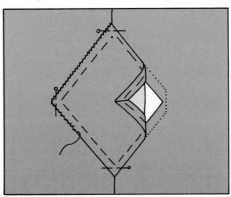

**8.** Alternatively, insert gusset by reinforcing WS of garment as in (**3**) or (**5**). Turn in gusset edges along seam lines, baste and press. Place gusset WS down on RS of garment to cover opening. Pin at corners. Baste round gusset so turned-in edges lie along seam line at opening. Hem or work a small slip stitch all round. Remove basting. Press. Work prick stitch from RS of gusset $3\,\text{mm}/\frac{1}{8}\,\text{in}$ inside join for extra strength. Overcast turnings together.

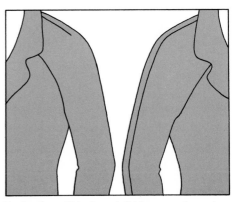

**Raglan sleeve** This sleeve is fairly easy to insert, but there are often fitting problems at the neckline. The excess width at the top of the sleeve is often drawn in with a dart. If the fullness at the point of the dart shows as a bulge on RS of garment, lengthen dart to help eliminate this. A raglan that has a seam running all the way from neck to wrist generally fits much better than a darted sleeve, and adjustments can be made easily on this seam.

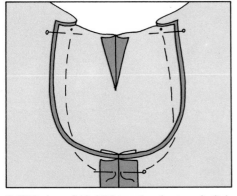

**2.** With sleeve folded RS together, baste and stitch underarm seam and dart or top seam. Remove basting. Press seam or seams. Cut dart and press open. At underarm place sleeve underarm and bodice seams RS together with raw edges level and pin. Place edges together at neck and pin; remember that all edges are on bias and likely to stretch. On each side of armhole in turn, baste from neck to seam at underarm, holding armhole as for curved seam.

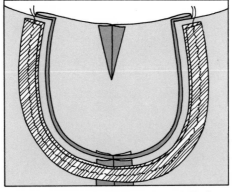

**3.** Remove pins. Machine round armhole from garment side and remove basting. If garment is of knitted fabric, which may stretch in wear, reinforce seam with a piece of bought bias binding, pressed out flat and then folded in half, or lining material cut on bias or true cross and folded in half. Baste binding down on garment side centred over seam line, and machine along on top of seam line, using a slight zigzag stitch. Remove basting.

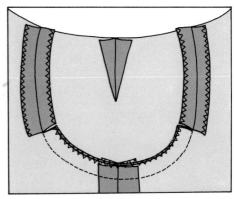

**4.** On WS press upper sections of seam open from neck downwards for the whole section that will be visible during wear. Press stitching of lower part of seam on WS so that turnings stand up together as for a plain set-in sleeve; neaten these underarm edges together. Snip outer, garment, turning down to just above machining and neaten the opened parts of the seam separately.

# Yokes

Attractive style details, yokes provide a good position for decorative stitching and also the opportunity to introduce fullness into the adjoining section either as a fashion feature or for freedom of movement. Other reasons for making a yoke include the need to economize on fabric—the resulting smaller pattern pieces may fit more easily on to the fabric than one large skirt or bodice piece—and the desire to take out other seams—the saddle yoke, for example, is a one-piece yoke that joins the front and back sections and eliminates shoulder seams.

Yokes can be made in matching or contrasting fabric and are often backed with interfacing. Double yokes, backed with self-fabric, thin cotton or lining fabric, give added body and support to the adjoining section. The lining also conceals the yoke seams.

The shape of a yoke varies according to its position and to the style of the garment. When sewing a curved or angled yoke, handle the seams as shaped seams.

*Edwardian little girls wore pinafores, usually made from strong white cotton, to protect heavier clothes beneath. The pinafores were designed with a yoke to give maximum room for movement and growth. These children celebrating a school holiday, right, were photographed in 1902 by Sir Bernard Stone. The holiday was granted to them by the townspeople of Hungerford, Berkshire, on the occasion of Hocktide, an ancient festival held shortly after Easter.*

*Modern washable materials make separate pinafores unnecessary, but the loose yoked dress is still an unbeatable design for young children, below. Charming and practical, it is an easy style to make, wear and look after.*

*The rustic character may be pure music hall, but the roomy smock is authentic, its deep, gathered yoke making it comfortable wear for heavy farm work.*

*Taken up by high fashion, the yoke, here rounded and buttoning at the sides, makes a soft, comfortable yet sophisticated dress.*

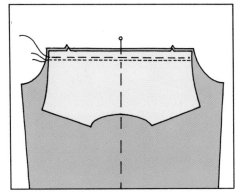

**Attaching plain yoke** Mark centre and balance marks on yoke and adjoining garment section. Place the two pieces RS together, matching centres and raw edges, and pin vertically at centre. Pin at balance marks and at each end. Baste pieces together along seam line, easing garment on to yoke if there is slight shaping. Leave centre pin in position and remove other pins. Stitch beside basting from end to end. Remove basting and centre pin.

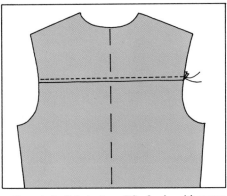

**3.** Top stitch, if desired, on RS of yoke, either very close to the yoke seam or a little way up from it, depending on the effect required. Press the stitching. If the turnings have been pressed open before top stitching, press lower turning up towards yoke.

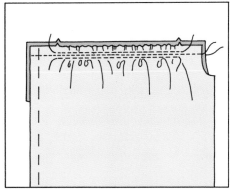

**2.** Gently pull up gathering threads until gathered section lies flat on yoke and anchor thread ends round a pin. Even out or bunch the gathers in groups to achieve the desired effect and fit. Working from gathered side, baste along seam line. Remove pins. Machine beside basting with gathered piece uppermost. Stitch slowly, making sure the gathers do not pleat or become uneven—adjust with points of small scissors. Remove basting and gathers.

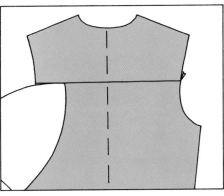

**2.** On WS of garment press the stitching flat and press seam turnings up towards yoke. If yoke is to be top stitched and is in medium or heavy fabric, press turnings open to lessen bulk. Turn yoke so that RS is uppermost and press.

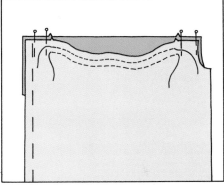

**Attaching gathered section to yoke** On section that is to be attached to yoke, insert two rows of gathering threads between balance marks indicating extent of gathered area. If you are introducing this feature into a pattern or not using a pattern, gather required length. Place yoke on gathered section, RS together. Match balance marks and ends and pin vertically. If whole width of adjoining section is gathered, pin together at ends only.

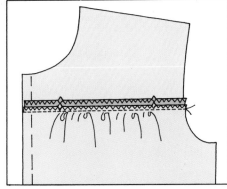

**3.** Trim the gathered seam turning only to 5 mm/¼ in. Press the turnings up into the yoke, taking care not to flatten the gathering. Neaten the seam turning on the yoke piece. Zigzag or oversew the gathered edge, catching it down to the yoke seam turning beneath. ▶

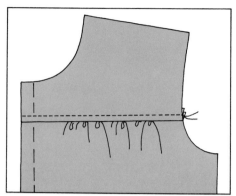

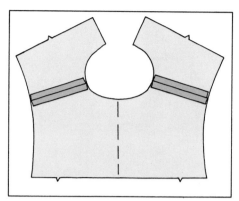

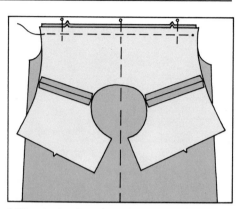

**4.** If you want to top stitch a yoke with a gathered adjoining section, there is no need to press turnings open as for a plain yoke, even on heavy fabric, as bulk is reduced when the gathered edge is trimmed in (3). Top stitch on RS of yoke as for a plain yoke, but work about 3 mm/⅛ in from the edge of the yoke. If the top stitching is right on the edge it will not hold up the seam turnings.

**Double or lined yoke** Cut out of garment fabric two sets of yoke pieces for front and back or cut out one set in fabric and one in thin cotton or lining material. Mark centres and balance marks on yokes and garment. Join shoulder seams with RS together on both sets of yoke pieces. Press shoulder seams open and trim turnings to 5 mm/¼ in.

**2.** Place back yoke to lower back section of garment with RS and raw edges together. Match centres and balance marks and pin, inserting pins vertically. Baste along seam line.

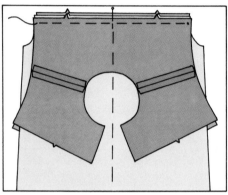

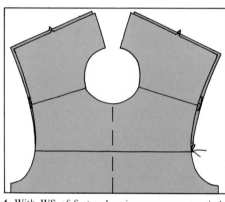

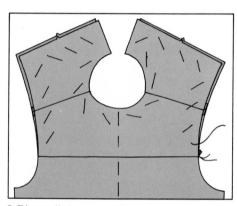

**3.** Take second, or lining, section for back yoke and place with RS of yoke to WS of garment so that yoke edge is level with the basted edges of first yoke and garment section. Match centres and balance marks and pin vertically. Baste along seam line through all layers. Leave centre pin in position to hold centres together, but remove other pins. The garment edge is now sandwiched between the two yoke pieces.

**4.** With WS of first yoke piece uppermost, stitch beside basting through all three layers. Remove basting and centre pin. Trim seam turnings to 5 mm/¼ in. Smooth both yokes upwards and garment section down. On WS press stitching flat and press seam turnings up towards yoke. If yoke is to be top stitched and is in medium or heavy fabric, press turnings open to lessen bulk. Turn yoke to RS and press. Top stitch as for plain yoke if desired.

**5.** Diagonally baste raw edges of the yokes, or yoke and lining, to hold them together while working other sections. Leave at least 2 cm/¾ in free of basting at the front yoke edges for attaching to the garment front sections.

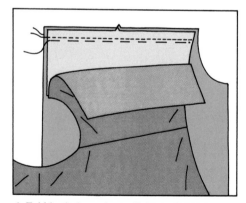

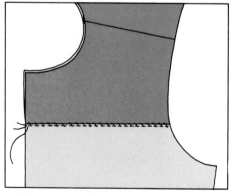

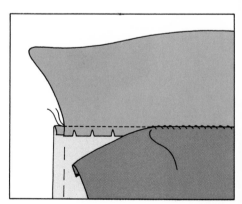

**6.** Fold back the under, or lining, yoke sections on the front yoke pieces. Place the front yokes on to the front garment sections with RS together. Pin and baste along seam line. Stitch beside basting through yoke and garment. Remove basting. On WS press seam up towards yoke and trim turnings to 5 mm/¼ in. If you want to add top stitching to the front yoke, as for a plain yoke, work it at this stage before stitching down under, or lining, yoke.

**7.** Bring under, or lining, yoke down on to seam. Turn under raw edge and baste. Press and finish by hemming into the seam stitching. Remove basting. This type of yoke is generally used on a shirt, so finish collar, sleeves and neck opening as usual, taking in both raw edges of yoke.

**8.** If a collar is to be added to a lined yoke, the lining can neaten neck edge instead of a facing. Join outer yoke to garment as before. Baste collar to RS of neckline. Stitch and remove basting. Trim and snip turnings and press into yoke. Make up yoke lining and press. Place lining on yoke WS together. Baste on shoulders and diagonally on body of yoke. Trim lining edges to 3 mm/⅛ in. Turn in, baste and hem lining round neck, opening and base of yoke.

## ADAPTING A PATTERN TO INCLUDE A YOKE

Draw a line on the existing pattern to mark the extent of the yoke. The yoke line should fall above the level of the bust, the shoulder blades or hips. It may be straight, curved or square (**1**). Make the

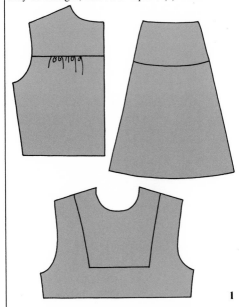

balance marks by pencilling across the line about 2.5 cm/1 in from each edge of pattern piece (**2**). Cut pattern on yoke line (**3**). Make a note on both sections to add seam turnings to edges when cutting out the fabric.

If the yoke is being added as a style feature or merely to economize on fabric, the pattern is now

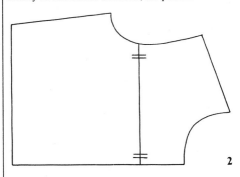

ready. Cut out the two pieces in fabric and make up as for a plain yoke.

If you decide to gather the section adjoining the yoke, cut the pattern top to bottom at the middle of where the gathers are to fall. Pin the two pieces to a sheet of paper, allowing extra width between

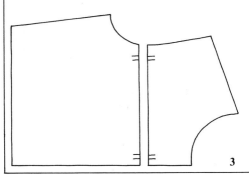

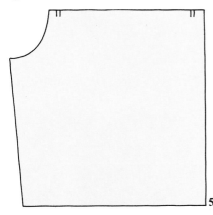

them for the gathers (**4**). Cut out a new pattern and mark balance marks (**5**) and turnings. Using new pattern piece, cut out yoke and adjoining section in fabric and make up in the usual way as for yoke and gathered section.

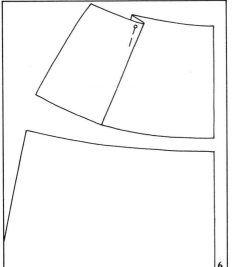

Remove darts if they appear wrong when the pattern is adapted to include a yoke, or if they have become unnecessary because gathers are providing the fullness. If a skirt pattern has been cut to make a yoke and a dart falls in the yoke area, fold and pin the dart on the pattern to remove it (**6**). Folding the dart curves the lower edge of the yoke

and provides shaping for this edge when it is joined to the lower part of the skirt.

If a bodice is cut to make a yoke and gathers are to be inserted in the lower section, the bust dart must be removed. Fold and pin the bust dart

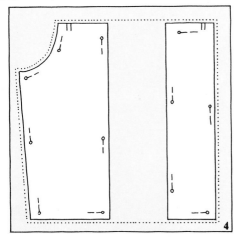

upwards on the pattern to remove it (**7**). Cut the lower section of pattern from top edge down past tip of bust dart to the lower edge (**8**). Spread pieces on another piece of paper and pin, allowing extra width between them for gathers. Cut a new pattern and mark balance marks and turnings.

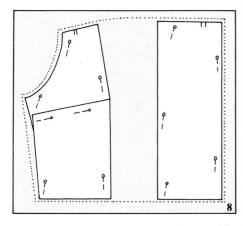

To transform an ordinary yoke into a saddle yoke, overlap shoulder turnings of back and front yoke patterns and pin (**9**). Place pattern on double fabric with centre back to fold if opening is at front, with centre front to fold if opening is at back. Cut out and attach as for plain yoke.

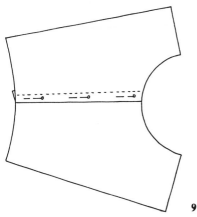

# Pleats

Pleats are folds of fabric treated in different ways to produce characteristic pleat types. Folds all pressed in one direction are knife pleats, while a single knife pleat that is left open below hip level on a skirt is called a kick pleat. Two knife pleats placed close together and pressed away from each other on the wrong side form an inverted pleat; if pressed towards each other they form a box pleat. Sunray pleats are concertina-like pleats graduating in width from almost nothing to about 2 cm/¾ in.

Pleats are most commonly used to create style and fullness in skirts, but can also be used as decoration on the back of bodices, shirts and jackets and on pockets. Most skirt pleats are stitched down for part of their length and pressed flat. However, the pleat folds can be held in position at the waist but left unpressed below the waistband. Decorative pleats are usually pressed flat and then anchored at top and bottom so the pleat can open.

When choosing fabric for pleating remember that all thick, spongy or hairy fabrics are bulky when pleated. For such fabrics restrict pleats to one or two knife, inverted or box pleats. Nearly all closely woven fabrics of light and medium weight pleat well; light synthetic jersey is the exception.

Sunray pleats should be permanently pleated professionally, but this is effective only on very fine or lightweight fabrics and is completely permanent only in synthetics. Always allow plenty of fabric. Shallow knife pleats can be done at home, but good results are difficult.

Success with pleats depends on accuracy, thorough pressing while the fabric is flat and before seams are joined, and a good fit. Choose a pattern for a pleated garment by its hip measurement and fit with pleats basted in place. Pleats should not provide body room: they should hang closed when the body is still.

*As practical and as insulating as porridge, pleated layers of the tartan of the Camerons of Erracht protect a lone piper, left, from Glencoe's chilly blasts.*

*A seductive swirl of diaphanous sunray pleats replaces the traditional seven veils usually favoured by Salome, seen above in her 1914 incarnation.*

# TYPES OF PLEATS

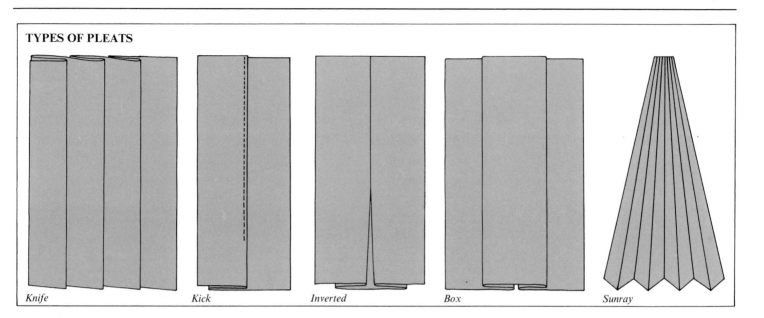

*Knife*    *Kick*    *Inverted*    *Box*    *Sunray*

## PLEAT WIDTHS AND FOLD LINES

The width of a pleat—the width of the concealed fold of fabric on the wrong side of a garment—depends on the type of pleat, the number of pleats, the design of the fabric and the amount of fabric available. As a general guideline, knife pleats may be up to $7\,cm/2\frac{3}{4}$ in wide if single, but if continuous or arranged in groups should be about $2$ to $4\,cm/\frac{3}{4}$ to $1\frac{1}{2}$ in wide. A kick pleat should never be less than $3\,cm/1\frac{1}{4}$ in wide. Inverted and box pleats should be at least $6$ to $8\,cm/2\frac{1}{4}$ to $3\frac{1}{8}$ in wide if used in the back of a skirt, but narrower if in groups because the folds at the backs of adjacent pleats must not overlap. It is most important to mark the width of all types of pleat accurately.

On checked or striped fabric make sure the pattern matches at pleats by avoiding joins except at garment seams. Decide both the width and arrangement of pleats for the best effect on the fabric. Ideally, a pattern of checks should remain unaltered after pleating, but this is difficult to achieve and may involve alterations in pleat width. Striped fabric may be pleated so that part of the design is concealed in the pleat shaping to give a diagonal effect.

Most pleats are stitched down to a depth mark, or release point, whose position varies according to the style of the garment. If you make the pleats narrower than suggested on the pattern, lower the depth marks—this will help stop the pleats opening during wear.

All pleats, apart from sunray, are marked out in the same way: an outer fold line, an inner fold line and a placement line on to which the outer fold line is brought. If more than one piece of fabric is used in a pleated section, place seams at the inner folds so the joins are invisible. The part under the fold between the inner fold and placement lines is the pleat backing. (For inverted and kick pleats a pleat backing cut in fabric of the same weight but of contrasting colour or pattern can produce a variety of attractive pleat effects.) How these lines are combined depends on the pleat type. To distinguish among them, mark fold lines with chalk or basting and placement lines with tailor's tacks.

**Inverted and box pleats** Both have two inner folds, **B**, and two outer folds, **A**; mark these and the centre line of the pleat backing, **C**, on which, for an inverted pleat, the two outer folds will meet on RS, for a box the two inner on WS.

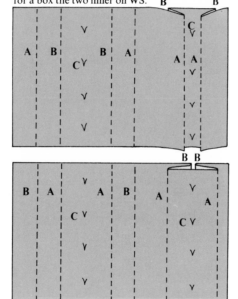

**Knife and kick pleats** Place outer fold, **A**, on placement line, **C**. Inner fold, **B**, falls between them.

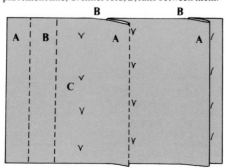

**Separate backing** If a separate backing, **D**, is used on inverted or kick pleats, seams should fall on inner fold lines, **B**. The advantage of a separate backing is that the pleat can be shaped so that it is wider at the hem than at the waist. Because the joins are not on the straight grain the skirt hangs well, and the waist shaping can be taken out of the pleat rather than with darts. If a separate backing is not used, only small adjustments can be made at the waist during fitting.

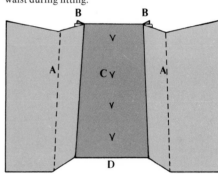

**The part of the backing** above the release point where a kick pleat opens may be cut from lining material if there is not enough fabric, as it will not show during wear. The two parts of the backing should be joined with an open seam. The backing of a kick pleat should always extend up to the waist or the pleat will drop, particularly if the backing hangs loose at the hem.

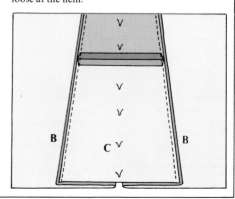

# Pleats

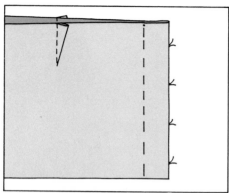

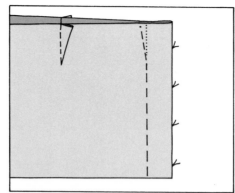

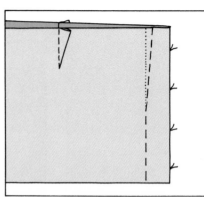

**Knife and kick pleats** Make all markings on garment pieces. Fold fabric RS together so that outer fold line of pleat meets placement line (see pleat widths p. 113). Baste the two layers together from hem to waist along lines. For more than one pleat continue to fold and baste in same way. Baste any darts. Baste side seams. Try on. To fit skirt across hips and thighs adjust side seams, not pleat width.

**2.** Adjustments at the waist can be made by altering the line of pleat basting (the pleat stitching line). To tighten waist, take in pleat stitching line a little at waist and then gradually run new line out to meet original line well above hip level. For grouped pleats, take in a little in this way equally on each pleat. For adjustment of continuous pleats see zip insertion method, p. 116.

**3.** If the pleat stitching line is shaped and the skirt is too tight across the stomach, release basting down to hip and baste a new line up to the waist. Unless the skirt is much too small, never let out the pleat right to the hem because the narrowed pleat will not hang well. If pleats are grouped, alter each one a little and by an equal amount. For adjustment in continuous pleats see zip insertion, p. 116.

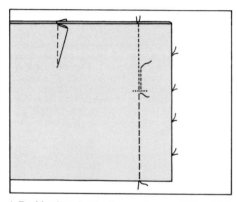

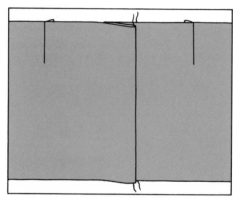

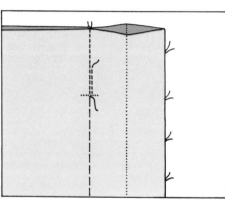

**4.** Decide pleat depth (distance from waist to which pleat will be stitched) during fitting, but do not use pleats to give figure room below waist: make skirt larger at sides instead. Mark depth of each pleat with chalk at release point. Machine from this mark up to waist along basted pleat line, reversing for a few stitches at start. Work large machine stitch from each release point down marked line to hem. Remove basting. Repeat for all pleats.

**5.** On WS press stitching flat and press fold (the pleat) to one side. The direction depends on the style; groups of pleats can be pressed in different directions. Press again from RS. Repeat for all pleats. Pressing must be very thorough to guarantee a crisp pleat fold. Remove large machine stitches. For unpressed pleats complete stages (**1**) to (**4**), but stitch only within seam allowance at waist where waistband will be attached. Press stitching only.

**Inverted pleats** Make all markings on garment pieces. Fold fabric RS together along centre line of pleat backing, matching inner fold lines and outer lines (see pleat widths p. 113). Baste fabric together along outer fold lines. Repeat for any other pleats. Baste any darts and side seams. Fit, adjust, mark pleat depth and machine along basted line with small and large stitches above and below release point as for knife pleats (**2**) to (**4**). Remove all pleat basting.

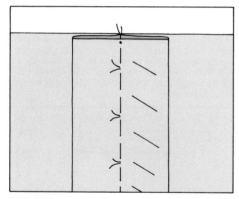

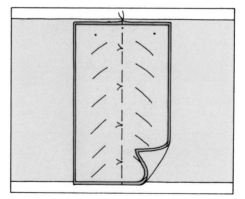

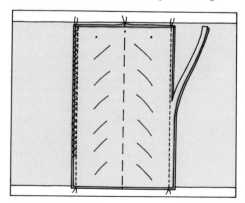

**2.** On WS press stitching flat. Open out the fold of fabric that forms the pleat and press centre line of pleat backing down on to stitched fold lines beneath. On RS smooth pleat seam flat with the fingers, all the way down the pleat, and press. Baste marked placement line to stitched folds. Repeat for any other pleats. Press lightly on RS. Baste diagonally along both folds of each pleat. Press all pleats thoroughly from both WS and RS. Remove basting.

**3.** If separate pleat backing has been cut (see pleat widths p. 113), baste and stitch along outer fold line on garment piece as in (**1**). Remove basting and press open on both WS and RS. Mark centre line on pleat backing. Place pleat backing RS down on WS of pleat with centre line of backing on pleat seam. Baste down. Lift raw edges of pleat and backing and hold together with diagonal basting. Repeat for all pleats.

**4.** With tailor's chalk mark seam line down raw edges of pleat backing. Machine along seam line through backing and pleat edges only. Trim raw edges and neaten. Finish neatening just above where the top of hem turn-up will come to as turning edges in hem area will be finished with the hem. Remove basting.

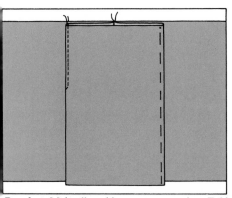

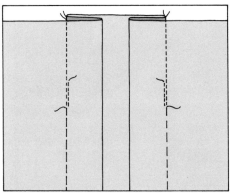

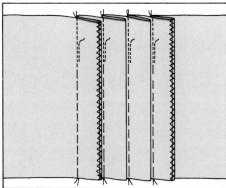

**Box pleats** Make all markings on garment piece. Fold WS of fabric together, match, baste and stitch fold lines as for inverted pleats. Press stitching on RS. Open each pleat out on RS and press so stitched folds are under centre of pleat. Baste pleat edges to garment from waist to hem. Press well. On RS machine or saddle stitch basted edges to garment starting at the waist and finishing at pleat release points. Repeat for all pleats. Remove basting.

**2.** Alternatively, make up two separate knife pleats, but press folds towards each other on WS to form box pleat. Press well on RS and WS. Repeat for all pleats.

**Joins** For an even better fit, the skirt may have a join or several joins in a group of pleats. Place joins at inner fold lines. Make up and press pleats in garment pieces according to type of pleat. Join raw edges on seam line and neaten together. These seams are often shaped into the waist edge, especially if pleats are grouped, as it prevents them overlapping. The distance from the waist at which the seams are shaped depends on the garment style.

## PLEAT FINISHES

Pleats may be finished with decorative stitching or with arrowheads, which provide both decoration and strength at points of strain. Top stitching is added on the right side of the pleats after they have been stitched and pressed, but before the waist finish is completed. The pressed fold of the pleat can be edge stitched, but this stitching should never be used to keep the pleat in place or as a substitute for pressing. Its disadvantage is that it is worked after the hem has been completed and so the stitching may wobble as it has to be worked over uneven thicknesses of fabric.

**Top stitching** Machine from RS, using machine foot as a guide to keep stitching straight. Start at waist and slope stitching in towards pleat release point for the last 5 mm to 1.25 cm/¼ to ½ in (**1**). Repeat for all pleats, making sure that stitching begins to slope at exactly the same level for each one. The size of the stitching and its distance from the pleat edge should match the position of any other top stitching on garment. If preferred, saddle stitch by hand.

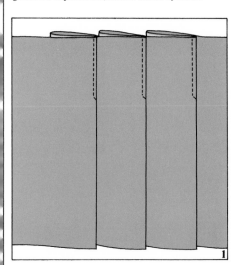

**Edge stitching** Unpick about 2 cm/¾ in of pleat stitching on WS above release point. (If edge stitching is decided on before pleats are machined, when machining leave long ends of thread that can easily be undone and then re-sewn on WS.) Edge

stitch on RS along fold of pleat from release point to hem (**2**). Finish edge stitching at hem by sewing in thread ends on WS by hand. On WS backstitch long threads from pleat stitching down to release point one at a time.

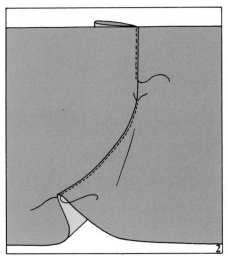

**Arrowhead** Using tailor's chalk, accurately mark out a triangle on RS of garment; make each side about 1 cm/⅜ in long and draw the base line so that the pleat release point lies just inside its centre. Thread a needle with buttonhole thread or top-stitching thread to match thread used for any other top stitching on garment and knot one end of thread. With RS of work uppermost, bring needle up to RS from WS at top of triangle, slightly to the left of its point (**3**).

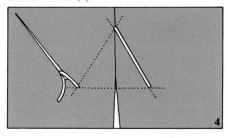

Take needle down to bottom righthand corner of triangle and insert. Bring needle up again at bottom lefthand corner (**4**).

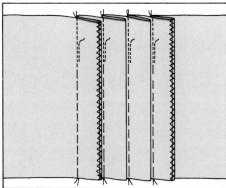

Insert needle slightly to right of top point of triangle and bring up again at top left just below position of first thread (**5**).

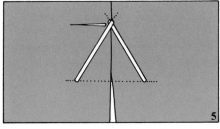

Continue in this way until whole triangle is filled, keeping stitches very close together, so that threads within triangle touch, making sure that stitches are in a straight line along base of triangle and working gradually down its sides (**6**). Fasten off on WS with backstitches and cut off thread end. Press arrow-head with RS down on a towel to preserve its raised appearance.

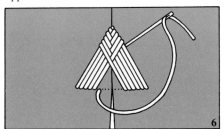

# *Pleats*

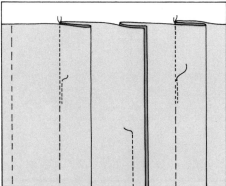

**Inserting a zip in continuous knife pleats** Cut out skirt with wide seam turnings at zip opening (at side seam) so seam position can be adjusted and to ensure even pleating at zip. On skirt back leave two or three pleats unstitched for fitting adjustments after zip is inserted; stitch and press pleats on either side of zip, except final pleat (the one at the zip opening) on skirt front. Baste and stitch side seam up to zip opening. Remove side seam basting.

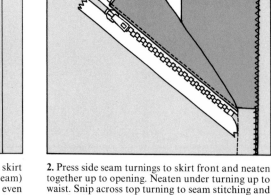

**2.** Press side seam turnings to skirt front and neaten together up to opening. Neaten under turning up to waist. Snip across top turning to seam stitching and turn back raw edge towards skirt back. Press along fitting line. Baste along fold. With work still WS up, set in first side of zip on turned back edge and then remove the basting from this edge.

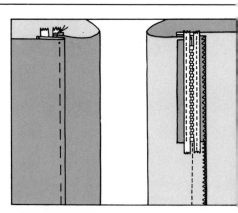

**3.** Baste and press fold of final pleat on RS of skirt and baste pleat down to other side of opening to cover zip. On WS of garment baste second side of zip tape to pleat edge along seam allowance. Do not take basting through to RS of skirt. Backstitch or machine zip tape to pleat edge only. Remove basting and press. Pleat is held in place by waist finish. Fit skirt by adjusting and stitching the last few pleats at back of skirt on WS as for knife pleats (**2**) to (**4**).

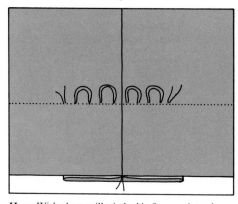

**Hems** With pleats still stitched in from waist to hem, stitch darts and side seams and complete waist. Try on garment and mark hemline in usual way with chalk or basting. Where a pleat occurs, mark through all layers with tailor's tacks, leaving long loops so that the three layers can be parted and loops snipped.

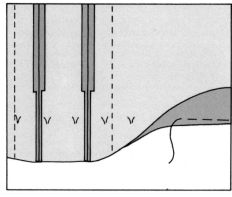

**2.** Unpick large machine stitches holding pleat edges together. Snip tailor's tacks and open out hemline. On WS fold up hem along marked line and baste near fold. Press well. If any stitching holes are still visible in fabric press on RS using a damp cloth. Where a seam occurs in a pleat—for example, when an inverted pleat has a separate backing—press seam open and trim edges to $5\,mm/\frac{1}{4}$ in within hem area before basting and pressing fold.

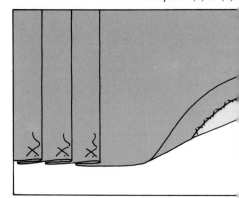

**3.** Trim raw edge of hem to a depth suitable for fabric, but keep hem as deep as possible—up to about $5\,cm/2\,in$—to add weight and so help pleats to hang well. Neaten raw edge. Baste to garment. Finish with catch stitch. On RS fold pleats back into position and work double diagonal basting to form a cross shape across each pleat and through all layers. Press well.

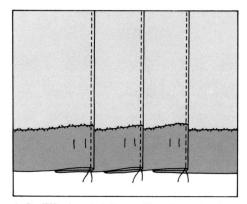

**4.** On WS edge stitch by machine along pleat fold only, from hem to as near waist as possible. If fabric is very bulky, backstitch through hem section by hand. Remove all basting.

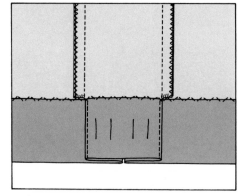

**5.** If pleat backing is separate, backs of pleats will have seams rather than folds. Snip seam edges at top of hem after hem has been completed to allow turnings to extend beyond hem edge. Overcast raw snipped edges. Pleats with a separate backing do not need edge stitching along their whole length, but the pleat fold at the hem must be edge stitched by machine or with backstitch.

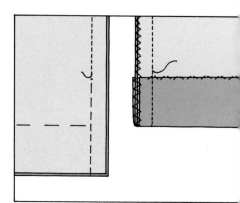

**6.** If a pleated skirt is cut in separate sections, the hem can be finished separately on each. Baste all seams and stitch to within about 13 cm/5 in of raw hem edge. Press seams to one side. Remove basting except in lower, unstitched part of seams. Try on. Mark hemline as in (**1**). Remove lower basting. Turn up and stitch hem on each section. Baste seams again up to end of seam stitching and stitch very slowly. Remove basting. Neaten turnings together.

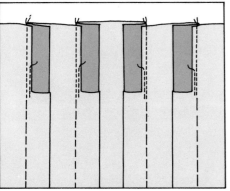

**Reinforcing pleat backs** Several pleats placed close together may produce excess bulk at the waist; if this happens or if pleats overlap, cut away top layer of fabric in pleat on WS from inner fold to within 1.5 cm/⅝ in of stitching and to 1.5 cm/⅝ in above pleat depth marks, leaving under-layer supporting pleat.

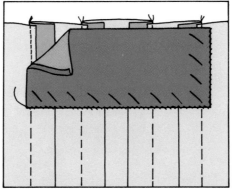

**2.** To reinforce, cut a piece of lining fabric to cover length of pleat section and depth from waist edge to pleat release point, plus allowance for turnings on all but waist edge. Baste diagonally in position to cover raw edges. Turn under lining edges and hem to pleats round three sides, leaving raw edge at the waist. Complete waist finish to include edge of lining.

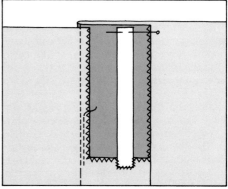

**3.** To reinforce single pleats or pleats in jersey or other fabrics likely to stretch or drop, cut away top layer of pleat as in (**1**). Neaten raw edges where pleat was trimmed away. Cut a thin strip of seam binding or tape the length of stitched pleat depth. Turn under raw edge at base of tape and hem to back of pleat just below where top layer was trimmed away. Pin or baste other edge at the waistline and include it in waist finish.

---

## MAKING A KILT

A traditional adult's kilt requires 3.75 m/4 yd of fabric 145 cm/54 in wide, but a kilt-style skirt can be made with 1.8 m/2 yd of fabric of the same width if the check is small. Cut off a piece for fringe 3 cm/1¼ in wide across whole width of fabric. Cut remaining fabric in half lengthways. Join one end of each piece, RS together, with an open seam to form one long piece, matching selvedges and checks so that check pattern is not altered. Press seam open and neaten.

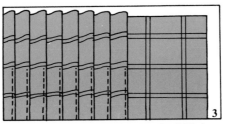

At each end of fabric measure and mark off amount to be left unpleated for the apron overlap and underlap—to extend right across the front of the body. Turn up hem if desired (traditionally, the selvedge is used as a hem). If hem is not turned up, mark top or waistline edge with a chalk cross. Fold fringe in half lengthways WS together and press. Fold under raw edge of apron overlap at the point where fringe will be attached; baste and press. Place this basted edge RS up over folded edge of fringe. Baste and hem or machine down. Make fringe by fraying out extending double raw edges (**2**).

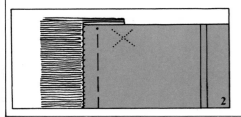

Turn under narrow hem on raw edge of underlap and machine. On RS measure to hip depth and pleat fabric at this level, pinning pleats until pleated section plus one apron equals hip measurement plus 5 cm/2 in for ease. Baste pleats from hip to hem and remove pins (**3**). Traditionally, pleats do not interrupt the tartan pattern, but on shorter lengths fold pleats over evenly on checks.

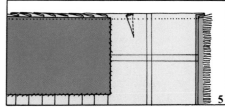

Working on RS, from hip line to waist, fold pleat along same check as below but wrap each pleat over a little farther. Pin all pleats between hip and waist (**4**). Try on. Reduce or increase pleat overlap until waist fits; use a piece of petersham cut to waist size plus one apron width to check easily. It may be necessary on women's kilts to insert small darts near pleats as well. Baste pleats from hip to waistline. Press all pleats well from RS and WS. Hold pleats by working felling stitch along each one on RS from hip to waist. Remove basting.

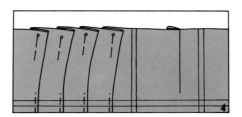

Cut a piece of firm lining material to hip depth and as long as pleated section, allowing for turnings on all but waist edge (see Reinforcing pleats). Diagonally baste lining to WS of pleats, turn under raw edges and hem, except at waist (**5**). Remove basting and try on. Pin apron overlap in place. Traditionally, aprons wrap from left to right, but women's may wrap from right to left. Ensure kilt is hanging level and mark position of overlap. Remove kilt. Place a length of petersham right round waist of kilt, leaving

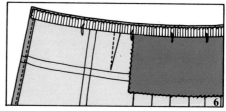

1.25 cm/½ in extending at each end. Mark waist by chalking just below level of petersham all round. Baste petersham to RS of waist edge. Turn in ends level with apron edges and hem. Hem top edge of petersham to kilt. Remove basting holding petersham to waist. Fold petersham over to WS

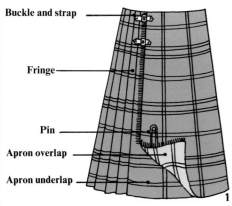

along marked line and press. Hold petersham to kilt at intervals with bar tacks (**6**). Remove remaining basting. Fasten traditionally with buckles, straps and eyelets (stitch straps with leather needle), or wrap apron over and fasten with large hooks and eyes, trouser hooks and eyes or Velcro placed on both parts of apron (**7**). For hooks or Velcro, add straps and buckles as decoration. On all kilts insert a large kilt pin through apron.

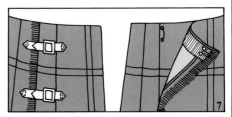

# Collars

The collar is so often the focal point of a garment that it must be made and attached with care for a professional result. This is not always an easy task. Most difficulty with collars arises from the shape of the collar pieces. The neck edge of the collar, that is, the edge that is attached to the neck edge of the garment, may be straight or curved in a slightly convex or concave shape. The concave edge—as on a flat collar, for example—is the easiest to attach because it is nearest in shape to the shape of the neck edge. The slightly convex edge often found on a tailored, classic collar with revers or on a shirt collar is the most difficult to attach because, when placed against the neck edge of the garment, it curves away from it and does not follow its line.

The variation in the shape of the neck edge of the collar also determines whether it lies flat or stands up against the neck. The less the neck edge of the collar follows the shape of the neck edge of the garment, the more the finished collar will stand up.

The outer edge of the collar is shaped in a variety of ways according to the style of the garment, and a paper pattern can easily be altered at this edge without affecting the fit of the collar. The neck edge of the garment may also vary in shape, but is usually slightly shorter than the collar neck edge. Position ease at the shoulder seam areas.

*Although now well over 40 years old, Donald Duck has never forsaken his unmistakable, square-collared American sailor shirt for anything more fashionable or practical, whatever the occasion. (© Walt Disney Productions.)*

*The epitome of sissiness to right-thinking boys, but a paragon of filial virtue to the adoring mamas of the Victorian era, Little Lord Fauntleroy inspired this costume with its ostentatious lacy collar.*

## FITTING, ADJUSTING AND PRESSING

Always attach a collar at the latest possible stage in making a garment, after you have finished fitting and have made any necessary adjustments to the neckline. If the garment has a zip at the neck, insert it before attaching the collar. If an alteration is made to the length of the neckline, alter the collar pattern accordingly. Lengthen a collar pattern by cutting it in two places on either side of the centre back or centre front line and

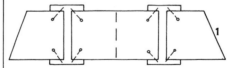

inserting extra paper (**1**). Similarly, shorten it by taking out a small pleat on either side of the centre back or centre front line (**2**). When all adjustments have been made, cut out the collar in fabric.

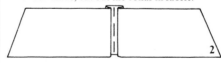

If you are uncertain about the fit or shape of the collar, or its effect on the finished garment, cut out a trial piece in spare fabric or interfacing and attach it at the fitting stage. If adjustments prove necessary, this piece can be altered and used as the collar pattern. Provided the length of the neck edge remains the same, any adjustment to collar shape or style can be made.

When attaching a collar always press the work well at every stage and never resort to top stitching instead of pressing to obtain a sharp outer edge. Press the neckline join as a curve over a pad, towel or sleeve board. If a dressmaker's dummy is available, put the garment on the dummy to press RS of neck join. If the collar has a roll line, keep

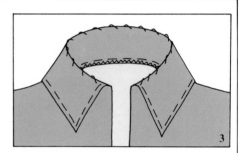

the collar in its rolled shape after basting the roll (**3**). Use the dummy when pressing to establish the roll line that the collar will adopt during wear.

## FACINGS

Although neck facing pieces are usually included in paper patterns the facing generally makes the collar too bulky. To eliminate this unwanted bulk, omit facings wherever possible.

If the collar stands up all round the neck, as in a stand or bias roll collar, or if the garment fastens up to the neck, as with a shirt, the neck join will not be visible and so no facing need be used. For a flat collar a simple alternative to a facing is to use a bias strip to conceal the neck join. However, if any part of the neck join is likely to be visible during wear, as in a classic collar with revers, it must be faced to conceal the join.

A facing is also required on a shawl collar, which usually stands up at the back of the neck, and the neck join at the front of the garment must also be concealed. This is sometimes achieved with a separate facing, but it is generally better to cut the top-collar and facing in one piece in order to avoid a join.

Where a collar is to be placed at a faced opening, always attach the facing or fold back and finish a facing cut as part of the garment after the collar has been attached.

## INTERFACING

All collars require some form of interfacing throughout the whole collar or in particular areas. If even more stiffness is needed in some parts of the collar, as at the points of a shirt collar, an extra layer of interfacing can be inserted.

The choice of interfacing depends on the style of the collar and the fabric. Select heavy, crisp, soft or thin interfacing accordingly. Always try out iron-on interfacing on a small piece of fabric first to ensure that it is not too crisp. Firm iron-on interfacing can be used, however, on stand-up collars, which do not fold over at the neck.

Always interface the section of the collar that is attached first to the neckline of the garment. For most collar styles this is the under-collar—the section that lies against the garment and does not show in wear. However, on stand-up collars it is the outer collar section that is interfaced, and often on men's shirts a better result is obtained by interfacing the outer collar.

Before attaching any type of collar, always make sure that the centre lines of both top- and under-collar pieces are marked with basting and that all turnings and any fold lines are appropriately marked. Also check that all markings on the neck edge of the garment have been made.

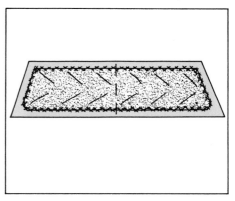

**Cut lightweight or thin interfacing** using collar pattern. If using iron-on interfacing, trim off 2 mm/$\frac{1}{16}$ in from all edges, to prevent interfacing sticking to ironing surface, and press on WS of under-collar. For sew-in interfacing, diagonally baste to WS of under-collar. The edges of both types of interfacing are later stitched into seams and light sew-in interfacing is trimmed close to the machining.

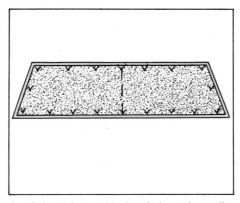

**2.** Mark turnings and centre front and centre back on garment. Attach suitable interfacing to WS of collar, to extend from one edge to 5 mm/$\frac{1}{4}$ in past fold line. Mark all turnings on collar pieces and mark centre and fold lines.

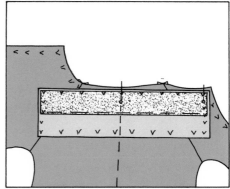

**Cut heavyweight or thick interfacing** to finished collar size using collar pattern. Either cut round collar pattern and then carefully cut off 1.5 cm/$\frac{5}{8}$ in all round interfacing, or trim turnings off pattern and then cut interfacing. According to type of interfacing, press or diagonally baste it in position on WS of under-collar. Cut off corners of interfacing at outer points of collar. Herringbone sew-in interfacing into place.

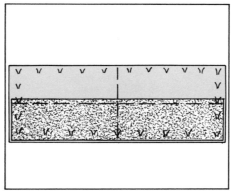

**3.** With RS of garment uppermost, place RS of collar down on RS of garment, with interfaced section towards neck edge. Match centre line of collar with centre back (or front) line of garment. Insert a pin across fitting line. Bring centre front (or back) markings at collar ends to meet centre front (or back) markings at opening on garment neckline. Pin across fitting line at each end, picking up fabric on this line only.

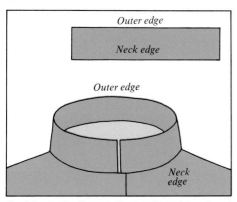

**Straight stand collar** stands away from the neck and is usually fairly narrow. If the edges are together at the front of the garment the collar is Chinese in style; if they meet at the back it is Victorian, a style often used on children's clothes, with tucks or lace. Cut a straight piece of fabric to twice the finished depth of the collar, plus two 1.5 cm/$\frac{5}{8}$ in turnings.

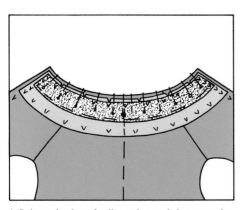

**4.** Snip neck edge of collar at intervals between pins to help collar lie flat against neckline. Lift neckline to keep it curved and pin collar to neckline. Use plenty of pins, inserting them across fitting line and picking up fabric on this line only. Baste with small stitches on fitting line. If any pleats or folds form, take smaller stitches. Remove pins.

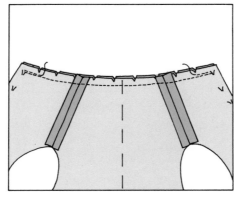

**5.** Snip neck edge of collar and garment together, ending snips halfway between raw edges and basting line. Turn work over so that neckline of garment is uppermost and machine close to basting. Stitch slowly and stop frequently to examine underside to make sure that pleats or folds are not being sewn in. Fasten off machining at each end exactly on centre front (or back) lines by reversing for a few stitches. Remove basting.

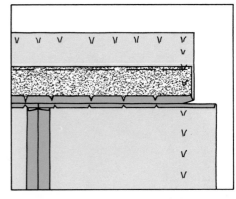

**6.** Arrange neckline on a sleeve board, pad or towel with RS of garment uppermost and run toe of iron round neck join, between collar and bodice. On WS trim garment edge at neck join to 3 mm/$\frac{1}{8}$ in and collar edge to 5 mm/$\frac{1}{4}$ in. If light or thin sew-in interfacing has been used, trim its edge very close to machining to help reduce bulk within turning. On WS of garment press neck join open. Turn to RS of garment and press join again.

▶

# Collars

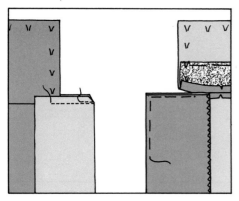

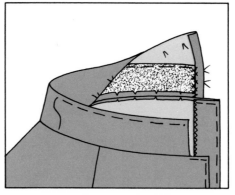

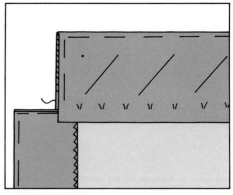

**7.** If facing is cut as part of garment, fold along marked line to RS and baste and machine top edge from collar fitting line to folded edge. For a separate facing, place it RS down on RS of garment and attach. For both types of facing, trim turnings along top edge and outer corner, and trim down the front on a separate facing. Turn through as for a normal facing. Baste and press edges so that join is 2 mm/$\frac{1}{16}$ in to WS. Neaten outer edge of facing.

**8.** With garment WS up, fold in collar ends along marked lines from neck join to 1 cm/$\frac{3}{8}$ in past centre fold line on collar. Baste folded ends. Press. Trim edges of turned-in ends to no less than 3 mm/$\frac{1}{8}$ in and, if fabric is springy, herringbone these edges down to hold in place. Remove basting. Turn garment so that RS of collar is uppermost and fold collar in half along fold line. Baste along fold. Press.

**9.** On WS finish collar ends by trimming raw edges of inner (unfolded) sections to no less than 3 mm/$\frac{1}{8}$ in. Fold in ends of inner sections so that they lie 2 mm/$\frac{1}{16}$ in to WS of collar and are invisible from RS. Baste. Press and slip stitch ends. Work a row of diagonal basting along centre of collar through both layers to hold them together.

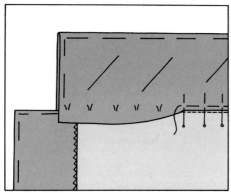

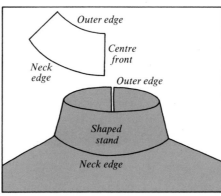

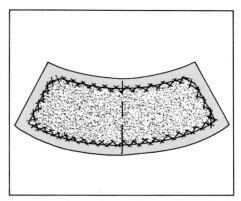

**10.** If fabric is lightweight, press all neck join turnings towards collar on WS of garment. Turn under raw edge of collar and pin vertically to neck edge on WS of garment, starting at centre. Baste. Remove pins. Finish by hemming into machining of neck join. Oversew end of facing to collar edge at top corner. For all other types of fabric, complete neck edge as for shaped stand collar (**8**) by prick stitching from RS into neck join. Remove all basting. Press.

**Shaped stand collar** A slightly curved collar that fits well up against the neck and can be made to any reasonable depth. The garment usually fastens at the back with the collar standing above the zip. Because of the shaping, two pieces of fabric are cut and then joined along their outer edges. The neck edge of the collar is the same length as that of the garment but the top, outer, edge is shorter, producing a closer fit than a straight stand collar.

**2.** Mark turnings and centre front and centre back on garment. Insert zip. Cut collar with straight grain running down centre front. If fabric is bulky, use lining material or cotton lawn for inner collar. Attach interfacing to outer collar as appropriate (see p. 119). Mark all turnings and centre front line on top and inner collar pieces.

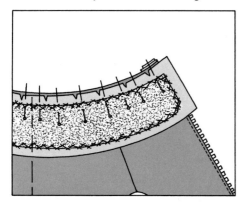

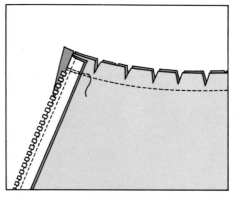

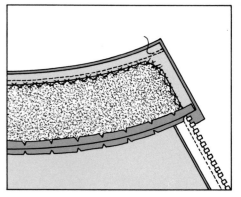

**3.** Place RS of outer collar on RS of garment neckline, matching centre front line on garment to centre line of collar. Pin across fitting line. Snip collar at neckline edge to bring collar and garment together at centre back, matching turnings at centre back exactly. Pin at each end. Pin frequently between centre front and centre back across fitting line, picking up fabric on this line only. Baste on fitting line. Remove pins.

**4.** If necessary, snip collar and neckline edges together halfway into turnings to make sure that the collar lies flat. With garment side uppermost, machine close to basting. Fasten off machining at each end exactly at centre back lines by reversing for a few stitches. Remove basting. To layer turnings, trim neck edge to 3 mm/$\frac{1}{8}$ in and collar edge to 5 mm/$\frac{1}{4}$ in. Trim lightweight or thin sew-in interfacing close to machining.

**5.** From WS of garment, press join open, making more snips if necessary so join lies flat. Press again on WS and RS. With RS of garment uppermost, place lining or inner collar against outer collar, RS together, matching centre front and fitting lines. Baste along outer edge at collar top on fitting line. Check depth of collar stand is equal all round—for accuracy use an adjustable marker. Machine from interfaced side beside basting. Remove basting.

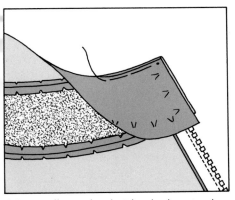

**6.** Layer collar turnings by trimming inner turnings to 3 mm/⅛ in and outer to 5 mm/¼ in and then trim interfacing close to machining if appropriate. Snip well. Roll inner collar to WS of garment, bringing join 2 mm/1/16 in over to WS. Baste along fold to hold join in place, leaving ends of collar free to be turned in. Press basted fold.

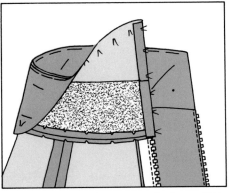

**7.** Baste diagonally along centre of collar on RS to hold lining flat. With WS of garment uppermost, turn in ends of collar along fitting lines to 1 cm/⅜ in past join at top edge of collar and then slightly more so that inner collar edge lies 2 mm/1/16 in to WS of collar. Slip stitch ends as far as the marked seam line on neck edge.

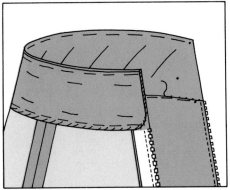

**8.** Trim raw edge of inner collar to 5 mm/¼ in and neaten. Neaten raw, snipped edge of garment only with overcasting. Baste edge of inner collar flat over neck join. Press. To prevent ends of inner collar from being visible beside zip, either trim collar edge at an angle and neaten or turn under and hem to zip tape. Turn to RS of collar and work prick stitch through into neck join. Remove all basting.

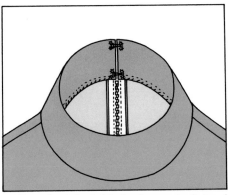

**9.** The ends of the finished collar can be fastened with hooks or Velcro. If using Velcro attach both pieces to inner collar on WS of garment, but arrange one piece so that it protrudes sufficiently to be fastened invisibly during wear, as for bias roll collar (7). Similarly, place hooks and eyes on WS, or work thread loops instead of eyes, just to inside of collar.

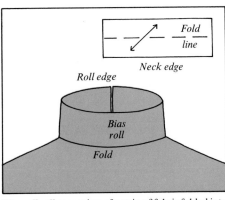

**Bias roll collar** consists of a strip of fabric folded into a double roll. The collar can be of any reasonable depth, but a finished roll of less than about 3 cm/1¼ in will not remain in rolled position during wear. Cut fabric on true cross to four times finished width of roll, plus two 1.5 cm/⅝ in turnings. It should be slightly longer than neck edge of garment. A garment with this type of collar usually fastens with a zip at centre back.

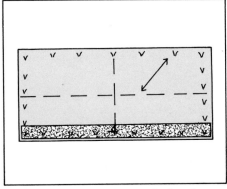

**2.** Mark all turnings and centre back and centre front on garment. Insert zip. Interface WS of collar along neck edge with a strip of iron-on interfacing of appropriate weight (see p. 119) and 2.5 cm/1 in wide (or proportionately wider for a deep collar). This interfacing is sufficient to support the collar against the neck. Mark all turnings, fold line and centre front line on collar piece.

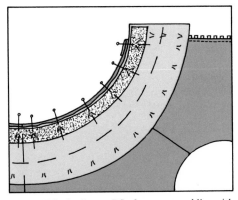

**3.** Place RS of collar on RS of garment neckline with interfaced section at neckline edge. Match centre front lines and pin across fitting line. Match centre back lines on collar ends and garment and pin across fitting line. Pin at intervals round neck, picking up fabric on fitting line only and easing in any fullness in the collar to fall near shoulder seams. On firm fabrics it may be necessary to snip the garment neckline to ensure the collar lies flat.

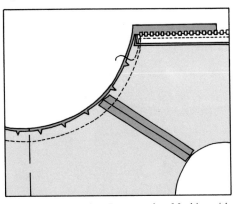

**4.** Baste on fitting line. Remove pins. Machine with garment side uppermost and fasten off machining by reversing for a few stitches, exactly at centre back lines above zip. Remove basting. Snip turnings in garment neckline only. Press join open from WS and press again on RS.

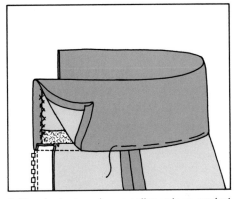

**5.** Turn in, baste and press collar ends on marked lines along their whole length. Trim raw edges of ends to 3 mm/⅛ in. On springy fabrics herringbone over raw edge of turning on inner part of roll to hold it in place. Remove basting. On fine fabrics, press turnings at neck join into collar, bring raw edge down, turn under, baste and hem into machining. Slip stitch ends so that inner edge is 2 mm/1/16 in to WS of garment. Remove all basting.

▶

121

# Collars

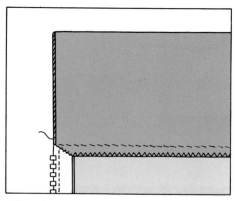

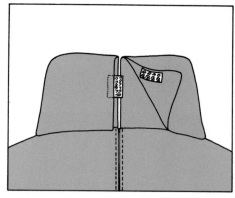

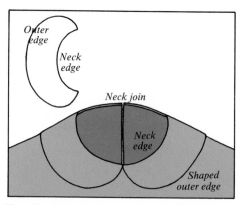

**6.** For all other fabrics, keep neck join open. Neaten raw edges of collar and baste flat over neck join. Beside zip, trim collar edge at an angle and neaten or turn under and hem. On RS of garment, prick stitch into join between collar and garment as for shaped stand collar (**8**). Slip stitch collar ends as in (**5**) so that the join is 2 mm/$\frac{1}{16}$ in to WS of garment. Remove all basting.

**7.** Place fold edge of collar on pressing surface. Hold one end of collar and stretch edge with iron. This ensures that the collar falls over and covers the neck join. Roll collar to RS of garment, allowing it to find its own roll line. Fasten collar with small hooks and eyes placed under outer part of roll or with a small piece of Velcro hemmed in a similar position, but with one part extending slightly from edge of roll.

**Flat collar** Neck edge is curved in a similar shape to garment neck. If both edges are exactly the same shape the collar lies completely flat with no stand. However, few flat collars are cut without a stand. The collar is usually in two parts, each made from two pieces of fabric, with outer edges curved to form a Peter Pan style. It can also be in one piece and the outer edge any shape. A very long outer edge will produce a fluted collar.

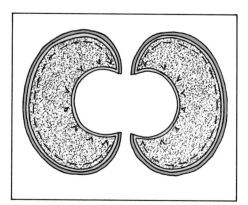

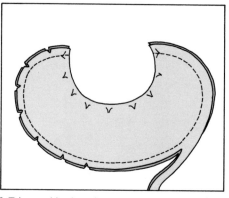

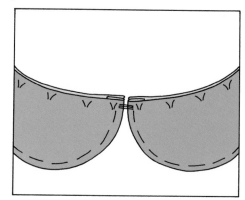

**2.** Mark turnings and centre front and centre back on garment. Cut out collar pieces. Interface whole of two under-collar pieces on WS as appropriate (see p. 119). Mark all turnings on collar pieces. Place under-collar pieces against top-collar pieces, RS together. Baste and machine round all except neckline edges, working from interfaced side and following turning lines exactly. Remove basting.

**3.** Trim machined turnings to no less than 3 mm/$\frac{1}{8}$ in. Trim interfacing close to machining if appropriate. Snip curved sections of machined outer edges of collar pieces every 5 mm/$\frac{1}{4}$ in.

**4.** Turn collar pieces RS out. Roll edges so that join is 2 mm/$\frac{1}{16}$ in to underside of each collar piece. Baste rolled edges. Press well. Place two collar pieces together at centre front and work a bar tack to hold them together, exactly on fitting line of neck edge.

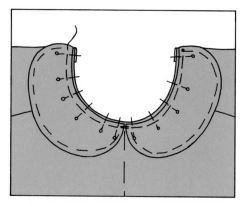

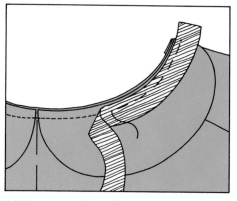

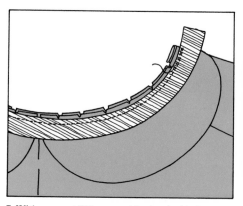

**5.** Place under-collar down on RS of garment neckline. Match centre front of garment and collar and pin across fitting line. Similarly, pin ends of collar to match centre back lines of garment. Insert more pins at intervals across fitting line, picking up fabric on this line only. Snip garment neckline if necessary so collar lies flat. Baste. Remove pins. With collar side up, machine on fitting line, reversing at collar ends. Remove basting.

**6.** Unless garment is to be faced as in (**10**) or lined as in (**11**), cut a bias strip of fabric or bought bias binding 2.5 cm/1 in wide to length of neckline, plus a 1.5 cm/$\frac{5}{8}$ in turning at either end. On RS of garment centre strip RS down over machine stitches so an equal amount extends at each end of collar. Taking a 5 mm/$\frac{1}{4}$ in turning on strip, baste along neck fitting line on top of machining joining collar to neckline.

**7.** With garment WS up, machine just inside first row of stitching exactly from centre back edge to centre back edge, starting and finishing by reversing for a few stitches. Remove basting. To layer turnings, trim edge of bias strip to 2 mm/$\frac{1}{16}$ in, trim garment neckline edge to 5 mm/$\frac{1}{4}$ in and collar edges to 3 mm/$\frac{1}{8}$ in. Trim interfacing close to machining if appropriate. Snip edges of garment and collar at intervals of 5 mm/$\frac{1}{4}$ in.

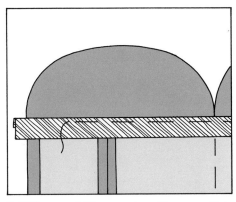

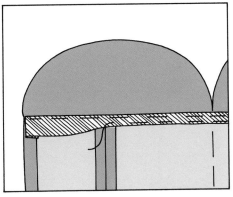

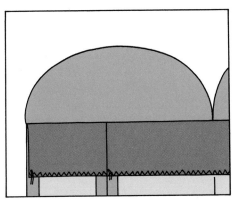

**8.** With garment RS up, run toe of iron round join under collar, and then place collar alone, RS up, on pressing surface and run toe of iron along join under edge of bias strip. With WS of garment uppermost, hold collar upright, smooth down bias strip over neck join to WS and baste just below join through turnings and garment. Press on WS.

**9.** Turn under both ends of bias strip so that they lie 2 mm/$\frac{1}{16}$ in from centre back edge. Baste. Trim 5 mm/$\frac{1}{4}$ in off remaining raw edge of bias strip, turn under and baste to garment. Press. Slip stitch ends of bias strip and slip hem turned-in edge to garment. Remove basting.

**10.** A flat collar may be neatened with a facing rather than a bias strip, but this adds unnecessary bulk and on children's clothes, where the facings are small, a faced collar can be fiddly to cope with in laundering. Treat as a normal facing after attaching collar. Place RS down on RS of garment over collar, machine from garment side with garment WS up, trim and snip. Roll facing to WS, neaten lower edge and anchor with bar tacks at shoulder seams and centre back.

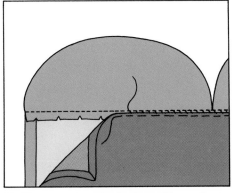

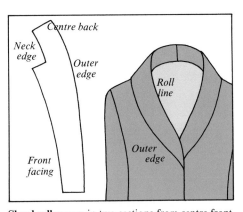

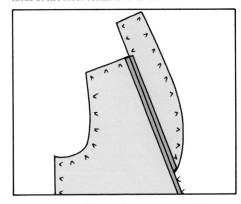

**11.** If garment is to be lined, machine collar to neckline, snip and layer turnings, trimming garment edge to 5 mm/$\frac{1}{4}$ in and collar edge to 3 mm/$\frac{1}{8}$ in. Press turnings towards bodice. Insert lining and neaten neck join by turning in edge of lining, basting it down and hemming into machine stitches at neck join. Remove basting.

**Shawl collar** runs in two sections from centre front opening or seam to centre back, where it is joined. Garment neck is usually V-shaped and, as collar neck edge is straighter than garment neck, the collar has a stand at back of neck. Under-parts are usually cut in one with front bodice, but may be cut separately and joined to bodice before shoulder seams are joined and collar is attached. Outer edge may be curved, pointed or scalloped.

**2.** Mark all turnings and centre front and centre back on garment. If separate pieces are to be attached to bodice for under-collar sections mark all turnings. Place front bodice and under-collar pieces RS together from shoulders down centre front bodice edges as far as collar extends, leaving back neck section of collar extending. Baste and machine along fitting lines and press seam open. Make all markings on top-collar.

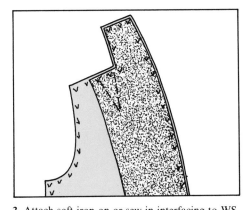

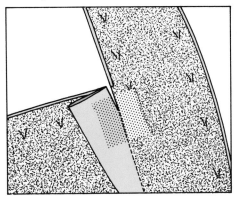

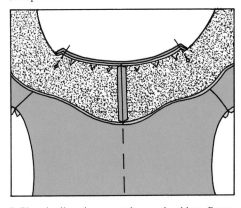

**3.** Attach soft iron-on or sew-in interfacing to WS of under-collar area of garment, extending it down centre front of garment if there is a front opening or fastening. If under-collar is cut in one piece with front bodice, make all markings on top-collar pieces and under-collar sections. Whether under-collar is separate or attached, on some patterns a dart is taken out of each side of collar neckline to improve its shape. Mark darts.

**4.** On WS of each under-collar, baste darts. Machine from fitting lines (not raw edges) to points. Remove basting. Trim away interfacing within dart to reduce bulk. Press darts towards armholes. If necessary, attach small pieces of paper-backed adhesive to WS of fabric at raw neck edges below base of dart to prevent fraying; snip fabric from neck edge to beginning of dart stitching.

**5.** Place bodice pieces together at shoulders. Baste and machine shoulder seams. Remove basting. Press seams open and neaten. Turn garment RS out and bring back neck edges of under-collar sections round to match back neck of garment. Pin to garment across fitting lines at back neck and between shoulder seams. Baste and stitch centre back ends of under-collar RS together. Remove basting. Press seam open and trim to 5 mm/$\frac{1}{4}$ in. ▶

# Collars

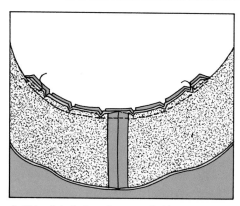

**6.** Trim interfacing close to stitching. To attach under-collar between shoulder seams along back of neck, baste, remove pins and machine with collar side up. Start and finish machining exactly at ends of shoulder seam stitching to avoid leaving a hole. Remove basting. Snip both turnings and layer them, trimming garment edge to 5 mm/$\frac{1}{4}$ in and collar edge to 3 mm/$\frac{1}{8}$ in. Trim interfacing close to machining. Press seam open.

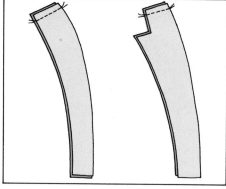

**7.** If top-collar is wide at shoulders, make darts in top-collar pieces as in (**4**). Place pieces together at centre back, RS together, baste and machine. Remove basting. Trim join to 3 mm/$\frac{1}{8}$ in and press open. The top-collar does not correspond in shape to the under-collar as the front facing is cut in one piece with it—it may extend over shoulder seams, above right. If garment is unlined, neaten outer edges of facing and, on all but fine fabrics, top-collar.

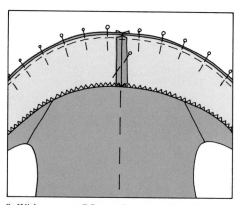

**8.** With garment RS up, place top-collar RS down on RS of under-collar. Match collar seams at centre back and pin across fitting line, picking up fabric on this line only. Match darts and pin. Pin round outer edge of collar and down centre front. Baste, remove pins and machine along fitting line. Trim turnings on garment to 5 mm/$\frac{1}{4}$ in and on top-collar to 3 mm/$\frac{1}{8}$ in. Trim interfacing close to machining. Snip turnings together frequently.

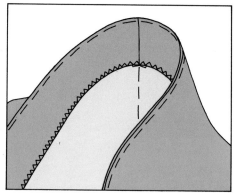

**9.** Press seam open up front edges and as far round outer edge of collar as possible. Turn top-collar to WS of garment. Roll edge and baste so join is 1 to 3 mm/$\frac{1}{16}$ to $\frac{1}{8}$ in to underside, depending on the fabric. Adjust position of top-collar and front facings so fitting lines match on WS of garment.

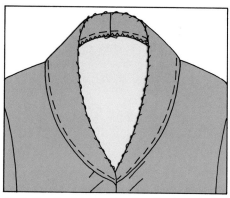

**10.** Roll collar into position it will adopt during wear. Work a row of diagonal basting over roll. Diagonally baste rest of front facings flat to WS of garment. Baste inside back neck between shoulder seams of top-collar flat to under-collar just above neatened edge.

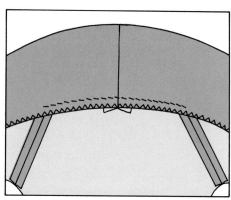

**11.** On all but fine fabrics, neaten raw edges of collar and garment seam at back of neck and from RS of garment prick stitch into neck join between shoulder seams. If facing ends extend over shoulder seams, herringbone ends to seam turnings on WS. Remove all basting.

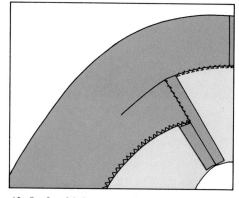

**12.** On fine fabrics, press snipped turnings at neck join up into collar, turn under raw edge of top-collar and hem across back of neck between shoulder seams. If facing ends extend over shoulder seams, turn them under and hem to seam turnings. If desired, hold down rest of facing on fine and bulky fabrics with small pieces of adhesive strip—if the strip will not show through on RS. Insert strip at intervals on WS of facing. Remove basting.

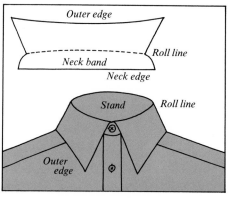

**Shirt collar** Made from two pieces of fabric joined at outer edges so collar points can be shaped. Neck edge is straight or slightly convex to give collar a stand at back of neck. Roll line is high at back but runs down to neck edge at centre front. For a higher, neck-hugging collar, a neck band can be cut as part of the collar or attached separately. Attach facings at centre front opening and turn them to WS in the usual way before attaching collar.

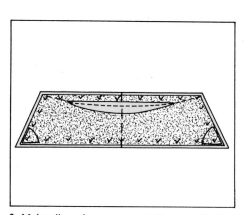

**2.** Make all marks on garment. Cut out all collar pieces. Interface under- or top-collar as appropriate (see p. 119). Add additional triangles of stiffening of a crisper type to collar points if desired. To achieve a good roll line with very stiff interfacing cut interfacing away on roll line. If collar has a neck band, interface band twice. Mark turnings, roll line and centre back line on collar pieces and turnings and centre back line on band if separate.

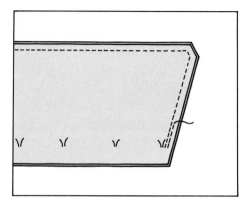

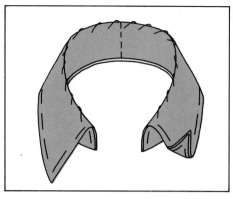

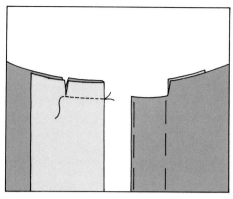

**3.** For collar without band, place top- and under-collar pieces RS together, matching centre back lines. Baste and machine round all but neck edges, starting and finishing exactly on centre front turning lines and working one machine stitch across each point to aid turning through. Trim and layer turnings to no less than $3\,mm/\frac{1}{8}$ in. Trim interfacing close to machining. Cut off corners at points and snip any curves on outer edges.

**4.** Place collar, still WS out, on pressing surface and run toe of iron inside it, along seam line. Turn collar RS out. Ease out points with a pin or collar point turner. Roll outer edges and baste so that join is $2\,mm/\frac{1}{16}$ in to underside of collar. Press. Fold collar into rolled position it will adopt in wear and baste diagonally across roll line.

**5.** Fold front facing to RS. Machine along top edge from fold to centre front mark. Snip turnings down to machining at centre front mark and trim off corner. Turn RS out. Baste facing down to WS.

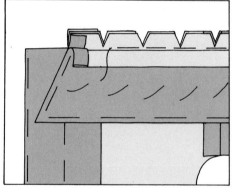

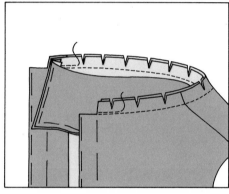

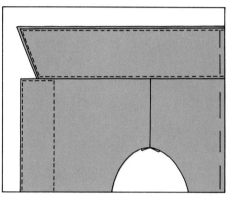

**6.** Opening collar out slightly, place RS of under-collar on WS of garment neckline, matching centre back lines. Pin across fitting line at centre back, picking up fabric on this line only. Pin centre front ends of under-collar to centre front lines of garment across fitting line. Snip edges of under-collar and garment so that collar lies flat. Baste under-collar to garment along fitting line at neck. Remove pins.

**7.** Machine from garment side with garment RS up, making sure that top-collar is not sewn in. Start and finish stitching exactly at collar ends and fasten off well here. Remove basting round neck edge. Trim turning on under-collar to $3\,mm/\frac{1}{8}$ in and turning on neck edge to $5\,mm/\frac{1}{4}$ in. Trim interfacing close to machining if appropriate (see p. 119). Press turnings up into collar. Press neck join from WS of garment.

**8.** Trim top-collar edge to $5\,mm/\frac{1}{4}$ in. Turn it under and baste in position so that it covers machine stitching. Machine on edge round neck with under-collar side up. Remove basting. Top stitch collar and front facing if desired from RS of collar and garment. Remove basting on facing.

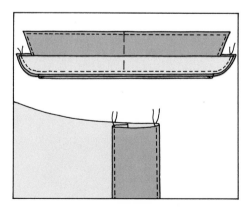

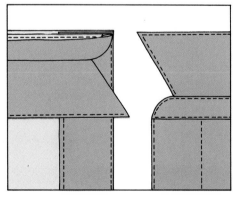

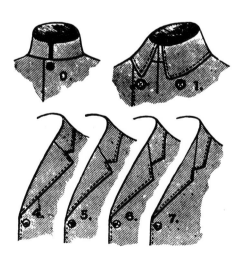

**9.** If collar has a separate band, make up collar as in (**2**) to (**4**). Turn to RS and top stitch. Place two band pieces RS together and, matching centre back markings, insert neck edge of collar between two band pieces until raw edges of collar are level with shaped edges of band pieces. To join, baste and machine along marked turning line on band from end to end. Remove basting. Turn front garment facings to WS and machine.

**10.** Trim one band turning to $2\,mm/\frac{1}{16}$ in, one collar turning to $4\,mm/\frac{1}{8}$ in, the second to $2\,mm/\frac{1}{16}$ in, and the other band turning to $4\,mm/\frac{1}{8}$ in. Snip turnings. Turn band RS out. Attach under-piece to neck as for under-collar in (**6**) to (**8**), but take ends to edges of centre front opening. On RS stitch along edge of top band piece on neck join; top stitch all round rest of band. If band is cut in one with collar, attach as for basic shirt collar, but take ends to centre front edges.

*Collar styles in 1907, selected from* The Tailor and Cutter *magazine, reflect the popularity of military styles like the stand up (0) and flat collar (1) and demonstrate the surprising number of variations possible on the classic lapelled jacket (4,5,6,7).*

# Collars

## Classic collar and revers

This collar, which is one of the most difficult to attach successfully, has a neck edge that is slightly convex in shape. The shape of the outer edge may vary widely—some collars have short points, for example, while others have wide or long points. The roll line of the collar runs from the back of the neck, where there is a stand, to the centre front edge of the neckline, where it lies flat against the bodice. The easiest way to ensure that the collar is evenly set and that equal steps and revers, or lapels, are produced is to finish the collar from the right side of the garment by hand.

The revers is formed by attaching a facing to the garment bodice front or by folding back a facing that is cut in one with the bodice front. In this way it has not changed since its inception during the 14th century when gentlemen had borders or facings, often of fur, on their outer garments. The revers, the upper part of the border, showed only when the coat was opened. Subsequently the term came to mean the turned-back edge of a coat, waistcoat or bodice. Revers varied in style according to fashion, first assuming a shape close to that of today at the end of the 1700s when the English riding jacket became the model for the dress coat worn by the European middle classes.

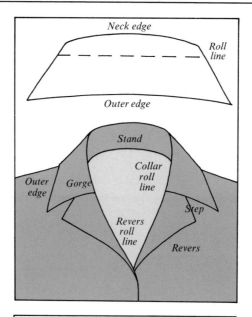

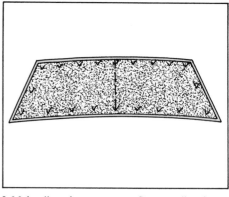

**2.** Make all marks on garment. Cut out collar pieces. Attach interfacing to whole of under-collar as appropriate (see p. 119), but if fabric is jersey or tweed, or is soft, use stretch or woven interfacing. Mark all turnings and centre back lines on top- and under-collar pieces. Interface WS of front opening area of garment with interfacing of the correct weight and, if fabric is heavy, interface shoulder area of garment as well.

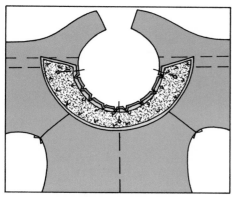

**3.** With garment RS up, place under-collar RS down on neck edge, matching centre back lines. Pin across fitting line, picking up fabric on this line only. Snip both edges if necessary to help collar lie flat and bring centre front ends of collar exactly to centre front lines of garment. Pin across fitting line. Baste and remove pins.

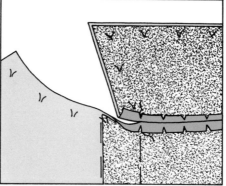

**4.** With garment WS up, machine on fitting line, starting and finishing exactly at centre front lines. Fasten off thread at start and finish by reversing. Remove basting. Snip edges a little more and trim garment edge to 5 mm/$\frac{1}{4}$ in and collar to 3 mm/$\frac{1}{8}$ in. Trim interfacing close to stitching if appropriate (see p. 119). Press join open from WS and RS.

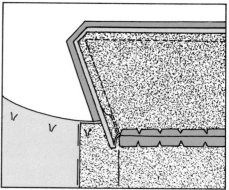

**5.** Place top-collar on under-collar, RS together, matching centre back lines and easing any fullness into outer edge. Baste and machine round outer edge of collar, ending stitching exactly at end of neck join stitching, and working one stitch across each collar point. Remove basting. Layer edges, one to 5 mm/$\frac{1}{4}$ in, one to 3 mm/$\frac{1}{8}$ in, and trim interfacing close to machining if appropriate. Snip outer edge of collar. Trim corners diagonally.

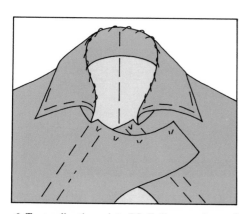

**6.** Turn collar through to RS. Roll outer edge until join is 2 mm/$\frac{1}{16}$ in to underside of collar, baste join in position and press. Arrange collar as it will fall during wear and baste diagonally over roll line. Place garment RS out on a dressmaker's dummy, sleeve board, pad or rolled-up towel and press roll line. Collars in woollens and other soft fabrics may be shaped into a good position with the fingers while they are still warm from pressing.

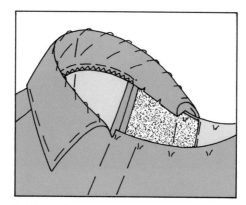

**7.** At back of neck between shoulder seams, baste top-collar flat to under-collar with diagonal stitches below roll and above raw edge. On all but fine fabrics, neaten raw edge of under-collar along back neck edge between shoulder seams. Baste under-collar flat over neck join, again between shoulder seams. On fine fabrics, press neck join turnings up into collar and turn under raw edge of under-collar between shoulder seams before basting.

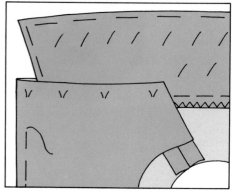

**8.** Fold front facings over to WS of garment on fold line or, if facings are separate, attach and fold back as for normal facings. With garment WS up, baste each centre front edge near fold to within about 2 cm/$\frac{3}{4}$ in of neck edge. If facings are separate, roll joins so they are 2 mm/$\frac{1}{16}$ in to WS, and so invisible in wear, before basting.

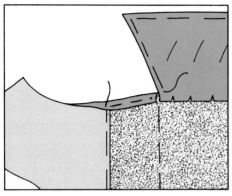

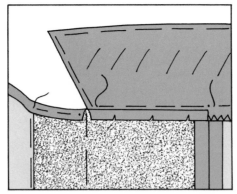

**9.** Turn work so that garment is RS out and open out the part of the facing that has not been basted down at centre front edge. Turn in top edge of each facing to WS from end of collar to marked point at centre front corner. Baste and press turnings. On WS of garment, trim raw edges of basted facing turnings to 2 to 4 mm/$\frac{1}{16}$ to $\frac{1}{8}$ in—the amount depends on the bulkiness of the fabric and also on how much it frays.

**10.** Trim edge of top-collar to 5 mm/$\frac{1}{4}$ in between centre front lines and shoulder seams on either side— these are the sections not basted down to the neck edge in (**7**). Turn under these trimmed edges exactly on join of seam pressed open at neck. Baste and press.

*The ultimate in nautical chic, boating pyjamas were a 1930s fashion worn either in midshipman style with a modified sailor collar or double-breasted, officer fashion in impractical white flannel.*

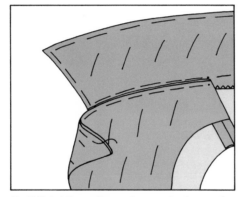

**11.** Turn remainder of facing back on centre fold line to WS of garment so edge of shoulder section of facing covers shoulder seam. Hold this section of the garment over one hand so that both collar and revers are in the wearing position. Baste facing down diagonally over its entire area.

**12.** Still holding collar and revers in the wearing position, turn in remainder of raw edge of facing from centre front corner to where it ends at shoulder seam. Folded edges of facing and bottom of collar must meet exactly to form the gorge. At the step, the part extending from the collar, fold top layer of facing under so fold protrudes above edge of fold basted in (**9**). Baste and press.

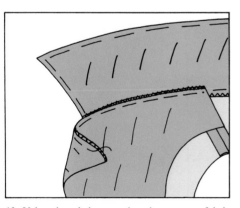

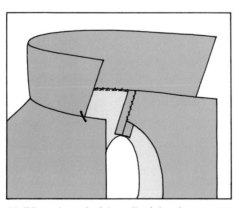

**13.** Using thread that matches the garment fabric perfectly, slip stitch folds of gorge together between facing and collar. Turn back revers and slip stitch step from underneath so that stitching is invisible on RS of revers during wear.

**14.** Where the end of the collar joins the garment, work a bar tack between underside of collar and garment, to hold collar in place during wear. At back of neck, on all but fine fabrics, prick stitch into seam from RS of garment as in shaped stand collar (**8**). In fine fabrics hem turned-in edge on WS into machining. On WS of garment catch stitch ends of facings to shoulder seams. Remove all basting. Press thoroughly on WS and RS.

*Collars on little girls' street dresses in the 1880s ran to the large size, often expanding into small capes. Older girls wore broad, puritan styles, plain or discreetly trimmed, while an excess of frills—to echo those on the cuffs and the rest of the outfit—was thought more suitable for younger children.*

# Pockets

*Exaggerated pockets, Bette Davis style, were popular in the early 1940s. They were usually more ornamental than functional, like this strategically placed pair decorated with sunbursts.*

Pockets may be decorative or functional or both. There are two basic types—patch pockets and bag pockets (see pocket types panel). Whatever the style, the pocket should be well made, neat and, if it is to be used, strong.

Always make pockets as early as possible in the construction of a garment and decide their position at the first fitting. The size of all visible pockets should be proportioned to both the garment and the wearer's figure. Most visible pockets create emphasis by breaking the line of a garment, so position them carefully. When choosing fabrics remember that emphasis is increased if the pocket fabric is a contrasting colour or design, or is cut on the cross.

## Size and strength

A functional pocket must be placed so that the hand can be inserted easily and be big enough for you to feel into all parts without disturbing the opening, but not so large that objects are lost in the bottom. Unless pocket size is dictated by the style of the garment, as in a jacket, calculate the dimensions by measuring the size of your hand and adding 2 to $4 \, cm/\frac{3}{4}$ to $1\frac{1}{2}$ in all round for ease.

For all pockets the wrong side of the garment fabric should be reinforced, especially if it has been cut to make the opening. Pocket bags must also be strong. Calico and pocket fabric are the toughest, but if strength is not essential use lightweight self-fabric or cotton, lining fabric or poplin.

## POCKET TYPES

**1.** A patch pocket is a finished piece of fabric applied to RS of garment. It may be shaped.

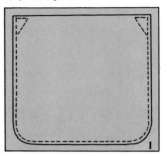

**2.** A seam pocket is formed from a bag, which is either cut out as part of the garment on garments in light-weight fabric, or attached to turn-ings of side or panel seams on those in heavy- or medium-weight. A gap is left in the seam for inserting the hand.

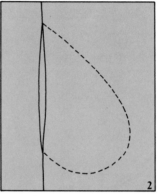

**3.** On a jetted pocket narrow bind-ings, or jettings, of even width neaten each side of the opening on RS of garment. If fabric is checked or striped, the jettings may be cut on the cross for decorative effect. The pocket is formed by a bag placed on WS of garment.

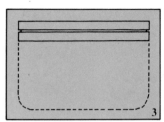

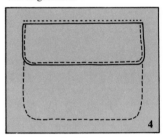

**4.** A flap pocket has a shaped flap attached on RS to upper edge of opening. The lower edge of it is finished with a jetting, or binding, which is concealed by the flap during wear. The pocket has a bag placed on WS of garment.

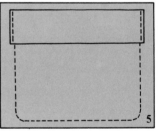

**5.** A welt pocket is formed by attaching a folded piece of fabric, or welt, to lower edge of pocket opening on RS of garment. The welt is then turned upwards so its folded edge forms top of opening. The welt may be cut on the cross for decorative effect. A pocket bag is placed on WS of garment.

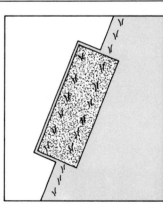

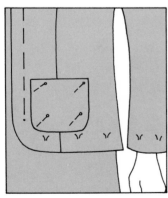

**Positioning** Try on basted garment and fit. Make any adjustments affect-ing pocket position. Except for seam pocket, cut fabric to size of visible part of finished pocket. Pin on garment so that top of pocket is not lower than wrist when the arm is hanging down. Mark correct position of seam pockets with pins or chalk.

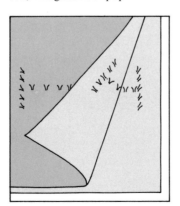

**Marking** Remove basting in garment pieces near pocket position and lay out garment section RS up. For two pockets of matching position pin paired garment sections WS together with all edges level. Chalk marks exactly to length of pocket opening and across ends. Tailor tack lines. Remove pins. Snip tacks.

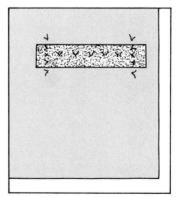

**To reinforce position** of a cut pocket opening on WS, or behind opening of a patch pocket on WS of garment (this is always advisable), cut a piece of iron-on interfacing, of weight appropriate to fabric, 5 cm/2 in wide and 4 cm/$1\frac{1}{2}$ in longer than pocket opening. Centre over marked line on WS of garment and press on.

**2.** For a seam pocket in garment of medium- or heavyweight fabric, press iron-on interfacing 3 cm/$1\frac{1}{4}$ in wide over both side seam fitting lines on WS of garment. Interfacing should end 3 mm/$\frac{1}{8}$ in from raw edges. For light-weight fabric adhesive web only is used for reinforcement; it is applied at a later stage (see seam pocket).

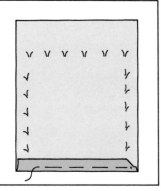

**Patch pocket** Mark pocket opening on garment. Cut pocket with side and bottom turnings of 1.5 cm/⅝ in, but slightly more at top. Mark turnings. On WS of pocket turn up a single hem along base. Baste 3 mm/⅛ in from fold. Press. Trim corners diagonally, from edge to line of basting.

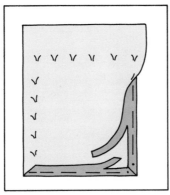

**2.** Fold side edges on marked lines to WS. Baste 3 mm/⅛ in from fold to top hem fold line. Press and trim bottom corners as in (**1**). Trim 3 to 5 mm/⅛ to ¼ in off turned-in edges; if desired, top stitch them and remove basting from them. Press. Snip side turnings at top hem fold line in to very near basting or top stitching.

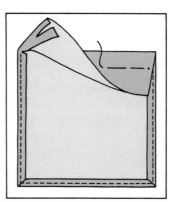

**3.** Turn in ends of top hem at an angle to WS and trim away extra fabric to reduce bulk. Turn down double or single hem along top edge and baste. Machine double hem once or twice with straight or zigzag stitch. Neaten raw edge of single hem and hold down with catch stitch, machining or adhesive web. Remove top hem basting.

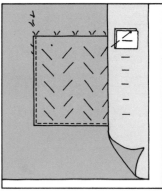

**4.** Place pocket in position RS up on RS of garment. If WS of garment has not been reinforced, pin pieces of cotton tape of appropriate length and width folded in half on WS of garment where top corners of pocket fall. Baste diagonally along top edge of pocket and round sides, matching pocket edges to tailor's tacks. Remove pins.

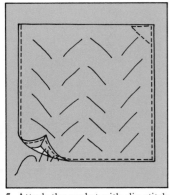

**5.** Attach the pocket with slip stitch worked under its edges or into top stitching. For strength, slip stitch for 5 mm/¼ in along each side of top edge and work concealed bar tacks under edge at ends of stitching, or machine small triangles or rectangles on corners, sewing in machining threads on WS. Remove basting. Press.

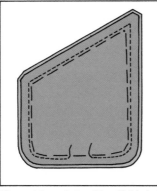

**Line patch pockets** with self-fabric if lightweight, or lining, cotton lawn or nylon jersey. Cut pocket and lining with 1.5 cm/⅝ in turnings. Mark pocket turnings. Trim 2 mm/1/16 in from lining edges. Baste pocket to lining, RS together and all raw edges parallel. Machine, leaving a gap of about 4 cm/1½ in for turning through.

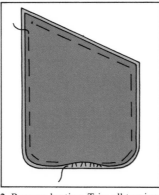

**2.** Remove basting. Trim all turnings to 4 mm/⅛ in, but if lining is in self-fabric, trim it to 2 mm/1/16 in. Trim corners and snip curves. Turn pocket through gap to RS. Roll and baste edges so that join is 2 mm/1/16 in to WS. Press well. Slip stitch gap. Press again. Baste pocket in position and attach as in (**4**) and (**5**).

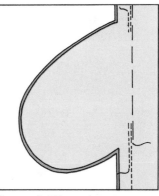

**Seam pocket** For pocket cut as extension of garment, make all markings and place garment pieces RS together. Baste whole of side seam. Machine seam, leaving gap for pocket opening between marks and reversing stitching at each end of opening. Remove basting from machined section and press seam open.

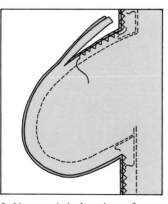

**2.** Neaten stitched sections of seam. Baste the bag pieces RS together. Machine round bag from top of opening, finishing about 5 mm/¼ in below opening at bottom. Reverse stitching at each end. Trim edges of the bag a little and neaten together. Remove basting. Press pocket in correct direction for use.

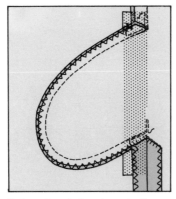

**3.** At each end of pocket snip diagonally into garment seam turning (on side pocket faces away from) to allow seam and pocket to lie flat. Loop stitch or overcast cut edges. On WS slip adhesive web 3 cm/1¼ in wide, and 1 cm/⅜ in longer at each end than opening, into fold between pocket and garment. Press.

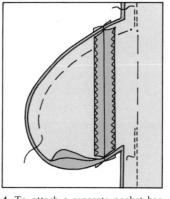

**4.** To attach a separate pocket bag for seam pocket (to reduce bulk or economize on fabric), prepare as in (**1**) and baste pocket pieces to extending seam edges, RS together, at correct position. Machine, remove basting, press open and neaten edges. Construct and finish pocket exactly as for an attached seam pocket (**2**) and (**3**).

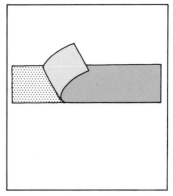

**Jetted pocket** Mark pocket opening on garment. Cut two fabric strips (jettings) on straight grain (or true cross for special effects) 3 cm/1¼ in wide and at least 5 cm/2 in longer than pocket opening. Press on paper-backed adhesive to cover whole of WS of each jetting. Peel off paper backing from adhesive strip. ▶

129

# Pockets

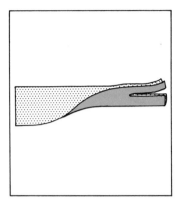

**2.** Fold each jetting in half WS together and press. Trim to twice desired width of finished jetting. Beginners should practise making jettings so that they are as narrow as possible.

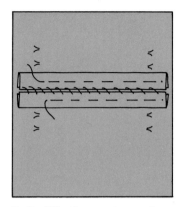

**3.** On WS of garment press down iron-on interfacing 5 cm/2 in wide and 4 cm/1½ in longer than opening. On RS centre jettings against line of opening with raw edges touching. Baste in position and hold their raw edges together by oversewing across them. This prevents the jettings pulling apart in later stitching.

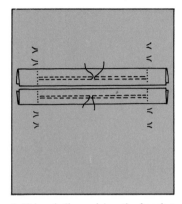

**4.** Using chalk, mark length of pocket opening accurately across jettings. Machine along centre of each jetting exactly between marks, starting and finishing at centre of each to give a double row of stitches. Cut off thread ends. Remove basting and the oversewing between jettings.

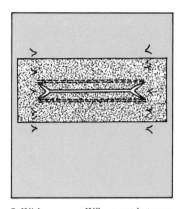

**5.** With garment WS up, cut between rows of machining to within 1 cm/ ⅜ in of ends and then cut out diagonally to ends of rows of stitching.

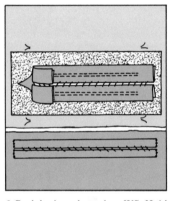

**6.** Push jettings through to WS. Hold folds of jettings together by oversewing on RS. Tuck triangles of fabric at each end of pocket opening back between garment and ends of jettings. Press from WS and RS. From RS stab stitch across ends of pocket.

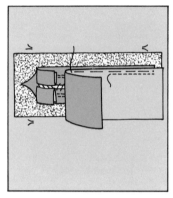

**7.** Cut a fabric strip on straight grain 4 cm/1½ in wide and 5 cm/2 in longer than pocket opening. On WS of garment place top edge of strip level with raw edges of upper jetting. Baste raw edges together. Machine just above machining joining jetting to garment. Remove basting. To finish, see pocket bags.

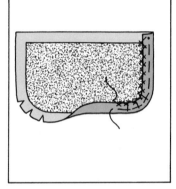

**Flap pocket** Mark opening on garment. Cut flap, allowing 1.5 cm/⅝ in turnings. Mark turnings. Interface as appropriate. Snip curves and turn in all but top edge to WS along marked lines. Baste. Check flap length equals length of opening; adjust side turnings if necessary. Press, trim turnings a little and herringbone edge.

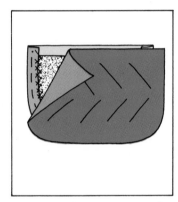

**2.** Cut flap lining to same size as flap piece. Use self-fabric if this is light-weight, lining material or plain cotton. Trim the lining edge by 3 mm/⅛ in all round. Diagonally baste lining to flap, WS together, along centre line and round, but not too close to, all edges.

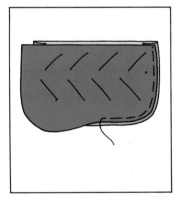

**3.** Turn in lining on all but top edge, snipping curves. Baste folded edges to lie 1 mm/1/16 in from finished edges of flap, press and fell stitch down. Remove basting except along top. Trim top of flap and lining to leave 6 mm/¼ in seam allowance. Cut fabric strip 2.5 cm/1 in wide and 5 cm/2 in longer than flap.

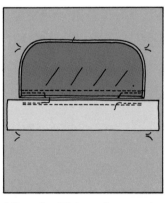

**4.** Baste flap RS down above opening on RS of garment with raw edges touching marked line. Centre strip below flap and baste RS down to garment with raw edge touching flap edges. Machine flap 6 mm/¼ in from edge and strip 3 mm/⅛ in from edge; finish strip stitching 3 mm/⅛ in from ends of flap stitching.

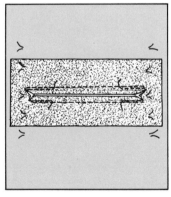

**5.** Remove basting. On WS of garment cut carefully between rows of stitching. Then, 1.5 cm/⅝ in from ends of shorter row of stitching, cut out to ends of rows of machining.

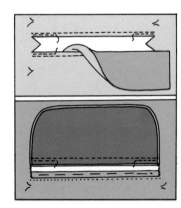

**6.** Push strip (jetting) through slit to WS. Fold it over the turnings and roll it tightly. Baste jetting down and on RS prick stitch in join between jetting and garment. Press with toe of iron. Push triangles of fabric at ends of pocket slit through to WS and stab stitch across pocket ends as for jetted pocket (**6**).

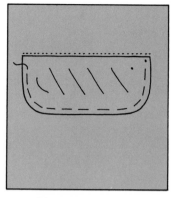

**7.** On RS of garment pull flap over pocket opening. Baste to garment, using straight stitches round edge and diagonal ones across centre. Prick stitch or machine 3 mm/⅛ in above join between flap and garment, stitching through garment and all turnings. Remove basting. Press. To finish, see pocket bags.

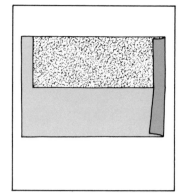

**Welt pocket** Mark opening on garment. Cut out welt piece, allowing 1.5 cm/⅝ in turnings. Mark turnings and fold line. Interface top half of welt piece from top edge to fold line, but within turnings at sides. Turn in sides so welt length equals that of opening. For best results fold in sides at a slight angle on lower half of welt.

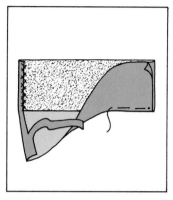

**2.** Trim 3 mm/⅛ in from the turned-in edges. Press and hold in place with herringbone stitch. Fold welt WS together at centre fold line. Baste fold. Baste folded ends together (angled fold falls on WS of finished welt). Baste raw edges of welt together. Press well. Slip stitch ends.

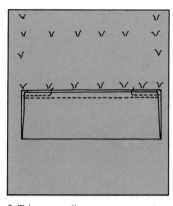

**3.** Trim seam allowance on raw edges of welt to 6 mm/¼ in. On RS of garment mark a line to depth of welt below pocket opening. Place welt RS down on garment below this line, with raw edges touching it. Baste and machine 6 mm/¼ in from edge. Remove all basting and press well. To finish, see pocket bags.

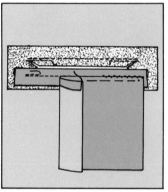

**Pocket bags** For each pocket cut two fabric rectangles wider than length of opening, plus a turning at top and bottom. For flap or jetted pocket press under top edge of one piece on seam allowance and place RS up on WS of garment with fold against machining on lower jetting. Baste in position and hem into machining. Remove basting.

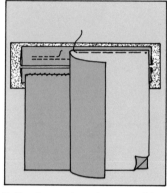

**2.** For flap pocket, place second bag piece RS down on top of first, with lower edges level and top edge level with raw edges of fabric of upper part of flap. Baste and machine to raw edges, taking a 6 mm/¼ in turning. Remove basting.

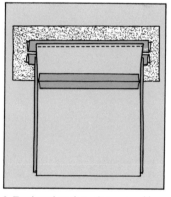

**3.** For jetted pocket, place second bag piece RS down over first, with top edge level with lower edge of attached strip forming pocket backing. Baste and machine second piece to strip, RS together, about 6 mm/¼ in from raw edges. Remove basting. Press seam open. Trim away any excess fabric at lower edge to make bag pieces equal.

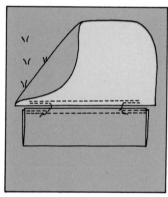

**4.** For welt pocket, cut two bag pieces as in (**1**). On RS of garment place one bag piece above marked opening, RS down, with lower edge touching raw edges of welt. Baste and machine 6 mm/¼ in from edge, but make stitching on bag piece 2 mm/1/16 in shorter at each end than stitching on welt. Remove basting.

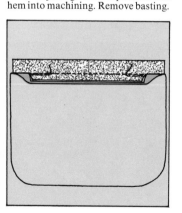

**5.** On WS cut the garment to make opening as for flap pocket (**5**). Push bag piece through to WS and allow to hang down inside.

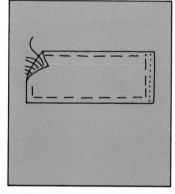

**6.** On RS fold welt up. Baste flat to garment. Press well. On WS of garment attach second bag piece as for first bag piece of a flap or jetted pocket. On RS slip stitch each end of welt to garment. Then prick stitch ends from RS, stitching no more than 4 mm/⅛ in from edges. Remove basting. Press.

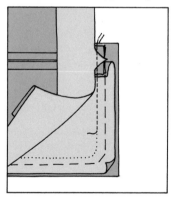

**7.** To finish any pocket bag, baste bag pieces RS together. Leaving about 1.25 cm/½ in seam allowance, mark final shape with chalk, rounding corners. Machine on chalk line, stitching as close as possible to original machining at pocket ends. Stitch again 5 mm/¼ in outside first row of machining. Remove basting. Press.

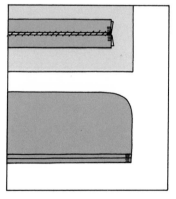

**8.** On a jetted pocket work satin stitch bar tacks on WS of garment across ends of jettings. On a flap pocket work similar bar tacks on RS of garment under flap, as near ends as possible but so they are invisible during wear. On an unlined garment trim all raw edges close to machining on WS and neaten over machining.

131

# Belts

A belt should be planned as an integral part of an outfit rather than added as an afterthought. Its effect must be considered when fitting a garment; a belt should never be used to disguise or draw in poor fitting. It can, however, be a useful means of disguising or emphasizing a figure point. One that circles the waist completely emphasizes a neat waist, while a half belt at the back, or one round to the front panel lines of a garment, appears to break up a thicker one. Choose belt width, position and fabric according to figure type. A wide, tight, high belt, for example, suits a long-waisted figure, a narrow, low, loose one a short-waisted figure.

When selecting belt fabric remember that self-fabric provides least emphasis, and contrasting fabric the most. Belts may be made from one fabric or a combination of two. They may be left plain or decorated with stitching, motifs, leather thonging or braid; or they may be shirred, quilted or made from three lengths of rouleau plaited together. A self-fabric belt can be fastened with a matching or contrasting buckle. To reduce emphasis, however, use a concealed overlap at the left side seam.

All belts except very soft tie belts need either a backing or an internal stiffening (interfacing) to prevent them from creasing. Widths are limited for bought belt backing so choose the backing before the buckle. These backings are, however, very difficult to sew: hand sewing is virtually impossible. Other stiffenings which are easier to handle include heavy or pelmet non-woven interfacing. These can be cut and so used for very wide shaped belts. Buckram can also be cut, but is difficult to sew. Petersham, which may be straight or shaped, is the easiest stiffening to use and may be enclosed by the belt fabric or used to back it.

### Belt carriers

The position of belt carriers is most important as it affects the comfort of a garment. The correct position varies with the individual and the garment. If the waist is small and emphasized by a tight belt, both belt and carriers should be exactly on the waistline. A thicker waist usually needs carriers placed higher to accommodate a looser belt. A loose-fastening outer garment such as a coat needs carriers placed to allow for body movement.

Choose carriers according to the strength required and to the garment fabric and style. Straight fabric carriers, for example, are stronger than thread loops, but more noticeable and, unlike rouleau carriers, cannot be inserted into garment seams.

Before attaching carriers, put on the garment, fasten the belt comfortably and use pins to mark each edge of the belt at the side seams (or centre back). For each carrier move pins out to add a total of 5 mm/$\frac{1}{4}$ in for ease.

### Buckles

A conventional buckle has a central shaft over which the belt passes. If the belt has a metal

In the early 20th century eyecatching buckles in the *Louis XV and* art nouveau *styles drew attention to the fashionable waist, then resting at its natural level.*

prong fastener on this shaft, eyelets must be worked in the belt or the prong removed. With an unpronged buckle, the belt extension is fastened in place with hooks or Velcro, unless the belt is much wider than the buckle and so gripped automatically.

It is advisable to buy a buckle after buying the garment fabric. Choose one to suit the wearer's figure. A large or fancy buckle will emphasize a trim waist, whereas a small matching buckle is preferable for a large one. For a special buckle, however, such as an heirloom, it may be worth selecting garment fabric to enhance it or making a plain, classic belt that can be worn on several garments. A fabric-covered buckle can be purchased or made at home from a kit that includes a metal buckle mould.

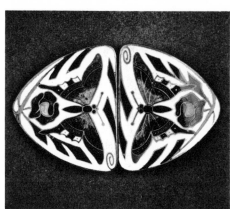

*Ancient Celtic art, typified by curvilinear designs taken from nature and often worked in enamel and silver, greatly inspired* art nouveau *jewellery and ornament, such as this enamel butterfly-clasp buckle. The butterfly was a characteristic* art nouveau *motif.*

## CALCULATING BELT LENGTH

It is important to calculate belt length correctly: a belt that is too short will not meet round the waist, while one that is too long will look ugly and, if it is a tie belt, upset the balance of the garment.

**Tie belt** Tie a tape measure or length of tape round waist. Loop ends over once (if belt is to be fastened with a press stud or Velcro), or tie a knot or a bow. Length of ends varies with garment, but the belt looks better if one end is 5 to 10 cm/2 to 4 in longer than the other. Allow for any fringing to be added.

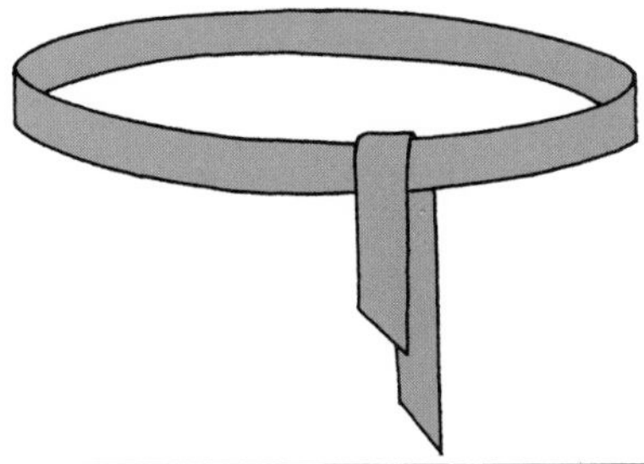

**Normal buckle** Measure waist and add 2.5 cm/1 in for ease (more if belt is wide), 3 cm/$1\frac{1}{4}$ in for attaching buckle and 20 cm/8 in for extension.

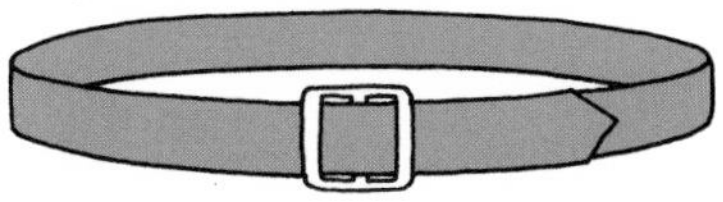

**Concealed overlap** Measure waist and add at least 10 cm/4 in for overlap, plus 2.5 cm/1 in ease. Use a concealed fastening at left side seam.

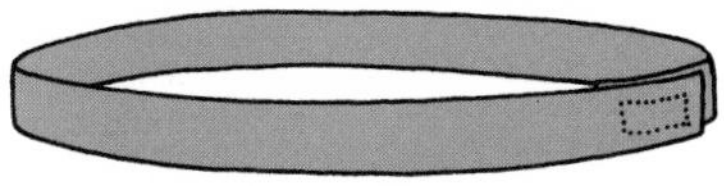

**Clasp** Purchase clasp. Measure waist and add 2.5 cm/1 in for ease, plus at least 5 cm/2 in for joining clasp; then subtract width of joined clasp.

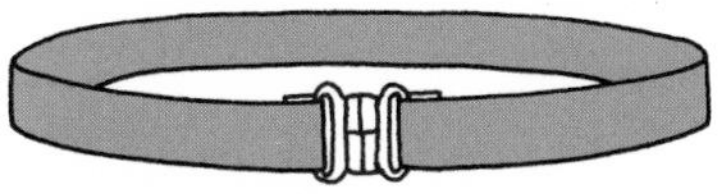

**Ring fastening** Suitable for an adjustable, wide, soft belt. Measure waist and add 2.5 cm/1 in for ease and 10 to 15 cm/4 to 6 in for joining to ring and adjusting its fit. Subtract width of ring.

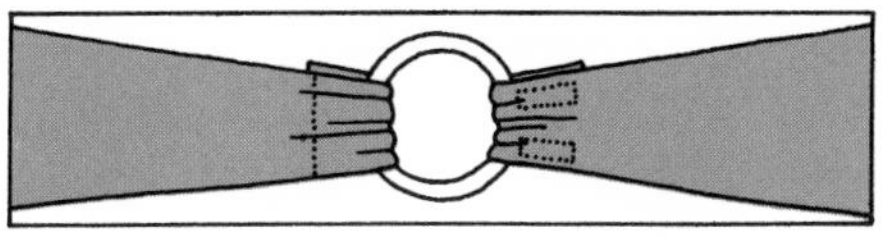

**Buckle or clasp with hook** The hook attaches to thread or rouleau loop on belt. To waist measurement add 2.5 cm/1 in ease and 3 cm/$1\frac{1}{4}$ in for joining buckle or clasp and deduct width of buckle. For a shirred belt use a strip about twice waist measurement, join one end to buckle or clasp and fit before placing and making loop.

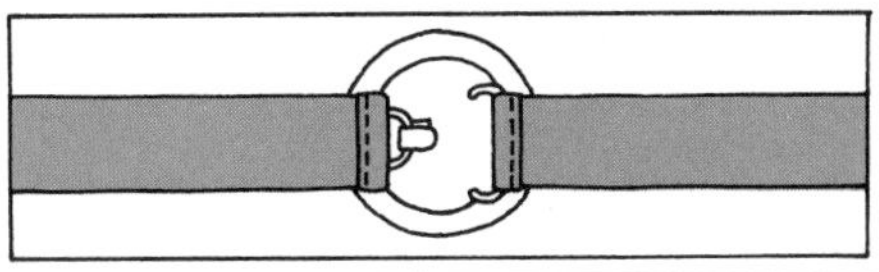

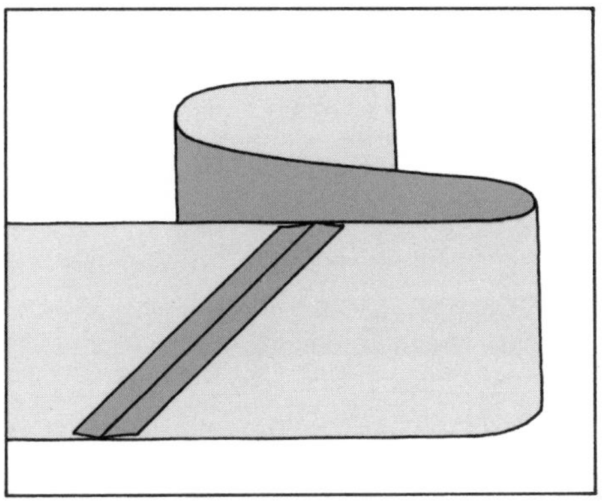

**Joining fabric** If belt cannot be cut from one strip of fabric, position joins at side seams or centre back of garment to make them less conspicuous. Cut diagonally across ends of strips and baste RS together, matching patterns, stripes or checks perfectly. Machine. Remove basting and trim seam to 5 mm/$\frac{1}{4}$ in. Press seam open. Because it is on the cross this seam will be less bulky, less visible and lie flatter than a straight join.

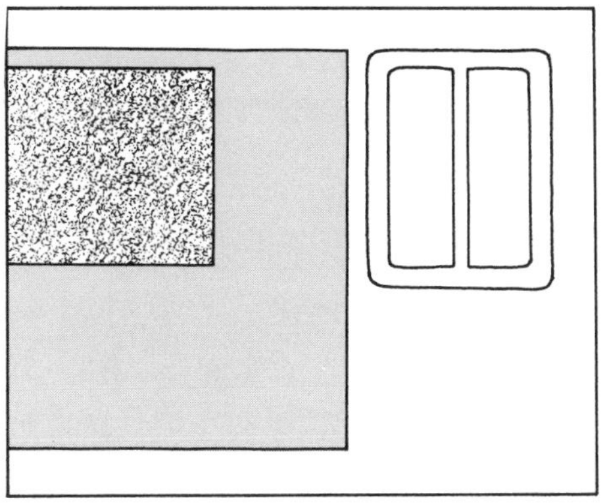

**Cutting interfacing** For a straight belt, buy belt backing or petersham to fit the buckle, allowing 3 mm/$\frac{1}{8}$ in for thickness of fabric, or cut interfacing to the finished width and length of belt, without turnings. To find interfacing width, experiment first: pin fabric to a small piece of interfacing and position buckle at one end. Then draw a straight pencil line on interfacing to the correct length. Measure and pencil another parallel line the right width. Cut out.

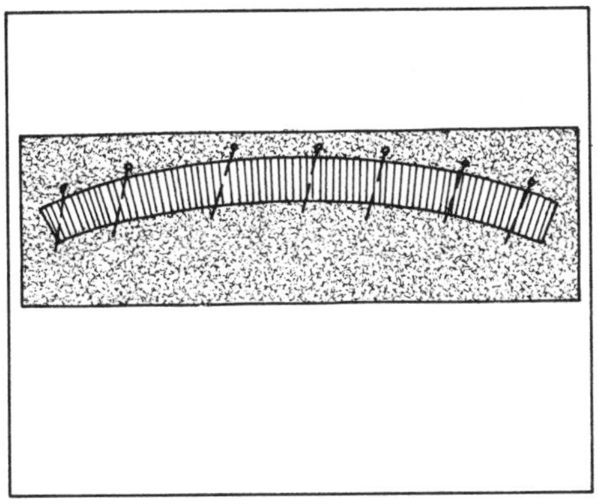

2. For narrow curved belt, cut curved petersham to width and length of finished belt. For wide belt, pin petersham the right length to interfacing. Pencil concave curve on interfacing. Mark ends. Remove petersham. With adjustable marker set to finished belt width, mark second curve at even distance from first. Cut out. For a pointed end on any belt, fold interfacing in two lengthways and cut to a point at required angle (try out first).

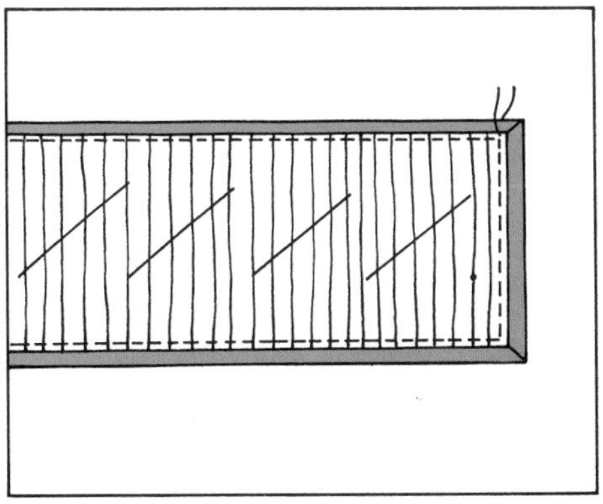

**Attaching stiffening** For belt backing or petersham backing, turn in all fabric edges so that fabric is 3 mm/$\frac{1}{8}$ in wider and longer than backing. Place fabric WS down on backing and baste diagonally down centre. If impossible to insert a hand needle, machine in place without basting. With backing side up, machine at even distance from backing edges. Stitch petersham close to edge; stitch inside stiff double edge of belt backing. Remove basting.

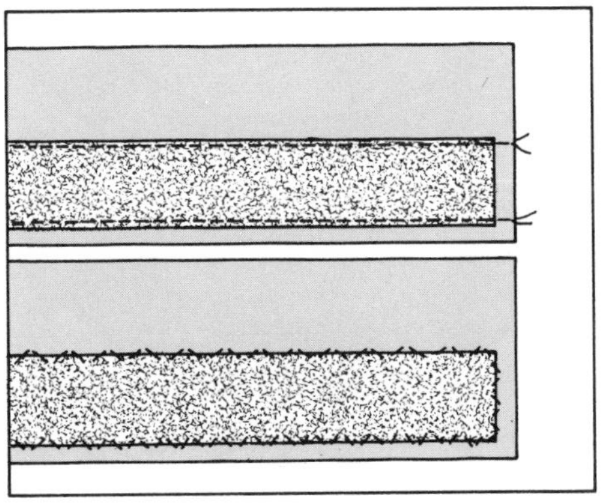

2. For internal stiffening (interfacing), place stiffening on WS of fabric as appropriate (see individual belt types) and baste. With stiffening side up, machine 2 mm/$\frac{1}{16}$ in from top and bottom edges and right out to raw fabric ends. Use a straight, blind hem or embroidery stitch; work several rows if desired. For a finish invisible on RS of belt, attach stiffening edges with herringbone or catch stitch, or with adhesive strips. Remove basting.

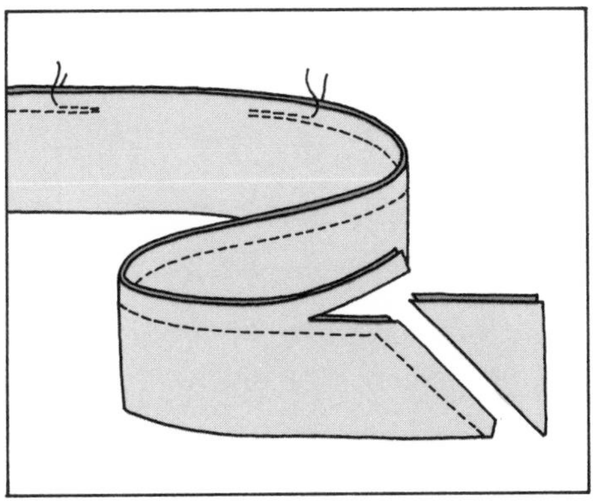

**Tie belt** Cut fabric to correct length on straight or cross grain and twice finished width of belt, plus 1.5 cm/$\frac{5}{8}$ in turnings on all edges. Attach interfacing if desired. Fold lengthways, RS together, and baste along raw edge and across ends, which may be pointed. Machine close to basting, leaving a gap of at least 10 cm/4 in centrally on one side to turn belt through. Trim raw edges to 3 mm/$\frac{1}{8}$ in except at gap. Trim corners diagonally. Remove basting and press. ▶

# Belts

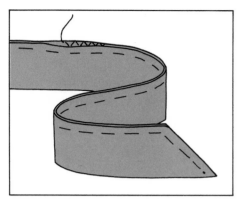

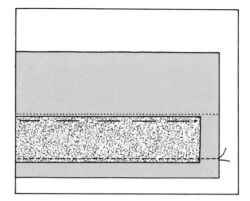

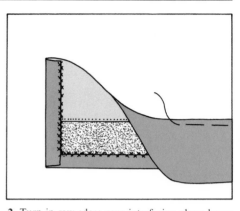

**2.** Turn belt RS out by pushing end of a knitting needle against stitched ends. Pull ends out through gap. Ease out corners. Roll edges so that join is on edge. Baste along stitched edges. At gap, turn in raw edges on seam line and baste. Press basted edges and then folded edge. Slip stitch gap. Remove basting. Press again. For looped belt attach fastenings at desired position.

**Straight belt in double fabric** For all but very bulky fabrics, cut interfacing to correct dimensions and cut a length of fabric on straight grain to twice width of interfacing, plus 1.5 cm/⅝ in turnings on all edges. Mark centre of fabric on WS with chalk. Place interfacing against but not over this line. Baste in position. Attach along edges right to fabric ends (but not across ends) by desired method, see p. 133. Remove basting.

**2.** Turn in raw edges over interfacing along lower edge and across ends (interfaced half is RS or outside of belt). Baste in position. Press. Hold down with herringbone stitch. Remove basting. Fold fabric down over interfacing and baste in position along top fold. Press.

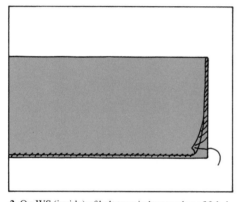

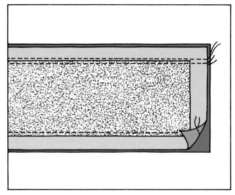

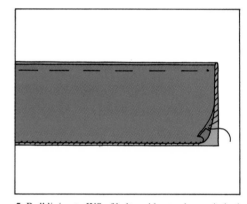

**3.** On WS (inside) of belt turn in lower edge of fabric that has been folded down over interfacing and baste along lower edge. Keep the edge 2 mm/1⁄16 in above lower belt edge so join does not show on RS. Slip stitch ends of belt and hem along lower edge. If interfacing was not machined into place, machine stitching may be worked all round belt at this stage. Remove basting and press.

**4.** For bulky fabric, cut fabric to the width of the interfacing, plus 1.5 cm/⅝ in for turnings on all edges. Cut another piece in lining fabric or nylon jersey to same size. Make any joins for length. Centre interfacing on WS of fabric piece and attach as desired right to fabric ends; see p. 133. Place lining and fabric strips RS together. Baste together just above top edge of interfacing and machine close to basting. Remove basting and press stitching.

**5.** Roll lining to WS of belt and baste along stitched top edge. Turn in fabric at each end of belt and then all edges of lining so that they lie 2 mm/1⁄16 in back from edge of belt and are invisible from RS. Baste and press. Slip stitch ends and hem along lower edge. Remove all basting. Press.

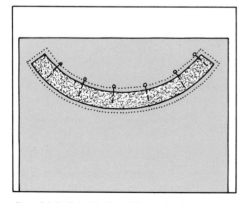

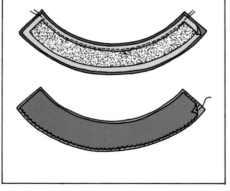

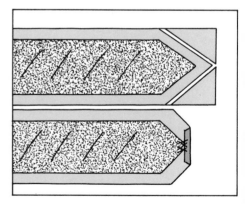

**Curved belt** Suitable for all but striped or checked fabrics. Place curved petersham or interfacing cut to correct dimensions on fabric and pin so curve is evenly placed across grain. Cut out round stiffening, allowing 1.5 cm/⅝ in for turnings on all edges. For patterned fabric, allow for a join at side seams. If belt fabric is light- or medium-weight, cut out two pieces, if heavyweight, cut out second piece in lining to reduce bulk.

**2.** Make any joins. Centre interfacing on WS of fabric and attach. Place two fabric strips or lining and fabric RS together, baste and machine along concave edge beside interfacing edge. Remove basting. Roll lining to WS of belt and baste top edge. Turn in fabric edges all round and herringbone; then turn in lining edges and baste so folded edges are 2 mm/1⁄16 in to WS of belt. Slip stitch ends and hem along lower edge. Remove basting. Press.

**Mitred end** If belt has a pointed end, reduce bulk at the end by mitring. Cut interfacing to correct dimensions and cut one end of it to a point. Baste diagonally along centre to WS of belt fabric and attach as desired; see p. 133. Cut end of fabric to shape, allowing 1.5 cm/⅝ in turnings. Fold end of fabric over point of interfacing and cut off so turning on point is 3 mm/⅛ in. Where trimmed fabric edge crosses interfacing, herringbone it down.

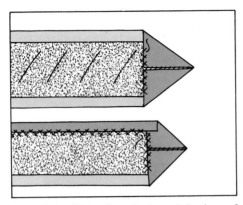

**2.** Fold in fabric along both angled edges of interfacing point. Press. Trim away excess fabric on overlapping folds and double layer at point. Slip stitch folded edges together to point. Herringbone down any raw edges that cross interfacing. Press well. Turn in raw edges along sides and herringbone to interfacing. To finish belt, cover with separate backing, but, if raw edges overlap and fabric is fine, turn under and hem second side to first side.

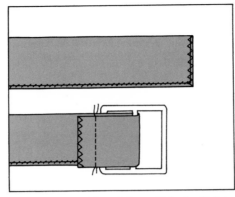

**Buckled belt** If making a belt to which a buckle is to be attached, do not turn in and slip stitch the buckle end of the belt. Instead, trim raw edges and neaten by overcasting or with a zigzag stitch. This helps reduce bulk. For unpronged buckle, thread belt over shaft and fold back surplus to WS. For strength, hold in place by machining across whole width. If the belt is a little short, fold back a minimum of 1 cm/$\frac{3}{8}$ in and hem in place.

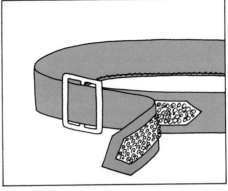

**2.** Hold belt extension down neatly to rest of belt with Velcro. This can be 13 mm/$\frac{1}{2}$ in wide and 8 cm/3 in long, or 3 cm/1$\frac{1}{4}$ in wide and 5 cm/2 in long, depending on width of belt. Fasten belt and mark position of extension end on main part of belt. Hem Velcro into position behind this mark and at extension end; it should be invisible on RS of belt. For pointed belt end trim Velcro to match.

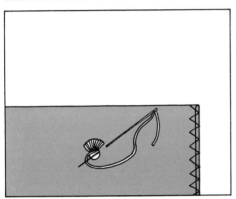

**3.** For a pronged buckle, mark central point on RS of belt 3 cm/1$\frac{1}{4}$ in from buckle end. On RS of belt make an eyelet here. For metal eyelet use an eyelet tool kit. For handworked type, make a hole with a punch tool or stiletto and loop stitch round. If using a stiletto, stitch quickly and reinsert stiletto during stitching to re-form hole. If stiletto will not pass through interfacing, use the points of small scissors and loop stitch hole.

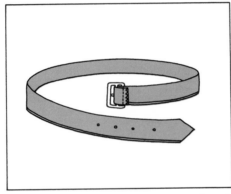

**4.** Thread belt through buckle, insert prong through eyelet and fold back to WS of belt the 3 cm/1$\frac{1}{4}$ in between eyelet and end of belt. Machine across whole width. Do up belt comfortably round waist. Mark position of prong in centre of belt extension. Work an eyelet as in (**3**) at this point, another 4 cm/1$\frac{1}{2}$ in behind it (for a tighter fit) and two more at intervals of 4 cm/1$\frac{1}{2}$ in towards belt end. These should be sufficient to allow for waistline fluctuations.

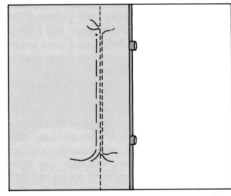

**Rouleau carriers** Measure between pins marking positions of carriers. Cut rouleau to this size, adding 1.5 cm/$\frac{5}{8}$ in for ease and 4 cm/1$\frac{1}{2}$ in for insertion at seams. On WS of garment measure equally from underarm to waist at side seams, or transfer marks from RS at centre back seam, to re-mark positions. Remove pins, unpick seam stitching between marks, insert ends of rouleau and baste. Restitch seam. For strength, stitch again. Remove basting.

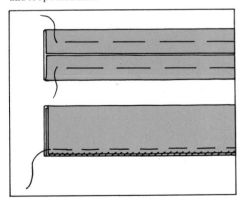

**Straight carriers** Cut a fabric strip on straight grain four times the finished carrier width, 2 to 4cm/$\frac{3}{4}$ to 1$\frac{1}{2}$ in wide and long enough to make all loops. Measure for loops as for rouleau carriers but allow only 5 mm/$\frac{1}{4}$ in for ease. Fold in sides of strip to meet in centre on WS. Baste. Fold again so folded edges meet. Baste, press and slip stitch folded edges of strip together.

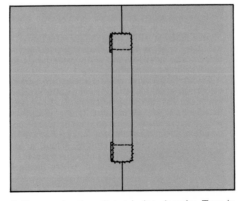

**2.** Remove basting. Cut strip into lengths. Turn in ends to obtain required loop length (make turnings as small as possible). Baste loop to RS of garment in pinned positions. Remove pins. Hem round three outer edges of ends and backstitch across base of turned-in edge of strip, stitching through to garment. Remove basting.

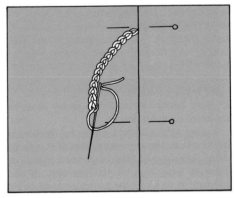

**Thread loops** Measure for loops as for rouleau carriers; allow 5 mm/$\frac{1}{4}$ in for ease, more for a thick belt. For a chain stitch loop, work stitches between pins, holding chains away from fabric; see also p. 33. For strength make a loop-stitched bar (see pp. 62–3), working four or five strands between pins and backstitching through all layers at strand ends. Use strong thread on heavy fabric or for a heavy belt. Remove pins.

# Fitting and Altering

Fitting depends not only on body shape but also on the style of the garment and the fabric. Good fitting produces a garment that is comfortable and looks pleasing: a garment that has been fitted properly is never too tight or too loose.

Always spend as much time as necessary to achieve a good fit. Because fitting can be learned only by experience, and because new fitting problems arise from changes in the shape of the body with increasing years and from alterations in fabrics and styles, it is worth compiling a chart of possible faults to be identified.

When fitting, consider the way of life of the wearer and the occasions on which the garment will be worn, but always make sure that there is room for normal everyday movements. Knitted fabrics can help fitting problems as they allow for movement.

The main principles of fitting apply to all types of garments for people of all ages. They can also be used to improve the fit of bought clothes, provided that only minor changes of shape, such as lengthening or shortening a dart and taking in, are involved. Do not attempt, for example, to raise a neckline or to let a garment out, and avoid lifting at the shoulders if this makes the skirt too short. Collar alterations are generally unsuccessful.

Trousers are often the most difficult garments to fit, especially on women. It is often impossible to determine your shape until the trousers are cut out and basted, and by then it may be too late to correct faults. Choose women's trouser patterns by their hip size, men's and children's patterns by their waist size. Before cutting out trousers, measure the inside leg seam of existing trousers and add 8 cm/3 in for lifting (less for a child), plus a hem allowance.

## Number of fittings

Few garments can be made satisfactorily without at least three fittings, and if the garment is close fitting or complicated in style many more will be needed. Use your body measurements as a guide and use a dress model to help with fitting, shaping and positioning. To determine how much ease is needed always try the garment on.

## Fitting techniques

If you fit a garment on yourself, it will take longer than if you have someone to help, but it is perfectly possible to achieve a good fit by standing still in front of a mirror to identify faults. Restrict yourself, however, to styles and fabrics that will accommodate problems. When fitting any garment follow these guidelines:

● Do not fit the garment too closely—remember that you are standing still.

● Fit and correct only one area at a time, not the whole garment.

● Attach interfacing before fitting to avoid stretching fabric edges during fitting.

● Allow extra turnings in known problem areas and for the hem.

● Until final fitting, fit the garment without a belt.

● Do not fit a problem area too tightly. Make sure that the fabric does not cling to bulges and so emphasize them. It should brush against them and curve gently into hollows.

● Keep all seam lines even. Shoulder and side seams should not be visible from the front.

● Choose a style with seams or darts over known problem areas.

● Large areas of fabric are difficult to fit unless broken up by features such as gathers.

● If your figure is lop-sided in any part, do not make the same alteration on both sides.

● Fit elbow darts with sleeves basted in position and arms slightly bent.

● For large busts do not make bust darts too large.

● Straining in any area indicates too little shaping.

● Before fitting baste centre front opening diagonally below and almost to waist and pin it securely above waist to neckline.

● If both back and front of neckline are lowered, shoulder seams may need lifting to prevent garment slipping off shoulders.

● Always check armhole fit before inserting sleeves, but remember that faults may not show until sleeves are basted in.

● To fit a waisted dress, try on bodice only.

● If natural waist is very low at back, do not fit too accurately.

● If abdomen is high and protrudes, choose an empire-line style or raise whole waistline above bulge.

## How to fit

The following equipment is necessary for fitting: a full-length mirror; a back-view mirror or another mirror propped up on a chair for viewing the back; pins; tailor's chalk; a tape measure; hem marker or long ruler. Equally essential is plenty of time, and a bonus, if you are making a garment for yourself, is someone to help who knows your fitting problems.

## Preparation

Tailor tack and interface the first part of the garment to be fitted, such as the bodice. Never prepare a whole garment before fitting. Mark centre back and centre front lines. Baste together the part to be fitted, but if fitting a bodice or dress with a back opening on yourself, baste up this opening but leave open left shoulder and side seam (or right if left-handed), which are easier to pin up for fitting than the back (1). For an overlapping opening,

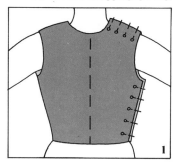

fold back the facing to the marking and baste. Stitch up any pleats. Wear correct undergarments and shoes and comb your hair into its usual style. If fitting a skirt or trousers, wear a close-fitting waist-length jumper, not a blouse. Never fit trousers with a dress or skirt bunched up.

Put on the garment and pin up any openings securely. It may help, at the first fitting, to put the garment on inside out so that alterations can be accurately marked, but try it on RS out for subsequent fittings.

Stand still and look front on in the mirror. Turn sideways, stand still again, and move the head only to view the side and some of the back. Turn and check the other side, then look in the back-view mirror. Consider each area in turn.

First check and adjust any darts or other shaping. Then proceed to the next area of fitting, usually the seams near the shaping that has already been corrected, then to seams such as waist joins that hold major sections of the garment together. When you are sure that these seams are correctly adjusted, check the shoulder seams, armholes, sleeves and, finally, the hem.

As few areas of a garment are completely isolated, when one fault is corrected another may be caused or cured elsewhere. Watch the overall

effect of alterations and, throughout the fitting process, try to maintain the original balance of the garment design and remember that shortening an opening or raising a waistline may upset buttonhole spacing. Slip on part of a garment, such as a sleeve, yoke or trouser leg, or at least hold it up against you, to check the general effect after basting the initial seams but before basting the main garment sections together.

## What folds indicate

Loose vertical folds indicate that the garment is too wide. To correct, take in the side seams, but if the garment is much too wide it may be necessary to take in a pleat down the centre front or back of the appropriate pattern piece and then recut.

Tight vertical folds or wrinkles are a sign that the garment is too short between two points, for example between shoulders and waist or, in trousers, between waist and crutch. Correct these faults by lengthening as necessary.

Loose horizontal folds indicate excess length in a particular area, for example between bust level and waist, between back of waist and bottom, or between front of waist and hips. Correct these faults by shortening at the nearest seams.

On a pear-shaped figure a horizontal fold of surplus fabric may occur above the waist of a dress and on a top-heavy figure below the waist. If the dress has a waist join, it may help to alter this, but it may also be necessary to alter the centre front seam. This seam must be altered if the dress has no waist join. If no seam is included in the pattern, it is often possible to insert one by cutting out two separate pieces for the front, each with a seam allowance, rather than folding the fabric in two. Careful fitting of the centre front seam can also disguise a lop-sided figure.

Tight horizontal folds or wrinkles indicate a tight garment and can be corrected by letting the garment out at the nearest seams.

## Marking and checking alterations

Whenever possible, mark alterations with tailor's chalk. Mark the end of a dart with a cross, mark basting lines with chalk lines and use chalk crosses to indicate where to start and finish any alteration. Use pins for taking out excess fabric.

After chalking these marks, take off the garment. If the garment has been fitted WS out, baste alterations and refit. If the garment has been fitted RS out, turn the fabric over where pins are inserted and insert pins between the original ones, picking up one layer of fabric only (2). Turn back to the first side and slide the points of the first pins out of the double layer and

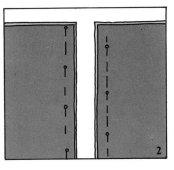

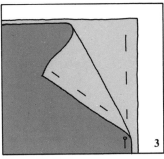

reinsert through the top layer only. Open out the fabric to reveal two adjusted lines (3). If chalk shows up sufficiently, mark both sides of alteration and remove pins. If not, leave pins in. Remove any tailor's tacks that are no longer needed.

Fold the garment in half, matching up the new lines, or place corresponding garment pieces together correctly and arrange them so they lie flat on the working surface. Mark new chalk or pinned line with tailor's tacks and snip tacks in the usual way. Baste the garment pieces together, try the garment on and check the alteration. Finally, before stitching, check the length of corresponding seams and darts to make sure that they are equal and mark dart lengths with chalk lines. Do not make any corrections to the length if your figure is lop-sided.

## Shaping

Darts, gathers and released tucks all contribute to shaping. A dart creates an area of fullness at its point and darts are placed to provide shaping for the bust, shoulder blades, elbows, abdomen and bottom. The dart should point towards the area being shaped, running right on to it for a close fit, or stopping short for a looser, more comfortable fit.

If the dart does not provide enough fullness, enlarge it or insert an extra one and make a compensatory adjustment in the nearest seam. If the dart creates surplus fullness, make it smaller or remove it altogether. If a dart is not in line with the bulge on the appropriate body area, move it to the correct position. For example, back darts in skirts and trousers usually fall midway between centre back and side seams, but if necessary, to improve fit, move them at the first fitting nearer to

the centre back, above the bottom. If a dart is altered to adjust the amount of shaping, the width of its wider, base, end is automatically altered. This may affect other areas: for example, the size of the waistline may be reduced or expanded, or seam edges on the back and front of the garment may no longer be equal in length. The same applies if an extra dart is added. Correct discrepancies at the seams nearest the darts.

Gathers, like darts, provide shaping for bulges and the fullness they create should be sufficient to accommodate these. On small areas of gathering, such as on a yoke, the gathers should be above or below the bulge. Excess fullness in gathers can be removed in the nearest seam. A small amount of extra fullness can be obtained by letting out the nearest seam, but a correct fit is usually guaranteed by repositioning gathers.

For all shaping alterations your helper can snip any basting where faults occur and repin the shaping correctly. If fitting yourself, make a chalk mark or insert a pin to mark the position of a fault and estimate the size of the adjustment needed. Take off the garment. Mark and baste the alteration and try the garment on.

## Seams

Functional and decorative seams also contribute to shaping. Check functional, fitting seams for position as well as fit. Make sure that shoulder seams run along the tops of the shoulders and slightly to the back and that side seams hang vertically. If side seams slope, either the front or back will have to be lifted or dropped to straighten them. If they wobble, the basting may be inaccurate, the garment may have been cut on the wrong grain or, more usually, is too tight. If the abdomen is very large or the back very narrow, an uneven alteration may be needed at the side seams. Trouser seams should hang straight and not twist. Yoke seams should run horizontally without dropping near the armholes. If the figure has one very exaggerated point, do not fit too closely over this area or a crooked seam will result.

Side seams may be used to alter the width of a dress bodice that is too loose or too tight round the back, bust or diaphragm. The front of the pattern is usually slightly wider than the back, which may not always be correct for the figure, and side seams may have to be adjusted by unequal amounts from the front and back. Skirts and trousers can also be altered by taking in or letting out the side seams.

Like other seams, decorative seams may need moving or altering after other fitting adjustments have been made. They should, however, always be attractively placed.

## IDENTIFYING THE PROBLEMS—SIDE VIEW

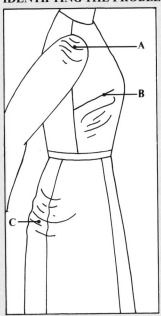

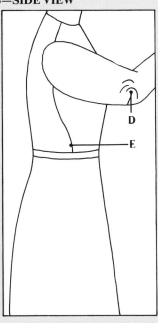

**A. Sloping shoulders** On a long sleeve horizontal wrinkles occur on sleeve head; on a short one hems drop.

**B. Bust darts too low** Garment too loose over bust with unfilled fullness below bust.

**C. Too much shaping in shaped seam over bust, bottom or shoulder blades**

An unfilled bulge of surplus fabric appears in the seam area.

**D. Elbow darts too high** Unfilled pockets of surplus fabric appear at the end of the dart.

**E. Back or front shoulder needs lifting** Side seams slope to front or back instead of hanging vertically.

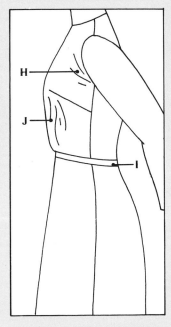

**F. Armholes too low** Entire garment is lifted when arms are raised.

**G. Bust darts too high** Fabric strains across bust and may ride up.

**H. Armholes too tight** Armholes may cut into the body at the front, especially on a fleshy figure.

**I. Low natural waistline at back** Waistline on waisted dress follows natural line and becomes uneven.

**J. Small bust** If bust dart is too wide at the base, unfilled fabric results below bust.

# Fitting and Altering

## IDENTIFYING THE PROBLEMS—BACK VIEW

**A. Sloping shoulders** Folds of excess fabric appear just below shoulders, starting near neck and increasing towards armhole edges.

**B. Narrow-backed figure** Centre back seam stands away from the body, possibly with folds on each side.

**C. Shoulder darts wrongly placed** If back is flat, surplus fullness occurs at end of darts.

**D. Back bodice too loose** Vertical folds form in armhole and underarm areas of bodice.

**E. Shoulder seams need lifting** Horizontal folds of fabric form above waist or below bottom.

**F. Hollow back—skirt** Folds form below back of waistband. In trousers waist appears too high at the back.

**G. Skirt or trouser side seams too loose** Vertical folds of fabric form down centre; on a very straight-hipped figure folds form at sides.

**H. Flat bottom—skirts and trousers** Unfilled fullness occurs at the points of back darts.

**I. Hollow back—dress** In a one-piece dress fabric droops above the waist or below bottom. In a waisted dress folds form above waist or waist join dips at the back.

**J. Sleeves set in too far back** Vertical wrinkles appear at back of upper part of sleeve.

**K. Trousers too loose** Excess fabric may hang in folds below bottom.

**L. Elbow darts too low** Garment wrinkles and strains on upper arms and across back.

**M. Neckline too tight or too high** Will be uncomfortable and may cause horizontal wrinkling at back or front of neck.

**N. Overtight fit/poor assembly/uneven shoulder seams** Centre back seam wobbles or sits at a bad angle.

**O. Bodice back too tight** Horizontal folds form on bodice back and on upper part of sleeves.

**P. Side seams too tight—skirt or trousers** Horizontal wrinkles appear in seam area.

**Q. Skirt or trouser darts too long or too narrow at base** Garment strains over large bottom.

**R. Bodice darts too wide** Garment feels tight round midriff and horizontal folds may result.

**S. Bodice darts too long** Garment feels tight at base of armholes.

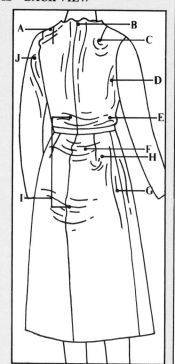

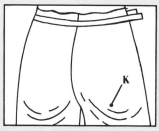

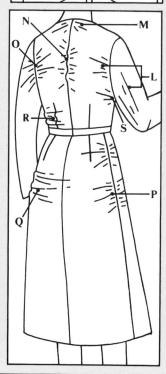

## IDENTIFYING THE PROBLEMS—FRONT VIEW

**A. Tight fit over bust or below armholes** Neckline gapes. This problem may also be caused by a narrow chest or prominent bust.

**B. Shoulder seams too long** Garment is uncomfortable and on a sleeveless bodice armholes gape; on a sleeved bodice the sleeve heads drop.

**C. Small bust** Sometimes bodice darts are unsuitable for the figure and empty pockets of fabric are produced above bodice dart point at bust.

**D. Hollow abdomen** Unsightly fullness may appear at points of waist darts on trousers and skirts.

**E. Centre front opening too short** Diagonal folds occur on each side of opening, running down to hem.

**F. Wrongly placed darts—skirt or trousers** Pockets of fullness show below or on the abdomen.

**G. Sleeves set in too far forward** When your arms are by your sides folds appear at front of upper sleeves.

**H. Bodice darts too short** Too much fullness is produced below bust.

**I. Too much fabric in shaped area** Gathers or released tucks create excess fullness or bulkiness or over-emphasize parts of the figure such as large bust, hips or thighs.

**J. Bodice darts too wide** Garment too tight at waist.

**K. Skirt or trouser darts too wide** Waist is too tight and garment may wrinkle on both sides of the darts.

**L. Centre front opening too long** Diagonal folds run up skirt and out towards side seams.

**M. Bodice darts too long** Bodice will be too tight across the bust and, if very tight, horizontal wrinkles will occur above and below the bust.

**N. Square shoulders** Fabric drags from armhole level to outer ends of shoulder seams.

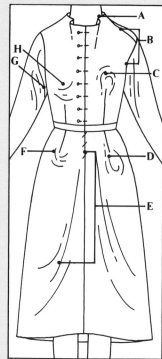

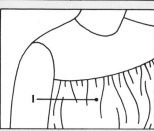

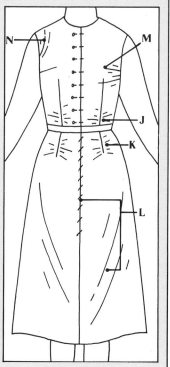

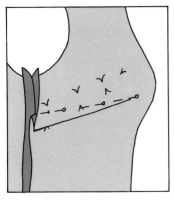
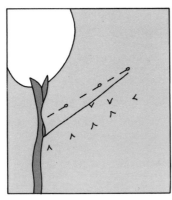
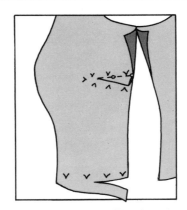
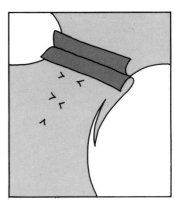

**BUST DARTS To lower darts** snip basting of darts and side seams. Pick up fabric of each dart and adjust angle by pinning from base of original dart, a little below bust level, to bust point. Mark new dart, baste and fit.

**To raise darts** snip basting of darts and side seams. Pick up fabric of each dart and, starting at base of original dart, repin dart at appropriate angle. Mark new dart, baste and fit.

**To take in surplus unfilled fabric** in bust area, snip basting of darts and side seams. Repin darts, making them narrower and, depending on the figure, shorter. Cut away surplus fabric at garment waist so edge of front bodice aligns with bottom edge of back bodice. Mark all corrections, baste and fit.

**BACK SHOULDER DARTS If shoulder blades are flat** remove darts and trim away surplus fabric at armhole edge.

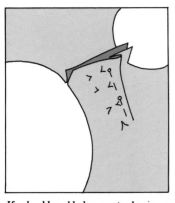
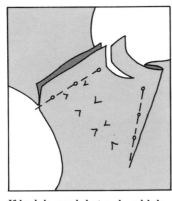
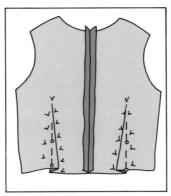
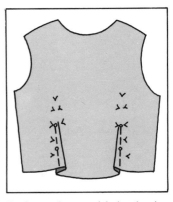

**If shoulder blades protrude** in a different place from where darts end, unpick the dart and shoulder seam basting. Move darts to appropriate place, pin, mark and baste. Pin and baste shoulder seams along original seam lines and refit.

**If back is rounded at neck and below** unpick the dart and shoulder seam basting. Move darts into neckline and repin shoulder seams, starting at outside sleeve edge. Mark and baste alterations. Trim excess fabric on back neckline to reshape. Refit.

**BACK BODICE DARTS To reduce width of darts** unpick basting and repin darts, taking up less fabric at base of each one. Mark new darts, baste and refit.

**To shorten darts** unpick dart basting and repin darts to correct length. Darts should end at least 2.5 cm/1 in below armhole level, but they should be lower than this for a good and comfortable fit if the figure has any surplus fat in the midriff area or above or below the bra fastening. Mark new darts, baste and refit.

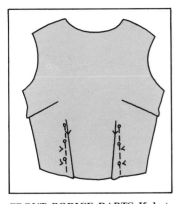
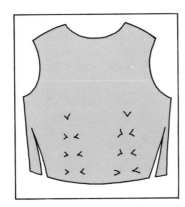
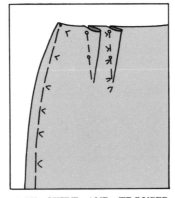
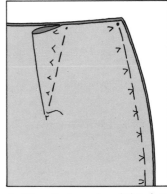

**FRONT BODICE DARTS If darts are too short** unpick dart basting and repin, lengthening darts as much as necessary so they provide or add to bust shaping. Mark, baste and fit. If darts are too long or too wide, shorten them or reduce width at base as for back bodice darts.

**For a small bust** remove darts and trim away excess fabric at side seams to bust level to compensate. However, if front bodice darts are the only means of bust shaping, they must be retained. Correct their length and position to give a smooth, comfortable fit. Pin, mark and baste darts and refit the bodice.

**BACK SKIRT AND TROUSER DARTS For a large bottom** insert another dart on each side, positioned and balanced for a good fit. Pin new darts, mark and baste. Unpick side seams to depth of dart, repin and baste, reducing width of turnings by appropriate amount to keep waist size correct. Refit.

**2.** Alternatively, make existing darts wider at base, and shorten if necessary. (Darts should end at the start of the rise of the bottom.) Pin, mark and baste darts and adjust side seams as in preceding method. Refit.

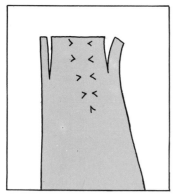

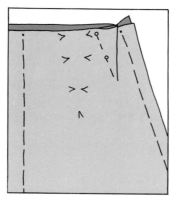

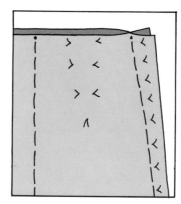

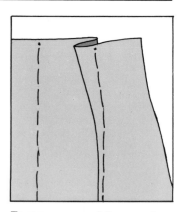

**For a flat bottom** make darts narrower at base as for back bodice darts. For a low bottom, lengthen darts as for front bodice darts. Alternatively, remove darts altogether. Unpick side seam basting and, on trousers, that of crutch seam to depth of darts; trim away excess fabric, repin, mark and baste. Refit.

**FRONT DARTS IN SKIRTS AND TROUSERS For a flatter effect** move these darts at the first fitting from their usual marked position midway between centre front and side seams nearer to side seams, make them shorter and slope them towards seams. Pin, mark and baste all corrections and fit again.

**If front darts are too wide** at the base, making the waist too tight, remove darts and take any extra fabric out of side seams by pinning and then basting; taper new line to meet original seam line below level of original darts. Refit.

**To remove excess fullness** continue darts as panel seams from waist to hem. Pin, mark and baste seams and try on again to check alteration.

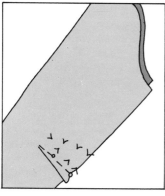

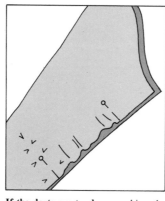

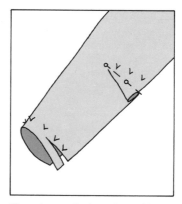

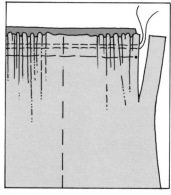

**ELBOW DARTS If darts are too high**—they should be just below the elbow—unpick dart basting and move whole dart down to appropriate level. Pin new dart, mark and baste. If darts are too low unpick dart basting and move whole dart up to appropriate level. Pin new dart, mark and baste. Refit sleeve for both alterations.

**If the darts are too long**, making the sleeves feel tight, shorten darts as for back bodice darts. If the sleeves are still uncomfortable, remove darts altogether and ease back seam turning of underarm sleeve seam on to front turning when remaking sleeve seam, placing ease above elbow.

**If arm is very slender** reduce width of elbow dart at its base, as for back bodice darts, and trim off equivalent surplus fabric at sleeve wrist. Pin and mark dart, baste and refit.

**GATHERS To reduce bulkiness** or fullness created by gathers, undo basting and detach shaped section. Reduce gathering by flattening fabric along gathering thread and rearrange gathers in correct position. Baste altered section to remainder of garment and trim away excess fabric of gathered section at ends of seam.

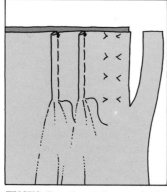

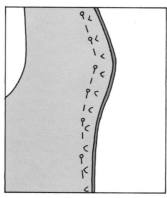

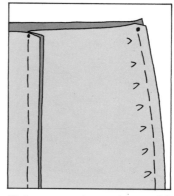

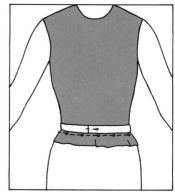

**TUCKS To reduce fullness** or bulkiness created by tucks, reduce the number and/or depth of stitching. Remove excess fabric at side seams. Generally tucks over the bust should be fairly long, those from the waist down fairly short.

**SHAPED SEAMS To remove excess shaping** or to introduce more shaping, the curves or angles of shaped seam edges may be adjusted in the same way as darts. To remove any excess, take up surplus fabric on seams with pins and mark new lines. Baste and stitch new lines to produce smooth seams without bulges.

**If the garment is too tight** unpick shaped seam at point of strain only and allow seams to open up as much as necessary. Pin in correct position, tapering alteration to meet original seam line. Mark and baste again. Stitch new lines to produce smooth seams without bulges.

**SIDE SEAMS On bodice of a waisted dress** side seams from underarm to waist should be long enough to allow for body movement but should not cause wrinkles or bulges. To fit, tie a tape round waist, over bodice, and mark waistline all round, level with bottom of tape, using pins or chalk. Check length of side seams.

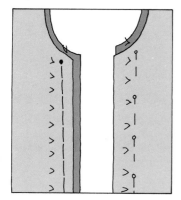
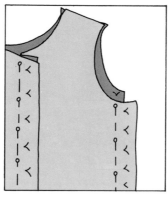
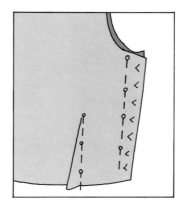
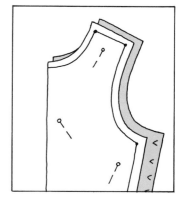

**To widen bodice** let out side seams, letting more out of back turning than front for a broad-backed figure. To tighten, pin out surplus at side seams. Mark and baste all adjustments and refit the bodice.

**For a narrow-backed figure** take more out of back turning of side seam than front and, if necessary, a little out of centre back seam. Pin, mark and baste alterations and refit.

**If shoulder blades are prominent** adjust side seams and, if necessary, add a waist dart on either side of centre back. Pin alterations, mark and baste them and refit.

**For a big reduction at bodice side seams** position pattern on fabric so pattern seam line aligns with new seam line. Pin pattern to fabric and recut armhole and, if necessary, shoulder. On outside leg seams of trousers run any large alterations down to the hem to avoid a wedge effect in the finished seam.

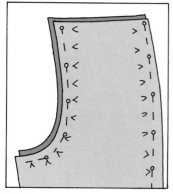
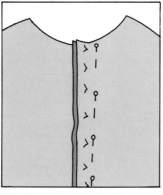
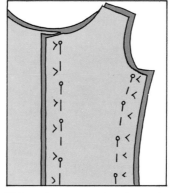
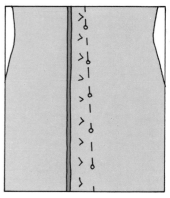

**To let out trousers or skirt** snip side seam basting in tight area and open up seams. Pin, mark and baste, as for shaped seams. Allow extra ease for a large bottom. For a large alteration let out centre back seam too. If necessary, unpick waist darts and move as appropriate. Reverse procedure for a loose garment.

**CENTRE FRONT SEAM For a pear-shaped figure** alter seam to correct loose fit above waist on a non-waisted garment. On a waisted garment alter seam as well as waist join if necessary. Unpick seam above waist and pin out surplus fabric, tapering alteration to meet original seam line. Mark new seam line, baste and refit.

**If the grain or pattern of the fabric** will be altered detrimentally by taking in centre front seam, take in a little at centre front and remainder at side seams. Pin, mark and baste new seam lines and refit.

**For a top-heavy figure** correct loose fit below waist by unpicking basting of centre front seam below waist. Take in appropriate amount from below waist area, tapering new seam line to meet original one above waist. Pin and mark new seam line, baste and refit.

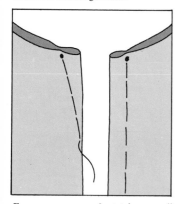
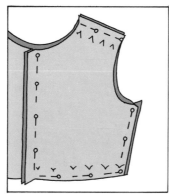
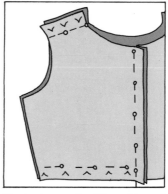

**For a very narrow chest** take a small amount from centre front to make a short dart at neck only. Alternatively, pin a tuck from neck edge all the way down centre front. Cut tuck open and treat as centre front seam. Mark and baste alterations. Refit.

**CENTRE FRONT OPENING To lengthen opening** drop position of waist seam on bodice and skirt by same amount and/or raise shoulder seams by letting out seams until folds disappear. Take care not to alter the balance of the garment style detrimentally. Pin and mark all altered seams, baste and try on again.

**To shorten opening** lift position of bodice and skirt waist seam by same amount and/or shoulder seams by taking in seams until folds disappear. Take care not to alter the balance of the garment style detrimentally. Pin and mark all altered seams, baste and try on again.

**CENTRE BACK SEAM To tighten seam,** if zip has been basted in, pin out surplus in a small fold on each side of zip. Remove zip. Mark and open out. Measure excess and incorporate excess into seam turnings. Rebaste zip and refit. If there is no zip, pin out surplus at centre back seam as for centre front seam.

143

# Fitting and Altering

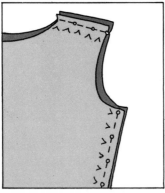

**To correct a badly angled seam** unpick basting of side and shoulder seams and adjust seam lines, making sure shoulder seams are even in width. Pin, mark and baste. To loosen seam, release basting and let out seam where necessary as for side seam; pin, mark and baste again. Refit.

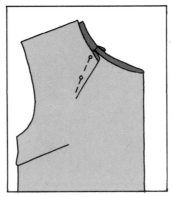

**NECKLINE If chest is narrow** and neckline gapes, pin out excess fabric in a tuck all down centre front (see p. 143). Alternatively, insert darts or small gathers in neck. Lifting the shoulders can help (see p. 146), but may not cure the fault. Pin, mark and baste all adjustments and refit.

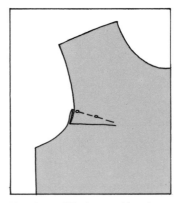

**If gaping neckline** is caused by a large bust, insert an extra dart in armhole. If armhole is then too tight, refit and release side seams (see p. 143). Pin, mark and baste all adjustments. Refit.

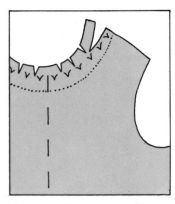

**To lower neckline** mark a possible new neckline with chalk on one half of WS of bodice, starting at original shoulder seam. Allow 2.5 cm/1 in for seam allowance and error. Snip raw edges of neck to release strain. Refit and, if correct, mark other half of neckline at same level. Trim 1 cm/$\frac{3}{8}$ in at a time until neckline is correct.

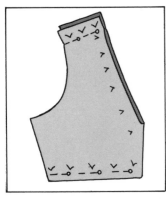

**To raise neckline** raise shoulders by necessary amount (see p. 146) and, in waisted garments, lower waistline accordingly. Pin, mark and baste adjustments and refit. When finishing neck edge take very small turnings.

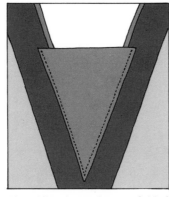

**If neckline is too low on finished garment** make an insert the desired shape and size from two pieces of matching or contrasting fabric. Stitch pieces WS together, leaving a gap, turn through to RS and slip stitch gap. Backstitch insert into position on front facings on WS of garment.

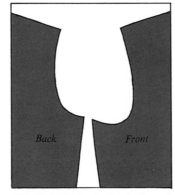

**ARMHOLES** Both the back and front of a correctly shaped armhole should run in a fairly straight line from the shoulder. The back curves gently towards the underarm seam, the front scoops in a deeper curve and then turns up slightly towards the seam. This shaping allows width at the back for arm movement.

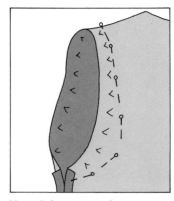

**If armholes are too loose** remove sleeves and unpick side seams. Starting at underarm seam, pin and mark new, deeply curved seam line on front of bodice armhole to meet original seam line at top of armhole. Baste in sleeve on new seam line and try on bodice. Trim away fabric to follow curve, leaving seam allowance.

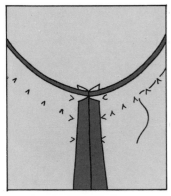

**If armholes are too tight** remove basting joining sleeve to armhole at underarm and release side seam in bodice and sleeve seam to allow more room. Pin, mark and baste altered seams and then refit.

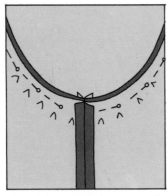

**If armholes are too low** correct by lifting shoulders (see p. 146), but check neck and darts afterwards. Alternatively, take very small turnings in underarm sections when setting sleeves into armholes.

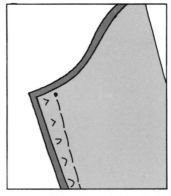

**If a large lifting alteration is made** the sleeves will be too big for the armholes. Adjust by taking them in at top of underarm seam. Pin and mark alteration, tapering it to meet original seam line. Baste and refit.

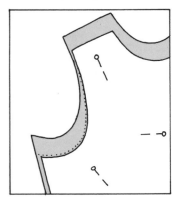

**If armhole is too high** (this generally occurs only if shoulders have been lifted) unpick shoulder and side seam basting and lay fabric pieces flat WS up. Place paper pattern on fabric with pattern armhole at required depth below fabric armhole. Redraw armhole round pattern. Trim excess fabric on marked line.

*Although all good dressmakers used tailor's dummies, and a plaster of Paris model was often made for regular clients, personal fittings were, and still are, an integral part of garment making. These sessions sometimes lasted several hours and could be as tiring for the customer as the needle-woman. This illustration is from the French magazine* Nos Femmes, *1900.*

*Bearing a certain resemblance to Gyro Gearloose's bright side-kick in Walt Disney's Donald Duck comics, this elegantly finished tailor's dummy had a somewhat eccentric selling point—the dressmaker of 1906 now burnt more than the midnight oil. A gas-powered bulb could be attached at the neck of the dummy to illuminate the seamstress's late working hours.*

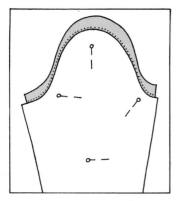

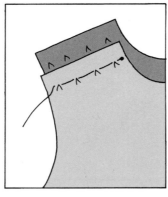

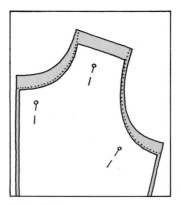

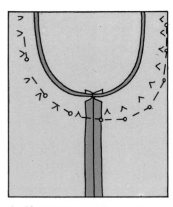

**If sizeable scoops of fabric** are removed from armholes, adjust sleeves accordingly. Position pattern on sleeves so pattern armhole is at required depth below fabric armhole. Using pattern as a guide, redraw sleeve armhole and head and cut along marked line.

**SHOULDERS To lift shoulders** remove basting and lift back or front of shoulder seams until folds disappear. Lifting is usually needed only at the back, but if pouches of fabric form at garment front, lift only the front. Pin, mark and baste alteration. On one-piece dresses lifting the shoulders is a useful alteration for a hollow back.

**2.** Unpick bodice and shoulder seams and pin pattern on fabric so shoulder seam on pattern aligns with new seam line. Recut neck, armhole and shoulder length round pattern piece.

**3.** If necessary, before setting in sleeves, scoop out armhole a little on front or back of bodice, depending on which parts of shoulder seams were lifted. Taper alteration to meet original seam line. Pin, mark, baste and fit corrections.

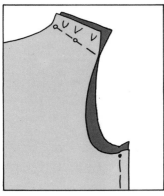

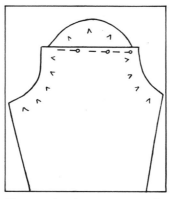

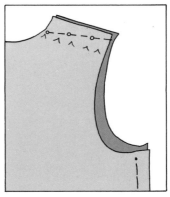

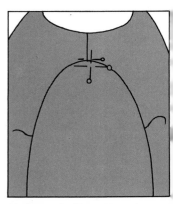

**If figure has sloping shoulders** unpick and repin shoulder seams to follow line of figure and to take out excess fabric. If figure is round-shouldered it may be necessary to take more out of the front of each seam than the back. Mark and baste alterations and refit.

**If garment has sleeves** compensate for altered shoulder seams by pinning a small pleat in each sleeve pattern piece 2 cm/$\frac{3}{4}$ in below centre top of sleeve head; trim edge to follow curve. Recut sleeve accordingly.

**To fit square-shouldered figure** snip basting at ends of each shoulder seam and allow seam to open sufficiently for alteration to be made. Pin and mark seam, angling it across from neckline edge up to outside edge. Baste. On some figures this alteration is needed only at either the front or back of each shoulder seam. Refit.

**To shorten shoulder seams** so they may finish exactly on top of bone at top of arms, snip basting over each sleeve head and lift pinned fold of sleeve head turning farther on to shoulder. Pin. Mark position reached by fold on shoulder seam with a pin.

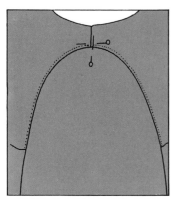

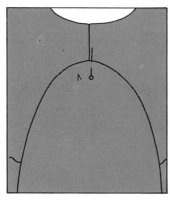

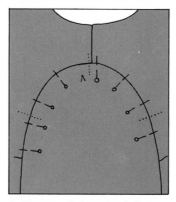

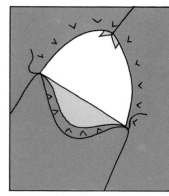

**2.** After removing garment, mark a new fitting line for each sleeve on bodice round edge of sleeve head. The new line should rejoin original marking above level where underarm curve begins. Baste and fit.

**SLEEVES If sleeves are too far forward** unpick basting at each sleeve head and pin fold of sleeve head turning to garment at shoulder, placing sleeve head marking slightly to the back of the shoulder seam. If sleeves are too far back, place sleeve head marking slightly to the front of the shoulder seam.

**2.** Pin rest of sleeve head, but not underarm, ensuring sleeve is hanging straight. Elbow darts may cause lower parts of sleeves to hang at an angle, but above elbow level sleeves should hang straight. Make three chalk marks across each sleeve head. Unpin and set sleeve in again, matching up marks. Fit.

**To correct wrinkles in sleeve head** first check whether they are caused by a sleeve that is too tight or a bodice that is too narrow at the back. If they are, undo the appropriate seams and release them as much as necessary. If not, unpick basting in each sleeve head, fold raw edge under a little farther and pin in position.

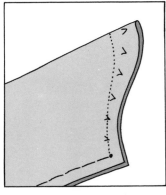

**2.** Unpin and mark new fitting line on sleeve head. Remove sleeve from garment and set in again, following new line and making a smooth curve over sleeve head only. Fit.

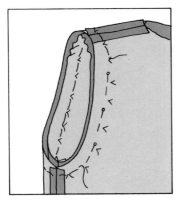

**Tightness blamed on sleeves** is often due to a narrow garment back. In area of strain only, unpick basting in back seams joining sleeves and garment. Pin new seam line, tapering it to meet original seam line and letting out appropriate amount, mark and baste again. Refit.

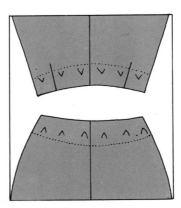

**WAISTLINE On a waisted dress** correct fit for a hollow back by separating bodice and skirt and marking a curved waist turning on back of skirt below original marking. Bodice may need similar alteration above first marking. To correct fit for a hollow back on a one-piece dress, lift shoulders (see p. 146).

**On a skirt or trousers** smooth fabric above waist, pin a tape round waist over fabric and, using chalk or pins, mark new back waistline level with bottom of tape. Finish waist following new line. Refit.

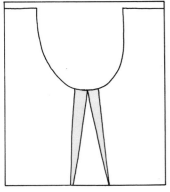

**TROUSERS Before cutting out** place both pattern pieces together at inside leg and check the width of the crutch. If pattern does not appear wide enough, extend back and front of crutch at top of inside leg 1 to 4 cm/⅜ to 1½ in when cutting out. For a large bottom make extension larger on back leg piece than front.

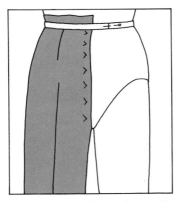

**2.** Alternatively, if crutch is too wide at fitting, take in inside leg by required amount. When the crutch width is correct, baste up one leg, press in crease and turn up and baste hem. Try trouser leg on, pin tape round waist and fit shaping of waist, hips and thighs as for a skirt.

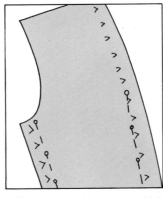

**3.** If legs are too wide, take two-thirds of excess from outside leg seam, from just below thigh level to hem. On inside leg, take in other third, from crutch if thighs are thin or, if not, from below thigh level to hem. Reverse procedure if leg is only slightly narrow. A big alteration must be done on the pattern.

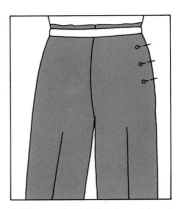

**4.** If trouser leg is twisted, unpick and rebaste vertically. After adjusting inside and outside leg seams baste crutch seam to join both legs and unpick left side seam enough for trousers to be put on. Try on, pin tape round waist and pin up unpicked seam securely. Mark and baste pinned seam and refit.

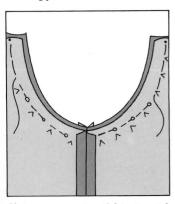

**If trousers are too tight at crutch** unpick basting at base of front and back crutch seams. Repin seams, letting out front of crutch and a little at the back. Taper alteration to meet end of basting on either side. Mark new curves. Baste and try on again.

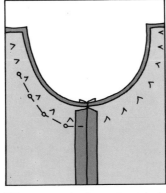

**If trousers are too loose at crutch** pin out surplus in back crutch and mark. Take off trousers and scoop out back of crutch seam on WS below original marking, tapering alteration to meet original seam line at inside leg. If trousers cut under crutch, scoop out seam a little in same way at back and front of crutch seam. Fit again.

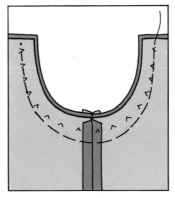

**Mark a level for waistline** as for a skirt (see Waistline) and lift trousers as much as necessary. If waistline is still too low, lower crutch curve the amount needed to lift the trousers. Pin, mark and baste alteration, tapering it to meet original seam line on front and back seam.

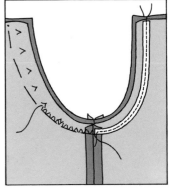

**If waist is too big** take excess out of centre back crutch seam from waist downwards. This improves the appearance as it makes the centre back seam lie more on the cross. Zigzag this seam for extra give. Reinforce front crutch seam, which is on straight grain, by stitching tape into seam or insert zip here.

147

# Curtains and Blinds

Professional-looking curtains are well within the scope of even a complete novice. The two basic requirements are a sewing machine and the ability to stitch in a straight line.

Start by choosing a fabric to go with your colour scheme and décor and decide on the style of curtain heading before buying the fabric, as the heading governs the amount you need. Remember to add extra for matching patterns and for shrinkage. Never skimp on the amount of fabric allowed for fullness. Styles such as pencil pleats will not hang well if the full amount of fabric is not used and the appearance of the curtains will be spoiled.

Most curtain fabric is 120 cm/48 in wide, although wider fabrics are also available; curtain lining is a little narrower so that it does not have to be trimmed before being made up.

Modern lightfast chemical dyes have minimized the problem of fading, but some fabrics such as printed cottons still have a tendency to fade, so avoid using them in a very sunny room. As strong sunlight also weakens fabric fibres, line the curtains to prolong their life in addition to preventing fading.

As well as thinking about colour, pattern and texture, bear in mind, when choosing the fabric, that curtains give privacy, help to reduce noise, prevent draughts, and, if heavy and lined, add to the warmth and comfort of the room. If you have draughty windows, it is well worth spending extra money on specially treated lining fabrics that provide insulation.

Remember, too, that curtains are not only for windows. Sheers and semi-sheers, hung from ceiling tracks, can make attractive room dividers, while a simple curtain in front of low shelving makes an instant cupboard and can hide a multitude of odds and ends.

## Blinds

An economical and easy way of covering small windows, blinds are traditionally made from Holland, a coarse linen fabric, but canvas, printed cotton, linen union and many of the medium-weight synthetics as well as PVC-coated cottons can be used.

Straighten the fabric before cutting out as it must be cut on the straight grain or the blind will hang crookedly. Roller blind fabric can be stiffened to give a smooth crisp finish. Apply spray-on stiffener before cutting out as it may shrink the fabric a little. Press the fabric well first, spray and allow to dry flat. As stiffener prevents fraying, no side hems are needed. However, if stiffener is not used, make the side hems narrow and not too bulky. A single turning, zigzagged, gives a much neater finish than a double hem.

Roller blinds with a spring roller are the most popular type. Another widely used type is the pleated blind, which folds up into soft pleats as it is drawn up by cords. Pleated blinds do not need stiffening and can be made with heavier fabrics and with more textured ones than those for roller blinds.

## MEASURING CURTAINS

If possible, install tracks and rods before measuring for curtains. They are fitted in different positions depending on the window shape and the style of the curtains.

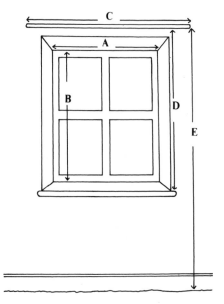

### Inside the window recess

Spring wires, rods and tracks for net and sheer curtains are generally fitted inside the window recess, **A**, and should be close to the top. Multiply measurement **A** two and a half or three times (depending on the desired style of the curtain heading) for the fullness of the curtains. Take measurement **B** for the length and add about 20 cm/8 in for hems.

If a straight track is fitted on a dormer window, the curtains may cover too much of the window and block out the light when they are drawn back. To prevent this, if the recess walls on either side of the window are deep enough, buy a track about 15 cm/6 in longer than the width of the window and at each end carefully bend 7.5 cm/3 in to fit round the recess. The curtains can then hang against the side walls.

Measure for half-length café curtains fitted inside the recess in the same way. Their length depends on the height of the rod from the window sill; extra fabric may be needed for a fancy heading or if the curtains extend outside the recess.

### Outside the window recess

Where possible, a wall-mounted track or rod should extend a little to either side of the window to allow for maximum daylight when the curtains are open. The amount of the extension depends on the overall proportions of the window and the thickness of the fabric when bunched together.

For sill-length curtains take measurement **C** and multiply according to the type of curtain heading to be used. Take measurement **D** for length and add about 20 cm/8 in for hems. Sill-length curtains should hang clear of the sill by about 2.5 cm/1 in to prevent wear along the bottom. Or if draughts are a problem, let the curtains hang slightly below the sill.

For floor-length curtains take measurement **C**, and multiply for fullness, and measurement **E**, adding on 20 cm/8 in for hems. Floor-length curtains should clear the floor by about 2.5 cm/1 in.

For floor-to-ceiling curtains, the track can be fixed to the top of the wall or to the ceiling. Neat, unobtrusive ceiling tracks are obtainable, but be sure to fix them securely—a batten screwed into the ceiling joints gives good support. Measure the length of the track **C**, and multiply for fullness; measure from track to floor and add about 20 cm/8 in for hems. With ceiling tracks use a tape with pockets at the top; special hooks may also be needed, depending on the style of heading and weight of the fabric.

### Headings

Curtain headings can be straight or gathered or have pencil or pinch pleats. For a straight heading no extra fullness is needed; make it with cotton heading tape. Special tape is available for all three shaped styles.

Gathered headings are the simplest and usually the most economical on fabric. Allow at least one and a half times the track length for fullness.

Pleated headings are particularly suitable for floor-length nets and sheers. Pencil pleats normally need about two and a half to three times the track length for the best result. Wide pleating tape is available with pockets nearer to one edge than the other. If you want a firm stand-up heading to cover a plain track (the pockets are nearer the bottom edge), add the depth of the tape to the length of the fabric required.

The various tapes for single, double or triple pinch pleats differ in fabric requirements. As estimating the amount required can be complicated, take the track measurements with you when buying the tape and fabric and ask the shop assistant for advice on the amount needed for fullness. When estimating the length of the fabric, decide whether you want the hook pockets at the top or bottom of the tape, as for pencil pleats.

If draw cords are to be used for any of these curtains, the curtains must fit the width of the track exactly.

## MEASURING BLINDS

Only two measurements are needed, the width, **A**, and length, **B**. Blinds are usually fitted inside the window recess. If there is no recess the blind should not extend too far beyond the edge of the window and should not drop below the sill.

### Roller blinds

Buy a roller blind kit to measurement **A** or longer. Remove metal cap from end opposite spring and cut off surplus on wooden part of roller. When the cap is replaced the complete roller should be about 1.25 cm/½ in shorter than the width of the recess (the pins, fitted into the brackets, make up the rest). Trim batten to fit.

Cut fabric measuring **B**, plus about 30 cm/12 in, by **A**, if fabric needs side hems. Cut fabric 2.5 cm/1 in narrower than **A** if stiffened or PVC-coated and so will not need the sides neatening.

### Pleated blinds

Cut two pieces of dowelling the length of **A**. Cut fabric measuring **A**, plus 2.5 cm/1 in, by **B**, plus 30 cm/12 in, joining fabric lengths if necessary.

### Joining widths and placing patterns

For curtains, join pieces of fabric selvedge to selvedge, to obtain the required width. The cut edge should be to the outside of the window. Join plain, colour-woven fabrics with a narrow open seam, snipping selvedges to allow fabric to drop evenly. If the selvedge is wide and a different colour, trim off and join widths with French seams. Match patterns carefully at seams; when the curtains are closed they must also match up where curtain edges meet.

Avoid joins for roller blinds as seams tend to interfere with the free running of the roller. Choose instead an extra wide fabric or make two blinds. If you have to join widths for any type of blind, make a central panel with an extension on either side, not a central seam. Keep seams flat and straight and trim and neaten seam turnings.

# CURTAIN FITTINGS

Select curtain fittings and accessories that are right for the weight and fullness of the curtain, as well as giving the effect required. Curtain tracks, for example, are made in many different styles and finishes: for straight runs or bay windows, for heavy or lightweight curtains, for use with or without pelmets. A wide variety of poles, rails and wires is also available. Below is a selection of standard fittings and accessories.

*Metal track with wall brackets and gliders; mainly for heavy curtains. Can be fitted with draw cords and a 7.5 cm/3 in overlap extension track, below, at the centre of the window. An alternative form of extension, for use with two separate rails, each longer than half the width of the window, consists of two plastic end stops for the track and a central metal bracket. The bracket has two grooves into which the tracks are slotted; it can be fixed to the top or side of the window recess.*

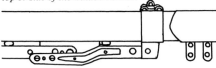

*White plastic track with gliders; unobtrusive and ideal for curtains without pelmets. Obtainable in different clip-on or stick-on finishes such as teak, silver, gold and other colours.*

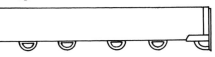

*Slimline track in plastic or metal with ceiling fitting; for curtains fixed to the ceiling or to inside top of the window recess. Ideal for lightweight nets and sheers.*

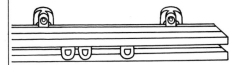

*Traditional wooden café curtain pole with wooden rings and wall-mounted brackets. Available in different wood finishes and colours.*

*Traditional brass rail with brass rings and wall-mounted brackets. Made in many designs and diameters for all weights of curtain.*

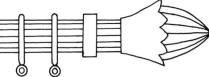

*Imitation brass pole with a concealed track; the gliders look like rings from the front. Can be fitted with draw cords.*

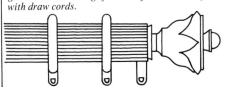

*Plastic-coated spring wire attached by hooks and eyelets within the window recess. Generally used for net and other lightweight curtains.*

*Brackets for fixing slimline wooden or brass rails to the inside of a window recess. Can be face-fitting (fixed to the wall behind the curtain), below left and centre, or end-fitting (fixed to the wall on the side of the window), below right. Various sizes take different diameter rails. Generally used with lightweight or café curtains.*

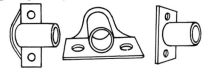

*For narrow rods or spring wires use small nylon or plastic rings (1), which are non-corrosive and washable. The ring is sewn on to the curtain. Alternatively, slot a split brass ring (2) through pocket tape or through the fabric instead of hooks. For wooden poles use a heavy wooden ring (3). A curtain hook is passed through the small eyelet at the ring base. Hollow brass rings (4) for brass rails are made in a range of sizes and fixed to the curtain in the same way as wooden rings. Hang shower curtains with metal pin rings (5) inserted through sail eyelets (6) at top of curtain. The eyelets are sold with instructions and a tool for inserting them.*

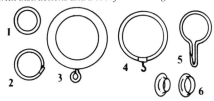

Special tapes and hooks are available for making different styles of curtain heading and for hanging the curtains. Headings can also be shaped by hand using standard heading tape. Below is the equipment for the most popular styles of heading.

*Cotton heading tape; white and coloured available.*

*Gathering tape for a gathered heading; available in cotton, nylon or polyester, in white, cream or a variety of colours.*

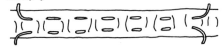

*Pencil pleat tape for a pencil pleat heading; available in cotton/nylon or nylon/polyester. Sheer pleating tape is also available for sheers and nets.*

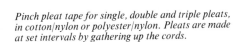

*Pinch pleat tape for single, double and triple pleats, in cotton/nylon or polyester/nylon. Pleats are made at set intervals by gathering up the cords.*

*Metal pronged hook for use with pinch pleat tape without cords for triple pleats at variable intervals.*

*Cotton lining tape.*

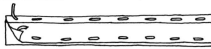

*Standard hooks for use with gathering and pleat tapes. Left, clear plastic, white plastic; right, brass, steel.*

*Pin hook for gathered and pleated headings made with standard heading tape; the point pierces fabric.*

*Plastic cord tidy keeps the ends of the cord out of the way behind the curtain and prevents tangling. It is hung by a hook from one of the tape pockets at outside edge of curtains.*

*Cording set with draw cords for straight runs of curtain (and some shallow bay windows) saves wear and tear and soiling of the curtains. Available in a range of sizes and styles to fit different tracks. The draw cord is joined to the two gliders at inside edges of curtain and draws the curtain open or closed.*

Double pulley fitting          Weighted ends

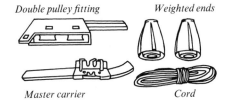

Master carrier          Cord

*Weighted tape, below left, consists of small pieces of lead encased in a fabric tube. Insert in bottom curtain hem for a better hang. Curtain weights, below right, are small button-like pieces of lead. Attach at intervals to bottom of ruched nets.*

*Pelmet bracket and rail for simple gathered pelmets. Can be fitted to most windows over the curtain track.*

*Right-angled brackets, below left, or "glass" plates made of brass, below right, can be used to fix the sides of a box pelmet frame to the wall. The plates screw into the sides of the frame.*

# Curtains

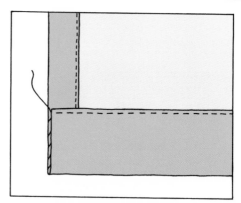

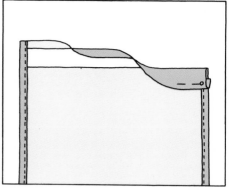

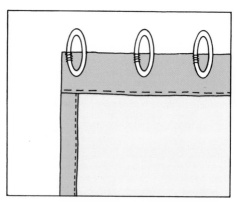

**Simple unlined curtains** Measure window according to shape and length of curtains required and cut fabric. Turn in 1.25 cm/½ in double hem down each side of curtain, snipping any selvedges, and baste. On most fabrics the hem can be machined, but hand sew satins and velvets. At bottom edge press up a 1.25 cm/½ in turning and turn fabric up again to form a double hem. Stitch by hand or with large machine stitch. Slip stitch folded edges at hem corners.

**2.** For a crisper look, stiffen top of curtains with iron-on interfacing. Cut interfacing 1.25 cm/½ in narrower than intended depth of top hem and iron it on to WS of fabric 1.25 cm/½ in from raw edge. Do not overlap ends on side hems. Turn down the 1.25 cm/½ in over it and turn down, pin and baste hem. (If using gathering tape for the heading—see Headings panel—cut interfacing to same depth as top hem and place it along fabric edge.)

**3.** Stitch hem by hand or machine, depending on fabric. If the heading is not to be gathered (leave fabrics such as tapestries and heavily patterned sheers ungathered to show off their design), sew hooks or rings to top edge of curtain.

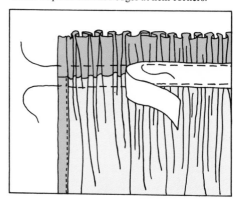

## CURTAIN HEADINGS
There are three ways to shape a curtain heading using tape specially prepared for each method.

**Gathered heading**
Cut a piece of standard gathering tape about 7.5 cm/3 in longer than the top edge of the curtain, draw out 4 cm/1½ in of the cords at one end of the tape and knot them together. Trim off surplus tape and fold end over knotted cords on WS (**1**). Turn

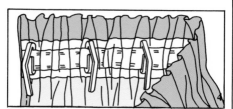

down and baste a single hem at curtain top. Place tape RS up with folded end on one side of curtain and over raw edge of hem (**2**). Baste in

place, leaving about 4 cm/1½ in extra tape at the other end. Unpick cords from extra tape back to curtain edge; trim end of tape and fold under, leaving ends of cord free. Sew tape to curtain, stitching close to top and bottom edges and avoiding cords (**3**). Fasten off thread securely and

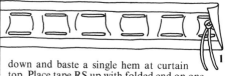

press curtains well. Draw up cords until the curtain measures half the track width and knot free ends of cord together. Repeat for second curtain, leaving loose cords at opposite side of curtain. The cords on both curtains should be at the outside of the window. Place hooks in tape at intervals of about 7.5 cm/3 in (**4**).

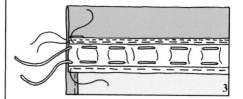

**4.** To make a gathered heading without gathering tape, work a row of gathering along top of curtain, about 2.5 cm/1 in above turned-down edge, and another row 2.5 cm/1 in below. Draw up threads until the curtain is the right width and distribute gathers evenly. Pin, baste and machine ordinary 2.5 cm/1 in tape along rows of gathering over edges of top hem. Remove gathering threads and insert pin hooks or split rings in tape.

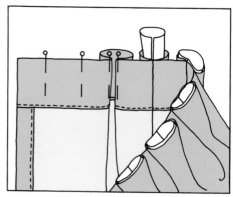

**5.** Simple pleats can be made without pleating tape. Decide on width of pleats and spaces between them. Measure and mark pleats on WS along top hem. With curtain WS up, bring marks together and on RS baste and stitch down them at right angles to top of curtain for 5 to 7.5 cm/2 to 3 in. Make cartridge paper tubes the width and depth of the stitched pleat and insert into each pleat to hold the shape. Insert pin hooks in back of alternate pleats.

**Pencil pleats**
Turn down top hem 2 cm/¾ in. Draw out 4 cm/1½ in of cord at both ends of tape; knot cords at one end only. At this end, trim off surplus tape and turn under as for gathered heading. Place tape close to top of hem (**5**) and attach as for gathered heading.

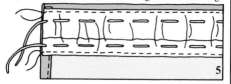

If you want to hang the curtains from a decorative rail without obscuring it, apply tape with pockets towards the top. Use the other way up for a firm stand-up heading to cover a plain track. Draw up pleats evenly and insert hooks every 5 to 7.5 cm/2 to 3 in (**6**), depending on the weight of the fabric.

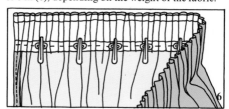

**Pinch pleats**
Attach tape to curtains as for pencil pleats (**7**).

*Creamy, cotton-lace, tie-back curtains and a pale, slubbed, dress cotton blind shade a westerly window. The blind is trimmed with antique lace to echo the curtains, which are tied back with crescents of blind material covered with lace and looped up on hooks in the wall behind the curtains to give a soft, draped effect.*

# Curtains

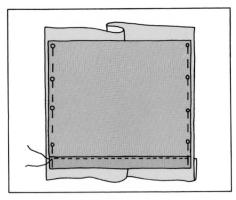

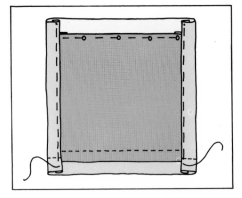

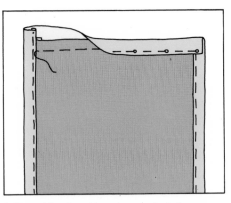

**Simple lined curtains** Cut curtains as for unlined method and cut lining 15 cm/6 in shorter than curtain and about 12.5 cm/5 in narrower. Turn up double hem of 7.5 cm/3 in at bottom of curtain and of 5 cm/2 in at bottom of lining and machine with a long loose stitch. With RS together, pin lining 5 cm/2 in from top edge of curtain so bottom of lining hem overlaps top of curtain hem by about 2.5 cm/1 in.

**2.** Baste and stitch side edges of curtain and lining together, leaving 1.25 cm/½ in seam allowances. Snip selvedges and press seams open. Turn curtain RS out and lay it RS down. Fold in equal turnings on both sides so lining is centred on back of curtain. Baste, making sure neither fabric nor lining is creased or puckered. Pin and baste top edge of lining to curtain.

**3.** Press side edges. Turn down a single hem at top of curtain over lining edge, pin and baste. Attach curtain tape (see Headings panel). Alternatively, turn down double hem, stitch and hand pleat as desired. Remove all basting. As the lining fills the top hem, interfacing is not usually necessary. For a very stiff hem for hand pleating, attach interfacing to top hem allowance of curtain before turning down hem as for unlined curtains (**2**).

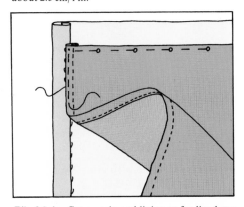

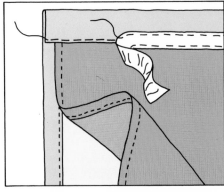

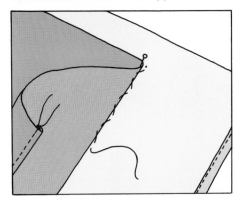

**Pile fabrics** Cut curtain and lining as for lined curtains, but make them up separately, with side and lower hems as for unlined curtains. Stitch curtain hems by hand to avoid marking the pile. With WS together, centre lining on curtain and pin top of lining 5 cm/2 in from top edge of curtain. Baste and slip hem lining to curtain down side hems. Finish heading by machine (see Headings panel).

**Stretch or loosely woven fabrics** Cut curtain and lining as for lined curtains. Make up separately, with side hems as for unlined curtains. Turn up and stitch double hem along bottom of lining. Baste lower, double hem of curtain. Join curtain and lining together and finish heading as for lined curtains. Hang curtain for a few days to drop. Adjust lower curtain hem if necessary and machine. Slip hem lining to curtain down side hems.

**Extra wide curtains** Linings may need anchoring at intervals. Make up curtain and lining separately, with side and lower hems as for unlined curtains. Place curtain RS down with lining centred, RS up, 5 cm/2 in from top. Pin lining to curtain down centre, turn back one side along pins and catch down with large, loose slip hemming. Repeat at intervals between centre and edges. Slip hem side hems together and finish as for lined curtains (**3**).

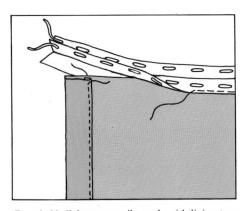

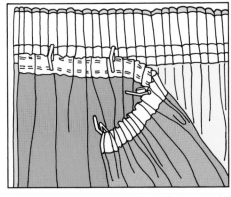

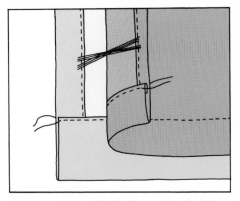

**Detachable linings** are easily made with lining tape and can be used with most heading tapes with pockets. Not all linings need be as full as curtains, e.g. on pencil- or triple-pleated curtains. Cut out the lining fabric as for unlined curtains and stitch a double hem along sides and bottom so lining is 2.5 to 5 cm/1 to 2 in shorter than curtain. Slip top edge between bottom edges of tape. Baste and machine along bottom of tape.

**2.** Knot cords of tape at one end and draw up at the other as for curtain tapes. Distribute gathers evenly. Join lining to curtains by curtain hooks, pushing hooks through slots in top of lining tape, up into pockets of main curtain tape and through into rings or gliders on track.

**3.** To keep linings neatly in place at sides of curtains, work long catch stitches between lining and curtain at intervals down sides. This allows some give and stops the edges puckering. Alternatively, slip stitch edges of lining and curtain loosely together, or, for a quicker release, sew on press studs at intervals, placing them on the side hems and stitching them to the turnings only so they cannot be seen from RS.

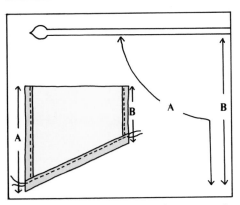

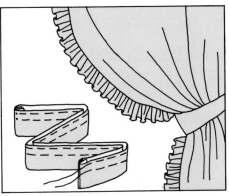

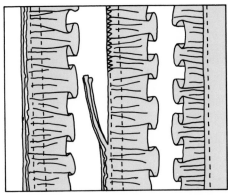

**Draped curtains** If the curtains are to be permanently drawn back, make the inside edge **A** longer than the outside edge **B** so hemline appears straight. Take measurement **A** from where open curtain will fall on rail and loop tape measure loosely up to side and then down to hem length. Take measurement **B** from rail to hem length for outside of curtain. Cut curtain twice desired width to allow for fullness and make, with sloping hem, as for unlined curtains.

**Frilled edge for drawn back curtains** Measure longer side of curtain. Cut strip of fabric one and a half times this length and double the width of the finished frill (2.5 to 4 cm/1 to 1½ in), plus two 1.25 cm/½ in seam allowances. Fold frill in half lengthways RS together, stitch across ends to neaten and turn RS out. Keeping raw edges level, work two rows of gathering close to seam line. Draw up gathering threads until frill fits curtain.

**2.** Distribute gathers evenly and, with RS together, pin and baste raw edges of strip to edge of curtain. Stitch along seam line. Stitch again, halfway between raw edge and seam; then trim away fabric close to second line of stitching. Zigzag all raw edges together with closely set stitches; press seam towards curtain so frill extends out from curtain and on RS top stitch along middle of seam allowance.

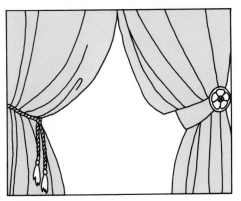

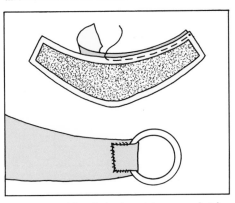

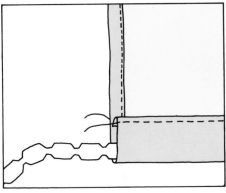

**Tie backs** For maximum daylight, curtains can be drawn back and fixed to hooks or brackets on the wall with matching fabric tie backs, chains or even a tasselled dressing-gown cord. Some brackets have chains to go round the curtain, others stand out from the wall so the curtains fit behind. For a simple tie back, fix a hook in the wall behind the curtain, thread a dressing-gown cord over it and tie the cord round the front of the curtain.

**2.** For a matching tie back, cut two curved strips of curtain fabric long enough to go loosely round curtain. To WS of one, attach iron-on interfacing 1.25 cm/½ in smaller all round than fabric. With RS together, join long curved edges of fabric strips with a 1.25 cm/½ in seam. Press, RS out. Slip a curtain ring over each end, turn down 1.25 cm/½ in to WS and hem. To fasten curtain back, hang rings on wall hooks behind or at side of curtain.

**Weighted hems** All curtains, except very heavy ones, and nets and sheers in particular, hang better if the bottom hem is weighted down with weighted tapes. The tapes consist of small pieces of lead enclosed in a fabric tube, which is passed through the bottom hem when the curtain is finished. Available in different grades, the tapes are very flexible and can be used even on full-gathered curtains.

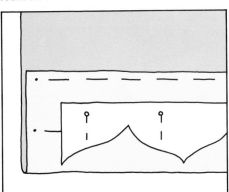

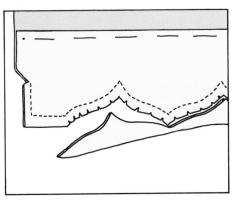

**Shaped hems** Prepare hem before stitching the lining to the curtain. From a piece of concertina-shaped paper cut a repeat pattern to the desired shape for a section of the hem. Cut curtain to required size, allowing pattern depth plus 5 cm/2 in for bottom hem. Turn lower hem allowance up on RS of fabric and hold with several lines of basting. Place pattern 1.25 cm/½ in from fold on hem and 5 cm/2 in from one end. Pin in place.

**2.** Chalk round shaped edges of pattern. Remove pattern. Baste and stitch along shape. Also stitch a 1.25 cm/½ in vertical seam at each end of curtain the depth of the pattern. Snip into side seam allowance at top of stitching. Trim turnings to 5 mm/¼ in, snip on curves and turn RS out. Finish hem in usual way and proceed as for simple lined curtains, cutting lining to finish 2.5 cm/1 in above top of decoration.

**Draw rods** Draw the curtains without handling them by easy-to-reach draw rods fitted to the two inside curtain edges. To make the rod, hold a split curtain ring against end of a length of thin dowelling with a piece of tape and bind tape ends tightly with string. Attach rod to curtain by passing ring through end pocket of heading tape at inside edge. Bind rod with bias or ribbon to match curtain, or decorate with braid and trim bottom with a tassel.

155

# Curtains

## NETS AND SHEERS

There are many suitable natural and synthetic fabrics, the choice ranging from fine, almost transparent net to the heaviest textured, patterned and coloured weaves. Many nets, especially cotton ones, shrink so buy extra material if necessary. If the fabric is not too bulky and there is not too much of it, wash the net before cutting it out. Otherwise, baste generous hems in place until after the first wash. Then adjust and sew permanently.

Net curtains are hung from tracks or poles if they are to be opened, spring wires if they are to stay closed. They are made in the same way as simple unlined curtains except for a few minor differences. For example, if you are using several drops of fabric for one window, leave them separate. The selvedges are less conspicuous lost in the folds than seams and the curtains are easier to wash. Eliminate vertical seams on plain nets for shallow windows by using the length of net sideways.

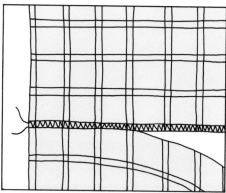

**Cutting nets level** Carefully follow the line of the weave to ensure the cut edge is level. Prevent excess fraying on cotton and some synthetic nets by zigzagging along cutting line first, and then cut fabric outside the stitched line. With a large-holed pattern cut along the solid part of the design, to give a definite edge to turn in and hem.

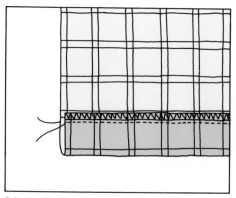

**Stitching the hem** Sometimes only a single turning is needed, especially if you have stitched before cutting. Fold fabric along centre of a pattern repeat or between patterns, whether the hem is to be single or double. This makes the hem neater and less noticeable as the holes in the pattern on the turnings fall exactly over those on RS. Use a longish stitch and a loose tension and keep fabric taut.

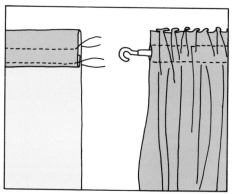

**Self-heading** The easiest heading for nets, it can be used with a spring wire on narrow windows or dowelling or a slim brass rod on wider ones. Allow about 5 cm/2 in top hem for a spring wire, a little more for a rod, depending on its thickness. Turn down 1.25 cm/½ in and turn down fabric again to make a 4 cm/1½ in hem. Stitch close to hem edge and then about 2 cm/¾ in from it. Insert wire or rod in lower channel of hem to leave top edge as a frill.

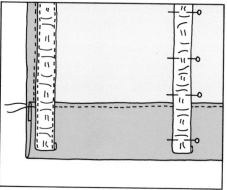

**Ruched nets** Cut and join fabric so it is one and a quarter times the track width, plus side hem allowances, and about two and a half times the desired length. Hem curtain, with self-heading at top. On WS below heading stitch lightweight gathering tape in vertical lines every 15 cm/6 in, starting at side hem and finishing 1.25 cm/½ in from bottom. Knot cords and turn under tape at lower end as for gathered headings. Leave cords free at top.

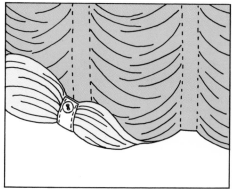

**2.** Draw up cords so curtain fits length of window and distribute gathers evenly down each tape. Tidy away ends of cords on cord tidies or by winding them round small pieces of card and pinning these on WS of top hem. For a better hang on very lightweight nets, sew curtain weights to lower end of each piece of tape before hanging the curtains.

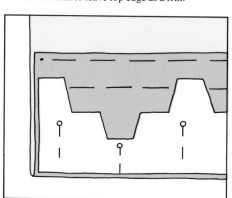

**Fancy hems** can be made on net or sheer curtains by using doubled fabric to create the design. The hem bottom is straight, but the top edge is stitched to form a pattern. Work out a fairly simple pattern on paper. Turn up a single hem slightly deeper than the pattern shape and hold in place with several lines of basting. Pin pattern to fabric and mark shaped edge on fabric with tailor's chalk, pencil or basting. Remove pattern.

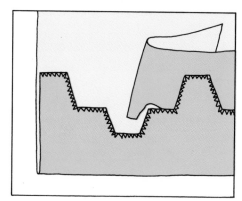

**2.** Set the machine to a medium-width, fairly close zigzag with a loose tension and stitch carefully along marked lines. Keep fabric taut while you stitch and do not allow it to pucker within the zigzag. A coloured thread adds to the decorative effect. Carefully trim away surplus hem allowance above stitching with small sharp scissors.

## LENGTHENING CURTAINS

Insert a lengthening band just above the hem rather than letting the curtains down, since the old hemline generally shows. If the curtains are only slightly short, insert wide braid. Free bottom of lining from curtain; measure from bottom of curtain the depth at which you want to insert braid, cut along line and zigzag raw edges. Overlap braid on edges and stitch in place. Let down lining.

## CAFÉ CURTAINS

The perfect screen, café curtains hang across the lower half of a window from a rod or pole, to which they are attached by rings or fabric loops. The spacing of the loops and rings, the width of the loops and the size of the gap between the top of the curtain and the rod depend on the thickness of the rod, the size of the window and the finished effect desired.

*In more contracted living spaces clever use of colour can separate a room into different areas. Here crisp greens in a variety of shades and checks make a fresh-looking dining area. The unlined café curtains give privacy while admitting the maximum light. Their hems are bound in a smaller matching check, cut on the true cross, as are the loops. The white, turned-wood curtain pole complements the look.*

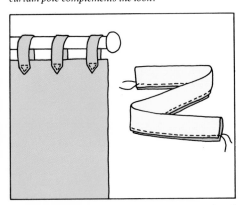

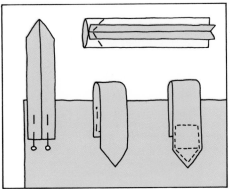

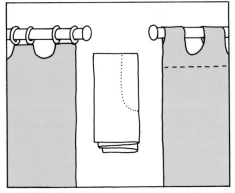

**Simple unlined café curtains** Hem a rectangle of fabric the required size. To make the loops, cut a long strip of fabric twice the finished width desired, plus two 1.25 cm/½ in seam allowances. Fold in half lengthways and stitch with RS together.

**2.** Cut strip into lengths, twice as long as finished loop. Press seam open down centre of each length and stitch a right-angled point at one end, trimming excess fabric from point. Turn RS out. Starting flush with one side of curtain, pin and baste unstitched end of one loop to RS of curtain top, so about two-thirds extends at top, and turn down shaped end over this to cover raw edge. Pin and baste; stitch to curtain through all thicknesses as shown.

**Scalloped-top café curtains** Decide on number and width of tabs and width of curved spaces (the scallops) between them. To length of curtain add depth of scallop, plus 1.25 cm/½ in seam allowance and a little extra if curtains are to be hung with rings. For fabric tabs extending from curtain, allow enough to go up over rod and down to 2.5 cm/1 in below base of scallop. From concertina-folded paper cut a pattern of about four tabs in a row.

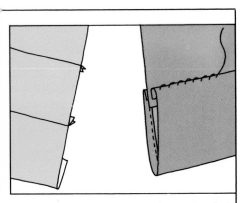

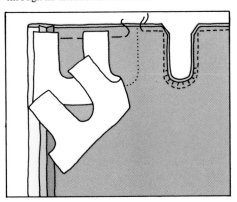

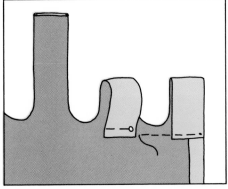

**2.** If the curtains are very short, insert a band of contrasting fabric. Cut a strip the width needed, plus 2.5 cm/1 in for seam allowances. Cut bottom as before and join raw edges of strip and curtain, RS together. Press seams towards strip. Let down lining and join lining fabric twice the extra width needed to the bottom, RS together. Press. Turn up new fabric and hem to seam line.

**2.** Cut curtain to required size and cut lining as for lined curtain. Stitch double hem on bottom of curtain and lining and, RS together, join sides as for lined curtains. Baste layers together along top. Pin pattern along top of lining, starting with a tab at one side, and mark outline with chalk or pencil. Baste and stitch through both layers along marked line. Trim seam to 5 mm/¼ in; snip round curves and trim corners. Turn curtain RS out and press.

**3.** If curtains are to be hung with rings, stitch one at each corner of each tab; if with fabric tabs, fold tops of tabs over to WS, pin in place 2.5 cm/1 in below base of scallops, and baste across back of curtains. Stitch in place, either by hand to lining only, or through all thicknesses by machine, in a straight line of stitching across whole width of curtain. Press curtain and thread rod through loops or rings.

# Curtains

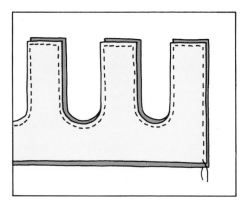

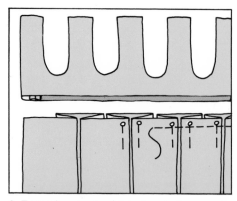

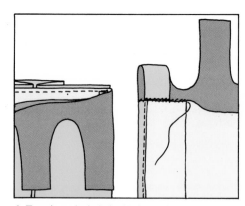

**Pleated café curtains** For shaped top band, cut fabric the length of the finished width of the curtain, plus 2.5 cm/1 in for seam allowances, by the depth required for the band, plus seam allowances of 2.5 cm/1 in. Line band as for lined curtains. Make pattern for band and cut band to shape as for scalloped-top café curtains.

## SHOWER CURTAINS

The ideal fabric for waterproof shower curtains is PVC-backed material, but it requires extra care in making up as pins, needles and unpicking leave marks. To avoid the marks showing, pin the fabric within the seam allowance or hold it together with paper clips, clothes pegs or adhesive tape.

The plastic coating of the fabric tends to cling to the smooth underside of the machine foot when the fabric is stitched on the right side so, if you intend to sew a lot with PVC, invest in a special foot with a small roller set into it. Otherwise, place tissue paper over the stitching line and tear it away after sewing. Sew plastic that has no woven backing with a large stitch to prevent tearing along the seam lines. Clean out the bobbin area of the machine thoroughly after sewing PVC or plastic; bits of fabric tend to lodge in the works and can cause the bobbin to jam.

## PELMETS

As a result of improvements in the design of unobtrusive curtain tracks and of smaller windows in most modern homes, pelmets are not used as often as they used to be. Some windows, however, need pelmets to set them off to the best advantage. In high-ceilinged rooms particularly, pelmets help to give the impression of height and width to a window.

The size and shape of a pelmet depend on the style of the window, but leave enough space between the pelmet and the curtain track behind to give access to the track and allow the curtains to run freely. Illustrated, right, are four of the most popular styles of pelmet.

For lightweight gathered pelmets there are special extension supports to carry a standard type of track several inches in front of the curtains. The heavier, shaped, box pelmet needs a wooden frame, which should extend at least 30 cm/12 in on either side of the window.

**2.** To work out extra fabric for pleating curtain, decide on width of pleat and double this measurement. Multiply doubled pleat measurement by number of tabs in top band, excluding the two end ones, and add to window measurement. Cut fabric to these dimensions. Mark pleats, arranging them so they fall from centre lower edge of tabs. Pin and baste them in place 1.25 cm/½ in from top. Work second row of basting 2.5 cm/1 in below first row.

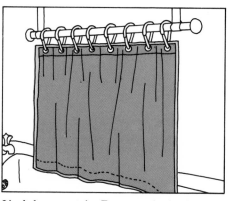

**Lined shower curtains** For a curtain that is waterproof on the inside and attractive outside, use towelling, lined with PVC-coated fabric, or plastic shower curtaining. Make up as for simple lined curtains with towelling as main fabric and allowing for 10 cm/4 in to hang down inside bath edge. To save on fabric, do not gather curtains but hang them straight using sail eyelets inserted through top hem and pin rings.

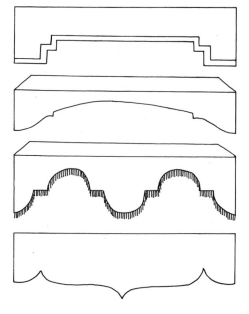

**3.** Turn in and stitch double hems down each side of curtain and at bottom edge. With RS together, leaving band lining free, join lower edge of band to top edge of curtain. Turn in seam allowance along lower edge of band lining and baste along machining to WS of curtain. If fabric loops are allowed for, turn them over and baste lining and loops in place at the same time. Stitch lining and loops by hand or by machine.

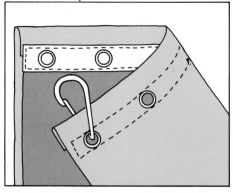

**2.** Sail eyelets are sold with an instruction leaflet and tool for inserting them. To make a sail eyelet heading, turn down a 5 cm/2 in single hem over lining edge and baste. Baste wide standard tape over hem edge to cover it and stitch close to tape edges and across ends. Insert eyelets along centre of tape about 7.5 to 10 cm/3 to 4 in apart. Pass pin rings through eyelets and over hanging rail.

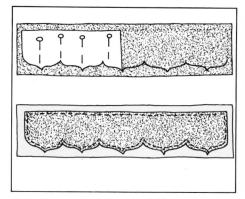

**Box pelmet to match curtains** Add length of front and sides of pelmet together and make a paper pattern to the required style for a section of the total length. Cut shape for entire pelmet round pattern from buckram interfacing. Cut two strips of curtain fabric the length and width of interfacing, plus 1.25 cm/½ in all round for turnings. Centre interfacing on WS of one strip and baste and machine to fabric close to edges of interfacing.

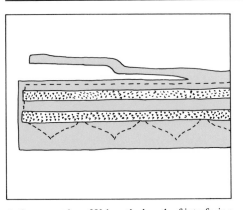

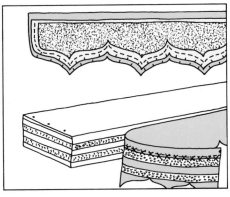

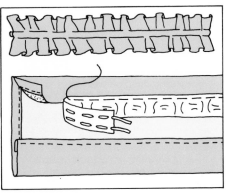

**2.** Cut two strips of Velcro the length of interfacing and glue hooked sections along top and bottom of front and side sections of pelmet box frame (before fixing box to wall if possible). Turn buckram-backed strip RS up and position the two loop sections of Velcro on fabric to correspond with those on pelmet. Machine in place down both edges of each strip. Trim top edge of fabric level with top of buckram.

**3.** Place strip, RS down, on a second, matching fabric strip and baste and stitch at ends and along bottom edge, following decorative shape of buckram. Trim fabric 5 mm/$\frac{1}{4}$ in from stitching; snip curves and turn RS out. Turn down top hem of second strip over first strip and buckram and cross stitch to Velcro. If decorating with braid, sew it to side without Velcro. Fasten fabric to pelmet frame by pressing the sections of Velcro together.

**Frilled pelmet** Cut a strip of fabric about three times the length of the pelmet by the depth required, plus 7.5 cm/3 in for both top and bottom hems. Stitch double hems along bottom and sides. Cut a strip of 7.5 cm/3 in iron-on interfacing as long as the fabric and iron to WS of top edge. Turn down top hem 7.5 cm/3 in and baste. Stitch gathering tape over raw edge, draw up cords, and hang from track as for gathered curtains.

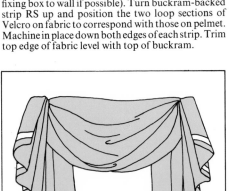

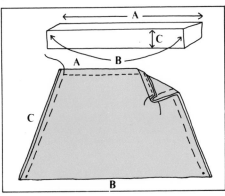

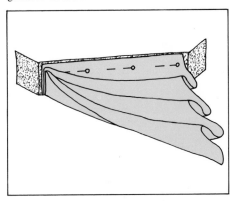

**Draped pelmet** A luxurious heading for long formal windows. This simple style has only three shaped pieces of fabric, used double so that each piece is self-lined. Braid or trimming can be added to side drapes.

**2.** To make the centre loop, measure length of front of pelmet, **A**, and then drape the tape measure loosely across the front to estimate length of drape's lower edge, **B**. Multiply depth of pelmet, **C**, four times to allow for the folds and cut a piece of double fabric based on these dimensions and to this shape, with folded edge at bottom. Baste side edges WS together. Turn down and stitch a narrow single hem along top edge.

**3.** Cut a strip of buckram the length and depth of pelmet front and sides. Cut and attach bands of Velcro to pelmet and back of buckram as for box pelmet (**2**). Taking pleats of equal depth on each side, and keeping side edges level, fold fabric up to either side of front section of buckram. Pin folds in place and stitch by hand through all layers along top edge of buckram. The stitches and basting at side edges will be hidden behind the side drapes.

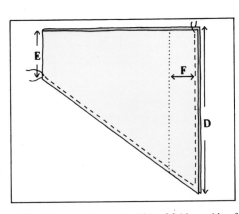

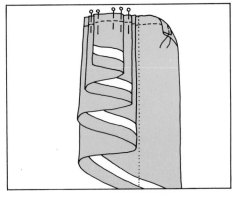

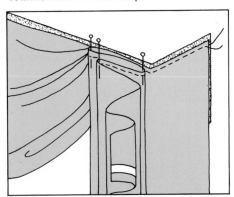

**4.** Decide on number and width of folds at side of pelmet and to this total width add length of pelmet side, **F**. Decide length of longest edge, **D** (roughly half length of curtain), and shortest edge, **E**, and add 5 cm/2 in to both for hems. Fold fabric in half and cut shape based on these dimensions with level top edge and slanted lower one. Mark extent of **F**. With RS together, join lower edge and long edge, **D**, with a 2.5 cm/1 in seam. Turn RS out and press.

**5.** If using braid or trim, sew approximately 2.5 to 5 cm/1 to 2 in away from lower edge. Turn down 2.5 cm/1 in to WS along top edge and machine. With RS (trimmed side) facing you, arrange and pin fabric in slightly decreasing concertina folds so top fold is the narrowest. Keep top edge level and leave enough of it unpleated at the widest end to pin along side of pelmet. When effect is right, mark folds and open out fabric.

**6.** Pin and stitch top of unpleated section, RS up, to top edge of one buckram side extension. On one side of centre section, pin and stitch first, widest fold through all thicknesses and, if possible, buckram to cover ends of centre drape. Work stitches so they are covered by next fold. Continue like this until narrowest fold and slip stitch this fold down each side about 2.5 cm/1 in. Make drape for other side. Attach to pelmet frame along Velcro strips.

# Blinds

## BLIND FITTINGS

Roller blind kits are available containing instructions and the following fittings: a spring-loaded roller with a flat pin at the spring end and a round pin at the other; top-fitting or face-fitting brackets; stretcher batten for base; nylon or cotton pull cord with two end fittings. In addition, the kit may contain small tacks and glue for fixing the blind to the roller and screws for the brackets.

For pleated blinds you need two lengths of dowelling, or one length for the bottom and a slim brass rod for the top; face-fitting brackets; a cord, heavier than that for a roller blind and without end fittings; a cleat to hold the cord ends when the blind is pulled up; and screw-in eyelets or metal pulleys with a plastic roller disc. The cleat is attached to the side of the window recess just above the cord end; pulleys or eyelets carry the cord and are fixed to the top and side of the window recess. The pulleys facilitate raising and lowering heavy pleated blinds.

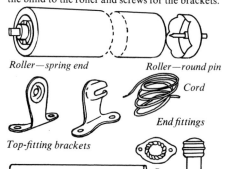

Roller—spring end          Roller—round pin
Cord
End fittings
Top-fitting brackets
Batten

Screw-in eyelet          Pulley          Cleat
Dowelling

**Roller blind** Cut roller and batten to size and fix brackets to recess wall. Straighten fabric grain and stiffen if desired. Cut out fabric (see Measuring panel p. 150) and, if not stiffened, stitch 1.25 cm/½ in side hems. Turn up and stitch double lower hem to take batten. Insert batten. Turn top of fabric over roller, glue and tack down. On WS attach cord to batten centre with fitting provided. Place roller on brackets and work to adjust spring tension.

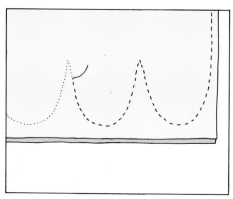

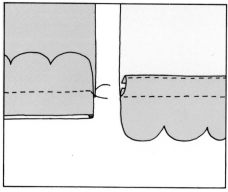

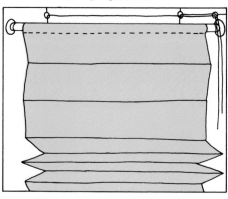

**Shaped decorative hem** Instead of a plain bottom hem cut two straight bands of fabric the length of the finished blind width, plus 2.5 cm/1 in, by the depth of the shaped motif, plus batten width and 2.5 cm/1 in. Trace decorative shape on WS of one band, leaving 1.25 cm/½ in seam allowances, and, with RS together, sew both bands along tracing line and at both ends. Trim seams, snip curves and turn band RS out.

**2.** Invert band over RS of blind base, with batten allowance extending over raw edge at bottom of blind, and stitch to bottom seam line of blind. Press shaped hem to extend below blind and press turnings up to WS. Turn under raw edges on batten allowance and stitch to WS of blind.

**Pleated, or Roman, blind** Folds into soft accordion pleats as it is drawn up and hangs straight when down. Cut two pieces of dowelling the width of the blind or, for the top of the blind, choose a slim brass rod the required size. Fix brackets at either side of window recess. Cut a rectangle of fabric on straight grain to fit window measurements **A**, plus 2.5 cm/1 in for side hems, by **B**, plus 30 cm/12 in for top and bottom hems (see Measuring panel p. 150).

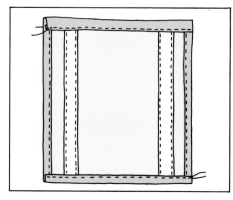

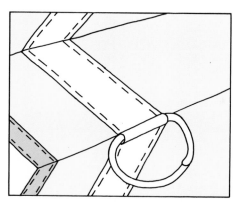

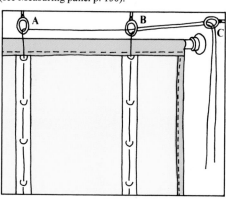

**2.** Turn in double hems down sides and stitch. Press under 1.25 cm/½ in along top and bottom edges and then turn in hems wide enough to take dowelling, or, at top, brass rod. On WS, about 10 cm/4 in from each side of the blind, stitch two lengths of narrow tape vertically between top and bottom hems, sewing down both edges of tape.

**3.** Work out width of pleats (10 cm/4 in is average width), mark pleats, fold fabric at marks and press pleats, one by one. Mark both pieces of tape at back edge of each pleat and push a small split brass curtain ring between tape and fabric at each mark, inserting last two rings at top edge of bottom hem. Fit two lengths of dowelling, or brass rod and dowelling, into top and bottom hems. Slip stitch bottom hem ends together.

**4.** Fix two screw-in eyelets or pulleys, **A** and **B**, to top of window recess in line with rings on WS of blind, and one, **C**, at top of one side of recess. Hang blind. Thread a cord through **C** and **B**, down through rings on one tape and up through those on the other. Take cord through **A**, back through **B** and down through **C**. Adjust ends, cut level and pull both together to raise blind. Attach cleat to side of recess near bottom of cord and wrap cord ends round it.

# Tablelinen

Create the perfect setting for every meal by making your own tablelinen. For a sophisticated dinner party make matching place mats and napkins and set them on a polished wood table. For afternoon tea try a pretty flowered cloth to complement your tea service, with a set of napkins in the predominant colour. Or, for brightening up breakfast on a dull morning, try a gingham or colourful non-iron seersucker cloth and napkins.

Tablelinen can also be used to conceal or disguise. Give an old or damaged table a new lease of life by hiding it under a floor-length cloth; hide improvised board and trestle tables for a buffet lunch or supper under attractive long cloths.

Choose washable fabric for all tablecloths and napkins. Linen is the traditional choice for table-linen that is likely to be in regular use. It is, however, fairly expensive and cotton or a cotton and synthetic mixture is equally suitable. Braid, appliqué and other forms of decoration should also be washable, colour-fast and shrink resistant.

If your table is fairly large and you want to avoid joining pieces of fabric to obtain the required width, it is worth looking for extra wide fabric such as polyester and cotton sheeting, which is now available in many colours and designs.

Napkins can be in the same fabric as the tablecloth or can contrast in colour or design. Table mats for daily use should be made from a heavy washable fabric, or one that can be wiped clean; PVC-coated fabrics are ideal for children's place mats. If you want to make matching mats in the napkin fabric, make them double or line them with a thicker material for extra protection. For square or rectangular napkins, follow the method for a rectangular cloth; for table mats follow the appropriate method for the shape required.

*Appliqué motifs are a simple yet effective way to decorate a tablecloth. They can be in plain or patterned fabric, to match or contrast with the cloth. Or, for a particularly striking effect, co-ordinate the appliqué motifs with your crockery.*

# Tablelinen

## MEASURING

For all shapes of tablecloth measure the area of the table top plus the depth of the side overhang.

For a square or round table there is only one top measurement, **A**; for an oval or rectangular table, measure the width, **A**, and the length, **B**. For all shapes of cloth add twice the overhang, **C**, plus two double hem allowances, to the top measurement. The standard double hem allowance is 2.5 cm/1 in, but it can be wider if desired. The depth of the overhang depends on personal preference, but generally a cloth ends just above the dining-chair seat; a long cloth on a side table can come to within a short distance of the floor, **D**.

### Joining fabric

Preferably try to find a fabric that is as close as possible to the width required for the cloth. However, if it is necessary to join fabric to make up the width needed, buy a piece of fabric twice the estimated length of the finished tablecloth; remember to allow extra for hems and for matching up the pattern when joining the pieces. Fold the fabric in half crossways and cut on the fold. One piece forms the centre top panel. From the second piece cut two pieces of equal size to make up the width (**1**), leaving a centre offcut, and join one to each side of the main part of the cloth, selvedge to selvedge and with any pattern motifs matching (**2**). The joins should, ideally, be placed in the overhang as seams across the table top are ugly and can unbalance crockery. Open seams are adequate for a cloth on a side table, but for cloths such as dining cloths that will be in more frequent use, stitch a fell seam or, if you do not want the stitching to show on the right side, a French seam. (The centre offcut, if wide enough, can be used to make matching table napkins.)

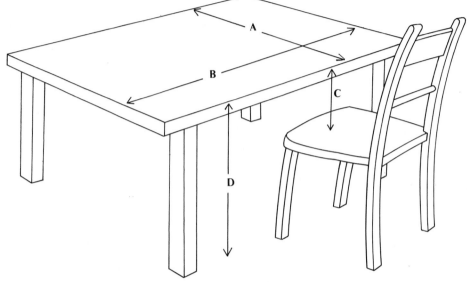

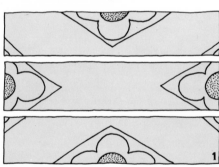

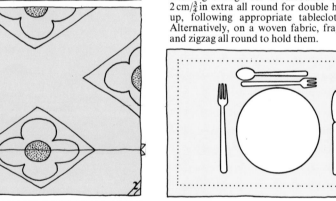

### Table mats

For everyday use table mats are generally made from heavier fabric than that used for tablecloths, since they should protect the table surface from hot dishes, spills and cutlery scratches.

Estimate the size required for mats by setting a place on the table. Measure the area it takes up, allowing enough for a surround. To this add 2 cm/$\frac{3}{4}$ in extra all round for double hems. Make up, following appropriate tablecloth method. Alternatively, on a woven fabric, fray the edges and zigzag all round to hold them.

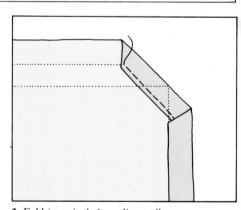

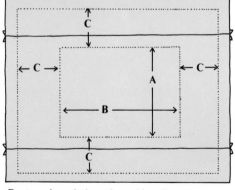

**Rectangular cloth and napkins** For square or rectangular napkins cut fabric to desired size, plus hem allowances of approximately 2 cm/$\frac{3}{4}$ in all round. For a cloth, measure **A** and **B**. To both measurements add twice the overhang, **C** or **D**, and two hem allowances. Cut a rectangle of fabric to these dimensions, joining widths if necessary. For both cloth and napkins, mark top and centre of hem allowance with tailor's chalk on WS.

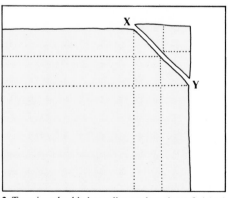

**2.** Turn in a double hem all round to give a finished hem of about 1.25 cm/$\frac{1}{2}$ in for a cloth, slightly less for a napkin. Press fold lines. Open out folds and cut off a triangle of fabric diagonally across each corner from **X** to **Y**.

**3.** Fold in a single hem diagonally across corners. Press the folds and baste them down across corners. Taking each corner in turn, fold in first fold of hem on one side of the fabric.

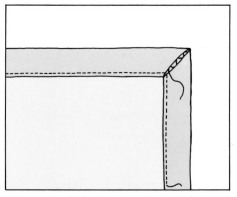

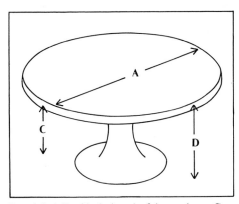

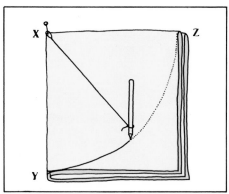

**4.** Turn in first fold on the other side and then second fold on each side. Pin and baste folds in place. Machine close to inner folded edge all round, pivoting stitching at corners. For neatness, slip stitch folds together at corners on wide hems. Remove basting and press cloth well.

**Round cloth** Double the length of the overhang, **C** or **D**. Add to it the diameter of the table top, **A**, plus two 1.25 cm/½ in single hem allowances. Cut a square of material based on this dimension, joining widths of fabric if necessary.

**2.** Fold square into quarters. To obtain a circular shape, measure length of one folded side from **X** to **Y**. At **X**, pin a piece of string and tie a pencil to it at the distance of **Y** from **X**. Using the pencil and string as a compass, draw a curve between the two diagonally opposite corners **Y** and **Z**. Be careful not to wrinkle the fabric as you draw and keep the string taut. Cut through all four layers of fabric along the pencil line and open the fabric out.

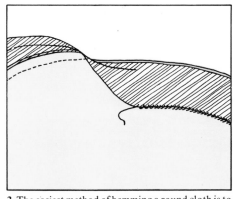

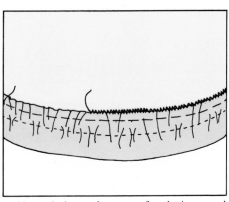

**3.** The easiest method of hemming a round cloth is to attach a length of single or double bias binding. With RS together, stitch binding round edge of cloth, roll binding and seam to WS and stitch in place by hand or machine.

**4.** Alternatively, work a row of gathering round cloth about 6 mm/¼ in from edge. Turn up a single hem and press, drawing up gathering thread to ease in fullness round edge. Baste hem in place and machine satin stitch round raw edge to neaten and hold hem. Remove basting and press.

**Octagonal cloth** An attractive shape for a round table, it is also easier to hem than a round cloth. To the diameter of the table top, **A**, add two side overhangs, **C** or **D**, and two double hem allowances. Cut a square of fabric based on this dimension, joining widths of fabric if necessary. The fabric must be exactly square to make an even-sided octagon. Make sure the sides of the square are exactly in line with the grain of the fabric. Fold square into quarters.

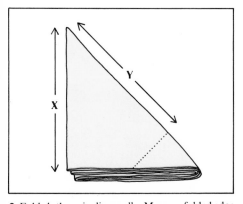

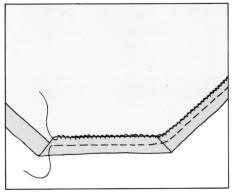

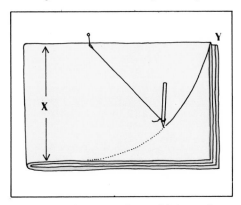

**2.** Fold cloth again diagonally. Measure folded edge **X** and, measuring from the top corner, on folded edge **Y** mark the length of **X** with a pin. At right angles to folded edge **Y** cut off the corner below the pin, taking care to cut in a straight line. (This gives a cloth with eight equal sides.)

**3.** Unfold fabric and trim edges to neaten. Turn up narrow single hem all round, overlapping corners and pressing them in place. Turn up a second, wider hem in the same way. Pin, baste and stitch in place by hand or machine. For a decorative finish stitch a tasselled braid to the hem.

**Oval cloth** Measure and cut fabric as for a rectangular cloth and fold it into quarters as for a round one. Measure width, **X**, of folded fabric and on one of long edges mark this distance from corner of raw edges, **Y**. At marked distance pin a piece of string. Measure length of **X** along string and tie on a pencil at this point. Using the pencil and string as a compass, draw a curve between corner and lower raw edges. Proceed as for a round cloth.

# Bedlinen

By making your own bedlinen you can not only save money, but you also have the greatest possible flexibility in the choice of colour, design and fabric, enabling you to co-ordinate your bedlinen with the colour scheme and décor of your room.

As bed shapes and sizes vary considerably, check the dimensions of your bed before buying the material. Sheeting is usually sold in widths of 175 cm/70 in and 230 cm/90 in for standard single and double beds. Extra wide fabric for king-size beds is not as easily available, but well worth while searching for as it avoids uncomfortable joins. As a general rule, a plain sheet should be long enough and wide enough to cover the mattress and also to tuck in all round.

Easy-care polyester and cotton mixtures are the most practical form of sheeting. Available in a wide range of colours and patterns, these mixtures are particularly useful for fitted bottom sheets, which can be difficult to iron. They are also ideal for valances, which cover the base of the bed, and for covers for the increasingly popular duvets. Duvet covers can also be made to match printed cotton curtains, providing the curtain fabric is smooth, washable and colour-fast.

Whatever the style of valance, it will stay in place more securely and with the minimum of pins if joined to a piece of fabric, ideally an old sheet, large enough to cover the bed base.

The main considerations in choosing fabric for pillowcases are that it should be washable, colour-fast and preferably non-iron. It can be plain or patterned and can match or contrast with the sheeting. Give a plain fabric added interest by decorating the pillowcase with embroidery or appliqué.

Of all items of bedlinen, bedspreads can be the least utilitarian and most eye-catching. Although heavier materials hang better than lighter weight ones, almost any material can be used. Accentuate the lines of a tailored cover with piping or braid. Highlight a plain fabric with appliqué motifs or embroidery in contrasting colours. Or try luxury quilted or lacy fabrics, or ornate jacquard weaves, for a simple yet stunning effect.

*Bold use of furnishing fabric, combined with toning sheeting fabric, can create a stunningly individual effect in any bedroom. The tops of the duvet and pillow covers, right, are made of soft, satin-finish furnishing fabric—two different coloured fabrics are stitched together on the duvet; the underneath is made of easy-care sheeting, as is the fitted bottom sheet. The valance has a trim of white sheeting.*

## SHEETS

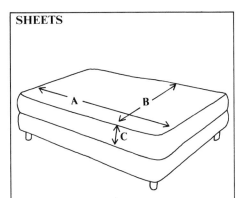

Take the following measurements:
**A** length of mattress top
**B** width of mattress top
**C** depth of mattress
In addition to these measurements allow 25 cm/10 in for hem turnings and tuck-in on a single bed, 30 cm/12 in for a double bed.

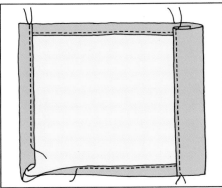

**2.** If the sheeting is the correct width for the bed, leave selvedges or stitch a single hem down each side. If the fabric is too wide, trim to size and stitch a double hem down each side. Stitch a double hem 7.5 cm/3 in wide at the top of the sheet and another at the bottom 2.5 cm/1 in wide. On the top hem a zigzag or machine embroidery stitch may be used for decorative effect. Slip stitch folded edges together at ends of double hems.

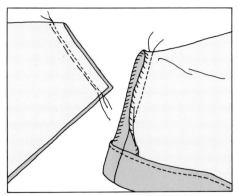

**2.** Join edges at each corner, RS together, with an open seam, taking 1.25 cm/½ in seam turnings. Alternatively, for extra strength, join edges with French seams. Turn in and stitch a 2.5 cm/1 in double hem round all edges of fabric.

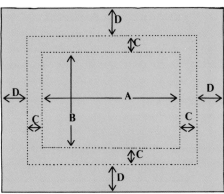

**Plain sheet** For the width of sheeting required, add **B** to twice **C**, plus two tuck-in and hem allowances, **D**. For the length, add **A** to twice **C**, plus two tuck-in and hem allowances, **D**.

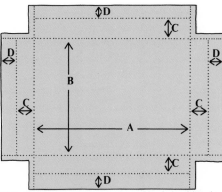

**Fitted bottom sheet** This is shaped and elasticated at all corners to fit round the mattress. For the width of sheeting required, add **B** to twice **C**, plus two tuck-in and hem allowances, **D**. For the length, add **A** to twice **C**, plus two hem and tuck-in allowances, **D**. Trim fabric to size if necessary and cut into corners as shown, leaving 1.25 cm/½ in hem allowance on each edge of corners.

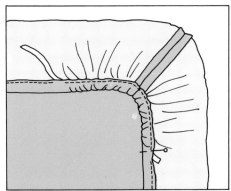

**3.** Unpick a small section of hem, wide enough to take a bodkin, on both sides of each corner, approximately 25 cm/10 in from corner seam. Cut four 20 cm/8 in lengths of strong elastic and with a bodkin thread each through hem section at corners, holding free end in place with a pin while threading the rest of the length through. Stitch both ends of elastic firmly in place. Remove pins. Sew in threads of unpicked hem sections.

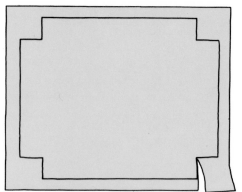

**To convert a flat sheet** into a fitted one, take measurements for a fitted sheet as in previous method and compare with those of flat sheet. If existing sheet is too small, unpick one or more of the hems, as necessary; if it is too large, trim it to required size. Mark out shape with chalk or pins, cut out and proceed as for fitted sheet.

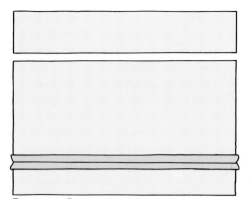

**Duvet cover** Cut two pieces of sheeting the length of the duvet by its width, adding 2.5 cm/1 in to both measurements. If joins are necessary, place them centrally or on either side of central panel, matching patterns and placing selvedge to selvedge. Join widths with open seams and press seams open.

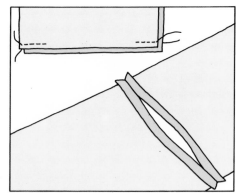

**2.** Place fabric RS together and, leaving a central opening approximately 45 cm/18 in shorter than the length of the edge, stitch along bottom edge from each end, taking 1.25 cm/½ in seam allowance. If the cover is to be fastened with a zip, press under seam allowance on opening and, with fabric RS up, insert zip by an even hems method. Stitch remaining three seams, RS together, and turn cover to RS through opening. Insert duvet.

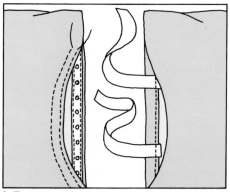

**3.** For a cover fastened with snap fastener tape or pieces of tape, leave opening and stitch remaining three seams. Turn cover to RS and press under seam allowance on opening. Apply fastener tape to each turning so one edge aligns with fold of turning and the fittings on both tapes coincide. Stitch along both edges of tape. Alternatively, stitch 15 cm/6 in pieces of tape every 10 cm/4 in under neatened turnings as you hem turnings down.

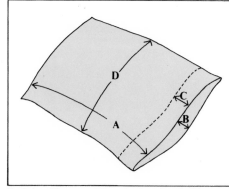

**Tuck-in pillowcase** Measure length of pillow **A**, double it and add 20 cm/8 in for tuck-in **B** and 7.5 cm/3 in for top hem **C**. Measure width of pillow **D** and add 2.5 cm/1 in for seam allowances. To both length and width measurements add another 2.5 cm/1 in to ensure that the pillow can be removed easily from the cover. Cut fabric to size.

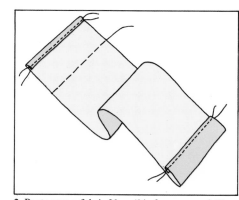

**2.** Baste across fabric 20 cm/8 in from one end. Turn down and stitch a narrow double hem across this end. At the other end, which will be the top hem, turn in 1.25 cm/½ in and press; turn in a further 6 cm/2¼ in and stitch in place. If you wish to decorate the top hem, do so now before joining side seams.

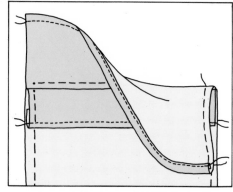

**3.** Working on a flat surface, RS together, fold top hem up to basted line and baste fabric together down both sides. Fold other end of fabric along basting line to cover top hem and baste it down through all layers. Stitch down entire length of each side, leaving 1.25 cm/½ in seam turnings. Turn cover RS out and press well.

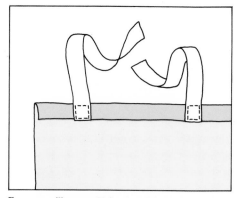

**Economy pillowcase** Takes less fabric than tuck-in pillowcase. Measure pillow length, double it and add 15 cm/6 in. Measure width and add 5 cm/2 in. Cut fabric to these dimensions. Turn in 1.25 cm/½ in single hem on short edges and press. Cut four 24 cm/9 in lengths of 1.25 cm/½ in tape and position two tapes on each side 10 cm/4 in from ends of turnings, with one end of tape on turning edge. Sew tape to turnings in a square.

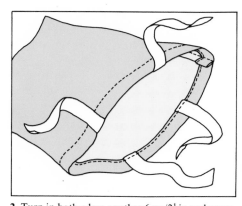

**2.** Turn in both edges another 6 cm/2¼ in and press, flipping tapes back over fold of hem. Hem turnings by hand or machine, stitching through tapes. Fold fabric in half crossways, WS together, and join two long sides with French seams.

# BEDCOVERS

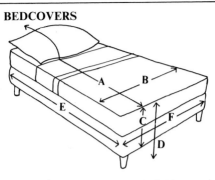

Before measuring, make up the bed. Measure **A** length of mattress top, including extra for pillow; **B** width of mattress top; **C** depth from mattress top to bottom edge of bed base; **D** depth from mattress top to within 2.5 cm/1 in of floor; **E** length of bed base; **F** width of base. Take 1.25 cm/½ in for seam allowances, 2.5 cm/1 in for single hem allowance, 4 cm/1½ in for a double hem.

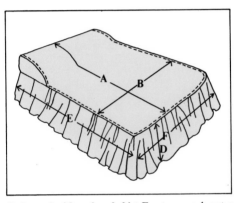

**Bedspread with gathered skirt** For top panel, cut a rectangle **A** by **B**, adding two seam allowances to both measurements. If necessary, join widths as for throwover cover. Take measurements for skirt: for skirt length, add twice **E** to **F**, plus half their combined length for fullness; for skirt depth, take **D**, plus one double hem and one seam allowance. Different fabrics can be used for the skirt and top panel, but choose one that drapes well for the skirt.

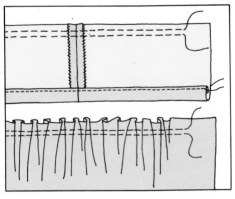

**4.** The skirt will have to be made up of several sections. Cut sufficient lengths of fabric to make a strip of dimensions taken, adding seam allowances for joining strips. Join lengths with open seams and press seams open. Turn up and stitch a double hem along bottom edge of skirt. Leaving double hem allowance at both ends of skirt, work two rows of gathering stitches along top. Draw up threads until skirt fits sides and foot of main panel.

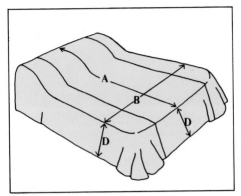

**Simple throwover cover** The easiest and quickest bedcover to make. For the length of fabric required, take **A** plus **D**, and add two double hem allowances, or more if the fabric is very heavy. For the width, add **B** to twice **D**, plus two double hem allowances. If necessary, join widths of fabric as for duvets, using one whole width for centre panel and joining two side panels.

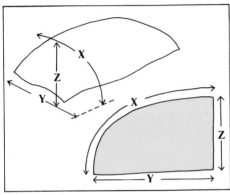

**2.** With pillow still in position, loosely measure length from bedhead over pillow to mattress at bottom edge of pillow **X**. Measure under pillow from bedhead to same point on mattress **Y** and measure thickness of pillow **Z**. Add seam allowances to **Y** and **X** and a double hem allowance to **Z**. Make a paper gusset with two straight sides the dimensions of **Y** and **Z** and a curved side as shown, approximately the length of **X**.

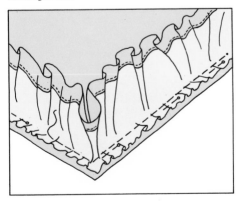

**5.** Measure and mark centres of gathered edge and foot of main panel. With RS facing, pin centres together and, working outwards to corners and then along sides of main panel to head end, pin rest of skirt to panel, distributing gathers evenly, and baste. Join with an open seam, pivoting stitching at corners, and press seam turnings towards panel.

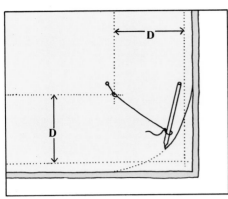

**2.** Fold fabric in half lengthways. At one end, on either side of corner, measure **D** plus hem allowance from raw edges and mark with chalk lines. At intersection of the two lines (this point is the top corner of the mattress) anchor a pin attached to a length of twine. Tie a pencil or chalk to twine and, with twine taut, draw an arc from edge to edge. Cut through both layers along curve. Double hem all fabric edges.

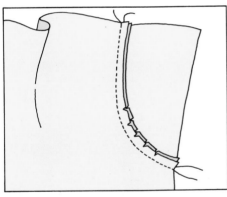

**3.** With fabric RS together, cut two gussets from pattern. If cutting them on single fabric, reverse pattern for the second. With RS together, join curved side of gusset to edge of top end of main panel with an open seam, keeping edges level and easing fullness round curve. Snip turnings round curve and press seam towards gusset.

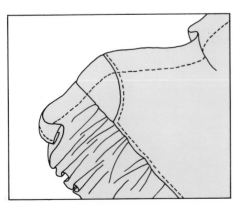

**6.** On RS top stitch near seam join to secure seam, sewing through seam turnings underneath. Press stitching. At top end of cover, turn in and stitch double hem along unstitched skirt edges, gussets and main panel.

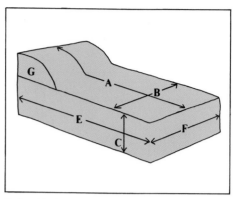

**Tailored bedspread** Cut main section measuring **A** by **B**, plus seam allowance on three sides and double hem allowance at top edge. Cut two gussets **G** as for bedspread with gathered skirt (2) and (3), and two side sections measuring **C** by **E**, adding one seam and double hem allowance to each dimension. For the foot section, cut a rectangle measuring **F**, plus two seam allowances, by **C**, plus one seam and double hem allowance.

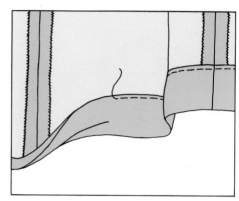

**2.** If necessary, join widths for main panel as for simple throwover cover and decorate with piping or braid if desired. Join pillow gussets to main panel as for bedspread with gathered skirt (3). With RS facing, join foot and side sections with open seams and press seams open. Turn up and stitch double hem on lower edge of this strip.

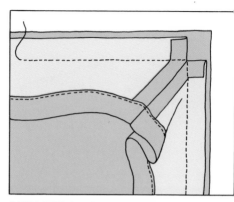

**3.** With RS facing, join strip to top panel and gussets with an open seam. Before stitching the corners, unpick seams of strip the depth of the seam allowance so fabric lies flat. Pivot stitching round corners. Press seam towards panel. At top end of cover, turn in and stitch double hem along unstitched skirt edges, gussets and main panel as for bedspread with gathered skirt (6).

## VALANCES

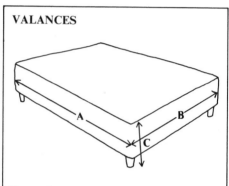

For a valance with two side skirts and one end skirt, measure **A** length of bed base; **B** width of base; **C** depth from top of base to within about 2.5 cm/1 in of floor. For a divan side-on to the wall, make two end skirts and one side one. Take 1.25 cm/½ in for seam allowances, 2.5 cm/1 in for single hem, 4 cm/1½ in for a double hem. Cut a fabric cover for bed base, with seam allowances on three sides and double hem allowance at top.

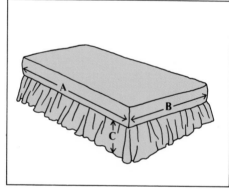

**Simple gathered valance** For the length, add twice **A** to **B**, plus two double hem allowances and half as much again for fullness. For the width, add one seam and one double hem allowance to **C**. Cut valance, joining pieces of fabric with open seams to make the required length. Press seams open.

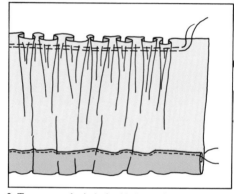

**2.** Turn up and stitch double hem along lower edge of valance and work two rows of gathering stitches along top, leaving double hem allowance un-gathered at both ends. Draw up thread until valance fits round sides and foot of base cover. Measure and mark centres of gathered edge and foot of cover.

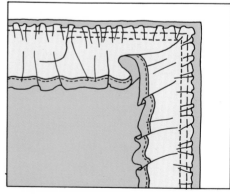

**3.** With RS facing, pin centres together and, working outwards to corners and then along sides, pin rest of strip to cover, distributing gathers evenly, and baste. Join with an open seam, pivoting stitching at corners, and press seam towards cover.

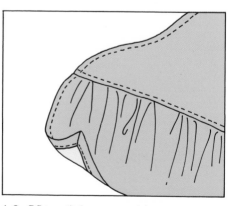

**4.** On RS top stitch near seam join to secure seam, sewing through seam turnings underneath. Press stitching. Turn in and stitch double hem along unstitched valance edges and top end of base cover.

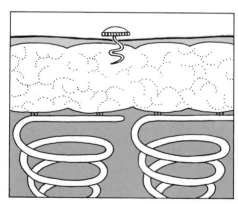

**5.** Place valance on bed base. To anchor it securely to a sprung-edge divan base, insert loose-cover pins at intervals along top edge of base, twisting them down through valance fabric into padding of base. To anchor a valance on a firm-edge divan base, insert a tack at each corner through the valance into the wooden corner block of the divan and insert loose-cover pins at intervals along top edges of base through valance into padding.

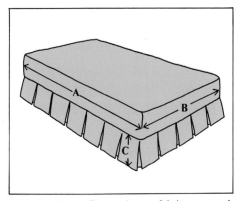

**Pleated valance** Choose heavy fabric to match bedcover. Pleats are distributed so bottom corners of the bed come between pleats. (Adjust pleat size towards top end of the bed if necessary.) For the width of the valance, take **C**, plus one seam and one double hem allowance; for the length, add twice **A** to **B**. To this add the extra length needed for the type of pleat used, plus two double hem allowances.

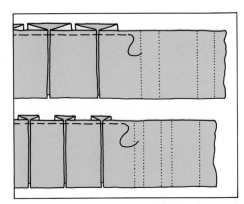

**2.** For deep box pleats (same width for front and concealed back folds), treble the length of valance. For shallow pleats (back fold half the width of front), double the length. Ideally, front folds of shallow pleats are 10 to 15 cm/4 to 6 in wide. Cut valance, joining lengths if necessary. Mark pleats and press in place, basting along both top and bottom edges of pleats as you press.

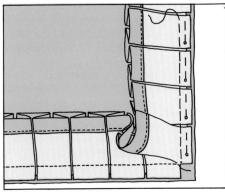

**3.** Find centre of pleated strip and on each side measure outwards half **B**. Pin the pleats at these points to bottom corners of base cover, RS together and taking usual seam allowance on sides of cover. Fit and pin rest of pleats along foot. Join with an open seam, snipping seam allowance of strip at corners. Swing valance round at right angles to stitched edge, pin pleats along sides of cover, baste and join. Finish and attach as for gathered valance.

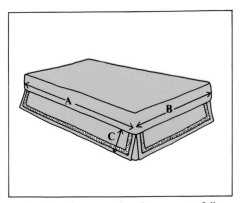

**Plain valance** An economic style as no extra fullness is required. Decorate skirt with braid or team valance with a tailored divan cover. Measure length of side **A** and deduct 1.25 cm/½ in; measure depth **C**. Cut two sections to these measurements, adding a seam allowance for top edge and double hems on other sides. Measure length of foot **B** and deduct 2.5 cm/1 in; measure depth **C**. Cut one section with same seam and hem allowances as for sides.

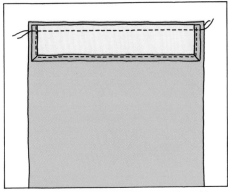

**2.** Turn in and stitch double hem along side and lower edges of skirt sections, mitring corners. If using braid, attach it to sides and lower edge of skirt, mitring corners. With RS facing, centre foot section of skirt on foot of base cover so that ends of foot section are 1.25 cm/½ in from edges of cover; baste and stitch in place, continuing the stitching to edges of cover.

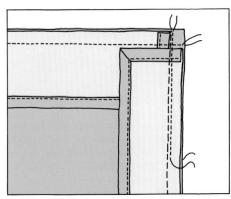

**3.** With RS facing, pin one of side sections of skirt to base cover, so bottom end is 1.25 cm/½ in from bottom edge of cover. Baste and join with an open seam, taking care not to catch foot section of skirt in seam and stitching to bottom edge of cover. Join other side section to cover in the same way. Turn in and stitch narrow double hem along top edge of base cover.

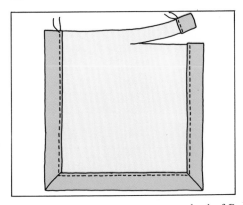

**4.** Measure two square corner gussets to depth of **C**, add double hem allowance on three sides and cut gussets out. Turn in and stitch hems, mitring corners. Trim off about 1.25 cm/½ in from top edge of each square so it will not hang below skirt sections.

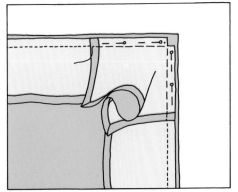

**5.** With base cover RS up, centre gussets RS down over bottom corners. Snip into seam allowance in centre of top edge of gussets and, working out from snipped centre of gussets, pin gussets to foot and sides of skirt and cover and baste. Join with open seams, pivoting stitching at corners so it forms a right angle and aligning it with previous rows of machining. Trim off bottom corners of base cover diagonally.

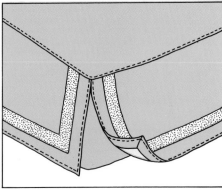

**6.** Press seams towards cover and top stitch as for gathered valance. Position valance on bed base, pull it firmly into place at corners and edges and attach to base with loose-cover pins as for gathered valance. Crease centre of gusset vertically between thumb and finger to help it to hang well.

# Loose Covers

A set of well-fitting loose covers can give a motley collection of sitting-room furniture a new lease of life. Chairs of different shapes and styles can be covered in matching or complementing fabrics to form a co-ordinated group, or a single chair can be covered in a different fabric from the main suite to add variety and interest.

Choose a sturdy, firmly woven fabric to ensure the cover wears well and retains its shape. A medium weight is best as heavy fabrics can be difficult to handle on intricate sections. Make sure the fabric is shrink-resistant if it is to be washed, or shrink it before making up. Also check that it is colour-fast.

Linen union—a tough blend of linen and cotton fibres—is traditionally used for loose covers and lasts well. Chintz is also popular, but is not quite as hard-wearing. Synthetic fabrics can be used if they are the correct weight and firmly woven. Avoid silky fabrics, which show marks easily, and also stretch fabrics, which sag. Most furnishing fabrics are 122 cm/48 in wide.

If there are old loose covers on the furniture that fit well, use them as a pattern, but do not remove any fixed upholstery fabric as this helps keep padding in shape. Try out and adjust each section as you work to ensure a good fit. Open and piped are the most suitable seams, and corded piping can be made in contrasting or matching fabric. For the latter allow an extra 50 cm/20 in of fabric on an average chair; offcuts can also be used.

The basic methods may be adapted for different chair and sofa shapes. Some of the more common variations are included at the end of this section. To avoid wasting fabric, make patterns as instructed for armchair covers for any awkward shapes. For all covers use the machine as much as possible, as machine stitching is stronger and more durable.

## EQUIPMENT

*Few special items of equipment are needed for loose covers. Suitable fasteners are Velcro, which can also be used to keep the cover in place, extra long zips with metal or nylon teeth—the strongest type of fastener—and press stud tape.*
*Use T-pins, below, to hold fabric to chair while fitting as they are easier to insert into and remove from padding than ordinary pins.*

*Two types of loose-cover pins are available to keep the cover in place: twist-in pins, below right, and double-pronged pins, below left.*

*Use screw-in press studs, below, to attach cover to a wooden base. Insert screw half into base and sew other half to fabric.*

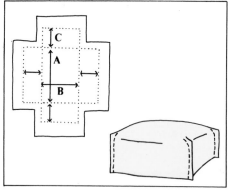

**Simple one-piece stool cover** Measure length **A**, width **B** and depth **C** of stool seat. Make a cross-shaped paper pattern, as shown, to these dimensions, adding 1.25 cm/$\frac{1}{2}$ in seam allowances in angles of cross and 5 cm/2 in to each arm of cross to turn under base. Use this pattern to cut out fabric. Baste and stitch each corner seam of cover RS together, tapering seams slightly at top of cover to give a rounded edge to seat. Press seams open.

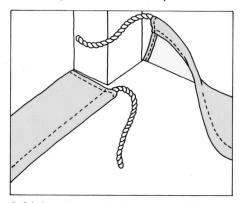

**3.** Stitch each corner in the same way. Turn up a 4 cm/1$\frac{1}{2}$ in double hem along base of each side of seat. Baste and stitch. Place cover on stool RS up. Take a length of cord or string and thread it through the hem at the base of each side in turn, taking it to inside of legs at corners. Pull ends of string firmly so that cover fits stool tightly, knot them together and tuck ends down under hem of cover.

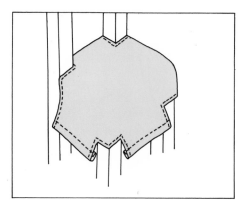

**2.** Replace cover on chair and pin side hems so they lie neatly on each side of inside angle of upright. Remove cover and trim away excess fabric at side hems. Stitch double hems if there is sufficient fabric; if not, stitch single hems and neaten edges. Finish lower edge of cover and insert cord and secure as for basic stool cover (**3**).

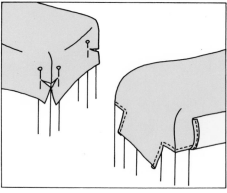

**2.** Place cover RS up on stool. At each corner insert two pins to mark position of stool leg either side of seam. Unpick base of seam to just below seat level and snip diagonally to pins. Turn under and pin centre section between pins level with base of stool seat to give a neat straight edge across each side of leg. Remove cover and baste and machine central single hem. Trim and turn in a narrow single hem down both sides; baste and machine.

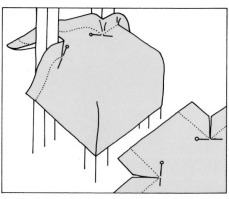

**Padded dining chair seat** Adapt the stool cover slightly to make allowances for the uprights at chair back. Make pattern and cut fabric as before. Stitch front corners. Place cover RS out on chair and pull back section out between uprights. Starting at front edge, smooth cover over seat. Mark position of uprights on fabric with pins across inside angles. Remove fabric from chair and snip it diagonally from edge of angle to pins.

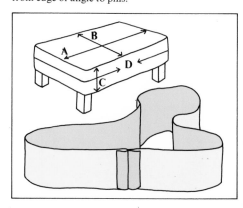

**Piped-edge stool cover** For top piece, the seat of the stool, measure length **A** and width **B** of stool top. Add 2.5 cm/1 in seam allowance to each measurement and cut fabric to these dimensions. Measure depth of seat **C** and add 10 cm/4 in, measure girth of seat **D** and add 2.5 cm/1 in seam allowance and cut gusset to these measurements. Place ends of gusset RS together and baste and stitch 1.25 cm/$\frac{1}{2}$ in seam. Press seam open.

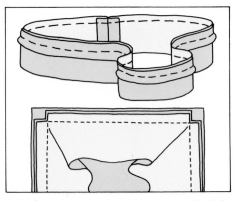

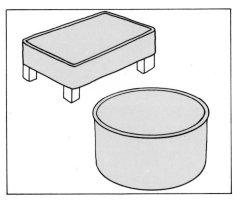

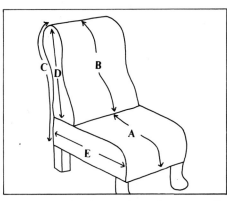

**2.** Make a piece of corded piping the length of the gusset. Baste piping to top edge of RS of gusset and pin seat section RS down over gusset. Baste and stitch as for piped seam, snipping into seam allowance of gusset and piping at corners and pivoting stitching.

**3.** Finish lower edge as for one-piece stool cover (**2**) and (**3**), dealing with legs in same way. If suitable use elastic in the hem instead of cord or string. Adapt this cover to fit any shape of stool or pouffe, but, if the top is not square or rectangular, make an accurate paper pattern for it, adding seam allowances as for standard piped-edge stool cover.

**Armless chair** There is no need to make a pattern. To estimate the amount of fabric needed, divide chair into three main sections: seat **A**, inside back **B** and outside back **C**. Side gussets **D** and **E** can often be cut from offcuts of main pieces; otherwise allow extra fabric. Measure **A**, **B** and **C** at longest and widest points and add 1.25 cm/½ in seam allowances all round. Add an extra 10 cm/4 in to length of seat and inside back for tucking in.

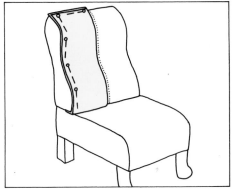

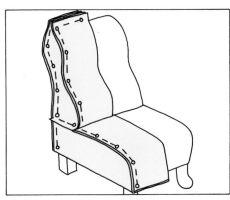

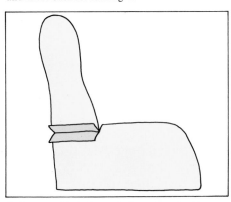

**2.** Cut out the three main pieces to these measurements. If chair seat and back are shaped, trim fabric pieces to fit exactly. Draw a chalk line down centre of inside back of chair. Fold inside back piece down centre and place on chair with fold on chalk line. Pin to side and top of chair and tuck extra 10 cm/4 in down back of seat. Trim to fit, allowing exactly 1.25 cm/½ in extra for seams at top and sides. Leave fabric pinned to chair.

**3.** Mark centres of seat and outside back of chair. Fold other main sections and pin to chair as in (**2**). Tuck extra 10 cm/4 in on seat section down back of seat. Measure longest and widest points of **D** and **E**, adding 2.5 cm/1 in seam allowances to length and width. With fabric on straight grain cut one strip for **D** and one strip for **E**. Pin both gussets to main fabric sections and trim to fit, allowing 1.25 cm/½ in seam turnings.

**4.** Remove fabric from chair and unpin. Reverse gussets left to right and use as patterns to cut another set. Place one set RS together, the base of back side gusset **D** to top of seat side gusset **E**, so that back gusset aligns with back of seat gusset. Baste and stitch 1.25 cm/½ in seam. Snip seat gusset beside end of stitching and press seam open. Join other set. Make enough piping if required to fit all edges of gussets.

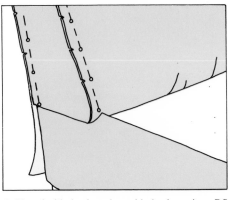

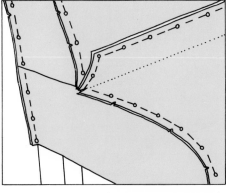

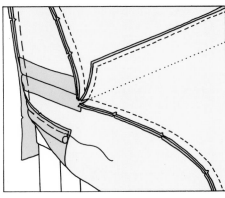

**5.** Place inside back and outside back sections RS together and baste and stitch seam at top edge of back. Press. Place back section RS out on chair, tucking extra on inside back down back of seat. Pin back side gussets RS out to main pieces, fitting fabric as close to chair as possible. Trim again if necessary, making sure seam allowances are exactly 1.25 cm/½ in and notching them at intervals to help rematch them exactly.

**6.** Fit seat gussets to seat cover in same way. Snip tuck-in allowances of **A** and **B** where they meet—level with join of back and seat gussets. Pin round edge of tuck-in allowance. Remove fabric from chair and unpin gussets from main sections. If using piping, pin and baste it to outside back, inside back and to seat edges of gussets on RS.

**7.** Pin main sections to gussets RS together and matching notches, but leave one outside back seam open for fasteners to about three-quarters of way up chair or to its widest part. Arrange snipped turnings of inside back and seat so they fall exactly at corner where gussets join and tuck-in fabric extends from seam. Join gussets to main sections. Baste and stitch seam for tuck-in between seat and inside back, pivoting stitching at corners. Neaten and press seams. ▶

171

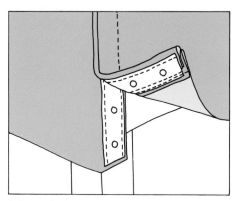

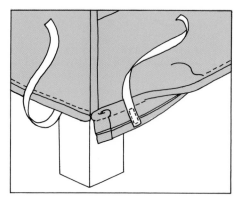

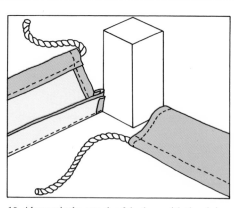

**8.** Insert zip, head downwards, in unstitched outside back seam, treating piped edge as fabric edge. Or on RS of turning without piping place one half of Velcro or press stud tape within seam allowance. Stitch down both edges. Attach second half within seam allowance on RS of opposite turning so it overlaps first half when turning is folded to WS on seam line and piping extends from edge. Top stitch this section to hold turning in place.

**9.** Finish lower edge with piping. Baste and stitch piping to RS of edge on fitting line, turning ends under towards cover so they meet. Press seam so piping extends down from lower edge and press turnings up towards cover. At edge of leg on each side stitch a length of tape to WS to tie round back of legs and so keep cover in place. Top stitch all round edge just above piping through tapes and turnings.

**10.** Alternatively, attach a false hem with the piping. Cut four fabric strips about 10 cm/4 in deep by length of each side of chair plus 2.5 cm/1 in for turnings. Stitch narrow double hem at each end of strips and baste and stitch a double hem on bottom of strips. Baste piping and then strips to edge of cover, RS together, and machine. Turn false hem to underside of chair and thread cord or string through as for one-piece stool cover (**3**).

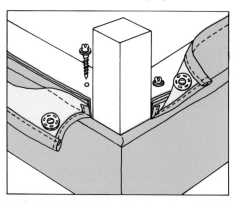

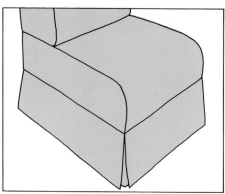

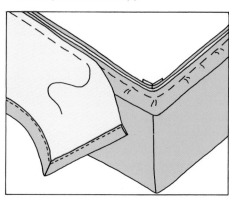

**11.** On chairs with wooden frames covers can be held in place with special screw-in press studs. Attach a false hem as in (**10**) and turn to underside of chair. Attach well half of press stud to underside of fabric hem. Screw stud half into timber beneath. Fasten stud to well to hold fabric down. Use several press studs on each side of chair depending on size.

**Valances** The base of the chair cover can be finished with a valance, which softens the outline and disguises ugly or damaged legs. For a plain valance with pleats at the corners, measure from lower edge of cover to within 1.25 cm/½ in of floor and add 4 cm/1½ in for a bottom hem and a 1.25 cm/½ in seam allowance. Measure length of each side of chair, adding 7.5 cm/3 in hem allowance to each side. Cut four strips of fabric to these measurements.

**2.** Turn in double hems on lower and side edges of all four strips. Make a length of piping to extend round lower edge of cover. Starting at fastened edge, baste piping to lower edge of cover along seam line, turning in ends as in armless chair (**9**). Place raw edge of each valance section on edge of cover, RS down, over piping. Make sure hemmed side edges of valances meet at corners. Baste and stitch through all layers.

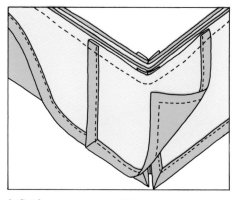

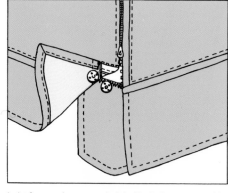

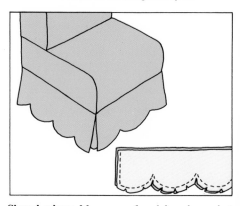

**3.** Cut four square pieces of fabric the same depth as the valance, plus double hem allowances on three sides, to make pleat backings. Turn up and stitch hems. Trim about 1.25 cm/½ in from top edge of each square so it will not hang below valance edges. Centre a pleat backing over all except fastened corner of valance, placing each square RS down on WS of valance. Baste along seam line and stitch in position through all thicknesses.

**4.** At fastened corner stitch half of pleat to one side of cover so that other half extends beyond fastened edge. Neaten top edge of turning and stitch one section of a press stud to top of extending half. On valance press seam allowance upwards into cover and top stitch above piping if desired, stitching through seam turnings. Mark position of second section of press stud on seam allowance on WS of valance and attach stud.

**Shaped valance** Measure as for plain valance, but add 1.25 cm/½ in seam allowances all round. Cut two strips for each side. Make a paper pattern of the shape (such as scallops) for the bottom edge and use pattern to mark shape on WS of one section on each side. Place sections RS together and stitch along shaping line and each end, snipping at curves. Trim turnings to 6 mm/¼ in, press seam and turn sections RS out. Join to cover as for plain valance.

*Keep loose covers simple so there is freedom to change their decorative effect. Here a tailored cotton-canvas cover, with a plain valance and plump, piped seat cushions, has floral cushions and an Eastern runner for summer. In winter richer coloured, plush-textured cushions warm the room.*

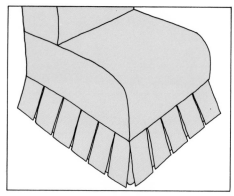

**Pleated valance** Box pleats are generally used, with the same width for front and concealed back folds. Calculate depth of valance as for plain valance. For the length, measure right round base of cover and treble the measurement. Add an extra 2.5 cm/1 in for hemming ends of valance. Cut a strip of fabric to these measurements, joining pieces if necessary.

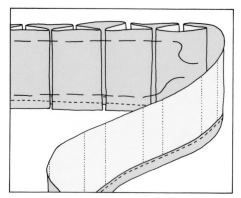

**2.** Turn in and stitch double hem on lower edge and side ends of valance. Work out size and number of pleats to fit side of chair so that corners of chair come between pleats. Mark pleats and press in place, basting along top and bottom edges as you press. Make a length of piping to extend round lower edge of cover. Remove cover from chair.

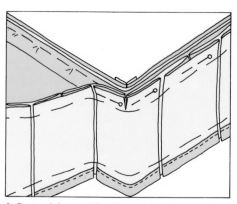

**3.** Baste piping to RS of lower edge of cover along seam line. Starting at the fastened seam on the cover, place valance RS down over piping and edge of cover, matching raw edges. Pin in place, positioning valance so that corner seams of cover come between pleats on RS. Snip valance at corners. Baste and stitch seam. Press seam turnings upwards. Top stitch on RS of cover above piping if desired, stitching through seam turnings.

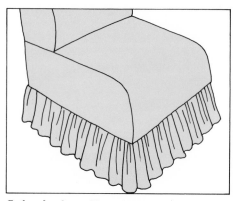

**Gathered valance** Use only on soft fabrics that drape well. This valance is most suitable on bedroom furniture or cottage-style chairs and stools. Calculate depth as for plain valance and measure length, allowing one and a half times the measurement around base of cover for fullness. Cut the valance strip, joining pieces if necessary, and stitch a double hem on lower and side edges. Make a length of piping to extend round base of cover.

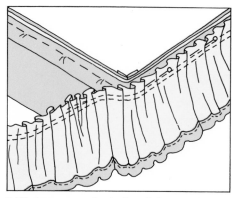

**2.** Work two rows of gathering stitches round top of valance. Draw up threads until valance fits base of cover exactly and distribute gathers evenly. Remove cover from chair. Baste piping strip to RS of lower edge of cover along seam line. Starting at fastened corner, pin valance RS down on cover, matching raw edges. Make sure gathers are well distributed on all sides of chair. Baste and stitch valance to cover through all layers.

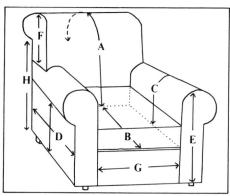

**Armchair** Unless you are very experienced at making loose covers, make a fabric pattern, according to the following instructions, for each area of the chair marked on the diagram. Use old sheets or curtains or cheap calico, as a paper pattern would not stand up to the fitting and pinning. Although the final seams are only 1.25 cm/½ in, add seam allowances of 2.5 cm/1 in all round so there is room for adjustment if the pattern is not correct.

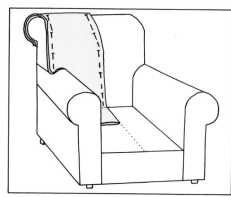

**2.** Remove seat cushion from chair. Chalk a line down centre of back **A** and seat **B**. Measure length and width of **A** and cut pattern about 7.5 cm/3 in wider than **A** and at least 20 cm/8 in longer. Fold in half down centre and place on chair with fold on chalk line, leaving about 2.5 cm/1 in extra at top and rest of extra length at bottom. Pin fabric to chair and trim to 2.5 cm/1 in at top of back and down side to seat, following shape of arm.

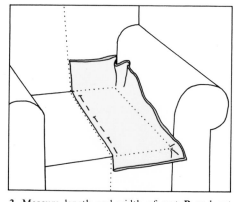

**3.** Measure length and width of seat **B** and cut pattern at least 20 cm/8 in longer and 25 cm/10 in wider. Fold in half and position on chair with fold on chalk line and all extra length except about 2.5 cm/1 in at back of seat. Pin to chair. If necessary trim turning to 2.5 cm/1 in along front edge of seat and at front of sides so pattern piece **B** extends gradually to full width at back edge. (The extra fabric is later tucked in round the seat.)

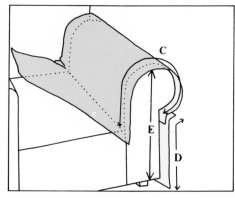

**4.** The chair arm is in three sections: inside arm and over curve **C**, outside arm beneath curve **D**, and shaped front gusset **E**. The seam joining **C** and **D** falls just below the curved part of the outside arm. Measure length and width of **D** and cut pattern 2.5 cm/1 in larger all round. Measure **C** and cut pattern, adding 12.5 cm/5 in to length of back edge and 10 cm/4 in extra to width for tucking in, tapering to 2.5 cm/1 in extra elsewhere.

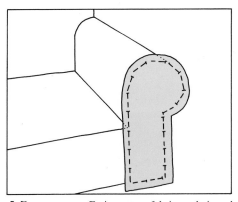

**5.** For arm gusset **E** pin pattern fabric to chair and mark gusset shape with chalk. Cut out pattern, adding 2.5 cm/1 in all round. Cut back gusset pattern **F** in same way. Mark the two gussets to differentiate between them.

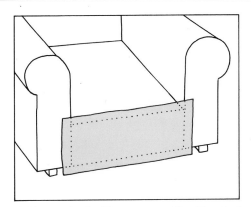

**6.** Measure depth of front seat area **G** and length of **G** across to inside edge of gusset **E**. Cut pattern 2.5 cm/1 in larger all round. For outside back **H**, pin pattern fabric to chair, mark shape with chalk and cut out pattern 2.5 cm/1 in larger all round. Sections **G**, **D** and **H** should fall to the same distance from the floor. Decide on the type of valance, if desired, and estimate measurements and amount of fabric required as for armless chair.

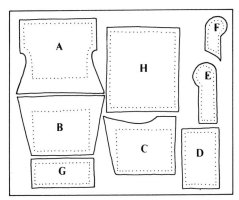

**7.** To estimate the amount of fabric needed for the eight pattern pieces, lay them out on the floor within the width of the fabric to be used and measure the length needed. Remember that sections **C**, **D**, **E** and **F** must be cut twice. Add extra for the valance and for matching patterns if the fabric is patterned.

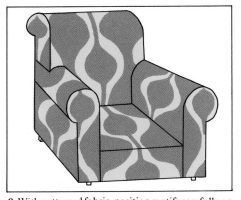

**8.** With patterned fabric, position motifs carefully on the chair—a badly placed motif can ruin the appearance of the cover. Centre a large motif on inside back, seat and outside back and, if possible, on the inside and outside of each arm. Centre a motif, not necessarily the main one, on the arm and back gussets. Avoid placing patterned fabric so there is half a motif on one half of a section and nothing on the other half.

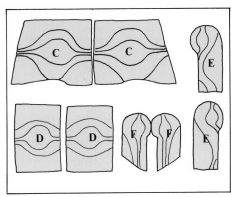

**9.** To ensure that any fabric motifs are fully visible and can be well positioned, place all pattern pieces on single fabric and on the straight grain. Place gussets **E** and **F** so warp runs vertically top to bottom. Cut out all pieces; reverse **C**, **D**, **E** and **F** to cut a second piece for each. Mark seam lines and centres on all sections.

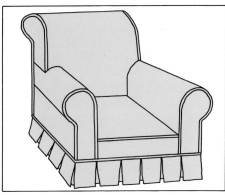

**10.** For piping, measure the length of the seams that emphasize the shape of the chair and give definition to its edges—top of seat front, arm front gussets down to valance, between base of cover and valance and from top of arm around back gusset and down to valance at back. Make separate lengths of piping for each seam.

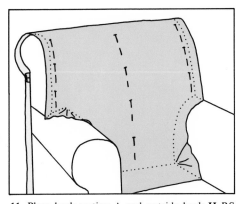

**11.** Place back section **A** and outside back **H** RS together and baste and stitch 2.5 cm/1 in open seam along top edges. Trim turnings to 1.25 cm/½ in and neaten this seam and all subsequent seams. Press seam open. Place back sections on chair RS out and pin in place down sides and centre, making sure top back seam is straight and any fabric motif is centred.

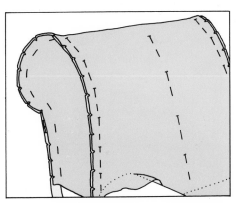

**12.** Position gussets **F** RS out on chair. Pin to edges of main back sections **A** and **H**, fitting fabric as close to chair as possible. Adjust until fabric fits chair tightly and then carefully trim seam allowances to exactly 1.25 cm/½ in beyond pins. Notch seam allowances at intervals to help match seams at next stage. Unpin and remove fabric from chair.

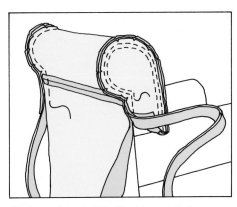

**13.** Baste piping to RS of back gussets **F** along seam lines, snipping piping round curves to fit. At back edge of gussets leave piping long enough to reach to top of valance as it will later be inserted in back seam. Do not pipe lower edge of gussets. With RS together, pin and baste gussets **F** to back sections **A** and **H**, placing main sections over piping and matching notches. Remove pins and stitch as for a piped seam; press turnings towards gusset. ▶

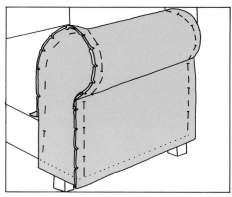

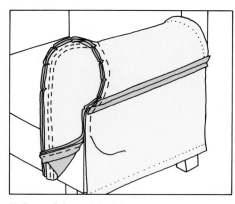

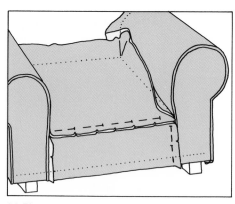

**14.** Join sections **C** and **D**, RS together, with a 2.5 cm/1 in open seam. Trim turnings to 1.25 cm/½ in. Place joined sections RS out on chair and pin in place, checking that the seam is straight and that it falls just below the curved part of the outer arm. Fit front arm gussets **E** in same way as back gussets (**12**), trimming and notching seam allowances. Remove all pins and take fabric off chair.

**15.** Baste piping to RS of front arm gussets **E** along seam lines, snipping piping round curves to fit. Do not pipe lower edges. With RS together, pin and baste gussets **E** to joined arm sections **C** and **D**, placing arm sections over piping and matching notches. Stitch as for a piped seam and press turnings towards gusset.

**16.** Place arm covers on chair RS up and place seat cover **B** RS up in position. Pin front seat strip **G** to seat cover **B**, matching centres, and pin **G** to front arm gusset **E**. Adjust pins for a good fit, and trim and notch seams as in (**12**). Unpin and take **B** and **G** off chair, leaving arm sections in place. Baste piping to RS of top edge of seat front **G** on seam line. Place seat cover RS down on seat front, matching notches, and stitch as for a piped seam. Press.

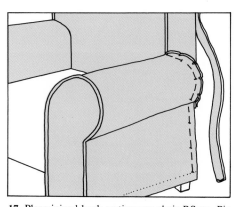

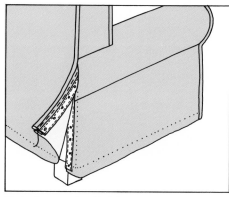

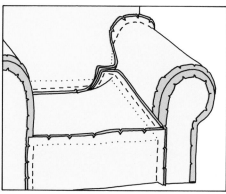

**17.** Place joined back sections on chair RS up. Pin seams between arm sections **C** and **D** and back sections **F** and **H** on each side, starting at inner edge of back gusset **F**. Adjust pins so fabric fits well, trim and notch seam allowances as in (**12**). Unpin and remove fabric from chair. On one side of chair only baste seam RS together, sandwiching end of piping extending from **F** in seam. Stitch as for a piped seam and press.

**18.** At the opposite side join arm section **C** to back gusset **F** only. To complete seam between **D** and **H**, baste end of piping to edge of **H**. Choose a zip to extend three-quarters of the height of the chair or to the widest part. Insert zip in back seam with head at base of cover as for armless chair (**8**). Alternatively, attach Velcro or press stud tape as for armless chair (**8**). Baste and stitch sides of seat front **G** to front of arm gusset **E**, RS together, as for piped seam.

**19.** With RS together, baste and stitch seam on each side between **A** and back edge of **C**. No fitting is necessary as seams are later tucked in round seat. With RS together, join sides and back of seat **B** to seat edge of arms **C** and of inside back **A**. Trim edges if necessary to help them fit together, but make sure there is still sufficient surplus for tucking down back and sides of seat.

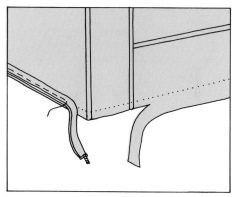

**20.** Place cover on chair. Smooth it into place, pulling it down well all round and tucking it in firmly round seat. Close fastener. Trim lower unfinished edge so it is level all round. Baste piping to RS of lower edge. To finish with a valance, check required depth of valance and attach valance to edge of cover. Alternatively, finish base as for armless chair. Cover loose cushions as for box cushion (see p. 180). Make sure all seams are neatened. Press.

*A consequence of the upholstered furniture introduced in the late 17th century, loose covers were at first made from strong, plain linen. Gradually, the urge to fancify took over and covers became as decorative as the fabrics they protected, although the method of tape fastening remained the same. This unusually well-preserved 18th-century example comes from Ham House, Surrey.*

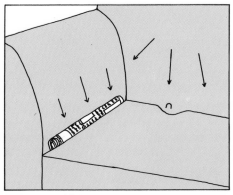

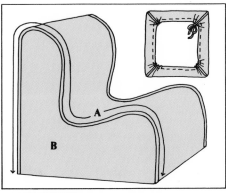

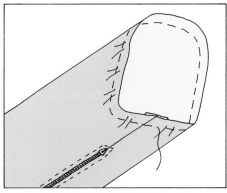

**21.** For a good finish, pull cover into place firmly and anchor it by inserting loose-cover pins through fabric into padding down sides and back of seat. Alternatively, push rolled-up newspaper down into tuck-in round seat to wedge cover down. Disguise any lumpy areas in the chair padding by arranging a layer of upholstery wadding on the chair before putting on the cover.

**ADAPTATIONS**
**Foam unit seating** This type of furniture is very easy to cover as there are only three sections: one long centre piece **A** extending down the back and front and two side gussets **B**. Cut out the sections, allowing about 15 cm/6 in extra fabric on all lower edges for turning under base of seat. Join with piped or open seams. Double hem lower edges and thread with elastic or cord to hold them under base of chair.

**Foam-filled furniture** For a softer look on this type of furniture omit piping and gather fabric into shape. Measure each cushion and cut fabric, adding 7.5 cm/3 in at each end. Cut out two gussets for each cushion, 5 cm/2 in smaller in diameter than ends of cushion. Stitch base seam of each cushion, inserting in the centre of the seam a zip long enough to enable the cushion to be removed easily. Run a row of gathers round each end of cover.

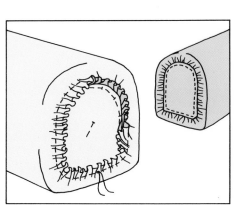

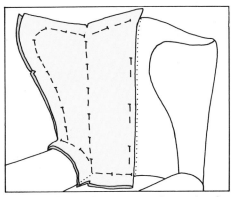

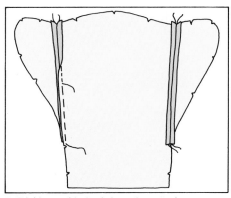

**2.** Place cover WS up on cushion. Pull up gathers so fabric fits round end of cushion. Place each gusset RS down on gathered end and pin to cushion in centre. Tuck gusset into gathered end and, pulling out edge of gusset as you work, pin gusset edge to gathered edge RS together. Open zip and remove cover. Baste and stitch gussets to cover and press seams towards gussets. Top stitch through both layers close to edges of gussets to hold gathers.

**Wing chair** Cut inside back pattern in one piece for back and wings. Chalk a line down centre back of chair, fold pattern and place it on chalk line, with tuck-in allowance at bottom of seat and about 2.5 cm/1 in extra at top as for armchair (**2**). Pin pattern fabric together round edges. To fit pattern, pin it very close to chair down inside angle of wing and chair back. If insufficient fabric is allowed here, the cover will be too tight and pull away from the angle.

**2.** Divide outside back into three sections: centre back and two wings. Cut and fit all three. Stitch one wing to centre back and baste the other in place. Fit and pin outside back to inside back round top and side edges and trim and notch seam allowances. Unpin the two back sections. Starting at the top, stitch 10 cm/4 in of the second wing seam on outside back. Choose a zip long enough to extend from end of stitching to bottom of outside back.

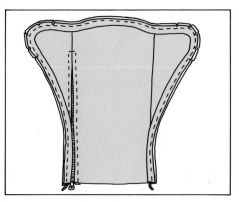

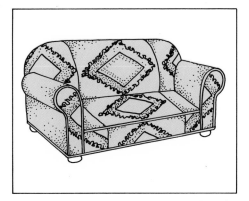

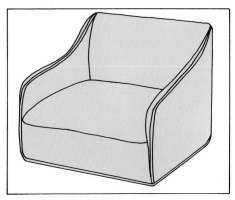

**3.** Insert base of zip into seam just below stitching. On centre back edge stitch zip down entire length. On other edge stitch down to bottom of wing. Baste piping round top and sides of outside back, treating unstitched side of zip as outer edge of outside back. Join inside and outside back along top and down sides as for piped seam and matching notches. Finish cover as for basic armchair cover.

**Sofa** Adapt the basic armchair instructions by adding an extra central panel of fabric to the inside back, outside back, seat and front of seat. Place any fabric design centrally on these panels. If the sofa is wide enough, use the whole width of fabric for the central panels and match the side panels to them. Allow extra fabric on each panel for seams. Join panels and proceed as for the armchair.

**Narrow-armed chair** No back opening is needed for a fastening and an arm gusset is unnecessary as inside and outside arm sections are joined along top of arm. Join outer arm to outer back and then join inner arm to inside back, allowing enough extra between them for tucking in. Join inner and outer sections with or without piping round top of arms and back. Add front and seat pieces, allowing tuck-in at sides and back of seat.

177

# Cushions

A few cushions can quickly transform the plainest chair or sofa, garden bench or hammock, and help to make a setting, whether indoor or outdoor, attractive and welcoming. Not only do they add comfort but they can also be used as decorative accents in a colour scheme, tying together colours and textures.

If your furnishings are fairly restrained, make a feature of the cushions. Design your own shapes and styles, making a paper pattern to cut round if the shape is irregular. (It is also advisable to make a pattern for cutting out circular cushions.)

Most fabrics can be used for cushion covers, including leather, suede, handicraft felt, PVC-backed fabrics and fake fur. Bear in mind whether the fabric can be washed or has to be dry cleaned and try to avoid those that shed pile or fluff. Covers with zips can be easily removed for washing and cleaning. Alternatively, stitch the opening by hand so that it may be unpicked easily.

### Choosing a filling

There are many suitable fillings for cushions. The most luxurious are feather and down; among the cheaper range, foam chips, foam slabs and kapok are the most widely used; and the most convenient of all are ready-made cushion pads.

Foam chips can be bought loose or in bags. They must be enclosed in a fairly thick inner cover and packed tightly or the cushion will flatten and become lumpy. Wear an overall when filling a cushion, as the chips are full of static electricity and cling to clothes and skin.

Slabs of latex or polyether foam for box cushions are available cut to size, or they can be cut to shape at home. (Dip the knife in water occasionally as you cut to help it slide through the foam.) Latex foam tends to be heavier and bouncier than polyether, but the latter is made in various densities. Ask advice when buying foam since different types of cushions require different densities.

Kapok, a vegetable fibre, is used mostly for lightweight cushions. Buy it by weight, packing the covers well or they may flatten.

### Inner cover

It is important to have a strong inner cover to facilitate cleaning and to keep the filling in place (this is particularly important if the cover is made from a knitted or stretchy fabric that may lose its shape). Calico is the most widely used material, particularly for foam slabs, which eventually tend to crumble. Any similar closely woven fabric can also be used, or even old sheets. Make inner covers in the same way as the outer ones, using open seams but omitting a zip or piping. For speed, turn in and machine zigzag the opening.

*Decorate cushions with piping, embroidery or appliqué, frills or fringes to create an eye-catching array that will lend style as well as comfort to any setting.*

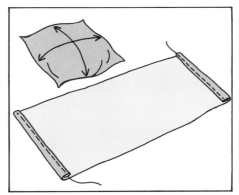

**Quick cover** Transform an old squashy cushion with this flapped cover. Cut a strip of material 2.5 cm/1 in wider and two-and-a-half times the length of the cushion. Turn both short edges under 1 cm/⅜ in, baste and press. Turn both edges under another 1.25 cm/½ in to make double hems, baste, press and slip hem or machine on WS.

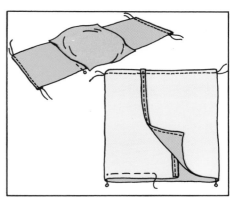

**2.** Centre cushion on RS of fabric, marking fabric at each end of cushion with a pin. Remove cushion and fold over both hemmed ends on the pins so that they overlap. Remove pins. Making sure raw edges are level, baste and stitch both side seams through all layers, leaving 1.25 cm/½ in turnings at each side. Turn cover RS out and insert cushion through overlapped opening.

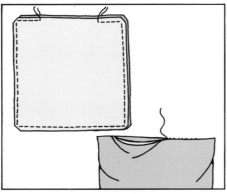

**Simple cover** Needs less fabric than the quick cover, but takes slightly longer. Cut two pieces of fabric the same size as the cushion, plus 1.25 cm/½ in seam allowance all round. With RS together, baste and stitch round three sides and a little way along each end of fourth. Press stitching and trim off corners diagonally. Turn cover RS out through gap. Press under 1.25 cm/½ in turnings on unstitched edges, insert cushion and slip stitch edges together.

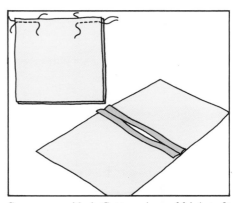

**Square cover with zip** Cut two pieces of fabric to fit cushion, plus 1.25 cm/½ in seam allowance on all sides. Choose a zip about 7.5 cm/3 in shorter than side of cushion and centre it along one edge of one piece of fabric, marking ends with chalk or pins. Remove zip, place fabric RS together and baste and stitch from ends of zip opening to edge of fabric. Press stitching and press seam open.

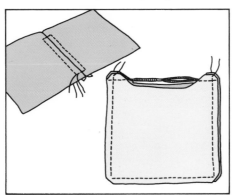

**2.** Place zip RS up under opening. Working from RS baste and stitch zip in place, using an even or un-even hems method and stitching across both ends. Remove basting and press; open zip enough to put your hand through and allow you to turn the cover through when stitched. Refold cover with RS together and baste and stitch remaining three side seams. Trim excess fabric diagonally at corners and turn cover through zip opening to RS. Insert cushion.

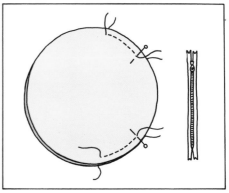

**Round cover with zip** Cut two circles the diameter of the cushion, plus 1.25 cm/½ in seam allowance. With direction of fabric grain matching, place circles RS together and position zip on edge, easing it round curve. The zip should measure approximately one-third of circumference. Mark ends of zip and baste and stitch 5 cm/2 in from each end. Press seam open. ▶

# Cushions

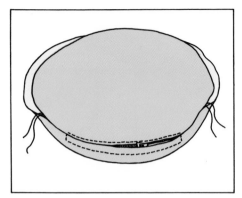

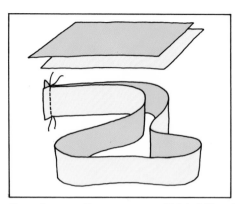

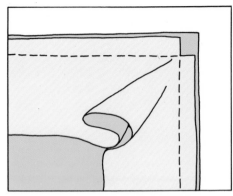

**2.** Turn fabric RS out and insert zip in opening by an uneven hems method, sewing across both ends. Turn fabric back again to WS, leaving zip partly open, and baste and stitch seam round the rest of the cover. Turn cover through opening to RS and insert cushion through opening.

**Square box cover** Cut two squares of fabric 1.25 cm/½ in larger all round than top of the cushion, and cut a side gusset the thickness of the cushion, plus 2.5 cm/1 in, by twice the combined length and width of the cushion, plus 2.5 cm/1 in. (Join pieces of fabric to make gusset if you do not have a large enough single piece.) Join ends of gusset RS together, leaving 1.25 cm/½ in turnings, to make a continuous band. Press seam open.

**2.** With RS facing and raw edges together, pin and baste one edge of gusset to all sides of one square. Ease corners by snipping into gusset seam allowance. Stitch with gusset uppermost, leaving 1.25 cm/½ in turnings and pivoting stitching at corners. Press seam down towards gusset.

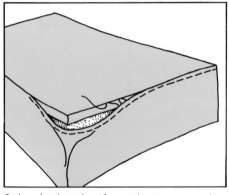

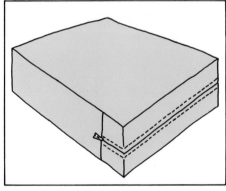

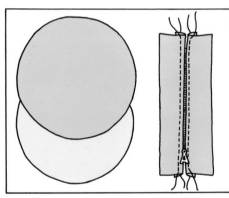

**3.** Attach other edge of gusset in same way to three sides of second square, leaving fourth side and about 7.5 cm/3 in of the two adjoining seams unstitched. Turn in seam allowance of unstitched gusset, baste and press. Turn fabric RS out and insert cushion. Smooth down seam allowance of unstitched section of square over edge of cushion and slip stitch it to basted turning of gusset.

**4.** For a square box cover with a zip, choose a zip that matches the colour of the fabric and measures about 15 cm/6 in longer than one side of the cushion. (It is easier to insert the cushion if the zip extends along the whole of one side and a few inches along the adjoining sides.) Cut gusset, insert zip and make up cover as for round box cover with zip.

**Round box cover** Cut two circles 2.5 cm/1 in larger in diameter than cushion. For a cover without a zip, cut a gusset and make up the cover as for square box, making sure that the fabric does not stretch as you slip stitch the opening. For a cover with a zip, use a zip measuring about one-third of cushion circumference. Cut two gusset strips 2.5 cm/1 in longer than zip and half the cushion thickness plus 2.5 cm/1 in. Attach strips to zip by an even hems method.

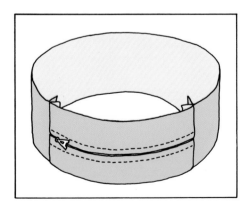

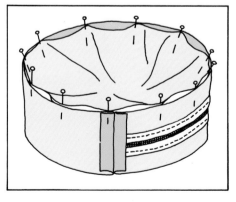

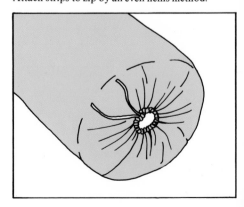

**2.** Cut another strip 2.5 cm/1 in wider than cushion thickness and long enough to complete the gusset, adding an extra 2.5 cm/1 in to the length for seam allowances. Join ends of strip to ends of zip section, RS together, taking 1.25 cm/½ in turnings. Press seams open.

**3.** With RS together, pin one circle to one edge of gusset, matching raw edges. Baste and stitch in place. Open zip enough to put your hand through. Attach second circle to other side of gusset, matching direction of fabric grain on both circles. Press seams towards gusset. Turn cover RS out through zip and insert cushion.

**Bolster cover with gathered ends** Cut a rectangle the length plus the diameter of the bolster by the circumference plus 2.5 cm/1 in. Fold in half lengthways, RS together, and join, taking 1.25 cm/½ in turnings. Press seam open, turn in and stitch 1.25 cm/½ in at ends of fabric. Turn cover RS out and insert bolster. With a bodkin run tape the length of the circumference through each hemmed end, draw up tape ends, tie and tuck in. Cover gap with a patch.

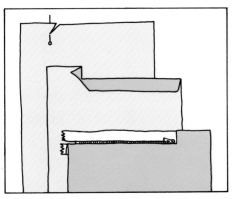

**Bolster cover with zip** Cut a rectangle the length of the bolster by the circumference, plus 1.25 cm/½ in seam allowance all round. Cut out two circles 2.5 cm/1 in larger in diameter than bolster. Place zip, measuring about three-quarters of circumference, along a short edge of rectangle and mark end with a pin. Snip diagonally into seam allowance to pin and fold under along zip section. With RS up, place zip so teeth centre under folded edge.

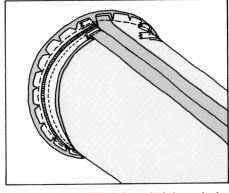

**2.** Baste zip tape to folded edge and stitch, continuing across top of zip. Fold rectangle in half lengthways, RS together, and join to make a tube, taking 1.25 cm/½ in seam turnings. Press seam open. With RS together, pin circle to edge of rectangle, treating exposed zip tape as fabric edge. Baste and stitch. Attach other circle of fabric to other end of rectangle and finish as for round box cover (**3**).

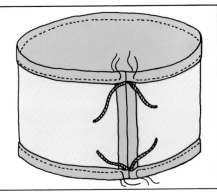

**Powder puff cushion** An easy way to cover a round cushion pad. Cut a rectangular strip the length of the circumference of the pad, plus 2.5 cm/1 in, by the width from the centre of the top side of the pad to the centre of the bottom. Join short sides RS together, taking 1.25 cm/½ in turnings. Press seam open. Turn in top and bottom edges 2.5 cm/1 in and stitch. Thread tape, about 10 cm/4 in longer than circumference, through each hem, leaving ends free.

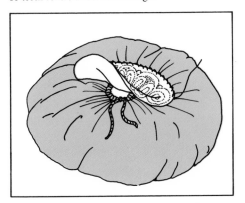

**2.** Turn cover RS out and insert cushion. Draw up tapes as far as possible and knot securely. Cover small central hole on each side with a circle of fabric, oversewing it in place.

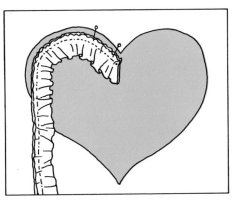

**Fancy cushion with frill** Cut two pieces of fabric to shape of cushion, plus 1.25 cm/½ in seam allowance all round. For the frill, cut a strip twice the intended finished width, plus 1.25 cm/½ in, and at least one and a half times the cushion's circumference. Fold strip in half lengthways, RS together, and stitch across ends. Press seam open and turn strip RS out. Work gathering on seam line. Pin one end of frill to cushion and draw up gathers evenly to fit.

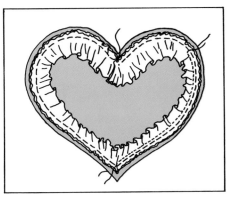

**2.** Pin and baste strip to one of fabric pieces, RS and raw edges together, adjusting the gathering if necessary so that it is full at each corner. Stitch together for approximately one-third of cushion's circumference.

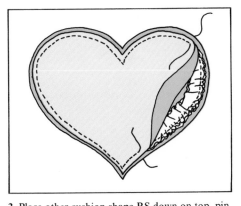

**3.** Place other cushion shape RS down on top, pin, baste and join remaining two-thirds of circumference where frill is not stitched to first cushion shape, stitching through all three layers. Turn to RS and press under 1.25 cm/½ in turnings on unstitched edges, insert cushion and slip stitch edges together.

## PIPING
Improve the appearance of a plain cushion with corded piping. This is particularly effective if the piping is in a contrasting colour to the cushion

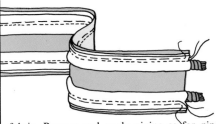

fabric. Prepare and apply piping as for piped seams, using a piping or zip foot and stitching as close as possible to cord. Follow the methods outlined below for a piped box cushion or a piped bolster.

For a box cushion, above, attach piping to RS of gusset strip along top or bottom edge, or both, as desired. Proceed as for a box cover, using piped seams when attaching gusset and piping to cover.

For a bolster, below, stitch side seam of cover to make a tube. On RS, pin and baste piping, the length of the circumference, round each end of tube, starting at seam line and placing raw edges together. Leave a short piece extending at both ends and join piping at seam line as for piped seam. Finish bolster as for round box cover.

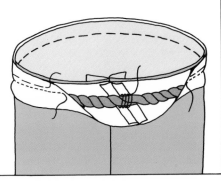

# Embroidery

Embroidery is one of the very oldest forms of decoration and one that has undergone remarkably few changes over the centuries. The Egyptians were embroidering as early as 3400 BC and evidence survives to show that civilizations as diverse as the ancient Maoris and classical Greeks were familiar with embroidery. Basic stitch construction has remained the same from the beginning. The versatile and ubiquitous cross stitch, originating in the Greek Islands, is the earliest known stitch, but others, such as stem, tent, satin and chain, have also been in use for centuries.

European embroidery came into its own in the 12th century. Like most medieval arts, its impetus and finance came from the Church, and much sumptuous gold and silk ecclesiastical work was produced, mainly by men. Even that most famous piece, the Bayeux tapestry, was Church inspired, commissioned by Bishop Odo of Bayeux, William's half-brother. The "tapestry"—a misnomer as it was not woven—was worked in wool on linen, a method known as crewel work, from the Old English *cleow*, ball of thread.

By the 16th century, embroidery had become domesticated. Bedcovers and wall hangings were decorated with needlepoint—canvas worked in silk, wool or precious metal thread. Mary, Queen of Scots covered prodigious amounts of canvas in this way during her imprisonment. The wealthy embroidered their clothes with silk thread, one of the luxuries resulting from the expanding trade with the East. Poorer people stuck to traditional forms of work on linen.

In the 17th century, crewel work expanded its stitch repertoire to include French knots, backstitch and various filling stitches. Stump work—raised figures on a satin ground—decorated such genteel trifles as purse lids and mirror frames.

In the 18th century, embroidery became an "accomplishment", and young ladies all over Europe and America worked samplers for practice, reference and display. Canvas work, particularly the distinctive chevrons of Italian bargello work, embellished chair backs and seats. It remained popular in the 19th century, culminating in the craze for Berlin work, a brighter version of crewel done on canvas. (This was so called after its place of origin.)

Embroidery is currently enjoying a renaissance. Materials and the scope for the application of embroidery may have improved, but the stitches remain the same, and some of the most lastingly popular working methods are explained on the following pages.

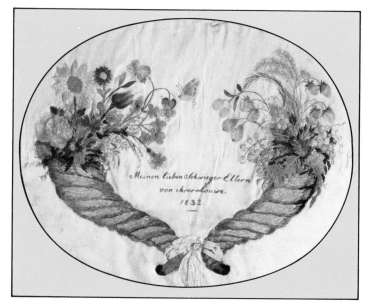

*Carefully embroidered cornucopias in crewel work from the 19th-century Biedermeier period, the German equivalent to the Victorian era. The piece, which is a dutiful New Year's greeting from a wife to her parents-in-law, is now in the possession of the Stadtmuseum, Munich.*

**A Thousand Birds Congratulate the Emperor,** *an 18th-century screen from China richly embroidered in silk on a silk ground. A birthday present to an unknown imperial recipient, the screen is now in the Museum für Völkerkunde, West Berlin.*

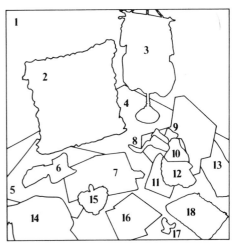

Embroidery can be used to decorate practically anything as the selection, left, from the 19th and 20th centuries shows. Some of the domestic items are almost too exquisite to be used, such as the Persian inspired silk-embroidered tablecloth (**1**), made in Europe in the 1930s, or the cushion (**2**) from the same period, but in traditional counted thread work and trimmed with bobbin lace. More practical are the all-purpose fine canvas cloth (**14**) from central Europe, decorated with cross stitch, and the modern hand towel with an appliquéed embroidered monogram (**13**). Once useful, but now collectors' items, are the canvas-work handscreen (**3**) and the cross-stitch sampler (**5**), both from the late 19th century. The chinoiserie craze of the 1920s produced such things as the imported Chinese shawl (**4**) and the Western-made evening bag (**18**) in imitation Chinese embroidery. Other personal items include embroidered detachable collars (**6** and **12**), beloved by smart ladies of the 1930s, and machine-embroidered ribbon (**8**). Tiny canvas-work sachets (**9, 10, 15**) are still made today, but it is unlikely that the handkerchief wallet (**11**) would be made even by the most conservative. Especially unusual are the counted thread cards (**16**) for French sailors in World War I, and the embroidered frontispiece for a Victorian album (**7**). The tiny silk bird (**17**) is the epitome of an object whose sole function is to be embroidered upon.

*Lemons worked in silk tent stitch on a canvas ground, a typical piece of English needlepoint, or canvas work, from c. 1600. Such pieces, called slips, were appliquéed to bedcovers and wall hangings.*

*The sampler was an essential record of embroidery stitches for all needlewomen. The meticulous one above is from the American Museum in Britain, Bath.*

*Art needlework, a 19th-century phenomenon, often decorated objects of doubtful utility. Suitable items suggested by Queen magazine in 1888 included a photograph frame and a "cosy".*

# Embroidery Equipment

Crewel and tapestry needles are the most commonly used needles for embroidery. Crewels have long eyes and sharp points for stabbing through fabric. Tapestry needles, with larger eyes and blunt tips, are used for canvas and drawn thread work. Both are available in a range of sizes.

Silk, cotton and wool are used for embroidery. Use stranded cotton or silk or woollen yarns for crewel work and crewel or tapestry wool for canvas work. Coton à broder, a twisted lustrous thread, and pearl cotton, a corded thread, are suitable for drawn, counted and pulled thread work. Soft embroidery cotton is a thick matt thread used for bold embroidery designs and counted thread work. A mercerized cotton is used for machine embroidery.

Work with threads no longer than 46 cm/18 in to prevent fraying. Single strands of cotton or silk should be only 30 cm/12 in or they tend to knot. The number of strands or the thickness of the thread depends on the fabric and the effect desired. A sharp pair of scissors and a thimble are also essential pieces of equipment.

## Fabrics

Suitable fabric must be used for embroidery. Crewel embroidery is traditionally worked on linen and twill. Today, however, many other fabrics can be used, provided they are firmly woven and the threads can be separated easily by a needle. Drawn and pulled thread embroidery are also traditionally worked on linen, but other evenweave fabrics can be used. Counted thread embroidery is worked on evenweave fabrics.

There are two main types of canvas for canvas embroidery which can also be used for counted thread work: single thread, or mono, and double thread, or penelope. Both are available in different sizes of mesh and are made in linen, cotton and acrylic. There is also a plastic mono canvas. Use fine canvas for detailed designs and a larger mesh for bold ones. Mono canvas is probably more versatile and easier to work on, but the advantage of penelope is that the double threads may be separated and used as a single mesh, thus giving a choice of a small or large mesh on one canvas.

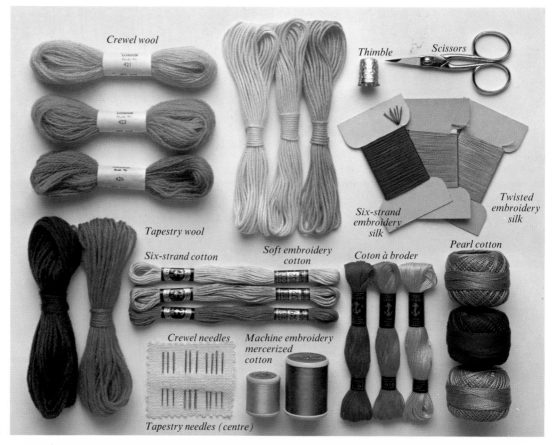

Crewel wool
Thimble    Scissors
Tapestry wool
Six-strand embroidery silk
Twisted embroidery silk
Six-strand cotton
Soft embroidery cotton
Coton à broder
Pearl cotton
Crewel needles
Machine embroidery mercerized cotton
Tapestry needles (centre)

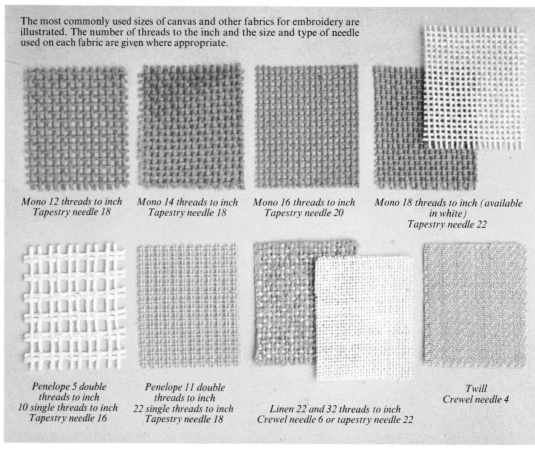

The most commonly used sizes of canvas and other fabrics for embroidery are illustrated. The number of threads to the inch and the size and type of needle used on each fabric are given where appropriate.

Mono 12 threads to inch
Tapestry needle 18

Mono 14 threads to inch
Tapestry needle 18

Mono 16 threads to inch
Tapestry needle 20

Mono 18 threads to inch (available in white)
Tapestry needle 22

Penelope 5 double threads to inch
10 single threads to inch
Tapestry needle 16

Penelope 11 double threads to inch
22 single threads to inch
Tapestry needle 18

Linen 22 and 32 threads to inch
Crewel needle 6 or tapestry needle 22

Twill
Crewel needle 4

## FRAMES

Although an embroidery frame is not essential, it gives a neater result and makes for easier and faster work. The fabric is stretched taut on the frame and kept flat, so that an even tension can be maintained. There are two types of frame: square and hoop, both available in different sizes.

Square, or rectangular, frames, made of wood, are ideal for large pieces of embroidery. The fabric is sewn on to the frame so that the whole expanse can be seen.

Hoop frames, although smaller, are more versatile as fabric of any size can be fitted on them in sections. They consist of two wooden hoops which fit over each other, clamping the material taut between them. A very small piece of embroidery can be mounted on linen and then framed. Delicate fabric can be marked by a hoop. Cover it with tissue paper before pushing the top ring down. Tear away the bulk of the paper to leave it just between the hoops.

Many frames are supplied with a floor or table stand, which leaves both hands free to stitch.

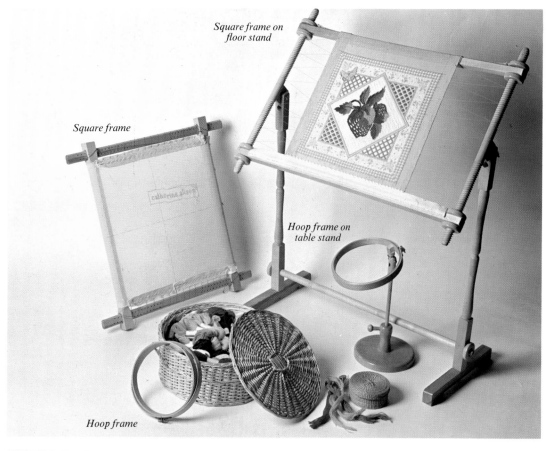

*Square frame on floor stand*

*Square frame*

*Hoop frame on table stand*

*Hoop frame*

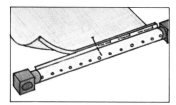
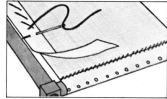
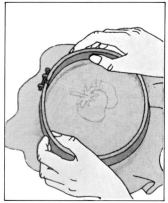
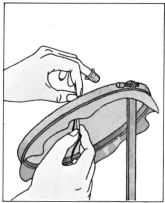
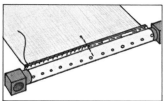

**Inserting canvas in a square frame** Prepare canvas by turning up 6 mm/¼ in hems all round. Mark centre of each edge with a pin. Mark centre of webbing attached to top and bottom stretchers of frame. Matching centres and edges, pin canvas to webbing, working from centres outwards to side edges to keep canvas straight and even. Using a strong needle and buttonhole twist, oversew canvas to webbing, again starting in centre and working outwards to each side in turn. Turn stretchers until canvas is pulled taut.

**2.** Insert vertical arms of frame and secure with the pegs or screws provided. Cut lengths of webbing to fit sides of canvas. Overlap webbing on to canvas and stitch firmly together diagonally. Using fine string or carpet thread and a very large needle, thread string through webbing and around vertical arms of frame. Pull ends of string until canvas is as taut as possible and secure round arms of stretchers. To remove work from frame, unpick stitching and undo stretchers.

**Inserting fabric in a hoop frame** Lay fabric, with design side facing upwards, over inner ring of frame so that area to be worked is in centre. Position outer ring over inner. If adjustable—many hoop frames have a screw on the outer ring for adjusting the diameter to accommodate different thicknesses of fabric—turn screw so that outer ring fits snugly over inner one and fabric. Gently pull the fabric taut and push outer ring firmly down over inner to hold fabric in place. Frequent adjustment may be necessary to maintain an even tension. When adjusting or removing fabric, press down on inner ring and lift off outer one. Hoop frames are not suitable for canvas embroidery.

**Working on a frame** When the fabric is securely held by a frame on a stand, both hands are free to work stitches. One hand should always be above the work and the other underneath to guide the needle through accurately. The steadier hand should be beneath the work. Wear a thimble on both hands. Use alternate pushing and pulling motions, stabbing the needle down into the canvas and pulling it through on the underside. Push the needle back up through the fabric and pull it through from above. When using a frame without a stand, work with these same stabbing movements.

Try to keep an even tension throughout the work—this will improve with practice as will working speed. Always embroider in a good clear light, particularly when working tiny stitches or delicate shading.

# Crewel Embroidery

**Enlarging or reducing a design** To adapt a design to the desired size for embroidery, draw a squared grid lightly in pencil over it or on tracing paper laid over it. To enlarge, mark out the shape on larger squares following outline on first squared grid. To reduce, mark out design in same way on smaller squares.

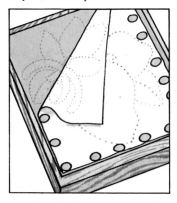

**Tracing a design on to linen** Trace design and, with a fine needle, prick holes along outline at 3 mm/⅛ in intervals. Matching centres, lay tracing on fabric and pin both to a board. With a rolled felt pad rub powdered charcoal over design. Remove tracing and paint along charcoal outlines as for canvas tracing.

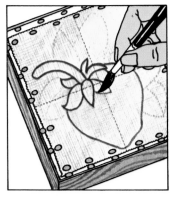

**Transferring a design to canvas** Trace design with a fine black felt-tip pen. Fold tracing into four to find centre and pin to a piece of board. Pin canvas in place over tracing, matching centres. Using black oil paint mixed with a little turpentine and a very fine brush, paint outlines of design on to canvas.

Crewel embroidery can enhance and decorate any reasonably soft pliable articles such as cushions and clothing. Wall hangings and embroidered pictures are among the numerous other items for which crewel is suitable. Imaginative use of the large variety of different threads available for crewel embroidery greatly increases the range of effects that can be achieved. Although linen and twill are the best fabrics for crewel, many other fabrics can be used successfully.

The stitches worked in crewel embroidery are all basic embroidery stitches suitable for all types of work. Even relatively few stitches can create an attractive effect, as the above sampler illustrates, and many decorative vari-ations can be worked on the basic stitches. Ordinary sewing stitches such as buttonhole, running stitch and backstitch can also be used in crewel as well as the following basic crewel stitches.

**Starting and finishing**

To start a stitch make a knot in the end of a length of thread and work two small running stitches inside the shape to be filled and close to the area to be worked. Do not begin on an outline as this makes it difficult to embroider on that line. When the thread is firmly held snip away the knot. Finish off the thread with two running stitches.

1. *Buttonhole*
2. *Chain*
3. *Cross*
4. *Double chain*
5. *Fishbone*
6. *French knot*
7. *Laced back*
8. *Long and short*
9. *Roumanian*
10. *Satin*
11. *Stem*

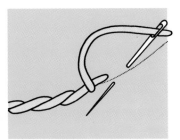

**Stem** Also known as outline, stem is one of the most commonly used stitches. Work it to outline and define shapes with a poor edge or work rows of stem to fill shapes. The slanting stitches are worked from left to right.

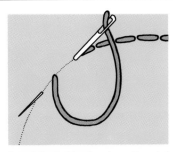

**Satin** Used to fill shapes, this stitch requires practice for a perfect result. Begin working at the centre of the shape to be filled and work outwards to either end of it. Try to keep an even edge, although stem may be worked round the shape afterwards.

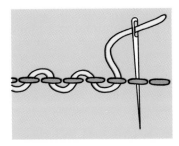

**Laced back** Use laced or threaded backstitch as a decorative edging or as a filling between two lines of stitching that are fairly close together. Work a line of backstitch from right to left. Weave a thread alternately through top and bottom of

stitches from left to right. The stitch is very effective worked in two contrasting coloured threads or in two shades of the same colour.

**Chain** Use to fill shapes or as an outline stitch, or work single stitches to form flower petals. Work stitches from top to bottom or curving from right to left.

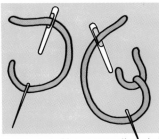

**Double chain** Use as an outline stitch only. Work from top to bottom and use one or two threads depending on the thickness of line required. Make an open chain stitch and continue stitching, looping thread alternately left and right, to make a double row

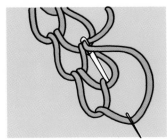

.of chain stitches. Keep an even tension so that each link of the chain is the same size.

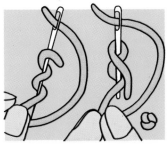

**French knot** Work in clusters or singly. Bring needle up at **A**. Holding thread taut, to left of **A**, take needle behind and under thread and pick up thread twice. Reinsert needle beside **A** still holding thread taut, and pull thread to WS to form knot.

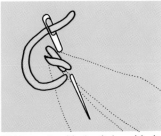

**Fishbone** An ideal stitch, with its realistic centre vein effect, for filling small shapes such as leaves or flower petals. For a neat edge, always push the needle down through edge of shape and bring it up again at centre. Begin with a straight stitch at point of

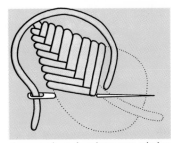

shape and work subsequent stitches left and right of centre alternately. Each stitch overlaps centre. Fishbone may be worked to fill either a vertical or a slanting shape.

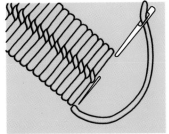

**Roumanian** Worked in a similar way to satin stitch, but each stitch is anchored in the centre by a small slanting stitch. Useful for filling large shapes as the size of the stitch can be increased and more than one central anchoring stitch worked. Variations

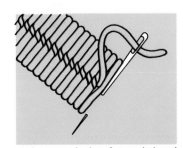

are known as janina, figure stitch and roumanian couching, depending on the direction of the stitch and the number of anchoring stitches worked.

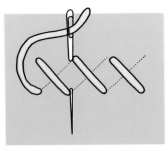

**Cross** One of the oldest decorative stitches, cross is a versatile stitch and forms the basis of many other stitches. Work first slanting stitches from right to left and then work crossing stitches from left to right over the first stitches.

**Split** Use to define outlines of shapes to be filled with long and short stitch. It may also be used as a filling where a flat surface is desirable. Work left to right, splitting the thread of each stitch with the needle.

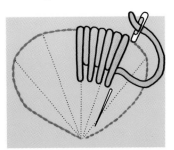

**Long and short** Work with different coloured threads to create a realistic shaded effect. Stitches follow direction lines marked on shape—these lines should relate to the shape's structure. Outline shape with split stitch. Begin in centre and work

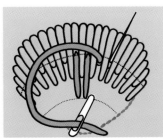

outwards to edges, placing stitches over outline. Start with a long stitch and work long and short stitches alternately; the short stitch should be two-thirds the length of the long one. On second row bring needle up one-third of the way along short stitch.

# Machine Embroidery

A variety of embroidery stitches can be worked on a sewing machine. Embroidery attachments are available for straight stitch and zigzag machines, but a larger range of stitches can be worked on a zigzag. Some machines work automatic embroidery patterns—follow the machine handbook instructions.

Transfer any design markings to the right side of the fabric and stitch on this side. On some fine or sheer fabrics it may be necessary to baste tissue to the wrong side to prevent the fabric slipping, and pulling while stitching. Always do this when working satin stitch.

The sampler, right, is worked mainly in free-style embroidery, which is almost a form of drawing with the machine.

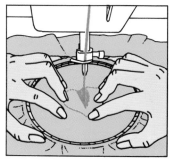

**Free-style embroidery** may be worked on a machine, using straight and zigzag stitches and a hoop frame to keep fabric taut. Place fabric RS up over outer ring; push inner ring down until slightly below outer so fabric lies flush with machine. Thread machine, remove foot and lower or cover feed teeth. Work on RS, moving hoop round under needle in direction of stitching to position stitches.

### Machine embroidery stitches

**Satin stitch** Use embroidery foot and zigzag stitch. Set stitch length to almost 0 so stitches lie side by side.

**Faggoting** is a decorative stitch which joins two pieces of fabric. Use on items such as blouses and tablelinen.

**Couching** Stitch down a length of cord or wool with straight or zigzag stitch, or with an automatic pattern, to form a decorative line.

**Twin-needle** embroidery is worked by the same method as satin stitch, but two rows of stitching are made at the same time by the two needles.

**Pin tucks** are made by using the twin needle and a pin tuck foot.

**Hem stitch** Use a special double hem stitch needle—twin needles, one of which is a flat spear shape. This flat needle makes the holes which give the stitch its open effect. Use straight or zigzag stitch or an automatic embroidery pattern.

**Drawn thread** Use a fine needle and thread. Best worked on pure linen, this is most suitable for tablelinen.

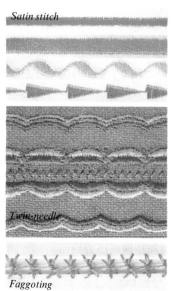

*Satin stitch*

*Twin-needle*

*Faggoting*

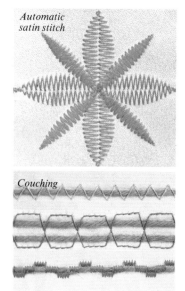

*Automatic satin stitch*

*Couching*

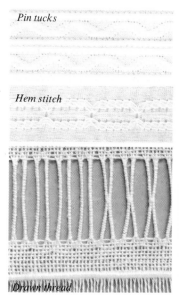

*Pin tucks*

*Hem stitch*

*Drawn thread*

# Smocking

Smocking is a decorative and practical way of arranging fullness. The word smock derives from Old English *smoc*, meaning a chemise, or loose shirt. Later, this working garment was gathered to allow room for movement and it became customary to work decorative stitching on the gathers.

Gather the fabric first and draw up the threads to form even pleats. Do not pull them up too tightly as there must be room to insert the needle between the pleats or gathers. Use the gathering threads as a guide when working embroidery. When the work is complete press it gently and remove these threads. Work smocking on the right side of the fabric, securing each thread with a backstitch on the wrong side.

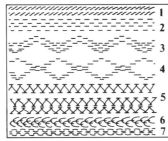

1. *Stem*
2. *Honeycomb*
3. *Stem (wave variation)*
4. *Stem (diamond variation)*
5. *Surface honeycomb*
6. *Feather*
7. *Cable chain*

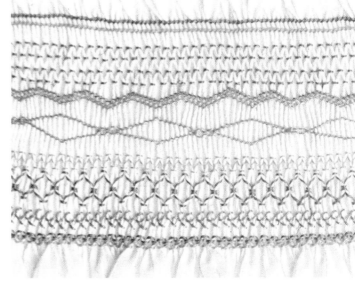

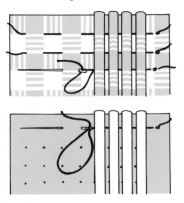

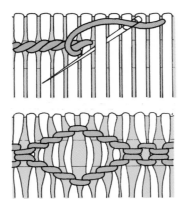

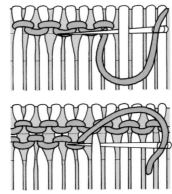

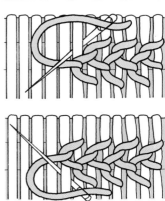

**Gathering** Insert rows of small, even gathering stitches over area to be smocked. Secure each thread with a knot and two small backstitches. If gathering fabric with checks or spots, use these as a guide. On plain fabric, apply dots to WS with a smocking transfer and use as a guide for gathers.

**Stem** Useful to set gathers. Stitches are worked from left to right along one row of gathering. One pleat is picked up with each stitch. Variations known as wave and diamond, shown above, are worked between two rows of gathers by stepping the stitches up and down to create patterns.

**Cable chain** An alternative outline stitch to stem, cable is worked left to right, along one row of gathers. Each stitch joins two pleats, the second pleat of one stitch becoming the first pleat of the next one. Work stitches with thread placed above and below the needle alternately.

**Feather** Worked from right to left. One pleat is taken up with each movement of the needle.

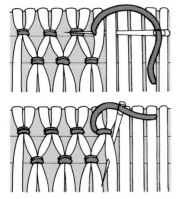

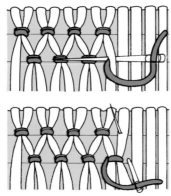

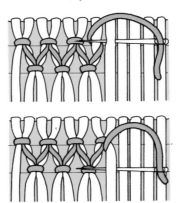

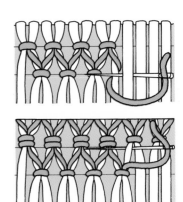

**Honeycomb** As this stitch has more elasticity than most smocking stitches it is often used on children's clothes, maternity wear and other items that need to have a reasonable amount of stretch or allow for growth. Work stitches left to right over two rows of gathering threads, alternating stitches between the two rows. Each stitch

is made twice and is worked over two pleats. Unlike surface honeycomb, the diagonal threads lie on WS of garment.

**Surface honeycomb** This stitch is worked from left to right over two rows of gathers. Each horizontal stitch is worked over two pleats. As the name implies, the stitches are made on the surface of the fabric; the thread is not taken through to WS. Work several rows of stitches to give an attractive honeycomb effect on the body of the

smocking. Make top horizontal stitch of next set of stitches directly beneath bottom stitch of first set, so that the two stitches lie against each other.

# Canvas Embroidery

Canvas embroidery is very attractive on many different articles. As it is so closely stitched, it is tough and hard-wearing and, therefore, ideal for making such items as rugs and chair seats.

Tent stitch is the basic canvas embroidery stitch. It is often known as gros, demi and petit point, which simply mean large, medium and small tent stitches. There are many other canvas stitches and variations upon them; crewel stitches may be used where suitable. Each stitch is worked over a number, or count, of threads of the canvas. The basic method is illustrated, but once you have mastered it, experiment with stitches.

Before beginning to embroider, note the details about the colours and the types of stitches on a diagram of the design.

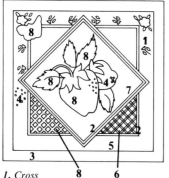

1. Cross
2. Crossed corners
3. Cushion
4. French knots
5. Hungarian
6. Milanese
7. Oriental
8. Tent

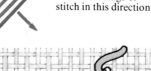

Canvas mesh of threads on which stitches are worked

Work first stage of stitch in this direction

Work second stage of stitch in this direction

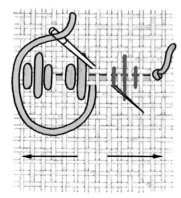

**Starting** Knot yarn and take needle through to back of canvas about 4 cm/1½ in away from intended position of first stitch. Push needle up again in position for first stitch. Work stitches back towards knot, weaving in thread at back of canvas. Snip off knot when thread is secure.

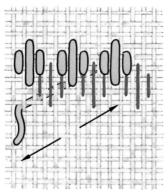

**Finishing** Pull end of thread through to RS of canvas about 4 cm/1½ in away from last stitch and level with next row of stitching. Weave in thread end when working the stitches on the next row. When secure, cut off end. At end of embroidery run 5 cm/2 in of thread through last row of stitches.

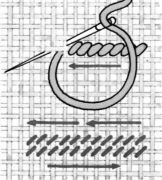

**Tent stitch** Versatile and easy, this is the basic canvas stitch used as a background stitch and for shaping. Work it in rows right to left and left to right alternately across the desired number of canvas threads. Tent stitch may also be worked in vertical rows from top to bottom and bottom to top alternately.

**2.** Tent stitch can be used for shading as well as long and short. Use as many shade variations as possible to create a realistic three-dimensional effect. Work lightest outer areas first and work down into the shape in order indicated on diagram above.

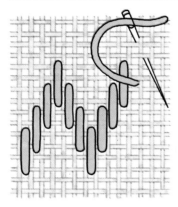

**Florentine or bargello** This is a simple, straight stitch and most effective. It is worked vertically over four threads, each stitch beginning two threads higher or lower than the previous one, depending on the pattern. Create patterns and fill large areas by working rows in varying colours. The count can be varied if desired.

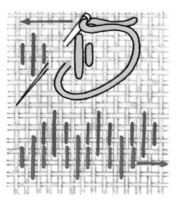

**Hungarian** A straight vertical stitch worked in groups of three. Working right to left, make first stitch over two horizontal threads, second over four and third over two. Leave two vertical threads between each group. Work next row left to right, setting long stitches into spaces between groups in first row.

## SPECIAL EFFECTS

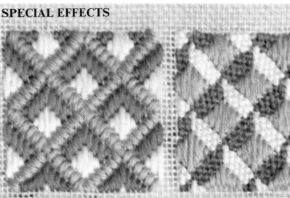

The same basic pattern can be greatly changed by using different stitch combinations and placing colours differently. The sample above left is worked with tent stitch over three threads of canvas for the diagonal lines and milanese for the insides of the squares. On the sample above right the diagonal

lines are worked in tent stitch over two threads of canvas and the squares in cushion stitch.

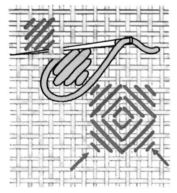

**Cushion** Useful for borders and square patterns, cushion stitch is worked over a square of three threads. Work the five slanting stitches over one, two, three, two and one thread of canvas respectively. Work squares slanting left to right and right to left to create patterns. The count can be increased.

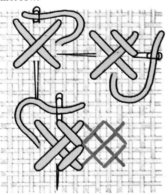

**Crossed corners or rice** A square stitch useful for geometric shapes and for borders. Work cross stitches over four threads of canvas in area to be filled. Then, over two threads of canvas, work diagonal stitches at right angles over corners of each cross stitch. When the design is complete, the small stitches also form crosses.

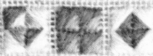

The sample above shows a border of different shading techniques all worked with cushion stitch.

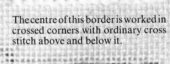

The centre of this border is worked in crossed corners with ordinary cross stitch above and below it.

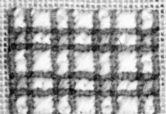

An example of how to make an attractive check pattern using three simple stitches: tent stitch for the horizontal and vertical lines; cushion and cross stitch for the contrasting check fillings.

Florentine stitch is used in the sample above to demonstrate how an attractive pattern can be created simply by varying the number of stitches in the blocks of colour.

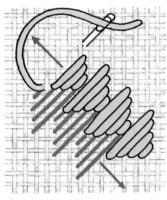

**Milanese** Work blocks of four slanting stitches in diagonal rows. The four stitches in each block are made over one, two, three and four threads of canvas respectively. Work first row from bottom right to top left and next row back from top left to bottom right, fitting stitches against those in first row. Continue working alternating rows.

**Oriental** Work first row as for milanese. On either side of milanese row, work groups of three slanting stitches over two threads next to and into same holes as three, two and one thread milanese stitches. Work these bottom right to top left. Work next row of milanese top left to bottom right beside groups of slanting stitches.

## STRETCHING THE CANVAS

Canvas can be pulled out of shape even in a frame. To restore the original shape and give the embroidery a professional finish, stretch, or block, the completed work. The canvas should measure 7cm/2¾in more than the design to allow a margin for stretching.

Nail canvas RS up on a board, pulling mesh as taut as possible so that sides are straight and corners are true right angles. Insert nails or tacks at intervals of 2.5cm/1in. Dampen canvas thoroughly with a sponge and cold water and leave to dry for between 24 and 48 hours. If canvas is still out of shape when dry, repeat process.

To stretch crewel embroidery on fabric, lay cotton sheeting between the embroidery and the board before nailing down the fabric. Stretch, dampen and dry as for canvas.

Although it is simple, stretching requires care and patience and it can

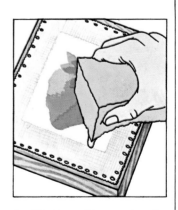

be difficult to achieve good results. Consequently, it may sometimes be better to have the canvas or crewel work stretched professionally rather than attempt it yourself. Many needlework shops offer this service.

# Drawn, Counted and Pulled Thread Work

There are three types of embroidery that rely, in different ways, on the background threads of the fabric they are worked on. These are drawn, pulled and counted thread embroidery. They can be effectively combined, as the sampler shows.

Drawn thread embroidery is worked on the loose threads remaining in the fabric when one set of threads is withdrawn. The decorative stitches pull the loose threads together into patterns. It is often worked in a rectangle to form an attractive border round items such as tablelinen.

Stitches in counted thread embroidery are worked over an exact number of fabric threads; the instructions for these stitches specify the number, or count.

The open effect of pulled thread, or drawn fabric, work is created by pulling all the stitches firmly so that the threads of the fabric are drawn together. A lacy pattern is formed by the spaces left between the threads. No threads are actually withdrawn from the fabric so the work is quite strong.

These three forms of embroidery should all be worked on even-weave fabrics. Crewel embroidery stitches can be used where suitable as well as the specific stitches for these types of work.

To start stitching, leave the thread end on the wrong side of the fabric and weave it into subsequent stitches until firm. To finish, weave the thread end into stitches on the wrong side.

*A 17th-century English example of drawn thread work on linen.*

*A 17th-century Italian band in counted thread embroidery.*

*A 17th-century Portuguese border in pulled thread work.*

1. Chain
2. Diamond filling
3. French knot
4. Hem stitch
5. Maltese filling and inside section
6. Needleweaving
7. Portuguese border
8. Raised stem
9. Satin stitch and eyelet
10. Spider's web
11. Stem
12. Step stitch filling
13. Wave

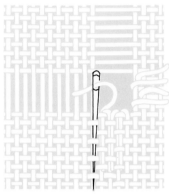

**To withdraw threads** for drawn thread embroidery, cut across the required number of warp or weft threads and remove them carefully. Do not withdraw threads right across the fabric. Leave each cut end long enough to be darned into the fabric. Decorative stitches are worked over remaining loose threads.

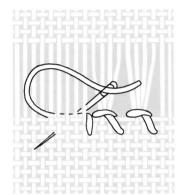

**Hem stitch** A drawn thread stitch, worked right to left. The needle is brought out two threads below area of drawn threads and four loose threads are caught together by the stitch. The number of loose threads in each stitch can be varied to suit the design. If hem stitch is used to edge a hem, stitch through folds of fabric.

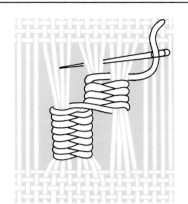

**Needleweaving** A drawn thread stitch, worked from bottom left to top right. Stitches are woven over groups of eight threads. Four threads of the first group become part of the second, and so on. Work an even number of stitches in each block of weaving, but the size of the blocks may be varied to suit the design.

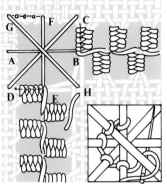

**Spider's web** A useful filler for corners of a rectangle of drawn thread work. Make eight stitches for spokes in order shown, weaving thread through fabric between stitches. To fill, or partially fill, web, weave thread round forward under two spokes and back over one. Weave end of thread into back of web to finish.

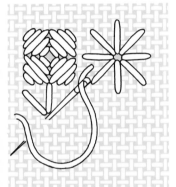

**Satin stitch and eyelet** A counted thread stitch. Work satin stitch squares containing four squares of five diagonal stitches. Each small square is worked over three threads so together they form a square over six. Alternate satin stitch blocks with eyelets of eight stitches over three threads from the same central hole.

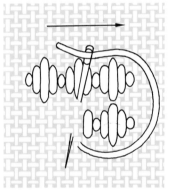

**Diamond filling** A counted thread stitch. Diamond is a geometrical pattern consisting of groups of five vertical stitches worked over one, three, five, three and one thread of canvas respectively. Do not pull the stitches; allow them to lie flat on surface of fabric. Work rows left to right and right to left alternately.

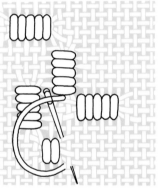

**Step stitch filling** A pulled thread stitch. Work blocks of satin stitches with five stitches to a block over an even number of threads. Alternate horizontal and vertical blocks to create a step-like effect. Pull stitches firmly so fabric threads are drawn together, to give the open look typical of this type of embroidery.

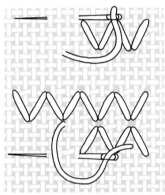

**Wave stitch** A pulled thread stitch, useful for filling. Each diagonal stitch is worked over four horizontal threads and two vertical threads of fabric. Several rows may be worked, placing stitches into holes formed by row above. Pull all stitches firmly. Work from right to left.

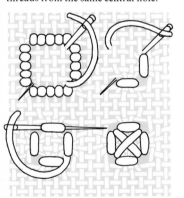

**Maltese filling** A pulled thread stitch. Over a square of six threads work a square of satin stitches—each stitch over two threads as before, and five stitches on each side of square. This gives an enclosed square of four threads. Work four backstitches round inside this square and work a cross in the middle over four threads.

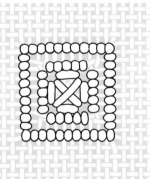

**2.** Work a border of satin stitches round whole square, taking each stitch over two threads as before and taking inside edges down into same holes as outside edges of first satin stitches. Pull all stitches firmly. On both inner and outer satin stitch squares work vertical stitches on horizontal rows and horizontal stitches on vertical rows.

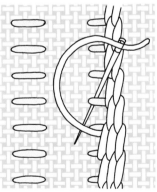

**Raised stem** An all-purpose outline or border stitch, worked on stitch bars not more than 6 mm/$\frac{1}{4}$ in apart. Work a row of stem stitch upwards over bars, picking up one bar with each stitch. Continue working rows of stem stitch close together until bars are completely covered. Always keep thread to same side of needle.

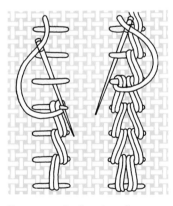

**Portuguese border** An all-purpose outline or border stitch, worked upwards over horizontal stitches as for stem. The stitch length for each bar depends on number of rows of surface stitches to be worked. With thread to left of needle work stitches over two bars at a time; work next row with thread to right of needle.

# Quilting

Quilting is a satisfying combination of utilitarian purpose and decorative result. Its insulating and protective qualities have long been appreciated. The Egyptian Pharaohs were wearing quilted mantles *c.* 3400 BC; in the 1st century AD quilting was even considered durable enough to be used for floor coverings; and in the Middle Ages it enjoyed an un-domestic vogue as armour. Today, however, it is most familiar as the bedcover to which it gives its name.

All quilting, whatever its ultimate function, is based on the same sandwich principle—two pieces of material enveloping one layer of wadding. (The only exception is flat quilting.) The incidental patterns that emerged when the layers were stitched together were later elaborated until the pattern dominated.

There are several forms of quilting. Wadded, commonly called English or American quilting, is the most straightforward and functional. It has a worldwide following but has always been considered a peasant tradition. The upper classes practised the more elaborate techniques of stuffed and corded quilting. Corded, or Italian, quilting developed later than stuffed, or trapunto, work and became extremely popular for bedcovers and hangings in the 17th century. Apart from providing extra weight to give a better hang, the stuffing for both varieties is purely decorative. Tied quilting can be even more ornamental, with non-structural buttons and bows. In contrast, flat quilting, beloved for heavy-duty wear in People's Republics, incorporates no stuffing at all; instead two pieces of fabric are held together by all-over stitchery.

For all forms of quilting choose closely woven, smooth materials, preferably natural fabrics such as cotton, linen or silk. Synthetics are usually too springy to give the soft, undulating surface characteristic of good hand work. Synthetic wadding, however, is a vast improvement on traditional materials, as it is lighter and easier to wash.

For quilting large articles by hand, a special quilting frame is a good investment. Otherwise it is essential to baste all of the layers together securely before beginning the quilting. Extra large articles can be made up in sections and then sewn together.

Like many other "cottage" crafts, quilting is today enjoying the revival it rightly deserves, as a relatively cheap yet effective way of providing strong, warm clothes and bedclothes.

*A simple, traditional way of making quilts is to work individual sections and join them to horizontal and vertical strips of fabric, as on this child's seashore quilt. The fabrics are curtain lining and satin and the quilting of the motifs is a mixture of stuffed, corded and wadded, worked by hand and machine. Some of the motifs were appliquéed to sections of the quilt and then stuffed.*

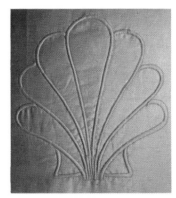

**Wadded quilting** has a top fabric and a backing, which can be of similar material to the top fabric if the article is to be reversible, or of muslin if lined. Between these is a filling, which can vary from a layer of fluffy domette, a knitted interlining, to several layers of wadding, depending on the thickness required for the article.

**Tied quilting** is a form of wadded quilting. The layers of fabric, with wadding between them, are held together at intervals by a knot rather than stitching. A bow or bead can be attached on RS for decoration. Use a strong thread such as linen thread, buttonhole twist, pearl cotton or coton à broder.

**Stuffed quilting** is essentially decorative as only parts of the design are stuffed—with teased wool or small pieces of wadding. The article must be lined, with lining fabric. The backing fabric should be loosely woven muslin or scrim.

**Corded quilting** is linear, with padding inserted between parallel rows of stitching. Use cotton cord or thick wool for padding. The quilting can be worked on single fabric or on fabric backed with muslin. If it is worked on backed fabric, line the quilting with lining fabric.

---

## BASIC QUILTING

The following processes are common to wadded, stuffed and corded quilting and also to flat quilting, the most basic form and the only one that is not padded. Instead, two layers of fabric are held together by an all-over pattern of stitches.

**Marking the design**
On RS of top fabric mark design with an embroidery transfer, dressmaker's carbon or crayon. Or, after the layers have been basted together (see below), mark design on top fabric round a metal, wooden or card template with a tracing wheel (**1**) or by indenting a line on the

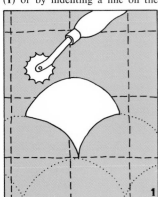

fabric with a blunt needle—it may be necessary to mark small areas at a time. The design for stuffed quilting must be composed of small enclosed shapes; for corded it must be linear. For quilting by machine, with the quilting foot and gauge, mark only one line in each direction for repeating patterns such as diamonds and squares.

**Basting**
Iron top fabric and backing. Stretch backing in a square embroidery frame, or spread it flat on a table or on the floor. Place filling over it (for

wadded and tied quilting) and then top fabric, RS up. Baste large pieces in a vertical and horizontal grid (**2**) and smaller ones radially from centre (**3**), smoothing out creases.

If, however, you wish to combine stuffed quilting with wadded in order to emphasize or highlight a part, or parts, of the design, work

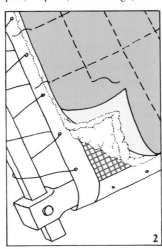

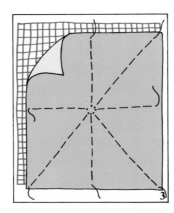

all of the stitching for the stuffed area and stuff before basting the filling and backing into position for the wadded quilting.

**Stitching**
Work stitching along design lines. The most common stitches for hand quilting are running stitch (**4**) and backstitch (**5**), although any line stitch is suitable. To stitch wadded quilting start with a knot hidden between layers. Work all stitches

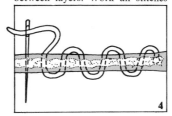

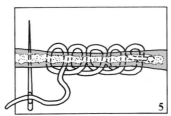

with a stabbing motion to ensure needle penetrates all layers of material—this is much easier if the quilting is framed.

**Quilting by machine**
For corded or stuffed quilting, use a normal foot as only two layers of fabric are being stitched. For wadded quilting, attach a quilting foot and gauge, or bar. The foot has a short front and moves over thick layers of material easily. Adjust gauge so it is required distance from foot (**6**). Use it as a stitching guide, to maintain even spacing between rows of stitching or adjust it for

each row as required. Set machine to medium-length stitch for all fabrics except PVC, which needs a long stitch to stop fabric tearing.

Choose thread to match top fabric—silk on silk, synthetic on synthetic—and a needle suitable for

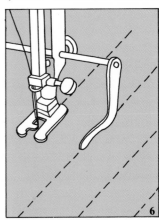

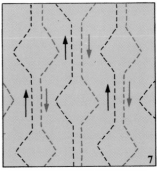

both the top fabric and the filling.
Stitch alternate lines in opposite directions (**7**) to counteract any tendency for top fabric to ride over filling. For a bold effect use satin stitch (with satin stitch foot) or automatic stitches.

# Quilting

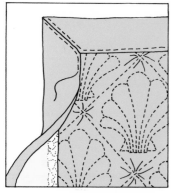

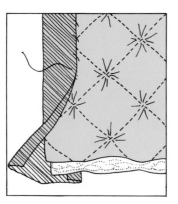

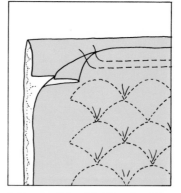

**Wadded** Prepare and stitch as for basic quilting. There are several ways of finishing the edges. If the backing is of a good material, cut out a piece slightly larger than the top fabric and bring it over to RS of finished quilting to form a neat border. Turn in edges, mitre and stitch corners and all round border.

**2.** Wadded quilting can also be finished with binding. Use strips of suitable fabric in a matching or contrasting colour and apply to all edges as for single or double binding.

**3.** For a traditional finish, end quilting pattern slightly away from edge (distance depends on scale of work) and fold in edges of top fabric and backing. Work one or two rows of stitching close to edge.

**4.** Alternatively, work buttonhole or machine satin stitch along edge of quilting pattern. Trim away surplus fabric and filling.

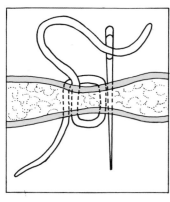

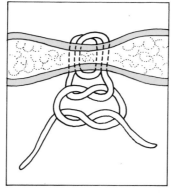

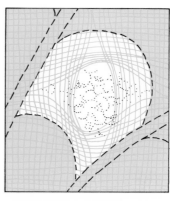

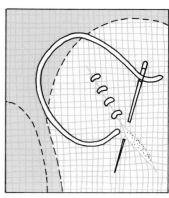

**Tied quilting** Prepare work in a frame as for basic quilting (there is no need to mark a design). Thread needle with a fairly short length of thread and bring through to RS, leaving thread end of about 5 cm/2 in on WS. Work two small backstitches over each other and take needle through to WS.

**2.** On WS tie both ends of thread together to form two or three firm knots and, on RS, a small hollow. Trim off ends close to last knot. Repeat knots at intervals (these do not have to be regular) to create desired pattern.

**Stuffed** Prepare as for basic quilting. Stitch round shapes by hand or with a fairly short machine stitch. Finish off ends securely. Remove basting. For small shapes, part warp and weft threads of backing sufficiently to insert desired amount of filling. Stroke threads of backing fabric into place with a needle.

**2.** For larger shapes, make a slit in backing and push filling into every point or corner of the design with a knitting needle, taking care not to puncture the top fabric. Oversew slit to keep filling in place.

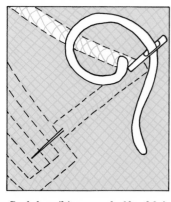

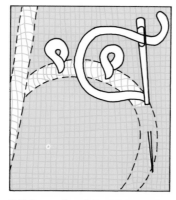

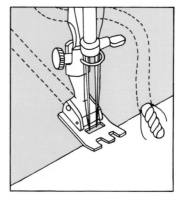

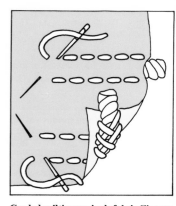

**Corded quilting on double fabric** Prepare and stitch as for basic quilting. Secure thread ends and remove basting. With backing uppermost, insert tapestry or rug needle, threaded with cotton cord or wool, through muslin and push between parallel stitching lines, drawing cord or wool with it.

**2.** Bring needle out at corners or curves and insert at same place, leaving a small loop of cord or wool projecting. This prevents puckering and allows for shrinkage. Where lines intersect, cut filling to leave short end and start a new length.

**Corded quilting** can be worked on the machine with the twin needle and cording foot, through which the cord is threaded. Cut off surplus cord at ends of channels when filling is inserted. Narrow lines of corded quilting can also be simulated—no filling is inserted—by using the twin needle and a tight bottom tension.

**Corded quilting on single fabric** Choose firm cotton cord the desired width for the filling. Hold it under fabric and backstitch alternately above and below the cord to secure it to the fabric. Cut off surplus cord at end of channels.

## SPECIAL EFFECTS

Create a wide range of original and attractive effects by combining different forms of quilting such as corded and stuffed, or by working them in special ways, as for shadow or contour methods. Quilting is also very effective when used with appliqué or patchwork.

### Contour quilting

A quick and easy method of wadded, flat, stuffed or corded quilting, this involves stitching round the design motifs in a patterned fabric, and round

the contours within them if desired. This method does away with the need to make and mark on designs, but choose a fabric with a simple pattern or the quilting effect will not show. Baste layers of fabric together and stitch as for basic quilting. Stuffed motifs look most effective worked in this way, either on their own or in conjunction with wadded quilting.

### Stuffed motifs on a corded ground

A decorative method popular in America, this is traditionally worked on white fabric so that the stuffed motifs stand out against the solidly corded background. It provides a similar warmth and weight to wadded quilting. Prepare work as for basic quilting and complete all stitching

before inserting filling as for corded and stuffed quilting.

### Shadow quilting

In contrast to most other forms of quilting, shadow quilting uses colour as an intrinsic part of the design. It can be wadded, corded or stuffed. The effect is achieved by quilting through two layers of transparent fabric such as organdie, and inserting a strongly coloured filling. No separate backing is used. Insert felt shapes between the layers as a filling for wadded quilting,

baste them in place and work quilting stitches round them. Use knitting wool in one or more thicknesses for corded quilting and tease it out for stuffed quilting.

### Tied quilting

For a decorative effect, attach a bead or button on RS when working second small backstitch. Alternatively, start

on RS and take needle through to WS and back to RS, leaving ends of thread long enough to tie into a bow on RS.

Use ribbon, threaded through a large needle, for more conspicuous bows.

### Appliqué quilting

Appliqué combines easily with all forms of quilting. For stuffed quilting (1) baste and machine satin stitch motifs to RS of fabric. Slit fabric carefully behind motif, making slit as small as possible; do not cut right to edges of motif. Insert padding and oversew slit. No backing is needed as the main fabric acts as a backing.

Apply braids or ribbons to RS of top

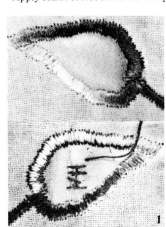

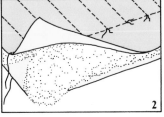

fabric and machine along both edges to form channels for corded quilting (2). Or, for wadded quilting, work an automatic stitch down centre of braid and a quilting stitch round it.

For motifs on wadded quilting, baste motifs to RS of top fabric before basting fabric to backing and filling. Proceed as for ordinary wadded quilting, stitching round the motifs with satin stitch through all layers of fabric and so working appliqué and quilting together.

### Quilted patchwork

Also known as Swiss or raised patchwork, this is an effective way to give patchwork extra warmth and bulk. Put any two matching patchwork shapes, e.g. hexagons or diamonds, RS together and sew round all but one side. Turn through to RS, stuff and slip stitch remaining side. Join prepared patches by oversewing.

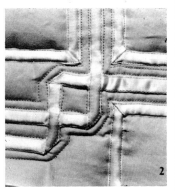

---

## MAKING UP A QUILTED GARMENT

Making up a garment from ready-made quilted fabric poses problems because of the bulk of the fabric. Choose a simple pattern without pleats, gathers or fullness and, if possible, a style with loose sleeves such as the kimono as the bulky fabric makes it difficult to achieve a good fit for set-in sleeves. Alternatively, design quilting to fit the pattern pieces of a garment. Bear the following rules in mind, particularly if you are using a conventional dress pattern:

### Ready-made quilted fabric

● Do not cut out pattern pieces with fabric double or folded, as the bulk

of the fabric causes distortion.

● When the pattern pieces are cut out and the seam lines are marked, unpick

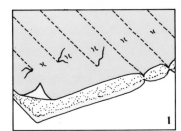

quilting stitches from the seam allowance (1), remembering to finish off all ends securely.

● Remove wadding up to seam line (2) to eliminate bulk in the seams. Do the same for any other areas that are likely to be bulky, such as darts, openings and facings.

● Never turn up a double hem on quilted fabric. Either remove wadding up to hemline, as above, and turn up a single hem, or bind edge of fabric and make a single turning.

● Set the sleeve head into the armhole before stitching the sleeve underarm seam and the garment side seam, so that any surplus fabric can be accommodated in these seams rather than being eased into the armhole and so creating unwanted bulk.

### Designing for pattern

● The entire garment need not be quilted. A quilted hem may be incorporated for weight; quilted sleeves may be added for warmth. Quilt details such as collars and cuffs to make them more hard-wearing as well as more decorative. The quilting can be wadded, corded, stuffed, flat or any combination.

● Place pattern pieces on fabric and work tailor's tacks at a slight distance beyond pattern edges to allow for shrinkage during quilting. Mark seam lines and remove pattern.

● Mark quilting design on RS of fabric, keeping within seam lines. Back fabric appropriately for the kind of quilting and stitch by hand or machine.

● When the quilting is complete, cut out garment pieces, using tailor's tacks as a guide, and make up the garment in the usual way.

# Appliqué

Appliqué has a long and ancient history and was probably first used by the Persians in the 9th century BC. The term is derived from the French "appliquer", to put on, and it denotes the attachment of one piece of fabric to another, traditionally by hand with fine hemming stitches. Motifs can be attached equally effectively by imaginative use of other hand stitches or by machine with both straight and swing, or zigzag, stitches.

Throughout its history appliqué has offered a wide scope for individual expression. Wall hangings and tents made by the Egyptians in the 8th century BC showed a subtlety of design far removed from the bold and colourful use of appliqué for both the tunics and banners of the knights of the Crusades. On medieval church banners and vestments appliqué achieved a new dimension of beauty and delicacy, whereas the early American settlers, with their quilts embellished with appliqué motifs, introduced the more personal, homely effect that is still popular today.

Appliqué motifs should ideally be strongly defined and the designs simple. Buildings can be broken down into a series of rectangles and trees shown as silhouettes. Basic shapes can be grouped to suggest leaves on a branch or petals on a flower. Add detail with surface stitching.

The choice of fabric is an important feature of the design. Virtually any type of fabric can be used, the only consideration being the use to which the article will be put—on a child's garment, for example, do not apply fabrics that are not easily washable. On a picture or banner, however, there are no such restrictions and the choice of fabric is much freer. Take into account the texture of fabrics as well as their pattern. A scrap of gingham may suggest a dress; a piece of velvet may be just right for a soldier's jacket. If you are starting from scratch rather than applying a motif to an existing garment, choose a background fabric that will complement the design without dominating it and group a selection of fabrics of different textures and colours on the background before choosing the final pieces.

The method of applying the fabrics depends on those used. Felt and leather do not fray and, therefore, do not need turnings, whereas fine fabrics need the edges turned under, or need backing with iron-on interfacing. Wherever possible, except for appliqué pictures, cut motifs to follow the same grain line as the background fabric. Material cut on the bias has a tendency to pull and pucker when attached.

Press all fabric motifs before applying. After the appliqué is completed, press gently, but as little as possible, on the wrong side to avoid flattening the work.

No special equipment is needed —only a sharp cutting knife, scissors, needles and matching or contrasting thread, depending on

*Hemmed, machined, persé and inlay appliqué have been combined in these panels for a folding screen. Ingenious use of brocade, braid, lining material and furnishing fabric is highlighted by the decorative machine and hand stitching.*

the type of appliqué and the effect desired. Mercerized cotton or a polyester thread is ideal for all types of appliqué. For planning the design you will need a soft pencil and drawing or tracing paper or stiff card for the templates for each motif. If necessary, pin the templates in place on the background fabric to arrange the design satisfactorily.

Appliqué has a wide range of uses, from decorating clothing, home furnishings and banners to making pictures and wall hangings. With the correct amount of care and preparation any of the basic types of appliqué on the following pages—hemmed, machined, persé, découpé, inlay, lace or reverse—will be a satisfying reflection of your imagination.

**Hemmed appliqué** is particularly suitable for a design based on colour and shape alone. The motifs are attached by hand, by hemming; the stitches should be almost invisible on RS. The material for the motifs should be lightweight and closely woven; fine cotton is ideal.

**Machined appliqué** is hard-wearing and, therefore, particularly suitable for household articles and children's wear. It is particularly important that the fabric for the motifs should be similar in fibre content and weight to the background fabric, especially if the article is to be washed.

**Appliqué persé** motifs are cut from patterned fabrics, traditionally chintz, which is still ideal for its bold patterns and close weave. Avoid fabric with highly intricate patterns and try to create something original rather than copy the fabric motifs. As chintz is liable to shrink, wash the fabric before applying it.

**Inlay appliqué** is used for banner and church work, box tops and stools. The motif is inserted into an area of identical shape cut out of the background fabric. Choose fabrics that contrast in colour with that of the background and that do not fray; felt, suede and leather are ideal.

**Découpé** is a simple form of inlay and can be worked by machine. The main, or surface, fabric is cut away to reveal applied motifs of contrasting colour underneath. The designs should be simple and bold and planned to ensure that the surface fabric holds them together adequately.

**Lacework appliqué,** with its lacy and openwork effect, is most suitable for lingerie and gives semi-transparent fabrics such as fine lawn, silk and georgette a delicate and luxurious appearance. Choose designs with a simple naturalistic outline and avoid very sharp curves as the fabric tends to fray when stitched.

**Reverse appliqué** produces a padded, multicoloured effect and is ideal for table mats, yokes or cushions. The design is created by cutting through layers of different coloured fabric to reveal the different colours beneath. The number of layers of fabric depends upon how many colours are required for the design.

## STITCHES

A variety of ordinary sewing stitches can be used to attach motifs: hemming—ideal for catching down the turned-in edge of closely woven fabrics; slip hemming, if decorative stitching is to be added; running stitch; loop stitch—excellent for wools and felts and very effective if worked in contrasting thread; buttonhole—ideal, closely worked, for covering the raw edge of fine fabric to give a decorative but firm edge; fishbone, particularly suitable for inlay appliqué where two edges are butted together; three-sided punch stitch (see diagrams, right), which gives an openwork effect to the edge of the motif and is ideal for lingerie; and both straight and zigzag machine stitches. Many interesting effects can be obtained by the careful use of the various automatic embroidery patterns that can be worked on some machines.

For decorative surface stitching the following stitches can be worked: stem, which gives a continuous line—the thickness can be varied by using different types of thread; chain; running stitch; couching—a thread is laid on the edge of a motif and held down with loop, herringbone or cross stitch worked in a matching or contrasting thread; French knots; and, for a heavier effect, spider's web, or wheel, and star stitches—star is the first, spoked stage of the wheel. Machine embroidery can also be worked.

### Three-sided punch stitch
Use fine thread—mercerized or polyester 50 is ideal—and a tapestry needle 18 or 14. Thread needle and tie end of thread round eye to prevent it slipping. Work right to left along edge of motif. At each stage work two stitches.

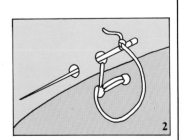

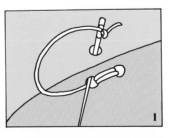
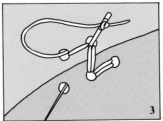

# Appliqué

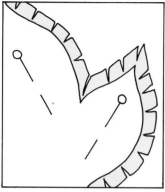

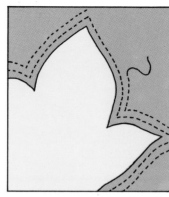

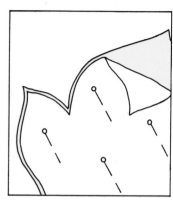

**Hemmed** Cut a paper template for each motif. Pin template to fabric and cut round it with sharp scissors, adding 5 mm/$\frac{1}{4}$ in for turnings all round. On curves snip into design line so that the turnings can be tucked in smoothly and stitched easily.

**2.** Place the motif, RS up, on RS of background fabric. Baste diagonally down centre and then work out to edges to avoid puckering. Using a fine needle and thread to match motif, hem round shape, tucking in turnings. Mitre points or fold them in carefully, keeping outline of motif as sharp as possible to give a neat finish.

**3.** The finished design should have a soft, raised appearance. Emphasize individual shapes by working running stitch (any number of rows) round them on the background fabric, using thread that contrasts with the motif. Do not press too heavily or the design will lose some of its freshness.

**Machined** Cut a paper template for each motif. Pin template to fabric and cut round it; no turnings are needed.

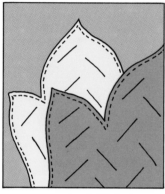

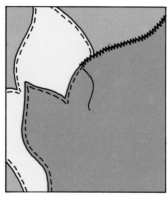

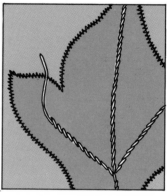

**2.** If fabric for motif is very fine or frays badly, back it with iron-on interfacing. Place the motifs, RS up, on RS of background fabric, overlapping them if necessary for the design. Baste diagonally in place as for hemmed appliqué. Work a row of straight machining round each motif, as close as possible to edge.

**3.** Insert satin stitch foot and fine sewing thread or machine embroidery cotton to match or contrast with background fabric or motif. Set for satin stitch—for most motifs to half the full zigzag. Using straight machining as guide, work satin stitch round motif over raw edges and machining.

**4.** If desired, work surface stitching or embroidery by hand or machine to add details such as features on a figure or veining on leaves and petals. Experiment with threads that match and contrast with the colour of the motif.

**Persé** Cut out motif from chintz or other suitable patterned fabric, using small sharp scissors for a clean outline. Place motif, RS up, on RS of background fabric and press carefully on RS. Baste diagonally in place as for hemmed appliqué.

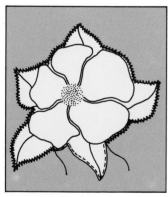

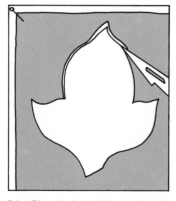

**2.** Work straight machining and satin stitch as for machined appliqué; use a thread to match background fabric for working satin stitch.

**Inlay** Pin main fabric RS up to a board. Cut template of stiff card to required shape for motif and place on fabric. Hold it down with one hand and, with a sharp knife, cut round template and through fabric to make appropriate shaped hole; no turnings are needed. Cut motif from contrasting coloured fabric in same way.

**2.** Working on a flat surface or in a circular embroidery frame, diagonally baste a backing fabric such as calico with RS to WS of main fabric. Diagonally baste motif RS up to RS of backing fabric over cut-out shape, matching raw edges with raw edges of main fabric.

**3.** Using a fine needle and a thread that blends with the colour of both the main fabric and the motif, work fishbone stitch through motif and main fabric only. Remove calico or, for a stiffer effect, leave it in place.

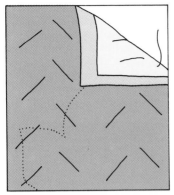

**Découpé** With tailor's chalk, mark design on RS of surface fabric. Cut a piece of contrasting coloured fabric slightly larger than required (it can be a rectangle and does not have to be cut to the shape of the motif). Baste diagonally, as for hemmed appliqué, with RS to WS of surface fabric.

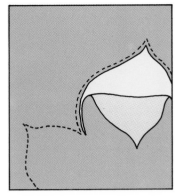

**2.** On RS of surface fabric, work straight machine stitching along chalk line. Cut away surface fabric just inside stitching.

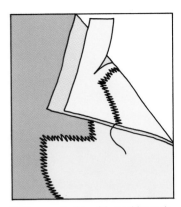

**3.** Cover cut edge with machine satin stitch worked as for machined appliqué. On WS cut away surplus contrasting fabric, leaving a small margin outside satin stitching.

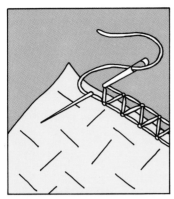

**Lacework** Using a paper template, cut out motif as for hemmed appliqué, but do not add turnings. Diagonally baste motif RS up to RS of garment, keeping it flat. With fine thread to match motif work three-sided punch stitch as close to raw edges of motif as possible. Pull each stitch to achieve the lacy effect.

**2.** Alternatively, set machine for zigzag at half full width of swing and at stitch length 1½ and insert hem-stitching needle. The flanges on the needle make holes in fine fabrics, so giving a lacy appearance. Stitch over raw edges of motifs.

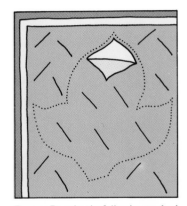

**Reverse** Practise the following method on three layers of fine cotton first. Diagonally baste layers together, RS up. On top layer mark design with tailor's chalk. Cut away all areas of design where top fabric is not required about 5 mm/¼ in within chalk line; cut slightly nearer to chalk line on a corner or tight curve.

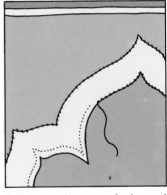

**2.** Snip round curves as for hemmed appliqué. Turn cut edges of first layer under to WS and hem down, working small neat stitches. Mark design on second layer of fabric, undoing basting if necessary. As for top layer, cut away second layer where this fabric is not required for the design and turn under and hem edges.

**3.** Proceed as for practice piece, using as many layers of fabric as required. If desired, in some areas of the design cut middle layers back to design line on top layer so that top layer can be hemmed to any layer beneath those that have been cut back. (The raw edges of the middle layers are encased when the top layer is hemmed down.)

**Appliqué pictures** give plenty of scope for the imagination, both in the composition and in the choice and mixture of fabrics.

The background fabric should not detract from the picture; a dull surface with a pleasing but not dominant texture is ideal. The straight grain should run the length of the picture. Allow enough fabric to be turned over the backing.

Design ideas can be taken from a wide variety of sources including children's books, posters and greetings cards. Trace the design on tracing paper for each shape and enlarge or reduce if required (see Embroidery p. 188). Cut shapes out, allowing for turnings where necessary (this depends on the type of appliqué to be worked), and pin shapes to chosen fabrics, to RS or WS as appropriate. Attach by hand or machine, by any of the above methods.

Hand embroider extra detail on attached motifs if desired. A variety of beads, buttons, sequins and paillettes

can also be sewn on to add interest.

To back picture, cut a piece of hardboard to size of picture. Stretch picture, RS up, over board and turn edges of background fabric over board. Mitre corners and glue edges to board. Glue a piece of strong paper or fabric to back of board to cover it. Alternatively, use a fabric backing such as calico. Turn in raw edges of background fabric, mitre corners and hem edges down to backing.

Fabrics of contrasting textures are combined to great effect in the appliqué picture *School class* by Ursula Ahrens. Surface stitching has been used to create the wide range of extremely boyish facial expressions and the master's equally magnificent moustache and hairstyle, as well as to break up the background patches to form a brick wall. The picture, dating from 1975, is in the Gallery for Folk Art, Munich.

# Patchwork

The ideal craft for anybody who enjoys hand sewing, patchwork is the formation of a new piece of fabric by joining small scraps of fabric in different colours and designs.

Patchwork is an ancient craft that probably began both as a thrifty way of using otherwise useless scraps of material and as a pleasant occupation. Little is known of its early history, but some years ago pieces of patchwork were found in a walled-up chapel in India which date back to the 6th and 9th centuries and were made by the same methods as patchwork today. In general there are few extant examples of patchwork which date back to before the 19th century.

Europeans who left their countries to settle in America from the 17th century onwards were certainly familiar with the craft and most probably carried patchwork quilts with them across the Atlantic as well as their knowledge of the craft. Patchwork remained particularly well loved in America and became an important feature of domestic life. In country districts, quilting parties, where friends and relatives met to join patchwork pieces or to finish a special quilt, were enjoyable social occasions.

Patchwork patterns were often peculiar to certain regions and many have fascinating names, such as "Bear's paw", "Rocky road to California" and "Duck's foot in the mud", reflecting local events and the environment. The same pattern may have different names according to where it is made. Many patterns popular in North America are identical to traditional patchwork designs in the North of England, which illustrates the continuity of the craft. Patchwork has remained

*Different shapes and fabrics are cleverly combined in this 19th-century patchwork picture to portray an attractive Stratford-upon-Avon shop. The half-timbered frontage is depicted in minute detail with light and dark squares of fabric and decorative stitching. Even the shadow beneath the upper-storey overhang is included. Full of ingenious ideas—scraps of lace become lace curtains, patterned fabric forms an amusing window display—the picture demonstrates the interesting and varied effects that can be achieved with patchwork.*

very much a home craft, as the time involved in stitching the individual pieces together has always prevented it from becoming a commercial proposition.

The appearance of patchwork depends on the shapes being meticulously stitched together so that they link perfectly to form the pattern. There are two basic methods of making patchwork. In the first, prepared patches, with seam allowances turned over the backing papers, are stitched together one by one. In the second method, overlapping patches are laid out on another piece of fabric, the foundation fabric, and stitched down.

The equipment needed for patchwork is readily available: a pair of sharp scissors for cutting fabric accurately; a sharp craft knife or scalpel for cutting backing papers; white basting cotton; fine sewing thread—use cotton on cotton fabrics, all-purpose or synthetic thread on synthetic fabrics and silk on silk; needles, sharps or betweens, sizes 8, 9 or 10 depending on the fabric; fine pins; a thimble; a soft pencil for marking shapes on the fabric; and templates for cutting out shapes. Patchwork pieces may also be joined by machine. It is often helpful to have an old cork mat or cork tile to hand when planning a design, so that when you have arranged the patches satisfactorily you can pin them down in position for the patchwork until needed.

For some patchwork designs firm paper is required for cutting the backing shapes for patches. Papers hold the patches firmly in shape until they are stitched together and are usually removed when the patchwork is complete. Alternatively, if an article needs extra body, cut backing shapes in iron-on interfacing and attach to the wrong side of the patches. These can be left in place when the patchwork is finished.

It is important to choose suitable fabrics for patchwork as its durability depends on the material used. Do not combine fabrics of different weights and thicknesses as the stronger fabrics tend to pull and strain the lighter. If mixing different fabrics, make sure they have the same washing and wearing qualities. Old and new fabrics can be used together, but check the old fabric is still strong by tugging it firmly in both directions, and wash new fabric before using it in patchwork in case of any shrinkage or colour loss.

Cotton and cotton mixtures are the best fabrics for a beginner as they combine well. Velvets and silks are more difficult to work with than other fabrics and should be used only when you are more experienced. They look splendid, however, on mounted patchwork such as crazy work, where they can be used together as the foundation fabric helps bear the strain of wear and tear.

Patchwork can be used to make a huge variety of items. Although the term is often thought of as referring only to quilts many other items, such as cushions, table-cloths, garments, bags and other accessories, can look very attractive in patchwork.

Successful patchwork depends not only on good technique but on a well-balanced design and a pleasing colour scheme. Many different shapes can be used, such as triangles, hexagons, diamonds, circles and squares. Experiment with new shapes to create unusual patterns. By the clever combination of different shapes and imaginative use of fabric patterns and colour, you will be able to create an infinite range of aesthetic and individual designs.

**Honeycomb** This rosette pattern is based on the hexagonal patch—a popular shape as its blunt angles make it easy to combine with other shapes. Seven hexagons are joined together to make a rosette.

**Diamond** A star pattern, each star being made with six diamonds. Diamonds also combine well with other shapes.

**Crazy** Different shapes and fabrics are stitched to foundation fabric. Detail from 1884 quilt by permission of the American Museum in Britain, Bath, and the Welsh Folk Museum.

**Log cabin** This pattern is made in separate squares which are then sewn together. Each square consists of strips of fabric stitched round a central square on foundation fabric.

*In America, as in Europe, every girl was expected to be a proficient seamstress. By the time of her betrothal it was customary for her to have twelve everyday patchwork quilt tops and a special bridal one. A quilting "bee", or party, was arranged and relatives gathered to celebrate and finish the bridal quilt as illustrated in this 19th-century American painting by an unknown artist.*

# Patchwork

## TEMPLATES

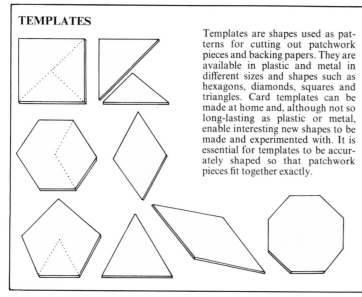

Templates are shapes used as patterns for cutting out patchwork pieces and backing papers. They are available in plastic and metal in different sizes and shapes such as hexagons, diamonds, squares and triangles. Card templates can be made at home and, although not so long-lasting as plastic or metal, enable interesting new shapes to be made and experimented with. It is essential for templates to be accurately shaped so that patchwork pieces fit together exactly.

Templates are often sold in pairs: one solid shape the exact size of the finished patch, used for cutting the backing papers, and one larger window template, for cutting fabric patches with seam turnings (**1**). The window template is 5 mm/$\frac{1}{4}$ in larger all round than the solid template and is shaped like a frame—the turning allowance is a solid border round a space the size of a finished patch. When the template is placed on the fabric any motif is visible as it will appear on the patch.

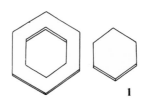

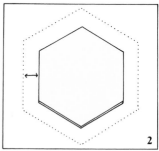

If you have only a solid template the size of the finished patch, make a window template to use with it for cutting backing papers. Place the solid template on a piece of card and draw round the outline. Draw a second outline 5 mm/$\frac{1}{4}$ in away and cut round both outlines to form the window template (**2**).

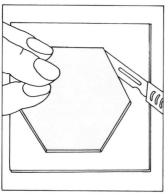

**Honeycomb** Prepare backing papers using a solid template the size of finished patch. Place template over one or two pieces of paper on a board. With a sharp knife cut firmly along each side of hexagon. Do not cut more than two papers together or the shapes will be inaccurate. Continue until required number is prepared.

**2.** Cut material patches using a window template. Place template on fabric with one side of hexagon on straight grain of fabric and make sure any fabric design is well positioned. Draw round outer edge of template with a pencil and cut out patch on this line with scissors.

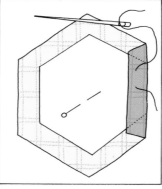

**3.** Place a backing paper exactly in centre of fabric hexagon on WS and pin. Hold patch with paper towards you. Fold turning allowance of one side over edge of paper, but do not fold paper. Crease fold and, beginning near centre of turning, take a long basting stitch through fabric and paper, leaving end of thread loose.

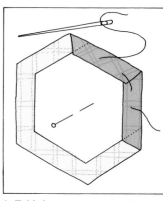

**4.** Fold down next turning in same way, overlapping corners. Make a basting stitch across corner with first turning and bring needle up again near next corner. Continue folding and basting down turnings in this way until sixth side is reached.

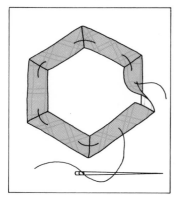

**5.** On sixth side, fold fabric and crease as before. Lift corner of first turning and tuck corner of sixth turning underneath. Secure with last basting stitch. Cut off thread leaving loose ends—this makes basting easier to remove. Remove pin. Press patch lightly on WS. Prepare required number of patches as above.

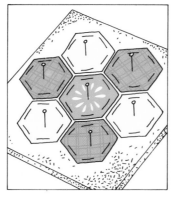

**Joining** Use the same basic method for joining most geometric shapes except diamonds and triangles. A good start for many articles is a rosette of honeycomb patches. Take seven patches which complement each other in colour and pattern. Arrange on a cork tile until satisfied with the design and then pin down to cork.

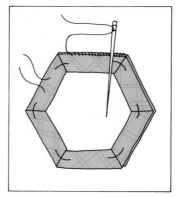

**2.** Place centre patch and one other RS together with corners matching exactly. With a fine needle and thread, oversew patches along one side, taking small stitches—16 to 18 to the inch. Take needle through edge of fabric only as the paper must be easy to remove. Start and finish stitching very securely.

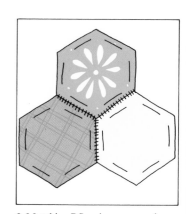

**3.** Matching RS and corners as above, join third patch to first two patches. When joining patches, take care to stitch whole length of seam and secure corners. Oversewing appears as straight stitches on RS and is part of the character of patchwork. Continue until all patches are attached round central patch.

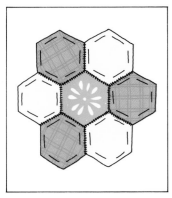

**4.** When the rosette is formed, remove basting and paper from central patch. As the basting is not held by knots or backstitches it is quickly removed. Leave other papers in position until the patches are surrounded on all sides. Press seams lightly on WS.

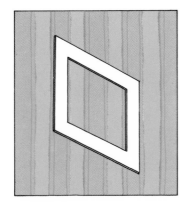

**Diamond** The lozenge diamond is based on the hexagon and measures the same across its width as along each side. Six of these diamonds make a six-pointed star. Cut backing papers as for hexagon using a diamond template. Cut fabric patches, placing template so that two opposite sides are parallel with straight grain of fabric.

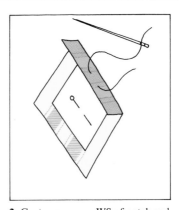

**2.** Centre paper on WS of patch and pin. Because some angles are sharper than those of hexagon, the folding procedure is different. Fold top right fabric turning over edge of paper, taking care not to roll paper. Hold with a long basting stitch, leaving a loose end, and bring needle out near top of diamond.

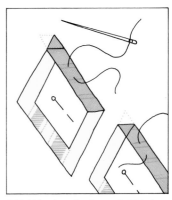

**3.** Fold back projecting end of fabric at top of diamond so that fold lies parallel with left side of diamond. Fold over the top triangular point of diamond and crease firmly.

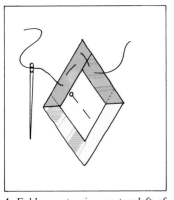

**4.** Fold over turning on top left of diamond, tucking folded point underneath. Secure with a basting stitch. Take another basting stitch and bring needle up near next angle. Fold turnings one under the other here as for honeycomb and baste to secure.

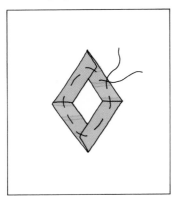

**5.** Fold bottom point of diamond in the same way as top and fold turnings one under the other as for honeycomb at fourth and last angle. Baste to secure and leave end of thread loose. Press each patch lightly on WS.

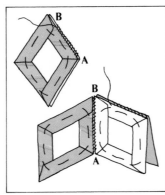

**Joining** Take six prepared patches and arrange design on cork as for honeycomb. Place two patches RS together, matching angles. Oversew from **A** to **B**. Open out and join third patch to central patch in same way. Make sure points meet exactly at centre. Lower sides of outside patches should form a straight edge.

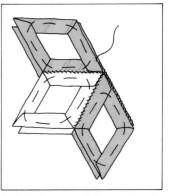

**2.** Join three remaining patches by same method. Place the two sets of patches RS together with points matching. Oversew along central join, checking that all six points meet neatly at centre of star.

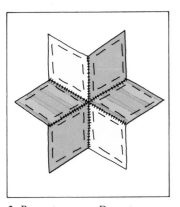

**3.** Press star open. Do not remove papers and basting until diamonds are stitched on all sides. This method applies also to triangles.

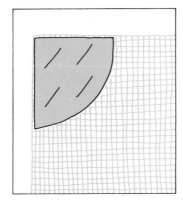

**Crazy** No templates or papers are required. Use fine cotton or muslin as foundation fabric and cut out whole shape, allowing about 4 cm/1½ in extra on required finished size. Cut patches of any size, shape and colour. At one corner of foundation fabric diagonally baste a right-angled patch into place, matching raw edges.

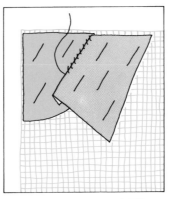

**2.** Place a second patch of different shape and colour so it overlaps or underlaps first patch. Diagonally baste in position. Turn under and hem or work running stitch on any raw edges not to be covered by other patches, to anchor them to foundation fabric. Finish thread securely. Patches may also be machined in place.

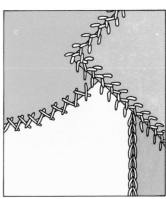

**3.** Continue overlapping and underlapping patches until foundation fabric is covered. Traditionally, crazy work is finished by embroidery such as herringbone, feather and chain stitches in matching or contrasting thread round each shape to cover joins. Embroidery may also be worked by machine. Press work on WS. ▶

207

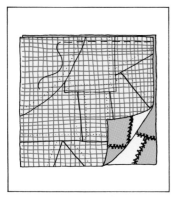

**4.** If making a large item such as a quilt, it may be easier to cut the foundation fabric into smaller squares. Stitch patches to squares. When squares are complete, place them RS together and stitch by hand or machine. Make sure colours and patterns are well distributed between squares.

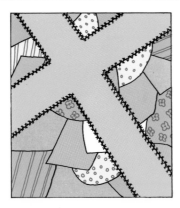

**5.** Alternatively, blocks of patchwork may be appliquéed separately to a large piece of background fabric which complements the patchwork in colour. Arrange patches at regular intervals so that background fabric forms a border round them. Fold under edges of background fabric and hem invisibly to make a border.

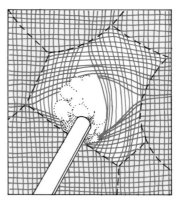

**6.** Small finished articles can be padded from the back with synthetic wadding or cotton wool. When cutting out fabric add about 5 cm/2 in to desired finished size to allow for extra fabric taken up by padding. Using a wooden skewer, push threads of foundation fabric apart in centre of shape and push in padding.

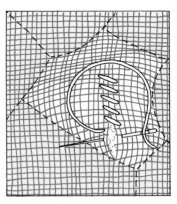

**7.** Work stuffing into corners of shape until it is well padded. Push parted threads of foundation fabric together again with wooden skewer. Alternatively, cut a small hole in back of shape to insert stuffing. Oversew hole neatly when shape is padded.

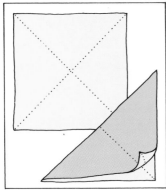

**Log cabin** Make a square template for foundation squares about 30 to 40 cm/ 12 to 15 in square if desired. Allow 1.25 cm/½ in all round for joining squares to make finished item. Cut foundation squares round template in firm cotton. Fold and press diagonally to find exact centre.

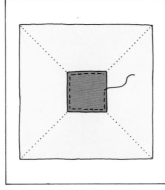

**2.** Cut small squares in patchwork fabric about 4 cm/1½ in square or slightly larger if desired. Matching centres pin a small square RS up on foundation square. Stitch round small square 5 mm/¼ in inside raw edges by hand, with running stitch, or by machine. Raw edges will be covered by patchwork strips.

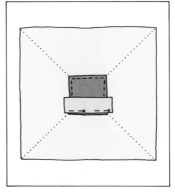

**3.** Cut strips of fabric on straight grain no less than 2.5 cm/1 in wide. Make some contrast, such as light fabrics on two sides of the square and dark on two sides. Cut a dark strip 2.5 cm/1 in longer than central square. Pin RS down on bottom edge of square, matching raw edges, with 1.25 cm/½ in protruding at each side.

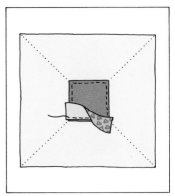

**4.** Allowing 5 mm/¼ in seam turnings, backstitch strip down, working through strip, central patch and foundation fabric. Roll strip towards you over stitching; do not pull it too tight. Press lightly and pin down to foundation fabric. Strips may also be attached by machine.

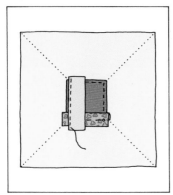

**5.** Cut a second strip in dark fabric long enough to extend over side edge of central square and end of first strip. Place RS down over side of square, matching raw edges and overlapping first strip. Pin, stitch and finish second strip as in (**4**).

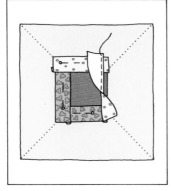

**6.** Cut a third strip in light fabric, long enough to cover top edge of central square and end of second strip. Attach to top edge as in (**4**). Cut a fourth strip in light fabric long enough to overlap both first and third strips. Pin to remaining free side of square, stitch and finish as first strip.

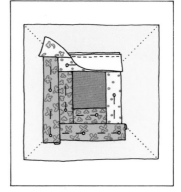

**7.** Attach second row of strips. Cut each strip to overlap in same way as first row of strips. Place light and dark fabric at the same sides each time. Place each strip RS down, matching raw edges with strip beneath. Remove pins from first row. Stitch strips with 5 mm/¼ in turnings as before, roll back and press. Pin down.

**8.** Continue until foundation square is covered. Fold final strips so that raw edges lie on edges of foundation square. To join foundation squares, place them RS together and backstitch or machine, making sure corners of squares correspond exactly and are securely stitched.

## FINISHING AND LINING

Perfect a beautiful piece of work and make it strong and long-lasting by finishing it well and lining it. Choose a weight of lining which is suitable both for the patchwork fabric and for the item: cotton poplin, linen and calico can be used to line quilts and coverlets, for example.

On some patchwork designs such as honeycomb, simply turn in the edges and hem them to the lining to give an

attractive shaped edge (1). Alternatively, turn the patch in half to give

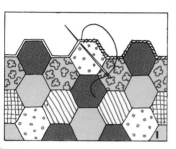

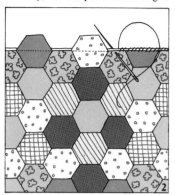

a straight edge and hem to lining (2). Quilts may also be finished by turning in the patchwork and lining so that the folded edges match exactly. Work a

row of neat running stitches 5 mm/¼ in from folded edge (3).

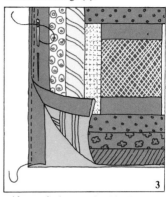

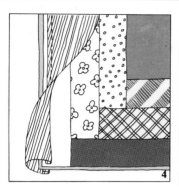

Alternatively, attach a binding strip to finish patchwork and lining edges (4). Covered piping cord can also be used and gives a strong finish.

To line a patchwork garment, lay patchwork on lining fabric and pin from centre, smoothing out lining to avoid creases. Cut out lining, allowing for seam turnings, and make up garment in usual way. If you have a pattern for the garment, use this to cut out the lining.

## SPECIAL EFFECTS

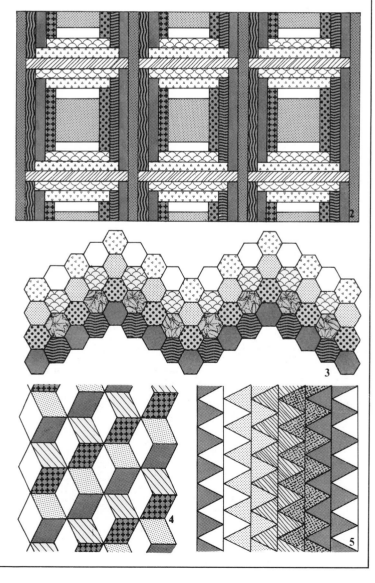

With imaginative use of colour and design, beautiful and interesting effects can be created in patchwork.

**1.** "Starburst", also referred to as "Star of Bethlehem", is made with the long diamond, which is narrower than the lozenge diamond. Eight long diamonds are needed to make a star. More diamonds are arranged in circles around the central star. The circles move from light to dark tones to create a radiating effect.

**2.** In this variation of log cabin blocks are arranged in a pattern known as "Courthouse steps". Light and dark strips are placed at opposite ends of

each square so, when the pattern is complete, the light strips stand out to create a pattern of their own.

**3.** This wave-like pattern is created by hexagons arranged in undulating lines. Light and dark tones are placed to accentuate the pattern.

**4.** The lozenge diamond based on the hexagon is used in this pattern known as "Baby blocks". Light and dark diamonds are arranged to give a three-dimensional cube-like effect.

**5.** Triangles in light and dark fabrics are juxtaposed to create attractive zigzag patterns.

# Beading

Beadwork, attaching beads to fabric in decorative patterns, is an attractive, traditional way of enhancing everyday and evening clothing and accessories. There are many ways of applying beads that, imaginatively worked, produce a beautiful effect and transform an ordinary garment into an original and individual one. For example, simple lines of beads can add interest, or more elaborate effects can be created by outlining or filling in shapes with beads and sequins. Period costumes, particularly those of the Elizabethan and Victorian eras, embroidery and even knitting patterns are some of the many sources of inspiration for beading designs.

Use the same methods for transferring a design to the fabric as for embroidery, but do not use embroidery transfers, which are difficult to remove. Avoid making permanent marks when transferring designs. Use an embroidery hoop to keep the fabric taut while attaching the beads. Always begin by securing the thread with a small backstitch on the wrong side of the fabric and fasten off in the same way. Do not make any of the stitches too tight or the fabric will pucker and the finished beadwork will be stiff and unattractive.

Many kinds of beads and sequins are available; choose those most suitable for the type and weight of the fabric to which they are to be attached. Before starting to bead an article, experiment on a scrap of the fabric with beads of different sizes, surface finishes and colours until a satisfactory effect is obtained.

Press beaded fabric carefully, as the finish of some beads may be dulled by heat and others are so delicate that heat and pressure may break them. Always press on the wrong side of the fabric, using a pressing pad or folded towel. If possible avoid pressing directly over the beads.

*From left to right: a fringed handbag from the 1920s, brightly decorated with rocaille and ceramic beads; the thirties clutch purse is made up in rocaille and bugle beads; dress trimming with crystal, bugle and rocaille beading.*

## EQUIPMENT

A selection of the many different types of beads available is illustrated. To attach beads, use a beading needle and a length of double thread coated with beeswax to prevent tangles. Match thread to the fabric: use synthetic threads for synthetic and other manmade fabrics, natural for natural fabrics.

*Beading needles are long and fine with a long eye. They are available in different sizes: use size 10 or 12 for attaching small beads and bugle beads, and size 9 for attaching larger beads and sequins.*

*Rocaille, or seed, beads are small glass beads slightly oval in shape. They are available in several different finishes, including opaque, transparent and metallic.*

*Bugle beads are long beads, some with a cut surface. Small bugle beads are also known as cut embroidery beads. Many bugle beads have a shiny or metallic finish.*

*Wood, pearl, ceramic and crystal beads can also be used to create interesting effects on beaded articles by imaginative use of their different textures.*

*Sequins are available in many different finishes, shapes and sizes and in a wide range of colours. They have a central hole through which they are stitched in place.*

*Paillettes are very large sequins, but have a hole at the edge instead of at the centre for attaching to fabric.*

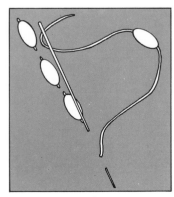

**Beads** For a scatter effect attach each bead individually. Secure thread on WS of fabric and take needle to RS. Pick up bead and make a backstitch, bringing needle into position for next bead and leaving bead on fabric. Attach heavy beads by this method even if not making a scattered pattern.

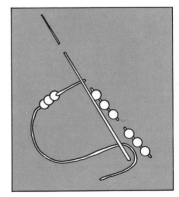

**2.** Make straight lines of small beads by picking up several beads at once. Secure thread on WS and take needle to RS. Pick up beads and make a running stitch, bringing needle into position for the next length of beads. The number of beads picked up depends on the size and weight of beads and the type of fabric.

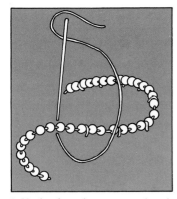

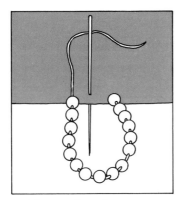

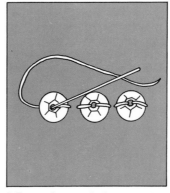


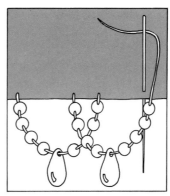

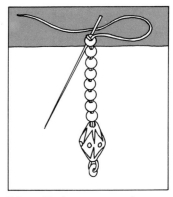

**3.** Use beads ready strung on a length of thread for making long, flowing lines in a design. To couch the beads on the surface of the fabric, secure thread on WS and take needle to RS. Stitch over the bead thread at intervals: between each bead if beads are large, or between every three beads if they are small.

**Bead loops** make scallop patterns or attractive edging. Secure thread on WS and bring needle to RS. Pick up beads, counting the number each time to ensure even loops, and place needle back into fabric to make the required width of loop. Do not pull thread too tight when making loops as they should not be rigid.

**2.** Overlap loops or space them out according to the effect desired. To accentuate the shape of the loops, place a larger bead in the centre of each loop.

**Fringes** Use in same way as loops or combine with loops. Secure thread on WS and take needle to RS. Pick up required number of small beads plus one larger bead. Take a small bead as an anchor for end of fringe, pass needle through it horizontally and back up through other beads. Secure thread at top of fringe on WS.

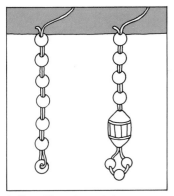

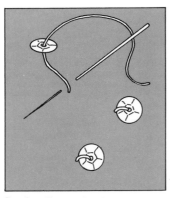

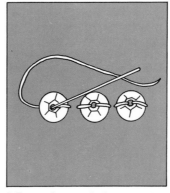

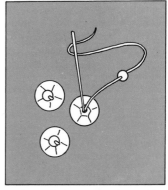

**2.** Vary fringes by omitting the large bead and using small beads only. Alternatively, attach three small anchor beads in a group at the base of the fringe for an attractive effect.

**Sequins** To apply single sequins, secure thread on WS, take needle to RS and pick up a sequin. Make a backstitch and, leaving sequin lying flat on fabric, bring needle up into position for next sequin. When all sequins are attached fasten off thread on WS of fabric.

**2.** To attach a row of adjacent sequins, secure thread on WS, bring needle to RS and pick up a sequin. Make a backstitch to right of central hole, bringing needle up to left of sequin. Replace needle in hole and make another backstitch, bringing needle up in centre of next sequin. At end of row fasten off on WS.

**3.** Alternatively, use a small matching or contrasting bead slightly larger than central hole to hold sequin. Secure thread on WS and bring needle up through central hole of sequin. Pick up bead and pass needle back into central hole. Secure thread on WS and proceed to next sequin.

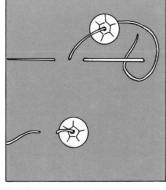

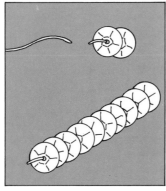

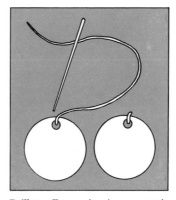

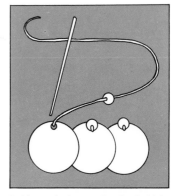

**Overlapping sequins** Secure thread on WS, take needle to RS and pick up sequin. With sequin on thread, make a backstitch half the diameter of the sequin and bring needle forward the same amount into position for next stitch. Pull thread through so sequin lies on fabric with stitch to left of central hole.

**2.** Attach next sequin in same way so that it overlaps the first and conceals the holding stitch. Continue until required area is covered and fasten thread off on WS.

**Paillettes** For overlapping rows apply as for sequins. To attach singly, secure thread on WS and take needle to RS through hole near edge of paillette. Take a stitch over edge of paillette into fabric and secure on WS.

**2.** Alternatively, use a bead to hold the paillette. Secure thread on WS and bring needle to RS through both paillette hole and bead. Replace needle into fabric at edge of paillette and secure thread on WS.

# Repairs

Repairing becomes necessary either because an area of fabric has given way as a result of constant wear or washing or because of accidents such as burns, tears or shrinking.

Wear in certain clothes, for example trousers and jackets, can often be foreseen and vulnerable areas such as knees and elbows can be reinforced with patches, either on the wrong side or, decoratively, on the right side. All repairs to worn areas are easier to manage before holes have formed in the fabric. Part of the good fabric must, however, be covered as well as the worn area; otherwise, the repair is stronger than the rest of the garment and creates more worn areas. It is not usually worth making a careful repair in one area if the fabric is weakening all over.

When repairing, use fabric that has already been washed and even worn. Old garments can often be cut up for this purpose. If a repair is needed at a point of strain, try to reinforce the whole area to stop the problem recurring. Use thread that is the same or finer than that used originally and take plenty of stitches. Generally, repairs intended to be unnoticed should be hand stitched rather than machined, but on furnishings machined repairs are stronger and look more professional.

The choice of repair depends on the degree and area of wear. Very small areas can be darned, but, except on knitwear, darning is not strong. Larger areas should be patched, or complete sections,

## SUEDE, LEATHER AND FUR

Suede, leather and fur are produced from animal skins or manufactured synthetically. The natural versions are limited in size and come in odd shapes that may have to be adapted to meet your requirements; the synthetic versions are manufactured in standard widths, usually between 145 and 160 cm/58 and 64 in, and have straight edges.

For easy sewing and professional results certain pieces of special equipment are needed, as well as the usual items.

**Leather needles** Available for both machine, below, and hand sewing, bottom, these needles have points that cut the fabric rather than force

holes. Use for real and synthetic leather and suede and real fur.

**Trimming (Stanley) knife or razor blade** Use to cut real fur. Place fur WS up and slice carefully through the skin only.

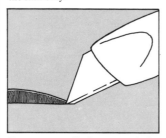

**Transparent adhesive tape, clothes pegs and paper clips** Use these aids instead of pins and basting on real and synthetic suede and leather and on real fur to avoid making holes that will show in the skins.

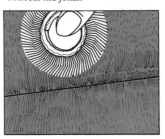

**Teazle brush or suede shoe brush** Use to raise the surface of fur fabric after stitching open seams and so conceal the joins.

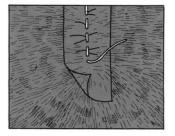

**Cellophane** If machining is necessary on RS of fur or fur fabric, place cellophane between fur and machine foot to prevent the pile being caught up.

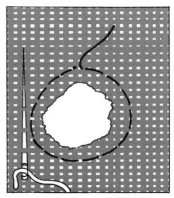

**Adhesive** Stick down seam turnings and hems in leather and suede with adhesive. If possible, try out the

adhesive on a piece of material to make sure it does not show on RS.

**Chalk, scissors and thread** For real or synthetic suede or leather or fur fabric, spread pattern out on WS of the material, placing all pieces in one direction so the pile is facing the same way, and mark round them with tailor's chalk to avoid using pins. Use large scissors for cutting out, cutting each piece singly and reversing the pattern to cut a second piece. Cut bulky fur fabric with extra seam allowances. Before stitching real or synthetic fur, trim the pile from seam allowances with small scissors to reduce bulk. For machining all types of leather, suede and fur, use synthetic thread for strength; use beeswaxed thread for hand sewing. Attach buttons with ordinary button thread.

Use open seams for fur fabric and open or welt seams for real or synthetic leather or suede. There is no need to neaten the seam edges, but trim them level after pressing. No seam allowance is needed for real fur; join edges by oversewing. Press real suede and leather on WS of garment only, using a dry iron over brown paper. With synthetics, experiment on a spare piece of fabric — try a steam iron on WS. Fur should not need any pressing, but some bulky fur fabrics may benefit from light pressing, on WS only, using a damp muslin pressing cloth.

Choose fastenings to suit the material. Large hooks and eyes are available for fur. Other suitable fastenings for fur, suede and leather are large zips with plastic teeth or zips that are totally concealed (keep fur pile well away from the teeth); Velcro; metal-capped stud buttons; eyelets and laces; frogs or buttons and worked loops of millinery elastic. Avoid buttonholes as they are difficult to work on fur, suede and leather garments.

such as trouser hems, may be removed and replaced with matching or contrasting fabric.

Repairs to burns and tears are more difficult to deal with. If they cannot be made invisible, make features of them by using contrasting fabric or adding items such as cuffs or pocket flaps in the same or contrasting fabric. If clothes and furnishings have shrunk, it is often better to lengthen them with contrasting fabric rather than to let down the hem, because hemline marks may show. Press all finished repairs to improve their appearance.

## DARNING BY HAND

Select thread that matches perfectly the colour of the item to be darned. It should be slightly thinner than the original thread as the darn will be thicker than its surround. Darning wool is thinner than ordinary wool. On woven fabrics it may be possible to use yarn pulled from spare fabric or from the hem. This gives a perfect colour match although it makes a thicker darn. Use a long piece of thread and a long needle — a sharps or, for wool, a darning or tapestry needle. Spread the area to be darned over your fingers or over a darning mushroom. Darn on the right side.

*Douglas Tempest's unliberated tot repairs frenziedly, perpetuating the myth that a woman's place is behind a man.*

**Darning fabric or knitting** Work a circle or oval of running stitches round the worn area or hole to mark its extent and cut off thread. Beginning at left of worn area, just outside marking stitches, work running stitches in vertical line to just beyond marking on opposite side. weaving needle in and out of fabric.

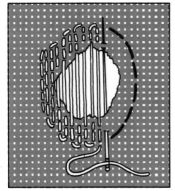

**2.** Leave a loop of thread at end of row, so darn is not too tight, and continue weaving backwards and forwards across hole, keeping threads parallel. At beginning of rows insert needle over and under raw edge of hole alternately. Work each row to slightly beyond the marked area.

## DARNING BY MACHINE

Machine darning is most often used for repairs on household linen, but is also suitable for garments and socks. This method is ideal for worn areas, but on holes the machining has to be worked so closely that it can produce a hard area. Use darning foot, below, and machine embroidery thread.

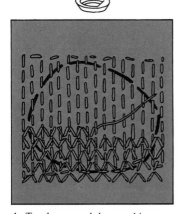

**4.** To darn wool by machine, use woollen thread and work first rows of stitching as for normal machine darning. Work second set of stitching in zigzag stitch and do not work a third set of stitching, even if darning a hole.

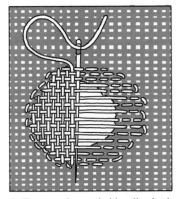

**3.** Turn work so stitching lies horizontally. Starting at point where needle has emerged, weave needle alternately over and under each of the previously laid threads, starting and finishing each row as in (**2**). Work over whole area. To finish, take thread to WS and run it in and out of fabric beside darn until secure.

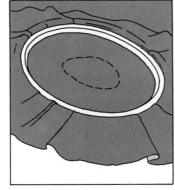

**1.** Lower feed teeth mechanism and set stitch length indicator to 0. Insert fabric RS up in an embroidery hoop by placing it over outer ring of hoop and pushing inner ring down slightly below outer one so fabric lies flush on machine bed. Mark area to be darned with a circle or an oval of running stitches in matching thread.

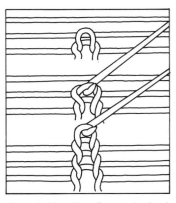

**Jersey ladders** Use a fine crochet hook or a special latched hook. On RS catch loop at base of ladder and loop it over bar of yarn above it. Catch that bar, loop it over next bar, and so on. If ladder ends in a hole, anchor final loop firmly in darn. If not, pull final loop to WS and anchor with several backstitches.

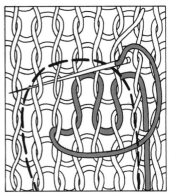

**Swiss darning on knitting** Use to repair a worn area before hole has formed. Mark extent of worn area as for standard darn. Start with two running stitches on RS just outside worn area, working towards top of area. Starting at top and working horizontally from right to left, pick up loops following formation of knitting.

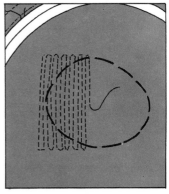

**2.** Place hoop under machine foot, lower needle into edge of worn area and lower foot. Hold outside of hoop with thumbs and little fingers. Machine to opposite edge, moving hoop to position each stitch. Use other fingers for additional control within hoop. Work further parallel rows fairly close together.

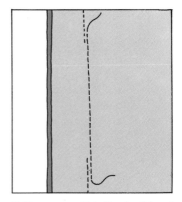

**Split open seam** Cut off ends of thread if stitch has broken. Machine seam up, overlapping original stitching by at least 5 cm/2 in at each end. Fasten off firmly. On jersey fabric restitch split area of seam using synthetic thread and a small zigzag stitch.

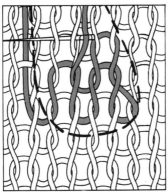

**2.** At end of first row turn work upside down so end of first row is on the right. Again following the knitting loops, work a second row to link with the first, as shown. Continue until whole area is reinforced. Finish off thread on WS with a row of running stitches beside darn.

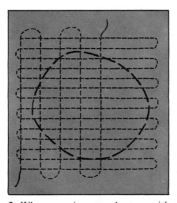

**3.** When area is covered, stop, with needle in fabric. Raise foot, turn hoop and lower foot again. Stitch back and forth across the first rows but allow more space between lines. If darning a hole, turn fabric again and work a third, vertical set of stitching over hole. Remove work, take fabric out of hoop and cut threads.

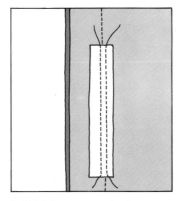

**2.** If fabric seems weak where seam has broken or if fabric has split, baste a strip of narrow tape or seam binding along seam, overlapping original stitching by 3 cm/1¼ in at each end. Stitch through tape and seam. Work two rows of stitching for strength.

# Repairs

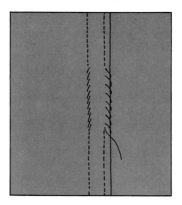

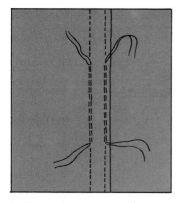

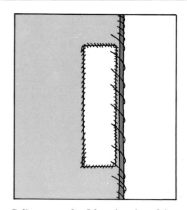

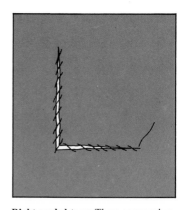

**Split machine fell seam** A repair often needed on jeans. On old jeans the easiest method is to hem the seam edges closely by hand on both RS and WS. If thread from original stitching is hanging loose, thread it into a needle and backstitch to match original stitches.

**2.** On new jeans or to repair a very visible split, thread machine with heavy top-stitching thread in matching colour or with two reels of normal sewing thread and machine split section on RS with a large stitch. Take all thread ends through to WS and finish by threading them into a needle and working backstitches.

**Split seam on fur** Often the edge of the skin gives way rather than the thread. Unpick any more of the seam that appears weak. Place a length of seam binding or tape over weak seam area on WS. Turn under tape ends and hem tape in position. Oversew seam edges RS together, taking needle through fur and tape.

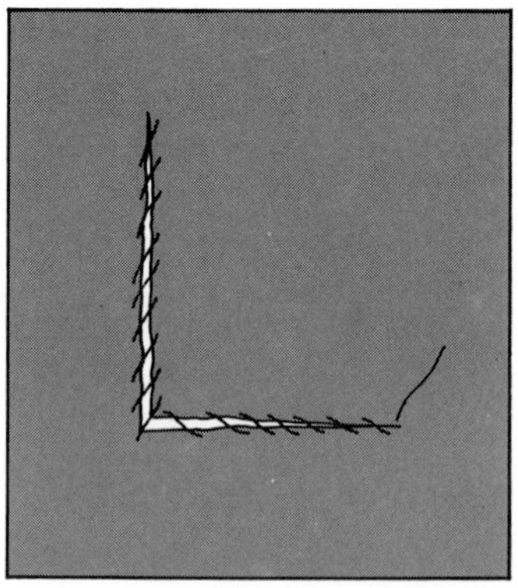

**Right-angled tears** These occur when the fabric catches on something sharp and both warp and weft threads give way. If the fabric is not very worn, the edges can be drawn together by running stitch. Use matching thread and begin by loosely oversewing the two raw edges together on RS.

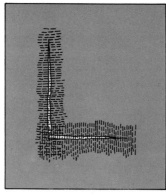

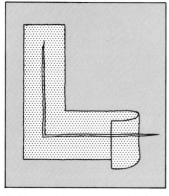

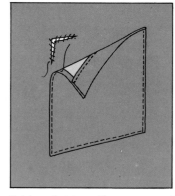

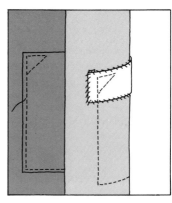

**2.** On RS work horizontal rows of close running stitch from top of tear down to angle and a little beyond. Vary length of rows to make darn less obvious. Fasten off thread on WS and begin again on RS at other end of tear. Work rows of running stitches as far as corner and a little beyond and fasten off thread.

**3.** On an old garment, work a large close zigzag stitch on RS to draw edges together. Alternatively, diagonally baste raw edges of tear together and press lightly. Remove basting and press to ensure edges meet. Cut an L-shaped piece of adhesive interfacing slightly larger than tear and iron on to WS.

**Patch pocket tears** Frequent use of these pockets often results in a hole in the garment fabric at the top corners. Unpick stitching at these corners. Darn tear or, if it is small, oversew raw edges together. Cut a strip of seam binding, tape or firm interfacing 3 cm/1¼ in longer than width of pocket.

**2.** Place strip on WS of garment level with pocket top. Turn in ends and attach by hemming all round or, if using iron-on interfacing, press in position. Restitch pocket corners firmly by hand or machine, working through pocket, garment and tape reinforcement.

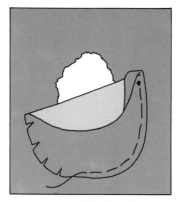

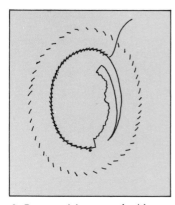

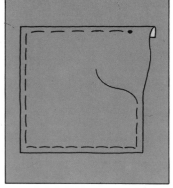

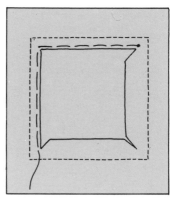

**Garment patch** Take fabric from hem or modify style to provide spare fabric. Cut patch at least 3 cm/1¼ in larger than needed, matching grain of fabric and pattern, if any, with garment area. Trim patch to a square or an oval. Place RS up over RS of hole or worn area. Baste, turning in edges 5 mm/¼ in and snipping curves.

**2.** Press, and hem round with very small stitches. On WS trim away surplus fabric within patch to a width of 4 mm/⅛ in. Overcast raw edges to neaten them.

**Household patch** Ideal on bedlinen, tea towels and other household items, this patch is machined for strength. Take fabric from another similar article for patch or use new fabric that has been washed. Cut a rectangular patch 3 cm/1¼ in larger than worn area. Baste in position, turning in edges 3 mm/⅛ in. Press.

**2.** Machine close to edge all round patch, using straight or zigzag stitch. Remove basting. On WS trim surplus worn fabric within patch to 1.5 cm/⅝ in. Make 1.25 cm/½ in snips into corners. Turn in raw edges and baste. Press. Machine on fold. Remove basting and press.

**Quick hard-wearing patch** Apply purchased patches of adhesive-backed denim or motifs. Press patch or motif RS up into position on RS of fabric and work loop stitch or machine zigzag round the edge. Trim away surplus fabric on WS and loop stitch, overcast or zigzag raw edges to neaten.

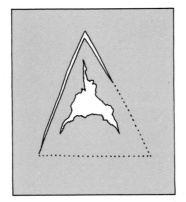

**Patching fur** On WS mark round hole or worn area with chalk in a triangular or oval shape. Using a trimming knife or razor blade, cut out this shape on WS. Lay it WS down on WS of new piece of fur and, matching colour and grain, cut out a new shape.

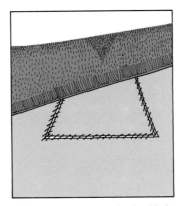

**2.** Slot this RS up into back of hole and apply impact adhesive to cut edges to hold them in place. When adhesive is dry oversew edges together on WS.

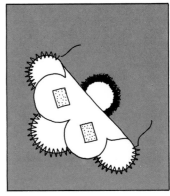

**Burn holes** For an effective yet attractive repair, cover hole with a form of decoration suitable for garment, such as rows of braid or pieces of appliqué. Attach appliqué motifs with pieces of fabric adhesive, press in place and embroider by hand or machine round outer edge. Attach braid by hand or machine.

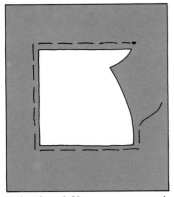

**Tailored patch** Use on garments such as suits and coats. Cutting exactly on straight grain, trim away worn area of fabric into a rectangular shape. On checked fabric cut exactly on line of check. Make snips of 1.25 cm/½ in into corners, turn edges under to WS, baste and press.

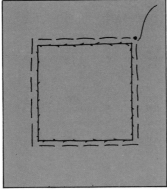

**2.** Cut a piece of fabric 3 cm/1¼ in larger all round than hole, with grain and pattern, if any, exactly matching garment area. Place patch RS up behind prepared hole and baste in position. Using basting thread, slip stitch on RS between patch and folded garment edge to hold patch in place. Remove basting.

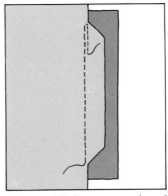

**3.** Turn to WS. Open out raw edges of garment and patch where slip stitching appears. Join edges by hand or machine on slip stitching, sewing each edge separately and reversing at end of each edge.

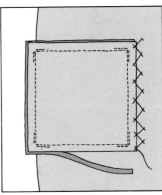

**4.** On WS trim edges to 5 mm/¼ in and then trim underneath edge a little more. Press flat and press turnings outwards from patch. Herringbone on WS to hold down raw edges.

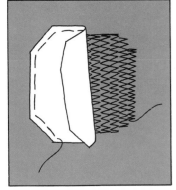

**Reinforcing knees** Apply decorative patches to RS of new clothes. Use shaped motifs, quilted fabric or make patch pockets. If a hole has formed, patch on WS before patching RS. If area is worn, reinforce with rows of zigzag machining parallel with straight grain of fabric before adding decorative patch to RS.

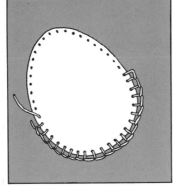

**Reinforcing with suede and leather** An ideal method for worn jacket elbows. Pre-cut patches are available, often with holes round edge to aid sewing. Alternatively, cut oval patches and machine round edge without thread to make holes. Position patch and, using buttonhole thread, loop stitch patch to sleeve through holes.

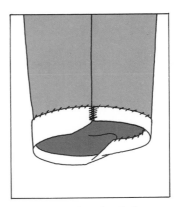

**2.** To reinforce frayed cuff edges on a jacket, cut a strip of leather about 2 to 2.5 cm/¾ to 1 in wide for each cuff. Apply to RS of cuff first, starting level with sleeve seam and hemming along top edge. Trim ends of leather level and oversew together. Fold leather over to WS of cuff so it encases cuff edge and hem in place.

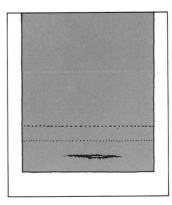

**Worn trouser hems** On trousers with turn-ups unpick turn-ups and press out all hem and turn-up creases. Try trousers on and turn up to correct length. Trim surplus fabric and finish with conventional hem. ▶

# Repairs

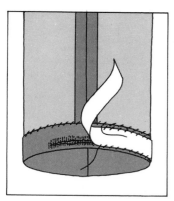

**2.** If trousers are worn because they are too long, unpick hems and press flat. Draw together fraying edges with hand or machine darning. Turn up hem so trousers are 3 to 5 mm/$\frac{1}{8}$ to $\frac{1}{4}$ in shorter than before. Reinforce WS with trouser kick tape. Position tape 2 mm/$\frac{1}{16}$ in from bottom of trouser hem and hem all round.

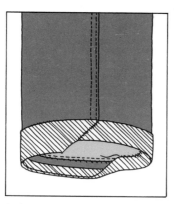

**3.** On casual trousers or jeans repair worn hems by binding bottom edge with purchased binding. Apply binding so it encases worn edge.

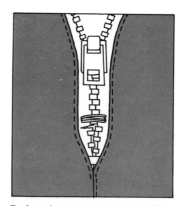

**Broken zip**—temporary repair. If zip teeth part, take slider to zip base. On side that has come away from slider snip into tape below last visible tooth. Lift that tooth and slot it firmly into top of slider. Move slider up to close teeth. At top of remaining gap work a strong bar tack into tape across teeth.

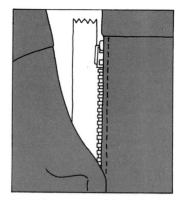

**Zip replacement** Unpick broken zip, noting how it was inserted. Remove old thread ends. Press opening edges, keeping them folded under. Baste in new zip and machine or prick stitch following original stitching lines. Work any extra rows of stitching needed to hold layers together. Remove basting. Press.

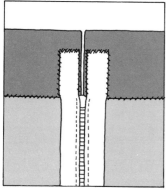

**2.** If tape ends of original zip were included in waistband, cut off old zip at base of band. When inserting new zip, lay it in position with tape ends on back of band and hem ends into position all round.

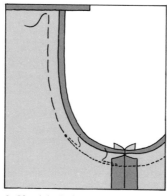

**3.** If original zip was curved and a replacement curved zip is unobtainable, buy a straight zip that is slightly shorter than the original one. Remove old zip, baste opening and sew up bottom, curved part of seam by machine or with prick stitch. This will leave a straight seam into which the new straight zip can be inserted.

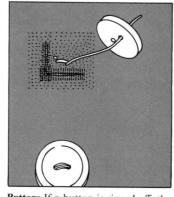

**Buttons** If a button is ripped off, the fabric may also tear. Remove button and all adhering thread. On a lined garment, slip a piece of iron-on interfacing through tear, bring edges of tear together and press interfacing in place. Repair tear by right-angled tear method. Replace button.

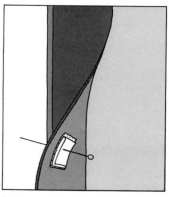

**2.** If garment is unlined, lift or unpick outer edge of facing and pin a piece of interfacing and a square of folded tape or seam binding on WS of facing at button position. Settle button on RS, remove pin and sew on button through interfacing, tape and facing.

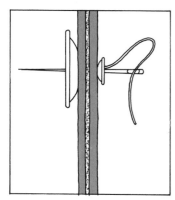

**3.** If several buttons have come off, remove all buttons. Lift or unpick facing and insert a strip of iron-on interfacing down opening on WS of facing. Replace facing, machining if necessary. Sew on all buttons; on leather or suede add a small button on WS behind each top button and sew through both.

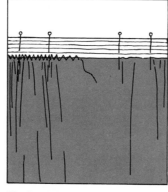

**Elastic edging** Unpick worn elastic and attach open-weave or ribbed elastic with a plain edge, measured and cut to required length. Join ends with zigzag stitch. Stretch elastic and pin bottom edge at intervals to RS of garment. Zigzag over bottom edge of elastic, keeping it stretched as you stitch. Remove pins.

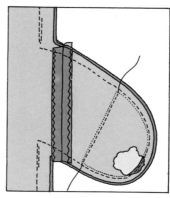

**Pocket bag** To mend a hole in the bottom, buy a pack of replacement bag sections, which are usually nylon with cotton edges. With garment WS out, slip new bag piece WS out into pocket. If new piece is adhesive, press it into place; if not, turn under top edges and machine or hem to pocket. Trim away worn part.

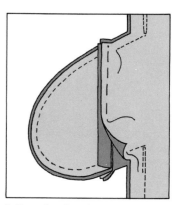

**2.** To replace bag, buy a pack of new bags. With garment WS out, unpick stitching joining worn bag to pocket edging. Remove bag. With new bag WS out, turn top edges back to WS. Place pocket edging over turned-back edges and baste together. Turn pocket RS out and hem bag to edging on basted join. Remove basting.

# Machine Faults

If your machine fails to operate correctly, the fault may be electrical or mechanical, but it is far more likely to be caused by the needle or thread, and can, therefore, be easily remedied. The main faults are given below with, where appropriate, a general remedy. If this remedy does not overcome the problem, check each point listed until the fault is diagnosed. All remedies are listed in italics.

## MOTOR DOES NOT RUN BUT LIGHT FUNCTIONS
*Power is reaching the machine if the light comes on so the problem is caused by motor failure, which must be dealt with by a dealer.*

## NEITHER MOTOR NOR LIGHT WORK
● Plug into machine, foot control or wall socket may not be fully pushed home.
● Faulty fuse or wiring in plugs.
● Main house fuse has blown.
● Area power failure.
*If power is still not reaching the machine, consult a dealer.*

## EXCESSIVE NOISE IN SEWING
*Insert a new or smaller needle.*
● Poor-quality oil or oil not intended for sewing machines may have solidified.
*Clean and oil thoroughly, but if noise continues, have poor oil flushed out by a dealer.*

## MACHINE WORKS TOO SLOWLY
*Open up machine and oil it.*
● On two-speed machines, speed indication may be on minimum.
*Check and regulate if necessary.*
● Machine out of use for some time, or stored in a cold room.
*Keep running until it warms up.*
● Something, e.g. reel of thread, may have rolled under foot control, so preventing you pushing it right down.
● Tension belt too tight.
*Must be corrected by dealer.*
● Motor not running properly.
*Consult a dealer.*

## NEEDLE DOES NOT MOVE
*Tighten wheel, which may have been loosened for bobbin winding.*
● An end of thread or dust may be caught in bobbin case.
*Remove dust or thread and check bobbin is correctly inserted.*

## MACHINE JAMS AFTER MAKING ONE OR TWO STITCHES
● Ends of thread or fluff trampled in and tangled under needle plate.
*Clean out plate area thoroughly.*
● Thread caught in bobbin case.
*To release it, remove plate and bobbin unit and gently rock hand wheel back and forth until you can see the thread. Pull the thread out.*
● Machine incorrectly threaded up.
*Check handbook and rethread.*
● Fibres of fraying material tangled under needle plate or in bobbin socket.
*Clean out plate area thoroughly.*

● Fabric not completely under presser foot.
*Adjust so fabric edges farther under foot.*

## MACHINE RUNS BUT NO STITCHES FORM
● Needle has come unthreaded.
*Make sure take-up lever is at high position to start and rethread.*
● Needle is wrong way round, or not tight up in socket.
*Unscrew and adjust.*
● Bobbin has run out.
*Remove and fill.*

## FABRIC DOES NOT FEED THROUGH
● Incorrect foot inserted for stitch (satin stitches get caught up if wrong foot is used).
*Change to correct foot.*
● Teeth may accidentally have been lowered.
*Raise to usual sewing position.*
● Machine bed damp, causing fabric to stick.
*Polish bed and sprinkle talcum powder on it.*

## WRINKLED STITCHING
*Place tissue paper or thin typing paper over teeth and over top of fabric.*
● Needle bent, too large for fabric, of poor quality and roughly finished, or ball-point needle being used on woven fabrics.
*Replace with new, correct needle.*
● Thread too coarse for fabric.
*Replace with suitable thread.*
● Incorrect foot inserted for stitch.
*Replace with correct foot.*
● Stitch too wide or too long for fabric.
*Adjust stitch size until it suits fabric.*
● Top tension too tight.
*Adjust tension screw if the machine has one. Otherwise check handbook for method of adjusting tension.*
● Pressure too great for thickness of fabric.
*If machine has a pressure screw, loosen slightly. If there is no screw, the machine should be self-adjusting; consult a dealer.*
● Teeth set too high.
*As a temporary measure, lower teeth slightly by turning knob towards darning position; have the setting adjusted properly by a dealer.*

## OCCASIONAL MISSED STITCHES
*If sewing on fine silky jersey, try a ball-point needle; lower the teeth very slightly; change to a different type of thread; or put tissue paper or typing paper under fabric.*
● Needle blunt, bent or too fine for fabric.
*Replace with new, correct needle.*
● Needle incorrectly inserted.
*Check handbook and reinsert.*
● Top tension too tight.
*Adjust tension screw if the machine has one. Otherwise check handbook for method of adjusting tension.*
● Pressure too high for fabric.
*If machine has a pressure screw, loosen slightly. If there is no screw, the machine should be self-adjusting; consult a dealer.*
● Starting off too violently.
*Use hand wheel.*

## NEEDLE BREAKS
● Needle bent or too fine for fabric.
*Replace with new, correct needle.*
● Needle loose.
*Unscrew and insert firmly.*
● Knot in thread.
*Cut off knotted section and rethread machine.*
● Bobbin case incorrectly inserted.
*Check handbook and reinsert.*
● Presser foot loose.
*Tighten screw attaching it to machine.*
● Zigzag stitch worked with unsuitable straight stitch foot, e.g. zip foot.
*Use zigzag foot or general straight stitch foot.*
● Pulling out fabric without raising needle.
*Always raise both needle and presser foot at end of stitching before removing fabric.*
● Pins left in fabric.
*Sew over them slowly if they are at right angles to stitching line or remove completely.*
● Approaching a thick area too fast (this cannot happen with an electronic foot).
*Slow down and, if area is very thick, use hand wheel to bring needle into layers of material.*
● Pulling material and bending needle.
*Do not pull fabric faster than machine sews.*

## TOP THREAD BREAKS
● Needle blunt, rough, or incorrect for fabric.
*Insert new, correct needle.*
● Needle inserted wrongly.
*Unscrew and adjust position.*
● Knot in thread.
*Cut off knotted section and rethread machine.*
● Thread caught twice round take-up lever or other part.
*Rethread.*
● Wrong thread for fabric.
*Replace with suitable thread.*
● Thread has dried out due to long storage in unfavourable conditions.
*Rethread with new thread.*
● Hole in needle plate rough.
*Ask dealer to smooth it or supply new plate.*
● Top tension too tight.
*Adjust tension screw if the machine has one, or check handbook for method of adjusting.*

## BOTTOM THREAD BREAKS
● Bottom thread caught up.
*If the bobbin is the two-piece type, check that the pieces are properly aligned and joined. Otherwise remove bobbin and reinsert as it may have been wrongly inserted.*
● Knot in thread.
*Cut off knotted section and rethread.*
● Top or bottom incorrectly threaded.
*Check handbook and rethread.*
● Bobbin overfilled.
*Cut off surplus thread.*
● Tension on bobbin case too tight.
*Adjust screw on bobbin case.*
● Bobbin wound unevenly.
*Rewind.*
● Fluff in bobbin case.
*Remove and brush out case and bobbin area.*
● Rough edges on bobbin case.
*Buy a new one.*

# Natural Fibres

| FIBRE | CHARACTERISTICS | USES | CARE |
|---|---|---|---|

**Cotton** Fibres have been extracted from the boll, or seed pod, of the cotton plant for several thousand years. Cotton is still the most widely used textile fibre.

Various types of cotton yarn are produced depending on such factors as climate and soil. Length of staple fibre varies between 2 cm/$\frac{3}{4}$ in and 5 cm/2 in. Egyptian and Sea Island fibres are generally long; North American and Indian fibres are short. All cotton fibres are thin, fairly smooth, soft to wear, absorbent and very strong (their strength increases by 25 per cent when wet). Can be dyed, glazed and mothproofed, as well as given many other finishes. Flammable and creases easily unless specially treated.

Sporting and warm-weather attire, underwear, towels, shirts, dresses, sheets, children's clothes and protective clothing.

Hard-wearing so can be washed frequently. White cotton can be bleached and boiled. Iron slightly damp with a hot iron until quite dry. Do not leave cotton damp as it is subject to mildew.

**Linen** An ancient fibre taken from the stem of the flax plant. Grown principally in the Soviet Union, Ireland, Belgium and Holland.

Length of staple fibre varies from 15 cm/5$\frac{1}{2}$ in to 1 metre/1 yard, depending on length of flax plant stem. Slightly uneven texture and dull in appearance. Expensive, but is very strong and highly absorbent. A good conductor of heat, it feels cool to the touch. Fabrics crease easily, so dress linens should be treated to make them crease resistant. Burns easily.

Tea towels, tablelinen in evenweave or damask fabric, best-quality bedlinen, shirts, dresses, suits and men's tropical suits.

Wash often, bleaching white linens. Iron fabric while evenly damp with a hot iron.

**Silk** An ancient and expensive fibre, produced by the silkworm. Although the cultivated silkworm can spin almost one mile of continuous filament on one cocoon, the filament has to be carefully unwound and spun into yarn. Primarily produced in Japan, China, the Soviet Union, India and Italy.

Removal of sericin, a gummy substance in the raw filament, gives silk its expensive lustrous appearance and may reduce its weight by as much as one-third. Weight loss is compensated for by addition of metallic salts. Some silk, such as taffeta, is heavily weighted, some, such as crêpe de Chine, less so; the amount of weighting gives the fabric its firmness. Spun silk is made from shorter, waste lengths of filament and is less expensive. Wild silk is reeled from the tusser moth and produces a rough, irregular filament. All silk is very strong, soft, smooth and comfortable next to the skin. It is extremely elastic and does not tear easily. A poor conductor of heat, it feels warm to the touch.

Scarves, dresses, suits, shirts, evening wear and ceremonial dress, nightwear and underwear. Fabrics made from silk fibre include crêpe de Chine, georgette, chiffon, twill and jersey.

Wash gently in warm water and pure soap flakes or dry clean before it is very soiled. Creases easily so do not squeeze or wring out. Iron cultivated silk when damp with a warm iron; iron wild silk when completely dry.

**Wool** The wool from the fleece of sheep has been used for clothing since earliest times. The best wool comes from the shoulders of the sheep. Australia supplies one-third of the world's wool.

Cylindrical but scaly, with a natural crimp; still air is trapped under the scales insulating the body against heat loss and making the fibre feel warm to the touch. Fibre length varies from 4 cm/2 in to 40 cm/15 in; it is fine or coarse depending on the type of sheep. Extremely resilient and absorbent.
   There are two kinds of yarn: woollen and worsted. Woollen yarns, made mainly from the shorter fibres, are thick and fluffy with a hairy surface. Worsted yarns, made only from the longer fibres, produce a smoother, clearer pattern when woven and can be printed. Both can be woven in any pattern, and mix and blend well with all other fibres. The label pure new wool indicates that the yarn has not been reprocessed or reclaimed, either by combing and carding old woollen cloth, or by using the combings and scraps left over from the processing of the fleece.

Woollen yarn is made into dress-, skirt- and coat-weight fabrics, and into blankets and furnishing fabrics. It is excellent for overcoats and raincoats. Worsted yarn is made into expensive men's suitings.

The scales on the fibre become entangled during frequent and incorrect washing. Woollen cloth varies in its finish; much of it is now processed so that it is machine washable. Follow label instructions carefully. To wash by hand, wash, rinse and squeeze gently in warm water. Do not soak or bleach. Dry without stretching the garment. If necessary, press lightly with a warm iron on WS.

*Alice and the wool-knitting sheep, in Sir John Tenniel's illustration for* Alice Through the Looking Glass.

*Watermelon grins cruelly belie the backbreaking reality of cottonpicking.*

# Manmade Fibres

| FIBRE | CHARACTERISTICS | USES | CARE |
|---|---|---|---|
| **Acetate** One of the cellulosic group of fibres. Not available in fibre form until 1918. Made by dissolving cotton linters—short cotton fibres—or nowadays generally wood in chemicals. The result is extruded to form an acetate yarn. | Can be a filament or staple yarn. Has low rate of absorbency and does not conduct heat readily—acetate garments are cool in summer and warm in winter. Dyes readily and can be embossed with patterns easily. Soft and pliable; drapes well. Weaker when wet and not hard-wearing; tends to tear at seams. | The first acetate was referred to as "artificial silk" and was a good, cheaper substitute for silk. Made into woven dress fabrics such as satins, taffetas and brocades and knitted fabrics such as jerseys for blouses, dresses, nightwear, underwear, men's ties, shirts, socks and suits. | Wash often in warm water; do not wring as creases can be permanent if the fibre cracks. Iron on WS with a medium iron and damp cloth. |
| **Acrylic** A synthetic fibre widely available since 1950. Contains at least 85 per cent acrylonitrile, a liquid derivative of oil refining and coal carbonization. | Can be filament but mostly produced in staple form, which tends to be warmer and woollier than the other synthetics, polyester and polyamide. Fairly strong and hard-wearing. Feels warm and soft and is thermoplastic, so can be permanently pleated by heat. Has a fairly low rate of absorbency and is moderately flammable. | The discovery of acrylic made it possible to produce less expensive, wool-like fabrics. Used in all kinds of clothing, knitwear, blankets and carpets. Blends well with other fibres, especially polyester. | Washes well in warm water, although the early yarns tended to stretch. Avoid wringing. Ironing not usually necessary, but if it is, use a cool iron. Take care, especially on jersey fabrics, to avoid stretching when pressing. |
| **Cuprammonium** One of the original rayon fibres, first produced commercially in Germany in 1919. Now widely known as cupro. The basic raw material, wood or cotton, is dissolved in copper sulphate, soda and ammonia—hence the fibre's name. Cupro has never been widely manufactured as it is expensive to produce. | Produced in filament form only. Fine, soft and lustrous and so closely resembles silk that the best hosiery and underwear were made from it until nylon came into general use. Quite difficult to distinguish from silk. Absorbent, drapes and wears well, but burns readily. | Sometimes blended with acetate and usually made into fine, soft, woven fabrics for sportswear, curtains, lining material and upholstery fabrics. Also found in soft, expensive, luxury dress fabrics such as chiffons, satins, ninons and nets. | Dry clean only unless the garment or fabric label indicates otherwise. |
| **Modacrylic** A modified acrylic yarn containing less than 85 per cent acrylonitrile (see acrylic); other synthetic ingredients, their percentage varying according to the manufacturer, make up the balance. | Very similar to acrylic but almost completely flame resistant. | Because of its flame resistance particularly suitable for children's nightwear and fabrics with excessive pockets of air in the surface such as fake fur. | As for acrylic. |
| **Modal** A cellulosic fibre. It is polynosic, a term used to describe a higher strength viscose that is stronger when it is wet. | Produced only in staple form, the fibre is soft and fuzzy, not shiny. Very strong and similar to cotton but more absorbent. Cool and soft, so pleasant to wear in the heat. Like cotton, it burns readily. | Mainly blended with cotton or polyester to produce a softer, less expensive fabric, suitable for blouses, shirts, nightwear, bedlinen, dresses, children's clothes and some furnishing fabrics. | As for cotton, wash in hot water and iron with a hot iron. |
| **Polyamide** A synthetic fibre more commonly known as nylon, the name it was given after its discovery in 1938. Polymer chips, produced from a nylon salt composed of benzine, oxygen, hydrogen and nitrogen, are melted and then extruded into yarn. | Initially mainly a filament yarn used for stockings and subsequently for parachutes and overalls because of its resistance to abrasion and its immunity to rotting and dampness. Now also produced in staple form. Very strong and highly elastic. Not very absorbent and so accumulates static electricity. Polyamide melts but does not burn. | Makes up well into fine materials such as chiffon, organza, surah and brushed and knitted nylon, for light garments, scarves, hosiery and underwear. Mixes well with other fibres and used in a wide range of fabrics from taffeta to laminates for protective clothing such as anoraks. Also used for carpets and upholstery. | Wash often, as nylon attracts dirt particles. White and light-coloured nylon may pick up tints from other fabrics, so wash separately. Needs little or no ironing; if necessary, use a cool iron. |
| **Polyester** A synthetic fibre. Experiments for making polyester yarn from petroleum and other chemicals were being made as long ago as 1938, but polyester was not in general production as a fabric until 1946. | Can be made in continuous filament form, which produces a smooth fabric, or in short staple lengths, producing a fuzzier, often thicker fabric. Very strong, resilient and hard-wearing. Has low moisture absorbency and so dries fast. Melts when heated, but does not burn. | Mixes well with, and often improves the performance of, other fibres. Can be knitted or woven into a wide variety of weights of cloth from voile, georgette, dress and knitted fabrics to suitings, furnishing fabrics and wadding for quilting. Also used to make sewing thread. | Attracts dirt particles, so wash often. Do not boil. Needs little or no ironing. If necessary, press with a warm iron. Can build up static electricity, especially in dry weather; rinse in fabric softener to reduce this tendency. |
| **Triacetate** Fabrics were first produced from triacetate in 1954. It is hard to distinguish triacetate from acetate although it is more lustrous. The initial processing of wood pulp or cotton is the same for both, but the final processing of the chemical flakes differs. | Can be a filament or staple yarn. Moderately strong but gives way at the seams. Drapes extremely well and feels crisp and firm. Not absorbent and dries quickly. Thermoplastic so can be permanently pleated by heat. Melts and burns readily. | Woven and knitted into various fabrics of different thicknesses. Can be mixed with nylon, especially in jersey fabrics, cotton, viscose or wool. Used for underwear and lingerie, and in weaves and knits that do not shrink. Also found in some pile and furnishing fabrics. | Wash often in warm water, but do not wring or squeeze, as the fibres can crack. Almost drips dry. Press while damp with warm iron on WS. |
| **Viscose** One of the cellulosic fibres formerly known as rayon. Produced by making sheets of cellulose from wood or cotton and soaking them in caustic soda to form crumbs of cellulose. Widely available from 1910 onwards and the first manmade fibre to be produced on a large scale. | Can be a staple or filament yarn. Fairly strong but loses as much as half its strength when wet. Feels soft, cool and limp against the skin. Burns very easily and is not hard-wearing. Viscose fabrics are often dull in texture. | Woven viscose fabrics are available in dress and blouse weights. Brushed viscose is useful for children's clothes, nightwear, housecoats and long casual wear. Also often used for furnishing fabrics, carpets, tyre cord and surgical dressings. Combines well with other fibres. | Wash in warm water. Use a medium-hot iron when slightly damp. |

# Index

# Index

# Acknowledgements

## PHOTOGRAPHY

The Publishers wish to acknowledge the kind co-operation of the following archives, photographic agencies and collections:
American Museum in Britain, Bath **185** centre bottom, **205** centre left (courtesy The Welsh Folk Museum, St Fagans)
The Bamforth Marketing Company **70** right, **212** bottom left
Barnaby's Picture Library **112** left
Bettmann Archive **90** centre top, **148–9**, **205** bottom
Bildarchiv Preussischer Kulturbesitz **72** top left
Anne S.K. Brown Collection, Rhode Island **53** right
Bruce Coleman **17** bottom left (Photo: Dr Sando Prato)
Butterick Fashion Marketing Company **72** centre
Colorific/Agence Top **9** bottom right (Photo: Jean-Philippe Charbonnier)
Colour Library International **104** bottom
Cooper-Bridgeman Library **16** bottom, **127** top right
Courtaulds **17** bottom right
Walt Disney Productions Ltd **118** top right (from *Donald's Gold Mine*)
Flick Ekins **101** centre left
Mary Evans Picture Library **6–7**, **8** bottom left, **8–9** bottom, **9** top left and centre right, **19** centre bottom, **21** top, **70** centre, **72** right (from *The Delineator* October 1915, courtesy Butterick Fashion Marketing Company), **104** top, **112** right, **118** bottom left, **127** bottom right, **145** bottom left, **224**
Giraudon **80** right
Susan Griggs Agency **65** bottom left (Photo: John Garrett)
Haddon Hall, courtesy The Duke of Rutland **19** centre left
Claus and Liselotte Hansmann **101** bottom left, **184** right and bottom left, **203**
Michael Holford **15** bottom right
Angelo Hornak **22**
Imperial War Museum **18** bottom left
IMS **157**
John Johnson Collection, Bodleian Library, Oxford **16** top right and bottom left, **185** bottom right, **218** bottom right
Mansell Collection **19** bottom right, **65** bottom right, **80** bottom left, **90** top right
Museum of Fine Arts, Boston **27**
The National Magazine Company **76**, **90** bottom left, **128** left
National Portrait Gallery, London **80** top left
Radio Times Hulton Picture Library **19** top right, **23**, **65** bottom centre, **70** left, **104** centre, **125** bottom right, **132** top, **145** bottom right
Ann Ronan Picture Library **9** second from left in top row and top right, **19** bottom left, **65** top right
Royal Shakespeare Theatre, Stratford-upon-Avon **204** (Photo: Joe Cocks)
Scala **90** centre right, **97** bottom left, **100** bottom right
The Singer Company **8** centre bottom, **9** third from left in top row
Snark International **132** bottom
Stone Collection of Photographs, Birmingham Reference Library **108–9** top
Sun Gravure (*100 Idées*) **16** bottom right, **108** bottom right, **109** bottom left
Talon **53** left
Unilever **18**, **19** top left
Henry Vyner, courtesy the Trustees of (Fountains Hall, Ripon) **43** (Photo: D.T. Atkinson)
Waring & Gillow, London **80** centre bottom
Frederick Warne & Co., courtesy The National Trust (from *The Tale of Mrs Tiggy-winkle* by Beatrix Potter) **29** bottom left
Welbeck Gallery, London **108** bottom left
Elizabeth Whiting **173** (Photo: Michael Nicholson)

**Original Photography:**
Philip Dowell **14**, **26**, **186** top
Flick Ekins and Val Hobson **153**
Melvyn Grey **Cover**, **68–9**, **161**

Nigel Heed **20–1**, **28** bottom centre and bottom right, **178–9**, **182–3**, **186** bottom, **188**, **190**, **191**, **192–3**, **194**, **196–7**, **199**, **200**, **201**, **205** top left, top right and centre right, **210** (bags courtesy Dorothy Johnson and Fiona Wood)
Angelo Hornak **8** top left and centre top, **9** centre bottom (all three photographs courtesy The Science Museum, London), **54** bottom, **65** centre right (courtesy The Button Queen, London), **71**, **146** bottom, **176** (courtesy The Victoria and Albert Museum, London, and Ham House), **185** bottom left
Rob Matheson **185** top, **187**
Malcolm Robertson **164–5**

## ARTISTS

Olivia Beasley **1**, **3**, **5**

*The Basics of Sewing* and *Perfect Dressmaking*: Diagrams, with the following exceptions, by Jill Shipley: Pamela Hardman **31–5**; Studio Collins International **10–11**, **13**, **54**; Anne Winterbotham **13**, **138–47**; Lyn Gray **139–40**. Colour realization **108–9** Sally Slight.

*Sewing for the Home*: Diagrams by Janet Sparrow. Colour realization **148–9** Val Hobson.

*Decorative Sewing*: Janet Sparrow **197–211**; Anne Winterbotham **187–95**.

*Repairs*: Anne Winterbotham.

The following furnishings and decorative sewing articles were specially made for the book:
Curtains **153**, tablelinen **161**, bedlinen **164–5**, cushions **178–9** Jeanne Argent
Embroidered picture **182–3** Prue Johnson
Crewel embroidery sampler **188** Daisy Collins
Machine embroidery sampler **190** Ann Harris
Smocking sampler **191** Flick Ekins
Canvas embroidery sampler **192** Kathie Chapman
Drawn, pulled and counted thread sampler **194** Jane Stevens
Quilt **196** Sue Thompson
Quilting samples **197** Flick Ekins
Quilting samples **199** Eirian Short
Appliqué screen **200** Elizabeth Manley
Appliqué samples **201** June Thorpe
Patchwork samples **205** Jenny Morgan
Cover by Eirian Short and Kathie Chapman

## SUPPLIERS

The Publishers are particularly grateful to David Wexper for supplying the irons for p. 28 and to John Cronk and Gloria Bradley for their loan of the tailor's dummies for pp. 68–9. They would also like to acknowledge the kind co-operation of the following: Anything Lefthanded; Bernina; The Button Queen; J. and P. Coats Ltd; Danasco Fabrics Ltd; Dickins & Jones (Harrods) Ltd; Habitat Designs Ltd; The Needlewoman; Mrs Millicent Nicoll, Butterick Archives; Mary Peacock.

## CONSULTANTS

David Bowers, Bedding Federation; Malcolm Hedges; John O'Gorman, British Man-made Fibres Federation; Christopher Thompson.

The Publishers also acknowledge the right to reproduce on p. 7 the first verse of a poem by Dorothy Parker entitled *The Satin Dress* from *The Collected Dorothy Parker* published by Gerald Duckworth & Co. Ltd, England, and first published under the title *The Portable Dorothy Parker* by The Viking Press, New York. © 1973 by National Association for the Advancement of Colored People.

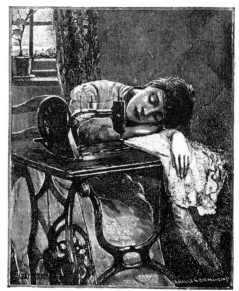

*"... Weariness Can snore upon the flint when resty sloth Finds the down pillow hard ..." (Shakespeare, Cymbeline). Although this exhausted seamstress undoubtedly agreed with Shakespeare, it is unlikely that she ever emitted such stertorous sounds.*